Financial Warnings

Financial Warnings

Charles W. Mulford
Eugene E. Comiskey

JOHN WILEY & SONS, INC.

New York • Chichester • Brisbane • Toronto • Singapore

Copyright © 1996 by John Wiley & Sons, Inc.

Library of Congress Cataloging-in-Publication Data:
Mulford, Charles W.
     Financial warnings   /   Charles W. Mulford, Eugene E. Comiskey.
       p. cm.
     Includes bibliographical references and index.
     ISBN 0-471-12044-8 (cloth :   alk. paper)
      1. Corporate profits—Accounting. 2. Financial statements.
     3. Assets (accounting). I. Comiskey, Eugene E. II. Title.
     HF5681.P8M85   1996
     657'.48—dc20   95-48809
                                              CIP

10 9 8 7 6 5 4 3 2 1

To Debby and Marlene. They understand.

Contents

Preface

It is hard to say exactly when the topic of financial warnings initially captured our interest and began to consume our attention. Certainly by the time the last recession was painfully present, it was very much in our consciousness. Leading up to that difficult time in 1991, and continuing thereafter to the present, certain corporate acts, such as the recording of restructuring charges and asset write-offs, the accrual of unrecorded liabilities, and earnings restatements for accounting irregularities or inflated profits, have been all-too-familiar occurrences. Moreover, rather than slowing with better economic times, their pace is accelerating as more and more companies announce special charges for restructurings, asset write-offs, and liability accruals. These special charges and restatements are taken in response to circumstances that often have been unanticipated and have led to unexpected reductions in corporate earnings and forecast cash flow. Affecting both lenders and equity investors, such changes may be accompanied by reduced debt-service capacity and lower share prices.

As we took notice of these earnings surprises, so did the bankers across the country with whom we worked. Striving to stay on top of debt-service capacity, the pervading question among them was "How could we have anticipated these surprises?" It is the search for an answer to that question that brought this book to life.

Financial Warnings identifies the financial characteristics of firms that typically precede such special charges and restatements, helping the informed financial statement reader anticipate their occurrence and their accompanying negative earnings surprise. We developed these characteristics from two primary sources. The first was through the examination of the financial statements and footnotes of firms reporting earnings surprises in the years preceding and leading up to those surprises. We looked for financial statement clues that helped to indicate that something was amiss. Some of the clues that we found to be effective, measures such as a declining gross margin or a lengthy collection period for accounts receivable, are commonly used by lenders and equity investors. Our experience indicates that others are less popular. For example, the company's revenue-recognition policy, its capitalization policy for costs incurred, or its reported investments in property and equipment relative to the level of sales, are less commonly employed and can be useful in anticipating earnings surprises. The second source involved in-person questioning of a large cross-section of experienced lenders. We wanted to learn from these important financial statement users just what clues they have found to be useful in the anticipation of earnings surprises. These lenders provided us with many useful insights that complemented our early warnings developed from the financial statements and footnotes. We did not, however, limit our research to earnings surprises from a lender's viewpoint. Also included in our work were developments that posed surprises for equity analysts in their forecasts of earnings per share.

Thus, we wrote *Financial Warnings* for both lenders and equity investors. Both groups rely on financial statements to formulate earnings and cash flow expectations as part of their decision processes. By raising their awareness of the financial characteristics of firms that often precede earnings surprises, more timely and profitable action can be taken.

It is our belief that the targeted reader will not only find the book to be interesting and informative reading, but also a useful reference source. To this end, checklists designed to focus attention on developing problems are provided as exhibits in several of the chapters. In addition, a sustainable earnings worksheet is provided and its use is demonstrated to help the reader uncover nonrecurring items of income and expense and derive an earnings base from which to begin formulation of an accurate earnings forecast. Finally, a collection of key accounting guidelines that provide background that some readers may be missing is provided in an appendix.

We strongly believe that *Financial Warnings* will provide serious help for those who rely on financial statements and footnote disclosures in their credit-granting and investment decision making.

Acknowledgments

We received assistance from many sources in making this book a reality. At John Wiley, Joanne Palmer, assistant managing editor, and Alice Cheyer, copy editor, have been exceptionally supportive and helpful. We thank Claire Greene, editor of the *Commercial Lending Review*, who over the past decade has taught these two professors much about expositional parsimony and keeping the target audience in mind. We also express our debt to the several thousand lenders who were participants in training programs we have conducted, and from whom we have learned much about the use of financial information. We especially thank the approximately 200 lenders who completed the lender survey that provided invaluable information about earnings surprises. When meeting the agreed-upon date for delivery of the manuscript looked more and more like an impossibility, we derived inspiration from that old Marine Corps maxim: "The difficult we do immediately, the impossible takes a little longer." Finally, while acknowledging inanimate objects is probably a bit unusual, the creation of this book benefited immeasurably from modern technology. We thank the following: our PCs, our laser printers, our copying machines, our faxes, and last, but far from least, the compact disk and its capacity to place the financial data of 10,000 companies at our fingertips.

Chapter 1

What Is an Earnings Surprise?

To be forewarned is to be forearmed.[1]

It is the rare day when at least one item in the financial press does not characterize a company's results as falling sharply below expectations. Consider the following examples:

> AST Research, Inc., struggling to regain its footing after failing to get new products out on time, said it had a loss of $22.3 million in the fiscal second quarter ended December 31. The Irvine, California, maker of personal computers said that the 69-cent-a-share loss for the quarter compares with net income of $17.9 million, or 54 cents a share, a year earlier. Revenue sank 6%, to $640.1 million from $677 million a year ago.[2]

> Fred Meyer, Inc., Portland, Ore., posted a deeper-than-expected net loss of $36.6 million in its fiscal third quarter because of a labor strike that has been settled and a one-time charge.[3]

> Datapoint Corp. posted an $85 million fiscal fourth-quarter loss and said its auditors are raising doubt about the technology company's future. . . . The biggest factor in the latest quarter's loss is a $57.7 million write-off of all of the company's goodwill.[4]

> Collins Industries, Inc., said its chief financial officer has resigned and two staff accountants have been suspended as an investigation indicates net income for fiscal 1992 was overstated by an estimated 72%. . . . The investigation to date has indicated that $1.2 million of fourth-quarter vendor payables were not properly recorded, causing an overstatement of net by about $762,000.[5]

> Jacobson Stores, Inc., . . . today reported sales for the third quarter ended October 29, 1994, of $86,501,000, down 4% from the same period in 1993. For the quarter, Jacobson's reported a net loss of $1,816,000, or 31 cents per share, compared to earnings of $1,186,000, or 21 cents per share, for the same period last year.[6]

> Comptronix Corp. suspended three of its top officers and began an internal investigation of its accounting procedures, saying that the three men had apparently caused

the company to overstate profits since 1989. . . . Comptronix said the three officers . . . apparently helped inflate profits by "improperly recording certain assets" and "either overstating current sales or understating current cost of sales on [the company's] income statement."[7]

Leslie Fay Companies, Inc., said it is investigating "alleged accounting irregularities" that, when corrected, could wipe out its 1992 net income and force the company to restate its 1991 earnings. . . . The company's corporate controller . . . indicated Friday during a year-end audit that he and another employee had made some "false entries" in the company's records.[8]

Gibson Greetings, Inc., said the Securities and Exchange Commission is investigating whether its employees violated securities laws while engaging in derivatives transactions or in overstating inventory at the company's Cleo, Inc., unit.[9]

Presidential Life Corp. will restate several years of financial results to reflect a mark-down of some junk securities in its portfolio as part of a settlement with the Securities and Exchange Commission. . . . The SEC . . . calls for Presidential to restate the results in order to comply with generally accepted accounting standards for valuing investment securities.[10]

To varying degrees, each of these items represents a deviation of income or earnings from expectations held by financial statement users. While different user groups employ financial statements in varying decision settings, earnings are typically a key decision input. This book focuses on the decisions of two broadly defined user groups: lenders and equity investors.

Lenders, including other financial statement users establishing a credit relationship with a company, such as suppliers or bond investors, form earnings expectations in deciding whether to extend credit and in designing the terms (repayment schedule, interest rates, security, etc.) of a credit facility. An actual earnings result that falls significantly below expectations can threaten prospects for repayment or call for modifying the terms of the credit to increase the likelihood of repayment.

The anticipation or avoidance of earnings surprises increases the likelihood that the original credit arrangement is designed to weather such downturns, and the pricing and loan structures are consistent with the risk inherent in the arrangement. Improving the quality of the original earnings expectation or forecast is an obvious first step in attempting to avoid earnings surprises. Beyond this, lenders try to avoid being surprised by a careful monitoring of signs, early warnings, that increase the likelihood of a shortfall of earnings in relation to expectations. Within limits, early warnings, for example, an unusual buildup in inventories or accounts receivable, a change in outside accountants, or an expansion into unrelated businesses, may provide the basis for recommendations to management of the borrower aimed at taking early corrective action so that an earnings surprise can be avoided.

Equity investors, or those who advise others on making equity investment decisions, place considerable reliance on earnings expectations. The prospects for and the uncertainty surrounding future earnings are pivotal in evaluating the appropriateness of an investment for a given investor. Investors and analysts place considerable reliance on earnings expectations in assessing current valuations of equity securities. Once an equity security has been purchased, dramatic losses can result if actual earnings fall short of expectations. Such losses may be avoided if such adverse developments can be anticipated. Alternatively, profits can be earned by investors who take short positions in securities in anticipation of earnings surprises that drive down the market value of equity securities.

Each of the examples provided earlier are actual cases where earnings were sharply reduced because of a variety of events, actions, or conditions. The position of this book is that at least some of these cases could have been anticipated, and that it is in the interests of lenders and equity investors to build the knowledge base and skills required to minimize these earnings surprises. The central goal of this book is to help financial statement users to develop skills that will permit them, to the extent possible, to avoid earnings surprises. Emphasis is placed upon those cases where actual results fall short of expectations. Such negative surprises can potentially lead to declines in the capacity of firms to remain current on their debt service obligations and endanger their ability to repay financings, and result in substantial losses on positions in equity securities.

AN EARNINGS SURPRISE REQUIRES AN EARNINGS EXPECTATION

An earnings surprise results when there is a material difference between actual and expected earnings. Thus, there must have been an earnings expectation for there to be an earnings surprise. In some cases, this earnings expectation will be explicit, resulting from the application of a careful, systematic procedure. It is, in essence, an earnings forecast. Explicit forecasts of earnings per share are available from a number of different sources, including Value Line, I/B/E/S, and Zacks.[11] In other cases, the earnings expectation may be only implicit. An implicit earnings expectation typically rests on the assumption that earnings either will not be significantly different from the most recent year or might simply grow or decline at a rate consistent with recent experience. For example, a company that has reported a 10% increase in revenue and net income in each of the last three years might lead one to implicitly expect a similar result in the fourth year.

Not All Deviations from Expectations Are Earnings Surprises

The concept of materiality is an important component of all earnings surprises. Seldom will actual results conform to expectations. It is possible to have a forecast error, a difference between expectations and actual results, without having an earnings surprise. Moreover, for two different firms or industries, the same percentage difference between actual results and expectations may represent an earnings surprise in one case and not the other. This is because of sharp differences in the general level of uncertainty associated with earnings expectations for different firms.

Consider the distributions of earnings per share forecasts for the two companies presented in Exhibit 1.1. There is a high level of consensus among the analysts forecasting earnings for Air Products and Chemicals, Inc. Two-thirds of the forecasts for this firm are expected to fall within the range of $2.62–$2.68, computed as the mean forecast of $2.65 plus and minus the standard deviation of 0.03.[12] An actual earnings result for 1994 of $2.56 would represent a forecast error of $0.09, which would be three standard deviations from the mean forecast of $2.65. The likelihood of such a deviation from the mean is less than 1 in 100, qualifying the actual result as an earnings surprise, even though it is only 3% from the mean forecast of $2.65.

An identical $0.09 forecast error in the case of Canadian Pacific Ltd. is far less likely to be seen as an earnings surprise, even though the actual result would be 10% below forecast versus 3% in the case of Air Products. There is considerable dispersion or disagreement among the forecasts for Canadian Pacific; the standard deviation of its forecasts is $0.18. The range within which two-thirds of its estimates fall is $0.69–$1.05, computed as the mean forecast of $0.87 plus and minus the standard deviation of $0.18. When there is greater disagreement among analysts, as with Canadian Pacific, larger forecast errors are not as surprising. Thus, a forecast error of $0.09, which is 10% of the mean forecast of $0.87, would fall within the range comprising two-thirds of the forecasts for the company and would not be considered an especially surprising result.

Forecast uncertainty, illustrated in Exhibit 1.1 for individual firms, also differs significantly across industries. Selected information on industry differences in earnings predictability is presented in Exhibit 1.2. The predictability statistic ranges in value from 0 to 100, and higher scores represent greater predictability.[13]

The industries in Exhibit 1.2 were chosen to illustrate a broad range of differences in predictability. The differences in predictability will probably strike most readers as quite plausible. For example, while being somewhat sensitive to weather and economic conditions, electricity consumption should have a fairly stable and predictable component based upon its essential nature. Thus, the high level of earn-

Exhibit 1.1   Examples of Variations in Forecast Uncertainty (Estimates of 1994 earnings per share)

	No. of Forecasts	Forecast Mean	Forecast Range	Coefficient of Variation
Air Products and Chemicals	21	$2.65	$2.55–$2.75	2.3%
Canadian Pacific Limited	13	.87	.4–1.10	42.0

Note: Data are drawn from the December 16, 1993, issue of *I/B/E/S Monthly Summary Data* on earnings forecasts. This document defines coefficient of variation as: "The standard deviation of the estimates expressed as a percent of the mean estimate; indicates the percent range within which about two-thirds of all estimates fall."

Exhibit 1.2   Selected Industry Differences in Earnings Predictability

Industry	Mean Predictability Score	No. of Companies in Industry	Range of Scores
Electric utility (East)	82	35	40–100
Beverage (alcoholic)	73	6	30–100
Bank (Midwest)	58	21	5–100
Auto parts (replacement)	46	8	25–95
Home appliance	43	5	15–65
Air transport	29	11	5–75
Auto and truck	12	5	5–40

Source: *Value Line Investment Survey* (New York: Value Line Publishing, 1994), from September, October, and November issues.

ings predictability of electric utilities is not surprising. At the other extreme, it seems reasonable that earnings predictability in the auto and truck industry would be quite low in view of the degree of competition in the industry and the cyclical nature of the demand for these major consumer durables. However, while the range in average predictability across the industries, 12–82, is substantial, it is exceeded by the range of 5–100 within the bank (Midwest) industry. Thus, even within relatively stable industries, companies with very uncertain earnings can be found.

Selected Causes of Earnings Surprises

The earnings surprises mentioned earlier have a number of different explanations. Each of these cases is characterized as representing an earnings surprise because it involved earnings that were well outside any reasonable explicit or implicit expectation or range. AST Research's earnings surprise resulted from a very common source— a failure to introduce a new product on a timely basis. Fred Meyer's earnings were lowered by the effects of a strike and an additional one-time charge. Strikes are subject to limited management influence or control, and anticipation or avoidance of this source of earnings surprises is difficult. The goodwill write-off of Datapoint presumably reflects a combination of deterioration in the prospects of a company previously acquired by Datapoint and the requirements of generally accepted accounting principles (GAAP). GAAP require that assets not be carried forward if their recovery from future revenue is not reasonably assured. Further, in recent years there has been increased pressure from the Securities and Exchange Commission to evaluate goodwill's realizability on an ongoing basis and to book write-downs when recoverability becomes unlikely. The cases of Collins, Comptronix, Leslie Fay, Gibson, and Presidential Life all involved misrepresentations of financial performance. It is unclear in each of these cases whether such misrepresentations were deliberate or inadvertent. The Gibson case also involved losses from alleged violations of company policies with respect to the use of derivative instruments. A contributing factor in the

Gibson case was a sharp change in interest rate levels, something beyond the company's control and anticipation. Finally, the earnings surprise of Jacobson Stores appeared to result simply from an unanticipated decline in sales.

The sources of earnings surprises are many and varied. Some of the factors or conditions associated with earnings surprises are given in the following list. Others will be identified in subsequent chapters, together with explanations of how they cause earnings surprises.

- Unexpected changes in general or industry economic activity
- Unexpected changes in prices, interest rates, currency values
- Natural disasters
- Wars
- Errors
- Nonrecurring gains and losses
- Fraud or fraudulent financial reporting
- Loss of a major customer
- Delays and difficulties with the introduction of a new product or process
- Mismanagement
- Unauthorized actions
- Unhedged risk associated with interest rates, exchange rates, or other prices
- Emergence of new competitors or competitive products or services
- Changes in accounting policies or accounting estimates
- Excessive buildups in inventories and accounts receivable
- Disruption in the supply of a major raw material
- Misapplication of generally accepted accounting principles
- Impact of government or regulatory action
- Discontinued operations
- Bad (for business) weather

As a general rule, surprises are something that people prefer to avoid. Surprises generally rule out anticipatory activities such as prevention or planning and preparation. Central to the avoidance of an earnings surprise, or any other form of surprise, are early warning signs or indicators. Such early warnings are often characterized as red flags. A more appropriate label in the area of earnings surprise anticipation would be yellow flags, since here early warnings are more in the nature of cautionary indicators that call for investigation and inquiry. They do not necessarily indicate that something is amiss.

An early warning of an earnings surprise, referred to in this book as a financial early warning, is defined as a measurement, event, condition, circumstance, development, or action that has historically been associated with a subsequent deviation of earnings from an expectation. This definition will guide our work throughout the book and provide focus in identifying those events to be anticipated and the manner of their anticipation and avoidance.

There is little direct evidence on the likelihood of an earnings surprise being associated with any particular early warning. Most of what we report in this area is anecdotal. However, it is based upon a very extensive review of the literature of finance and accounting as well as on the accumulation and analysis of numerous examples of earnings surprises from the financial press. The items that we have uncovered have historically been related to earnings surprises. Moreover, in Chapter 4, we add the results of a survey of lenders on the early warnings that they have found to be associated with earnings surprises. Their responses are consistent with the financial early warnings accumulated from other sources.

FORECAST SURPRISES IN NONEARNINGS AREAS

Reviewing the role of surprises in other settings may help in a consideration of the value of early warnings in the earnings area. Examples of early warnings from nonearnings settings are provided in Exhibit 1.3. These represent areas in which early warnings, or diagnostics, are commonly used to anticipate, moderate, or eliminate surprises and their potentially adverse consequences.

Note the parallels between the activities in Exhibit 1.3 and the roles played by lenders and equity investors. Physicians take various readings and measurements and infer from this information what therapy, if any, is called for. An elevated blood pressure reading may indicate an underlying pathology calling for treatment, or it might simply be the result of some transient phenomenon that requires no attention. Treatment is designed to ward off the surprise, such as a stroke or other event. Lenders and equity investors take many diagnostic readings as well. Common examples include inventory days, receivables days, and gross margin. Deviations from norms, or industry averages for such financial statistics, are reviewed to determine whether a condition calling for some intervention is evident. On occasion, preplanned intervention is provided for. Financial covenants in loan agreements permit lenders to

Exhibit 1.3 Activities Aimed at Preventing or Anticipating Surprises

Area	Activity	Objective
Medicine	Blood pressure monitoring	Identify treatment needs in order to avoid a stroke or other adverse event
Weather	Monitoring and predicting weather conditions	Identify conditions calling for travel warnings in order to protect citizens
Military	Monitoring troop movements and buildups	Prevent or prepare to respond to hostile acts

take action in cases where a borrower's financial statistics deviate from agreed guidelines. Similarly, deterioration of financial statistics may cause equity investors to alter their investment positions.

THE PLAN OF THIS BOOK

The goal of this book is to help lenders, equity investors, and other users of financial information build skills that will help them reduce earnings surprises. It is important to stress reduction and not the total elimination of earnings surprises. Some of the causes of earnings surprises are by their nature difficult if not impossible to anticipate. For example, the earnings of many firms were sharply affected by the Gulf War—in most cases, but not all, the impact was negative. Various natural disasters have also had a major negative effect on the earnings of firms in recent years: flooding in the South and Midwest, fires and earthquakes in California, and hurricanes in the South. It is unlikely that lenders and equity investors will ever be successful in anticipating much in advance the negative impact on earnings of such events. The anticipation of other classes of earnings surprises is also very difficult. For example, in recent years, cases of improper or fraudulent financial reporting have been a steady source of earnings surprises. These cases have involved such acts as inventory misstatements and the improper booking of sales. Such activities have proved very difficult to detect, especially when the active collusion of a number of top officers is involved. There are many classes of earnings surprise, however, including some frauds, that can be successfully anticipated. Helping users of financial information to anticipate these events and reduce earnings surprises as much as possible is the goal of this book.

Chapters 2 and 3 provide a starting point. In Chapter 2 we describe the steps taken to discover the actual earnings surprises used in developing our financial early warnings. These surprises, identified by the financial press and from our own comparison of actual results with both explicit and implicit earnings expectations, provided the raw material for our work. We sought to uncover the indicators that were available prior to the observed surprises. In Chapter 3 we classify the discovered earnings surprises according to the factors that appeared to cause them. In our view, a careful classification is an important first step in providing the reader with a better understanding of the causative factors of earnings surprises. The more one understands about the causative factors, the better one is prepared to avoid the associated earnings surprises.

Chapter 4 builds on the large-scale data analysis of Chapters 2 and 3 by reporting the results of a survey of lenders designed to identify financial early warnings that have been found to be useful in anticipating declines in earnings and avoiding earnings surprises. This large body of information is organized into detailed categories of early warnings that should prove useful for those attempting to anticipate and avoid the negative impact of earnings surprises.

Chapters 5 and 6 are designed to aid the statement user to perform a thorough analysis of recent historical earnings. The approach taken in this book is that the most important initial step in avoiding earnings surprises is to improve the quality of the earnings expectation or forecast. This improvement in forecast quality is achieved through a process aimed at identifying a firm's sustainable earnings base. The goal of this process is to identify the most reliable base upon which to formulate an earnings expectation. In security analyst terminology, the process is sometimes characterized as assessing the quality of earnings.

The sustainable earnings base represents a historical earnings series that has been purged of the effects of all nonrecurring items of revenue or expense and gain or loss. This has become an increasingly difficult task in recent years as income statements have become cluttered with a wide range of nonrecurring items such as restructuring charges, accounting changes, changes in estimates, gains and losses on asset sales, LIFO (last in, first out) liquidation effects, foreign exchange gains and losses, discontinued operations, nonrecurring tax charges or benefits, extraordinary items, and so on.

Chapter 5 presents and illustrates the current GAAP requirements that guide the construction of the income statement and associated disclosures. It will become clear that a complete analysis of earnings calls for a systematic approach to the examination of the income statement, statement of cash flows, and many other notes and disclosures. Chapter 5 provides a step-by-step search sequence that is designed to maximize the location of material nonrecurring items in the most efficient manner possible.

Chapter 6 presents a worksheet designed to summarize the analysis outlined in Chapter 5. Application of the worksheet is illustrated with two complete case studies that apply and evaluate the search sequence outlined in Chapter 5. The product of the completed worksheet is a sustainable earnings base, a historical earnings series that has been comprehensively restated to exclude all nonrecurring items. All statement users should find the sustainable earnings worksheet and recommended search sequence to be of considerable value in improving the quality of their earnings expectations or forecasts and, as a result, avoiding earnings surprises.

In the same spirit, a balance sheet–oriented approach to anticipating earnings surprises is outlined in Chapter 7. This material draws on the concept of financial position quality, an analytical procedure that stresses deviations of the book or carrying value of assets and liabilities from their market or liquidation value, along with the existence of off–balance sheet assets and liabilities. The principle underlying this analysis is that differences between the book and market values of assets and liabilities eventually work their way into profit determination, often as unexpected revenue or expenses and gains or losses. This process represents the balance sheet parallel to the income statement–oriented process of assessing earnings quality, discussed in Chapters 5 and 6.

Following this work on forecast improvement, the book focuses on key sources of earnings surprises and the associated early warnings that should prove effective in anticipating them. The key elements of this treatment involve a focus on overstated revenue in Chapter 8, understated expenses in Chapter 9, misreported assets and liabilities in Chapter 10, and earnings management in Chapter 11. Early warning checklists are provided at the end of each of these chapters to serve as guides for financial statement users in their review of company financial statements and other relevant information.

The focus in this book is on earnings surprises and their anticipation and avoidance. This focus is consistent with the central role played by earnings in both public and private markets for debt and equity. However, in recent years, various measures of cash flow have become popular analytical tools. This is true for both lenders and equity investors. Most of the key indicators of potential cash flow difficulties also have implications for possible earnings declines and surprises. Chapter 12 introduces cash flow–oriented analytical procedures and illustrates the role that they can play in anticipating earnings declines so as to avoid or prepare to respond to earnings surprises.

With the apparent growth in earnings surprises over the past decade, there has been a rising tide of complaints and legal actions directed at the auditing profession. Especially troubling have been instances of bankruptcy filings or equivalent actions by firms within short periods of time after the receipt of clean or unqualified audit reports. The expression "audit failure" has been coined to apply in such instances. Chapter 13 provides an overview of the various roles that outside accountants and auditors play in providing different levels of assurance to financial statement users. Some very useful research findings on circumstances conducive to and indicators of fraudulent financial reporting are summarized in this chapter in a series of exhibits.

Our expectation is that this book should be well within the reach of interested readers with a basic background in financial accounting acquired either in a formal academic setting or from experience. However, to broaden the accessibility of the material in the book, we provide an appendix, which gives a brief discussion on a range of financial reporting topics that provide additional background for material in earlier chapters. The appendix should prove useful to those whose financial reporting background requires some review or updating. Moreover, readers with relatively limited backgrounds may find it useful to preview the appendix prior to reading the earlier chapters. The appendix may also be used on a selective basis as readers feel the need for a stronger foundation in dealing with specific accounting and financial reporting matters.

Earnings expectations are important in the assessment of the repayment potential of a loan or the intrinsic value of an equity security. It is our belief that the financial early warnings provided in this book will be helpful to both lenders and equity investors in formulating better earnings expectations and avoiding unwanted earnings surprises.

ENDNOTES

1. Derived from "Forewarned forearmed" in Miguel de Cervantes, *Don Quixote de la Mancha* (1605–1615), III, 10, p. 502.
2. *The Wall Street Journal*, January 26, 1995, p. B6.

3. Ibid., December 2, 1994, p. A4.
4. Ibid., November 15, 1994, p. A19.
5. Ibid., March 5, 1993, p. B3.
6. Jacobson Stores, Inc., press release, November 21, 1994.
7. Ibid., November 27, 1992, p. A3.
8. Ibid., February 2, 1993, p. A4.
9. Ibid., November 16, 1994, p. B10.
10. Ibid., March 2, 1993, p. B3.
11. The *Value Line Investment Survey* (New York: Value Line Publishing, 1994) includes both quarterly and annual forecasts of earnings per share. I/B/E/S (Institutional Brokerage Estimate System) provides an extensive database of earnings per share forecasts from a large number of analysts. Zacks Investment Research, Inc., provides forecast information comparable to I/B/E/S.
12. The statistical properties of a normal distribution, assumed to be appropriate for earnings forecasts, lead us to expect actual earnings to fall within this range.
13. This earnings predictability index is defined in the guide *How to Use the Value Line Investment Survey*, 1985, p. 63, as follows: "Earnings predictability index—a measure of the reliability of an earnings forecast. Predictability is based upon the stability of year-to-year comparisons, with recent years being weighted more heavily than earlier ones. . . . The earnings stability is derived from the standard deviation of percentage changes in quarterly earnings over a five-year period."

Chapter 2

Identifying Earnings Surprises

Punished by marketing mistakes, weakness in the apparel market and theft, 50-Off Stores, Inc., said it expects to post a net loss for its fourth quarter ended Jan. 28 [1994] of between $2.2 million and $2.7 million, or up to 27 cents a share, based on preliminary results.

The loss, sharply below consensus analysts' estimates of earnings of 7 cents a share for the quarter, as compiled by Zacks Investment Research, sent 50-Off common shares down 62.5 cents to $5.75 in Nasdaq Stock market trading.[1]

We sought to develop a collection of financial early warnings preceding such earnings surprises as the 50-Off Stores, Inc., example. We began by reviewing the financial statements of firms reporting earnings surprises in the years preceding and leading up to each surprise. Our objective was to find financial statement items and characteristics that consistently preceded such earnings shortfalls. For example, we searched for such clues as an unexpectedly high level of accounts receivable days, or a particularly long depreciation period for fixed assets. Other candidates included certain balance sheet accounts, such as capitalized marketing costs or unamortized goodwill. Still others consisted of off–balance sheet disclosures of commitments and contingencies. While we had certain preconceived notions about what warnings or indicators to look for in the periods preceding the earnings surprises, we tried to be open and let the financial statements tell us what appeared to be awry. With this approach, we felt that we would be less likely to miss something.

For our financial early warnings to be complete and effective, they needed to be developed from as broad a collection of earnings surprise examples as possible. We felt that the more past examples we could identify and use, the more confident we could become that some warnings were not slipping by our notice. We sought earnings surprises from two sources: the financial press and our own comparison of actual results with expectations based on prior-year trends and analyst forecasts.

This chapter was co-written with Stacey R. Nutt, Assistant Professor of Accounting, Virginia Polytechnic Institute and State University, Blacksburg, Virginia. The authors greatly acknowledge the contribution of I/B/E/S International, Inc., for providing earnings per share forecast data, available through the Institutional Brokerage Estimate System.

There was some overlap between the two sources, but not much. We tended to use the financial press to identify the more sensational examples of earnings surprises—those receiving more prominent press attention. Such cases often involved active manipulation of earnings by management and sometimes outright fraud. In contrast, the earnings surprises identified by comparing reported results with prior-year trends and analyst forecasts were more often caused by declining economic fundamentals. This latter group was not ignored by the financial press but did not receive the same prominent attention given to situations of active earnings manipulation or fraud.

There is, however, another, more fundamental reason that helps explain why the earnings surprises obtained from the two sources were different. When the more egregious cases of earnings manipulation and fraud are discovered and corrected, a restatement of prior-year results is typically required. Prior years are adjusted downward to remove the accounting error effects, and afterwards current year earnings do not provide as strong a contrast. Accordingly, our comparison of actual results with expectations based on restated prior-year trends would not pick up such a surprise, resulting in examples of earnings surprises that differ from those identified in the financial press. Similarly, to the extent that analyst forecasts are adjusted to remove accounting error effects, our comparison of actual results with expectations based on adjusted analyst forecasts would also fail to pick up such surprises.[2]

REVIEWING THE FINANCIAL PRESS

The financial press, including books, journal articles, and newspaper accounts, provided a rich collection of earnings surprises. In reviewing these outlets, we looked for articles or chapters about companies that implied that some group of investors or creditors was clearly surprised by developments at that firm. Consider the following announcement from Leslie Fay Companies, Inc.:

> As you may know, an investigation has been instituted by the audit committee of the Board of Directors into alleged accounting irregularities. False entries have been made in the company's books and records which would affect the accuracy of some of the information contained in these documents.[3]

We first became aware of problems at Leslie Fay from reports in the financial press. In the announcement, the company referred to "false entries" made in its books and records. To the extent that earnings expectations had been built on prior-year results boosted by "false entries," actual results would fall below those expectations, resulting in an earnings surprise. We obtained financial statements for Leslie Fay for the years preceding the earnings surprise and examined them for potential clues of the impending decline in earnings. It was from clues like this that we developed our financial early warnings.

Another example is that of The Topps Co., Inc. In early 1993 the company made the following announcement:

Shipments of sports cards during the fourth quarter ending February 27, 1993, will be significantly lower than the company anticipated. As a result of lower shipments, as well as the company's decision to increase provisions for obsolescence and returns, the company will report a net loss for its fourth quarter.[4]

With this announcement, the company was declaring that shipments would fall below levels that had been expected. As a result, revenue would decline, hurting earnings. Providing an additional reduction in earnings, however, was a special provision or expense to cover the anticipated effects of increased obsolescence and returns of the company's cards. Once we located this announcement of an earnings surprise, the company's financial statements in the immediately preceding years and quarters became a natural source of information warning of the impending event.

It should be noted that in locating earnings surprises, our primary focus was on industrial firms. Financial firms, such as banks, thrifts, and insurance companies were, for the most part, excluded. This is not to say that financial firms do not have their share of earnings surprises. One needs only to consider historically recent events, including dramatic increases in interest rates and crises surrounding Mexico and, in particular, the devaluation of the peso, to be reminded that earnings surprises occur at such institutions. For example, in early 1995, Bankers Trust New York Corp., a financial firm, made the following statement accompanying its release of financial results for 1994:

During the fourth quarter of 1994, $423 million of leveraged derivative contracts were reclassified as receivables in the loan account and placed on a cash basis. Of this amount, $72 million was subsequently charged off to the allowance for credit losses.[5]

Derivatives are financial instruments that derive their value from other, underlying financial contracts or indices. A stock call option giving its holder the right to buy stock in a specified company at an established price and by an established date is a derivative, deriving its value from its terms and the value of the underlying stock. The derivatives in question in the Bankers Trust case were primarily interest rate swap agreements. These are agreements entered into with other companies whose value is tied to the level of interest rates. Swaps, used by many firms to hedge interest rate risk, can also be used to speculate on interest rate movements. Bankers Trust entered into interest rate swaps with some of its customers that chose to speculate on interest rate movements. Rapid increases in interest rates during 1994 created significant losses for many of them. With its announcement, Bankers Trust was charging off losses on some of these agreements due to defaults by some of its customers.

Also in early 1995, the following article regarding Chemical Banking Corp. appeared:

Chemical Banking Corp. said it would incur a $70 million pre-tax trading loss for the fourth quarter because one of its New York–based currency traders made unauthorized transactions involving the Mexican peso.

Chemical said the loss, which will sharply reduce overall trading revenue, will result in an after-tax charge against earnings of about $40 million, or about 15 cents a share.

Chemical said the trader, whom it did not identify, concealed positions in the peso that were in violation of the bank's authorized risk limits. . . .

The bank said the losses came to light when the value of the peso fell sharply about two weeks ago.[6]

In this instance, a trader took large, speculative bets that the Mexican peso would appreciate in value. Instead, it declined in value dramatically, creating large losses for Chemical Banking.

Such examples of earnings surprises notwithstanding, we chose to exclude financial firms because the structure of their financial statements is very different from that of industrial companies. In developing financial characteristics of firms that precede earnings surprises, it was important that the firms in question have similar financial statements. Financial firms, for example, do not report either inventory or a gross margin on sales or services. In addition, they do not report accounts receivable nor classify their balance sheets into current and noncurrent sections. We found that these items can play an important role in identifying earnings surprises for industrial firms. Moreover, as a group, financial firms are affected differently by such macroeconomic factors as interest rates and inflation than are industrial firms. We did not, however, ignore the financial firms entirely. With some surprises, especially those involving off–balance sheet commitments and contingencies, we found that financial firms provided unique and insightful examples that could also affect industrial firms. As a result, we occasionally refer to a financial firm as we develop our financial early warnings.

To help keep the scope of our project manageable, we did not use examples of all the earnings surprises identified. When several earnings surprises were caused by the same underlying factor, we considered the size and timeliness of the surprise as well as the anticipated level of general reader interest in selecting examples. Thus, the examples discussed in this book should not be considered to be a complete collection of all earnings surprises occurring over the last 25 years or so. A reader's favorite example of fraud or aggressive application of generally accepted accounting principles (GAAP) may be omitted. If it is, the issues and the financial early warnings were likely highlighted by another source.

COMPARING ACTUAL RESULTS WITH EXPECTATIONS

Having developed a substantial collection of earnings surprises located in the financial press, we wanted to make an additional sampling of earnings surprises to see if there was something we might have missed. That is, we wanted to supplement the financial press material with a second sample. Our objective was to examine the financial statements of those 200 companies whose earnings since 1980 had fallen below expectations by the greatest amount.

Earnings Expectations

In order to compare actual results with expectations, we needed a definition of earnings expectations. We used two. The first was an implicit expectation based on prior-year results. The second was an explicit expectation based on analyst forecasts.

The first definition is an expectation that an established income trend will continue. In this setting, a significant negative deviation from an established trend, often referred to as an earnings reversal or turning point, is defined as the earnings surprise. For the period 1980–1993 we searched Standard & Poor's Compustat database to identify those 100 industrial firms with the largest percent drop from the prior year in income from continuing operations (after income taxes) after four or more years of steady or increasing income.[7] This drop in income from continuing operations was defined as the earnings surprise. Four years of steady to increasing income was considered sufficient to influence investors and creditors into expecting a continuation of same. It would seem that a significant earnings reversal after such an established trend would represent to most an earnings surprise. Compustat proved to be a useful source for collecting the needed data. The database contains income statement and balance sheet data for virtually thousands of firms over a 20-year period. The period since 1980 was used so that the sample would comprise more recent earnings surprises. Examples located using this first definition of earnings expectations were termed trend-based earnings surprises.

The second definition of earnings expectations used the consensus or mean of financial analyst forecasts. Unlike a simple prior-year trend, analysts can incorporate turning points into their forecasts at any time. They can use prior-year results as a starting point and then incorporate other general macro and micro information to develop more accurate forecasts. By using mean or average forecasts, the highly divergent forecasts of some individual analysts are smoothed to give more meaningful earnings expectations. The extent to which actual income from continuing operations differed from the mean analyst forecast was defined here as the earnings surprise. For the period 1981–1989, the years for which data were available to us, we searched the 1989 Institutional Brokerage Estimate System (I/B/E/S) database to identify those 100 industrial firms with the largest negative deviation in income from continuing operations from mean forecast.[8] A negative deviation in income from forecast was one in which reported income from continuing operations fell below forecast. Our interest was exclusively on such negative surprises.

The I/B/E/S database provides a collection of mean analyst forecasts and actual earnings for thousands of firms. To ensure significant deviations from forecast, we used a nine-month forecast horizon. That is, forecast data were collected nine months prior to the end of each firm's fiscal year-end. Because forecasts tend to be adjusted toward actuals as quarterly results are released, we wanted no actual results to be incorporated into the forecasts. At nine months prior to year-end, previous-year results are typically available. However, first-quarter results for the new year have not as yet been released. Examples located using this second definition of earnings expectations were termed analyst-based earnings surprises.

One important difference between the trend-based and the analyst-based earnings surprises is in how the analyst data are adjusted. That is, I/B/E/S strives to exclude the effect on reported differences between actual earnings and forecast earnings of nonrecurring events such as restructuring charges, asset write-downs, and special liability accruals. Accordingly, to the extent companies identify such nonrecurring items when actual results are reported, I/B/E/S removes their effect from the reported actuals. For example, assume that three months into the year, the 1996 mean analyst forecast for hypothetical Button Corp. is $5.50 per share. Further, assume that at year-end Button reports actual results for 1996 of $5.00 after taking a fourth-quarter after-tax restructuring charge of $0.50. After removing the effects of the restructuring charge, Button's actual results for 1996 are $5.50. As a result, there is no difference between the mean forecast and actual results. By this definition, there is no earnings surprise. Because of these adjustments, it was expected that nonrecurring items would play a less important role in identifying the reasons for earnings surprises for the analyst-based firms than for the trend-based firms, though whether this expectation is realized depends on the extent to which companies identify nonrecurring items at the time actual results are reported.

From the annual reports of 200 firms reporting earnings surprises, 100 trend-based and 100 analyst-based, we reviewed two key documents: the income statement and Management's Discussion and Analysis (MD&A). The objective was to use the income statement and management's observations to determine, to the extent possible, what happened.

The Income Statement

The income statement proved to be a valuable source of information. From that document, for the year of each earnings surprise, we took the following measures:

- Percent change from the previous year in revenue
- Change from the previous year in gross margin, or gross profit as a percent of revenue
- Change from the previous year in selling, general, and administrative expense as a percent of revenue
- Change from the previous year in research and development expense as a percent of revenue
- Nonrecurring items as a percent of pre-tax income from continuing operations
- Change from the previous year in effective tax rate on income from continuing operations.

The percent change in revenue from the previous year helped us determine if declining revenue may have contributed to the earnings surprise. Differences in the gross margin percent provided insight into the effect of changes in the general level of profitability of each company's product or service line. Variations in the selling, general, and administrative expense percent helped determine whether the firms were controlling operating expenses. Changes in the research and development expense percent, relevant for technology firms only, was designed to measure the effects of increases or decreases in this often material discretionary expenditure. Nonrecurring items as a percent of income from continuing operations enabled us to isolate the role of such nonrecurring losses as restructuring charges, asset write-downs, and special liability accruals. Finally, because earnings surprises were defined using after-tax income from continuing operations, it was necessary to measure the effects of changes in effective tax rates.

One might question why we did not consider the potential surprise effects of such significant nonrecurring items as discontinued operations, extraordinary items, and the cumulative effects of changes in accounting principles. Such events, many of which entail discretionary management acts, are normally excluded from models used to develop earnings expectations. As such, earnings forecasts typically focus on income from continuing operations, a measure of income that excludes such items. For consistency, we also focused on income from continuing operations as our forecast object and excluded discontinued operations, extraordinary items, and the cumulative effects of changes in accounting principles from our earnings surprise definition.

Management's Discussion and Analysis (MD&A)

MD&A is a report by management required of public companies by the Securities and Exchange Commission. The report's objective is to provide investors and creditors with management's analysis of the firm's financial position and performance from the standpoint of liquidity, capital resources, and results of operations. If material, an analysis of the effect of inflation is also required. By providing an analysis by management, an informed participant in the company's affairs, MD&A is designed to give investors and creditors a valuable insight into a company's financial condition, operating results, and cash flows. In conducting the analysis, management is required to focus on events, trends, and uncertainties that could cause past results not to be indicative of future performance.

Because MD&A is designed to help investors and creditors better understand why past results may not be indicative of the future, the report was viewed as an excellent complement to the income statement in understanding why the sample of chosen firms reported earnings surprises. For each firm, MD&A was read, with particular attention to the "results of operations" section. In particular, we were interested in determining why the measures taken from the income statement occurred, and what underlying factors caused them.

The Findings

Most of the earnings surprise examples discussed individually in this book were drawn from the financial press, not from our trend-based and analyst-based samples. However, we did not ignore the earnings surprises in our trend-based and analyst-based samples. Though we wanted to emphasize earnings surprises that were larger in amount and that might carry a higher level of reader interest, our objective was to base our financial warnings on as complete a collection of earnings surprises as possible.

While few of the individual trend-based or analyst-based surprises were alone significant enough to be afforded separate coverage, collectively these samples carried much information. For example, the data contained in these samples were useful in answering questions such as the following:

- What causes a company to report sharply reduced earnings or a loss after four or more years of steady improvement?
- How often is a special provision, such as an asset write-down or liability accrual present when a company's earnings fall below trend?
- What factors are present when financial analysts are most surprised?

Our review of these surprises is designed to help the reader better understand why such surprises occur. The findings are then incorporated into the conclusions reached in Chapter 3, "Causative Factors."

Trend-Based Earnings Surprises

The trend-based surprise firms, the year of their earnings surprise, and the percent decline in income from continuing operations (after-tax) from the final year of the four-year trend are provided in Exhibit 2.1. Also provided in the exhibit is other preliminary information on what may have caused each earnings surprise. This additional information includes the change in revenue, the change in operating profit margin, nonrecurring items, and the change in the effective tax rate.

The change in revenue, measured as the percent change from the last year of the four-year trend, indicates whether an unusual change in sales or service revenue, up or down, may have contributed to the earnings surprise. A drop in revenue could lead to a decline in income from continuing operations, even if profit margins were maintained. Even an increase in revenue, if accomplished at the expense of reduced profit rates, could lead to lower earnings. Operating profit is defined as revenue less cost of sales, referred to as gross profit, less selling, general, and administrative expenses and research and development expenses. Operating profit margin is operating profit as a percent of revenue. The change in operating profit margin, as presented in the exhibit, is the change in the operating profit margin in the surprise year from the last year of the four-year trend. This statistic captures the effect of changes in the company's fundamental profitability on its change in income from continuing operations.[9] Nonrecurring items include all separately disclosed, irregular items of income or expense included in income from continuing operations. These nonrecurring items are usually negative, that is, they represent losses, and are reported in the exhibit as a percent of the absolute value of income from continuing operations before taxes in

Exhibit 2.1 Trend-Based Earnings Surprises, 1980–1993

Company	Year	Change in Income from Continuing Operations	Change in Revenue	Change in Operating Profit Margin	Nonrecurring Items	Change in Effective Tax Rate
Acuson	1992	-37.08%	1.93%	-10.22%	0%	-.36%
Advanced Micro Devices	1982	-63.56	-8.99	-10.67	0	-197.21
Alberto Culver	1981	-42.31	28.39	1.04	-81.82	5.55
Aldus	1992	-71.43	3.94	-14.29	0	.21
Altera	1992	-35.39	-5.05	-8.25	0	.11
Amer. Business Products	1981	-13.58	12.49	-1.91	0	-1.40
Analog Devices	1981	-50.54	15.11	-4.66	-55.88	-.95
Anheuser-Busch	1993	-40.22	.94	-.15	-53.79	4.90
Arch Petroleum	1992	-99.03	4.35	-20.47	0	-30.70
ARX	1988	-13.33	43.07	-5.74	0	-7.56
Astrosystems	1985	-42.42	-18.26	-12.83	0	-1.38
Acxiom	1990	-32.58	8.92	-1.65	0	2.94
Becton, Dickinson	1983	-53.06	.50	-1.72	-96.14	-34.52
Bell Atlantic	1989	-18.40	5.23	-3.05	0	1.78
Best Lock	1982	-32.04	7.75	-6.95	0	.32
Biocraft Labs	1989	-43.84	-14.76	-13.27	18.70	-7.27
BioLogic Systems	1988	-33.91	5.75	-3.95	0	17.20
Brock Exploration	1982	-80.93	10.26	-16.55	-70.00	.24
Brooklyn Union Gas	1986	-25.62	-2.05	-2.19	0	-2.03
Caere	1993	-113.51	-22.97	-31.59	-38.10	16.18
Caesar's New Jersey	1981	-51.55	-.90	-6.16	-25.42	5.83
Caesar's World	1982	-69.55	-3.26	-1.55	-62.01	50.02

			-4.75%	-4.15%	-8,695.65%	-634.56%
California Microwave	1980	-93.42%	-4.75%	-4.15%	-8,695.65%	-634.56%
Central & South West	1988	-11.44	2.82	-3.26	0	-6.37
CLARCOR	1989	-60.78	4.61	-2.03	-45.26	20.19
Clothestime	1987	-45.38	11.48	-8.06	0	-6.52
Cogitronics	1981	-66.00	6.06	-7.47	0	.70
Comdisco	1980	-32.89	17.67	-2.53	0	-6.09
Computer Task Group	1989	-222.44	6.54	-3.25	-110.83	-8.13
Conolog	1985	-23.64	88.33	-8.81	-53.90	-12.72
Core Industries	1982	-24.09	-2.87	-2.83	0	-.63
Craig	1991	-47.20	0	-25.00	-82.45	5.82
Cray Research	1989	-43.10	3.76	-7.75	-37.71	-2.99
Daniel Industries	1983	-76.97	-21.35	-10.97	0	-55.27
Data General	1981	-25.23	12.69	-5.32	0	-.10
Dayton Power & Light	1984	-15.91	5.95	2.30	-23.19	9.31
Delta Natural Gas	1990	-20.00	5.45	-2.24	0	-.67
DeSoto	1985	-24.47	-.44	-.58	0	1.61
DH Technology	1991	-21.67	15.75	-5.04	0	-4.02
Diebold	1985	-46.75	-13.33	-10.86	0	-8.17
Digital Equipment	1983	-32.02	10.08	-6.57	0	0
Elgin Sweeper	1983	-39.83	18.14	-3.48	0	.93
Eli Lilly	1987	-24.19	9.67	-1.70	-45.70	-4.79
Federal Signal	1983	-39.83	18.14	-3.48	0	-.57
Food Lion	1992	-13.26	11.76	-1.11	0	-1.05
General Electric	1987	-14.97	10.31	-.42	-32.02	1.43
Great A & P Tea	1991	-53.25	1.75	-2.12	0	.52
Greentree Software	1989	-236.40	92.97	95.04	-92.55	0
HADCO	1991	-27.27	-5.03	-2.36	0	-3.12
Hathaway	1986	-98.15	15.07	-12.18	-122.70	65.56

(continued)

Exhibit 2.1 *(continued)*

Company	Year	Change in Income from Continuing Operations	Change in Revenue	Change in Operating Profit Margin	Nonrecurring Items	Change in Effective Tax Rate
Home Depot	1986	-41.84%	61.90%	-2.29%	-100.86%	-16.69%
Houston Industries	1982	-41.68	24.00	-.07	-129.85	.93
Hughes Supply	1989	-34.02	5.58	-.92	0	1.02
Idaho Power	1985	-15.20	5.45	-9.91	0	-4.05
Intel	1981	-71.77	-7.71	-17.68	0	-15.71
IPL Systems	1993	-180.65	-25.93	-19.17	0	2.80
Johnson Controls	1980	-25.44	4.73	-2.09	0	2.45
Kaman	1989	-65.61	4.39	-.48	-135.54	7.49
Lancer Orthodontics	1989	-235.57	2.17	-17.51	-50.71	-36.78
LDI	1992	-33.65	-5.24	-2.83	0	1.19
Lin Broadcasting	1989	-17.26	11.18	-.56	-67.26	4.80
LVMH Moet Hennessey	1992	-11.94	7.28	-1.02	-15.72	.24
M.S. Carriers	1990	-23.11	27.69	-5.15	0	.91
Mechanical Technology	1989	-235.71	-1.21	-10.83	0	-4.52
Medex	1993	-38.62	6.09	-3.43	-29.33	-1.41
Mobil	1981	-25.64	7.63	-2.43	4.52	-2.86
Montana Power	1984	-42.10	7.53	-.71	-9.59	8.62
National Convenience Stores	1985	-16.22	13.25	-.76	0	-2.36
New York Times	1989	-57.68	4.05	-5.21	-34.67	7.56
NYNEX	1989	-38.59	4.34	-.69	-47.51	2.67
Oakwood Homes	1987	-93.85	3.16	-1.65	-2,633.33	-75.43
Ohio Edison	1988	-46.98	20.40	6.29	-50.96	11.68
Pacificorp	1984	-11.73	11.74	.83	0	4.96

Panhandle Eastern	1982	-15.94%	3.83%	2.91%	-5.69%	-16.82%
Pharmaceutical Resources	1991	-153.52	49.34	26.85	-63.45	-32.67
Phillips Petroleum	1981	-17.85	19.35	-6.52	0	.90
Pinnacle West Capital	1987	-16.21	6.42	-7.93	0	-6.36
Playboy Enterprises	1982	-13.29	-5.19	2.81	-65.52	-7.72
QMS	1988	-183.10	28.58	-14.81	0	2.11
Revco, D.S.	1985	-52.03	7.54	-3.15	-56.39	-.36
Russ Berrie	1988	-20.00	-1.84	-6.82	0	-6.33
Saatchi & Saatchi	1989	-117.58	12.91	-4.37	-181.19	105.74
Schering-Plough	1981	-24.38	4.03	-3.21	-12.91	0
Southwestern Energy	1986	-36.19	-20.46	-4.28	0	-.27
Standard Products	1989	-15.84	9.95	-1.87	0	1.67
Stratus Computers	1993	-70.65	5.63	-2.09	-99.02	21.60
Sun Company	1982	-50.09	3.64	-2.48	0	1.11
Superior Industries	1990	-23.96	8.74	-.37	-24.66	1.00
SuperValu	1993	-15.38	18.21	.04	-32.52	.70
Syntex	1993	-39.00	3.21	-.77	-241.15	-130.11
Teradyne	1981	-62.28	-3.09	-7.63	0	-24.31
The Southern Company	1987	-37.21	2.39	-2.13	-38.64	-2.28
UpJohn Company	1982	-31.46	-3.54	-2.12	0	2.53
Thomas & Betts	1982	-29.64	-4.99	-5.24	0	-2.71
United States Surgical	1993	-199.86	-13.36	-15.54	-100.15	-28.94
UGI	1982	-26.60	4.72	-2.62	0	-19.25
Universal Health Services	1986	-48.39	31.83	-3.41	0	11.02
Vishay Intertechnology	1981	-50.00	.81	-3.03	0	-14.29
Wackenhut	1984	-128.13	16.91	-1.31	-957.14	316.24
Willcox & Gibbs	1991	-69.09	5.63	.43	-144.44	25.12
Samplewide mean		-54.97%	7.77%	-3.90%	-151.33%	-7.33%

the surprise year. Examples include typical nonrecurring items such as restructuring charges, asset write-downs, and special liability accruals. Also included is any expense that is significantly higher than prior years, making a major contribution to the earnings surprise noted that year.[10] This latter group might include foreign exchange losses or a sudden increase in interest expense, whether due to an increase in rates or to increased borrowings. The effective tax rate is computed as income tax expense divided by pre-tax income from continuing operations. As reported in the exhibit, the change in the effective rate is the change in the tax rate in the surprise year from the last year of the four-year trend. An increase in the effective tax rate could lead to a decline in after-tax income from continuing operations even if pre-tax income remained unchanged.

After four or more years of steady or increasing earnings, the companies reported in Exhibit 2.1 experienced the reported percent declines in income from continuing operations. The earnings declines experienced by these firms represent the 100 largest such declines, as defined, for the period 1980–1993. Their declines in earnings were significant. The percent decline in income from continuing operations in the year of the earnings surprise from the last year of the four-year trend averaged just under 55%.

In reviewing Exhibit 2.1, it can be seen that no firm appears on the list more than once. This is understandable given the requirement that a four-year or more trend of steady or increasing earnings was necessary before a company could be considered a candidate for an earnings surprise. Once a decline in earnings occurred, another four-year positive trend was needed before that firm could be considered a candidate for a second earnings surprise, and such a development is unlikely.

Macro-Factors

While our interest is primarily in micro-, or firm-specific, factors causing earnings surprises, the potential impact of such macro-factors as recessions or industrywide developments cannot be ignored. Because business activity turns down generally during a recession, such a period would seem to provide fertile ground for trend-based earnings surprises. Over the 14 years from 1980 through 1993, there were three recessions.[11] One started in 1979 and ended in mid-1980, a second ran from late 1981 through most of 1982, and a third started in mid-1990 and lasted into mid-1991. If we group the earnings surprises according to the years in which they occurred, the effect, if any, of recession years on trend-based earnings surprises can be seen. The results of this grouping are provided in Exhibit 2.2.

The recession of 1981–1982 had a significant association with the earnings surprises of the companies under review. A total of 24 firms reported earnings surprises during that period. This is a greater number than during any other two-year period under review, including the recession of 1990–1991, which was mild by comparison with the earlier recessions.

Of the period surveyed, the single year with the highest number of earnings surprises was 1989. A total of 15 trend-based earnings surprises were noted for that

Exhibit 2.2   Trend-Based Earnings Surprises by Economic Period, 1980–1993

Year	Economic Period	No. of Occurrences
1980	Recession	3
1981	Recession	12
1982	Recession	12
1983	Growth	5
1984	Growth	4
1985	Growth	7
1986	Growth	5
1987	Growth	6
1988	Growth	6
1989	Growth	15
1990	Recession	4
1991	Recession	6
1992	Growth	7
1993	Growth	8
Total		100

year. Interestingly, 1989 was a nonrecession year, though real growth in gross domestic product stayed below 2% for three of four quarters that year and fell to no growth during the third quarter.

Thus, there is some support for the view that recessions cause trend-based earnings surprises. However, as seen in Exhibit 2.2, recessions helped explain only a small proportion of the earnings surprises observed.

Other macro-determinants that could help explain earnings surprises include factors that are industry-specific. A sudden decline in business activity for an industry generally could result in the reporting of earnings surprises by a large number of firms belonging to that industry group. Exhibit 2.3 presents all industries represented by two or more firms reporting earnings surprises during the period under review.

The industry group with the greatest representation of firms reporting earnings surprises is the electric services industry. This group consists of pure electric utilities (Standard Industrial Classification 491) and other primarily electric utilities that also provide natural gas services (SIC 493). Given the stable nature of earnings for firms in this industry group, these firms readily met the first criterion of a trend-based earnings surprise: four years of stable or increasing income. However, it was unexpected that so many firms in this industry would report significant declines in profit.

We first expected that sudden increases in fuel costs or interest rates at certain points in time might have caused the industry as a whole to report disappointing results. If this were the case, then most of the electric services firms would have reported earnings surprises in the same year or two. However, we noted that no single year was overly represented. The year 1984 was the most popular, but only three electric utilities reported trend-based earnings surprises that year. And we could see

Exhibit 2.3   Trend-Based Earnings Surprises by Industry, 1980–1993

Industry	No. of Firms
Electric services	10
Electronic components	9
Computer and office equipment	8
Computer and data-processing services	7
Drugs	6
Medical instruments and supplies	6
Measuring and controlling devices	5
Crude petroleum and natural gas	4
Grocery stores	4
Telephone communications	3
Beverages	2
Communications equipment	2
Electrical goods	2
Gas production and distribution	2
Hotels and motels	2
Motor vehicles and equipment	2
Petroleum refining	2
Soap, cleaners, and toilet goods	2
Total	78

nothing in the financial statements of these companies that would relate their earnings declines to an event that could be tied to that specific year.

The single most common factor explaining the earnings surprises for firms in the electric services industry is one that could be considered an industry problem. It is not, however, a problem that could be related to any one year. Five of the ten electric services firms reported significant nonrecurring items in their earnings surprise years. These nonrecurring items were primarily write-downs of investments in power-generating plants due to an inability to have these investments included in permitted rate bases. These write-downs can be related to a general industry problem—one of excess generating capacity and a hostile rate-setting environment.

The electronic components industry (SIC 367), which includes the semiconductor manufacturers, was also well represented by earnings surprises during the period under review. The recession years hit this industry hard. Six of the nine earnings surprises occurred during recession periods, with four occurring during the 1981–1982 recession and two during the downturn of 1990–1991. Sales declined for four of the six firms reporting earnings surprises during recessions and were essentially unchanged for a fifth firm. Interestingly, all nine firms in the electronic components industry saw their operating profit margins decline in the earnings surprise year. These declines could be attributed primarily to declines in gross margins, defined as gross profit as a percent of revenue. There was very little increase noted in selling, general, and administrative expense as a percent of revenue or research and development expense as a percent of revenue. Finally, nonrecurring items were reported by three of the nine firms in the industry. Interestingly, all three were caused by a sudden increase in interest expense. In one instance, an increase in rates, occurring in 1981, was to blame. In the remaining cases, significant increases in borrowings to help finance asset growth and an acquisition caused the increase noted in interest charges.

The next two industries represented on our list, computer and office equipment (SIC 357) and computer and data-processing services (SIC 737) are related. The first group consists primarily of computer makers, while the second includes software firms. There was no period-related industry malaise noted for either group during the years under review. Moreover, most firms enjoyed increasing revenue in the years in which earnings surprises were reported. Operating profit margins did, however, decline for all eight of the computer and office equipment group firms and six of seven of the computer and data-processing services firms. For the computer and office equipment group, the declines noted in operating profit margins could be attributed first to declines in gross margins, followed closely by increases in selling, general, and administrative expense as a percent of revenue. As a percent of revenue, research and development expense changed very little. For computer and data-processing services firms, gross margins declined, but not by significant amounts. Increases in selling, general, and administrative expense as a percent of revenue were more to blame for the declines noted in operating profit margins. Here, too, research and development expense as a percent of revenue increased only marginally.

The drugs industry (SIC 283) and the medical instruments and supplies industry (SIC 384) were also well represented in the list of firms reporting trend-based earnings surprises. The earnings surprises noted in the drugs group were unrelated to any particular year. Five of the six drugs firms did report a decline in operating profit margins, explained primarily by a decline in gross profit margins and an increase in selling, general, and administrative expense as a percent of revenue. These declines, however, were not the primary reasons for the earnings surprises reported here. Nonrecurring items, including restructuring charges, the settlement of a legal proceeding, and a loss associated with a terminated business, were primarily to blame. Four of the six drugs firms reporting earnings surprises recorded such charges during the period under review.

Half of the firms reporting earnings surprises in the medical instruments and supplies industry did so in 1992 or 1993. Possibly, the disappointing results noted could be attributed to health care reform that was so much in discussion during those years. While revenue increased for most firms in this industry, operating profit margins declined. Causing the declines were increases in selling, general, and administrative expense as a percent of revenue. Also prominent in the earnings surprises of firms in this industry was the role played by nonrecurring items. Four of the six firms reported nonrecurring charges due to such factors as restructuring charges and asset write-downs.

The remaining industries noted in Exhibit 2.3 were not viewed as having sufficient representation to warrant separate attention. Of these remaining industries, the earnings surprises of only the measuring and controlling devices group (SIC 382) appeared to be caused by macro-factors. Three of the five firms represented by this industry reported earnings surprises in the recession years of 1980, 1981, and 1982.

Firm-Specific Factors

While macro-factors, such as recessions and general industry trends, did explain some of the earnings surprises noted in Exhibit 2.1, most of the surprises were due to firm-specific factors. Among the firm-specific factors, two that were not helpful in explaining the earnings surprises were revenue declines and changes in effective tax rate. In reviewing Exhibit 2.1, we note that the average firm actually reported an increase in revenue in the year of the earnings surprise. The mean increase in revenue was 7.77%, with 75 firms reporting revenue increases and 25 firms reporting revenue declines. Also in reviewing the exhibit, it can be seen that income taxes as a percent of pre-tax income declined by an average 7.33%. Exactly half of the firms experienced an increase in effective tax rate in the earnings surprise year, while half of them experienced a decline. The firm-specific reasons for the trend-based earnings surprises noted in Exhibit 2.1 are related primarily to two factors: declining operating profit margins and nonrecurring items.

Operating Profit Margins

Operating profit margins declined by an average of 3.9% of revenue in the earnings surprise year. A total of 90 of the 100 firms included in Exhibit 2.1 experienced a decline in their operating profit margins. As noted earlier, operating profit consists of revenue less cost of sales, referred to as gross profit, less selling, general, and administrative expense and research and development expense. The firms in Exhibit 2.1 reporting earnings surprises saw their operating profit margins decline primarily because of declines in gross margin, or gross profit as a percent of revenue, and secondarily because of increases in selling, general, and administrative expense as a percent of revenue. While 30 of 35 earnings surprise firms reporting research and development activities did see their research and development spending increase, the amount of increase was small and was not a significant contributing factor to the observed earnings surprises.

A total of 76 of the 90 firms in Exhibit 2.1 that reported declines in operating profit margins also reported declines in gross margins. MD&A was reviewed for each of these firms to determine why gross margins declined. The results of this review, for the 63 instances in which a clear and concise reason for the decline was provided, are presented in Exhibit 2.4.

Declining selling prices, a changing product mix, and excess capacity due to declining revenue volume topped the list of reasons for declines in gross margins. As sales prices decline, revenue declines even as the same physical volume of product or service is sold. Because production costs or cost of sales typically include some

Exhibit 2.4 Trend-Based Earnings Surprises: Factors Contributing to Declines in Gross Margin, 1980–1993

Factor	No. of Instances
Decreased revenue due to lower selling prices	13
Changing product mix to products with lower gross margins	13
Excess capacity due to declining revenue volume	12
Increased costs associated with general cost increases	11
Unfavorable foreign currency movements	6
Capacity expansion to meet anticipated increases in revenue volume	5
Increased costs associated with new product development	2
Lower gross margin of acquired company	1
Total	63

portion of fixed costs, they typically cannot be reduced proportionately to the decline in revenue, leading to a decline in gross margin. Closely related to the effects on gross margins of declining sales prices is the effect of declining revenue volume. Here fewer units are sold. Geared up for higher volume, the firm finds itself with excess production capacity. Unfortunately, many of the costs of carrying and maintaining this capacity are fixed. As revenue declines, production costs, including the fixed costs associated with excess capacity, cannot be reduced at the same rate, and gross margins decline. A changing product mix results in a decline in gross margin when a firm sells proportionately more of a product or service that carries a lower gross margin than in prior years. This is likely done to meet changing market demand.

Also leading to reduced gross margins is the effect of general cost increases. Here variable production costs increase because of general inflation effects. The firm is unable to pass along all of these cost increases to customers in the form of price increases, and gross margins decline.

Other factors leading to declining gross margins include unfavorable foreign currency movements and capacity expansion to meet anticipated increases in revenue volume. Foreign currency movements can affect gross margins in two ways. Firms with foreign customers might see revenue decline as the dollar appreciates relative to foreign currencies. With no accompanying decline in cost of sales for domestic production, gross margin declines. Alternatively, firms with foreign suppliers could see production costs increase when the dollar depreciates, leading also to a decline in gross margin. During the 1980–1993 sample period, there was ample movement in the value of the dollar to create significant losses. The dollar generally appreciated relative to foreign currencies from early in the sample period into 1985. Since 1985, the general trend in the dollar value has been down. Turning to capacity expansion, firms that increase capacity and fixed production costs to meet anticipated increases in revenue volume will experience declines in gross margin in advance of those sales increases. Gross margins should improve, however, once those anticipated revenue increases are realized.

Rounding out the list of reasons for declining gross margins are increased costs associated with new product development and the lower gross margin of an acquired company. New product development sounds like a discretionary move that may be short-lived. Gross margin should return to earlier levels when these increased expenditures are discontinued. A lower gross margin associated with an acquisition is very similar to the effects of a changing product mix: in this case, the acquiring company has sought to add a "product line" with a lower gross margin.

Seventy-five of the 90 firms in Exhibit 2.1 that reported declines in operating profit margins also reported increases in selling, general, and administrative expense as a percent of revenue. The increases, however, did not explain as much of the declines in operating profit margin as did the declines noted in gross margin. MD&A was again reviewed to determine why selling, general and administrative expense increased. The results of this review for the 62 instances in which clear reasons were provided are presented in Exhibit 2.5.

The exhibit indicates that increased spending on marketing and advertising was the primary reason for the increases noted in selling, general, and administrative expense as a percent of revenue. While the firms generally enjoyed revenue increases during the year, marketing and advertising expenses increased at a faster rate, leading to an increase in selling, general, and administrative expense as a percent of revenue. Also contributing to the increase in selling, general, and administrative expense were increases in administrative and miscellaneous expense, which included overhead charges like healthcare and other benefits for nonsales personnel, expenses of management information systems and management training, and property taxes.

In several cases, revenue declined faster than firms could reduce selling, general, and administrative expense. In others, firms increased selling, general, and administrative expense ahead of sales increases in an effort to build the infrastructure needed for sales growth. In both instances, selling, general, and administrative expense increased as a percent of sales.

Other reasons for increased selling, general, and administrative expense include higher legal costs, increased costs of acquired companies, and additions to customer

Exhibit 2.5 Trend-Based Earnings Surprises: Factors Contributing to Increases in Selling, General, and Administrative Expense as a Percent of Revenue, 1980–1993

Factor	No. of Instances
Increased marketing and advertising expense	25
Increased administrative and miscellaneous expense	14
Decreased revenue due to lower volume or prices	6
Costs of expansion ahead of sales growth	6
Increased legal expense	5
Increased expenses of acquired company	4
Increased customer service expense	2
Total	62

service departments. All these reasons, together with the number of instances in which each was noted, are listed in Exhibit 2.5.

Nonrecurring Items

Nonrecurring items include expenses or losses that are irregular in nature or at odds with a company's typical expense level. In reviewing Exhibit 2.1, it can be seen that 45 of the 100 firms reporting earnings surprises also experienced a nonrecurring loss in the same year. While two firms did report nonrecurring gains, the focus here is on the loss side. With nearly half the sample firms reporting such nonrecurring losses, identifying them is clearly important for our study of earnings surprises.

Many nonrecurring items, including restructuring charges, asset write-downs, and special liability accruals, are normally given separate line item treatment on the income statement. Such charges can be readily identified. For example, consider the income statements of Pharmaceutical Resources, Inc., Caere Corp., and Greentree Software, Inc. On its 1991 income statement, Pharmaceutical Resources reports a $12.5 million charge labeled "settlements of legal proceedings."[12] On its 1993 income statement, Caere Corp. reports a $0.8 million loss for "discontinuance of product line."[13] And on its income statement for 1989, Greentree Software includes a special $1.5 million charge for "stock option compensation."[14] In each instance, the nonrecurring item is prominently displayed. Other examples include Willcox & Gibbs, Inc., which reported a $6.5 million "restructuring charge" on its 1991 income statement, and Wackenhut Corp., whose 1984 income statement included a $6.7 million "loss on proposed disposition of subsidiary."[15]

In reviewing MD&A for other companies, we became aware of significant nonrecurring charges that were *not* given separate income statement treatment. Consider the following excerpt from MD&A in the 1990 annual report of Lancer Orthodontics, Inc.:

> Cost of sales as a percentage of sales increased from 54.0% to 57.6%. The increase can be primarily attributed to two unusual items: (1) The write-off of $133,000 (1.4%) of monies advanced to a vendor. . . . When it became apparent that the vendor would be unable to supply enough services to pay off the advances, the company discontinued doing business with the vendor. The company does not expect to recover any of the monies written off. (2) The incurring of $118,000 (1.3%) in material price variances on substitute parts. These parts were replacements for parts provided by a vendor that went out of business.[16]

As can be seen, the company included nonrecurring items in cost of sales. Similar examples can be found in the annual reports of Revco D.S., Inc., and Cray Research, Inc., where such nonrecurring items as inventory write-downs and product transition expenses were included in cost of sales. In collecting data for these companies, it was necessary for us to remove these special charges from cost of sales in calculating gross profit and report them as nonrecurring items.

In another instance, Oakwood Homes Corp. reported a provision for losses on credit sales on its income statement.[17] Typically, such a charge would not be considered a nonrecurring item. However, in 1987, that charge was 289% higher than it was in the previous year. We removed the increase in this charge from selling, general, and administrative expense and recorded it as a nonrecurring item.

Other examples of nonrecurring items that were not separately disclosed on income statements include a 1981 temporary increase in interest rates, which pushed up interest expense for Analog Devices, Inc., by 59%, and a provision for losses related to the termination of a business, listed by Schering-Plough Corp. under "other, net" on its 1981 income statement. In each instance, we used MD&A to identify the nature and amount of the nonrecurring item. The results of our search for nonrecurring items are presented in Exhibit 2.6.

In reviewing this exhibit, note that restructuring charges are the primary type of nonrecurring item. Restructuring charges are typically related to strategic moves on the part of management. With them, companies position themselves for a more profitable future. For example, plants are consolidated and closed, personnel levels are reduced, and unproductive assets are written down.

For example, in 1993, Syntex Corp. recorded a $320 million restructuring charge, which the company described as follows:

> Included in operating expense for fiscal 1993 is a restructuring charge of $320 million, which covers estimated costs resulting from the decision to completely or partially close several of the company's chemical and pharmaceutical manufacturing plants and two small research facilities and estimated severance costs associated with a reduction in the company's work force.[18]

Similarly, in the same year, United States Surgical Corp. recorded a restructuring charge that totaled $137.6 million. The company described the charge as follows:

Exhibit 2.6 Trend-Based Earnings Surprises: Nonrecurring Items, 1980–1993

Nonrecurring Item	No. of Instances
Restructuring events	10
Write-down of property, plant, and equipment and intangible assets	9
Write-down of inventory	6
Write-down of accounts receivable	5
Increased interest expense	5
Other nonrecurring events	5
Write-down of investments	3
Unfavorable foreign currency movements	2
Total	45

In the second half of 1993 the company adopted a restructuring plan designed to reduce its cost structure and improve its competitive position through property divestitures and consolidations and a reduction in its management, administrative, and direct labor work force. During the third and fourth quarters of 1993 the company recorded restructuring charges of $8.0 million and $129.6 million, respectively. . . . These charges consist primarily of write-downs of certain real estate to net realizable value ($79 million), provisions for lease buyout expenses ($24 million), severance costs ($30 million), and write-down of other assets ($5 million).[19]

Both the Syntex and United States Surgical examples are typical of the kinds of activities and costs included in the category "restructuring charges."

We saw numerous examples of asset write-downs in the sample under review. As shown in Exhibit 2.6, there were 23 examples of asset write-downs, including property, plant, and equipment (nine instances), inventory (six instances), accounts receivable (five instances), and investments (three instances). Assets are written down when they become value-impaired: the total undiscounted cash flows expected to be realized from the asset are less than the asset's book value.

Asset write-downs are closely related to restructuring charges. The latter is used to describe the charge when a major strategic move is associated with it. Note that in its restructuring charge described earlier, United States Surgical Corp. included write-downs of assets, including real estate and other assets. In the absence of any major change of direction that might be considered a corporate restructuring, the loss associated with an asset write-down would be reported more descriptively as just that—an asset write-down. An example of such a charge is provided on the 1987 income statement of The Southern Company, where a $357.8 million charge is described as "disallowed Plant Vogtl costs."[20]

Other nonrecurring items noted in the financial statements of firms with earnings surprises included increased interest expense and losses due to unfavorable foreign currency movements. Normally we would not think of interest expense as a nonrecurring item. However, in the five instances noted, interest expense increased markedly in the year of the earnings surprise, adding to the downturn. Increases in interest were due in some instances to sharply higher interest rates and in others to much higher borrowings. The foreign currency losses were due to the effects of foreign currency fluctuations on items unrelated to inventory acquisition. As discussed earlier, foreign currency losses related to inventory costs were included in the calculation of gross margin.

Other nonrecurring charges reported in Exhibit 2.6 comprise several items that were not prominent enough to warrant separate attention in the exhibit, such as accrued litigation losses, product transition expenses, and increased preopening costs.

Analyst-Based Earnings Surprises

As was the case for the trend-based earnings surprises, we provide descriptive statistics for the analyst-based surprise firms, in Exhibit 2.7. However, analyst surprise data are provided only for the period for which analyst forecasts were available to us: 1981–1989.

In addition to the same statistics as were provided for the trend-based earnings surprise firms, Exhibit 2.7 lists the "I/B/E/S surprise." This statistic is a measure of the difference of the mean forecasts of analysts from actual results divided by the standard deviation of the forecasts. It is essentially a measure of how far the analysts' forecasts were from actual earnings, standardized to remove the effects of size differences across firms. The negative amounts denote negative surprises: actual results were less than analyst forecasts.

An example would help demonstrate how the I/B/E/S surprise is calculated. Assume that five analysts forecast 1996 earnings per share (EPS) for hypothetical Antron Corp. Their forecasts, mean forecast, and standard deviation of forecast are shown in Exhibit 2.8. Antron's mean and standard deviation of forecasts is $6.04 and $0.671863, respectively. If Antron Corp. later reported actual EPS of $5.20, the I/B/E/S surprise would be –1.25, calculated as ($5.20 – $6.04) divided by $0.671863.

Over the period 1981–1989, the most notable analyst-based earnings surprise was related to actual income from continuing operations reported by the 100 firms presented in Exhibit 2.7. Note that the mean I/B/E/S surprise was –25.27, indicating that these firms reported earnings that were dramatically different from what analysts had predicted. Interestingly, 22 of the firms actually reported an increase in income from continuing operations in the earnings surprise year. Apparently, while positive, these firms' earnings were still less than analysts had expected. Consider, for example, Collaborative Research, Inc. In 1988, the company's revenue increased 30.5% over 1987. Moreover, the company's operating profit margin also improved. While the company did lose money in 1988, it had lost much more in previous years. Apparently, analysts were expecting much more from the company in 1988 and were surprised when actual results did not meet those expectations. Note that even with some firms, like Collaborative Research, reporting improving results in the earnings surprise year, collectively the analyst-based surprise firms experienced a mean decline in income from continuing operations of over 100% from the previous year.

Unlike the trend-based earnings surprise group, some of the analyst-based earnings surprise firms appear on the list more than once. This is due to our methodology: to be included in the analyst-based group, firms did not need to establish a four-year trend in positive or increasing earnings. There are eight such repeats of analyst-based earnings surprise firms.

Macro-Factors

During the time period employed for the analyst-based earnings surprises, there was only one recession, that of 1981–1982. However, as can be seen in Exhibit 2.9, analysts were not fooled by the commencement of a general decline in economic activity that accompanies a recession. It is interesting to note that consistent with the

Exhibit 2.7 Analyst-Based Earnings Surprises, 1981–1989

Company	Year	I/B/E/S Surprise	Change in Income from Continuing Operations	Change in Revenue	Change in Operating Profit Margin	Nonrecurring Items	Change in Effective Tax Rate
Acme-Cleveland	1988	-188.00	-714.58%	-.23%	.17%	-82.01%	-72.12%
Adage	1984	-26.30	38.71	37.99	-2.97	0	-.93
Advance Circuits	1986	-20.30	-175.56	-3.82	-20.62	0	10.81
Advance Circuits	1988	-40.60	-975.00	18.66	4.15	-126.58	-57.26
Air Midwest	1985	-44.30	-325.00	3.59	-12.83	0	-6.57
Alberto Culver	1985	-18.00	25.40	12.65	1.07	0	6.21
Allen Group	1987	-9.70	-85.05	-1.20	-5.57	0	44.47
Altron	1989	-21.00	5,284.62	26.90	4.54	0	23.03
Amdahl	1989	-7.30	-30.14	16.61	-7.44	0	-1.25
Amerada Hess	1985	-13.00	-253.00	-7.56	-3.91	-440.74	-154.98
American Mgmt. Sys.	1982	-13.50	50.00	6.10	3.87	-168.18	33.65
American Mgmt. Sys.	1989	-11.20	-16.22	5.63	-1.27	0	5.14
Analogic	1984	-20.00	9.27	9.70	-2.70	0	-1.90
Apache	1987	-23.50	-432.68	-5.19	-14.96	-69.69	-6.29
Applied Magnetics	1984	-12.10	-88.37	43.60	-6.92	0	-19.62
Arvin Industries	1988	-7.90	-65.55	.49	-2.37	-100.69	1.06
Atlantic Richfield	1985	-18.10	-75.75	-8.44	1.27	-517.53	-16.53
Avery International	1987	-20.30	-28.60	29.53	-.47	-32.09	10.96
Bairnco	1988	-7.50	44.36	21.28	1.05	0	-4.59
Baltimore Gas & Electric	1989	-8.10	-8.93	7.51	-2.91	0	-.60

(continued)

Exhibit 2.7 (continued)

Company	Year	I/B/E/S Surprise	Change in Income from Continuing Operations	Change in Revenue	Change in Operating Profit Margin	Nonrecurring Items	Change in Effective Tax Rate
Bell Atlantic	1989	-9.10	-18.40%	5.23%	-3.04%	0%	1.78%
Bindley Western	1987	-9.60	-64.81	48.41	-.29	0	.37
Bio-Medicus	1987	-40.00	233.33	91.84	10.81	0	33.33
Bolt, Beranek & Newman	1987	-132.00	-170.80	31.46	-.26	-574.36	258.13
Bolt, Beranek & Newman	1989	-89.70	-274.59	-4.42	-23.50	-10.67	.11
Bristol-Myers Squibb	1989	-10.00	-40.43	7.37	.41	-57.95	7.90
Builders Transport	1986	-13.60	-40.00	16.22	-3.05	0	7.95
Burlington Northern	1988	-11.20	-44.69	10.60	2.29	-108.38	7.59
California Microwave	1987	-52.70	-263.64	-6.42	-19.60	0	-1.50
Carolina Power & Light	1988	-9.40	-43.59	9.17	.36	-4.53	-1.82
Centocor	1986	-42.50	-1,214.29	77.27	7.51	-120.26	-42.20
Cerner	1988	-15.67	-12.50	21.73	2.25	0	-8.61
Cetus	1983	-14.30	55.56	27.05	.52	0	12.45
Cincinnati Gas & Electric	1985	-14.50	30.52	-8.65	-1.94	0	-9.32
Ciprico	1989	-71.00	-101.77	-5.17	-14.84	0	-33.00
Collaborative Research	1988	-13.00	43.75	30.51	8.56	0	0
Computer Identics	1986	-36.30	-1,246.67	-25.00	-18.06	-50.00	8.80
Cordis	1987	-22.60	-241.67	33.75	4.04	-222.22	243.14
Corporate Software	1989	-8.30	3.23	0	-1.40	0	0

Cross and Trecker	1987	-9.80	-755.56	5.69	-2.52	-32.45	-96.70
Cross and Trecker	1989	-11.60	-307.11	5.99	1.52	-47.53	28.22
Data Card	1981	-20.30	-8.57	13.73	-4.43	0	-4.77
Data General	1987	-14.20	-1,554.39	.50	-3.02	-76.31	-27.01
Datapoint	1982	-14.60	-87.23	13.13	-16.01	0	-2.70
Dennison Manufacturing	1989	-10.40	-22.83	6.79	-2.77	0	-5.95
Dravo	1987	-75.30	19.78	1.64	.28	-35.21	-11.56
Duplex Products	1983	-20.00	-2.22	-.32	-.93	0	-3.56
Duplex Products	1988	-17.30	-15.00	21.73	-6.68	0	-7.97
Eastman Kodak	1989	-15.80	-62.13	8.01	-3.10	-94.59	5.31
El Paso Electric	1982	-13.90	25.04	7.87	-7.20	0	-9.83
Eli Lilly	1987	-21.50	14.61	28.75	-1.00	0	7.94
Evans and Sutherland	1988	-9.20	-94.56	-2.99	-11.19	0	-138.03
Fair, Isaac	1989	-11.00	-13.04	10.48	-5.10	0	1.30
Flowers Industries	1989	-7.80	-28.67	6.10	-1.74	0	4.58
General DataComm	1988	-8.70	-2,400.00	-5.31	-6.50	-43.48	-61.90
General DataComm	1989	-7.90	51.09	2.55	3.28	-52.48	10.89
General Signal	1988	-11.10	-63.69	9.79	-1.72	-133.52	23.97
Geosources	1981	-14.40	42.58	35.59	1.97	0	3.07
Grace, W.R.	1986	-11.50	-528.54	4.85	-11.36	0	-58.50
HB Fuller	1989	-6.60	-25.59	9.99	-.65	0	7.16
Hercules	1988	-7.70	-88.86	4.05	-2.15	-27.85	-9.56
Hogan Systems	1984	-21.90	91.89	114.12	-4.80	-2.61	4.66
Honeywell	1988	-75.80	-271.42	6.88	-5.98	0	-154.78
House of Fabrics	1989	-13.00	7.62	4.81	-.07	0	-5.61
IBM	1986	-12.40	-27.27	2.40	-6.96	0	-.14

(continued)

Exhibit 2.7 *(continued)*

Company	Year	I/B/E/S Surprise	Change in Income from Continuing Operations	Change in Revenue	Change in Operating Profit Margin	Nonrecurring Items	Change in Effective Tax Rate
Internat. Kings Table	1986	-12.70	-6.67%	5.58%	-.90%	-13.43%	-.89%
Interstate Power	1987	-11.80	-38.96	-10.61	-2.18	0	4.96
Justin Industries	1986	-18.30	-66.89	-8.99	-5.03	46.67	-.77
Kellwood	1988	-9.40	18.97	22.03	.62	0	-1.74
KLLM Transport	1989	-10.25	-51.72	18.79	-2.83	0	-.54
Lamaur	1985	-12.40	-45.10	-.17	-3.66	0	-2.80
Lockheed	1989	-19.40	-98.69	-5.20	-6.17	0	91.20
Lone Star Technology	1989	-19.50	-359.20	2.27	-18.00	-22.37	-4.60
Louisiana Land & Ex.	1988	-12.30	-383.06	-12.32	-8.66	-84.54	-.34
McDonnell Douglas	1989	-12.27	-108.00	-5.51	-2.42	0	42.93
Medical Graphics	1987	-36.00	-466.67	-8.51	-22.66	0	-13.27
MNX	1988	-15.00	-38.46	-19.66	1.20	0	12.06
National Education	1989	-60.00	-163.99	-12.39	-18.08	-82.28	-17.54
New England Electric	1988	-12.10	-123.54	4.94	-4.67	-289.11	6.90
Norfolk Southern	1987	-11.50	-66.76	.89	.42	-138.60	-1.08
Northern Telecom	1988	-10.70	-47.24	10.03	-2.39	-85.14	-6.99
Oxford Industries	1987	-14.00	2.91	3.71	.14	0	2.84
Pacific Gas & Electric	1987	-13.50	-44.77	-8.07	-7.09	-.73	4.15
Pacific Gas & Electric	1989	-10.30	1,350.24	12.33	3.72	0	-44.51

	Year						
Park Ohio Industries	1985	−16.70	−66.67	−4.71	−3.07	0	−79.53
Park Ohio Industries	1988	−197.30	−10.53	7.08	−.43	0	−14.68
Petrolite	1986	−14.30	−22.32	−9.18	−2.42	0	−.50
Raymond	1987	−10.50	−92.86	−10.58	−11.45	0	−106.70
Scan Optics	1987	−14.30	−136.67	46.90	−24.74	0	7.10
Seven Oaks Int.	1988	−10.20	−148.21	10.34	−22.31	−235.29	−105.20
Stepan	1989	−8.30	−41.79	3.90	−2.89	0	−1.37
Sundstrand	1988	−33.10	−249.42	2.66	−7.69	0	−.59
TNP Enterprises	1986	−12.00	−7.06	−17.14	1.44	0	−.25
Transco Energy	1988	−12.80	6.57	−11.80	−.24	−57.09	30.06
United Industrial	1986	−21.70	−148.17	1.15	−4.10	−187.50	13.63
UTL	1987	−18.80	−119.61	−40.32	−39.15	−16.13	29.34
Warner-Lambert	1985	−179.80	−240.97	.71	.33	−260.04	−67.15
Whitehall	1987	−12.00	−390.91	−8.67	−7.02	−96.36	21.42
Xicor	1989	−13.80	−97.14	.11	−16.76	0	25.33
Zapata	1986	−20.10	−292.64	−23.87	−22.53	−53.94	−38.77
Samplewide mean		−25.27	−101.34%	8.27%	−4.79%	−48.08%	−4.42%

Exhibit 2.8   Analyst Forecast Data, Antron Corp., 1996

Analyst	EPS Forecast
A	$ 6.10
B	6.40
C	5.80
D	5.60
E	6.30
Mean of forecasts	$ 6.04
Standard deviation of forecasts	$.671863

trend-based earnings surprises results, the most analyst-based surprises occurred in 1989. This was a difficult, though nonrecession, year for the U.S. economy.

A breakdown of the number of firms reporting analyst-based earnings surprises for those industries with two or more representative firms is provided in Exhibit 2.10. Note that, again, the industry group with the greatest representation is the electric services industry (SIC 491 and 493). Over the period under review, there was a new level of volatility in the earnings of these firms. No particular year was overly represented by the electric service firms in the sample.

The computer and office equipment (SIC 357), drugs (SIC 283), computer and data-processing services (SIC 737), and electronic components (SIC 367) industries, which were prominently represented in the trend-based earnings surprise group, also caused problems for the analysts-based group. In none of these industries did any one year stand out, indicating that, as with general economic trends, industry trends did not fool analysts. Nor was the problem declining revenue, since the majority of the firms in these industries enjoyed increasing revenue during the period under review. With the exception of the drugs group, most firms in these industries suffered from

Exhibit 2.9   Analyst-Based Earnings Surprises by Economic Period, 1981–1989

Year	Economic Period	No. of Occurrences
1981	Recession	2
1982	Recession	3
1983	Growth	2
1984	Growth	4
1985	Growth	8
1986	Growth	12
1987	Growth	21
1988	Growth	23
1989	Growth	25
Total		100

Exhibit 2.10   Analyst-Based Earnings Surprises by Industry, 1981–1989

Industry	No. of Firms
Electric services	10
Computer and office equipment	9
Drugs	6
Communications equipment	5
Computer and data-processing services	5
Electronic components	5
Medical instruments and supplies	4
Crude petroleum and natural gas	3
Metalworking machinery	3
Trucking and courier services	3
Aircraft and parts	2
Blast furnace and basic steel products	2
Manifold business forms	2
Measuring and controlling devices	2
Miscellaneous converted paper products	2
Miscellaneous plastic products	2
Petroleum refining	2
Railroads	2
Research and testing services	2
Soap, cleaners, and toilet goods	2
Total	73

declining operating profit margins. In the computer and office equipment industry, declining operating profit margins were attributable to declining gross margins and increasing selling, general, and administrative expense as a percent of revenue. The electronic components firms also suffered from declining gross margins, but these firms were better able to control spending on selling, general, and administrative expense. In contrast, firms in the computer and data-processing services industry maintained gross margins but saw increased selling, general, and administrative expense as a percent of revenue. While firms in the drugs industry were able to maintain operating profit margins, the primary factor present in the earnings surprise years for these firms was nonrecurring items.

It should be noted that as we review available data, we can only surmise why analysts were surprised. By contrasting each firm's actual results in the surprise year with that of the prior year, we can identify what appears to have been the problem for analysts. We cannot know for certain, however, how they formed their expectations or why they were surprised.

Also represented on the analyst-based surprise list were the communications equipment (SIC 366) and medical instruments and supplies (SIC 384) industries. The only time period concentration noted for either of these industries was in the medical instruments and supplies group of firms. Of the four analyst-based earnings surprises noted in this industry, three occurred during 1987. It is difficult to say what it was about 1987 that explains the high concentration of analyst-based earnings surprises in the medical instruments and supplies industry. However, given the prominent representation of that year and the fact that no single firm-specific factor seems to stand out in our data, an industrywide event that fooled the analysts cannot be ruled out in this instance.

In the communications equipment industry, no single year stands out. Apparently, analysts may have been surprised by declining revenue, which occurred at three of the five firms, and declining operating profit margins caused by both declining gross margins and increasing selling, general, and administrative expense.

Firm-Specific Factors

While there were a few exceptions, most of the surprises noted in Exhibit 2.7 appear to be the result of firm-specific factors, not macro-factors. While we cannot be certain about what specific factors caused the analysts to be surprised, we can surmise based on descriptive statistics from available data.

Neither changing revenue nor effective tax rate would appear to explain the analyst-based surprises observed. In reviewing Exhibit 2.7, it can be seen that 68 of 100 firms actually saw revenue increase in the earnings surprise year. The average firm enjoyed an increase in revenue of 8.27% in the earnings surprise year. This measure is comparable to the 7.77% increase experienced by the trend-based surprise firms. Less comparable with the trend-based firms is the change in effective tax rate. The trend-based firms experienced a mean decrease of 7.33% in effective tax rate in the earnings surprise year. The sample was split evenly between firms experiencing a decrease and those experiencing an increase. In the analyst-based sample, there was a mean increase in effective tax rate of 4.42%. Given this relatively small increase in effective tax rate and the fact that only 56 of the 100 analyst-based firms saw their effective tax rate increase in the earnings surprise year, changing tax rate would not appear to be the reason for the sizable earnings surprises noted in the sample.

In examining Exhibit 2.7, declining operating profit margins and nonrecurring items appear to be the primary factors explaining the sizable analyst-based earnings surprises reported. These factors were also primary in explaining the trend-based surprises.

Operating Profit Margins

As seen in Exhibit 2.7, operating profit margins declined by an average of 4.79% of revenue in the earnings surprise year. Seventy-three of 100 firms experienced declines in operating profit. Consistent with the trend-based surprises, declines in gross margin followed by increases in selling, general, and administrative expense as a percent of revenue were the primary reasons for the declines in operating profit margins. Research and development expense as a percent of revenue increased for 23 of the 34 companies reporting research and development expense. The increase was only marginal, however. Accordingly, attention here is focused on what managements see as the reasons for changes in gross margin and selling, general, and administrative expense.

A total of 58 of the 73 firms in Exhibit 2.7 that reported declines in operating profit margins also reported declines in gross margins. Exhibit 2.11 reports the factors noted in MD&A for the 57 instances where clear reasons were provided.

Many of the same factors that explained declines in gross margin for the trend-based firms also helped to explain declines for the analyst-based firms. Especially important here were general cost increases, a changing product mix, declining revenue volume, and lower gross margins of acquired companies.

Fifty-six of the 73 firms in Exhibit 2.7 that reported declines in operating profit margins also reported increases in selling, general, and administrative expense as a percent of revenue. The results of a review of MD&A where 30 clear reasons were identified are provided in Exhibit 2.12.

In reviewing the exhibit, it is clear that increased marketing and advertising was the primary reason for the increase noted in selling, general, and administrative expense as a percent of revenue. This was also the case for the trend-based firms. While revenue increased for both groups of firms, marketing and advertising costs increased at a faster rate. Increased spending on administrative activities was important, but a distant second.

Nonrecurring Items

In the analyst-based surprise group, nonrecurring items were important in helping to explain the earnings surprises observed. Forty-one of 100 analyst-based firms reported nonrecurring items. This is high, given the previously described I/B/E/S practice of

Exhibit 2.11   Analyst-Based Earnings Surprises: Factors Contributing to Declines in Gross Margin, 1981–1989

Factor	No. of Instances
Increased costs associated with general cost increases	14
Changing product mix to products with lower gross margins	11
Excess capacity due to declining revenue volume	9
Lower gross margin of acquired company	8
Decreased revenue due to lower selling prices	6
Increased costs associated with quality improvement	3
Capacity expansion to meet anticipated increases in revenue volume	2
Increased costs associated with new product development	2
Unfavorable foreign currency movements	2
Total	57

Exhibit 2.12   Analyst-Based Earnings Surprises: Factors Contributing to Increases in Selling, General, and Administrative Expense as a Percent of Revenue, 1981–1989

Factor	No. of Instances
Increased marketing and advertising expense	16
Increased administrative and miscellaneous expense	7
Increased customer service expense	3
Unfavorable foreign currency movements	2
Increased expense of acquired company	2
Total	30

adjusting analyst forecast data to remove separately disclosed nonrecurring items. However, recall that our definition of nonrecurring items was broadened to include many items that firms typically do not disclose separately. Items such as inventory write-downs, which might be included in cost of sales, or special provisions for uncollectible accounts receivable, on-going litigation, or stock option compensation, which might be included with selling, general, and administrative expense, may not have been identified as nonrecurring items by reporting companies. As a result, they would not have been adjusted for by I/B/E/S. Other examples might include foreign currency losses or even a sudden, nonrecurring increase in an operating expense. In addition, it is also possible that nonrecurring items were disclosed and adjusted for by I/B/E/S, but that the earnings surprises noted were due to other, unrelated factors. We can only say whether nonrecurring items were present in earnings surprise years, not whether those items actually caused the earnings surprises noted.

The primary nonrecurring items reported in the financial statements of the analyst-based earnings surprise firms are detailed in Exhibit 2.13. Asset write-downs, including property, plant, and equipment and intangible assets, inventory, investments, and accounts receivable were prominent among the nonrecurring items noted. The following disclosure provided by Bolt, Beranek & Newman, Inc., is representative:

> Cost of products and services as a percentage of revenue increased to 76.4% in 1989 from 60.9% in 1988. This increase is primarily due to $16 million in write-downs of inventory and related assets, reflecting lower than anticipated sales of certain communications and parallel-processing hardware.[21]

Also important were restructuring charges. For example, the Eastman Kodak Co. described a restructuring charge it took in 1989 as follows:

> Operating earnings for all segments were adversely affected by $875 million of restructuring costs, primarily for the write-off of inventories, capital and other assets, and the provision for separation costs for employees leaving the company. These restructuring costs were incurred as a result of actions taken by the company to sharpen its focus by restructuring or withdrawing from businesses and activities

Exhibit 2.13 Analyst-Based Earnings Surprises: Nonrecurring Items, 1981–1989

Nonrecurring Item	No. of Instances
Write-down of PP&E and intangible assets	14
Restructuring events	13
Write-down of inventory	5
Other nonrecurring events	4
Write-down of investments	3
Contract termination	2
Litigation	2
Write-down of accounts receivable	2
Work force reduction	2
Total	47

Note: The total number of nonrecurring items (47) exceeds the number of firms reporting nonrecurring items (41) because some firms reported more than one item.

that are not critical to the achievement of its business strategies or do not contribute to shareowner value. The company expects that these actions will favorably affect future results of operations and cash flow.[22]

In 1988, Arvin Industries, Inc., recorded a $28.7 million restructuring charge. The expense was described as follows:

In March 1988, the company announced a plan to restructure its automotive parts businesses. The restructuring is aimed at consolidating the Arvin and Maremont exhaust businesses and enhancing the company's overall competitive characteristics by eliminating certain redundancies through the integration of the manufacturing, distribution, and marketing operations of both.[23]

Finally, the other nonrecurring charges category consists of moving expenses, merger-related expenses, and lease termination costs. Also included in this category is the following item disclosed in the financial statements of Hercules, Inc.:

In addition to gross margin factors, 1988 and 1987 profit from operations were significantly affected by nonrecurring operating costs which include . . . environmental cleanup costs for a previously owned idle facility.[24]

SUMMARY

Most of the earnings surprise examples given individual attention in this book were first identified in the financial press. These surprises were more significant in amount and tended to carry a greater surprise effect. The financial early warnings included here, however, were developed not only from the earnings surprises that surfaced in the financial press but also from our own comparison of actual results with trend-based and analyst-based expectations. By developing our early warnings from such different sources, we were more confident that important factors would not be omitted.

The premise employed here is that early warnings of incipient earnings difficulties can be developed using firm-specific variables derived from a subject company's financial statements. In reviewing the earnings surprises of a sample of 200 firms, we noted a greater presence of certain firm-specific factors than macro-factors. This is not to say that macro-factors are not important in predicting earnings surprises well in advance of their occurrence. Such a statement would defy common sense. Indeed, in some instances, developing economic or industry trends may be the only available early warning. Rather, it is our position that firm-specific factors, developed from company-provided financial statements, can in most instances provide warnings of earnings surprises that are more focused on developments at individual firms than those derived from macro-factors.

Among the firm-specific factors examined in our review of the income statements and MD&A of 200 trend-based and analyst-based earnings surprise firms, declines in operating profit margins and nonrecurring items were particularly important. Thus, in subsequent chapters, we strive to ensure that predictors of such developments are included in our set of early warnings.

REFERENCES

Afterman, A. *SEC Regulation of Public Companies* (Englewood Cliffs, N.J.: Prentice Hall, 1995).

Briloff, A. *More Debits Than Credits* (New York: Harper & Row, 1976).

———. *Unaccountable Accounting: Games Accountants Play* (New York: Harper & Row, 1972).

Commerce Clearing House. *SEC Accounting Guide* (New York: Commerce Clearing House, 1989).

Schilit, H. *Financial Shenanigans: How to Detect Accounting Gimmicks & Fraud in Financial Reports* (New York: McGraw-Hill, 1993).

Thornhill, W. *Forensic Accounting: How to Investigate Financial Fraud* (New York: Irwin Professional Publishing, 1995).

ENDNOTES

1. *The Wall Street Journal*, February 16, 1994, p. C6.
2. It is our understanding from discussions with personnel at I/B/E/S, the source of our analyst forecasts, that steps are taken to remove differences between actual results and forecasts for separately reported nonrecurring items, including the effects of prior-year errors.
3. Leslie Fay Companies, Inc., announcement, February 1, 1993.
4. The Topps Co., Inc., press release, January 25, 1993.

5. Bankers Trust New York Corp., press release, January 19, 1995. While a charge to the allowance for credit losses would not entail an immediate reduction in earnings, it would reduce earnings when the allowance is subsequently increased to desired levels.

6. *The Wall Street Journal*, January 4, 1995, p. A8.

7. Compustat Services, Inc. (New York: Standard & Poor's Corp., 1993).

8. Note that a standardized measure of the negative deviation from forecast was used. This measure was calculated by taking the difference between actual results and mean forecast for each firm for which at least two forecasts were available and dividing by the standard deviation of the forecasts composing the mean. By using such a standardized measure, the confounding effects of large disagreements among analysts were controlled for. As a result, the calculated deviations served as meaningful earnings surprises.

9. While measures of gross margin, selling, general, and administrative expense, and research and development expense were analyzed separately, for brevity, only changes in the summary operating profit margin are reported in Exhibit 2.1.

10. We used judgment in deciding when expenses were significantly higher than in prior years. At a minimum, an expense had to increase over 10% of pre-tax income.

11. Recessions are defined here as periods during which real gross domestic product declines.

12. Pharmaceutical Resources, Inc., Form 10K annual report to Securities and Exchange Commission, September 1991.

13. Caere Corp., annual report, December 1993.

14. Greentree Software, Inc., annual report, May 1989.

15. Wilcox and Gibbs, Inc., annual report, December 1991, and Wackenhut Corp., annual report, December 1984.

16. Lancer Orthodontics, Inc., annual report, August 1990, p. 12. Lancer's MD&A refers to performance in 1989 as compared with 1988.

17. Oakwood Homes Corp., annual report, September 1987.

18. Syntex Corp., annual report, July 1993, p. 27.

19. United States Surgical Corp., annual report, December 1993, pp. 6–7.

20. The Southern Company, annual report, December 1987.

21. Bolt, Beranek & Newman, Inc., annual report, June 1989, p. 19.

22. Eastman Kodak Co., Inc., annual report, December 1989, p. 33.

23. Arvin Industries, Inc., annual report, December 1988, p. 18.

24. Hercules, Inc., annual report, December 1988, p. 43.

Chapter 3
Causative Factors

California Micro Devices Corp. said an internal audit has found "widespread" accounting irregularities that inflated reported earnings for the fiscal year ended June 30 by as much as $25 million.

The company said the findings will prompt restatements and write-downs that will result in the company posting a net loss of $12 million to $20 million for fiscal 1994. California Micro originally reported net income of $5 million, or 62 cents a share.[1]

In reviewing examples of earnings surprises, both from the financial press and from a comparison of actual results with expectations, we noted three general types of causative factors: (1) changing economic fundamentals, (2) aggressive application of accounting principles, and (3) fraudulent financial reporting. This classification scheme was based on the extent to which there was active manipulation of reported results by management in the years preceding the earnings surprise. If there was no such manipulation, indicating that earnings fell below expectations solely because of business and economic developments, the surprise was attributed to the first type of factor, changing economic fundamentals. If results in preceding years were manipulated, but that manipulation was not so egregious or willful as to reveal fraudulent intent, it was classified in the second category, aggressive application of accounting principles. Even proper application of accounting principles leaves much room for judgment and the reporting of different results in similar circumstances. Within the boundaries of what is acceptable accounting practice, earnings can be manipulated, or "managed," as these steps are more typically described, and adjusted to shed a more positive light on a company's performance. Unfavorable business and economic developments may also contribute to the earnings surprise.

When earnings in previous years were manipulated to the extent that fraudulent intent was attributable to the actions, we assigned the resulting earnings surprise to the third type of factor, fraudulent financial reporting. The California Micro Devices example can be classified in this category. Here again, changing economic fundamentals may also be present. Such surprises may also include losses due to asset defalcations on the part of management.

We found this classification scheme helpful for understanding why companies report results below expectations. With a better understanding of the causes of earnings surprises, we were able to devise early warnings that should be more effective in detecting them. Interestingly, we were able to use the same early warnings in anticipating earnings surprises caused by all three types of causative factors. The only real difference was in how each earnings surprise was reported in the companies' financial statements. For example, in some cases involving changing economic fundamentals, earnings surprises were reported with asset write-downs and special liability accruals, known as nonrecurring items. The same could be said for aggressive accounting that stayed within the boundaries of generally accepted accounting practices. But when aggressive accounting was found to fall outside those boundaries, whether or not with fraudulent intent, a restatement of affected years was needed. Such a restatement entailed changing prior-year results to remove any amounts that were, in hindsight, found to be outside accepted practice. More development of these factors, their causes, and the manner in which they are reported in financial statements are discussed in this chapter.

CHANGING ECONOMIC FUNDAMENTALS

Earnings surprises caused by changing economic fundamentals were the broadest and affected the largest number of firms in our study. Included in this category are the factors contributing to the majority of the trend-based and analyst-based earnings surprises discussed in Chapter 2.

The changing economic fundamentals category can include any number of events, from a decline in demand for a company's product or service to a general weakening in the credit quality of a company's customers and an accompanying decline in the collectibility of its receivables. It can also include the results of poor management decision making that affects corporate performance.

Urcarco, Inc., was a company that ran a chain of used car retail sales lots and also provided credit to customers who were unable to obtain traditional car financing. The company grew rapidly, and in its fiscal year ended June 1990, Urcarco reported sales and net income, respectively, of $150,417,000 and $15,802,000, up from $8,428,000 and $248,000 in 1988. However, the recession that developed in 1990 and continued into 1991 hit the company's customers very hard. Helped by sales early in the year, the company reported revenue of $155,924,000 in the fiscal year ended June 1991. But as the recession took hold, the company's customers were unable to service their outstanding loans. They defaulted on their car notes, causing the company to make a special provision for uncollectible receivables. Net income declined dramatically that year and became a loss of $47,226,000. Thus, the year ended June 1991, which broke a trend in earnings growth that had been established with the company's inception in 1987, can be viewed as an earnings surprise year. In this case, the earnings surprise was caused by a change in economic fundamentals.[2]

In its fiscal year ended August 1991, Machine Technology, Inc., a maker of semiconductor manufacturing equipment, reported sales and net income, respectively, of $30,996,000 and $3,335,000. However, in a press release dated March 24, 1992, the company provided the following insight:

> Machine Technology said the rate of incoming orders has continued to decline due to the continued weakness in the semiconductor processing equipment market and in the overall economy. Gary Hillman, president, said that because of this "regaining positive operating results during the balance of the fiscal year is unlikely."[3]

For the year ended August 1992, the company reported revenue of $21,119,000 and a net loss of $3,672,000, the first loss in several years. This, too, is an example of a change in economic fundamentals causing an earnings surprise. Of course, whether investors and creditors were surprised by the developments depends on the extent to which they were aware of economic developments affecting the company.

A listing of economic fundamentals noted in the review of financial statements of firms reporting earnings surprises is provided in Exhibit 3.1. Among the economic fundamentals listed are factors, such as declining revenue and increasing effective tax rate, that were not noted to be key among the trend-based and analyst-based earnings surprises reviewed earlier. We included them because they were noted to be the primary cause of at least a subset of the earnings surprises studied. Moreover,

Exhibit 3.1   Changing Economic Fundamentals and Earnings Surprises

---

Resulting in a decline in sales or service revenue
Decreased physical volume of sales or service activity
Decreased prices for sales or services
Increased sales returns

Resulting in a decline in gross margin on sales or service
Capacity expansion to meet anticipated increases in revenue volume
Changing product mix to products with lower gross margins
Decreased revenue due to lower selling prices
Excess capacity due to declining revenue volume
Increased costs associated with general cost increases
Increased costs associated with new product development
Increased costs associated with quality improvement
Unfavorable foreign currency movements
Lower gross margin of acquired company

Resulting in an increase in selling, general, and administrative expense as a percent of revenue
Costs of expansion ahead of sales growth
Decreased revenue due to lower volume or prices
Increased administrative and miscellaneous expense
Increased customer service expense

Exhibit 3.1 *(continued)*

Increased expense of acquired company
Increased legal expense
Increased marketing and advertising expense
Unfavorable foreign currency movements

Resulting in an increase in research and development expense as a percent of revenue
Declining revenue due to lower volume or prices
Increased research and development activities
In-process research and development acquired from another company and written off
at acquisition

Resulting in an increase in interest expense
Increased borrowing
Increased interest rates on variable-rate notes
Reduction in capitalized interest

Resulting in an increase in the effective tax rate
Expiration of loss and tax credit carryforwards
Higher proportion of expenses that are not tax-deductible
Increase in deferred tax asset valuation allowance
Increase in tax rate
Loss of tax credits
Loss of foreign tax advantages

Resulting in a nonrecurring charge against income from continuing operations
Write-down of accounts receivable
  Reduced collectibility
Write-down of inventory
  General value impairment
  Slow-moving or obsolete
Write-down of investments
  Decreased market value, recovery not expected
Write-down of property, plant, and equipment and intangible assets
  General value impairment
  Increased obsolescence
Restructuring events
  Plant consolidations
  Work force reductions
Other nonrecurring events
  Contract termination
  Environmental costs
  Increased warranty claims
  Product transition/termination
  Lease termination
  Litigation
  Mergers
  Moving
  Realization of contingent obligations
  Unfavorable foreign currency movements

they were present in other surprises highlighted by the financial press. While we strived to make the list as complete as possible, it should not be viewed as all-inclusive but rather as a reasonably representative list of such factors.

Some of the factors may result in negative earnings surprises for the year in question but have positive implications for the company's earning power in future years. Included in this category are research and development expense as a percent of revenue and restructuring events. To the extent that they yield marketable discoveries, increased research and development expenditures should serve to increase earnings in future years. Similarly, because a corporate restructuring can help reduce inefficiencies, future earnings may also benefit. Also included in this category would be, for example, a decline in gross margin attributed to an expansion in plant capacity designed to meet an anticipated increase in sales. When higher sales materialize, gross margin should improve.

One can argue that the underlying economic causes are more fundamental than the factors listed in the exhibit. For example, a decline in revenue volume may not be the real culprit; rather, a recession or a general change in tastes or demand may be at fault. It may not be selling, general, and administrative expense that increases faster than revenue, but rather the need to boost marketing expenses to offset soft demand, may be the ultimate problem. However, for our purposes, the analysis is best confined to the set of firm-specific explanations provided. Any number of underlying factors could have caused the observed changes in economic fundamentals listed in Exhibit 3.1. It is not, however, those real economic factors we are interested in as financial early warnings are developed, but rather company developments using disclosures provided in company reports.

In 1993, United States Surgical Corp. experienced an earnings surprise as net sales decreased 13%, gross margin decreased from 60% to 50%, and selling, general, and administrative expense increased from 39% to 43% of net sales. The company provided the following explanation:

> Sales in 1993 decreased compared to the prior year for the first time in the company's history. The company's principal competitor has made a major effort to gain market share through discount pricing, and a number of hospitals have asked their surgeons to evaluate competitors' products. Although surgeon support is strong for the company's products, sales revenue is lost during the time of the evaluation. . . . The increase in cost of sales percentage . . . resulted from higher per unit indirect production costs due to lower production volume and lower margins realized on sales through the JIT ["just-in-time"] program. . . . Selling, administrative, and general expense expressed as a percentage of sales was 43% in 1993. . . . The percentage increase . . . resulted primarily from higher depreciation and amortization charges related to the company's facilities expansion.[4]

With this discussion, the company identified the underlying economic changes that caused it to report a loss for the first time in several years. These underlying factors caused the changes in the income statement that resulted in the loss. As noted, our objective is to forecast the income statement changes regardless of what caused them.

Although, in some of the cases we review, knowledge of developing changes in the economy was helpful in judging the sustainability of reported results, references to macro-factors in this book will be the exception and not the rule.

Another way to consider the factors that are included in this economic fundamentals category is to note that this is the only category, of the three types of causative factors highlighted, that does not involve in some way the active manipulation of accounting results in years preceding the earnings surprise. In both the aggressive application of accounting principles and fraudulent financial reporting categories, management took active steps to improve reported results. Earnings surprises occur when actual results do not live up to expectations built on artificially overstated earnings. In the economic fundamentals category, though, generally no such active manipulation took place. Prior-year results are not fabricated, and the surprise is based solely on declines in fundamentals.

The financial impacts of changing economic fundamentals are accounted for as they affect results. Earnings decline as revenue drops and/or expenses increase. There is no restatement of prior-year earnings. For example, IPL Systems, Inc., experienced an earnings surprise in 1993 as sales dropped 26% and the company was unable to effect a similar reduction in cost of sales and selling, general, and administrative expense.[5] The effect of these developments, attributed by the company to competitive pricing, was reported in the year they occurred.

Very typical of earnings surprises in the economic fundamentals category are those involving nonrecurring items—special provisions or expenses such as restructuring charges, asset write-downs, or special liability accruals. In early 1993, Home Nutritional Services, Inc., made the following announcement:

> During the latter part of 1992, further changes in the reimbursement patterns of indemnity insurance carriers required an additional charge for doubtful accounts of $6.7 million after-tax. Many of the indemnity carriers either arbitrarily took discounts from our list prices or demanded discounts through case management. In many instances, discounts were even taken on invoices for services rendered in 1991. Despite our firm resistance to these pressures through threatened and actual litigation, we found our rates of collection for these types of accounts decreased to the point that additional reserves against our accounts receivable were considered necessary.[6]

What the company was saying was that the insurance companies it billed for covered health services began taking a very hard line regarding payment. As a result, the collectibility of amounts due the company and reported as accounts receivable became questionable. The company took a special charge, an expense, of $6.7 million after-tax to reduce the reported amount of accounts receivable to be more consistent with amounts likely to be collected.

Another example of a special provision is provided by Tektronix, Inc. Charged against the company's earnings in 1990 was a restructuring charge of $80 million. This charge was described in the notes to its 1991 financial statements as follows:

In 1990, the company provided for restructuring charges of $80.0 million for costs associated with downsizing of operations, consolidating facilities and the disposal, either through sale or abandonment, of certain product lines. The charges included severance costs, commitments to third parties, product line disposal costs, write-off of intangible assets, and relocation costs. A $0.6 million credit was recognized in 1991 as a further result of these restructuring activities.[7]

Here Tektronix described a one-time special expense reflecting the costs of downsizing operations, consolidating facilities, and disposing of certain product lines. Included in the charge are special liabilities for severance costs and other commitments to be paid in the future as well as the costs of disposing of product lines and the write-off of certain assets.

Of the three types of factors causing earnings surprises, changing economic fundamentals is arguably the most difficult to forecast using prior-year and prior-quarter company financial statements. This is especially true when the surprise does not involve a special provision or expense. As discussed in subsequent chapters, there are early warnings to help forecast the earnings effects of changing fundamentals that do not involve special charges. They are less reliable, however, than warnings preceding special income statement provisions or expenses to account for such items as restructuring charges, asset write-downs, or special liability accruals. They are also less reliable than early warnings used to predict when results are being affected by active earnings manipulation.

Before proceeding to the next category, we note that we specifically excluded from our discussion of earnings surprises those caused by acts of nature. The successful forecasting of fires, floods, earthquakes, and other natural disasters is clearly beyond the scope of what can be expected from the information available in corporate annual reports. However, we point out that insufficient insurance against such events sends a clear message that future losses may be incurred.

AGGRESSIVE APPLICATION OF ACCOUNTING PRINCIPLES

As noted, the application of generally accepted accounting principles leaves much room for judgment and the reporting of different results in similar circumstances. Consider the following amortization policies for goodwill taken from the footnotes of the 1993 annual reports of four medical instruments companies.

From the annual report of Biomet, Inc.:

Excess acquisition costs over fair value of acquired net assets (goodwill) are amortized using the straight-line method over periods ranging from eight to ten years.[8]

From the annual report of Diagnostic Products, Inc.:

The excess of cost over net assets acquired is being amortized over 20 years using the straight-line method.[9]

From the annual report of Allergan, Inc.:

Goodwill represents the excess of acquisition costs over the fair value of net assets of purchased businesses and is being amortized on a straight-line basis over periods from ten to thirty years.[10]

From the annual report of Healthdyne, Inc.:

The excess of cost over net assets of businesses acquired is being amortized using the straight-line method over periods of up to 40 years.[11]

All four companies, sharing the same general industrial group, have chosen different amortization periods over which to expense goodwill. The periods range from as short as 8 years to as long as 40 years. Generally accepted accounting principles require amortization of goodwill, but permit companies to choose their amortization period. The only stipulation is that the amortization period cannot exceed 40 years. The longer the amortization period, the lower the annual charge or expense. As a result, different companies can report different earnings for no other reason than a difference in the period of amortization. While most companies choose 40 years, that choice is not unanimous.

As another example, consider the accounting principles guiding the capitalization of software development costs. Generally accepted accounting principles stipulate that the costs of developing software are to be expensed as research and development costs until the software project reaches technological feasibility, basically when it is known that it will meet its design specifications. Once the project reaches technological feasibility, the costs of developing software are to be capitalized, or reported as an asset, and amortized to expense over time. Like the amortization period for goodwill, this definition is quite broad and leaves much to management judgment. As might be expected, in applying this principle, companies capitalize varying amounts of software development costs. In turn, earnings are materially affected. In 1993, Microsoft Corp. expensed all of its software development costs. That same year, System Software Associates, Inc., capitalized 38% of its software development costs, and American Software, Inc., capitalized 63% of its software development costs. As a point of reference, had American Software followed Microsoft's policy, its earnings in 1993 would have been reduced by 57%.[12]

The accounting policies for goodwill and software development costs are only two examples of the judgment calls available to management in compiling financial results. There are many more. One might question why financial results should be open to management judgment in this way. Should not all companies account for transactions in the same way? The appropriate response to this question is that all transactions really are not the same. Conditions and circumstances differ. Consider the goodwill example. Goodwill arises in an acquisition when management pays more than the fair market value for the net assets, assets less liabilities, of the company acquired. The acquired company is worth more than the sum of its parts. This goodwill may represent a recognized brand name or a distribution network.

The acquiring company anticipates earning above-average returns from the acquisition over some future period. In choosing an appropriate amortization period for this goodwill, management is to choose that period over which they anticipate earning these above-average returns. Not all acquired companies provide above-average returns over the same periods. Thus, differences in amortization periods result. A similar point can be made for software development. Different projects will meet their design specifications at different points in the development process. Requiring all companies to expense all their software development costs, or requiring all companies to capitalize 50% or 100%, would not be a step toward more meaningful financial reporting.

In the majority of cases, managements must use judgment to provide investors and creditors with a fair presentation of their results and financial position. They do not use the judgment calls available to them to consistently improve their results. However, there are exceptions. Some managements use these judgment calls to consistently make their firms look better. For years, Chambers Development Co., Inc., a solid waste management firm and developer of landfills, capitalized the costs of developing new landfills. These costs, including executive salaries for time spent on the projects, public relations, travel and legal expenses as well as interest incurred on monies borrowed during development periods, were reported as assets. Accounting principles permit capitalization of such costs when future periods clearly benefit. In this case, whether future periods clearly benefited could be questioned. The company was taking an aggressive stance that contrasted with its competitors. These competitors, such as WMX Technologies, Inc., and Browning-Ferris Industries, Inc., expensed these same costs when incurred. In 1992, Chambers Development was forced to reverse its position and expense these costs when the company's auditors decided that the capitalization policy had gone too far. Prior-year results were restated for consistency with this new policy. However, the damage, in the form of a dramatic loss of shareholder value, had been done. For years Chambers Development reported higher earnings and a stronger balance sheet that did not result from better fundamental performance but rather from an aggressive application of accounting principles.

Another case involves a financial firm, Presidential Life Corp. Presidential Life had been reporting its junk bond portfolio at cost even though the market value of its securities had declined and the company was holding a significant paper loss. At the time, accounting principles permitted firms to report investments in debt securities at cost when declines in market value were considered to be only temporary. Presidential Life took the position that the market value of its portfolio was impaired on a temporary basis only, avoiding a write-down and charge to earnings. This was an aggressive stance, stretching its interpretation of a permitted accounting rule to its own benefit. In 1993 the Securities and Exchange Commission forced the company to restate its results for 1991, 1990, and 1989, reducing its portfolio to market value and showing the effect on earnings.

As these examples show, the aggressive application of accounting principles can be used by management to shed a positive light on reported financial performance and position. Earnings are reported at amounts that overstate actual performance. To the extent that these earnings are used to form expectations of future results, investors and creditors are set up for an unpleasant surprise when the charade is discovered. The catalyst for discovery may be adverse fundamentals that make it clear to all that amortization periods were too long, or that amounts capitalized would not be realized, or that the decline in the market value of an investment was not a temporary phenomenon. Or the catalyst may be an outside agent like the company's auditors or a regulator like the Securities and Exchange Commission. Regardless of the catalyst, the result is an earnings surprise: current-year earnings do not live up to expectations built on prior-year results.

We are defining the aggressive application of accounting principles as falling short of a deliberate intent to defraud. In many cases, though, revising results that are due to the aggressive application of accounting principles and adjusting for the effects of a fraud are the same. Prior-year financial statements must be restated, removing the misleading amounts. However, while virtually all financial frauds involve the restatement of incorrect prior-year results, not all examples of aggressive accounting end in restatement. It is a matter of degree. When accounting principles have been applied in such an aggressive fashion that prior-year results are considered in error, a restatement is called for. Generally accepted accounting principles clearly call for a restatement when an error is committed. This is true whether or not the error was intentional. The discovery that in a prior year fixed assets had been inadvertently depreciated by an incorrect amount would call for restatement of earnings for that prior year.

Unlike frauds, some examples of the aggressive application of accounting principles do not go far enough to imply that prior-year results were incorrectly stated. Financial statements are a collection of estimates. If in future years it is determined that an amortization period was too long, that amortization period should be changed and taken into account with increased amortization over the asset's remaining useful life. This is a change in estimate and does not involve an error or restatement of prior years. Often, though, the aggressive application of accounting principles, when not considered to be in error, results in immediate charges to current-year earnings. Such charges are taken in an effort to catch up and typically take place when it becomes clear that on the balance sheet an asset is overvalued or a liability is undervalued. These adjustments are still viewed in the context of changes in estimate and do not entail the correction of an error.

In its 1989 annual report, Vista Resources, Inc., provided the following description of its amortization policy for goodwill:

Excess of cost over net assets of businesses acquired: For businesses acquired prior to 1971 the excess of cost over net assets ($1,744,075) is not amortized or written down except to the extent that in the opinion of management there has been a decrease in value.[13]

The company reported this goodwill in the amount of $1,744,075 on its balance sheet as an asset that was not being expensed over time. Generally accepted accounting principles permitted such practice for goodwill acquired prior to 1971.[14] In its 1990 annual report, Vista Resources provided the following disclosure:

> In 1990, the excess of cost over net assets of businesses acquired in the amount of $1,744,075 was written off because, in the opinion of management, such excess cost no longer has value.[15]

Here the company changed its opinion about the realizability of its investment in goodwill. When that happened, an immediate charge to earnings was taken, helping to push the company into a loss for the year. The asset was now viewed as being overvalued, necessitating a write-down. It is difficult to accept the premise that the goodwill became overvalued in one year. More likely, it declined over an extended period. By failing to amortize it, the company was taking an aggressive position, though one permitted by generally accepted accounting practices, and seeking to report earnings and financial position in as positive a light as possible. When sufficient evidence mounted indicating that the goodwill was no longer worth the amount at which it was reported, it was written off. An investor or creditor, unaware that the company was taking such an aggressive stance, would have been surprised by this development.[16]

In many cases, it is difficult to determine if a special charge against earnings is due to changing economic fundamentals or to the aggressive application of accounting principles. It may be due to a combination of the two. In its 1990 annual report, Bassett Furniture Industries, Inc., made the following disclosure:

> In the first quarter of 1990, the company recorded a provision for restructuring charges of $14.3 million ($11.2 million net of tax, or $1.38 per share).
>
> The restructuring plan was designed to bring the Casegood Division's plant capacity in line with market demands and to lower inventory positions in order to improve its competitive positioning, asset utilization, and work force efficiency.
>
> The provision for restructuring charges included primarily the costs to phase out the oldest Casegood plant, eliminate marginal suites, and write off related unproductive assets.[17]

A component of the company's restructuring charge was to write off unproductive assets. These assets likely did not become unproductive within one year. Rather, this was probably the result of changing economic fundamentals over several years. A better measure of income in prior years could have been provided by writing these assets down over time as they became less productive. By not doing so, one could argue, the company was aggressive in its application of accounting principles. However, applying such a standard in a situation like this would have been impractical. Instead, the company waited until it was clear the assets were unproductive and wrote them off that year, much like a change in estimate.

It would not be fruitful for us to so refine our classification of the factors causing earnings surprises that we attempted to identify whether a special provision was due to changing economic fundamentals or aggressive application of accounting principles. If in hindsight management has not actively adjusted its financial statements to incorporate changing valuations as they occur, then it can be said that it has been somewhat aggressive in its application of accounting principles. But to say so does not serve any useful purpose. The end result is the same, an unexpected charge against earnings. We seek to present early warnings of these charges, regardless of whether they resulted from changing economic fundamentals or from the aggressive application of accounting principles. And these warning signs are very much the same.

FRAUDULENT FINANCIAL REPORTING

Fraudulent financial reporting was identified as the cause of an earnings surprise when fraudulent intent was clearly involved in misreported prior-year results. Here, expectations are based on earnings of previous years that are fictitious and overstated. Changing economic fundamentals may also play a role in causing the earnings surprise, but fraudulently overstated results are the primary culprit.

Consider the case of Leslie Fay Companies, Inc. In 1992 the dressmaker saw its sales sagging because of high prices and out-of-date styles. To counter these difficulties, the company gave its buyers mark-down money in the form of merchandise discounts and ultimately cut prices 20%. However, it also fraudulently overstated the number of garments produced. This enabled the company to reduce its cost of sales by leaving a higher proportion of production costs in inventory. In this way, the company was able to maintain profit margins even as sales prices and revenue declined. While changing fundamentals may have caused the company to resort to fraudulent reporting, the real surprise occurred when investors and creditors learned that earlier results had been fabricated. A significant loss was reported as fictitious prior-year results were corrected.

Another example is that of Sequoia Systems, Inc., a manufacturer of fault-tolerant computer systems. This company fraudulently overstated fiscal 1991 revenue by 8% and net income by 60%. These actions were taken when revenue began to fall below plan. Among the actions perpetrated was the shipment of systems against canceled purchase orders. In so doing, it was able to record nonexistent revenue and accounts receivable.

Some cases of fraud involve asset defalcations on the part of management as well as fraudulent financial reporting. Consider, for example, the case of ZZZZ Best, Inc., a carpet cleaning and restoration firm. This company's results were fabricated almost from the start. In his book, Mark Stevens wrote:

> Minkow's [the founder] company indeed seemed well on its way to becoming "the GM of the cleaning business" but it was all a hoax. The insurance restoration business that Minkow touted as the linchpin of his company existed on paper only. The fire-scorched buildings ZZZZ Best claimed to be restoring, the teams of workers allegedly restoring smoke-stained carpets, the reported contracts with the Allstates, the Liberty Mutuals and the Prudentials of the world were figments of Minkow's

fertile imagination. In reality, the carpet-cleaning wizard had masterminded a complex Ponzi scheme, raising millions of dollars from unsuspecting lenders and investors only to shuffle the money among a series of dummy companies controlled by Minkow and his cohorts. . . . Even more shocking than Minkow's gall in fabricating an entire business and thinking he could get away with it was the fact that he did get away with it—long enough to bilk ZZZZ Best investors of at least $70 million and to hoodwink one of the largest . . . accounting firms in the world.[18]

In this case, fraudulent financial results were used to raise new debt and equity capital. The primary purpose of the capital raised, more than anything, was to support the lifestyle of the company founder. What is interesting to note about this company is that pre-tax earnings had grown from $152,192 for the *year* ended April 1984 to $1,834,707 for the *quarter* ended July 1986, based mainly on the stroke of a pen.[19] Investors and creditors who based their earnings expectations on these fabricated results were surprised (shocked is probably a better description) when, during the company's audit for the year ended April 1987, the fraud was uncovered.

Correcting financial statements for financial frauds entails the restatement of prior-year results. Reported earnings are considered to be in error, necessitating a restatement for their correction. However, whether an earnings surprise is communicated with a restatement, as is the case with frauds; a special charge, as is the case with some instances of aggressive application of accounting principles; or simply a decline in earnings or the reporting of a loss due to changing fundamentals, it is something to be avoided.

CLASSIFYING EARNINGS SURPRISES

Exhibit 3.2 summarizes the classification scheme for earnings surprises developed in this chapter. It lists the three factors causing earnings surprises, the extent to which active earnings manipulation is present, and the method in which each is reported in the financial statements.

Exhibit 3.2   A Classification of the Causes of Earnings Surprises

Cause of Earnings Surprise	Extent of Earnings Manipulation	Method of Reporting
Changing economic fundamentals	None	Reduced revenue Increased operating expenses Special provisions
Aggressive application of accounting principles	Present but lacking fraudulent intent	Special provisions Restatement
Fraudulent financial reporting	Present and attributable to fraudulent intent	Restatement

In Chapter 1 we listed several earnings surprises caused by varying factors. At this point, we revisit those earnings surprises and use the classification scheme developed here to categorize them.

> AST Research, Inc., struggling to regain its footing after failing to get new products out on time, said it had a loss of $22.3 million in the fiscal second quarter ended December 31. The Irvine, Calif., maker of personal computers said the 69 cent-a-share loss for the quarter compares with net income of $17.9 million, or 54 cents a share, a year earlier. Revenue sank 6%, to $640.1 million from $677 million a year ago.[20]

The AST Research earnings surprise can be included in the changing economic fundamentals category. There is no evidence of active earnings manipulation. The earnings decline, due primarily to declining revenue associated with a late product introduction, was reported without a special provision.

> Fred Meyer, Inc., Portland, Ore., posted a deeper-than-expected net loss of $36.6 million in its fiscal third quarter because of a labor strike that has been settled and a one-time charge.[21]

The Fred Meyer earnings surprise is also an example of changing economic fundamentals, with no apparent earnings manipulation. The loss reported for the quarter is due primarily to higher costs and lost revenue associated with a labor strike. The one-time charge referred to in the example is a special provision to account for the company's decision to exit markets in northern California.

> Datapoint Corp. posted an $85 million fiscal fourth-quarter loss and said its auditors are raising doubt about the technology company's future. . . . The biggest factor in the latest quarter's loss is a $57.7 million write-off of all of the company's goodwill.[22]

This example appears to include elements of changing economic fundamentals and aggressive application of accounting principles. It is likely changing fundamentals that focused the firm's attention on the impaired value of its goodwill. In retrospect, the company had been aggressive in the period chosen to amortize its goodwill. Had the goodwill been amortized more quickly, reducing earnings in prior years, the company could have avoided much of the large provision it found necessary to take in one year.

> Collins Industries, Inc., said its chief financial officer has resigned and two staff accountants have been suspended as an investigation indicates net income for fiscal 1992 was overstated by an estimated 72%. . . . The investigation to date has indicated that $1.2 million of fourth-quarter vendor payables were not properly recorded, causing an overstatement of net by about $762,000.[23]

Certain managers at Collins Industries appear to have erred in their calculation of net income. That is, by excluding from their calculations certain vendor payables and associated inventory purchases, cost of sales was understated, overstating net income. To our knowledge, no fraudulent intent has been attributed to these actions. Thus, the example would not be properly classified with fraudulent financial reporting. Examples of inadvertent errors in financial reporting are fairly infrequent and insufficiently numerous to support a separate category of earnings surprise. Accordingly, we classify them with other examples of aggressive application of accounting principles. Because an error was committed, a restatement of erroneous results would be needed.

> Jacobson Stores, Inc., . . . today reported sales for the third quarter ended October 29, 1994, of $86,501,000, down 4% from the same period in 1993. For the quarter, Jacobson's reported a net loss of $1,816,000, or 31 cents per share, compared to earnings of $1,186,000, or 21 cents per share, for the same period last year.
>   Jacobson's third-quarter performance was negatively affected by higher markdowns.[24]

The Jacobson Stores example can be included with others in the changing economic fundamentals category. Higher markdowns, likely due to soft demand, reduced revenue and resulted in a loss for the quarter. The loss was reported without any special provision.

> Comptronix Corp. suspended three of its top officers and began an internal investigation of its accounting procedures, saying that the three men had apparently caused the company to overstate profits since 1989. . . . Comptronix said the three officers . . . apparently helped inflate profits by "improperly recording certain assets" and "either overstating current sales or understating current cost of sales on [the company's] income statement."[25]

This example clearly illustrates fraudulent financial reporting. Management at the company had purposefully overstated revenue and profits for several years, presumably in an effort to artificially inflate the market value of the company's stock. When the fraud was discovered, it was corrected with a restatement of prior-year reported results.

> Leslie Fay Companies, Inc., said it is investigating "alleged accounting irregularities" that, when corrected, could wipe out its 1992 net income and force the company to restate its 1991 earnings. . . . The company's corporate controller . . . indicated Friday during a year-end audit that he and another employee had made some "false entries" in the company's records."[26]

The Leslie Fay example also involves fraudulent financial reporting. False entries were made in an effort to boost net income. Note the reference to restatement of the 1991 results.

> Gibson Greetings, Inc., said the Securities and Exchange Commission is investi-

gating whether its employees violated securities laws while engaging in derivatives transactions or in overstating inventory at the company's Cleo, Inc., unit.[27]

The Gibson Greetings example involves two earnings surprise causes. Because alleged violation of securities laws is involved, we include the two earnings surprises in the fraudulent financial reporting category. It should be noted, however, that these accusations are to date unproved.

In the first example, the company is being investigated to determine whether it violated securities laws while engaging in derivatives transactions. Apparently, in an effort to speculate on interest rate moves, the company entered into certain risky interest rate swap transactions that generated significant losses. While company reports disclosed that it had entered into interest rate swap agreements, disclosures provided implied that these agreements were being used to hedge against the potential negative effects of interest rate moves and not to speculate. Consider the following footnote provided in the company's 1993 annual report:

> The difference between the amount of interest to be paid and the amount of interest to be received under interest rate swap agreements due to changing interest rates is charged or credited to interest expense over the life of the agreements. The fair value of interest rate swaps (used for hedging purposes) is the estimated amount that the company would receive or pay to terminate the swap agreements at the reporting date, taking into account current interest rates and the current creditworthiness of the swap counterparties.[28]

Note how the disclosure refers to the use of interest rate swaps for hedging purposes but provides no indication that the company was speculating on the movement of interest rates. The Securities and Exchange Commission was likely concerned that the company had not provided adequate disclosure of the risks it was undertaking. If upon review by the Securities and Exchange Commission, the company were found not to have violated any laws, the earnings surprise would be properly classified with those in the aggressive application of accounting principles category. The company did not fully disclose the risks of the transactions it had entered into and misled investors and creditors as to its exposure to interest rate movements. The losses occurred when changing fundamentals, that is, increased interest rates, forced the company to make significant payments in accordance with the terms of its contracts. These losses were reported in the period the payments were made and, as such, did not entail special provisions. Even if it is found that securities laws were violated, there will likely be no restatement of prior-year earnings because amounts reported on the financial statements in prior periods were not in error.

The overstatement of inventory does have a clearer fraudulent intent, as the following excerpt indicates:

> Regarding the inventory overstatement, Gibson said the SEC is looking at the public statements the company made regarding the overstatement and also scrutinizing the company's accounting systems. Gibson said it believes the Cleo overstatements

are the result of "a deliberate attempt by one or more Cleo personnel to overstate income."[29]

This misstatement of inventory resulted in an overstatement of the company's 1993 net income by about 20%. As would be expected, earnings for that year were restated.

> Presidential Life Corp. will restate several years of financial results to reflect a mark-down of some junk securities in its portfolio as part of a settlement with the Securities and Exchange Commission. . . . The SEC calls for Presidential to restate the results in order to comply with generally accepted accounting standards for valuing investment securities.[30]

As noted earlier, Presidential Life provides a good example of aggressive application of accounting principles. The company was aggressive by not writing down the value of the portfolio of securities when its value declined due to more than a temporary condition. The SEC viewed prior-year results to be in error and forced the company to account for the new valuation of its securities portfolio with a restatement.

SUMMARY

While there are many causes of earnings surprises, they can be classified generally into three groups: changing economic fundamentals, aggressive application of accounting principles, and fraudulent financial reporting. Of the three, financial early warnings to anticipate earnings surprises arising from aggressive application of accounting principles and fraudulent financial reporting are clearer and more easily detected using prior-period financial statements. Changing economic fundamentals are more subtle and provide a more difficult target for avoiding earnings surprises. This is especially true for those that do not entail a special income statement provision for such items as restructuring charges, asset write-downs, and special liability accruals. Those that do not include special provisions are typically more accurately forecast using an appreciation of developing business and economic conditions along with financial statement disclosures.

Our objective is to provide financial early warnings for earnings surprises caused by all three of the categories identified. We do this using examples grouped by financial statement area. We start with revenue and work our way down the income statement. As we go, we identify the early warning role played by related balance sheet accounts. In fact, because the balance sheet serves as a repository for amounts that have not as yet been taken to the income statement, it provides a fruitful hunting ground for warnings of future earnings declines.

In those instances where a background understanding of accepted accounting practice is needed, that background is provided. However, such background information is kept to the minimum necessary to provide the reader with a working knowledge of the relevant rules. For more detailed background information, the reader is referred to Chapter 14.

ENDNOTES

1. *The Wall Street Journal*, January 10, 1995, p. B6.
2. Urcarco, Inc., annual report, June 1991.
3. Machine Technology, Inc., press release, March 24, 1992, and annual report, August 1992.
4. United States Surgical Corp., annual report, December 1993, pp. 22–23.
5. IPL Systems, Inc., annual report, December 1993.
6. Home Nutritional Services, Inc., press release, March 3, 1993.
7. Tektronix, Inc., annual report, May 1991, p. 23.
8. Biomet, Inc., annual report, May 1993, p. 17.
9. Diagnostic Products, Inc., annual report, December 1993, p. 23.
10. Allergan, Inc., annual report, December 1993, p. 34.
11. Healthdyne, Inc., annual report, December 1993, p. 26.
12. Data and accounting policies obtained from Microsoft Corp. annual report, June 1993, System Software Associates, Inc., annual report, October 1993, and American Software, Inc., annual report, April 1993, respectively.
13. Vista Resources, Inc., annual report, December 1989, p. 10.
14. Accounting Principles Board Opinion No. 17: *Intangible Assets* (New York: Accounting Principles Board, August 1970).
15. Vista Resources, Inc., annual report, December 1990, p. 12.
16. Because of the intangible quality of goodwill, creditors routinely deduct it from assets and equity. Then a sudden write-off by the company would not have the same surprising impact.
17. Bassett Furniture Industries, Inc., annual report, November 1990, p. 6.
18. Mark Stevens, *The Big Six: The Selling Out of America's Top Accounting Firms* (New York: Simon & Schuster, 1991), pp. 28–29.
19. ZZZZ Best Co., Inc., preliminary prospectus, October 1986.
20. *The Wall Street Journal*, January 26, 1995, p. B6.
21. Ibid., December 2, 1994, p. A4.
22. Ibid., November 15, 1994, p. A19.
23. Ibid., March 5, 1993, p. B3.
24. Jacobson Stores, Inc., press release, November 21, 1994.
25. *The Wall Street Journal*, November 27, 1992, p. A3.
26. Ibid., February 2, 1993, p. A4.
27. Ibid., November 16, 1994, p. B10.
28. Gibson Greetings, Inc., annual report, December 1993, p. 23.
29. *The Wall Street Journal*, November 15, 1994, p. C27.
30. Ibid., March 2, 1993, p. B3.

Chapter 4

A Survey of Lenders

We should be careful to get out of an experience only the wisdom that is in it—and stop there; lest we be like the cat that sits down on a hot stove-lid. She will never sit down on a hot stove-lid again—and that is well; but also she will never sit down on a cold one any more.[1]

This chapter reports on efforts to tap the experience of bank lenders in identifying financial early warnings. Since they are frequent users of financial statements, we felt it was important to learn from them what early warnings they found to be helpful in avoiding earnings surprises. While we did not include security analysts in our survey, a survey of that group's views on a related topic, earnings quality, was published in 1982.[2]

The information reported in this chapter was collected from 191 bank lenders during a five-month period ending March 1995. These lenders were employed by five different large regional banks with operations in the Southeast, Midwest, and North. The lenders were all participants in credit-training programs conducted by the authors, principally for experienced lenders. The average credit experience, typically in lending but also in credit examination or credit administration in some cases, was 11.4 years and ranged from 0 to 34 years.

After some brief prefatory information, the lenders were asked to list "the major early warning signs that you have found to be good indicators of earnings declines." Space was provided to list four indicators, though some provided as many as eight. A total of 870 indicators of potential earnings declines was provided by the 191 lenders, or an average of 4.5 each. As one would expect, many of the indicators appeared repeatedly. Common examples were (1) declines in gross margins, (2) increases in receivables days, (3) bank overdrafts, (4) changes in management, and (5) changes in outside accountants.

The lender early warnings have been grouped into categories in order to summarize this significant body of data. No set of categories is perfect, and some items could appear in more than one category. For example, two of the categories are liquidity and profitability. We elected to classify increases in inventory days in the liquidity category rather than in profitability. An increase in inventory days has a negative impact upon liquidity by reducing cash flow. A sufficient reduction in cash flow can lead to reductions in earnings by creating restrictions on the ability to secure funding, increasing financing costs, and creating difficulties in being able to purchase required inventory (being placed on a C.O.D. status). However, increases in inventory days can also affect future earnings in a different way. Underlying an increase in inventory days may be an inability to move inventory that has become stale, obsolete, or otherwise unattractive. Price reductions may be necessary to move the inventory, and write-downs may be required. Both of these actions will cause future earnings to suffer.

The lender early warnings are summarized in a series of exhibits. The early warnings included in the exhibits are typically those that appeared most frequently in the lender responses. However, occasionally an early warning was included because of its uniqueness or the potential insight it offers. More than a single example of some types of lender early warnings were included in the exhibits if the language or illustrations used aid in understanding their nature and importance. In every case, the early warnings are included using the wording provided by the lenders themselves. The major classifications used are (1) profitability, (2) liquidity, (3) management (behavior, quality, changes in), (4) external environment, (5) borrower/lender communications, (6) financial information (quality, timeliness), (7) strategy issues, and (8) miscellaneous.

PROFITABILITY-RELATED EARLY WARNINGS

Exhibit 4.1 contains a summary of profitability-related lender early warnings. Once again, the classification is based upon whether the potential earnings impact is direct or indirect, a first- or second-order effect. A prospective decline in margins, for instance, will have a direct impact on earnings. An increase in inventory days has a direct impact on liquidity (cash flow) but only a potential indirect impact on profitability.

The early warnings in Exhibit 4.1 and each of the subsequent exhibits should be seen as indicating only *possible* developments that could affect future earnings. In flag terminology, these are yellow rather than red. It is always necessary to investigate the circumstances surrounding or underlying early warnings. The link with future earnings is fairly evident for many of the items in Exhibit 4.1, and therefore our comments are selective.

Increase in Inventory Days

To provide more user background on early warnings, we asked a subset of the 191 lenders who participated in the survey to describe cases where early warnings proved to be benign. The most frequent case dealt with an increase in inventory days (ex-

Exhibit 4.1   Profitability-Related Early Warnings

1. Declining sales or declining margins—decreasing gross profit, especially in businesses with high fixed costs.
2. A slump in sales for a leveraged, capital-intensive company with high fixed costs.
3. Ever larger percentage of EBITDA (earnings before interest, taxes, depreciation, and amortization) coming from nonrecurring, nonsustainable, or nonoperating sources.
4. Relying on nonoperating sources of income, e.g., assets sales, securities gains, and accounting adjustments for net income.
5. Sale of assets with gains making up greater and greater percentage of income—with gain proceeds used to pay unrelated debt.
6. Order backlog declines in several consecutive reporting periods. Future revenue may fall to a point where future earnings will be affected if overhead costs are not reduced appropriately.
7. Increased fixed assets (trucking company) in anticipation of increased revenue. Did not materialize, leading to a huge loss.
8. Underestimating the amount of bad debt in the allowance account as receivables days increase.
9. High inventory levels over previous years. Increases in inventory days would indicate trouble moving the product, eventually becoming obsolete.
10. Buildup in inventory in a company operating in a dynamic high-tech industry—could signal obsolescence.
11. Contractors: a buildup in costs over billings, which could signal a loss on the contract.
12. Contractors: uncollected and unreserved receivables from customers disputing contract performance.
13. Deterioration in gross margin as a percentage of sales often signals price cutting as a result of attempting to hold market share. Sometimes signals poor job costing and an unexpected increase in a raw material price that cannot be passed along to customers.
14. A significant drop in gross margin usually indicates more competitive pressure or some other factor making it necessary to sell at a lower price.
15. Inventory slowness combined with pressure on margins indicates inventory may be obsolete and must be sold at a discount.
16. Unexpected adjustments to earnings, usually at year-end, that may just be the beginning of larger adjustments to come.
17. Discounts provided on contracts to customers.
18. Significant deterioration in financial stability of a major customer—high concentration.
19. Business expanding faster than expertise and infrastructure—often results in unforeseen problems and expenses.
20. Loss of good, long-time customer.
21. Badly overvalued assets, especially inventory.
22. Interim statements show decline in gross margin offset by lower operating expenses, usually achieved by reduction in owner's compensation to maintain the bottom line.
23. Accounts receivable aging begins to indicate more accounts over 90 days.

Exhibit 4.1   *(continued)*

24. Increase in raw materials cost and inability to pass price increases to customers quickly enough, lowering margins.
25. Declining gross margin, but unable to reduce operating expenses—primarily fixed costs.
26. Provisions to clean up, fix, adjust balance sheet and provisions for disposal of company segments. Often, the provisions taken this year are just not enough—more announced later.
27. Receivables days maintained by shifting stale receivables to notes receivable. Company was not recognizing losses in receivables.
28. Expiration of tax loss carryforwards.
29. Reliance on company prepared interims where you know the accounting ability of the preparer is questionable. Most often they do not properly match items, e.g., sales and cost of goods sold.
30. Inventory levels were not adjusted in interim statements.
31. Financial problems at main customer
32. Rising interest rates affecting highly leveraged borrower.
33. Sale of income-producing assets.

amples 9, 10, and 15 in Exhibit 4.1). The typical concern is that an increase in inventory days implies obsolescence and the potential for write-downs. However, lenders described circumstances surrounding increases in inventory days that resulted in no threat to future earnings. Three representative examples include (1) "buildup in inventory, only to be followed by a large sale with the contract signed prior to the buildup"; (2) "buildup in inventory at year-end due to ability to purchase additional vehicles at a lower cost"; (3) "company is expanding product lines, or a growing company has established a direct arrangement for purchasing inventory rather than through a wholesaler that requires larger minimum orders."

High Fixed Component to Cost Structure

Several participating lenders commented on the significance of a high degree of fixed costs in a firm's cost structure. Examples 1, 2, and 25 suggest that earnings will suffer more from declines in sales and margins in companies with high fixed costs. This circumstance, often referred to as the degree of operating leverage, produces exaggerated swings in earnings as sales and margins move up or down. Total costs move in closer harmony with revenue when variable costs rather than fixed costs dominate the cost structure.

Sustainability of Earnings

In Chapters 5 and 6, we focus on earnings analysis and the effect of nonrecurring or irregular sources of income or expense on sustainability. Earnings sustainability is a dimension of the quality of earnings. Examples 3–5, 26, and 33 raise the issue of nonrecurring items and their implications for future earnings. The thrust of examples 3, 4, and 5 is that one should expect future declines in earnings in cases where they are currently being propped up by nonrecurring gains. Example 26 suggests that certain charges, which might be expected to reduce earnings only temporarily, have a tendency to continue to reduce earnings in subsequent periods. Example 33 is a classic case of "eating your seed corn."

Example 18 also identifies a significant threat to sustainability in the form of a concentration of sales. Loss of such a customer could dramatically reduce future earnings. However, in the extended survey results, one respondent commented that customer concentration had not been a problem "due to the length and quality of the relationship." Another respondent noted little harm from loss of a significant customer "because the volume was very low margin and was actually depressing profitability on a percentage basis."

Decline in Gross Margin

Declining gross margin as a percentage of sales (revenue minus cost of sales or services as a percentage of revenue) was cited by 36 of the survey participants as a useful early warning. With the exception of references to changes in the range of days-type statistics, e.g., inventory days, receivables days, and payables days, a current decline in margins was the most frequently cited of the profitability- and liquidity-related early warnings.

Many of the survey participants pointed to the changes in underlying conditions that are reflected in the gross margin. Example 13 highlights possible price cutting to hold market share, suggesting a change in competitive conditions in the market. Examples 13 and 24 identify underlying increases in material costs that cannot be passed on to customers as sources of current margin reductions and future earnings decreases. The survey participants clearly see declining margins as something to be investigated closely and as a phenomenon that has proved to be a useful early warning.

As with the inventory days, some participants in the extended survey identified cases in which declining margins did not prove to be associated with decreases in future earnings. In one case, a margin decline in interim statements was simply "due to the effects of low-margin product runs in a single month for a year's production." In a case involving a contractor, the margin decline was likewise harmless: "Gross margin declined dramatically for a paving contractor, but it turned out that a large contract included a good portion of subcontract work, essentially passed through without markup."

Rapid Growth

Example 19 deals with the potential impact on future earnings of rapid growth. Rapid growth was a frequently cited early warning (14 times). Most of the high-growth cases are included in Exhibit 4.2, which deals with liquidity-based early warnings. In Exhibit 4.1, example 19, however, the emphasis is on the potential impact on future expenses and therefore earnings. In the more typical reference, the emphasis is upon the direct or first-order impact of growth on liquidity. However, significant liquidity problems related to growth often lead to reductions in future earnings as a second-order effect.

LIQUIDITY-RELATED EARLY WARNINGS

Exhibit 4.2 contains a summary of liquidity-related early warnings. The examples listed here could be characterized as liquidity/profitability early warnings. What begins as a liquidity problem may create a further problem that results in a reduction in earnings. That is, an increase in inventory and accounts receivable may be driven by rapid growth. This will create a need for careful management of the firm's liquidity. Alternatively, an increase in inventory and receivables days, in the absence of growth, may create both a liquidity problem and a reduction in future earnings if increases in bad-debt provisions and inventory write-downs become necessary.

The liquidity-related early warnings forecast earnings declines by playing the role of symptoms in diagnosis. For example, a sharply elevated blood pressure is a symptom that may suggest an underlying hypertensive condition. By the same token, an elevated blood pressure reading may simply be a transient phenomenon that is wholly benign. A deterioration in future health, and even death, may result should the elevated blood pressure be associated with a hypertensive condition that is not treated.

An elevated inventory days indicator is also a symptom. It may or may not be associated with an underlying pathology, such as inefficient inventory management, obsolete inventory, or fraudulently overstated inventory. An investigation of the reasons for the increased inventory days is necessary to establish whether a problem with the potential for having a negative impact on future earnings exists.

Some of the examples in Exhibit 4.2 have a somewhat more involved interpretation. For example, a bank overdraft is a problem in its own right. On the other hand, it can also be viewed as a symptom of an underlying condition that has reduced the capacity of the firm to generate adequate cash flow. That condition may be a buildup in obsolete inventory that reduces cash flow and may require a write-down that will reduce future earnings. Beyond this, the more fundamental problem may really be a failure to be responsive to a change in consumer preferences.

Overdrafts

Overdrafts were among the most frequently cited liquidity-related early warnings (39 times), but examples were offered where overdrafts proved to be benign. However, in most cases, overdrafts were simply identified as early warnings without comment. In one case, it was explained that a "book" overdraft was created by writ-

Exhibit 4.2   Liquidity-Related Early Warnings

1. Overdrafts.
2. Customers showing a buildup in inventory.
3. Increase in the frequency of book overdrafts at the bank in the customer's major checking account. Frequent overdrafts are an indication of a constrained working capital position that generally portends a decline in operating performance.
4. Inability to rest a seasonal line of credit despite a decrease in sales.
5. Do not clean up line as required.
6. Rapid growth and related expansion activities.
7. Dividends or withdrawals in excess of earnings where net worth is declining, leverage is increasing, and business is not growing.
8. Combination of increased fixed assets (new location) plus increased inventory in anticipation of price increases. Resulted in negative cash flow and a huge loss.
9. Working capital lines of credit of a business that continually become permanent working capital and have to be amortized out. Sometimes the companies are funding losses through these lines.
10. Riding of accounts payable—slow payment may indicate cash flow problems and hence lack of or downturn in sales.
11. Increased payables days with shrinking inventory.
12. Sales terms changed, i.e., extended.
13. Quick buildup in accounts receivable.
14. Significant increases in days receivables or inventories days in light of level or declining sales.
15. Accounts payable—bank receives more credit reference calls, agings show deterioration in payments, and vendors put them on C.O.D. terms.
16. Lengthening of payables, increase in accrued expenses over a period of time and borrowings at limit on revolving credit matched with growing level of permanent working capital.
17. Stagnant line usage at or near maximum permitted with delinquent borrowing-base reporting.
18. Drawing on line when in the past it was never used.
19. Higher than average usage of line of credit.
20. Higher than normal borrowing under line of credit not accompanied by growth in revenues.
21. Frequent calls from other creditors.
22. Request for small amounts of money.
23. Past due payroll taxes.
24. Payments begin to be made late.
25. Significant reductions in cash balances held at banks.
26. Increased loans from shareholders.
27. Constant loan requests, especially for working capital and evergreen loans.
28. Requests for funds to cover payroll.
29. Accrued expenses continue to grow beyond what is supported by operating growth—indicates that while company is recognizing the expenses, cash flow is not sufficient to pay expenses.
30. Inability of cash flow from operations to cover current maturities on long-term debt and interest expense.
31. Increasing frequency or questionable draws on construction loans.

Exhibit 4.2 *(continued)*

---

32. Fewer deposits made with bank.
33. Comparing the owner's personal financial statement from period to period reveals declining liquid assets that may indicate that he has to subsidize the business, whose operations are not really viable.
34. Overdrafts (negative cash) on year-end balance sheet. Lender thought it was how the borrower (compiled statements) accounted for uncollected funds. Borrower had actually bounced checks and had no cash to cover.

---

ing and holding checks at year-end as a device for reporting a smaller accounts payable balance. As the business had extended terms with two of their suppliers, there was no real problem with the status of their payables. In another example, it was reported that "overdrafts were the controller's way of managing cash and reducing borrowing." The survey respondent added, "The account officer added overdraft fees and showed the company's management how this was increasing costs. The overdrafts stopped."

Increase in Days Statistics

Increases in receivables, inventory, and payables days were cited as early warnings about as often as overdrafts. Some survey respondents identified changes in days that they saw to be inconsistent with other data. For instance, Exhibit 4.2, example 11, points to increased payables days in the face of a shrinking inventory. Example 14 identifies significant increases in inventory days and receivables days in cases where sales were level or declining. Riding the trade to excess can result in being put on C.O.D. terms, as example 15 explains.

In the extended survey, dealing with early warnings that proved not to be problems, respondents identified a number of examples: (1) increase in inventory days due to taking advantage of low lumber prices, (2) increase in payables days due to extended terms made available by a supplier, and (3) increase in inventory days that was overcome by aggressive marketing.

Performance of Lines of Credit

A failure to satisfy a cleanup period requirement in a line of credit was a frequently cited early warning: examples 4 and 5 in Exhibit 4.2. Various other features of line usage are included in Exhibit 4.2: examples 9, 16, 17, 18, and 20. Unusual borrowing patterns were a source of concern as well as lines of credit that end up funding increases in permanent working capital positions.

Inquiries from Other Creditors

Trade inquiries from suppliers and other creditors to banks concerning the financial status of their customers were fairly frequent. Such inquiries probably make it clear that there was a failure to pay bills in a timely basis and that it is a source of concern to the supplier-creditor.

MANAGEMENT-RELATED EARLY WARNINGS

The competence, integrity, judgment, and a host of other characteristics of management are clearly central to the success of firms and to their prospects for future profitability. Our survey revealed that lenders saw early warnings in a wide variety of actions and characteristics of management. A sampling of the most frequently cited or interesting responses from our group of lenders is provided in Exhibit 4.3.

Some of the more dominant areas of concern from the survey responses were changes in management, the failure of management to plan or meet projections, the presence of litigation, and management's lifestyle. Also listed are selected responses that reflect on the quality and wisdom of management. Aspects of management's communication with the lenders are dealt with later.

Changes in Management

Items 1–8 in Exhibit 4.3 provide examples of survey responses on changes in management. Respondents were seldom specific about the nature of the possible connection between changes in management and future earnings. In the case of unexpected changes in chief financial officer, a decline in results is a reasonable expectation. Example 8 in Exhibit 4.3 is a case in point. Changes in management may reflect a failure on the part of personnel to perform, where such failure has not yet been reflected in results. A number of survey respondents identified management changes as early warnings that had not proven to be problems. Unexpected change is clearly of greater concern than change that has been planned. However, change in senior management introduces an additional element of uncertainty that the survey respondents, based upon their experience, view with caution.

Failure to Make or Meet Projections

The failure of management to make or meet projections, generally on a more or less consistent basis, was also a frequent early warning and identified by 13 survey respondents. Comments ranged from simple failure to provide or meet forecasts to unrealistic forecasts of poor quality (see examples 9–12 in Exhibit 4.3).

Exhibit 4.3 Management-Related Early Warnings

1. Important management changes—often too late by the time the announcement is made.
2. New management or ownership.
3. Unexpected management turnover.

Exhibit 4.3 *(continued)*

4. Resignation of key management or owners.
5. Change in key managers respected by the bank.
6. Transition of management—parent to child.
7. Aging management and lack of management succession.
8. Sudden change in duties of company's CFO.
9. Management's projections of sales and earnings were well beyond past history—leveraged buyouts.
10. Inadequate forecasting of capital requirement and time it will take to turn a profit.
11. Failure to meet projections.
12. Management has not prepared any projections as to what future earnings would be.
13. Customer uses working capital loans to purchase fixed assets, e.g., cars, airplanes, and boats.
14. Owner or principal frequently away from premises.
15. Excessive perks for owners and employees.
16. Extravagance.
17. Lifestyle of owner not consistent with profitability of the company.
18. Owner indulges in lavish lifestyle.
19. Principal in company receiving extraordinarily large withdrawals, leaving capital accounts at marginal levels in order support extravagant lifestyle.
20. Divorces and other family problems.
21. Absentee management.
22. Slack or complacent business management style.
23. Lack of adequate reinvestment in core business, e.g., insufficient capital expenditures in a capital-intensive business.
24. Growth that stretches the ability of management.
25. Talk of rapid sales growth without knowledge to handle it—no systems and depth of people or financing lined up.
26. Overpaying for acquisitions.
27. Poor housekeeping.
28. Lack of interaction between management and labor.
29. Owner defers totally to CFO in contacts with bankers.
30. Change in attitude or behavior.
31. No backup management.
32. Management that does not recognize the cost of growth because of an inherent sales mentality.
33. Not keeping up with changes in technology.
34. Inflexible and dominant senior management coupled with a weak board of directors.
35. Litigation (both ways—that is the company being sued or suing someone else)—diverts management attention from day-to-day business, resulting in poor performance.
36. Tax fraud or evasion.
37. Wanting to be released from a personal guarantee for no apparent reason.

Management Lifestyle

Examples 13–20 in Exhibit 4.3 deal with matters related to management lifestyle or attitudes and behaviors that may not bode well for the firm's future. The fact that these matters were identified fairly frequently as early warnings establishes that the respondents' experience has shown them to be associated with subsequent declines in earnings. The most common theme in this class of early warnings is a lifestyle judged to be extravagant. In some cases, this extravagance has a direct effect on the firm by draining needed resources (example 19). An extravagant personal lifestyle may also be seen as reflecting negatively on values and judgment. Divorce and other family problems (example 20) are generally seen as posing a threat to the firm by deflecting energy and attention away from managerial responsibilities.

Other Management-Related Early Warnings

The balance of the management-related early warnings, items 22–37, raise issues of competence, effectiveness, and behavior of management. Of these items, litigation is the one that appeared with the greatest frequency (11 times). When survey respondents elaborated on this early warning, they pointed out that litigation was a potential problem regardless of whether the firm was the plaintiff or defendant. Further (example 35), litigation "diverts management attention from day-to-day business, resulting in poor performance." Also, "Lawsuits, regardless of merit, will almost invariably cause management to take its eye off the ball." While not stated directly, the potential direct financial costs or benefits of litigation must also be viewed as central to the early-warning status of litigation.

EXTERNAL ENVIRONMENT–RELATED EARLY WARNINGS

Most of the early warnings are rather inward-looking and firm-focused. However, a careful review of the 870 early warnings provided by the lenders revealed some that related to changes in the firm's external environment and how, directly or indirectly, these changes could affect future earnings. Examples of external environmental early warnings are provided in Exhibit 4.4.

References to external environmental early warnings were far less numerous than to profitability- or liquidity-related early warnings.

Example 1 in Exhibit 4.4 takes the position that early warnings related to changes in the external environment are among the best: "Oftentimes, the best early indicators of earnings declines are things outside of the company." These external indicators may, individually, be more powerful than firm-specific information because they tend to be aggregations that include information from a variety of different sources. Further, there may be a greater response gap between movement in an external indicator and a subsequent impact on the profits of firms. This may explain why some

Exhibit 4.4 External Environment–Related Early Warnings

---

1. Often the best early indicators of earnings declines are things outside of the company—for example, rapidly rising interest rates or changes in the industry in which a particular client operates, government regulation or new competitive advantages enjoyed by direct competitors. Even weather patterns could affect a company in the property and casualty insurance industry.
2. Changes in economic conditions.
3. Interest rates rise.
4. Rising interest rate environment for borrowers who have historically had marginal debt service capacity.
5. Effect of rising interest rate environment on a highly leveraged borrower.
6. Changes in technology.
7. Rapidly changing technology in an entire industry that is not being addressed. Either affects cost of production, efficiency, and quality, or results in obsolete inventory.
8. Industry downturns.
9. Changes in an industry—slow-down in home building.
10. Fundamental change in industry—deregulation in airlines and trucking.
11. Borrower operates in a declining competitive industry.
12. Regulatory considerations and their impact on operations and profitability.
13. Changes in competition and market share.
14. New competition.
15. Overproduction—too many in the business.
16. Changes in demand for products and services.
17. Tightening of competition, thus pressures on borrower to cut prices to retain or gain market share, change terms on receivables.
18. Local economic or industry trends.
19. Earnings drops of competitors or other negative announcements.

---

lenders view this external information as a better leading indicator than firm-specific information. As an example, there is apparently a close but lagged relation between carpet sales and new home starts. Forming an expectation of future earnings of a carpet company will be helped by employing information on significant changes in new home starts.

BORROWER COMMUNICATIONS–RELATED EARLY WARNINGS

The preceding section on management-related early warnings dealt with issues of management performance. But lender-survey responses also pointed to the nature and quality of communications between the borrower's management and the lender as an early warning. A summary of selected early warnings related to the borrower's communications with the lender is contained in Exhibit 4.5.

Recall that an extended version of the basic questionnaire was provided to a

Exhibit 4.5   Management Communications–Related Early Warnings

1. Information flow slows.
2. General change in attitude and accessibility of the customer toward the bank. Customer becomes negative, especially avoiding requests for information.
3. Principal of business is always unavailable for my calls.
4. Client doesn't return phone calls or is evasive.
5. Lack of contact, lack of communications, not returning calls, changes in contact person at company, "incommunicado," low-priority feeling given bank.
6. Company management becomes elusive—hard to get in touch with.
7. Customer visits bank personally less often.
8. They don't call us, or they have their secretary do the "bank work."
9. Management won't answer questions.
10. Vague answers are given to specific questions.
11. Management shows reluctance to discuss company trends or is not knowledgeable about why negative trends are occurring.
12. Borrower blames an employee for not sending debt-service checks on time.
13. Borrower telegraphs via conversations.
14. Comments from borrower on problems.
15. In discussions, customer focuses on sales growth but does not talk much about profitability.
16. Borrower extols the company and feels that the company has only positive characteristics, while brushing off weaknesses—when overall economic conditions indicate otherwise.
17. Customer saying the business is down when the economy is good.
18. Customer complaining about the difficulty of collecting receivables and experiencing higher bad debt.
19. Complaints about how tough things are getting.

subset of the overall group of 191 lender respondents. The additional questions included one designed to elicit examples of early warnings that were not associated with subsequent declines in earnings. Not a single such example was offered from the borrower/lender communications category. Apparently, the behaviors represented in this category, with examples in Exhibit 4.5, have a reliable association with subsequent declines in earnings.

Decline in Responsiveness

About 25 of the lender responses dealt with a decline in the borrower's responsiveness to the lender. Typically, the borrower stopped returning phone calls or returning them on a timely basis. One of the lenders, example 5, referred to management becoming "incommunicado." The borrowers in these cases appeared to be trying to avoid and distance themselves from their bankers. Notice that in examples 7 and 8 management avoids going to the bank personally. The words most commonly used by the lenders to describe these actions were "elusive" and "evasive."

Quality and Character of Communications

In addition to a decline in borrower responsiveness, the *quality* of some of the interactions was seen as an early warning. Note the references to the borrower becoming "negative" (example 2), "won't answer questions" (example 9), and "vague answers given to specific questions" (example 10). Some of the examples suggest a form of denial on the part of management regarding negative developments or a preference not to be candid about such trends. One respondent mentions management's "reluctance to discuss company trends" (example 11). Other examples include "focuses on sales growth but does not talk much about profitability" (example 15), "feels the company has only positive characteristics, while brushing off weaknesses" (example 16), and "complaints about how tough things are getting" (example 19).

As the lender in example 13 suggests, "borrower telegraphs via conversations." Examples 14, 18, and 19 could be seen as fitting this category. The lender, or any other interested party, could read these conversations as telegraphing possible declines in results without the borrower's stating this outright. These early warnings may be more subtle than some others, but lenders appear to find them useful in their efforts to avoid earnings surprises.

FINANCIAL COMMUNICATIONS–RELATED EARLY WARNINGS

The behaviors listed in Exhibit 4.5 are seen by lenders as often associated with subsequent declines in earnings. We elected to treat financial management communications separately from nonfinancial management communications because of the frequency of references to the former as sources of early warnings. Selected early warnings from the survey responses dealing with financial communications are provided in Exhibit 4.6.

Early warnings based upon various aspects of financial communication amounted to 103 out of a total of 870 early warnings in the lender survey. Lenders attach great value to a firm's financial information, its quality and manner of communication, as a basis for the anticipation of future declines in earnings. The dominant early warning in this category concerns delays in the receipt of financial information. Next to delays come changes in accountants/auditors and accounting methods.

Delayed Receipt of Financial Information

Whereas delays in providing financial information could prove to be benign, the frequency with which this was offered as an early warning indicates that lenders see delays as signaling that bad earnings news may be forthcoming. Examples 4–6 in Exhibit 4.6 suggest that a delay is likely to be associated with a reduction in earnings. Both 4 and 6 indicate that management may be hoping that a delay will permit subsequent improvements to ameliorate the impact of prior bad results when they are

Exhibit 4.6   Financial Communications–Related Early Warnings

1. Delay of financial statements.
2. Unexplained delays in providing financial information.
3. Customer is slow in getting financial information to me and gets too easily irritated about the request.
4. Delays in providing financial information—hoping to fix a problem before they let you know about it.
5. Delay in getting financial statements promptly—usually means something is wrong, i.e., losses or a large earnings decline.
6. Delays in getting financial statements. Usually indicates bad news in prior period. Could be waiting (hoping) for next interim to correct or overcome the bad period.
7. Borrower fails to provide financials in a timely manner. Often, they blame it on a new accounting firm they are using to prepare the statements.
8. Failure to produce interim statements on a timely basis.
9. Management that is not particularly interested in timely financial reporting or unconcerned about the quality of the financial reporting.
10. Change of accountants (CPA)—ask yourself why?
11. Change in accountants/accounting firms has often preceded earnings declines.
12. Frequent changes in auditors.
13. Despite disclosure requirements when changing accountants, behind the stated reasons for the dismissal or disengagement the actual truth almost never is well or clearly stated.
14. Change from a reputable CPA firm to an unknown firm.
15. Changes in accounting methods—makes several extraordinary moves that make analysis of statements difficult.
16. Frequent changes in accounting principles, estimates, or prior-period adjustments show a lack of consistency that should be fully examined.
17. Change in fiscal year-end.
18. Customer does not want to share interim financial information when they always have in the past.
19. Change in format of income statement, e.g., less detail on cost of sales.
20. Providing only compiled financial statements (versus statements with a higher level of outside accountant involvement such as reviewed or audited statements) is often a result of a borrower placing low importance on obtaining quality financial statements. This lack of financial sophistication has often signaled trouble during times of declining sales plus or minus other problems.
21. Going from audit to reviewed, or reviewed to compiled statements.
22. Lack of audited statements—should cause concern from day 1 of the relationship.
23. Compiled statements lacking footnote disclosures.
24. Inability to obtain financial information.
25. Reluctance to provide full tax returns.
26. Poor quality of financial information: weak internal controls, delays in getting numbers from CPA, inability of customer to explain numbers, and general lack of financial sophistication.
27. Re-signing and current dating of old personal financial statements and refusing to provide new ones.
28. Unusual accounting practices.

Exhibit 4.6   *(continued)*

29. Borrower (in the real estate business) fails to provide proof of payment of real estate taxes or insurance even though they show on the income statement as being expensed.
30. Audits performed by the bank for asset-based credits begin to reflect discrepancies between management reports and actual audit findings.
31. Loan covenants not met, loan covenants then amended by the lender and made less stringent, and still covenants are not met.
32. Accounts receivable aging. Accounts receivables aged over 90 days were "forgiven" and moved back to the 0–30 day aged category on the following month's aging.
33. Customer gives the bank "due date" accounts receivable agings rather than "invoice date" agings. The former can be manipulated by the bank's customer extending due dates, but the latter shows how many days have actually elapsed since goods were shipped.

finally disclosed. Explanations for the lateness of financial information, from the extended survey results of early warnings that proved to be benign, included illness or retirement of responsible individuals.

Changes in Accountants/Auditors and Accounting Methods

Examples 10–21 of Exhibit 4.6 involve several types of changes: in accountant/auditors, in accounting methods, in fiscal year-end, and in level of accountant/auditor service. The traditional concern with a change in accountants/auditors is that it may reflect disagreement over the amount or manner in which earnings have been determined. Example 11 expresses the concern that most lenders have when there is a change in accountants/auditors: an earnings decline. It will be a rare case when a change in accountant/auditor involves a disagreement in which the client's wish is to report a lower earnings number than the accountant/auditor. Beyond an immediate earnings issue, a change might suggest that the accountant/auditor is no longer comfortable with the conduct of the client's affairs from a legal or ethical standpoint. If the accountant/auditor's concerns are well founded, this could result in reductions in future earnings. However, there is always the possibility that the change is simply due to a lower fee being offered by a new accounting firm.

The presence of early warnings does not necessarily lead to reductions in future earnings. For example, from the extended survey results dealing with benign early warnings, a lender offered the following:

Often a change in accountants can be a red flag, especially if it signifies a change in past policies and practices. However, in the cases I have handled, a sit-down with management has always readily explained the reasoning for the change. This is not to say it should not be investigated promptly, just that in the cases I have seen there have been valid reasons.

Changes in accounting methods, especially where the result is to increase earnings, may be viewed as prompted by management's anticipation of reduced profitability. Changes in fiscal year-ends can make it more difficult to judge trends in performance. Our sense is that lenders see such changes as sometimes motivated to achieve just this result. This may account for its identification as an early warning.

The level or changes in the level of outside accountant or auditor service was also identified as an early warning. Many borrowers are smaller firms that do not provide audited financial statements. Rather, to the extent that outside accountants or auditors are associated with their statements, it may be in either a compilation or review capacity. These different levels of service are discussed in detail in Chapter 13. Compilations do not involve the application of any audit procedures. The statements are simply prepared from information provided by the firm's management. The accountant does not express any assurance about the statements. Reviews involve inquiries and other analytical procedures designed to provide a basis for expressing "limited assurance" about the statements. These levels of service fall far short of those involved in an audit. Examples 20–24 in Exhibit 4.6 are early warnings related to level of outside accountant/auditor service.

Notice that example 20 suggests that the provision of only compiled financial statements may signal that the borrower places little importance on providing financial information. Beyond this, compiled and reviewed financial statements result in financial information that is less reliable and less complete than audited data. For example, bank customers providing compiled financial statements typically omit the statement of cash flows and all notes to the financial statements. Example 21 points to a reduction in the level of accountant/auditor service as an early warning.

STRATEGY-RELATED EARLY WARNINGS

The lender survey responses identified a number of early warnings involving changes in the activities or businesses in which the firms were engaged. We have grouped these in the strategy-related early warnings category. Exhibit 4.7 lists examples from the lender survey.

The strategy-related early warnings in Exhibit 4.7 have been organized into two relatively homogeneous groupings: change and expansion, and diversification into unrelated businesses. The first category includes examples 1–8, and the second category, examples 9–17. As with all classifications of early warnings, the breaks between categories are never clear, and multiple classifications could easily be defended.

Change and Expansion

Change on any key dimension of a business, along with expansion, however defined, was seen by lenders as calling for caution. Their identification as early warnings suggests that in some cases lenders have found that they have preceded declines in

Exhibit 4.7 Strategy-Related Early Warnings

1. Substantial change in direction for the company. New product lines, new locations, vertical integration.
2. Major changes in business plan: marketing, product line, ownership, management; price place, product, and promotion.
3. Fundamental changes in business, e.g., switch from wholesale to retail mode of business or switch from catalog retailer to showroom retailer.
4. Management change in strategy or commitments, e.g., product or service delivery in the market declines in quality and efficient delivery.
5. Frequent changes in direction or target market.
6. Expansion at a time when the industry seems to be pulling back or becoming obsolete. Indicates a failure to recognize change or refusal to believe change in fundamentals.
7. Expansion into new markets, products, or locations with overly optimistic expectations.
8. Excessive expansion in cyclical business.
9. Diversifications are often an inflection point for a company and bear monitoring to track success.
10. Expanding into unknown industry.
11. Company expands in unrelated business, which takes a lot of management time.
12. Investment in unrelated or high-risk expansion.
13. Entering into related or nonrelated business segment.
14. Going into fields in which management has no particular knowledge, e.g., shoe company going into fashion ready-to-wear.
15. New product lines: gauze machines versus burn beds.
16. Entry into a related but new product line. Does the company have the expertise to produce the new product to the standards called for in the production contract? Example: circuit board manufacturer starts manufacturing laptop computers.
17. Foray into unrelated businesses. For example, an aggregates company starts up an asphalt paving business. It may seem like similar industries when in fact it is two completely different businesses with different requirements for success.

earnings. The labels used by the lenders to characterize the change and expansion that should be a source of concern include substantial, major, fundamental, frequent, and excessive. In addition, expansion based upon overly optimistic expectations, or at a time when an industry seems to be pulling back, are singled out.

The type of change that is a potential source of concern is quite broad. It includes direction, product lines, location, organization (vertical), marketing, ownership, management, wholesale versus retail, and target market.

Movement into Unrelated Businesses

The movement of companies into unrelated businesses is a significant cautionary event. An implicit theme of examples 9–17, which deal with this matter, is that the actual range of related businesses is frequently more narrow than management believes it to be. The examples that would probably be seen as related activities, but might prove not to be, involved shoes to fashion ready-to-wear (example 14), gauze machines to burn beds (example 15), circuit board manufacturing to laptop computers (example 16), and aggregates to asphalt paving (example 17). As stated in example 17, "It may seem like similar industries when in fact it is two completely different businesses with different requirements for success."

In gauging the early warning character of an expansion into a new line of business, lenders must decide whether the key skills and capabilities demanded in the new business are already present in their customer's current business. If not present, can they be acquired or developed on a timely basis?

MISCELLANEOUS EARLY WARNINGS

Those early warnings from the lender survey that did not fit into any one of the seven previous categories were classified as miscellaneous. Exhibit 4.8 provides a sampling of these miscellaneous early warnings.

Exhibit 4.8   Miscellaneous Early Warnings

1. Hiring of telemarketers.
2. When traditionally a contractor is in an underbilled or overbilled position at each fiscal year-end, then suddenly this position reverses.
3. Significant changes in any account: accounts receivable, sales, taxes. Here, historical information and industry averages help.
4. Significant increases in legal expenses.
5. A loan closing is lengthy. Usually this indicates problems later.
6. Stock price drops significantly in a very short period of time. Wall Street is the most efficient market in terms of disbursing information.
7. Loan is downgraded.
8. Wanting a guarantee to be released for no apparent reason.
9. No personal guarantee on a financing.
10. Talk of looking for an outside investor.
11. The company starts borrowing at other places.
12. Expanding bank relationships beyond a reasonable number.
13. Large purchases of equipment with long-term debt in a cyclical industry, e.g., grading contractors.
14. The owner/president of the company begins investing in other business ventures.
15. Industry crashes but company continues to perform.
16. Enlarged facilities.
17. Buying a new building.
18. Insurance cancellations.
19. What borrower's competitors are saying. A lot of it needs to be listened to with skepticism, but it should all be checked out.

Declines in stock prices made up five of the miscellaneous early warnings. Reductions in share prices may reflect expectations of declines in earnings that are not yet evident in the financial statement–based early warnings. Market prices for securities have generally proved to reveal new information in a very timely fashion.

There were also five miscellaneous early warnings involving personal guarantees for indebtedness. These were seen as early warnings in cases where borrowers were unwilling to serve as guarantors or had been serving as guarantors and now wanted to be removed from guarantor status. It would be reasonable to assume a possible negative development, known to the guarantor but not to the lender, in a case where the guarantor wants to be removed from this status and is unwilling to provide a reason.

SUMMARY

The results of the lender survey has provided a wide range of early warnings that lenders believe are predictive of future declines in earnings. The early warnings were grouped into seven different specific and one miscellaneous category. This organization of a large body of early warnings should make the information more useful for those attempting to avoid earnings surprises by improving the quality of their earnings expectations.

To provide a summary view of the sources of the early warnings, the 870 collected from the lender survey are broken down by category in Exhibit 4.9.

This breakdown is based solely on frequency of the early warnings by category. The ranking of early warnings by their numerical frequency does not indicate whether, for example, liquidity or profitability early warnings are individually more powerful predictors of earnings declines. Recall that the survey respondent providing example 1 in Exhibit 4.4 takes the position that external environment early warnings are among the best: "Oftentimes, the best early indicators of earnings declines are things outside of the company." The survey results do not provide any evidence on the relative value of a liquidity item, such as a significant increase in inventory days, versus something from the strategy classification, such as expansion into an unrelated busi-

Exhibit 4.9 Distribution of Early Warnings by Category

Liquidity	274
Profitability	177
Management	136
Borrower financial communications	125
Borrower communications	39
External environment	35
Strategy	35
Miscellaneous	49
Total	870

86

ness. It would be a mistake to place less reliance on the categories into which fewer early warnings fall.

To complete this recap of early warnings, some of the more frequently cited in each category are shown in Exhibit 4.10.

Exhibit 4.10 Most Frequently Cited Early Warnings by Category

Category	Early Warnings
Liquidity	Increases in working-capital days statistics Overdrafts Failure to satisfy line-of-credit cleanup period Inquiries to bank from borrower's creditors Late payments Rapid growth
Profitability	Declining gross margins Increases in working-capital days statistics Nonrecurring income Customer concentrations Loss of a major customer
Management	Failure to provide or meet projections Changes in management Management lifestyle Litigation
Borrower financial communications	Delayed receipt of financial statements Changes in accountants/auditors Changes in accounting policies Reduced quality of financial information
Borrower communications	Failure to respond to phone calls Management generally nonresponsive Evasive management communications
External environment	Rising interest rates New competition New technology Changing regulations
Strategy	Expansion into unrelated businesses Fundamental changes in business direction Fundamental change in industry
Miscellaneous	Lack of personal guarantees Declines in stock prices

While the results of the lender survey summarized in Exhibits 4.9 and 4.10 should prove to be useful, they do not demonstrate which of the specific early warnings are most effective. However, based upon the survey results and analysis in this chapter, it is possible at least to suggest some of the more desirable characteristics of early warnings.

The *timeliness* of an early warning is of great importance. In fact, virtually by definition, an early warning must be available prior to the earnings decline so that an earnings surprise can either be avoided or mitigated. The most useful early warnings will have *lengthy response intervals*. That is, the likelihood of avoiding an earnings surprise is increased the more the time between the emergence of the early warning and the potential earnings decline.

The section on early warnings related to the external environment provided a relevant example in the form of the approximately six-month lag between changes in housing starts and changes in carpet sales. This provides ample time to adjust earnings expectations so that a shrinkage in earnings does not come as a surprise. Medical diagnosis is replete with developments that are designed to expand the response interval during which appropriate therapy may either effect a cure or at least an improvement in outcome. Mammography and the relatively new prostate specific antigen (PSA) test are medical examples of efforts to increase the therapeutic response interval.

An early warning could have both the desirable characteristics of timeliness and lengthy response intervals and not be very effective if it does not display a reasonably *high correlation* with subsequent changes in earnings. Again, to use the medical diagnostics framework, a medical test with a high frequency of false positives (incorrectly indicates the presence of a disease) is presumably not an effective tool. The same is true of early warnings.

Finally, financial analysis, of which the identification and use of early warnings is a part, is an economic activity conducted under at least an implicit budget constraint. Therefore, *efficiency* in the identification and use of early warnings is a desirable characteristic. The high correlation characteristic will increase efficiency by reducing the time devoted to the investigation of false positives. Many of the profitability- and liquidity-related early warnings involve various days statistics that are often produced by commercial software products that provide a vast range of statistics on a very low cost basis. Whereas days-related early warnings probably yield a high percentage of false positives, the cost of their production is rather low. However, the employment of an analyst's time to explore the early warnings is costly.

ENDNOTES

1. Mark Twain, *Following the Equator. Pudd'nhead Wilson's New Calendar* (1897), frontispiece caption.
2. Joel Siegel, "The 'Quality of Earnings' Concept—A Survey," *Financial Analysts Journal*, March–April 1982, pp. 60–68.

Chapter 5

Avoiding Earnings Surprises by Improving the Quality of Historical Earnings Analysis

Users want information about the portion of a company's reported earnings that is stable or recurring and that provides a basis for estimating sustainable earnings.[1]

An earnings surprise results when there is a material difference between expected and actual results. Much of the work in this book is focused on how, once an earnings expectation is formed, a surprise can be avoided by careful attention to a range of financial early warnings. However, the focus in this chapter and in Chapter 6 is on reducing the likelihood of earnings surprises by improving the quality of the earnings expectation or forecast.

Exhortations to heed the lessons of history are among the popular bits of cautionary advice. This advice applies equally to distilling and using the information contained in historical financial results in forming earnings expectations. Unlike the once-fashionable zero-base budgeting, today's forecasts of earnings are seldom built from the ground up. Far more efficient is a process that employs carefully analyzed *past performance* as the forecast foundation. Critics sometimes dismiss the value of financial statements on the grounds that they are basically historical documents. The implication is that they would be of little value in forecasting because they describe where the firm has been, not where it is going. The weakness of such views is pointed up by studies of forecasting performance that demonstrate the rather surprising effectiveness of forecasting rules that employ nothing more than a no-change extrapolation of the most recent actual (historical) earnings.[2] That is, there is a tremendous amount of valuable information in the past financial performance of a firm that is useful in estimating future results. However, to be of maximum value for forecasting purposes, a reported earnings series must be purged of the effects of any revenue or gain and expense or loss that are *nonrecurring* in nature.

THE NATURE OF NONRECURRING ITEMS

It is difficult to provide a definitive definition of nonrecurring items. "Unusual" and "infrequent in occurrence" are characteristics often cited in defining nonrecurring items. Kieso and Weygandt, in their very popular intermediate accounting text, use the term *irregular items* to describe what most mean by nonrecurring items.[3] For our purposes, irregular or nonrecurring items are revenues or gains and expenses or losses that are not reasonably consistent contributors to results, either in terms of their presence or their amount. This is how we use the term *nonrecurring items* throughout this book.

From a security valuation perspective, nonrecurring items could be characterized as those having a smaller effect on share price than recurring elements of earnings. Some items can often be identified as nonrecurring simply by their very nature, e.g., restructuring charges, litigation settlements, flood losses, product recall costs, embezzlement losses, and insurance settlements. Other items may appear consistently in the income statement but vary widely in amount. For example, gains on the disposition of flight equipment were reported in recent years by Delta Air Lines, Inc.:[4]

1989	$17 million
1990	18 million
1991	17 million
1992	35 million
1993	65 million
1994	2 million

These above gains averaged about $44 million over the past 11 years and ranged from a loss of $1 million (1988) to a gain of $130 million (1984). The more recent six years typify the variability in the amounts for the entire 11-year period. It would be difficult to call these gains nonrecurring, but they are very irregular in amount. There are at least three different ways to handle this line item in revising results for the purpose of identifying sustainable or recurring earnings: (1) simply eliminate the line item based upon its highly inconsistent contribution to results; (2) include the line item at its average value ($44 million for the period 1983–1994) for some time period; or (3) attempt to acquire information on planned aircraft dispositions that might make possible a superior prediction of the contribution of gains on aircraft dispositions to future results. The last may appear to be the most appealing but may prove difficult to implement because of lack of information, and it may also be less attractive when viewed from a cost-benefit perspective. In general, we would recommend simply employing a fairly recent average value for the gains in projecting earnings.

Other examples of such irregular items of revenue or gain and expense or loss abound: temporary revenue increases or decreases associated with the Gulf War— "Sales to the United States government increased substantially during the Persian

Gulf War. However, sales returned to more normal levels in the second half of the year"[5]; temporary revenue increases associated with expanded television sales due to World Cup soccer; temporary increases in loan loss provisions resulting from economic downturns and problems in the financial services industry; foreign currency gains and losses; and temporary increases in warranty expense resulting from unique problems associated with selected automobiles or other products, e.g., the Pentium chip.

Identification of nonrecurring or irregular items is not a strictly mechanical process. It calls for the exercise of judgment and involves both line items and period-to-period amounts of individual income statement items.

THE PROCESS OF IDENTIFYING NONRECURRING ITEMS

Careful analysis of past financial performance, aimed at removing the effects of nonrecurring items, is a far more formidable task than one might suspect. The task would be fairly simple if most nonrecurring items were prominently displayed on the face of the income statement, but this is not the case. Recent work suggests that less than a quarter of nonrecurring items are likely to be found, individually disclosed, on the income statement.[6] Providing guidance to make possible the location of the remaining items is the goal of this chapter.

Our experience with this search activity suggests a sequence that has the highest cumulative yield of nonrecurring items in terms of both materiality and search cost. Search cost, mainly analyst time, is an important consideration because financial analysis is an economic activity that should be conducted in an efficient manner. Further, time devoted to this task is not available for another task, and therefore there is an opportunity cost to consider. The discussion that follows is organized in accordance with the recommended search sequence shown in Exhibit 5.1. Following only the first four steps in this search sequence is likely to locate almost 60% of all nonrecurring items.[7] Continuing through steps 5 and 6 will increase this percentage. However, the 60% discovery rate is undoubtedly higher if the focus is only on *material* nonrecurring items. The nonrecurring items disclosed in other locations, beyond steps 1–4, are far fewer in number and less likely to be material than those found through steps 1–4.

NONRECURRING ITEMS IN THE INCOME STATEMENT

Examination of the income statement, the first step in the search sequence, requires a thorough understanding of the design and content of contemporary income statements to aid in the location and analysis of nonrecurring components of earnings. This calls for a review of the generally accepted accounting principles (GAAP) that determine the structure and content of the income statement. Locating nonrecurring items in the income statement is a highly efficient, cost-effective process. Many

Exhibit 5.1 Efficient Search Sequence for Nonrecurring Items

Step and Search Location

1. Income statement
2. Statement of cash flows—operating activities section only
3. Inventory note—assuming that inventories exist, are significant, and that the firm employs the last in, first out (LIFO) method
4. Income tax note
5. "Other income (expense)" note in cases where this balance is not detailed on the face of the income statement
6. MD&A of financial condition and results of operations—a Securities and Exchange Commission requirement and therefore available only for public companies
7. Other notes revealing nonrecurring items:

Note	Nonrecurring Item Revealed
Property and equipment	Gains and losses on asset sales
Long-term debt	Foreign currency and debt retirement gains and losses
Foreign currency	Foreign currency gains and losses
Restructuring	Current and prospective impact of restructuring activities
Contingencies	Potential revenue or expense items
Quarterly financial data	Nonrecurring items in quarterly results

nonrecurring items will be prominently displayed on separate lines in the statement and be readily recognizable. Further, leads to other nonrecurring items disclosed elsewhere may be discovered during this process. For example, a line item summarizing items of "other income (expense)" may include an associated note reference detailing its contents. These notes should always be reviewed, step 5 in the search sequence, because they will typically reveal nonrecurring items.

Examples of the two principal income statement formats under current GAAP are presented in Exhibits 5.2 and 5.3. The income statement of Schering-Plough Corp., Exhibit 5.2, follows a single-step design, and that of Air Products and Chemicals, Inc., Exhibit 5.3, illustrates the multi-step format. An annual survey of financial statements conducted by the American Institute of Certified Public Accountants reveals that about one-third of the 600 companies in its survey use the single-step format and the other two-thirds the multi-step format. The distinguishing feature of the multi-step statement is that it provides an intermediate earnings subtotal designed to reflect pre-tax operating performance. In principle, operating income should be composed almost entirely of recurring items of revenue and expense that result from the main operating activities of the firm. In practice, it is common for numerous material nonrecurring items to be included in operating income. For example, where present,

Exhibit 5.2 Single-Step Income Statement: Schering-Plough Corp. and Subsidiaries, Consolidated Income Statements, Years Ending December 31, 1992–1994 (millions of dollars except per share data)

	1992	1993	1994
Sales	$4,055.7	$4,341.3	$4,657.1
Cost of sales	900.6	908.8	958.6
Selling, general, and administrative	1,629.8	1,747.4	1,828.9
Research and development	521.5	577.6	620.0
Other expense, net	49.9	29.1	36.4
Total costs and expenses	3,101.8	3,262.9	3,443.9
Income before income taxes	953.9	1,078.4	1,213.2
Income taxes	233.9	253.4	291.2
Income before items below	720.0	825.0	922.0
Extraordinary item	(26.7)	–	–
Cumulative effect of accounting changes	27.1	(94.2)	–
Net income	$ 720.4	$ 730.8	$ 922.0
Earnings per common share before items below	$ 3.60	$ 4.23	$ 4.82
Extraordinary item	(.13)	–	–
Cumulative effect of accounting changes	.13	(.48)	–
Earnings per common share	$ 3.60	$ 3.75	$ 4.82

Source: Schering-Plough Corp., annual report, December 1994, p. 20.

"restructuring charges," one of the most popular nonrecurring items of the 1990s, is virtually always included in operating income.

The Schering-Plough single-step income statement does not partition results into intermediate subtotals. For example, there is no preliminary result identified as "operating income." Rather, all revenues and expenses are separately totaled and "income before income taxes" is computed in a single step, as total expenses are simply deducted from total revenues. However, the Air Products multi-step income statement provides an intermediate profit subtotal identified as "operating income."

Nonrecurring Items Located in Income from Continuing Operations

Whether a single-step or multi-step format is used, the composition of income from continuing operations is the same. It includes all items of revenue or gain and expense or loss with the exception of those (1) identified with discontinued operations, (2) meeting the definition of extraordinary items, and (3) resulting from the cumulative effect of changes in accounting principles. Because it excludes only these three items, one can find in income from continuing operations all other nonrecurring items of revenue or gain and expense or loss in this key profit subtotal.

Exhibit 5.3 Multi-Step Income Statement: Air Products and Chemicals, Inc., and Subsidiaries, Consolidated Income Statements, Years Ending September 30, 1992–1994 (millions except per share data)

	1992	1993	1994
Sales[a]	$3,217.3	$3,327.7	$3,485.3
Other income (expense), net[a]	8.8	27.8	(1.5)
Total sales and other income	3,226.1	3,355.5	3,483.8
Cost of sales	1,936.7	2,029.9	2,111.5
Selling, distribution, and administrative	723.7	744.0	788.8
Research and development	85.2	92.3	97.4
Workforce reduction and asset write-downs [a]	–	120.0	–
Total costs and expenses	2,745.6	2.986.2	2,997.7
Operating income	480.5	369.3	486.1
Income from equity affiliates net of related expenses[a]	6.7	11.8	28.5
Gain on sale of investment in equity affiliates[a]	9.1	1.0	–
Loss on leverated interest rate swaps[a]	–	–	107.7
Interest expense[a]	89.3	81.3	81.6
Income before taxes	407.0	300.8	325.3
Income taxes[a]	130.0	99.9	91.8
Income before items below	277.0	200.9	233.5
Extraordinary item—loss on early retirement of debt, net of income tax benefit of $3.5[a]	6.0	–	–
Cumulative effect of accounting changes[a]	–	–	14.3
Net Income	$ 271.0	$ 200.9	$ 247.8
Monthly average no. of common shares outstanding	113.0	113.9	113.6
Earnings per common share before items below	$ 2.45	$ 1.76	$ 2.06
Extraordinary item	(.05)	–	–
Cumulative effect of accounting changes	–	–	.12
Earnings per common share	$ 2.40	$ 1.76	$ 2.18

Source: Air Products and Chemicals, Inc., annual report, September 1994, p. 8.
[a]The original report made reference to notes, which are not included here.

The Nature of Operating Income

Operating income is designed to reflect the revenue or gain and expense or loss that are a product of the fundamental operating activities of the firm. However, notice that the 1993 operating income of Air Products includes a charge for "workforce reduction and asset write-downs" of $120 million. In this case, operating income, as reported, is not that measure of sustainable earnings called for in the quotation from the report of the American Institute of Certified Public Accountants, Special Committee on Financial Reporting, that opened this chapter. Even at this early point in the operations section of the income statement, nonrecurring items have been introduced that will require adjustment in order to arrive at an earnings base "that provides a basis for estimating sustainable earnings."[8] Be aware that "operating income" in a multi-step format is an earlier subtotal than "income from continuing operations."

Nonrecurring Items Included in Operating Income

A review of current corporate annual reports reveals that the Air Products situation is not at all unusual. A sampling of nonrecurring items included in the operating income subtotal of multi-step income statements is provided in Exhibit 5.4. There are more instances of nonrecurring expense or loss than of nonrecurring revenue or gain. This may simply suggest that operating activities are far less likely to produce favorable than unfavorable nonrecurring items. However, fundamental accounting conventions such as the historical cost concept and conservatism may also provide part of the explanation. Many of the nonrecurring expense or loss items involve the recognition of declines in the value of specific assets. Restructuring charges have been among the most common items in this section of the income statement in recent years. These charges involve asset write-downs and liability accruals that will be paid off in future years. Seldom is revenue or gain recorded as a result of writing up assets. Further, unlike the case of restructuring charges, the favorable future consequences of a management action would rarely support current accrual of prospective revenue or gain.

Nonrecurring Items Excluded from Operating Income

"Other income (expense)" items, typically reported immediately below the operating income subtotal, are usually less closely associated with the basic operating activities of the firm. In addition to interest expense, Air Products included earnings from equity-accounted investments, gains on the sale of investments, and a loss on leveraged interest rate swaps. Of these items, the gains on the sales of investments and the loss on the interest rate swaps would typically be considered nonrecurring. A sampling of nonrecurring items found in the "other income (expense)" category of the multi-step income statements of a number of companies, is provided in Exhibit 5.5.

A comparison of the items in Exhibits 5.4 and 5.5 reveals some potential for overlap in these categories. Exhibit 5.4 should be dominated by items closely linked to company operations. The nonrecurring items in Exhibit 5.5 should fall outside the operations area of the firm. Notice that the USX Corp. litigation charge (Exhibit 5.4) is included in operating income but that of Sun Microsystems (Exhibit 5.5) is pushed out of operating income into "other income (expense)." The antitrust character of the USX charge must be viewed as more operations-related than the securities-related

Exhibit 5.4 Nonrecurring Items of Revenue or Gain and Expense or Loss Included in Operating Income

Company	Nonrecurring Item
Expense or loss	
Argosy Gaming (1993)	Flood costs
Burlington Industries (1994)	Provision for restructuring
Business Records (1993)	Purchased in-process R&D
Dual Drilling (1993)	Land rig write-down
Gaylord Container (1994)	Asset write-downs from plant relocation
Heart Technology (1992)	Product recall costs
Hitox (1994)	Inventory valuation charge
Meredith (1994)	Write-down of film assets
On The Border Cafes (1994)	Injury claim settlement (airplane crash)
Osmonics (1993)	Embezzlement loss
Pinkerton (1993)	Investment write-down
Southwest Airlines (1993)	Merger expenses
Universal Foods (1992)	Lease termination and related costs
USX (1993)	Litigation charge (antitrust action)
Worthington Foods (1991)	Write-down of nonoperating assets
Revenue or gain	
Air Products and Chemicals (1993)	Insurance settlement
Boise Cascade (1993)	Sales of assets
Federal-Mogul (1993)	Sale of business
Ingersoll-Rand (1993)	Restructure of operations benefit

Sources: Companies' annual reports. The year following each company name designates the annual report from which each example was drawn.

settlement of Sun Microsystems. However, the Baxter International, Inc., litigation settlements due to product-related suits and the Global Industries Ltd. fire loss on a marine vessel case were both excluded from operating income (Exhibit 5.5). Each of these items would seem to be closely tied to the operations of these two firms and therefore more properly included in operating income. The goal of the operating income subtotal should be to capture core operating profitability. Clearly, the range and complexity of nonrecurring items creates difficult judgment calls in implementation of this operating income concept.

Unlike the multi-step statement shown in Exhibit 5.3, the single-step income statement in Exhibit 5.2 does not include a subtotal representing operating income. As a result, the task of identifying core profitability is somewhat more difficult. Nonrecurring items of revenue or gain and expense or loss are either presented as separate line items within the listing of revenue or gain and expense or loss, or included in an "other income (expense)" line.

Exhibit 5.5   Nonrecurring Items of Revenue or Gain and Expense or Loss Excluded from Operating Income

Company	Nonrecurring Item
Expense or loss	
Air Canada (1993)	Investment write-downs
Baxter International (1993)	Litigation settlements (breast implants, etc.)
Becton, Dickinson (1994)	Foreign currency loss
Global Industries (1993)	Fire loss on marine vessel
Hollywood Casino (1992)	Write-off of deferred preacquisition costs
Imperial Holly (1994)	Work force reduction charge
Sun Microsystems (1993)	Securities class action lawsuits
Revenue or gain	
Amtran (1992)	Gain on sale of takeoff/landing slots
Ferro (1993)	Foreign currency transaction gain
Freeport-McMoRan (1991)	Insurance settlement (tanker grounding)
Lin Broadcasting (1992)	Litigation settlement
Meredith (1994)	Sale of broadcast stations
Noble Drilling (1991)	Insurance on rig abandoned in Somalia
Tandem Computers (1994)	Gain on sale of subsidiaries

Sources: Companies' annual reports. The year following each company name designates the annual report from which each example was drawn.

Nonrecurring Items Located Below Income from Continuing Operations

The area of the income statement below "income from continuing operations" has a standard organization that is the same for both single-step and multi-step income statements. The format is outlined in Exhibit 5.6. The income statement of Orange-co, Inc., shown in Exhibit 5.7, illustrates this format. Each of the special line items—discontinued operations, extraordinary items, and changes in accounting principles—is discussed, along with illustrative examples, in the following sections.

Discontinued Operations

The discontinued operations section is designed to enhance the interpretive value of the income statement through separation of the results of continuing operations from those that have been, or are in the process of being, discontinued. Only the discontinuance of operations that constitute a separate and complete segment of the business are to be reported in this special section. In addition, discontinued operations are presented net of their own separate income tax effects. In the case of Orange-co, which is primarily in the business of citrus production and the manufacture of juices and drinks, its discontinued operations involved disposal of its petroleum business.

Exhibit 5.6 Standard Income Statement Format

Income from continuing operations	$000
Discontinued operations	000
Extraordinary items	000
Cumulative effect of changes in accounting principles	000
Net income	$000

Exhibit 5.7 Disclosure of Discontinued Operations: Orange-co, Inc., Consolidated Income Statements, 1991–1993 (thousands of dollars)

	1991	1992	1993
Sales	$64,368	$79,890	$71,938
Cost of sales	56,003	59,618	62,279
Gross Profit	8,365	20,272	9,659
Other costs and expenses, net			
Selling, general, and administrative	(4,276)	(4,236)	(3,995)
Provision for restructuring and other nonrecurring items	(2,120)	(2,100)	–
Gain (loss) on disposition of property and equipment and property held for disposition	1,022	(104)	142
Other	(223)	(627)	(227)
Interest	(4,392)	(2,907)	(1,820)
Income (loss) from continuing operations	(1,624)	10,298	3,759
Income tax expense	272	2,109	1,539
Net income (loss) from continuing operations	(1,896)	8,189	2,220
Discontinued operations			
Loss from operations of discontinued Petroleum Division, net of applicable income tax (benefit) of $(13), $(127) and $(104)	(174)	(208)	(22)
Loss (estimated) on disposal of Petroleum Division, including provision of $30 for operating losses during the phaseout period	–	–	(513)
Loss from discontinued operations	(174)	(208)	(535)
Net income (loss) before items below	(2,070)	7,981	1,685
Extraordinary (loss)—early extinguishment of debt (loss net of applicable tax benefit of $366)	–	–	(597)
Cumulative effects of accounting change	(3,444)	–	–
Net income (loss)	$ (5,514)	$ 7,981	$ 1,088

Source: Orange-co, Inc., annual report, September 1993, p. 7.

Other examples of operations that have been viewed as separate segments, and therefore classified in the discontinued operations category are provided in Exhibit 5.8.

Extraordinary Items

Income statement items are considered extraordinary if they are *both* unusual *and* infrequent in occurrence.[9] Unusual items are those not related to the typical activities or operations of the firm. Infrequency of occurrence simply implies that the item is not expected to recur in the foreseeable future.

In practice, the joint requirement of "unusual and nonrecurring" results in very few items being reported as extraordinary. Generally accepted accounting principles do require that gains and losses associated with two particular transactions be classified as extraordinary without the need to satisfy the tests of being both unusual and nonrecurring: (1) gains and losses from the extinguishment of debt,[10] and (2) gains and losses of debtors resulting from "troubled debt restructurings."[11] Included here are either the settlement of obligations or their continuation with a modification of terms.

A tabulation of extraordinary items, based upon an annual survey of 600 companies conducted by the American Institute of Certified Public Accountants, is provided in Exhibit 5.9. This summary highlights the relative rarity of extraordinary items under current reporting requirements. Debt extinguishments represent the larg-

Exhibit 5.8   Discontinued Operations

Company	Principal Business	Discontinued Operation
Chiquita Brands (1991)	Fresh fruits, vegetables, and processed foods	Meat segment
Ecolab (1992)	Cleaning, sanitizing, and maintenance products and services	Lawn care
Ethyl (1993)	Chemicals	Insurance company
General Electric (1993)	Diversified manufacturing and financial services	Aerospace business
Kodak (1993)	Imaging	Chemical business
Owens-Illinois (1993)	Packaging products	Glass tableware
Quaker State (1992)	Petroleum products and related activities plus insurance	Coal operations
Tenneco (1992)	Diversified company	Minerals and pulp chemicals
Texaco (1993)	Oil and gas	Chemical operations

Sources: Companies' annual reports. The year following each company name designates the annual report from which each example was drawn.

Exhibit 5.9   Extraordinary Items

	1990	1991	1992	1993
Debt extinguishments	36	33	60	79
Operating loss carryforwards	24	20	17	9
Litigation settlements	2	1	2	1
Other	5	4	5	6
Total extraordinary items	67	58	84	95
Companies presenting extraordinary items	63	55	81	91
Companies not presenting extraordinary items	537	545	519	509
Total companies	600	600	600	600

Source: American Institute of Certified Public Accountants, *Accounting Trends and Techniques* (1994), p. 408.

est portion of the disclosed extraordinary items. Extraordinary items associated with operating loss carryforwards have now been eliminated under the new requirements of Statement of Financial Accounting Standards No. 109, "Accounting for Income Taxes."[12] This leaves only from five to seven *judgmental* extraordinary items per year among the 600 companies surveyed in Exhibit 5.9.

The small number of gains and losses classified as extraordinary is consistent with the definition of extraordinary gains and losses. However, this adds to the challenge of locating all nonrecurring items as part of a thorough earnings analysis. Few nonrecurring items will qualify for the prominent disclosure that results from display in one of the special sections, such as that for extraordinary items, of the income statement.

A review of recent annual reports highlights the variation in practice resulting from application of the "unusual and nonrecurring" test to determine extraordinary items. Exhibit 5.10 presents a number of nonrecurring transactions that were or were not treated as extraordinary. The similarity between the two groups highlights the degree of judgment involved in applying the classification rules. For example, Raychem Corp.[13] reported a charge from a class action litigation settlement as extraordinary, and Scientific-Atlanta, Inc.,[14] did not. Each case involved a class action securities suit. As each appears to be nonrecurring, the classification decision must have turned on whether or not the charges were unusual. It becomes more difficult to consider such items as unusual in today's litigious environment. Raychem's 1993 Form 10-K annual report to the Securities and Exchange Commission lists ten different legal proceedings.[15] However, they are all related to the operation of the business, not to relations with investors in Raychem. Material losses from these cases are more likely to be classified as part of operating results.

American Building Maintenance treated the results of a natural disaster, an earthquake, as extraordinary, but Alexander & Baldwin, Inc., did not classify its loss from a natural disaster, a hurricane, as extraordinary. Again, in the Bay Area of San Francisco, the location of American Building's loss, it would seem difficult to consider

Exhibit 5.10 "Extraordinary Item" Classification Decisions

Item or Event	Company
Reported as extraordinary	
Settlement of class action litigation	Raychem (1993)
Gain on insurance settlement due to damage to building from San Francisco earthquake	American Building Maintenance (1989)
Insurance settlement due to deprivation of use of logistics and drilling equipment abandoned in Somalia because of civil unrest	Noble Drilling (1991)
Gain on insurance settlement resulting from a drilling rig being subject to theft and vandalism	Noble Drilling (1989)
Reserve on Iraqi account receivable—from Iraq's State Enterprise for Tobacco and Cigarettes	Dibrell Brothers (1992)
Loss from accidental melting of radioactive substance used in steel operation	NS Group (1992)
Gain from a settlement with the government of Iran over the expropriation of Phillips' oil production interests	Phillips Petroleum (1990)
Not reported as extraordinary	
Settlement of securities class action litigation	Scientific-Atlanta (1994)
Hurricane loss	Alexander & Baldwin (1992)
Flood costs	Argosy Gaming (1993)
Insurance claim settlement (airplane crash)	On The Border Cafes (1994)
Gain from insurance settlement as a result of the loss of Rowan Gorilla I jack-up, which capsized and sank while being towed to the North Sea	Rowan Companies (1988)
Loss provision for costs associated with cleanup of oil spill in Valdez, Alaska	Exxon (1989)
Gain from a settlement with the government of Iran over the expropriation of Sun oil production interests	Sun Company (1992)

Sources: Companies' annual reports. The year following each company name designates the annual report from which each example was drawn.

earthquakes unusual. However, an earthquake of the magnitude of the one in 1989 is clearly an exceptional event.

The last examples in the two classifications, Phillips Petroleum and Sun, represent the sharpest contrast because the gains they reported appear to be identical. That is, each company received settlements from the government of Iran as a result of the expropriation of oil production interests during the Iranian revolution.

The judgmental character of the definition of extraordinary items, combined with the growing complexity of company operations, results in the diversity in classification revealed in Exhibit 5.10. The task of locating all nonrecurring items of revenue or gain and expense or loss is aided only marginally by the presence of the extraordinary category in the income statement, because it is employed so sparingly. Locating most nonrecurring items calls for careful review of other parts of the income statement, other statements, and notes to the financial statements.

Changes in Accounting Principles

Changes in accounting principles, for example, the adoption of newer accounting standards for income taxes and postretirement benefits, and changes in estimates, such as an increase in useful lives used in computing depreciation, are the principal types of changes that affect earnings analysis.

In changes from one accepted accounting principle to another, the most common reporting treatment is to show the cumulative effect of the change on the results of prior years as a single total, net of taxes, in the income statement for the year of the change. Less common is the retroactive effect approach whereby statements of prior years are restated on the new accounting basis. The effect on years prior to those presented in the annual report for the year of the change—usually three years— is treated as an adjustment to retained earnings of the earliest year presented. Recent accounting standards have sometimes required the use of one particular method of reporting a change in principle and in other cases have permitted use of either method.

Accounting changes in recent years have been influenced by the required adoption of new Financial Accounting Standards Board statements. Information on accounting changes, both in accounting principles and in estimates, is provided in Exhibit 5.11. This information is drawn from the annual financial statement survey conducted by the American Institute of Certified Public Accountants. The distribution of adoption dates for the same accounting standard results because some firms adopt the new statement prior to its mandatory adoption date. For example, the latest that Statement of Financial Accounting Standards (SFAS) No. 109 could be adopted was for fiscal years beginning after December 15, 1992, or calendar 1993 for firms with a December 31 year-end.

Most recent changes in accounting principle have been reported on a cumulative effect basis. The cumulative effect is reported, net of taxes, in a separate section of the income statement (see Exhibits 5.2 and 5.3 for examples of this disclosure). The cumulative effect is the effect of the change on the results of previous years. The effect of the change on the current year, i.e., year of the change, is typically disclosed in a note describing the change and its effect. However, it is not disclosed separately on the face of the income statement. An example of disclosure of the separate effects,

Exhibit 5.11   Accounting Changes

	No. of Companies			
Subject of the Change	1990	1991	1992	1993
Income taxes				
SFAS No. 109 adopted	–	16	244	233
SFAS No. 96 adopted	16	16	–	–
Pension costs				
Actuarial assumptions	122	151	121	224
SFAS No. 87 adopted	19	1	–	–
Postretirement benefits	2	39	198	176
Postemployment benefits	–	–	21	87
Investments (SFAS No. 115)	–	–	–	21
Inventories				
LIFO discontinued	3	3	4	6
LIFO adopted	1	2	3	1
Capitalization of costs formerly expensed	–	3	2	–
Other	3	3	–	2
Reinsurance contracts	–	–	–	7
Depreciable lives	5	4	6	6
Depreciation method	3	5	3	3
Reporting entity	6	1	5	5
Other—described	13	17	17	21
Total	193	261	624	792

Source: American Institute of Certified Public Accountants, *Accounting Trends and Techniques* (1994), p. 37.

current and prior year, of the adoption of SFAS No. 106, "Employers' Accounting for Postretirement Benefits Other Than Pensions," by Federal Mogul Corp. is provided in Exhibit 5.12.

The incremental as well as the cumulative effect of the adoption of SFAS No.

Exhibit 5.12   Separating the Current Period and the Cumulative Effect of an Accounting Change: Federal-Mogul Corp., 1992–1993 (millions of dollars)

	1992	1993
Incremental annual expense	$ 7.6	$6.6
Income tax benefit	(2.7)	(2.4)
	4.9	4.2
Cumulative effect of accounting change	135.7	
Income tax benefit	(47.6)	
	88.1	
Net effect of SFAS No. 106	$93.0	$4.2

Source: Federal-Mogul Corp., annual report, December 1993, p. 33.

106 is properly excluded, i.e., added back to results, if the objective is to compare 1992 results with those of 1991 on a consistent basis. However, if the goal were to arrive at a sustainable earnings base for purposes of forecasting future results, then the incremental annual expense is part of future results and should not be removed. The cumulative effect would still be added back in view of its nonrecurring character.

Changes in Estimates

Whereas changes in accounting principles are handled on either a cumulative effect basis or a retroactive restatement basis, changes in accounting estimates are handled on a prospective basis only. The effect of a change is included only in current or future periods; retroactive restatements are not permitted. For example, in its 1993 fourth quarter, Delta Air Lines, Inc., implemented two changes in estimate: (1) an extension of the useful life of its flight equipment from 15 years to 20 years and a reduction in estimated residual values from 5% to 10% of cost, and (2) an increase in the expected long-term rate of return on pension assets of from 9% to 10%. Delta reported that "flight equipment that was not already fully depreciated is being depreciated on a straight-line basis to residual values (5% of cost) over a 20-year period from the dates placed in service."[16] Delta disclosed that the changes in useful life and residual value reduced the level of depreciation for 1993 by $34 million. Since the change affected only the fourth quarter 1993, the size of the effect for the next full year would have been four times this amount, or $136 million. Prospective application of the change in estimate involved computing future depreciation based upon the new useful life and residual value estimates. Depreciation expense for 1993 was simply $34 million less than it would have been under the prior useful life and residual value assumptions. No separate identification of the effect of the change appeared in the 1993 income statement.

The increase in the pension return assumption reduced operating expenses by $13 million for the single quarter in 1993 for which the change was effective.[17] This amounts to an expense reduction of $52 million on an annualized basis: $13 million reduction per quarter × four quarters = $52 million. Pension expense is reduced by an amount equal to the return assumption multiplied by pension fund assets. If the assumed rate of return is increased, then so is the pension return deducted in arriving at net pension expense. The annualized effects of Delta's two estimate changes, $136 million from the depreciation change and $52 million from the pension return change, should have added $188 million to 1994 pre-tax results.

The implications for earnings analysis of changes in accounting principles, e.g., a switch from accelerated to straight-line depreciation, versus changes in estimates differ. A change in accounting principle reported on a cumulative effect basis places a clear nonrecurring item in the income statement. However, a change in estimate, e.g., Delta's extension of the useful life of its flight equipment, simply shifts the amount of an expense or revenue item to a different level on an ongoing basis. A comparison of Delta's financial performance in 1993 (year of the change) to that in 1992 must place 1993 net income on the same basis as 1992 net income. Therefore, 1993 net income should be reduced by the combined after-tax benefit of the depreciation and pension changes. However, a projection of Delta's 1994 net income, as distinguished from a comparison of 1993 with 1992, should employ 1993 net income with a further adjustment to put the benefits of both the depreciation and pension changes on a full-year basis.

NONRECURRING ITEMS IN THE STATEMENT OF CASH FLOWS

After the income statement, the operating activities section of the statement of cash flows is an excellent source of disclosure of nonrecurring items (step 2 in the search sequence). The diagnostic value of this section of the statement of cash flows results from two factors: (1) gains and losses on the sale of investments and fixed assets must be removed from net income in arriving at cash flow from operating activities, and (2) noncash items of revenue or gain and expense or loss must be removed from net income. All cash flow associated with the sale of investments and fixed assets is to be classified in the investment section of the statement of cash flows. This requires removal of the gains and losses, which are typically nonrecurring in nature, on the sale of such items in arriving at cash flow from operating activities. Similarly, many nonrecurring expenses or losses do not involve a current period cash outflow. This requires such items to be adjusted out of net income in arriving at cash flow from operating activities. Such adjustments, assuming that they are not simply combined in a miscellaneous balance, often highlight nonrecurring items.

The partial statement of cash flows of The Dow Chemical Co. in Exhibit 5.13 illustrates the disclosure of nonrecurring items in the operating activities section of the statement of cash flows. The nonrecurring items would appear to be (1) gains and losses on investments, (2) gain on sales of plant properties, (3) gains and losses on foreign currency transactions, and (4) special charges. Dow's income statement also disclosed, on separate lines, each of the nonrecurring items revealed in the operating activities section, with the exception of the gain on the sales of plant properties. The gains and losses on sales of investments and plant properties are removed from the computation of cash from operating activities because all cash from such transactions is classified in the investing activities section.

Gains and losses on foreign currency transactions are removed either because they are noncash or the associated cash flow is properly classified as either investing or financing. The adjustment for special charges reflects their noncash character at the time recorded.

Examples of nonrecurring items disclosed in the operating activities section of a number of different companies are presented in Exhibit 5.14. Frequently, nonrecurring items do appear in the operating activities section of the statement of cash flow. However, none of the nonrecurring items in Exhibit 5.14 were disclosed in the company income statement.

Exhibit 5.13 Nonrecurring Items Disclosure in Statement of Cash Flows: The Dow Chemical Co. Consolidated Cash Flow Statements, 1991–1993 (millions of dollars)

	1991	1992	1993
Operating Activities			
Income before cumulative effect of accounting change	$ 942	$ 276	$ 644
Adjustments to reconcile net income to net cash provided by operating activities			
Depreciation and amortization	1,465	1,487	1,552
Provision (credit) for deferred income tax	(177)	(295)	24
Undistributed (earnings) losses of 20%–50% owned companies	(64)	(27)	147
Minority interests' share in income	236	322	275
Net gain on investments[a]	–	–	(592)
Gain on the sale of Destec Energy, Inc. public stock offering[a]	(213)	–	–
Gain on sales of plant properties	(5)	(22)	(58)
Special charge[a]	370	433	180
Losses (gains) on foreign currency transactions	(70)	(11)	10
Other	(3)	10	13
Changes in assets and liabilities that provided (used) cash			
Accounts receivable	326	(17)	(8)
Inventories	200	195	207
Accounts payable	(70)	(275)	139
Other assets and liabilities[a]	(198)	(183)	(637)
Cash provided by operating activities	$2,739	$1,893	$1,896

Source: The Dow Chemical Co., annual report, December 1994, p. 29.
[a]The original report made reference to notes, which are not included here.

NONRECURRING ITEMS IN THE INVENTORY NOTE OF LIFO FIRMS

The carrying value of inventories maintained under the LIFO method are often significantly undervalued in relation to replacement cost. For public companies, the difference between the LIFO carrying value and replacement cost (frequently approximated by FIFO) is a required disclosure under Securities and Exchange Commission regulations.[18] An example of a substantial difference between LIFO and current replacement value is given in Exhibit 5.15. In discussing its liquidity and capital resources, Handy & Harman states that its precious metal inventories, consisting principally of gold and silver, "may be considered as an equivalent to cash."[19]

A reduction in the physical quantities of a LIFO inventory is called a LIFO liquidation. With a LIFO liquidation, a portion of the firm's cost of sales for the year

Exhibit 5.14   Nonrecurring Items in Operating Activities Section of Cash Flow Statement But Not in Income Statement

Company	Nonrecurring Item
ACX Technologies (1993)	Gain on sale of properties
Avon Products (1993)	Translation losses
Chrysler Corp. (1993/1991)	Reversal of a prior provision
Dresser Industries (1992)	Gain on business disposals
Fina (1993)	Gain on sale of assets
IBP (1993)	Loss on disposal of properties
Kellogg (1993)	Gain on sale of subsidiaries
Scott Paper (1993)	Gains and losses on asset sales
Sherwin-Williams (1993)	Provisions for disposition of operations and for environmental remediation
SCI Systems (1993)	Unrealized foreign exchange losses
Zycad (1993)	Gain on sale of Synopsys stock

Sources: Companies' annual reports. The year following each company name designates the annual report from which each example was drawn.

will be made up of the carrying values associated with the liquidated units. These costs are typically lower than current replacement costs, resulting in increased profits or reduced losses.

As with the differences between the LIFO cost and replacement value of the LIFO inventory, Securities and Exchange Commission regulations also call for disclosures of the effect of LIFO liquidations.[20] The following disclosure, from the statements of Wyman-Gordon Co., illustrates compliance with this requirement:

> Inventory quantities were reduced in 1993, 1992, and 1991 resulting in liquidations of LIFO inventories carried at lower costs prevailing in prior years compared with the cost of current purchases. The effect of lower quantities decreased 1993 loss from operations by $5,469,000, increased 1992 income from operations by $18,388,000, and decreased 1991 loss from operations by $1,529,000.[21]

The 1992 effect of the LIFO liquidation is quite dramatic. The $18,388,000

Exhibit 5.15   LIFO Inventory Valuation Differences: Handy & Harman, 1992–1993 (thousands of dollars)

	1992	1993
Precious metals stated at LIFO cost	$ 32,783	$ 32,797
LIFO inventory—excess of year-end market value over LIFO cost	$105,416	$141,273

Source: Handy & Harman, annual report, 1993, p. 31.

increase in 1992 income from operations amounted to 67% of the $27,275,000 of income from operations for the year. Even though Wyman-Gordon reported LIFO liquidations for each of the years 1991–1993, an analysis of sustainable earnings would consider the profit improvements from the liquidations to be nonrecurring. The LIFO liquidations result from reductions in the physical quantity of inventory. There are obvious limitations on the ability to sustain these liquidations in future years; the inventory cannot be reduced below zero. Moreover, the variability in the size of the effect on profits of the liquidations argues for the nonrecurring classification. The profit improvement resulting from the LIFO liquidation amounts to nothing more than the realization of the undervalued asset. It is analogous to the gain associated with the disposition of an undervalued security, piece of equipment, or plot of land.

The analyst cannot rely on the disclosure requirements of the Securities and Exchange Commission when reviewing the statements of nonpublic companies, especially where an outside accountant has done only a review or a compilation (see Chapter 13). However, one can infer the possibility of a LIFO liquidation through the combination of a decline in the dollar amount of inventory and an otherwise unexplainable improvement in gross margin. Details on the existence and effect of a LIFO liquidation should then be a subject for discussion with management.

NONRECURRING ITEMS IN THE INCOME TAX NOTE

Income tax notes are among the more challenging of the disclosures found in annual reports. However, mastering this challenge is worth the effort because they can be a rich source of information on important nonrecurring items. Fortunately, our emphasis here on the persistence of earnings permits us to focus only on a subset of the information found in tax notes.

Under the requirements of current GAAP related to tax disclosures, the location of nonrecurring tax items calls for mastery and review of only two elements of the tax notes. The first is a schedule that reconciles the actual tax expense or credit with the amount that would have resulted if all pre-tax results had been taxed at the statutory federal rate. An example of this disclosure for Biogen, Inc., is provided in Exhibit 5.16.

Notice that Biogen's tax expense is substantially reduced in each of the years 1991–1993 because of the utilization of losses from earlier years. Current U.S. tax law permits net operating losses to first be carried back for 3 years, providing a refund of prior taxes, and then, if not fully utilized, to be carried forward for 15 years, providing a shield against tax payments. Biogen's carryforward benefits have a substantial favorable effect on its current profitability. For example, the net operating loss carryforward benefits in 1992 and 1993 amount to 37% and 34%, respectively, of net income. However, these benefits are not a sustainable element of operating results. Biogen's tax note discloses the availability of $89 million of unused net operating loss carryforwards, plus $11 million of tax credit carryforwards. As a result, near-term projections of results should continue to assume that profits will be

Exhibit 5.16 Reconciliation of Statutory and Effective Federal Income Tax Rates: Biogen, Inc., 1991–1993 (thousands of dollars)

	1991	1992	1993
Income (tax) at statutory rates	$2,532	$13,577	$12,116
Foreign income (tax) at other than U.S. rates	56	(655)	(253)
Utilization of net operating loss carryforwards	(2.510)	(14,070)	(11,159)
Effects of losses not currently utilizable	–	2,562	1,187
Other	182	206	309
Reported income tax expense	$ 260	$ 1,620	$ 2,200

Source: Biogen, Inc., annual report, December 1993, p. 29.

substantially shielded from taxation. However, the amount of unused net operating loss and tax credit carryforwards should be closely monitored.

A strong indicator of nonrecurring tax benefits is an unusually low effective tax rate. This condition should first be noticed upon initial review of the income statement, step 1 in the search sequence in Exhibit 5.1. The percentage relations between Biogen's tax provision and its income before taxes for 1991 to 1993 are shown in Exhibit 5.17.

In addition to net operating loss carryforward benefits, a variety of other items may produce nonsustainable increases or decreases in total tax expense or tax benefit. These include

1. Tax reductions from other loss carryforwards and various tax credits and tax credit carryforwards such as capital loss carryforwards, research and development tax credits, alternative minimum tax credit carryforwards, and foreign tax credits.
2. Tax increases or decreases resulting from revaluations of deferred tax assets and liabilities as a result of changes in income tax rates.
3. Tax increases or decreases resulting from the resolution of disputes with tax authorities.
4. Tax increases or decreases attributable to changes in the deferred tax valuation allowance based upon (a) realization of previously unrecognized deferred tax

Exhibit 5.17 Effective Tax Rate: Biogen, Inc., 1991–1993 (thousands of dollars)

	1991	1992	1993
Total income tax provision	$ 260	$ 1,620	$ 2,200
Income before income taxes	7,446	39,931	34,617
Effective tax rate	3.5%	4.1%	6.4%

Source: Biogen, Inc., annual report, December 1993, p. 28.

benefits or (b) revised estimations of the likelihood of realization of deferred tax assets.

5. Tax reductions resulting from earnings taxed at reduced rates compared to the U.S. federal statutory rate. The persistence of such benefits relies on the continuation of this feature in the tax law and the company's ability to continue to avail itself of the benefit.

The reconciliation schedule of Mitchell Energy & Development Corp. in Exhibit 5.18 provides an illustration of cases 1 and 2 in the preceding list. An example of case 3 is the 3.4 percentage point reduction in the effective tax rate of Diebold, Inc., resulting from a tax court settlement.[22] Case 4 is illustrated in the reconciliation schedule of General Instrument Corp. in Exhibit 5.19.

Mitchell Energy's earnings benefited from tax reductions produced by tax credits and other carryforwards. However, it is important to understand that benefits associated with carryforwards will eventually cease when the carryforwards are utilized or expire prior to use. Continuation of the benefits from the federal tax credits, mainly the result of Section 29 of the Internal Revenue Code for natural gas produced from certain wells, requires that this feature of the tax law be maintained and that Mitchell Energy be in a position to continue to perform the activities that earn the benefit.

Exhibit 5.18 Reconciliation of Statutory and Effective Federal Income Tax Rates: Mitchell Energy & Development Corp., 1992–1994

	1992	1993	1994
Statutory federal income tax rate	34.0%	34.0%	35.0%
State income taxes, net of federal income tax benefit	10.6	(3.0)	2.3
Federal tax credits	(2.5)	(7.9)	(10.8)
Utilization of tax carryforwards	(6.6)	–	(2.3)
Increase in corporate statutory federal income tax rate	–	–	23.1
Other, net	(.4)	.2	(.1)
Effective federal income tax rate	35.1%	23.3%	47.2%

Source: Mitchell Energy and Development Corp., annual report, January 1994, p. 55.

Exhibit 5.19 Effective Tax Rate Reduced by the Realization of Previously Reserved Deferred Tax Assets: General Instrument Corp., 1993–1994

Statutory tax rate	35.0%
Valuation allowance benefit	(41.3)
State income taxes, net	2.9
Foreign operations	2.9
Nondeductible purchase accounting items	3.5
Other permanent items, net	0.8
Effective tax rate	3.8%

Source: General Instrument Corp., annual report, December 1994, p. 34.

In addition to tax reductions in each of the years 1992–1994, Mitchell's 1994 effective rate was increased by 23.1 percentage points as a result of a 1 percentage point increase in the federal statutory tax rate. SFAS No. 109, "Accounting for Income Taxes," requires that deferred tax assets and liabilities be revalued when tax rates change. Mitchell has a very large net deferred tax liability, and its cumulative revaluation required an offsetting increase in the tax provision for its fiscal 1994.

In contrast to Mitchell Energy's increased tax provision, Owens-Corning Fiberglas Corp. disclosed a 10 percentage point decrease in its 1993 effective tax rate due to the rate change.[23] Unlike Mitchell Energy, which had an overall deferred tax liability that had to be boosted to the 35% tax rate level, Owens-Corning had a substantial net deferred tax asset position. Offsetting the increase in this deferred tax asset was a reduction in the firm's 1993 tax provision. The resulting earnings increase is nonrecurring because it results in revaluations of deferred tax assets accumulated on the balance sheet in prior periods. It is comparable to the cumulative effect on earnings resulting from a change in accounting principles. There is, of course, a recurring feature to the increase in the rate to 35%. Future pre-tax results will be taxed at the new 35% versus the old 34% rate. Projections of future net income should be based upon this new higher tax rate.

Case 4 in the preceding list is illustrated by the tax disclosures of General Instrument Corp. (Exhibit 5.19). General Instrument reported an effective tax rate of only 3.8% in 1994. Because of uncertain profit prospects, General Instrument had previously written off, through a valuation allowance, most of its deferred tax assets. The generation of profits in both 1993 and 1994, plus a general improvement in its prospects, permitted General Instrument to lower its valuation allowance. This reduced its net tax provision and increased its net earnings.

General Instrument's remaining valuation allowance relates to deferred tax assets associated with capital loss carryforwards. Realization of these tax savings calls for the generation of a narrow class of income, that is, capital gains. As a result, realization of these benefits is quite uncertain. The benefits recognized in 1993 and 1994 are unlikely to be reproduced in future years, and projections of after-tax results should assume that future earnings will be fully taxable.

Finally, an example of case 5 is the tax reconciliation schedule of C. R. Bard, Inc., shown in Exhibit 5.20. The substantial reductions in Bard's effective rate will presumably be maintained only if Bard continues to conduct operations in Ireland and Puerto Rico, if the associated laws remain in effect, and if Bard's eligibility for these tax benefits continues. This series of ifs means that an important element of Bard's future net income is subject to a degree of uncertainty.

Expanding somewhat on the C. R. Bard example, we examine information from the 1993 annual report of Digital Equipment Corp. Digital's tax reconciliation schedule details tax benefits from the taxation of manufacturing operations in Puerto Rico (operations discontinued in fiscal 1993), Ireland, Singapore, and Taiwan. It discloses the nature of these arrangements as follows:[24]

Exhibit 5.20   Effective Tax Rate Reduced by Operations in Ireland and Puerto Rico: C. R. Bard, Inc., 1991–1993

	1991	1992	1993
Statutory tax rate	34%	34%	35%
State income taxes net of federal income tax benefit	2	2	3
Operations taxed at less than statutory rate, primarily			
Ireland and Puerto Rico	(9)	(10)	(11)
Justice Department settlement	–	–	7
Other, net	(1)	4	3
Effective tax rate	26%	30%	37%

Source: C. R. Bard, Inc., annual report, December 1993, p. 25.

Ireland: The income from products manufactured for export by the corporation's manufacturing subsidiary in Ireland is subject to a 10% tax rate through December 2010.

Singapore: The income from certain products manufactured by the corporation's manufacturing subsidiary in Singapore is taxed at approximately 3% through December 1993 and then at 13.5% through December 1995.

Taiwan: The income from certain products manufactured by the corporation's subsidiary operating in Taiwan is subject to a reduced tax rate of 20% through June 1997.

These data on Digital's tax benefits reveal that all the arrangements are for limited periods of time. Continuation of this boost to profitability is obviously not assured.

NONRECURRING ITEMS IN THE "OTHER INCOME (EXPENSE)" NOTE

An "other income (expense), net" or equivalent title, line item, or section is commonly found in both the single-step and the multi-step income statements. In the case of the multi-step format, the composition of other income and expenses is sometimes detailed on the face of the income statement. In both the multi-step and single-step formats, the most typical presentation is a single line item with a supporting note, if the items included in the total are material. Even though a note detailing the contents of other income and expense may exist, guidance is typically not provided as to its specific location. A note often exists even in the absence of a specific note reference. Where present, "other income (expense)" notes tend to be listed close to the end of the notes to the financial statements.

Small Net Balances May Obscure the Presence of Large Nonrecurring Items

Even if their net amount is small, the composition of other income and expense balances should be explored. For example, a small net balance may result from nonrecurring expense items offsetting recurring items of income. An illustration of this point is the "other income (expense), net" note located in the 1993 annual report of 3Com Corp. displayed in Exhibit 5.21. This item was listed as note number 12 out of 15 notes. In 1992 there was a nonrecurring increase of about $2 million in the level of the provision for doubtful accounts. The $1.7 million in "other" is a combination of losses on property and equipment dispositions and foreign exchange transactions. These should be viewed as nonrecurring. As a result, a net line item balance of only $347,000 masks nonrecurring charges of about $3.7 million. Thus, one should always look for details on the composition of other income and expense even when its net amount is small.

"Other Income (Expense)" Notes Typically Include Recurring and Nonrecurring Items

The 3Com note in Exhibit 5.21 details the composition of a single "other income (expense)" income statement line item. In contrast, Dresser Industries, Inc., provides some of the detail on the face of the income statement and then discloses the balance in a note. As with 3Com, the balance is a mix of recurring and nonrecurring items. Both the income statement display and the note information of Dresser are provided in Exhibit 5.22.

From the Dresser income statement, a nonrecurring item from the benefit plan curtailment is evident. The note disclosure reveals further nonrecurring candidates in the form of the "gain on business disposal" and "foreign exchange" line items. In addition to these disclosures, there is also commentary on the "other income" category in Dresser's MD&A of financial condition and results of operations. The value of this section of the annual report of public companies, as an aid in locating nonrecurring items, is discussed next.

Exhibit 5.21   Other Income (Expense) Note: 3Com Corp., 1991–1993 (thousands of dollars)

	1991	1992	1993
Interest income	$ 6,143	$ 5,080	$ 3,602
Provision for doubtful accounts	(1,691)	(3,683)	(1,995)
Other	(2,570)	(1,744)	(2,284)
Total	$ 1,882	$ (347)	$ (677)

Source: 3Com Corp., annual report, May 1993, p. 34.

Exhibit 5.22   Income Statement and Other Income (Expense) Note: Dresser Industries, Inc., 1991–1993 (millions of dollars)

	1991	1992	1993
From income statement			
Other income (deductions)			
Interest expense	$(38.6)	$(29.7)	$(27.4)
Interest earned	19.6	16.8	16.0
Retiree medical benefit plan curtailment	–	–	12.8
Other, net	16.7	30.8	30.9
Total other income, net	$ (2.3)	$ 17.9	$ 32.3
From note			
Composition of "Other, net"			
Gain on business disposal	$ 3.5	$ 18.2	$ –
Equity earnings	7.3	10.3	15.7
Other income	19.0	13.2	12.3
Foreign exchange	(13.1)	(10.9)	2.9
Total "Other, net"	$ 16.7	$ 30.8	$ 30.9

Source: Dresser Industries, Inc., annual report, October 1993, pp. 25 and 40.

NONRECURRING ITEMS IN MANAGEMENT'S DISCUSSION AND ANALYSIS (MD&A)

MD&A of financial condition and results of operations is an annual and a quarterly Securities and Exchange Commission reporting requirement. Provisions of this regulation have a direct bearing on our goal of locating nonrecurring items. As part of MD&A, the Securities and Exchange Commission requires registrants to

> Describe any unusual or infrequent events or transactions or any significant economic changes that materially affected the amount of reported income from continuing operations and, in each case, indicate the extent to which income was so affected. In addition, describe any other significant components of revenues and expenses that, in the registrant's judgment, should be described in order to understand the registrant's results of operations.[25]

Responding to this requirement means firms have to identify and discuss items that may have already been listed in other financial statements or notes. In reviewing MD&A with a view to locating nonrecurring items, attention should be focused on the section dealing with results of operations. Here is presented a comparison of results over the most recent three years, with the standard pattern involving discussion of, for example, 1994 with 1993, and 1993 with 1992.

Locating nonrecurring items in MD&A is somewhat more difficult than locating these items in other places. Typically, the nonrecurring items in MD&A are discussed in text and are not set out in schedules or statements.

A small number of firms do summarize nonrecurring items in schedules within MD&A. The information on nonrecurring items in Exhibit 5.23 is from the 1993 annual report of C. R. Bard, Inc. This schedule summarizes, in a single location, the after-tax effect of the listed nonrecurring items on Bard's 1993 results. We would have located most of these items in steps 1–5 of the search sequence outlined in Exhibit 5.1. Items not located in these five steps would have been the severance costs item, disclosed only in the report to shareholders by management, plus the Justice Department settlement provision, which was disclosed only in the note on commitments and contingencies.

The presentation of information on nonrecurring items in schedules within MD&A is still a fairly limited practice but appears to be on the rise. Though helpful for the task of locating nonrecurring items, such schedules must be viewed as useful complements to, but not substitutes for, the search process. A review of the scope of items presented in such schedules reveals that the displays are sometimes limited only to a subset of nonrecurring items. A sampling of omissions of nonrecurring items from schedules within MD&A is provided in Exhibit 5.24.

NONRECURRING ITEMS IN OTHER SELECTED NOTES

The preceding discussion has illustrated locating nonrecurring items through steps 1–6 of the search sequence outlined in Exhibit 5.1. Generally, most material nonrecurring items will have been discovered by proceeding through these first six steps. However, occasionally additional nonrecurring items will be located in other notes. It is possible for nonrecurring items to surface in virtually any note to the financial statements. Three selected notes, which frequently contain other nonrecurring items, are now discussed: foreign exchange, restructuring, and quarterly and segment financial data.

Exhibit 5.23 Nonrecurring Items Included in MD&A of Financial Condition and Results of Operations: C. R. Bard, Inc., 1993 (millions of dollars)

Gain on sale of Ventritex stock	$ 19.4
Gain on sale of MedSystems division and other one-time charges	6.0
Severance costs related to plant closing	(1.8)
Effect of accounting change for postretirement benefits	(6.1)
Provision for the Justice Department settlement agreement	(45.4)
Net income effect of nonrecurring items	$(27.9)

Source: C. R. Bard, Inc., annual report, December 1993, p. 19.
Note: Other firms providing similar presentations include Amoco Corp., Carpenter Technology Corp., Chevron Corp., Deere & Co., Halliburton Co., Maxus Energy Corp., Raychem Corp., and Unocal Corp.

Exhibit 5.24   Nonrecurring Items Omitted from Schedules But Included in MD&A of Financial Condition and Results of Operations

Company	Nonrecurring Item Omitted
Amoco (1993)	Tax credits
	Foreign exchange gains and losses
	LIFO liquidation gains
Carpenter Technology (1991)	LIFO liquidation gains
Deere (1993)	LIFO liquidation gains
Doskocil Companies (1993)	Impact of a strike
	Insurance gain
Halliburton (1992)	Foreign exchange losses
Maxus Energy (1993)	Charge for deferred tax valuation
	allowance increase

Sources: Companies' annual reports. The year following each company name designates the annual report from which each example was drawn.

Foreign Exchange Notes

Foreign exchange gains and losses can result from both transactions, e.g., accounts receivable or payable denominated in foreign currencies, and translation exposure from foreign subsidiaries. They can also result from the use of various currency contracts such as forwards, futures, options, and swaps used for purposes of hedging and speculation. It is not uncommon to observe foreign exchange gains and losses year after year in a company's income statement. However, it is also the case that the amount and nature, a gain versus a loss, of these items will typically be very irregular.

To illustrate, a portion of a note titled "foreign currency translation" from the 1993 annual report of Dibrell Brothers, Inc., is reproduced here:

> Net gains and losses arising from transaction adjustments are accumulated on a net basis by entity and are included in the Statement of Consolidated Income, Other Income—Sundry for gains, Other Deductions—Sundry for losses. For 1993 the transaction adjustments netted to a gain of $4,180,000. The transaction adjustments were losses of $565,000 and $206,000 for 1992 and 1991, respectively, and were primarily related to the company's Brazilian operations.[26]

The Dibrell gains and losses disclosed appear as adjustments, reflecting either their noncash or nonoperating character, in the operating activities section of Dibrell's statement of cash flows. The effect of the 1993 currency exchange gain is also referenced in Dibrell's MD&A as part of the comparison of earnings in 1993 to those in 1992.

While appearing in each of the last three years, Dibrell's foreign currency gains and losses are far from stable—two years of small losses followed by a year with a large gain. One way to gauge the significance of these exchange items is to compute their contribution to the growth in income before income taxes, extraordinary items, and cumulative effect of accounting changes. This computation is presented in Exhibit 5.25.

Dibrell's currency gain made a major contribution to its profit growth in 1993. This would explain the fact that a separate note to the financial statements is devoted to its discussion and disclosure. Following our recommended search sequence should have turned up this item at step 2, the statement of cash flows, or step 6, MD&A. If search failures occurred at steps 2 and 6, then examination of the foreign exchange note represents a backup procedure to ensure that the important information contained in this note is available in assessing Dibrell's 1993 performance.

Restructuring Notes

The 1990s have been dominated by the corporate equivalent of a diet program. Call it streamlining, downsizing, right-sizing, redeploying, or strategic restructuring—the end result is that firms have been recording nonrecurring restructuring charges of a size and frequency that are unprecedented in our modern economic history. The size and scope of these activities ensures that they leave their tracks throughout the statements and notes. Notes on restructuring charges are among the most common of the transaction-specific notes.

The 1993 restructuring charge of Kimball International, Inc., illustrates the variety of locations in which a restructuring charge and related commentary appear. The Kimball charge reduced operating income by $2,850,000, or 5.8%, in 1993. Kimball's operating income fell by a total of $2,563,000 in 1993. In the absence of the restructuring charge, Kimball would have had a small increase in operating income of $287,000. Kimball's restructuring charge, was extensively disclosed because

Exhibit 5.25   Contribution of Foreign Currency Gains to Pre-tax Income from Continuing Operations: Dibrell Brothers, Inc., 1992–1993

Pre-tax income from continuing operations	
1993	$58,259,560
1992	43,246,860
Increase	$15,012,700
Foreign currency gains and losses	
1993 gain	$ 4,180,000
1992 loss	565,000
Improvement	$ 4,745,000
Contribution of improvement in foreign currency results, 1993 over 1992, to 1993 pre-tax income from continuing operations: $4,745,000/15,012,700	32%

Source: Dibrell Brothers, Inc., annual report, 1993, p. 14.

of its material effect on operating income. A summary of this disclosure is provided in Exhibit 5.26.

Restructuring notes sometimes add *prospective* information to the current-period information in the income statement and statement of cash flows. This contributes to improving the quality of earnings expectations. A portion of a recent restructuring note of The Times Mirror Co. is reproduced here:

> The restructuring charges over this three-year period (1991–1993) have totaled $325.2 million, or $196.5 million after taxes, principally for severance and payroll-related costs for staff reductions and for expected losses on leased facilities. . . . The restructuring efforts have helped to improve operating results in newspaper publishing and are expected to improve results at the professional publishing companies over the longer term.[27]

While current results were reduced significantly by these restructuring charges, the company projected a favorable effect on future earnings from them. Another restructuring firm, Armstrong World Industries, also projected a favorable effect on future results: "Cash outlays for the 1993 restructuring charges will occur primarily throughout 1994 and should be fully recovered within two to three years."[28]

Quarterly and Segmental Financial Data

Quarterly and segment financial disclosures frequently provide information on nonrecurring items. In the case of segment disclosures, the goal is to aid in the evaluation of profitability trends by segments. For example, The B. F. Goodrich Co. disclosed the effect of restructuring charges on the operating income of its aerospace and specialty chemicals segments.[29] Firmwide restructuring charges for the affected years were already disclosed in Goodrich's income statements. Moreover, breakdowns of the restructuring charges by segment were also provided in MD&A and in a separate restructuring note.

Exhibit 5.26   Restructuring Charge Disclosures: Kimball International, Inc.

Location of Disclosure	Page in Annual Report
Separate line item in income statement	22
Separate line item in statement of cash flows, operating activities section	23
Separate note to the financial statement devoted to the restructuring charge	26
Disclosed and discussed in MD&A	18
Disclosed with quarterly financial information	29
Disclosed in an 11-year summary of operations	32
Disclosed in the management letter to shareholders	2

Source: Kimball International, Inc., annual report, June 1993.

Quarterly financial data of Scientific-Atlanta, Inc., disclosed the effect on earnings for the second quarter of 1994 from a litigation settlement and the effect on the first-quarter results of 1993 from the adoption of three new accounting standards.[30]

SUMMARY

This chapter provides background information designed to build the skills necessary to identify nonrecurring items of revenue or gain and expense or loss. The search sequence outlined in Exhibit 5.1 provides an efficient procedure to follow in the attempt to locate all material nonrecurring items.

The ultimate goal of the search for nonrecurring items is to identify a level of earnings that could be expected to continue into the future in the absence of change. This earnings amount is called the sustainable earnings base. The sustainable earnings base should be the most reliable point from which to build an earnings expectation or forecast for coming periods. The sustainable earnings for each of several recent years should also provide the best indication of the trends in fundamental operating performance, purged of the effects of nonrecurring, and often nonoperating, items of revenue or gain and expense or loss.

In many cases, the number of nonrecurring items found in the most recent several years will be large. A systematic procedure for accumulating this information is essential to determining the sustainable earnings base in each year. The following chapter provides such a procedure based on a sustainable earnings base worksheet and illustrates its application.

ENDNOTES

1. Special Committee on Financial Reporting, *The Information Needs of Investors and Creditors* (New York: American Institute of Certified Public Accountants, November 1993), p. 4.
2. R. Barefield and E. Comiskey, "The Accuracy of Bank Earnings Forecasts," *Business Economics,* May 1976, pp. 59–63.
3. D. E. Kieso and J. J. Weygandt, *Intermediate Accounting,* 8th ed. (New York: Wiley, 1995), pp. 145–153.
4. Delta Air Lines, Inc., annual report, June, 1994, pp. 38–39.
5. Geo. A. Hormel & Co., annual report, October 1992, p. 58.
6. H. Choi, "Analysis and Valuation Implications of Persistence and Cash-Content Dimensions of Earnings Components Based on Extent of Analyst Following." Unpublished Ph.D. thesis, Georgia Institute of Technology, October 1994, p. 80.
7. Ibid. The authors of this book served on Dr. Choi's thesis advisory committee.
8. *The Information Needs of Investors and Creditors,* p. 4.
9. Accounting Principles Board, Opinion No. 30, "Reporting the Results of Operations" (New York: American Institute of Certified Public Accountants, July 1973), para. 20.

10. Statement of Financial Accounting Standards (SFAS) No. 4, "Reporting Gains and Losses from the Extinguishment of Debt" (Stamford, Conn.: Financial Accounting Standards Board, March 1975).
11. SFAS No. 15, "Accounting by Debtors and Creditors for Troubled Debt Restructurings" (June 1977).
12. SFAS No. 109, "Accounting for Income Taxes" (February 1992).
13. Raychem Corp., annual report, June 1993, p. 22.
14. Scientific-Atlanta, Inc., Form 10-K annual report to the Securities and Exchange Commission, July 1994, pp. 17 and 22.
15. Raychem Corp., Form 10-K annual report to the Securities and Exchange Commission, July 1993, pp. 4–5.
16. Delta Air Lines, Inc., annual report, June 1993, p. 27.
17. Delta Air Lines, Inc., annual report, June 1994, p. 34.
18. Securities and Exchange Commission, Regulation S-X, Rule 5-02.6.
19. Handy & Harman, annual report, 1993, p. 21.
20. Securities and Exchange Commission, *Staff Accounting Bulletin No. 40.*
21. Wyman-Gordon Co., annual report, December 1993, p. 24.
22. Diebold, Inc., annual report, December 1993, p. 35.
23. Owens-Corning Fiberglas Corp., annual report, December 1993, p. 31.
24. Digital Equipment Corp., annual report, June 1993, p. 41.
25. Securities and Exchange Commission, Regulation S-K, Subpart 229.300, Item 303(a)(3)(i).
26. Dibrell Brothers, Inc., annual report, June 1993, p. 35.
27. The Times Mirror Co., annual report, 1993, p. 23.
28. Armstrong World Industries, Inc., annual report, December 1993, p. 41.
29. The B. F. Goodrich Co., annual report, December 1993, p. 16.
30. Scientific-Atlanta, Inc., annual report, July 1994, pp. 22–23.

Chapter 6

The Analysis of Sustainable Earnings

The best of prophets of the future is the past.[1]

The absence of romance in my history will, I fear, detract somewhat from its interest; but I shall be content if it is judged useful by those inquirers who desire an exact knowledge of the past as an aid to the interpretation of the future.[2]

In this chapter, we continue the effort, begun in Chapter 5, to understand past earnings performance as an aid to improving both the formation of earnings expectations and the avoidance of earnings surprises. The goals of Chapter 5 were to provide an understanding of current generally accepted accounting principles (GAAP) that guide the presentation of earnings, and to start building the skills required to identify and locate nonrecurring items of revenue or gain and expense or loss. Plato declared that "the life which is unexamined is not worth living"[3]; and we add: the unexamined earnings report is not worth using; in fact, its use could be dangerous.

The work of Chapter 5 laid important groundwork, but it is incomplete. Still needed is a device to summarize all the information on nonrecurring items so that new measures of sustainable earnings can be developed. The initial focus of this chapter is a worksheet designed to aid in assembling sustainable earnings base information about companies. Two different companies are employed as case studies to illustrate use of the worksheet. In addition, various examples of sustainable earnings presentations, provided by companies themselves, are analyzed. Finally, the treatment of income taxes in the preparation of the worksheet is discussed.

THE SUSTAINABLE EARNINGS BASE WORKSHEET

The sustainable earnings base worksheet is shown in Exhibit 6.1.[4] Instructions for completing it follow:

1. Net income (loss) is recorded on the top line of the worksheet.
2. All identified items of nonrecurring expense or loss, which were included in the income statement on a pre-tax basis, are recorded on the "add" lines provided.

Exhibit 6.1   Adjustment Worksheet for Sustainable Earnings Base

	Year	Year	Year
Reported net income (loss)	____	____	____
Add			
Pre-tax LIFO liquidation losses	____	____	____
Losses on sales of fixed assets	____	____	____
Losses on sales of investments	____	____	____
Loss on sales of other assets	____	____	____
Restructuring charges	____	____	____
Investment write-downs	____	____	____
Inventory write-downs	____	____	____
Other asset write-downs	____	____	____
Foreign currency losses	____	____	____
Litigation charges	____	____	____
Losses on patent infringement suits	____	____	____
Exceptional bad-debt provisions	____	____	____
Nonrecurring expense increases	____	____	____
Temporary revenue reductions	____	____	____
Other	____	____	____
Other	____	____	____
Other	____	____	____
Subtotal	____	____	____
Multiply by			
(1 – combined federal and state tax rates)	____	____	____
Tax-adjusted additions	____	____	____
Add			
After-tax LIFO liquidation losses	____	____	____
Increases in deferred tax valuation allowances	____	____	____
Other nonrecurring tax charges	____	____	____
Losses on discontinued operations	____	____	____
Extraordinary losses	____	____	____
Losses/cumulative-effect accounting changes	____	____	____
Other	____	____	____
Other	____	____	____
Other	____	____	____
Subtotal	____	____	____
Total additions	____	____	____
Deduct			
Pre-tax LIFO liquidation gains	____	____	____
Gains on sales of fixed assets	____	____	____
Gains on sales of investments	____	____	____
Gains on sales of other assets	____	____	____
Reversals of restructuring charges	____	____	____
Investment write-ups (trading account)	____	____	____

Exhibit 6.1   *(continued)*

	Year	Year	Year
Foreign currency gains	————	————	————
Litigation revenues	————	————	————
Gains on patent infringement suits	————	————	————
Nonrecurring expense decrease	————	————	————
Temporary revenue increases	————	————	————
Reversals of bad-debt allowances	————	————	————
Other	————	————	————
Other	————	————	————
Other	————	————	————
Subtotal	————	————	————
Multiply by			
(1 – combined federal and state tax rates)	————	————	————
Tax-adjusted deductions	————	————	————
Deduct			
After-tax LIFO liquidation gains	————	————	————
Reductions in deferred tax valuation allowances	————	————	————
Loss carryforward benefits from prior periods	————	————	————
Other nonrecurring tax benefits	————	————	————
Gains on discontinued operations	————	————	————
Extraordinary gains	————	————	————
Gains/cumulative-effect accounting changes	————	————	————
Other	————	————	————
Other	————	————	————
Other	————	————	————
Subtotal	————	————	————
Total deductions	————	————	————
Sustainable earnings base	————	————	————

Where a prelabeled line is not identified in the financial statement, a descriptive phrase should be recorded on one of the "other" lines and the amounts recorded there. In practice, the process of locating nonrecurring items and recording them on the worksheet would take place at the same time. However, effective use of the worksheet calls for the background provided in the previous chapter. This explains the separation of these steps in this book.

3. When all pre-tax, nonrecurring expenses and losses have been recorded, subtotals should be computed. These subtotals are then multiplied by 1 minus a representative combined federal and state income tax rate. This puts these items on an after-tax basis so that they are stated on the same basis as net income or net loss.

4. The results from step 3 should be recorded on the line labeled "tax-adjusted additions."

5. All after-tax nonrecurring expenses or losses, or comparable items, are next added separately. These items will typically be either tax items or special income statement items that are disclosed on an after-tax basis under GAAP, e.g., discontinued operations, extraordinary items, or the cumulative effect of accounting changes. The effects of LIFO liquidations are sometimes presented pre-tax and sometimes after-tax. Note that a line item is provided for the effect of LIFO liquidations in both the pre-tax and after-tax sections of the worksheet.

6. Changes in deferred tax valuation allowances are recorded in the after-tax additions (or deductions) section only if such changes affected net income or net loss for the period. Evidence of an income statement effect will usually take the form of an entry in the income tax rate reconciliation schedule. More background on this matter is provided later.

7. The next step is to subtotal the after-tax additions entries and then combine this subtotal with the amount labeled "tax adjusted additions." The result is then recorded on the "total additions" line at the bottom of the first page of the worksheet.

8. Completion of the deductions part of the worksheet, for nonrecurring revenue or gain, follows exactly the same steps as those outlined for nonrecurring expense or loss.

9. With the completion of the deductions part, the sustainable earnings base for each year is computed by adding the "total additions" line item to net income (loss) and then deducting the "total deductions" line item.

ROLE OF THE SUSTAINABLE EARNINGS BASE

The sustainable earnings base provides profitability information from which the distorting effects of nonrecurring items have been removed. Some analysts refer to such revised numbers as representing "core earnings." The sustainable earnings base is history analyzed rather than simply revealed. It provides a profit series that is a reliable depiction of the past.

Sustainable is used in the sense that earnings devoid of nonrecurring items of revenue or gain and expense or loss are much more likely to be maintained in the future if previous operating conditions persist. *Base* implies that sustainable earnings provide the most reliable foundation or starting point for projections of future results. The more reliable such forecasts become, the less the likelihood that frequent earnings surprises will result. Chevron Corp. captures the essence of nonrecurring items in the following:

> Transactions not considered representative of the company's ongoing operations. These transactions, as defined by management, can obscure the underlying results of operations and affect comparability between years.[5]

APPLICATION OF THE SUSTAINABLE EARNINGS BASE WORKSHEET: ACME-CLEVELAND CORP.

This first illustration of the application of the worksheet is based upon the 1992 annual report of Acme-Cleveland Corp. and its results for 1990–1992. To provide a realistic illustration of the process of comprehensive identification of nonrecurring items and the completion of the worksheet, the income statement, statement of cash flows, Management's Discussion and Analysis (MD&A) of financial condition and results of operations, and selected notes disclosing nonrecurring items are provided in Exhibits 6.2–6.9. Further, to reinforce the objective of efficiency in financial analysis, the search sequence outlined in Exhibit 5.1 is followed.

Exhibit 6.2 Acme-Cleveland Corp., Consolidated Income Statements, Years Ending September 30, 1990–1992 (thousands of dollars except per share data)

	1990	1991	1992
Net Sales	$199,493	$183,940	$177,594
Cost of products sold	144,708	137,228	131,096
Gross profit	54,785	46,712	46,498
Selling, general, and administrative expense	46,831	43,165	40,199
Earnings from operations	7,954	3,547	6,299
Other income (expense)			
Interest income	1,437	1,272	1,413
Interest expense	(1,067)	(828)	(760)
Other income	2,651	2,908	2,465
Other expense	(698)	(1,362)	(1,123)
Provision for facility consolidation	–	–	(1,750)
Provision for asset write-down	(3,384)	–	–
Total	(1,061)	1,990	245
Earnings from continuing operations before income taxes and extraordinary item	6,893	5,537	6,544
Income taxes	3,830	2,465	2,925
Earnings from continuing operations before extraordinary item	3,063	3,072	3,619
Discontinued operations, net of tax	–	(6,035)	–
Extraordinary item—tax benefit from utilization of net operating loss carryforward	2,050	–	1,700
Net earnings (loss)	$ 5,113	$ (2,963)	$ 5,319
Earnings (loss) per common share			
Continuing operations before extraordinary item	$.44	$.44	$.53
Discontinued operations		(.96)	
Extraordinary item	.33	–	.26
Net earnings (loss) per common share	$ .77	$ (.52)	$ .79

Source: Acme-Cleveland Corp., annual report, September 1992, p. 13.

Exhibit 6.3   Acme-Cleveland Corp., Cash Flow Statements (Operating Activities Only), Years Ending September 30, 1990–1992 (thousands of dollars)

	1990	1991	1992
Continuing operations			
Earnings before extraordinary item	$ 3,063	$ 3,072	$ 3,619
Noncash charges to earnings			
Depreciation and amortization	7,214	7,278	6,418
Provision for asset write-down	3,384	–	–
Deferred income taxes	289	195	57
Undistributed (earnings) loss of minority equity investments	78	373	(286)
Disposal of minority equity investments	1,377	–	–
Gains on sale of property, plant, and equipment	(422)	(25)	(241)
Cash provided by earnings and noncash charges before extraordinary item and changes in working capital	14,983	10,893	9,567
Extraordinary item—tax benefit from utilization of loss carryforward	2,050	–	1,700
Changes in operating assets and liabilities			
(Increase) decrease in marketable securities	387	(1,500)	1,500
(Increase) decrease in trade receivables	(591)	2,246	529
(Increase) decrease in inventories	1,997	3,357	8,087
(Increase) decrease in other current assets	1,196	(180)	385
(Increase) decrease in recoverable income taxes	(468)	280	90
Increase (decrease) in payables to banks	443	(198)	148
Increase (decrease) in accounts payable	(3,835)	(922)	232
Increase (decrease) in other accrued liabilities	(3,643)	3,572	(1,719)
Increase (decrease) in accrued compensation	(37)	11	544
Increase (decrease) in other accrued taxes	86	(80)	(185)
Increase (decrease) in income taxes payable	(443)	570	362
Increase (decrease) in unfunded pension and health care costs	(203)	(631)	44
Other, net	(800)	(13)	(174)
Cash provided by continuing operations	$11,122	$17,405	$21,110
Discontinued operations			
Net loss	–	$(6,035)	–
Adjustments to reconcile net loss to net cash used by discontinued operations: decrease in current liabilities of discontinued operations	$ (605)	(775)	$ (87)
Cash used by discontinued operations	(605)	(6,810)	(87)
Net cash provided by operating activities	$10,517	$10,595	$21,023

Source: Acme-Cleveland Corp., annual report, September 1992, p. 17.

Exhibit 6.4   Acme-Cleveland Corp., LIFO Inventory Note, 1990–1992

Inventories

Inventories are priced at the lower of cost or market. Inventories valued using the last in, first out (LIFO) method comprised 62% and 63% of consolidated inventories at September 30, 1992, and 1991, respectively. Inventories not valued by the LIFO method are principally on the first in, first out (FIFO) method. If the cost of all inventories had been determined by the FIFO method, which approximates current cost, inventories at September 30, 1992, and 1991 would have been greater by $30,388,000 and $36,765,000, respectively.

During 1992, 1991, and 1990, inventory quantities were reduced at certain locations. These reductions resulted in liquidations of LIFO inventory quantities carried at lower costs prevailing in prior years as compared with the cost of current purchases, the effect of which increased net earnings by $2,484,000, or $.39 per common share, in 1992 and $137,000, or $.02 per common share, in 1990 and decreased the net loss by $224,000, or $.04 per common share, in 1991.

Source: Acme-Cleveland Corp., annual report, September 1992, p. 18.

An enumeration of the nonrecurring items located in the Acme-Cleveland statements is provided in the completed worksheet in Exhibit 6.10, following the financial statements and other disclosures. (See page 132.) Each nonrecurring item that is found is recorded on the worksheet. When an item is found for the first, second, third, or fourth time, it is marked by a corresponding superscript. For purposes of illustration, all nonrecurring items have been recorded on the worksheet without regard to their materiality. We believe this to be the best procedure to follow. A materiality threshold could exclude a series of immaterial gains or losses that in combination could distort a firm's apparent profitability.

COMMENTS ON THE ACME-CLEVELAND WORKSHEET

The completed worksheet for Acme-Cleveland is presented as Exhibit 6.10.[6] Further, a summary of the results of the nonrecurring items search process is provided in Exhibit 6.11 (see page 134). As noted earlier, all nonrecurring items were recorded without regard to their materiality. If small nonrecurring items could be counted on to generally offset each other, then we would focus only on more material balances. Since an offsetting cannot be counted on, we believe that it is best to record all nonrecurring items, regardless of size. However, an effort is made to consider the possible effect of materiality in Exhibit 6.12. (See page 135.)

The tax rate assumed in the analysis in the Acme-Cleveland worksheet was a combined 40%. This rate is a blend of state, federal, and foreign taxes. A somewhat higher rate might have been used based simply on Acme-Cleveland's three-year average effective rate of about 48% (see Exhibit 6.5). However, when some nonrecurring elements, 16.6% and 2.0% in 1990, are adjusted out of the calculation, the

Exhibit 6.5 Acme-Cleveland Corp., Income Tax Note, 1990–1992 (thousands of dollars)

Note E–Income Taxes
The components of earnings from continuing operations before income taxes and extraordinary item are (in thousands):

	1990	1991	1992
Domestic	$4,259	$4,502	$7,361
Foreign	2,634	1,035	(817)
	$6,893	$5,537	$6,544

Income taxes for continuing operations, before extraordinary item, included in the statement of consolidated operations are as follows (in thousands):

	1990	1991	1992
Federal			
Current	$ 944	$1,425	$ 825
Deferred	–	–	–
	944	1,425	825
Foreign			
Current	496	795	168
Deferred	289	195	57
	785	990	225
State and local	51	50	175
Charge in lieu of income taxes	2,050	–	1,700
	$3,830	$2,465	$2,925

The 1992 and 1990 provisions for income taxes included charges in lieu of federal, foreign, and state and local taxes representing taxes which would have been provided in the absence of net operating loss carryforwards from prior years. Income tax benefits resulting from the utilization of net operating loss carryforwards for financial reporting purposes are presented as an extraordinary item.

At September 30, 1992, the corporation had available for federal income tax purposes net operating loss carryforwards of $580,000 which expire in 1999 through 2002, tax credit carryforwards of $2,630,000 which expire in 1995 through 2005, and capital loss carryforwards of $1,025,000 which expire in 1994 through 1996. For financial statement purposes, the corporation has domestic net operating loss and tax credit carryforwards of $6,100,000 and $8,100,000, respectively, which expire in 1995 through 2006, and capital loss carryforwards of $1,025,000 which expire in 1994 through 1996. For alternative minimum tax purposes, the corporation has domestic net operating loss and tax credit carryforwards of $220,000 and $5,025,000, respectively, which expire in 1995 through 2006, and a minimum tax credit carryforward of $960,000 which has no expiration date. The difference between book and tax carryforwards is due primarily to the write-down of asset values, restructuring, and inventory reserves not currently deductible for tax purposes. A reconciliation of the statutory federal income tax rate and the effective rate for continuing operations follows:

Exhibit 6.5   *(continued)*

	1990	1991	1992
Statutory federal income tax rate	34.0%	34.0%	34.0%
Effect of			
Foreign income taxes	.1	11.5	7.7
State income taxes	2.7	.6	3.1
Goodwill	2.1	2.5	1.7
Earnings from minority equity investments	(4.0)	(4.2)	(1.1)
Write-down of minority equity investments	16.6	–	–
Dividends from foreign subsidiaries	1.1	–	–
Loss carryback	(2.0)	–	–
Other items	5.0	.1	(.7)
	55.6%	44.5%	44.7%

The components of deferred income taxes from continuing operations are summarized as follows (in thousands):

	1990	1991	1992
Accelerated depreciation for tax purposes	$(408)	$(684)	$(741)
Inventory, employee benefits, and other reserves deducted for tax returns in periods different than for financial reporting purposes	458	1,166	1,528
Capitalized leases	29	8	–
Minority equity investments	(36)	(5)	23
Elimination of deferred items due to loss carryforwards	246	(290)	(753)
	$ 289	$ 195	$ 57

Source: Acme-Cleveland Corp., annual report, September 1992, pp. 20–21.

Exhibit 6.6   Acme-Cleveland Corp., "Other Income" Note, 1990–1992

Other Income
Other income included gains from sales of minority equity investments of $1,137,000 and $423,000 in 1991 and 1990, respectively, gains from sales of unused land and buildings of $919,000 and $352,000 in 1992 and 1990, respectively, and royalty income of $231,000, $423,000, and $429,000 in 1992, 1991, and 1990, respectively.

Source: Acme-Cleveland Corp., annual report, September 1992, p. 18.

average comes down to about 42%. Beyond this, we made two judgmental adjustments: an addition of 1% for the subsequent increase from 34% to 35% in the federal rate, and a reduction of 3% to deal with what appeared to be temporary elevations in the level of foreign taxes. Interestingly, Acme-Cleveland's average effective tax for the period 1992–1994 turned out to be 39%. More discussion of income taxes and the worksheet is provided later in this chapter.

Exhibit 6.7 Acme-Cleveland Corp., Discontinued Operations Note, 1990–1992

Note C–Discontinued Operations
In March 1991, the corporation agreed to a settlement of litigation initiated in 1987 by Vickers, Incorporated, which sought to recover damages for the alleged breach by the corporation of a contract for the sale of a fully automated flexible machining system. The corporation agreed to pay $4,000,000 in cash and to provide $4,500,000 worth of new and rebuilt multiple spindle machines in settlement of this litigation. The settlement resulted in a charge to discontinued operations of $6,035,000, net of $1,365,000 income tax benefit, or $.96 per common share.

Source: Acme-Cleveland Corp., annual report, September 1992, p. 20.

Exhibit 6.8 Acme-Cleveland Corp., MD&A of Financial Position and Results of Operations, 1990–1992

Consolidated Results
Earnings from operations improved in fiscal 1992 on 3% lower volume. Lower spending, productivity improvement programs, and increased income from the liquidation of inventories valued under the last in, first out (LIFO) method of accounting exceeded the impact from the decrease in sales volume and lower product margins. Further, this improvement was sufficient to offset a provision for one-time costs associated with consolidating cutting tool production.

The corporation earned $3.6 million, or $.53 a common share, from continuing operations before extraordinary tax benefit on sales of $177.6 million in fiscal 1992. This compares to earnings from continuing operations of $3.1 million, or $.44 a common share, on sales of $183.9 million in fiscal 1991 and earnings from continuing operations before extraordinary tax benefit of $3.1 million, or $.44 a common share, on sales of $199.5 million in fiscal 1990.

During fiscal 1992, the corporation determined that the number of cutting tool plants and associated manufacturing capacity would continue to exceed realistic volume expectations, and that the related structured cost placed the corporation at a competitive disadvantage. To address this issue, a decision was made to consolidate the production of Cleveland Twist Drill's Mansfield, Massachusetts, plant into other cutting tool facilities. The decision necessitated a charge against earnings of $1.8 million, or $.28 a common share, for the estimated costs in connection with the consolidation. Such costs include employee training, production disruption, machinery relocation, severance, and other miscellaneous expenses. Fiscal 1990 included a provision of $3.4 million, or $.54 a common share, to write down a minority equity investment. The write-down resulted from minority equity losses in discontinuing certain U.S. operations.

The utilization of net operating loss carryforwards increased net earnings in fiscal 1992 to $5.3 million, or $.79 a common share, and net earnings in fiscal 1990 to $5.1 million, or $.77 a common share. In fiscal 1991, the corporation incurred a net loss of $3.0 million, or $.52 a common share, due to a litigation settlement charge against a previously discontinued operation of $6.0 million, or $.96 a common share.

Exhibit 6.8   *(continued)*

Aggressive inventory reduction programs, which the corporation pursued at all operating locations, generated net earnings from the liquidation of LIFO inventories amounting to $2.5 million, or $.39 a common share, in fiscal 1992. This compares to LIFO earnings of $.2 million, or $.04 a common share, in fiscal 1991, and $.1 million, or $.02 a common share, in fiscal 1990.

Operations, Fiscal 1992 vs. Fiscal 1991
Earnings from operations for the Metalworking Products segment decreased by $2.1 million to $.6 million on sales of $115.0 million from $2.7 million on sales of $126.9 million. Factors contributing to the year-over-year earnings decrease were the lower sales volume, $3.7 million; lower product margins, $5.4 million; and higher retiree health benefits, $.5 million. These were mitigated by improved operational performance, $5.0 million; and increased LIFO income, $2.5 million.

The lower sales volume, mainly affecting cutting tools and machine tools, reflected the low backlog existing at the beginning and during most of fiscal 1992. The lower product margins resulted primarily from pricing pressures on cutting tools and master gauges. Product margins in fiscal 1992 were also impacted by unabsorbed fixed costs.

Earnings from operations for the Telecommunication and Electronic Products segment increased by $5.3 million to $8.3 million on sales of $62.6 million from $3.0 million on sales of $57.1 million. Factors contributing to the year-over-year earnings improvement included higher sales volume for telecommunication products, $2.2 million; favorable product margins, $.8 million; improved operational performance, $1.2 million; and increased LIFO income, $.3 million. Fiscal 1991 results also included unusual warranty costs of $.8 million; no such costs were incurred in fiscal 1992.

Income taxes for fiscal 1992 were $2.9 million on earnings of $6.5 million, for an effective tax rate of 45%, comparable to the effective tax rate for fiscal 1991. Provisions for foreign taxes accounted for most of the difference between the effective rate and the statutory U.S. corporate income tax rate of 34% in both years. Note E to the financial statements includes a reconciliation of effective tax rate to the statutory rate and a discussion of Statement of Financial Accounting Standards No. 109, "Accounting for Income Taxes."

Operations, Fiscal 1991 vs. Fiscal 1990
The $10.0 million decrease in Metalworking Products sales and the $5.6 million decrease in Telecommunication and Electronic Products sales resulted from lower orders during fiscal 1991 in most of the corporation's product lines. The decreased orders, in turn, resulted largely from economic slowdowns in major served markets, and not from a change in the corporation's competitive standing. Cost containment actions enabled the corporation to absorb most, but not all, of the decrease in sales. Earnings from operations in fiscal 1991 were also impacted by unabsorbed fixed costs, unusual warranty expenses, and unsatisfactory performances by our European operations.

Earnings from operations for Metalworking Products decreased by $3.6 million, to $2.7 million in fiscal 1991. The effects of the lower sales volume, $3.2 million; lower product margins, $5.2 million; and higher retiree health benefits, $.2 million were mitigated by savings from improved operational performance of $5.0 million.

Exhibit 6.8   *(continued)*

Earnings from operations for Telecommunication and Electronic Products decreased by $.4 million, to $3.0 million in fiscal 1991. The effects of the lower sales volume, $2.4 million, and unusual warranty expense, $.8 million, noted earlier, were mitigated by improved operational performance, $2.8 million.

Income taxes for fiscal 1991 were $2.5 million on earnings from continuing operations of $5.5 million, for an effective tax rate of 45%, compared to 56% in fiscal 1990. The nondeductible write-down of the minority equity investment, noted earlier, accounted for most of the higher effective tax rate in fiscal 1990.

Source: Acme-Cleveland, annual report, September 1992, pp. 10–11.

From a strictly bottom-line perspective, the reported net income or loss of Acme-Cleveland for 1990–1992 would suggest a profitable year (1990), followed by a loss year (1991), followed by a year of recovery (1992). However, the complete restatement represented by the worksheet conveys quite a different message. The income series reveals a decline in fundamental profitability over the period 1990–1992. Clearly, the number and magnitude of nonrecurring items in the Acme-Cleveland income statements alone would suggest a lack of reliability of the unanalyzed earnings data. However, until a comprehensive identification of nonrecurring items has been completed and summarized, the operating performance over the three-year period is

Exhibit 6.9   Acme-Cleveland Corp., Other Selected Notes, 1990–1992

Foreign Currency
Foreign currency transaction and translation gains of $150,000 in 1992 and $61,000 in 1991 and losses of $313,000 in 1990 were included in earnings from continuing operations before income taxes and extraordinary item.

Note B—Facility Consolidation
In September 1992, the corporation determined that its number of cutting tool plants and associated manufacturing capacity would continue to exceed realistic volume expectations for the foreseeable future and that the related structured costs placed the corporation at a competitive disadvantage. Accordingly, a provision of $1,750,000 was made for the estimated costs to be incurred to consolidate the production of our Mansfield, Massachusetts, plant into other company facilities. Such estimated costs include employee training, production disruption, machinery relocation, severance, and other miscellaneous expenses.

Note D—Provision for Asset Write-Down
During 1990, the corporation recorded a $3,384,000 write-down related to the permanent impairment of its minority equity investment in International Twist Drill (Holdings) Limited (ITD). The write-down of the investment and goodwill was necessitated by the substantial losses incurred by an ITD subsidiary in discontinuing its manufacturing operations.

Source: Acme-Cleveland Corp., annual report, September 1992, pp. 19–20.

Exhibit 6.10 Adjustment Worksheet for Sustainable Earnings Base: Acme-Cleveland Corp., 1990–1992 (thousands of dollars)

	1990	1991	1992
Reported net income	$5,113	$(2,963)	$5,319
Add			
Pre-tax LIFO liquidation losses			
Losses on sales of fixed assets			
Losses on sales of investments	1,377		
Losses on sales of other assets			
Restructuring charges			1,750
Investment write-downs	3,384		
Inventory write-downs			
Other asset write-downs			
Foreign currency losses	313		
Litigation charges			
Losses on patent infringement suit			
Exceptional bad-debt provisions			
Nonrecurring expense increases		800	
Temporary revenue reductions			
Other			
Other			
Other			
Subtotal	$5,074	$ 800	$1,750
Multiply by			
(1 – combined federal, state and			
foreign tax rates)	60%	60%	60%
Tax-adjusted additions	$3,044	$ 480	$1,050
Add			
After-tax LIFO liquidation losses			
Increases in deferred tax valuation allowances			
Other nonrecurring tax charges			
Losses on discontinued operations		6,035	
Extraordinary losses			
Losses/cumulative-effect accounting changes			
Other			
Other			
Other			
Subtotal		$ 6,035	
Total additions	$3,044	$ 6,515	$1,050
Deduct			
Pre-tax LIFO liquidation gains			
Gains on sales of fixed assets	$ 422	$ 25	$ 241
Gains on sales of investments	423	1,137	
Gains on sales of other assets	352		919
Reversals of restructuring charges			

Exhibit 6.10 *(continued)*

	1990	1991	1992
Investment write-ups (trading account)			
Foreign currency gains		61	150
Litigation revenues			
Gains on patent infringement suits			
Nonrecurring expense decreases			
Temporary revenue increases			
Reversals of bad-debt allowances			
Other			
Other			
Other			
Subtotal	$1,197	$1,223	$1,310
Multiply by			
(1 – combined federal, state and			
foreign tax rates)	60%	60%	60%
Tax-adjusted deductions	$ 718	$ 734	$ 786
Deduct			
After-tax LIFO liquidation gains	137	224	2,484
Reductions in deferred tax valuation allowances			
Loss carryforward benefits from prior periods	2,050		1,700
Other nonrecurring tax benefits			
Gains on discontinued operations			
Extraordinary gains			
Gains/cumulative-effect accounting changes			
Other			
Other			
Other			
Subtotal	2,187	224	4,184
Total deductions	$2,905	$ 958	$4,970
Sustainable earnings base	$5,252	$2,593	$1,399

difficult to discern. This is the value of the search process and the sustainable earnings base worksheet.

Chapter 5 focused on the reporting and disclosure of earnings under current generally accepted accounting principles, and an efficient search sequence was outlined in Exhibit 5.1. This search sequence was based upon the experience of the authors, supported by a large-scale study of nonrecurring items by Choi.[7] The efficiency of the search sequence is evaluated in Exhibit 6.12, based upon a summary of the location of nonrecurring items reported in Exhibit 6.11. While the recommended search sequence may not be equally effective in all cases, Exhibit 6.11 demonstrates that most of Acme-Cleveland's nonrecurring items could be located by employing only steps 1–5, a sequence that is very cost-effective. That is, the items located in these steps require reading very little text; the nonrecurring items are generally set

Exhibit 6.11 Summary of Nonrecurring Items Search Process: Acme-Cleveland Corp.

Step and Search Location	Nonrecurring Items Revealed
1. Income statement	Provision for facility consolidation (1992)[1] Provision for asset write-down (1990)[1] Loss on discontinued operations (1991)[1] Extraordinary items (1990 and 1992)[1]
2. Statement of cash flows	Provision for asset write-down (1990)[2] Loss on disposal of minority equity investments (1990)[1] Gains on property, plant, and equipment (1990–1992)[1]
3. Inventory note (LIFO firm)	LIFO liquidation benefits (1990–1992)[1]
4. Income tax note	Tax benefits of tax loss carryforwards, disclosed in the income statement as extraordinary items (1990 and 1992)[2]
5. "Other income (expense)" note	Gains on sales of minority equity investments (1990 and 1991)[1] Gains from sales of unused land and buildings (1990 and 1992)[1]
6. MD&A	Provision for facility consolidation (1992)[2] Provision for asset write-down (1990)[3] Tax benefits of tax loss carryforwards (1990 and 1992)[2] Loss on discontinued operations (1991)[2] LIFO liquidation benefits (1990–1992)[2] Unusual warranty costs (1991)[1]
7. Other notes revealing nonrecurring items:	
Foreign currency	Translation and transaction gains (1991 and 1992) and losses (1990)[1]
Facility consolidation	Provision for facility consolidation (1992)[2]
Discontinued operations	Loss on discontinued operations (1991)[3]
Provision for asset write-down	Provision for asset write-down (1990)[4]

Note: The superscripts 1, 2, 3, 4 indicate in how many search locations the nonrecurring item was found: for instance, "provision for asset write-down" was found in the income statement (first location); in the statement of cash flows (second location); in MD&A (third location); and in "other notes" (fourth location).

Exhibit 6.12   Efficiency of Nonrecurring Items Search Process: Acme-Cleveland Corp.

	Incremental Nonrecurring Items Discovered			
	(1) All Nonrecurring Items	(2) Cumulative % Located	(3) All Material[a] Items	(4) Cumulative % Located
Step and Search Location				
1. Income statement	4	21%	4	36%
2. Statement of cash flows	4	42	1	45
3. Inventory note	3	58	1	54
4. Tax note	0	58	0	54
5. "Other income" note	4	79	4	91
6. MD&A	1	84	1	100
7. Foreign currency note	3	100	0	100
8. Discontinued operations note	0	100	0	100
Total nonrecurring items	19	100%	11	100%

[a]5% or more of the amount of the net income or net loss, on a tax-adjusted basis.

out prominently in statements or schedules. With current belt-tightening measures extending to both security and credit analysts—statement users with the deepest interest in earnings analysis—cost-effective financial analysis is very important.

Exhibit 6.12 presents information on the efficiency of the search process. The meaning of each column in the Exhibit is as follows:

Column 1:   The number of nonrecurring items located at each step in the search process. This is based on all nineteen nonrecurring items without regard to their materiality.

Column 2:   The cumulative percentage of all nonrecurring items located through each step of the search process. Seventy-nine percent of the total nonrecurring items were located through the first 5 steps of the search process. All nonrecurring items were located by step 7.

Column 3:   Same as column 1 except that only material nonrecurring items were considered.

Column 4:   Same as column 2 except that only material nonrecurring items were considered.

For the case of Acme-Cleveland, Exhibit 6.12 reveals that 91% of all *material* nonrecurring items were located through the first 5 steps of the search sequence. This result is achieved very efficiently because most of the nonrecurring items are located in either statements or schedules, with little requirement to read more time-consuming text. Further, locating nonrecurring items in text is subject to a greater risk that a nonrecurring item will simply be overlooked.

APPLICATION OF THE SUSTAINABLE EARNINGS BASE WORKSHEET: THE E. W. SCRIPPS CO.

The same pattern as for Acme-Cleveland is followed here in presenting information on the sustainable earnings analysis of E. W. Scripps Co. Financial statements and other disclosures used in completing the worksheet are provided in Exhibits 6.13–6.20, on pages 137 to 146. The completed worksheet is shown in Exhibit 6.21, on page 146. Following the completed worksheet is Exhibit 6.22, on page 148, which enumerates the nonrecurring items located in following the search sequence outlined in Exhibit 5.1. Information on the efficiency of the search sequence is summarized in Exhibit 6.23, on page 149.

A tax rate of 42% was used in making tax adjustments to the E. W. Scripps nonrecurring items. As in the case of Acme-Cleveland, this rate is an average of the effective rates for the last three years, adjusted for nonrecurring items.

COMMENTS ON THE E. W. SCRIPPS WORKSHEET

The as-reported results of E. W. Scripps reveal a sharp profit improvement in 1993 followed by a small decline in results for 1994. The sustainable earnings base tells a quite different story: an earnings decline in 1993 followed by dramatic earnings growth in 1994. The management of E. W. Scripps appeared eager to emphasize this alternative perspective on performance. Management provided a revised earnings per share series for this same period as part of MD&A (Exhibit 6.18). The message of the Scripps sustainable earnings series is quite different from that of Acme-Cleveland. With Acme-Cleveland, the sustainable earnings base suggested an earnings decline instead of the recovery represented by as-reported results. With Scripps, dramatic profit improvement is revealed when earnings are comprehensively restated by removing all nonrecurring items.

The 19 nonrecurring items in the case of Acme-Cleveland and 17 in the case of E. W. Scripps would probably be on the high side for most companies. Nevertheless, even with a much reduced set of nonrecurring items, it quickly becomes difficult to pierce the sustainable earnings veil by a simple inspection of a limited set of data. It is essential to have a systematic and efficient approach to gauging the sustainability of results. This is the role played in financial analysis by the sustainable earnings base worksheet.

As in the case of Acme-Cleveland, a summary of nonrecurring items discovered at each step of the search process is provided (Exhibit 6.22), and a presentation dealing with the efficiency of the search process is presented (Exhibit 6.23).

Acme-Cleveland and E. W. Scripps have about the same number of nonrecurring items, but their disclosure pattern is quite different. With Acme-Cleveland, 58% of all nonrecurring items were revealed through search steps 1–4, and only 21% in step 5, the "other income (expense)" note. With Scripps, only 24% of all nonrecurring items were located through steps 1–4, but the "other income (expense)" note alone, step 5, disclosed 70% of the total. The location of nonrecurring items within

Exhibit 6.13 The E. W. Scripps Co., Income Statements (Partial), Years Ending December 31, 1992–1994 (thousands of dollars)

	1992	1993	1994
Operating revenue			
Advertising	$ 432,799	$ 401,247	$ 433,551
Circulation	123,375	116,413	116,684
Other newspaper revenue	52,513	50,394	52,703
Total	608,687	568,054	602,938
Broadcasting	277,287	284,294	288,184
Cable television	238,116	251,792	255,356
Entertainment	87,209	84,741	73,473
Other	44,172	8,126	–
Total operating revenue	1,255,471	1,197,007	1,219,951
Operating expense			
Employee compensation and benefits	417,090	375,846	359,972
Program rights and production costs	119,592	119,279	121,696
Newsprint and ink	90,044	89,062	94,160
Other operating expense	334,276	304,141	303,809
Depreciation	88,330	88,745	85,883
Amortization of intangible assets	33,599	32,133	30,384
Total operating expense	1,082,931	1,009,206	995,904
Operating income	172,540	187,801	224,047
Other credits (charges)			
Interest expense	(34,247)	(27,286)	(16,616)
Net gains and unusual items	74,483	94,374	11,151
Miscellaneous, net	(3,696)	(2,552)	(986)
Net other credits (charges)	36,540	64,536	(6,451)
Income before income taxes, minority interests, and cumulative effect of accounting change	209,080	252,337	217,596
Provision for income taxes	92,585	106,750	86,925
Income before minority interests and cumulative effect of accounting change	116,495	145,587	130,671
Minority interests	10,176	16,901	7,988
Income before cumulative effective of accounting change	106,319	128,686	122,683
Cumulative effect of accounting change— adoption of FAS No. 106 (net of deferred income tax of $15,533)	(22,413)	–	–
Net income	$ 83,906	$ 128,686	$ 122,683

Source: The E. W. Scripps Co., annual report, December 1994, p. 38.

Exhibit 6.14   The E. W. Scripps Co., Cash Flow Statements (Operating Activities Only), Years Ending December 31, 1992–1994 (thousands of dollars)

	1992	1993	1994
Net income	$ 83,906	$128,686	$122,683
Adjustments to reconcile net income to			
net cash flows from operating activities			
Depreciation and amortization	121,929	120,878	116,267
Deferred income taxes	16,873	37,308	2,743
Minority interests in income of			
subsidiary companies	10,176	16,901	7,988
Net gains and unusual items	(77,983)	(91,874)	(7,409)
Cumulative effect of an accounting change	22,413	–	–
Changes in certain working capital			
accounts, net of effects from subsidiary			
companies purchased and sold	5,987	4,168	3,769
Miscellaneous, net	19,819	9,485	2,816
Net operating activities	$203,120	$225,552	$248,857

Source: The E. W. Scripps Co., annual report, December 1994, p. 39.

Exhibit 6.15   The E. W. Scripps Co., LIFO Inventory Note, 1993 and 1994

Inventories
Inventories are stated at the lower of cost or market. The cost of newsprint included in inventory is computed using the last in, first out (LIFO) method. At December 31 newsprint inventories were approximately 58% of total inventories in 1994 and 25% in 1993. The cost of other inventories is computed using the first in, first out (FIFO) method. Inventories would have been $1,200,000 and $200,000 higher at December 31, 1994, and 1993 if FIFO (which approximates current cost) had been used to compute the cost of newsprint.

Source: The E. W. Scripps Co., annual report, December 1994, p. 42.

the first five steps of the search sequence will probably be quite variable across companies. However, our experience would suggest that a substantial majority of all nonrecurring items will be located in these initial five steps. A focus on the initial five steps in the search sequence stresses the importance of conducting financial analysis in as efficient a manner as possible. As noted in discussion of Acme-Cleveland, these first five steps involve reading relatively little text, and most of the nonrecurring items located in this stage of the search sequence are disclosed in either statements or schedules. This reduces the likelihood that nonrecurring items will be overlooked.

Though it was presented on an earnings-per-share basis, the sustainable earnings type of analysis performed by E. W. Scripps (Exhibit 6.18) should increase the analyst's confidence that most nonrecurring items have been located. Unfortunately, a relatively comprehensive restatement of actual results, such as that provided by E.

Exhibit 6.16 The E. W. Scripps Co., Income Tax Note (Partial), 1992–1994 (thousands of dollars)

	1992	1993	1994
Current income taxes			
Federal	$62,401	$ 55,295	$64,699
State and local	9,294	9,877	14,819
Foreign	4,017	3,745	4,412
Total current	75,712	68,917	83,930
Deferred income taxes			
Federal	13,384	47,672	(8,269)
Other	3,489	4,380	3,020
Total deferred	16,873	52,052	(5,249)
Total income taxes	92,585	120,969	78,681
Income taxes allocated to stockholders' equity	—	(14,219)	8,244
Provision for income taxes	$92,585	$106,750	$86,925
Statutory federal income tax rate	34.0%	35.0%	35.0%
Effect of			
State and local income taxes	4.0	3.6	4.5
Amortization of goodwill	4.3	1.4	2.0
Increase in tax rate to 35% on deferred tax liabilities	–	1.4	–
Change in estimated tax basis and lives of certain assets	–	(1.5)	(2.1)
Difference between foreign and U.S. tax rates, including foreign tax credits	.7	.3	.3
Miscellaneous	1.3	2.1	.2
Effective income tax rate	44.3%	42.3%	39.9%

Source: The E. W. Scripps Co., annual report, December 1994, pp. 45–46.

Exhibit 6.17 The E. W. Scripps Co., Note on Unusual Credits and Charges, 1992–1994

Unusual Credits and Charges
1994—The company sold its worldwide Garfield and U.S. Acres copyrights. The sale resulted in a pre-tax gain of $31,600,000, $17,400,000 after tax, $.23 per share.
The company's three television stations that had been Fox affiliates changed their network affiliation. In connection with the change certain program rights owned by those stations will be sold at an estimated loss of $7,900,000. Two of the stations are constructing new buildings to accommodate expanded local news staffs, and currently owned real estate will be sold at an estimated loss of $2,800,000. These estimated losses were recorded in 1994, reducing net income $6,600,000, $.09 per share.
The company made a special contribution of 589,165 shares of Turner Broadcasting Class B common stock to a charitable foundation. The contribution reduced pre-tax income by $8,000,000 and net income by $4,500,000, $.06 per share.
Management changed its estimate of the tax liability for prior years as a result of

Exhibit 6.17   *(continued)*

---

an audit by the Internal Revenue Service (IRS). The adjustment increased net income by $4,500,000, $.06 per share.[a]

The company accrued an estimate of the ultimate costs of certain lawsuits associated with divested operations. The accrual reduced net income by $5,800,000, $.07 per share.

1993—Operating results include net pre-tax gains of $91,900,000, $46,800,000 after-tax, $.63 per share.[a]

Management changed the estimate of the additional amount of copyright fees the company would owe when a dispute between the television industry and the American Society of Composers, Authors and Publishers (ASCAP) was resolved. The adjustment increased operating income $4,300,000 and net income $2,300,000, $.03 per share.

The company realized a $1,100,000 gain on sale of certain publishing equipment and received a $2,500,000 fee in connection with the sale of the Ogden, Utah, Standard Examiner. Net income increased $2,300,000, $.03 per share.

The company recorded a $6,300,000 restructuring charge. The charge reduced net income $3,600,000, $.05 per share.

Management changed its estimate of the tax liability for prior years.[a] The adjustment increased net income $5,400,000, $.07 per share. The federal income tax rate was increased to 35%. The effect on the company's deferred tax liabilities reduced net income $3,700,000, $.05 per share.

1992—Operating results include pre-tax gains of $78,000,000, $45,600,000 after-tax, $.61 per share.[a]

The Pittsburgh Press was not published after May 17 due to a strike. Reported 1992 results include operating losses of $32,700,000 and net losses of $20,200,000, $.27 per share, during the strike period.

The company reduced the carrying value of certain property and investments to estimated realizable value. The resultant $3,500,000 charge reduced net income $2,300,000, $.03 per share.

Source: The E. W. Scripps Co., annual report, December 1994, pp. 44–45.
[a]Original refers to notes, which are not included here.

W. Scripps Co., is very unusual. However, where available, even a partial restatement by management along the lines of a sustainable earnings base analysis is a valuable input to the process of earnings analysis.

The next section presents some examples of sustainable earnings base analyses found in selected company annual reports.

SUSTAINABLE EARNINGS BASE ANALYSIS IN COMPANY ANNUAL REPORTS

Our review of over 500 annual reports revealed only a small number of sustainable earnings base analyses. The case of E. W. Scripps is one of the most comprehensive.

Exhibit 6.18 The E. W. Scripps Co., MD&A of Financial Position and Results of Operations (Partial), 1992–1994 (thousands of dollars except per share data)

	1992	Change	1993	Change	1994
Operating revenue					
Newspapers	$ 508,690	8.5%	$ 551,902	9.2%	$ 602,938
Broadcast television	247,225	3.1	254,944	13.0	288,184
Cable television	238,116	5.7	251,792	1.4	255,356
Entertainment	87,209	(2.8)	84,741	(13.3)	73,473
Continuing operations	1,081,240	5.7	1,143,379	6.7	1,219,951
Divested operations	174,231		53,628		–
Total operating revenue	1,255,471	(4.7)	1,197,007	1.9	1,219,951
Operating income					
Newspapers	88,743	(13.7)	76,556	56.1	119,539
Broadcast television	61,606	12.1	69,071	36.9	94,560
Cable television	43,741	3.4	45,233	(12.0)	39,784
Entertainment	7,708	(58.0)	3,239		(7,083)
Corporate	(14,618)	11.0	(13,017)	(14.0)	(14,838)
Continuing operations	187,180	(3.3)	181,082	28.1	231,962
Divested operations	(14,640)		7,619		–
Unusual items	–		(900)		(7,915)
Total operating income	172,540	8.8	187,801	19.3	224,047
Interest expense	(34,247)		(27,286)		(16,616)
Net gains and unusual items	74,483		94,374		11,151
Miscellaneous, net	(3,696)		(2,552)		(986)
Income taxes	(92,585)		(106,750)		(86,925)
Minority interest	(10,176)		(16,901)		(7,988)
Cumulative effect of accounting change	(22,413)		–		–
Net income	$ 83,906	53.4%	$ 128,686	(4.7)%	$ 122,683
Per share of common stock					
Net income	$1.13	52.2%	$1.72	(6.4)%	$1.61
Note references					
(i) Garfield gain	–		–		(.23)
(ii) Net gains on sales of divested operations	(.61)		(.63)		–
(iii) TV programs/property write-downs	–		–		.09
(iv) Special charitable contribution	–		–		.06
(v) Change in tax liability	–		(.07)		(.06)
(vi) Lawsuits re: divested operations	–		–		.07
(vii) ASCAP adjustment and other items	–		.04		–

Exhibit 6.18   *(continued)*

	1992	Change	1993	Change	1994
(viii),(ix) Pittsburgh strike and write-downs	.30		–		–
(x) Cumulative effect	.30		–		–
Adjusted net income per share (excluding net gains and unusual items)	$1.12	(5.4)%	$1.06	45.3%	$1.54

In the third quarter of 1994 the company acquired the remaining 13.9% minority interest in Scripps Howard Broadcasting Company (SHB) in exchange for 4,952,659 shares of Class A Common stock. In 1993 the company purchased 5.7% of the outstanding shares of SHB and the remaining 2.7% minority interest in the Knoxville News-Sentinel.

The company's average debt balance decreased $202,000,000 in 1994 and $101,000,000 in 1993.

The effective income tax rate decreased in 1994 due to the change in estimate of the tax liability for prior years described in (v) below. Excluding the effect of that adjustment the effective income tax rate would have been 42% in 1994. The effective income tax rate in 1995 is expected to be approximately 42%.

Net gains and unusual items affecting the comparability of the company's reported results of operations include the following:

(i)   In 1994 the company sold its worldwide Garfield and U.S. Acres copyrights. The sale resulted in a pre-tax gain of $31,600,000, $17,400,000 after-tax, $.23 per share.

(ii)   The company divested the following operations: 1993—book publishing; newspapers in Tulare, California, and San Juan, Puerto Rico; Memphis television station; radio stations. 1992—The Pittsburgh Press; TV Data; certain other investments. These business units, and any related gains on the sales of the business units, are hereinafter referred to as the divested operations.

The following items related to divested operations affected the comparability of the company's reported results of operations:

	1992	1993
Net gains recognized (before minority interests and income taxes)	$78,000,000	$91,900,000
Net gains recognized (after minority interests and income taxes)	45,600,000	46,800,000
Net gains recognized per share (after minority interests and income taxes)	$.61	$.63

The Herald, a newspaper with a circulation of approximately 37,000 in Monterey, California, was acquired on December 31, 1992, in connection with the sale of The Pittsburgh Press.

Exhibit 6.18 *(continued)*

(iii) In late 1994 and early 1995 the company's three television stations that had been Fox affiliates changed their network affiliation. In connection with the change certain program rights owned by those stations will be sold at an estimated loss of $7,900,000. Two of the stations are constructing new buildings to accommodate expanded local news programming, and currently owned real estate will be sold at an estimated loss of $2,800,000. These estimated losses were recorded in 1994, reducing net income $6,600,000, $.09 per share.

(iv) In 1994 the company made a special contribution to a charitable foundation that reduced pre-tax income by $8,000,000 and net income by $4,500,000, $.06 per share.

(v) In 1993 management changed its estimate of the tax basis and lives of certain intangible assets. The resulting change in the estimated tax liability for prior years increased net income in 1993 by $5,400,000, $.07 per share. In 1994 the Internal Revenue Service proposed adjustments related to those intangible assets. Based upon the proposed adjustments management again changed its estimate of the tax liability for prior years, increasing net income in 1994 by $4,500,000, $.06 per share.

(vi) In 1994 the company accrued an estimate of the ultimate costs of certain lawsuits associated with divested operations. The accrual reduced net income by $5,800,000, $.07 per share.

(vii) Other items in 1993 include the following:

Management changed the estimate of the additional amount of copyright fees the company would owe when a dispute between the television industry and the American Society of Composers, Authors and Publishers was resolved. The adjustment increased operating income $4,300,000 and net income $2,300,000, $.03 per share.

The company realized a $1,100,000 gain on sale of certain publishing equipment and received a $2,500,000 fee in connection with the sale of the Ogden, Utah, Standard Examiner. Net income increased $2,300,000, $.03 per share.

The company recorded a $6,300,000 restructuring charge. The charge reduced net income $3,600,000, $.05 per share.

The federal income tax rate was increased to 35%. The effect on the company's deferred tax liabilities reduced net income $3,700,000, $.05 per share.

(viii) The Pittsburgh Press was not published after May 17, 1992, due to a strike. Reported 1992 results include operating losses of $32,700,000 and net losses of $20,200,000, $.27 per share, during the strike period. The company sold The Pittsburgh Press on December 31, 1992 (see (ii) above).

(ix) In 1992 the company reduced the carrying value of certain property and investments to estimated realizable value. The resultant $3,500,000 charge reduced net income $2,300,000, $.03 per share.

Exhibit 6.18   *(continued)*

(x)   In 1992 the company adopted Financial Accounting Standard No. 106—Employ-
       ers' Accounting for Postretirement Benefits Other Than Pensions. The cumulative
       effect of the accounting change decreased net income $22,413,000, $.30 per share,
       of which $18,000,000, $.24 per share, was associated with divested operations.

Operating results, excluding the divested operations and unusual items described above,
for each of the company's business segments are presented on the following pages. The
effects of the foregoing unusual items and the divested operations are excluded from the
consolidated and segment operating results because management believes they are not
relevant to understanding the company's ongoing operations.

Demand for advertising continued to improve in 1994. Advertising revenues increased
for all of the company's daily newspapers.

Newspaper revenues and expenses in 1993 were boosted by the fourth-quarter 1992
acquisition of three California daily newspapers.

Because the supply of newsprint exceeded demand, its price generally declined from
1988 through August 1992. Since the first quarter of 1994 prices have increased sharply.
The weighted average price of newsprint was $492 per metric ton in the fourth quarter of
1994. Based on price increases announced by suppliers, including an increase effective
May 1995, the weighted average price of newsprint in 1995 will be at least 40% higher
than in 1994.

Depreciation expense for 1992 includes a charge of $5,500,000 to reduce the book
value of certain equipment to estimated net realizable value.

Source: The E. W. Scripps Co., annual report, December 1994, pp. 26–29.

Exhibit 6.19   The E. W. Scripps Co., Note on Acquisitions and Divestitures (Partial),
1992 and 1993 (thousands of dollars except per share data)

The following table presents additional information about the divestitures:

	1992	1993
Cash received	$36,919	$140,509
Notes and preferred stock	14,150	–
Net assets of The Herald:		
Tangible assets	21,602	–
Liabilities assumed	(1,227)	–
Total proceeds	71,444	140,509
Net assets (liabilities) disposed	(6,539)	48,635
Net gains recognized (before minority interests and income taxes)	77,983	91,874
Net gains recognized (after minority interests and income taxes)	$45,600	$46,800
Net gains recognized per share (after minority interests and income taxes)	$.61	$.63

Included in net assets (liabilities) disposed in 1992 are pension and other postretirement
benefit obligations totaling $36,500,000.

Exhibit 6.19   *(continued)*

Included in the consolidated financial statements are the following results of divested operations (excluding gains on sales):

	1992	1993
Operating revenue	$174,200	$53,600
Operating income (loss)	(14,600)	7,600

Source: The E. W. Scripps Co., annual report, December 1994, p. 44.

Exhibit 6.20   The E. W. Scripps Co., Note on Segment Disclosures (Partial), 1992–1994 (thousands of dollars except per subscriber data)

CABLE TELEVISION—Operating results for the cable television segment were as follows:

	1992	Change	1993	Change	1994
Operating revenue					
Basic services	$163,069	5.3%	$171,703	(3.5)%	$165,682
Premium programming services	44,559	4.1	46,401	6.1	49,242
Other monthly service	13,002	12.4	14,611	19.2	17,422
Advertising	8,394	5.7	8,870	28.2	11,367
Installation and miscellaneous	9,092	12.3	10,207	14.1	11,643
Total operating revenue	238,116	5.7	251,792	1.4	255,356
Operating expense					
Employee compensation and benefits	38,332	2.4	39,237	5.4	41,343
Program costs	51,225	8.4	55,548	10.9	61,614
Other	47,394	9.2	51,747	6.8	55,264
Depreciation and amortization	57,424	4.5	60,027	(4.5)	57,351
Total operating expense	194,375	6.3	206,559	4.4	215,572
Operating income	$ 43,741	3.4%	$ 45,233	(12.0)%	$ 39,784
Other financial and statistical data					
Earnings before interest, income taxes, depreciation, and amortization (EBITDA)	$101,165	4.0%	$105,260	(7.7)%	$97,135
Percent of operating revenue					
Operating income	18.4%		18.0%		15.6%
EBITDA	42.5%		41.8%		38.0%
Capital expenditures	$ 58,299	15.0%	$ 67,019	(37.9)%	$ 41,616
Average number of basic subscribers	656.7	4.2%	684.3	4.9%	717.7
Average monthly revenue per basic subscriber	$ 30.22	1.5%	$ 30.66	(3.3)%	$ 29.65
Homes passed at December 31	1,128.8	1.6%	1,146.8	2.0%	1,170.0
Basic subscribers at December 31	673.1	4.1%	701.0	5.4%	739.2
Penetration at December 31	59.6%		61.1%		63.2%

Exhibit 6.20   *(continued)*

Re-regulation of the cable television industry significantly affected the company's cable television operations in 1994 and in 1993. The effects of price decreases resulting from re-regulation were partially offset by growth in subscribers in 1994. After declining year-over-year for five straight quarters, EBITDA increased in the fourth quarter of 1994.

Other operating expenses in 1994 include a $3,000,000 charge for special rebates to the company's Sacramento system customers and related legal costs. The rebate was awarded by a federal court in connection with litigation concerning the system's pricing policies in the late 1980s.

Source: The E. W. Scripps Co., annual report, December 1994, p. 33.

Exhibit 6.21   Adjustment Worksheet for Sustainable Earnings Base: The E. W. Scripps Co., 1992–1994 (thousands of dollars)

	1992	1993	1994
Reported net income	$83,906	$128,686	$122,683
Add			
Pre-tax LIFO liquidation losses			
Losses on sales of fixed assets			
Losses on sales of investments			
Losses on sales of other assets			
Restructuring charges		6,300	
Investment write-downs			
Inventory write-downs			
Other asset write-downs	3,500		
Foreign currency losses			
Litigation charges			
Losses on patent infringement suits			
Exceptional bad-debt provisions			
Nonrecurring expense increases			
Temporary revenue reductions			
Other—sale of TV stations			10,700
Other—charitable contributions			8,000
Other—strike loss	32,700		
Other—operating loss divested operations	14,600		
Other—special rebates, Sacramento cable system			3,000
Subtotal	$50,800	$6,300	$21,700
Multiply by			
(1 – combined federal and state tax rates)	58%	58%	58%
Tax-adjusted additions	$29,464	$3,654	$12,586
Add			
After-tax LIFO liquidation losses			
Increases in deferred tax valuation allowances			
Other nonrecurring tax charges			

Exhibit 6.21 *(continued)*

	1992	1993	1994
Losses on discontinued operations			
Extraordinary losses			
Losses/cumulative-effect accounting changes	22,413		
Other—lawsuit accrual			5,800
Other			
Other			
Subtotal	22,413		5,800
Total additions	$51,877	$3,654	$ 18,386
Deduct			
Pre-tax LIFO liquidation gains			
Gains on sales of fixed assets			
Gains on sales of investments			
Gains on sales of other assets		$1,100	
Reversals of restructuring charges			
Investment write-ups (trading account)			
Foreign currency gains			
Litigation revenues			
Gains on patent infringement suit			
Nonrecurring expense decreases			
Temporary revenue increases—fee on asset sale		2,500	
Reversals of bad-debt allowances			
Other—sale of Garfield and U.S. Acres copyrights			$ 31,600
Other—gain on divestitures	$78,000	91,900	
Other—increase in benefit of copyright dispute		4,300	
Other—operating income divested operations		7,600	
Subtotal	$78,000	$107,400	$ 31,600
Multiply by			
(1 – combined federal, state tax rates)	58%	58%	58%
Tax-adjusted deductions	$45,240	$62,292	$ 18,328
Deduct			
After-tax LIFO liquidation gains			
Reductions in deferred tax valuation allowances			
Loss carryforward benefits from prior periods			
Other nonrecurring tax benefits		9,100	4,500
Gains on discontinued operations			
Extraordinary gains			
Gains/cumulative-effect accounting changes	22,413		
Other			
Other			
Other			
Subtotal	22,413	9,100	4,500
Total deductions	$67,653	$71,392	$ 22,828
Sustainable earnings base	$68,130	$60,948	$118,241

Exhibit 6.22   Summary of Nonrecurring Items Search Process: The E. W. Scripps Co.

Step and Search Location	Nonrecurring Item Revealed
1. Income statement	Total for "net gains and unusual items," with no detail (1992–1994); not treated as a nonrecurring disclosure in the absence of detail (1992–1994) Cumulative effect of the adoption of SFAS No. 106 (1992)[1]
2. Statement of cash flows	Total for "net gains and unusual items," with no detail (1992–1994); not treated as a nonrecurring disclosure in the absence of detail (1992–1994) Cumulative effect of the adoption of SFAS No. 106 (1992)[2]
3. Inventory note (LIFO firm)	No nonrecurring items disclosed
4. Income tax note	Nonrecurring effect of increase in tax rate on net deferred tax liability (1993)[1] Change in tax basis and useful lives of some assets (1993–1994)[1]
5. "Other income (expense)" note	Gain on sale of Garfield and U.S. Acres copyrights (1994)[1] Loss associated with sale of program rights and real estate associated with three stations changing network affiliation (1994)[1] Special charitable contribution (1994)[1] Accrued lawsuit costs (1994)[1] Gains on divestitures (1993)[1] Additional ASCAP income accrual (1993)[1] Gain on sale of publishing equipment (1993)[1] Fee from sale of Ogden, Utah, Standard Examiner (1993)[1] Restructuring charge (1193)[1] Nonrecurring effect of increase in tax rate on net deferred tax liability (1993)[2] Change in tax basis and useful lives of some assets (1993–1994)[2] Gains on divestitures (1992)[1] Loss due to strike (1992)[1] Write-down of property and investments (1992)[1]

Exhibit 6.22 *(continued)*

Step and Search Location	Nonrecurring Item Revealed
6. MD&A	Each item found in "other income (expense)" note (Exhibit 6.17) was also found in MD&A[2]
7. Other notes revealing nonrecurring items:	
Acquisitions and divestitures	Gains on divestitures, 1992 and 1993[2]
	Operating income (loss) of 1992 and 1993 divestitures[1]
Segment disclosures	Loss associated with sale of program rights and real estate associated with three stations changing network affiliation (1994)[3]
	Additional ASCAP income accrual (1993)[3]

Note: The superscripts 1, 2, 3 indicate in how many search locations the nonrecurring item was found: for instance, "Additional ASCAP income accrual" was found in "other income (expense)" note (first location); in MD&A (second location); and in "segment disclosures" note (third location).

Exhibit 6.23   Efficiency of Nonrecurring Items Search Process: The E. W. Scripps Co.

	Incremental Nonrecurring Items Discovered			
	(1) All Nonrecurring	(2) Cumulative	(3) All Material[a]	(4) Cumulative
Step and Search Location	Items	% Located	Items	% Located
1. Income statement	1	6%	1	12%
2. Statement of cash flows	0	6	0	12
3. Inventory note	0	6	0	12
4. Tax note	3	24	1	25
5. "Other income (expense)" note	12	94	4	75
6. MD&A	0	94	0	75
7. Acquisitions and divestitures note	1	100	2	100
8. Segment disclosures note	0	100	0	100
Total nonrecurring items	17	100%	8	100%

[a]5% or more of the amount of the net income or net loss, on a tax-adjusted basis.

Other companies providing such analyses, with varying degrees of completeness, included Amoco Companies, Inc., C. R. Bard, Inc., Carpenter Technology Corp., Chevron Corp., Deere & Co., Doskocil Corp., Halliburton Co., Maxus Energy Corp., Mobil Corp., Raychem Corp., Shell Oil Co., TOTAL Petroleum (North America) Ltd., Union Texas Petroleum, and Unocal Corp. The high representation of oil companies in this set is notable. Perhaps the results of oil companies have a higher incidence of nonrecurring items and therefore there is a greater need to provide such guidance to users of their statements.

Amoco Corporation

Amoco presented a schedule of "unusual items affecting income" in its MD&A. The schedule, presented as Exhibit 6.24, is on an after-tax basis but does not, as in the case of E. W. Scripps, display a reconciliation of reported results to a new sustainable earnings base series. Amoco's reported results for 1992–1994 were $(74) million, $1,820 million, and $1,789 million, respectively. Based upon its analysis of the after-tax impact of its unusual items, Amoco drew conclusions regarding the effect on earnings comparisons for 1993–1994 and 1992–1993. It commented on the effects of its nonrecurring items: 1994–1993—"Excluding these items, 1994 earnings were about the same as 1993"; 1993–1992—"Adjusting for unusual items and accounting changes, 1993 earnings were 18%, or $256 million, above the 1992 level."[8]

Removing the unusual items from 1992, 1993, and 1994 net income results in a revised series, comparable to a sustainable earnings base, of $1,475 million, $1,740 million, and $1,728 million, respectively. The 1992 restatement also includes a $924 million income reduction from accounting changes. Comparison of Amoco's revised series to actual results led to Amoco's characterizations of its revised earnings performance.

Amoco's presentation of the information on unusual items in Exhibit 6.24 is

Exhibit 6.24 Display of Unusual Items: Amoco Corp., 1992–1994 (millions of dollars)

	Increase (Decrease) in Net Income		
	1992	1993	1994
Crude oil excise tax settlement	–	–	$270
Restructurings	$(805)	$(170)	(256)
Environmental provisions	–	–	(6)
Gains on dispositions	–	190	45
Tax obligations and other	90	60	62
Sharjah natural gas settlement	90	–	–

Source: Amoco Corp., annual report, December 1994, p. 29.

very valuable to an analysis of its performance. However, it does not represent a complete revision of reported results and therefore does not lead to sustainable earnings base series such as were developed for both Acme-Cleveland and E. W. Scripps. Two specific examples were the failure to exclude the following in its revisions: (1) the material income-increasing effects of LIFO inventory liquidations in 1993, and (2) foreign currency gains in each of the years 1992–1994. Amoco reported a $50 million increase in net income in 1993 from LIFO liquidations. The effects of LIFO liquidations in both 1992 and 1994 were not material. Foreign currency gains, pre-tax, amounted to $129 million, $47 million, and $24 million, respectively, in 1992, 1993, and 1994.

Further adjusting Amoco's results beyond the Amoco-supplied revisions in Exhibit 6.24, for the LIFO liquidations, and the foreign currency gains would result in the revised series in Exhibit 6.25.

Incorporation of the information on the LIFO liquidation and foreign currency gains alters somewhat the Amoco characterizations of the 1994–1993 earnings comparison. Earnings in 1994 are now more accurately described as somewhat improved over 1993. Amoco did not include the effects of the LIFO liquidation and foreign exchange gains in its set of unusual items. It may be that Amoco did not view these items as unusual in view of the nature of its operations. However, the same could probably be said of at least some of the items treated as unusual in Exhibit 6.24. Restructuring charges are among the more common income statement items in the 1990s, and Amoco treats them as unusual in each of the years 1992–1994. Amoco also reported restructuring charges in 1991.

The case for including the LIFO liquidation and foreign exchange gains in a sustainable earnings calculation turns more on irregularity in their amount than whether they qualify as unusual. Note that the LIFO liquidation added $50 million to 1993 net income, but LIFO liquidations were not material in either 1992 or 1994. Further, the foreign currency gain declined by $105 million, $63 million after-tax, between 1992 and 1994.

Our view is that adjustments should be made for both of these items in the calculation of the sustainable earnings base. The case for exclusion from sustainable

Exhibit 6.25   Additional Revisions to Earnings: Amoco Corp., 1992–1994 (millions of dollars)

	As Reported	Amoco Revised	Further Revised[a]	Difference
1992	$ 850	$1,475	$1,398	$77
1993	1,820	1,740	1,662	$78
1994	1,789	1,728	1,714	$14

[a]Further revisions: 1992—foreign currency gain of $129 × (1 − .40 tax rate) = $77; 1993—foreign currency gain of $47 × (1 − .40 tax rate) = $28; disclosed increase in income, after-tax, from LIFO liquidation $50; 1994—foreign currency gain of $24 × (1 − .40 tax rate) = $14.

earnings is strongest in the case of the $50 million LIFO liquidation benefit, both in terms of its materiality and its irregularity. However, there are foreign currency gains in each of the years 1992–1994 (Exhibit 6.25); there was a foreign currency loss of $20 million in 1991. An alternative treatment in a sustainable earnings analysis, especially when either gains or losses dominate the series over an extended period, would be to include some average amount of gain or loss in the development of a sustainable earnings series.

Other Petroleum Companies

It is useful to consider the items treated as special, nonrecurring, or unusual by other petroleum companies that provide some degree of sustainable earnings analysis. Exhibit 6.26 provides a summary of such items by five additional petroleum companies.

There is a great deal of similarity in the types of items treated as nonrecurring by Amoco and the five other petroleum companies in Exhibit 6.26. Most of these firms use the term *special items* to describe what most would consider to be nonrecurring items. Chevron defines special items as follows:

Transactions not considered representative of the company's ongoing operations. These transactions, as defined by management, can obscure the underlying results of operations and affect comparability between years.[9]

In arriving at sustainable earnings results, all the petroleum companies adjusted for the effects of changes in accounting policies and extraordinary items. These items are not included in the Exhibit 6.26 summaries.

Implementation of the definition of special items offered by Chevron requires the exercise of considerable judgment. The weakness of the terms *nonrecurring* and *unusual* has probably led to the use of *special.* For example, it would be difficult to employ the term *nonrecurring* and then single out restructuring charges for adjustment in the development of a sustainable earnings series or its equivalent. Three of the six petroleum companies discussed here had restructuring charges in each of the years 1992–1994. In each case, these charges were removed from net income or net loss to arrive at a sustainable earnings series. In Exhibit 6.26, Unocal identifies "major asset sales" as adjustment items. Distinguishing major asset sales from all other asset sales must, at times, be a rather subjective determination.

Whereas Amoco did not treat its LIFO liquidation gains as special items, Chevron, Mobil, and Shell did. TOTAL Petroleum disclosed no LIFO liquidations. Taxes, a topic discussed later in this chapter, were a major adjustment item for all the petroleum companies discussed.

The sustainable earnings type of analyses of these petroleum companies can be a significant aid to completion of the worksheet, illustrated earlier for Acme-Cleveland and E. W. Scripps. Company-prepared sustainable earnings analyses have a strength that results from the intimate knowledge of the company and its circum-

Exhibit 6.26   Nonrecurring Items and Sustainable Earnings Base Information
Provided by Petroleum Companies

Chevron Corp. (1994)
Prior-year tax adjustments
Asset dispositions
Asset write-offs and revaluations
Environmental remediation provisions
Restructurings and reorganizations
LIFO inventory gains and losses

Mobil Corp. (1994)
Asset sales and write-downs
Tax rate change
Inventory and supplies adjustments
Restructuring provisions
Environmental provisions
Property write-downs
LIFO and other inventory adjustments
Shutdown of solar energy program
Claim settlement
Tax adjustments
Hurricane Andrew property damages

Shell Oil Co.
Property write-offs
Litigation provisions and settlements
Tax adjustments
Natural gas contract settlement
Work force reduction charge
Environmental provisions
LIFO liquidation gain
Asset sales
Tax adjustments—rate change
Environmental remediation

TOTAL Petroleum (N.A.) Ltd. (1994)
Inventory valuation adjustments
Gains on asset disposals
Income tax adjustment

Unocal Corp.
Major asset sales
Litigation
Write-downs of assets
Restructuring costs
Tax benefit

Sources: Companies' annual reports.

stances. However, with this strength comes a potential weakness. Given the room for exercise of considerable judgment in the analysis, the absence of an outside, independent perspective has the potential to distort key classification decisions. Sustainable earnings analyses could become a new avenue for the practice of earnings management.

Non-Petroleum Companies

Sustainable earnings base analyses in other, nonpetroleum companies are briefly reviewed here. Their disclosures are much like those of the petroleum companies. Sustainable earnings base analyses of Carpenter Technology Corp. and Halliburton Co. are presented in Exhibits 6.27 and 6.28, respectively.

Carpenter Technology's sustainable earnings statement goes from reported to revised results, just like the worksheet in Exhibit 6.1. Halliburton employs just the opposite format, going from revised results, or net income before special items, to reported results.

A review of Carpenter Technology's statements and notes reveals at least two

Exhibit 6.27 Reconciliation of Net Income to Earnings before Accounting Changes and Special and Extraordinary Charges: Carpenter Technology Corp., 1991–1993 (millions of dollars)

	1991	1992	1993
As reported in the income statement	$30.1	$13.6	$(48.1)
Cumulative effect of adopting SFAS No. 106 and No. 109	–	–	74.7
Extraordinary charge—purchase of long-term debt	–	1.2	–
Earnings before accounting changes and extraordinary charge	30.1	14.8	26.6
Current year effect of adopting SFAS No. 106 and No. 109	–	–	6.1
Special charges—costs of salaried staff reductions; costs of closing Bridgeport, Conn. plant	4.3	4.9	–
Earnings before accounting changes and special and extraordinary charges	$34.4	$19.7	$32.7

Source: Carpenter Technology Corp., annual report, June 1993, p. 22.

Exhibit 6.28 Reconciliation of Net Income before Special Items to Net Income (Loss): Halliburton Co., 1990–1992 (thousands of dollars)

	1990	1991	1992
Net income before special items	$195.1	$90.4	$ 46.6
Special charges	–	(83.0)	(185.8)
Provisions for expected losses with respect to operations in Iraq and Kuwait	(16.6)	–	–
Gain on sale of Health Economics Corp.	–	–	9.0
Interest on tax refunds	–	19.2	6.7
Gain on sale of 23 marine construction vessels and associated assets	18.8		–
Changes in accounting methods			(13.8)
Net income (loss)	$197.3	$26.6	$(137.3)

Source: Halliburton Co., annual report, December 1992, p. 25.

additional items that should normally be included in a complete sustainable earnings analysis. Carpenter's inventory note disclosed a $13.4 million benefit to 1993 net income from a LIFO liquidation.[10] In addition, Carpenter's MD&A identified a benefit of $3.7 million from a patent suit award.[11] Recall that most of the petroleum companies that had LIFO liquidation effects, included them in their sustainable earnings revisions.

    Incorporation of the two items omitted by Carpenter changes the message of their sustainable earnings presentation. Applying Carpenter's 1993 combined federal and state tax rate of 38% to the patent award yields a net benefit of $2,294,000. No tax adjustment is necessary for the LIFO liquidation because it is already expressed on an after-tax basis. Deducting both the $2,294,000 after-tax patent income and the $13.4 million LIFO liquidation benefit from 1993 results produces the new sustainable earnings series in Exhibit 6.29.

The original revised series suggests a sharp profit improvement in 1993 over 1992. In contrast, additional adjustments for the LIFO liquidation and the patent award indicate a small decline. A complete sustainable earnings analysis, such as that performed for Acme-Cleveland and E. W. Scripps, is essential in order to produce the most reliable indicators of profit performance.

An additional feature of Carpenter's revised earnings information calls for comment. Carpenter adopted both SFAS No. 106 and SFAS No. 109 in 1993.[12] The cumulative effect of the adoption, $74.7 million, is a necessary adjustment in arriving at sustainable earnings. However, Carpenter also treated the separate, incremental impact of $6.1 million on the net loss for 1993 as an adjustment. The new accounting standards, especially SFAS No. 106, raised expenses to a new level, one that will be sustained in the future. A complete sustainable earnings analysis should not remove the current-year effect of these new accounting standards from earnings. Again, using a 38 % tax rate, $3.8 million [(1–0.38) × $6.1 million] should be deducted from the revised series (Exhibit 6.29). The new revised results for 1993 become $13.2 million in place of $17.0 million. Sustainable earnings for 1993 are weakened still further with this more complete analysis.

Halliburton's sustainable earnings analysis, presented in Exhibit 6.28, requires none of the additional adjustments called for in the Carpenter case. However, Halliburton does disclose a significant series of foreign currency losses for the period 1990–1992: $11.2 million, $11.1 million, and $32.7 million, respectively.[13] Halliburton explains that the 1992 increase in such losses resulted from various Latin American and, to a lesser degree, European and African exposures. The company further notes, "The Latin American and African currencies have been prohibitively

Exhibit 6.29   Results of Partial Versus Complete Sustainable Earnings Base Analysis: Carpenter Technology Corp., 1991–1993 (millions of dollars)

	1991	1992	1993[a]
Original revised earnings			
Earnings before accounting changes			
and special and extraordinary charges	$34.4	$19.7	$32.7
Fully revised earnings series			
Earnings before accounting changes			
and special and extraordinary charges	$34.4	$19.7	$17.0

[a]Only 1993 required further revisions.

expensive to hedge and losses there are likely to continue." If, indeed, the losses are likely to continue, then their complete removal in developing a sustainable earnings series is not called for. Adjusting the reported results by an amount that will include such losses at their average value for the three-year period is the best approach. The three-year average value for currency losses was $18.3 million. The actual loss for the next year, 1993, was $21 million. Use of the loss average in this case would be preferred to total removal of the currency losses in arriving at sustainable earnings.

The treatment of income taxes is an important and potentially complex matter in sustainable earnings analysis. This is especially true under the new tax accounting requirements of SFAS No. 109, "Accounting for Income Taxes." The next section of this chapter provides additional guidance on the treatment of income taxes.

INCOME TAXES AND SUSTAINABLE EARNINGS BASE ANALYSIS

Selection of an Average Effective Tax Rate

Most of the company-produced examples of sustainable earnings discussed in preceding sections are on an after-tax basis. For example, Halliburton's disclosed 1992 gain on its sale of Health Economics Corp. amounted to $13.6 million on a pre-tax basis.[14] However, in Exhibit 6.28 the gain appears as $9.0 million. The difference between these two amounts, $4.6 million, represents an assumed tax effect of about 34% (4.6/13.6 = 33.8%). In the same year, the tax effect on $264.6 million of special charges, or $185.8 after-tax, was computed using a tax rate of about 30%. These tax rates presumably represent the marginal tax effect of these transactions. The different tax rates used for various items within the same year result from differences between the book and tax return amount of the gain and special charges, respectively, and tax rates in the various taxing jurisdictions in which the charges and gains are reported.

The third instruction for filling out the sustainable earnings worksheet calls for tax adjustments to be based upon a representative combined federal and state rate. Where there is no state income tax, this rate should approximate the current federal statutory rate of 35%. With a state rate, the combined rate will generally range between 38 and 42%. A reasonable approximation should be the goal. Information on a company's tax rates is found in the required schedule that reconciles statutory, or expected, to effective, or actual, tax rates or amounts.[15] Exhibit 6.30 includes a schedule reconciling both dollar amounts of taxes and tax rates. Where only dollars amounts are provided, these amounts should be divided by income before taxes to convert to percentages.

The combined effective federal and state tax rates for Nalco Chemical Co. in Exhibit 6.30 are about 39%, 38%, and 37% over the three-year period. Absent information on significant changes in rates, use of an average rate of 38%–40% in the

Exhibit 6.30 Disclosure of Statutory and Effective Income Tax Rates: Nalco Chemical Co., 1992–1994

	1992	1993	1994
Statutory federal income tax rate	34.0%	35.0%	35.0%
State income taxes, net of federal tax benefit	2.6	2.7	4.5
Foreign taxes on formation and consolidation	–	–	5.7
Foreign earnings subject to higher (lower) rates	2.0	.6	(.4)
Other	.6	.6	.1
Effective income tax rate	39.2%	38.9%	44.9%

Source: Nalco Chemical Co., annual report, December 1994, p. 29.

sustainable earnings worksheet would be appropriate. The 5.7% effective rate increase due to foreign taxes in 1994 appears to be nonrecurring and should be excluded in selecting a representative rate.

Dealing with Changes in Valuation Allowances

The sustainable earnings base worksheet indicates that increases in deferred tax valuation allowances should be added back to net income and decreases subtracted. However, instruction for the worksheet cautions that changes in deferred tax valuation allowances are recorded in the tax-adjusted additions or deductions section only if such changes affected net income or net loss for the period. Evidence of an income statement effect will usually take the form of an entry in the income tax rate reconciliation schedule.

The deferred tax valuation allowance is required by SFAS No. 109, "Accounting for Income Taxes," in cases where the realization of deferred tax assets is unlikely[16]— a more expansive discussion of this matter is provided in Chapter 7. A change in the valuation allowance will be recorded on the worksheet when such an increase or decrease results in a corresponding increase or decrease in the deferred tax provision account, that is, when it decreases or increases net income. The best approach is to review the tax reconciliation schedule and determine if a change in the valuation allowance has affected the effective tax rate. If it has, then that portion of the change in the tax provision that appears in the reconciliation schedule should be recorded on the worksheet.

Valuation Allowance Change Recorded on Worksheet

To illustrate, Boston Chicken, Inc., disclosed a deferred tax valuation allowance of $3,847,000 at the end of 1993. As the disclosure in Exhibit 6.31 reveals, this valuation allowance was reduced to zero by the end of 1994.

To determine whether any of the valuation allowance reduction reduced the tax

Exhibit 6.31 Change in Deferred Tax Valuation Allowance: Boston Chicken, Inc., 1993 and 1994 (thousands of dollars)

	1993	1994
Deferred tax assets		
Accounts payable and accrued expenses	$ 78	$ 794
Deferred franchise revenue	1,992	3,469
Other noncurrent liabilities	623	262
Net operating losses	4,844	11,639
Other	52	173
Total	7,589	16,337
Less: valuation allowance	(3,847)	–
Net deferred tax assets	$ 3,742	$16,337

Source: Boston Chicken, Inc., annual report, December 1994, p. 36.

provision for the year, and as a result increased net income, reference is made to the tax reconciliation schedule presented in Exhibit 6.32.

Exhibit 6.32 reveals that $3,520,000 of the $3,847,000 reduction in the valuation allowance reduced the tax provision for 1994. In 1993 the amount was $626,000.[17] As a result, net income for 1994 would be increased by $3,520,000. In its MD&A, Boston Chicken highlighted this tax benefit and attributed it to "the increased level of operating income."[18] These increases in net income should be treated as nonrecurring and deducted from net income in the worksheet in arriving at sustainable earnings. Since the valuation allowance has been reduced to zero, it offers no further potential for earnings increases. The valuation allowance resulted from potential tax benefits that originated in earlier years—mainly net operating loss carryforwards. However, these tax benefits were not judged to be sufficiently likely to be realized and, as a result, were written off by recording the valuation allowance. As a result, these potential benefits were not previously recognized in the earnings of Boston Chicken. In retrospect, the earnings of prior periods were understated while losses were overstated.

Exhibit 6.32 Tax Reconciliation Schedule: Boston Chicken, Inc., 1993 and 1994 (thousands of dollars)

	1993	1994
Income tax expense at statutory rate	$ 560	$ 6,953
State taxes, net of federal benefit	66	818
Other	–	26
Change in valuation allowance	(626)	(3,520)
Provision for income taxes	$ –	$ 4,277

Source: Boston Chicken, Inc., annual report, December 1994, p. 37.

Valuation Allowance Change Not Recorded on Worksheet

North American Biologicals, Inc., recorded a $1,337,000 increase in its valuation allowance in 1994. However, its tax reconciliation schedule disclosed no associated increase in its tax provision. The schedule of deferred tax assets of North American Biologicals is provided in Exhibit 6.33.

Notice that the $1,337,000 increase in valuation allowance ($1,519,000 – $182,000) is virtually equal to the new deferred tax asset of $1,336,000 recorded in 1994 for the potential tax benefits of loss carryforwards. These carryforwards were acquired along with the 1994 purchase of Premier BioResources, Inc.

SFAS No. 109, "Accounting for Income Taxes," requires that deferred tax assets be recorded for all potential tax benefits. This holds even if their likelihood of realization is so low that an immediate write-off through the deferred tax asset valuation allowance is planned. Limitations on the utilization of acquired loss carryforward benefits frequently result in their full or partial write-off, as in the present case.

The growth in the deferred tax asset is exactly offset by the increase in the valuation allowance, a contra-asset account. The valuation allowance increase has no current effect on the tax provision. As a result, no worksheet adjustment is required in this case.

SUMMARY

Building on Chapter 5, this chapter introduced the sustainable earnings base worksheet as a device to summarize the effect of all nonrecurring items on net income or loss.

Exhibit 6.33   Change in Deferred Tax Valuation Allowance: North American Biologicals, Inc., 1993 and 1994 (thousands of dollars)

	1993	1994
Deferred tax assets		
Amortization	$ 409	$ 911
Bad debt	–	197
Depreciation	–	142
Inventory reserves	133	290
Inventory capitalization	145	162
Accrued vacation	207	151
Loss carryforward	–	1,336
Foreign tax credits	111	111
Other	89	61
Total	1,094	3,361
Less: valuation allowance	(182)	(1,519)
Net deferred tax assets	$ 912	$ 1,842

Source: North American Biologicals, Inc., annual report, 1994, p. 24.

The sustainable earnings base provides profitability information from which the distorting effects of nonrecurring items have been removed. As such, this series provides a sound foundation upon which to build earnings expectations or forecasts. The likelihood of earnings surprises is reduced by the improvements in earnings expectations made possible by sustainable earnings analysis.

The sustainable earnings base worksheet was applied to two case studies: Acme-Cleveland Corp. and The E. W. Scripps Co. In each case, the sustainable earnings series conveyed a quite different picture of earnings performance than the as-reported earnings. The E. W. Scripps Co. presented a sustainable earnings series that was apparently designed to aid the reader in evaluating its earnings performance. In addition, a selection of other firms were discussed that presented various examples of earnings information revised to exclude the effects of nonrecurring items. In each case, these efforts fell short of the comprehensive revisions that could be achieved with the sustainable earnings base worksheet.

In both the Acme-Cleveland and E. W. Scripps applications, the efficiency of the standard search process outlined in Exhibit 5.1 was evaluated. The recommended sequence resulted in the location of a very high percentage of all nonrecurring items in each case by moving only through the first five steps in the search sequence.

Finally, because of their importance to the entire process of computing sustainable earnings, additional technical background was provided on (1) selecting the required tax rate used in the revision process, and (2) determining when a change in a deferred tax valuation allowance is to be included in the computation of sustainable earnings.

ENDNOTES

1. Lord Byron, *Journal*, January 28, 1821.
2. Thucydides, *The History of the Peloponnesian War* (431–413 B.C.) Bk 1, Sec. 1.
3. Plato, *Apology*, 24.
4. An earlier version of this worksheet was published as E. Comiskey, C. Mulford, and H. Choi, "Analyzing the Persistence of Earnings: A Lender's Guide," *Commercial Lending Review*, (Winter 1994–1995), pp. 4–23.
5. Chevron Corp., annual report, December 1994, p. 24. This quotation appeared in Chevron's Glossary of Energy and Financial Terms. The description is actually for the term *special items*. However, it is clear that the term is being used to describe nonrecurring items as discussed in this book.
6. H. Choi, "Analysis and Valuation Implications of Persistence and Cash-Content Dimensions of Earnings Components Based on Extent of Analyst Following." Unpublished Ph.D. thesis, Georgia Institute of Technology, October 1994, chs. 5 and 6.
7. Ibid., chs. 5 and 6.
8. Amoco Corp., annual report, December 1994, p. 30.
9. Chevron Corp., annual report, December 1994, p. 24.
10. Carpenter Technology Corp., annual report, June 1993, p. 32.
11. Ibid., p. 23.

12. Statement of Financial Accounting Standards (SFAS) No. 106, "Employers' Accounting for Postretirement Benefits Other Than Pensions," (Norwalk, Conn.: Financial Accounting Standards Board, December 1990) and SFAS No. 109, "Accounting for Income Taxes" (February 1992).
13. Halliburton Co., annual report, December 1992, p. 32.
14. Ibid., p. 27.
15. SFAS No. 109, "Accounting for Income Taxes" (February 1992), para. 47.
16. Ibid., para 17.
17. It is common for portions of valuation allowance reductions to be credited (added to) shareholders' equity. This typically results when the benefits realized are related to stock options. Boston Chicken reported such increases in its additional paid-in capital balance in both 1993 and 1994. Boston Chicken, Inc., annual report, 1994, p. 32.
18. Ibid., p. 27.

Chapter 7
Financial Position Analysis

General Motors Corp.'s 1992 earnings were reduced by $20.8 billion as a result of recording a liability for previously unaccrued postretirement health care and life insurance benefits.[1]

Norfolk Southern Corp.'s 1993 earnings were increased by $467 million because of the reduction in the value of its net deferred tax liability to reflect lower current tax rates compared to those in effect when the obligations were originally recorded.[2]

LCI International, Inc.'s 1994 results benefited by $17.7 million based upon its recognition of the potential tax-saving of net operating loss and tax credit carryforwards that had previously been written off.[3]

In 1995, The Seagram Co. Ltd., sold its 24% interest in E. I. du Pont de Nemours and Co. [Du Pont] for an after-tax gain of approximately $3 billion dollars.[4]

The four cases cited above illustrate the eventual earnings effect of (1) an off–balance-sheet obligation (General Motors Corp.), (2) an overstated liability (Norfolk Southern Corp.), (3) an off-balance-sheet asset (LCI International, Inc.), and (4) an undervalued asset (The Seagram Co. Ltd.). The income statement creates a linkage between successive balance sheets; earnings, to the extent not distributed as dividends, increase shareholders' equity. This linkage means that earnings will ultimately be affected either when off-balance-sheet assets or liabilities exist or when assets or liabilities are undervalued or overvalued.

This eventual effect on earnings may result from a variety of internal or external forces. In the case of General Motors, the earnings reduction resulted from the mandatory adoption of a new accounting standard, SFAS No. 106, "Employers' Accounting for Postretirement Benefits Other Than Pensions," which required General Motors to record a liability for previously unaccrued expenses.[5] Similarly, Norfolk Southern's earnings increase resulted from the mandatory adoption of SFAS No. 109, "Accounting for Income Taxes."[6] However, LCI International's earnings increase resulted from the application of judgment, which is a feature of current generally accepted accounting principles (GAAP) that guide income tax accounting. Finally Seagram's gain resulted from a management decision to dispose of the Du Pont shares and to redeploy the proceeds in the entertainment business.

The eventual effect on earnings of off-balance-sheet and undervalued or over-valued assets and liabilities may take a very long time to surface. For example, SunTrust Banks, Inc., holds a large number of shares of the Coca-Cola Co. acquired over 75 years ago at a recorded cost of $110,000.[7] At the end of 1994, the investment was worth about $1.2 billion. This appreciation, net of associated deferred taxes, is now part of shareholders' equity. Recognition of this growth in value did not result from sale of the shares but rather from adoption of a new accounting standard, SFAS No. 115, "Accounting for Certain Investments in Debt and Equity Securities."[8] How-ever, it has yet to become part of SunTrust's earnings. This will occur only if and when SunTrust sells the shares and realizes the gain. As another example, Illinois Tool Works, Inc., in its adoption of SFAS No. 106, elected an option that permitted recognition of its unaccrued postretirement benefit obligation, an off-balance-sheet liability of $145 million, over a 20-year period.[9]

FINANCIAL POSITION ANALYSIS AND FINANCIAL FLEXIBILITY: THE EARNINGS SUSTAINABILITY CONNECTION

The thrust of both Chapters 5 and 6 was that earnings surprises can be reduced by a thorough analysis of historical earnings so that the most reliable foundation, the sustainable earnings base, can be employed in earnings projections. In this same spirit, thorough balance sheet analysis is required to identify circumstances where selected balance sheet information and relations can imply future earnings consequences.

Further, it should be clear that off-balance-sheet assets or liabilities and under-valued or overvalued assets and liabilities affect the financial flexibility of firms. Financial flexibility has been characterized by the Financial Accounting Standards Board as the "ability of an enterprise to take effective actions to alter the amounts and timing of cash flows so that it can respond to unexpected needs and opportunities."[10] Others have aptly pointed out the central implication of financial flexibility:

> An enterprise with a high degree of financial flexibility is better able to survive bad times, to recover from unexpected setbacks, and to take advantage of profitable and unexpected investment opportunities. Generally, the greater the financial flex-ibility, the lower the risk of enterprise failure.[11]

It also follows that the firm with more financial flexibility is more likely to maintain or sustain its profitability, thereby avoiding earnings surprises.

Pan Am Corp. is a classic case of a firm weathering financial storms by drawing on its sources of financial flexibility, though in the end it succumbed. The primary sources of Pan Am's financial flexibility were appreciated assets that could be liqui-dated to produce the cash necessary to sustain the core Pan Am business, i.e., the airline. Difficulties started late in the 1970s, and Pan Am successively played two appreciated-asset cards—the Pan Am Building in Manhattan and its Intercontinental Hotels. Towards the end, even though profit was an increasingly distant memory, Pan Am produced additional hundreds of millions of dollars in cash by selling its Airbus A320 order positions (1988, $101 million), selling Pan Am World Services (1989, $165 million), engaging in a sale and lease-back of aircraft (1988–1990, $411 million), selling IGS (1990, $150 million), and selling its London routes and other assets to United Air Lines, Inc. (1990, $90 million in the initial phase of a $400 million transaction).

This chapter provides an overview of a number of major reporting areas in which the analysis of financial position can help to identify balance sheet conditions with the potential for affecting financial flexibility and, as a result, future earnings. For each example, a limited critique of relevant GAAP is provided. More detailed reviews are provided in the appendix. The topics covered here include (1) investments, (2) income taxes, (3) LIFO inventories, and (4) pensions and other postemployment and postretirement benefits.

INVESTMENTS

The accounting for investments creates significant potential for the emergence of differences between their carrying, or book, value and their market, or fair, value. SFAS No. 115, "Accounting for Certain Investments in Debt and Equity Securities"(May 1993) has made important changes in the accounting for investments. This statement requires that many investments must now be carried at their fair, typically market, value with appreciation or depreciation in value being recognized either in earnings or directly in shareholders' equity. Whether investments are carried at fair value is based upon their classification into three different categories: held-to-maturity, trading, and available-for-sale. Equity investments not covered by SFAS No. 115 include voting stock interests of, typically, 20% or greater, and untraded stocks with no readily determinable market value. These investments remain subject to Accounting Principles Board, Opinion No. 18, "The Equity Method of Accounting for Investments in Common Stock."[12]

Held-to-Maturity Investments

Securities in the held-to-maturity category would necessarily comprise mainly debt instruments, given that equity investments generally have no maturity.[13] Securities classified as held-to-maturity are not marked to market or fair value but rather are carried at their amortized cost. Classification as held-to-maturity is proper only if "the reporting enterprise has the positive intent and ability to hold those securities to maturity."[14] Even though market and amortized cost may diverge over the life of the investment, upon maturity the investor will, barring severe financial difficulties, receive the carrying value of the investment, and neither a gain nor a loss will be recorded.

Financial institutions appear to be the main users of the held-to-maturity investments. They, unlike most nonfinancial firms, typically have substantial holdings of debt instruments that may be held to maturity. A disclosure of held-to-maturity investments from the financial statements of Peterborough Savings Bank is provided in Exhibit 7.1.

Peterborough's accounting policy for investment securities states, "Bond and note obligations are stated at cost, less amortization of premiums and accretion of discounts. . . . Bond and note obligations are carried at cost because it is management's intention to hold them until maturity."[15] Peterborough's balance sheet carries the investments at their total cost of $39,948,000 even though this amount exceeds their market value. The unrealized losses in Exhibit 7.1 indicate that current required yields exceed those of Peterborough's investments.

Trading Investments

Investments are to be classified as trading securities if they "are bought and held principally for the purpose of selling them in the near term."[16] Trading securities are carried on the balance sheet at their market value, and the period-to-period changes in value are included in the income statement. Once again, this feature is relevant mainly for financial firms, where it is common to maintain portfolios of securities for trading purposes. Moreover, the SFAS No. 115 requirement to mark the trading portfolio to market value, and take the gains or losses to the income statement, simply codifies what has long been the industry accounting practice.

BankAmerica Corp.'s accounting policy for "trading account assets" follows:

Trading account assets, which are generally held for the short term in anticipation of market gains and for resale, are carried at their fair value. Realized and unrealized gains and losses on trading account assets are included in net trading account related and foreign exchange trading related income.[17]

Exhibit 7.1 Held-to-Maturity Investments: Peterborough Savings Bank, 1994 (thousands of dollars)

	Amortized Cost	Unrealized Gains	Unrealized Losses	Fair Value
Bonds and obligations				
U.S. Treasury	$ 2,998	$–	$ (104)	$ 2,894
U.S. government agencies	31,383	–	(2,390)	28,993
SBA securities	2,177	–	(120)	2,057
Municipal obligations	2,390	–	(32)	2,358
Corporate and other	1,000	–	(23)	977
Total investment securities	$39,948		$(2,669)	$37,279

Source: Peterborough Savings Bank, annual report, December 1994, p. 23.

BankAmerica's SFAS No. 115 policy applied to trading account investments is also extended to interest rate and foreign currency derivative contracts that are part of its trading activities.[18] The accounting treatment applied to trading securities ensures that all changes in market value will affect the income statement as they accrue. As a result, earnings will not be jolted by the recognition of a backlog of appreciation or depreciation upon the subsequent sale of securities.

Available-for-Sale Investments

Debt and equity securities covered by SFAS No. 115 that do not fall into either the held-to-maturity or trading classifications are considered to be "available-for-sale." The SunTrust holding of Coca-Cola shares, cited previously, was accounted for as available-for-sale. Banks would rarely hold equity securities for trading purposes, and the lack of a maturity for equity securities rules out the held-to-maturity classification. As a result, holdings of marketable equity securities—untraded shares are not included within the scope of SFAS No. 115—below the levels that would call for use of the equity method or for consolidation, are treated as available-for-sale.

The Wiser Oil Co. adopted SFAS No. 115 at December 31, 1993, and classified its entire marketable securities portfolio as available-for-sale. Prior to adoption of the new standard, the cost and carrying value of the portfolio was $3,845,000. Upon adoption of SFAS No. 115, the portfolio was marked up to its market value of $34,781,000. The price appreciation of $30,936,000 [$34,781,000 – $3,845,000] was added directly to shareholders' equity, net of a deferred tax provision of $10,518,000.[19] A summary of the effect of adoption follows:

Assets increase to market value	$30,936,000
Liabilities increase—deferred tax liability	$10,518,000
Shareholders' equity increase—marketable securities valuation adjustment	20,418,000
Total	$30,936,000

Notice that the write-up of the securities does not affect the income statement. The deferred tax provision is deducted directly from the gross write-up, reducing the amount added to shareholders' equity, and does not appear in the income statement. Projections of future earnings should take account of the fact that sale of part or all of the Wiser portfolio could put significant gains into its income statement—Wiser's total net income for the three years from 1991 to 1993 was only about $4 million. Companies sometimes sell portions of appreciated security holdings to maintain profit at target levels or to support continued dividend payout policies. For example, Chemed Corp., a firm with a very high dividend payout, disclosed that during the first quarter of 1995 it "harvested $2.5 million of after-tax capital gains from its investments, as compared with $871,000 in the prior-year first quarter."[20]

Equity-Method Investments

Holding voting shares within the range of 20%–50% of outstanding shares generally calls for the use of the equity method of accounting.[21] Beyond a 50% holding of voting shares, the preparation of consolidated statements is the norm. Again, qualification for use of the equity method moves the investment beyond the reach of SFAS No. 115. In broad outline, the equity method is generally applied as follows:

1. The investment is initially recorded at cost by the investor.
2. If the cost of the investment exceeds the share acquired by the investor of the book value of the net assets, or shareholders' equity of the investee, then, if feasible, the premium is assigned to adjust the carrying value of assets and liabilities whose book values differ from their fair values. Any residual after this process is assigned to goodwill and amortized.[22]
3. The investor recognizes its share of the earnings or loss of the investee. A share of earnings is recorded by increasing the investor's investment account; a loss reduces the investment.
4. Depreciation and amortization required by the results of step 2 are added to or deducted from the share of investee earnings.
5. Dividends received by the investor are recorded by increasing cash and reducing the carrying value of the investment. That is, dividends received are treated as partial liquidations of the investment.
6. If the value of the investment is deemed to have suffered a decline that is other than temporary, then the investment is to be written down.

Chemed Corp.'s investment in Omnicare, a company traded on the New York Stock Exchange, provides a useful example of the application of the equity method. At the end of 1993, Chemed had a 27% interest in Omnicare. Chemed's note disclosures on the Omnicare holding showed that Omnicare had total net income of $9,014,000 in 1993 and that Chemed received dividends on this investment of $407,000. Chemed's beginning and ending investments in Omnicare were $28,501,000 and $30,656,000, respectively. An explanation of the change in investment balance is provided in Exhibit 7.2.

Chemed's disclosed ending investment balance was $30,656,000.[23] The small difference of $104,000 from the $30,552,000 shown in Exhibit 7.2 is probably due to a rounding effect in the percentage ownership used in the calculations. At the end of 1993, Chemed's actual ownership amounted to 27.266%. The annual report discloses a rounded 27% ownership.

Chemed's disclosures of its Omnicare investment reveal that the market value of the investment at December 31, 1993, was $81 million. This represents unrecognized appreciation of approximately $50 million. Such unrecognized appreciation will work its way through the income statement if part or all of the investment is sold. Expectations of future earnings should consider this possibility.

Exhibit 7.2 Change in Investment Balance: Chemed Corp., 1993 (thousands of dollars)

Chemed investment in Omnicare at the beginning of 1993, per Chemed balance sheet	$28,501
Chemed share of 1993 Omnicare net income: .27266[a] × 9,014	2,458
Chemed dividend received from Omnicare	(407)
Chemed investment in Omnicare at the end of 1993, as computed here	$30,552

[a]Computed from actual shares held at the end of 1993.

Chemed did, in fact, dispose of a significant portion of its Omnicare shares in 1994, and it reduced its ownership to 6%. These sales produced pre-tax gains of $43,606,000.[24] Further, because the remaining 6% holding was not sufficient to justify continued use of the equity method, Chemed now accounts for the investment as available-for-sale under the requirements of SFAS No. 115. This requires that the remaining shares be carried at market value and that the unrecognized appreciation, after-tax, be included in shareholders' equity. Chemed's 1994 balance sheet carries a shareholders' equity balance of $21 million, designated as "unrealized appreciation on investments." Most of this amount represents the after-tax appreciation of the remaining Omnicare shares.

Investments, Financial Flexibility, and the Sustainability of Earnings

In forming expectations for future earnings, the presence of appreciation or depreciation in the value of investments should be identified and monitored. Appreciation or depreciation on investments classified as held-to-maturity should vanish as the securities approach maturity. No gain or loss will make its way to the income statement. The premature sale, prior to maturity, of held-to-maturity securities could jeopardize maintaining the remainder of the portfolio at amortized cost, and call for marking the remaining investments to market value, with gains or losses being included in earnings. As a consequence, their potential contribution to financial flexibility is limited.

The appreciation or depreciation on available-for-sale investments will generally be included in earnings when the securities are sold. These gains or losses will be candidates for adjustment in the computation of sustainable earnings. Financial flexibility is realistically represented by the balance sheet because the investments are carried at their fair value.

Appreciation or depreciation on trading securities is included in the income statement on an ongoing basis as market values change. Their contribution to financial flexibility rests mainly in their potential as a quick source of cash.

Equity-accounted securities are generally not carried at their market value. Such investments, when they have appreciated significantly, can be sources of considerable financial flexibility. Kmart Corp.'s investment in Coles Myer Ltd., an Australian retailer, is a recent case in point. At the beginning of 1994, the year in which Kmart sold this investment back to Coles Myer, the 21.5% holding was carried on Kmart's books at $512 million.[25] Its market value was about $1.0 billion. Kmart drew on the financial flexibility represented by this appreciated investment by selling the shares and reinvesting the proceeds in its restructuring program and ongoing effort to restore and sustain profitability.

INCOME TAXES

From the perspective of financial position, the principal changes brought about by the current tax-accounting standard, SFAS No. 109, "Accounting for Income Taxes," are to value deferred tax assets and liabilities at current tax rates, and to recognize deferred tax assets and liabilities more completely—especially deferred tax assets. Both of these changes remove sources of book to fair value differences and off-balance-sheet items that could affect future earnings and contribute to earnings surprises.

While generally contributing to a reduction in the potential for earnings surprises, SFAS No. 109 did include a wholly new feature that has great potential to affect future earnings—in addition to providing a new tool for earnings management, a topic discussed at length in Chapter 12. SFAS No. 109 calls for the recognition of deferred tax assets and liabilities on all temporary differences. Most temporary differences result from variations in the timing of expense and revenue recognition in the books, or shareholder income statement, rather than in the tax return. In subsequent references, book income will refer to the shareholder income statement whereas tax income will refer to income on the tax return.

The most common source of deferred tax liabilities are differences between the recognition of depreciation in the books versus the tax return. Typically, through a combination of shorter useful lives and accelerated depreciation methods, tax depreciation exceeds book depreciation. This relation generally holds as long as the firm is growing or replacing fixed assets at ever-rising price levels. Should the firm plateau and prices stabilize, then there is the potential for tax depreciation to fall below the level of that on the books. In this case, deferred tax liabilities accumulated over prior years will be drawn down resulting in increased tax payments.

Deferred tax assets result most frequently from expense being recognized in the books sooner than in the tax return, or from revenue being recognized sooner in the tax return than in the books. In addition to these "temporary differences," a variety of losses, both operating and capital, and tax credit carryforwards are common sources of deferred tax assets. Deferred tax assets are reduced when (1) expense previously recorded in the books is deducted for tax purposes, (2) when revenue previously recorded in the tax return is included in the books, and (3) when tax credits and loss carryforwards are utilized for tax purposes or expire unutilized.

Deferred Tax Assets

Deferred tax assets have the greatest potential to produce unexpected increases or decreases in future earnings. It is important to have a clear picture of exactly how deferred tax assets make their way on and off the books of firms and in the process affect earnings. One of the most common sources of deferred tax assets today is restructuring charges. In most cases, these charges are recorded in the books before they are available as deductions in the tax return. Often the charges are made up of asset write-downs rather than revenues not yet recorded in the books, and expense accruals that are yet to be paid. Losses on the assets will be deductible in the tax return only when actually realized, i.e., when assets are sold, and expense accruals will generally be deductible when paid.

Amdahl Corp. recorded a $478 million restructuring charge in 1993. This entire amount was added back to net income in the statement of cash flows in arriving at cash from operating activities.[26] This treatment in the cash flow statement suggests that the charges are either noncash in nature, e.g., asset write-downs, or future cash items that have not yet required disbursements, e.g., work force reduction costs. Amdahl declared that most of the restructuring actions provided for in 1993 would in fact be undertaken in 1994. The composition of the restructuring charge, as well as its cash and noncash components, is detailed in Exhibit 7.3.

SFAS No. 109, "Accounting for Income Taxes," requires that deferred tax assets be recorded in these cases for the future tax savings that will result when the restructuring charges become deductible in the tax return. Among its scheduled deferred tax assets at the end of 1993, Amdahl listed $166 million due to "reserves." Most of this is attributable to the restructuring charge and amounts to about 35%, the current statutory federal tax rate, of the amount of the $478 million restructuring charge.

Exhibit 7.3   Restructuring Charge Composition: Amdahl Corp., 1993 (millions of dollars)

Workforce reductions	$120
Closing excess facilities and equipment write-downs	200
Write-downs of excess inventory	60
Vendor charges, cancellations of development programs	10
Other	88
	$478
Noncash asset write-offs	$298
Projected cash outflows	180
	$478

Source: Amdahl Corp., annual report, December 1993, p. 20.

Deferred Tax Asset Valuation Allowances

Once deferred tax assets are recorded, SFAS No. 109 requires that their ultimate realizability be assessed. Then, a valuation allowance must be established "if, based upon the weight of available evidence, it is *more likely than not*, a likelihood of greater than 50%, that some portion or all of the deferred tax assets will not be realized."[27] After performing this assessment, Amdahl recorded a valuation allowance of $152 million against its deferred tax assets, a major portion of which related to the deferred tax assets from the restructuring charge. Amdahl's schedule of deferred tax assets and liabilities is provided in Exhibit 7.4. Amdahl characterized the valuation allowance as composed of "worldwide operating losses, deferred tax assets, and tax credit carryforwards which may expire before the company can utilize them. The company believes sufficient uncertainty exists regarding the realization of these items, and accordingly, a valuation allowance has been established."[28]

Recording the $152 million valuation allowance against $235 million of deferred tax assets does not rule out the eventual realization of some or all of the $152 million tax benefit. Amdahl has a strong record of profitability in previous years—$340 million of net income over the period 1989–1992. Moreover, it made a significant return to profitability in 1994, earning a net income of $75 million. While there is apparently considerable uncertainty surrounding realization of the $152 million tax benefit, the likelihood is not zero. As a result, projections of future earnings should monitor improving prospects and the likelihood that deferred tax assets written off through the valuation allowance may be realized, increasing earnings in the process. Further, the prospective realization of these off-balance-sheet assets represents a source of financial flexibility. This in turn increases the likelihood of sustained profitability.

Exhibit 7.4 Schedule of Deferred Tax Assets, Liabilities, and Valuation Allowance: Amdahl Corp., 1993 (thousands of dollars)

Deferred tax liabilities	
Tax on foreign income	$ (46,094)
Depreciation	(42,273)
Other	(16,861)
Total deferred tax liabilities	(105,228)
Deferred tax assets	
Reserves	$ 165,578
Revenue timing	18,656
Net operating loss carryforwards	50,672
	234,906
Valuation allowance	(152,337)
Total deferred tax assets	82,569
Net deferred tax liability	$ (22,659)

Source: Amdahl Corp., annual report, December 1993, p. 28.

Recognition of Previously Reserved Deferred Tax Assets

Recognition in earnings of previously reserved, or written-off, deferred tax assets is rather common. There are a number of possible explanations: (1) Revisions in estimations are bound to result, given the difficulty of assessing the realizability of deferred tax assets; (2) the prospects of realization of the reserved deferred tax assets may have risen above the 50% threshold required for their recognition; (3) firms adopt an overly conservative posture, recording a larger valuation allowance than necessary in initially booking the valuation allowance; and (4) the valuation allowance may be employed by some firms as an earnings management tool. In some cases, all four of these possibilities could be present. Several case examples are discussed in the following sections.

Prospects Improved for Realization: UNR Industries, Inc.

UNR generated a substantial loss in 1992 and recorded a tax benefit of $110 million, net of a valuation allowance of $20 million. Of the net benefit of $90 million, $53 million was realized in the form of federal and state refunds from loss carrybacks. UNR realized—that is, used the carryforwards to shield profits in the tax return from taxation—tax benefits of previously recognized—that is, recorded as deferred tax assets and not written off through the valuation allowance—loss carryforwards in both 1993 and 1994.

Based on its generation of taxable earnings, UNR reduced the initial valuation allowance of $20 million to $10 million in 1994. The 1994 annual report observed, "The reduction in the valuation allowance to $10 million relates to management's judgment concerning the realizability of benefits arising from net operating loss and credit carryforwards. The remaining net operating loss carryforwards . . . may be recorded into income . . . at a future date."[29] This decline in the valuation allowance would be an adjustment in arriving at sustainable earnings, as discussed in Chapters 5 and 6. The tax benefit is nonrecurring.

The increase in UNR's earnings that resulted from the reduction in its valuation allowance is highlighted by its tax reconciliation schedule in Exhibit 7.5. Note that the 1992 tax provision was increased by the valuation allowance increase of $20 million but decreased in 1994 by the valuation allowance decrease of $10 million.

The UNR case involves a firm that recorded a valuation allowance and then experienced relatively strong operating performance. It is reasonable to anticipate an earnings increase, as the result of a valuation allowance reduction, in circumstances such as these. It should not come as a surprise if the remaining valuation allowance of $10 million is brought into earnings in 1995.

None of the four possible explanations offered earlier for the recognition of previously reserved deferred tax assets can be ruled out in the UNR case. In the case of the fourth possibility, earnings management, it is worth noting that the $10 million valuation allowance reduction contributed 80% of UNR's growth in earnings for 1994—a year characterized as "our best yet" on the cover of UNR's 1994 annual

Exhibit 7.5   Changes in Tax Reconciliation Schedule and Valuation Allowance: UNR
Industries, Inc., 1992–1994 (thousands of dollars)

	1992		1993		1994	
	Amount	%	Amount	%	Amount	%
Computed statutory provision	$ 15,100	34%	$11,000	35%	$13,800	35%
Trust payments	(12,100)	(27)	–	–	–	–
State taxes, net	1,600	4	1,800	5	2,000	5
Enacted tax rate change	–	–	(1,100)	(3)	–	–
QSF deduction (Sec. 468B)[a]	(110,000)	(248)	–	–	–	–
Valuation allowance	20,000	45	–	–	(10,000)	(25)
Total provision (benefit)	$(85,400)	(192)%	$11,700	37%	$ 5,800	15%

Source: UNR Industries, Inc., annual report, December 1994, p. 17.
[a]The Qualified Settlement Trust (QST) relates to a tax deduction obtained as a result of
a transfer of 29.4 million shares of UNR stock to the UNR Asbestos-Disease Claims Trust.
This deduction was made possible, in turn, by issuance of final Internal Revenue Service
regulations under Section 468B, "Special Rules for Designated Settlement Funds."

report. Some firms may find the valuation allowance irresistible should the need for
a source of profit increase, or decrease, arise.

Fully Reserved Net Operating Loss Benefits Being Realized: Chad Therapeutics Inc.

Chad Therapeutics had valuation allowances at the end of both 1993 and 1994 that
reduced its net deferred tax assets to zero. Its principal sources of deferred tax assets
were net operating loss and tax credit carryforwards. The complete write-off of its
deferred tax assets would suggest considerable doubt that these tax benefits would
be realized. Yet, Chad realized tax benefits from its loss carryforwards in each of the
years 1992–1994. Moreover, in an earnings release for the first quarter of its fiscal
year ending on March 31, 1995, Chad stated that its "remaining net operating loss
carryforwards of $715,000 for federal income tax purposes will be fully utilized during
the current fiscal year."[30]

   Chad Therapeutics realized a benefit from its net operating loss position of
$641,000 in its fiscal 1994. Yet, in the face of these very positive results, it still
maintained a valuation allowance that reduced its net deferred tax asset position to
zero. Chad Therapeutics' deferred tax asset schedule is presented in Exhibit 7.6. The
company disclosed no deferred tax liabilities.

   Chad Therapeutics had an off-balance-sheet tax asset of $411,000 as it entered

Exhibit 7.6   Net Deferred Tax Asset Schedule: Chad Therapeutics, Inc., 1994

The tax effects of temporary differences that give rise to significant portions of the deferred tax assets at March 31, 1994, are as follows:

Net operating loss carryforwards	$243,000
Other tax credits	84,000
Warranty and other	84,000
Total gross deferred tax assets	411,000
Less: valuation allowance	(411,000)
Net deferred tax assets	$ 0

Source: Chad Therapeutics, Inc., annual report, March 1994, p. 9.

its fiscal 1995. Its profit performance and record of previous realization of net operating loss carryforward benefits provided a strong indication that much of the off-balance-sheet asset, especially that related to the net operating loss carryforwards, would be realized in 1995. Chad Therapeutics' earnings release for the first quarter of fiscal 1995 sustains this expectation. The lesson here is that formation of an earnings expectation in situations such as this should include the likely movement of such off-balance-sheet value into earnings. Further, such off-balance-sheet value, with the cash flow saving represented by its realization, added to Chad's financial flexibility.

Improved Prospects Plus Realization of Carryforward Benefits: National Steel Corp.

National Steel incurred losses in each of the years 1991–1993. Upon adoption of SFAS No. 109 in 1992, the company wrote off most of its deferred tax assets in determining its net deferred tax asset position. The deferred tax assets not written off involved $43 million of benefits that it judged could be realized by the tax-planning strategy[31] of changing from the LIFO to the FIFO method of valuing inventories.[32] Later, in 1993 and 1994, National Steel "determined that it was more likely than not that sufficient taxable income would be generated to justify increasing the net deferred tax asset after valuation allowance."[33] As a result, the valuation allowance was reduced by $37.6 million and $20.7 million in 1993 and 1994, respectively.

Improved prospects moved $37.6 million and $20.7 million from off-balance-sheet asset status into the income statements of 1993 and 1994, respectively. These tax savings were recognized on the books of National Steel but had not yet been realized. In addition to these recognized benefits, National Steel also realized tax savings by using its loss carryforwards to shield profits from taxation in its tax returns. The 1994 deferred tax asset schedule of National Steel disclosed a decline of from $189.6 million to $105.5 million in its deferred tax assets for net operating loss carryforwards. In the same year, the tax reconciliation schedule disclosed an $84.1 million [$189.6 − $105.5 = $84.1] reduction in taxes due to benefits of operating loss carryforwards. Since $20.7 million of these benefits involve recognized benefits resulting from the 1994 reduction in the valuation allowance, the balance, $63.4 million, represents realized net operating loss benefits. As with Chad Therapeutics, the potential realization of this off–balance-sheet value increased National Steel's financial flexibility.

National Steel disclosed $286.9 million of unused net operating loss carryforwards at the end of 1994.[34] The deferred tax asset disclosed for these carryforwards is $105.5 million. Expiration dates of these carryforwards are $70.5 million in 2006, $99.4 million in 2007, and $117.0 million in 2008. In addition, National Steel reports that there have been no changes in the ownership of the company that could place limitations on use of the loss carryforwards.[35] As with Chad Therapeutics, the prospects are good that more of National Steel's unrecognized deferred tax assets will increase its future earnings. This likelihood is strengthened by the length of time remaining before the carryforwards expire. Earnings projections should take into account these possibilities.

Deferred Tax Assets, Financial Flexibility, and the Sustainability of Earnings

Deferred tax assets recognized should provide future tax savings when the following happen: (1) Expense deductions taken earlier in the books are subsequently taken in the tax return; (2) revenues or gains already included in the tax return are later included in the book income statements; and (3) net operating loss and tax credit carryforwards are used in the tax return to reduce tax payments. A summary of the effects of these occurrences on book earnings, tax return earnings, and tax cash flows when deferred tax assets are realized is provided in Exhibit 7.7 assuming that no valuation allowance had been recorded and in Exhibit 7.8 assuming that the deferred tax assets had been written off fully through a valuation allowance.

Exhibit 7.7 Deferred Tax Assets: Book Earnings, Tax Return Earnings, and Cash Flow with No Valuation Allowances

Source of Deferred Tax Asset Realization	Effect on Book Earnings	Effect on tax Return Earnings	Effect on Cash Flow
Expense deductions taken in the tax return	None	Reduced	Increased
Revenue or gain included in book earnings	Increased	None	None
Net operating loss and tax-credit carryforwards used in the tax return	None	Reduced[a]	Increased

[a]Technically, utilization of the tax credit carryforwards reduces taxes but not taxable earnings.

Exhibit 7.8   Deferred Tax Assets: Book Earnings, Tax Return Earnings, and Cash Flow with Full Valuation Allowances

Source of Deferred Tax Asset Realization	Effect on Book Earnings	Effect on tax Return Earnings	Effect on Cash Flow
Expense deductions taken in the tax return	Increased	Reduced	Increased
Revenue or gain included in book earnings	Increased[a]	None	None
Net operating loss and tax credit carryforwards used in the tax return	Increased	Reduced[b]	Increased

[a]The increase in book earnings here is greater than in Exhibit 7.7 by the amount of the deferred tax benefit not previously recognized because of the full write-off through the valuation allowance.
[b]Utilization of the tax credit carryforwards reduces taxes but not taxable earnings.

In each of the cases in Exhibit 7.7, the potential tax savings have been realized. In the first and third cases (expense deductions and net operating loss and tax credit carryforwards), there is no effect on book earnings. This is because the potential tax benefits were recognized earlier when the deferred tax assets were recorded. However, tax cash payments are reduced by (1) expense deductions taken in the tax return, (2) the shielding of tax return profits by the net operating loss carryforwards, and the reduction of tax payments through the use of tax credit carryforwards. In the second case in Exhibit 7.7 (revenue or gain now included in book earnings), book earnings are increased because revenue or gain previously included in the tax return, and taxed, are now treated as earnings for book purposes.

The sustainability of earnings is unaffected by the cases in Exhibit 7.7, where potential tax benefits were recognized as they accrued and were not subsequently written off through the deferred tax valuation allowance. However, where valuation allowances have been established, the tax benefits represent potential off-balance-sheet assets. Exhibit 7.8 recasts the cases in Exhibit 7.7 to show the differences that result when full valuation allowances have been recorded.

The write-off of deferred tax assets is based upon a 50% realization threshold. That is, deferred tax assets with a likelihood of realization below 50% are written off. There are numerous current examples of the realization of such off–balance sheet value. Even though realization may indeed be uncertain, a firm with fully or partially reserved deferred tax assets has a source of additional strength that adds to its financial flexibility and at the same time to the potential sustainability of its earnings.

LIFO INVENTORIES

The use of the LIFO (last in, first out) inventory method over a sustained period of time can result in significant differences between the carrying value and replacement or current cost of inventory. The disclosure of such differences in valuation, if material, is required for public companies by the Securities and Exchange Commission.[36] Replacement cost is frequently approximated by the disclosure of FIFO (first in, first out) valuation of the inventory, and far less frequently by average cost. Information on the frequency of use of LIFO is provided in an annual survey of 600 companies' annual reports conducted by the American Institute of Certified Public Accountants. Recent results are presented in Exhibit 7.9.

It is common for LIFO users to employ other methods as well. For the 348 LIFO firms in Exhibit 7.9, only 17 use LIFO for all inventories and 191 use it for 50% or more of all inventories.[37] High-use industries include beverages, paper products, petroleum, and rubber products. Lower use is found in electronic equipment, shoe manufacturing, business equipment and supplies, aircraft and equipment, and controls, instruments and medical equipment.[38]

As with investments and deferred tax assets, differences between LIFO and replacement values of inventories often work their way into the income statement. These valuation differences are disclosed in a number of different ways and employ diverse terminology.

Disclosure of LIFO Valuation Differences

Regulation S-X of the Securities and Exchange Commission requires disclosure of the excess of replacement or current cost over stated LIFO value. Disclosure may be parenthetically or in a note to the financial statements.[39] Some examples of these

Exhibit 7.9 Inventory Cost Determination

	No. of Companies			
Method	1990	1991	1992	1993
First in, first out (FIFO)	411	421	415	411
Last in, first out (LIFO)	366	361	358	366
Average cost	195	200	193	195
Other	44	50	45	44

Source: American Institute of Certified Public Accountants, *Accounting Trends and Techniques* (1994), p. 160.
Note: No. of companies does not reflect the 600 companies included in the survey, because many companies use more than a single inventory method.

disclosures are presented in Exhibit 7.10. This small set of disclosures reveals considerable diversity. Footnote disclosure rather than presentation on the face of the balance sheet is the most common practice.

The difference between replacement or current cost and LIFO cost is reported in a number of different ways. The term *LIFO reserve* is often used to denote the excess of replacement or current cost over the LIFO carrying value. Moreover, *LIFO reserve* is rather uniformly used by analysts to label this difference in inventory valuation, even when the LIFO statements being discussed do not employ the term. For

Exhibit 7.10   Disclosures of LIFO Valuation Differences

Company	Disclosure
Caterpillar (1994)	Inventory note disclosure: "If the FIFO (first in, first out) method had been in use, inventories would have been $2,035 million and $1,818 million higher than reported at December 31, 1994 and 1993, respectively.
R. R. Donnelley & Sons (1994)	LIFO reserve balance deducted from current cost of inventory in an inventory footnote.
Handy & Harman (1994)	LIFO inventory excess of year-end market value over LIFO cost disclosed in a footnote.
Philip Morris Companies (1994)	Inventory footnote disclosure: "The cost of approximately 48% of inventories in 1994 and 54% in 1993 was determined using the LIFO method. The stated LIFO values of inventories were approximately $870 million and $1.0 billion lower than the current cost of inventories."
UNR Industries (1994)	LIFO reserve deducted in the balance sheet.
Wolohan Lumber (1994)	Disclosure on the face of the balance sheet (thousands):

	1993	1994
Inventories—current cost	$64,385	$64,555
Reduction to LIFO cost	(13,280)	(14,549)
Inventories at lower of LIFO cost or market	$51,105	$50,006

Company	Disclosure
Wyman-Gordon (1993)	Inventory footnote disclosure: "If all inventories valued at LIFO cost had been valued at first in, first out (FIFO) cost or market which approximates current replacement cost, inventories would have been $33,448,000 and $41,365,000 higher than reported at December 31, 1993 and 1992, respectively."

Sources: Companies' annual reports. The year following each company name designates the annual report from which each example was drawn.

some firms, the LIFO reserve is an account balance, in addition to a disclosure, that is used to adjust results from FIFO, or average cost, to LIFO. FIFO, or average cost, is often employed for internal reporting and control purposes, and the LIFO reserve is then used to adjust results for purposes of preparing interim or annual financial statements.

Notice that among the firms in Exhibit 7.10 some, such as Caterpillar, disclose how much *higher* the inventories would be if FIFO had been used, while others, such as Philip Morris, indicate how much *lower* the inventories are as a result of their use of LIFO. Other firms simply disclose the current cost of LIFO inventories.[40] Given the potential effect of this inventory valuation difference, the key is to ensure that it is located. The review of balance sheets and notes should focus on language indicating differences between LIFO and replacement, current, FIFO, or average cost. No significance should be attached to the particular location of the disclosures or the manner in which the difference between LIFO and replacement or current value is described.

LIFO Valuation Differences: Out of the Notes and into the Income Statement

The most likely manner by which the inventory undervaluation represented by the LIFO reserve would affect earnings is through a LIFO liquidation. A LIFO liquidation is a reduction in inventory quantities. The costs assigned to the liquidated units are typically lower costs that existed when initial inventory levels were established or increased. These older costs are usually well below current inventory replacement costs.[41] The increase in pre-tax results from the LIFO liquidation is the difference between current replacement cost and the LIFO cost associated with the liquidated inventory quantities.[42]

A profit increase from a LIFO liquidation is similar to the realization of gains on the sale of any other type of undervalued asset, e.g., land or securities. One difference is that the effect of the LIFO liquidation might be seen more readily as an operations-related earnings increase than would gain from the sale of land and securities. Recall that in Chapter 6 Amoco Corp.'s earnings, which the company itself revised for the effects of unusual items, did not exclude the effects of its LIFO liquidations. However, the sustainable earnings base worksheet of Chapters 5 and 6 provides for the removal of the effects of LIFO liquidations on earnings. These gains, or rarely losses, may fall within the scope of operations, but they fail the test of longer-term sustainability. While firms could generate LIFO liquidation gains for a number of years, there is a limit to this source of earnings; the firm's LIFO inventories can only be reduced to zero.

The Size of LIFO Valuation Differences

LIFO valuation differences vary both over time and by type of firm. Exhibit 7.11 provides some examples of these valuation differences with size gauged in relation

Exhibit 7.11 Size of LIFO Valuation Differences

Company	Industry	Pretax % of Equity	After-tax %[a] of Equity
Armstrong World Industries	Wall/Floor coverings	16	10
Carpenter Technology	Blast furnaces/Steel mill	53	33
Caterpillar	Construction machinery	70	43
Cincinnati Milacron	Machine tools	38	23
Deere & Co.	Agricultural equipment	37	23
Gleason	Machine tools	56	35
Handy & Harman	Precious metals products	131	81
Kmart	Department stores	14	9
Lukens	Specialty steel	15	10
National Steel	Integrated steel producer	42	26
Teledyne	Diversified technology	69	43
Winn-Dixie Stores	Grocery stores	19	12

Sources: All information is drawn from the 1994 annual reports of the listed companies.
[a]After-tax percentage addition to shareholders' equity is computed using a combined federal and state income tax rate of 38%. Thus, 62% of the excess of current replacement cost over LIFO cost is the increase in shareholders' equity.

to potential pre-tax and after-tax effect on shareholders' equity. The examples in Exhibit 7.11 are not presented as typical of their size for the industries. They were simply chosen to illustrate firms that had substantial valuation differences in relation to their shareholders' equity.

LIFO Inventories, Financial Flexibility, and the Sustainability of Earnings

If undervalued LIFO inventories are reduced, earnings will include a component that is not sustainable. Such LIFO liquidation gains should be deducted from earnings in the computation of the sustainable earnings base. The implication of undervalued LIFO inventories for financial flexibility is not the same as in the case of other un-dervalued assets. No additional cash is produced simply because the LIFO method rather than the FIFO method is in use and inventory quantities are reduced. In fact, marginally less net cash flow is produced because the additional profit resulting from the LIFO liquidation results in a higher tax payment. The unrecognized value, which is real and is approximated by the size of the LIFO reserve, does not create any additional cash inflow when realized through a LIFO liquidation.

PENSIONS AND OTHER POSTRETIREMENT AND POSTEMPLOYMENT BENEFITS

The accounting for a wide range of employment benefits has been affected by a number of relatively recent FASB statements, particularly SFAS No. 106, "Employers' Accounting for Postretirement Benefits Other Than Pensions," and SFAS No. 112, "Employers' Accounting for Postemployment Benefits.,"[43] These statements continue the thrust of the earlier pension statement, SFAS No. 87, "Employers' Accounting for Pensions," and also break new ground.[44] In terms of the focus in this chapter on financial position analysis, the most important feature of SFAS No. 87 was the requirement to record previously off-balance-sheet pension obligations. Both SFAS No. 106 and No. 112 also call for recording such off-balance-sheet liabilities, and they mandate accrual, rather than cash basis, accounting for these benefits. Because the key accounting issues and terminology for postretirement and postemployment benefits are very similar to those for pensions, pensions will be used to illustrate the implications of this range of compensation-related programs on financial flexibility and the sustainability of earnings.

Pension Reporting and Associated Disclosures

The pension disclosures of Lincoln Telecommunications Co. illustrate the connection between the funded status of a firm's pension plan and its financial flexibility. The funded status of Lincoln Telecommunications' pension plan is presented in Exhibit 7.12. Funded status is judged by the relation between the plan assets and either the "accumulated pension benefit obligation" or the "projected pension benefit obligation." The accumulated benefit obligation is the most relevant gauge of funded status if a liquidation-oriented analysis is being conducted. The accumulated benefit obligation is the present value of the pension benefits earned by the employees to date. It approximates the legal obligation in the event of a plan termination. The vested

Exhibit 7.12   Pension Plan Funded Status: Lincoln Telecommunications Co., 1993 and 1994 (thousands of dollars)

	1993	1994
Actuarial present value of pension benefit obligation		
Vested	$ 97,040	$100,817
Nonvested	14,108	15,097
Accumulated pension benefit obligation	$111,148	$115,914
Projected pension benefit obligation	$127,884	$133,108
Less: plan assets at market value	185,197	177,196
Excess of plan assets over projected benefit obligation	$ 57,313	$ 44,088
Unrecognized prior service cost	5,924	4,888
Unrecognized net gain	(49,088)	(34,689)
Unrecognized net asset being recognized over		
15.74 years	(12,520)	(11,088)
Prepaid pension cost recognized in the consolidated		
balance sheets	$ 1,629	$ 3,199

Source: Lincoln Telecommunications Co., annual report, December 1994, p. 31.

amount is that portion to which the employee has a legal claim based upon years of service. This benefit will be received upon reaching retirement even if the employee has left the employment of the plan sponsor. The projected benefit obligation would be used in a going concern evaluation of funded status. If the firm continues to operate and the pension plan remains in effect, this measures the present value of the ultimate obligation that must be met. The projected benefit obligation incorporates assumptions, if the plan is pay-related, about expected increases in compensation.

Lincoln Telecommunications' pension plan is overfunded in 1994 against both measures of pension obligation: $61.3 million [$177.2 – $115.9], based on the accumulated obligation, and $44.1 million [$177.2 –$133.1], based on the projected obligation. This overfunded status adds to Lincoln's financial flexibility and also to the sustainability of its earnings.

An asset balance, "prepaid pension cost," of $3,199,000 is disclosed in Exhibit 7.12 and also appears on the balance sheet of Lincoln Telecommunications, the sponsor of the pension plan. The reason for the difference between the asset recognized on the balance sheet and the amount of the overfunding of the pension plan is explained by three line items: (1) unrecognized prior service cost, (2) unrecognized net gain, and (3) unrecognized net asset. This portion of the pension fund's statement functions exactly like a bank reconciliation.

Unrecognized prior service cost is *added* to the $44.1 million of overfunding because, while it has been recognized in the pension obligations of the pension plan, it has not been recognized in the books of Lincoln Telecommunications. Prior service cost results when retroactive improvements are made to pension benefits. This immediately increases the pension obligations of the plan. However, under SFAS No. 87, this increased obligation is amortized over future years in the books of the pension plan sponsor.[45]

Unrecognized net gain is *deducted* from the pension plan's overfunded amount in reconciling to Lincoln's balance sheet position. This gain has been recognized in the statements of the pension plan but not in the statements of Lincoln Telecommunications. The most common source of such gains are earnings on the pension plan assets that exceed the expected or assumed rate of return.

Finally, the unrecognized net asset is also *deducted* from the overfunded amount in the pension plan because it has not been recognized in the books of Lincoln Telecommunications. This balance represents the unrecognized (in the books of Lincoln) amount of overfunding of the pension plan at the date of initial adoption of SFAS No. 87. SFAS No. 87 requires that the underfunded or overfunded amounts at adoption be recognized in the books of the pension plan sponsor "over the average remaining service life of the employees expected to receive benefits under the plan."[46]

In each of the three cases just discussed, recognition in the books of Lincoln Telecommunications will take the form of inclusion in the computation of its periodic net pension cost.

Funded Status and Financial Flexibility: Overfunded Versus Underfunded Plans

In its summary of SFAS No. 87, "Employers' Accounting for Pensions," the Financial Accounting Standards Board offered the following view on overfunded and underfunded pension plans:

> The Board believes that an employer with an underfunded pension obligation has a liability and an employer with an overfunded pension obligation has an asset. The most relevant and reliable information available about that liability or asset is based on the fair value of plan assets and a measure of the present value of the obligation using current, explicit assumptions. [47]

Contrary to this, SFAS No. 87 calls for immediate recognition of an obligation in the case of underfunded plans but does not permit immediate recognition of an asset in the case of overfunded plans.

An Underfunded Case: Grossman's, Inc.

The 1993 disclosures of Grossman's underfunded pension plan are provided in Exhibit 7.13. Grossman's plan assets are compared to the accumulated, rather than

Exhibit 7.13   Liability Recognition in the Underfunded Case: Grossman's, Inc., 1993 (thousands of dollars)

Actuarial present value of projected benefit obligation	
Vested employees	$61,823
Nonvested employees	1,766
Accumulated benefit obligation	63,589
Impact of future salary increases	3,480
Projected benefit obligation for service rendered to date	67,069
Estimated market value of plan assets, primarily cash equivalents and publicly traded stocks and bonds	48,390
Projected benefit obligation in excess of plan assets	18,679
Items not yet recognized in earnings	
Unrecognized net transition asset	1,795
Unrecognized prior service cost	(1,410)
Adjustment required to recognize minimum liability	21,939
Unrecognized net loss	(25,803)
Pension liability	$15,199[a]

Source: Grossman's, Inc., annual report, December 1993, p. 23. While 1992 data were also presented, only the 1993 data are included in this exhibit.
[a]Failure to foot by $1 is due to rounding.

projected benefit obligation in determining the liability to be recognized. SFAS No. 87 requires that the plan sponsor, Grossman's, make whatever adjustment is necessary to establish a net pension liability equal to its underfunded amount. The plan assets of $48,390,000 fall short of the accumulated benefit obligation of $63,589,000 by $15,199,000. To produce this final net liability, Grossman's made an adjustment of $21,939,000 as Exhibit 7.13 reveals. The excess of the required adjustment, $6,740,000 [$21,939 – $15,199], over the underfunded amount of $15,199,000 indicates that Grossman's had a prepaid pension asset balance on its books of $6,740,000 before the adjustment.

To achieve a final net pension liability balance of $15,199,000 in the face of a pre-existing pension asset of $6,790,000 required a liability adjustment of $21,939,000.

In recording the additional minimum liability, it is important to note that earnings are not reduced. Rather, the charge that offsets the liability growth will be recorded as (1) an intangible pension asset, (2) a reduction in shareholders' equity, or (3) a combination of 1 and 2. If the minimum liability adjustment does not exceed the sum of unrecognized prior service cost and unrecognized transition obligation, then an intangible asset is recorded for the entire adjustment.[48] That is, an asset and a liability of equal amounts are recorded. If there were neither unrecognized prior service cost nor transition obligation, then shareholders' equity would be reduced by the entire amount of the liability recorded, net of taxes.

In Grossman's case, unrecognized prior service cost of $1,410,000 existed. However, it had an unrecognized transition asset and not an obligation. Therefore, only $1,410,000 of the $21,939,000 adjustment was recorded as an intangible asset and the balance was deducted directly from shareholders' equity.[49]

Both financial flexibility and future profitability are reduced by this underfunded status, even though a liability has been recorded.[50] The funding shortfall will eventually need to be dealt with, thus reducing the flexibility in the employment of future financial resources. Moreover, the funding shortfall increases future pension expense. The expected return on pension assets is treated as a reduction in pension expense. With a funding shortfall, a smaller expense reduction from the return on plan assets will result, and with it increases in future pension expense and a reduction in future earnings.

An Overfunded Case: Teledyne, Inc.

The 1993 disclosures of Teledyne's overfunded pension plans are provided in Exhibit 7.14. Teledyne has a very significant overfunding of its pension plans. Pension assets exceeded the accumulated obligation by $991 million and the projected obligation by $857 million. However, Teledyne's 1993 balance sheet only included a pension asset, "net prepaid pension cost," of $255 million. SFAS No. 87 does not permit immediate recording of an asset equal to either measure of the overfunding, the $991 million or the $857 million. This lack of consistency of treatment— underfunding requires booking a liability but overfunding does not permit recording an asset—appears to be explained simply as traditional accounting conservatism.

Exhibit 7.14 Asset Recognition in the Overfunded Case: Teledyne, Inc., 1993 (millions of dollars)

Plan assets at fair value	$1,893.2
Actuarial present value of benefit obligations	
Vested benefit obligation	893.8
Nonvested benefit obligation	8.6
Accumulated benefit obligation	902.4
Additional benefits related to future compensation levels	133.6
Projected benefit obligation	1,036.0
Plan assets in excess of projected benefit obligation	$ 857.2
Not included in balance sheet	
Unrecognized net gain due to experience different from that assumed and changes in the discount rate	353.4
Unrecognized net asset at adoption of SFAS No. 87, net of amortization	273.5
Unrecognized prior service cost	(24.7)
	602.2
Net prepaid pension cost asset included in the Teledyne balance sheet	$ 255.0

Source: Teledyne, Inc., annual report, 1993, p. 24. While Teledyne's pension disclosures included 1992 data, only 1993 data are presented in this exhibit.

Teledyne's annual pension accrual is detailed in Exhibit 7.15. More detailed discussion of the information in both Exhibits 7.14 and 7.15 is provided in the appendix. However, it is important to note that in the computation of the pension accrual Teledyne receives credit for an expected return on the assets in the pension plans. This is approximately equal to the pension assets at the beginning of the year multiplied by the assumed rate of return on the pension assets. Because of the significant overfunding of the plans, this credit results in overall pension income instead of pension expense.

In 1993, Teledyne's prepaid pension asset balance increased by $67 million. Notice that this is equal to the pension income for 1993. In this manner, there is a

Exhibit 7.15 Overfunded Pension Plans and Pension Income: Teledyne, Inc., 1991–1993 (millions of dollars)

	1991	1992	1993
Service cost of benefits earned during year	$ 36.8	$ 42.6	$ 29.6
Interest cost on benefits earned in prior years	65.6	67.6	68.4
Expected return on plan assets	(92.4)	(102.6)	(106.1)
Net amortization of unrecognized amounts	(39.3)	(41.8)	(58.9)
Pension income for defined benefit plans	$(29.3)	$(34.2)	$(67.0)

Source: Teledyne, Inc., annual report, 1993, p. 24.
Note: A small item of pension income and expense related to other plans is omitted from the schedule.

gradual recognition in the Teledyne balance sheet of the benefits of its overfunded pension plans. Over the period 1991–1993, Teledyne would have recognized a total of $129 million of pension income and recorded corresponding increases in the prepaid pension asset balance.

Exhibit 7.16 summarizes the contribution that Teledyne's pension income from its defined benefit pension plans has made to increasing earnings or reducing losses over the period 1991–1993.

Teledyne's $26.3 million [$113.3 million – $87.0 million] increase in earnings in 1993 would have been a small decrease in the absence of the $32.8 million [$67.0 million – $34.2 million] increase in pension income. Because the pension income is matched by a growth in the prepaid pension asset, there is no cash inflow associated with this portion of Teledyne's earnings. As the pension fund assets are held in trust to benefit the beneficiaries, no assets of the pension, short of a plan termination, could be paid to Teledyne.

Teledyne's financial flexibility and the sustainability of its earnings are both positively affected by the funded status of its pension plans. As long as the overfunded status of Teledyne's pension plans is maintained or increased, earnings will continue to benefit. Further, because of the overfunded status of the plans, Teledyne has made cash contributions to the pension plans of only $3.6 million for the entire 1991–1993 period. The absence of the need to make significant pension contributions improves Teledyne's cash flow and its financial flexibility.

Beyond the annual cash flow savings from its overfunded status, assets could be recovered through a termination of the pension plans. However, the recovery would be far less than the excess of pension assets over the accumulated benefit obligation. A combination of federal income and excise taxes, plus state income taxes if applicable, could drain off 60% or more of the recovered assets.[51] Teledyne has obviously given some thought to a plan termination because its pension note advises readers, "Any reversion of pension plans' assets to the company would be subject to federal and state income taxes, substantial excise tax, and other possible claims."[52]

Exhibit 7.16   Pension Plan Contribution to Earnings: Teledyne, Inc., 1991–1993 (millions of dollars)

	1991	1992	1993
Income (loss) before income taxes, extraordinary loss and cumulative effect of changes	$(31.8)	$87.0	$113.3
Pension income	29.3	34.2	67.0

Source: Teledyne, Inc., annual report, 1993, p. 24.

Reporting and Disclosure of Other Postretirement and Postemployment Benefits

The more recent accounting standards dealing with employment benefits focus on extending accrual accounting to other postretirement or postemployment benefits. Postretirement health care and life insurance are the principal items covered by SFAS No. 106. Postemployment benefits include items such as severance pay, disability-related benefits, salary continuation, and workers compensation. Benefits such as these, received during the period after employment but before retirement, are covered by SFAS No. 112. The thrust of each of these standards is the same: the benefits are earned and are to be accrued during the years the employee provides services. Both standards employ calculations and terminology that are very similar to that employed in pension accounting under SFAS No. 87. Given their similarity, only the reporting under SFAS No. 106, not SFAS No. 112, will be illustrated.

In the past, most companies simply recorded the expense of providing SFAS No. 106 and No. 112 benefits as cash payments were made. Both of these standards now require firms to adopt accrual accounting for such plans. In addition, upon adoption, the previously unaccrued obligations must be recognized. To ease the negative effect on financial statements of recording this obligation, both standards provide that recognition of these unaccrued obligations may be spread over future periods. The amortization period is the average remaining service life of active plan participants. However, if this period is less than 20 years, then a 20-year amortization period may be used.[53]

Immediate Charge Recorded for the Unaccrued Liability: General Motors Corp.

A previously off-balance-sheet obligation is brought into the balance sheet of firms that elect immediate recognition of the entire previously unaccrued amount. This represented a very large new liability for many firms. For example, upon adoption of SFAS No. 106, the cumulative effect amounted to an after-tax charge of $20.8 billion for General Motors Corp. In addition, "The incremental ongoing effect in 1992 of this accounting change increased the loss before cumulative effect of accounting changes by . . . $1,384.2 million after tax."[54] That is, in addition to recognizing a liability for the previously unaccrued benefits, the movement from a cash basis recognition of the expense to a full accrual treatment raises the future expense stream to a new higher level.

Unaccrued Liability Amortized over Future Years: Illinois Tool Works, Inc.

Illinois Tool Works avoided a large immediate charge to its income statement upon its January 1, 1993, adoption of SFAS No. 106 by electing to amortize the obligation of $145,500,000 over 20 years. The disclosures of its postretirement health care benefits are provided in Exhibit 7.17.

The similarities of these disclosures to the pension examples earlier in this chapter are substantial. A significant difference is the absence of plan assets and a return on plan assets in the computation of net postretirement benefit cost. Few of these plans are funded, but the number funded appears to be increasing. To highlight the sensitivity of both the obligation and the benefit cost to the health care cost trend assumption, the effect of a one-percentage-point increase in the rate is disclosed. For Illinois Tool Works, the effect would be to increase the obligation at December 31, 1994, by approximately $13,668,000 and the annual service and interest cost by approximately $1,666,000.

Exhibit 7.17   Postretirement Benefit Disclosures under SFAS No. 106: Illinois Tool Works, Inc., 1993–1994 (thousands of dollars)

The costs of postretirement health care benefits under SFAS No. 106 for the years ending December 31, 1993 and 1994 are as follows:

	1993	1994
Service cost	$ 2,312	$ 2,187
Interest cost on accumulated postretirement benefit obligation	11,912	10,715
Net amortization and deferral	6,968	7,519
Net postretirement benefit cost	$21,192	$20,421

The following table sets forth the amounts recognized in the company's statement of financial position at December 31, 1993 and 1994:

	1993	1994
Accumulated postretirement benefit obligation		
Retirees	$(112,876)	$ (91,691)
Active employees	(31,439)	(29,661)
	(144,315)	(121,352)
Unrecognized transition obligation	137,283	129,764
Unrecognized net gain	(3,470)	(28,689)
Accrued postretirement benefit cost	$ (10,502)	$ (20,277)

The significant actuarial assumptions at December 31, 1993 and 1994 were as follows:

	1993	1994
Discount rate	7.6%	8.5%
Health care cost trend rate		
Current rate	10.0%	8.0%
Ultimate rate in 1999	5.0%	5.0%

Source: Illinois Tool Works, Inc., annual report, December 1994, p. 32.

Illinois Tool Works disclosed its cash basis benefit cost in 1992 as $8.9 million. The benefit cost amounts under SFAS No. 106 were $20.1 million and $20.4 million for 1993 and 1994, respectively. This more than doubling of the benefit costs will continue to reduce earnings in future years. The increase in cost is greater because of the decision to amortize the accumulated obligation at adoption of SFAS No. 106 over 20 years rather than to expense this amount immediately.

Financial Flexibility and the Recognition of Other Postretirement and Postemployment Obligations

At the end of 1994, Illinois Tool Works had an unrecognized postretirement benefit obligation of $101,107,000 [$121,352,000 − $20,277,000]. Even though the company may not make any immediate changes in the pattern of its cash payments for benefits, this obligation does represent a requirement to make cash payments at some future date. This off-balance-sheet obligation reduces financial flexibility and with it the potential for growth and sustainability of future earnings.

General Motors elected immediate recognition of its benefit obligation and therefore does not have an off-balance-sheet obligation like Illinois Tool Works does. Also, because of immediate recognition of the unaccrued liability, the increase in future benefit costs for General Motors is relatively less than that for Illinois Tool Works. However, whether recognized immediately or over time, the unfunded obligation places significant demands on future cash flows.

OTHER ITEMS

The preceding discussion addresses some of the major topics in financial position analysis. Here we provide discussion of a selection of other items that should also be considered in conducting an analysis of financial position.

Undervalued Land

Seldom is any information provided on potential unrecognized gains associated with land that has been on the books of some companies for many years. The presence of such undervaluation often surfaces when portions of land are sold and gains reported. Not surprisingly, paper companies, with large land holdings, often disclose gains on land sales. For example, Union Camp Corp. reported gains on land sales in 1991–1993 of $8.3 million, $10.6, and $18.0 million, respectively.[55] Similarly, Champion International Corp. recorded gains of $93 million and $107 million in 1991 and 1992, respectively, on sales of portions of its West Coast timberlands.[56]

As with most off-balance-sheet or undervalued assets, these unrecognized values can be expected to eventually work their way into earnings. Further, position quality is strengthened and financial flexibility enhanced by this unrecognized appreciation in land values.

Sale and Leaseback Gains

Gains on sales in which the asset sold is immediately leased back generally require the deferral of part or all of the gain. The deferred gain is then amortized into earnings over the term of the lease.[57] For example, Specialty Paperboard, Inc., deferred a gain of $17 million on a 1994 sale leaseback transaction.[58] The unamortized gain at the end of 1994 was included among Specialty's long-term liabilities in its balance sheet.

This deferred gain is a delayed element of shareholders' equity rather than a liability. The gain, the result of unrecognized appreciation in the value of an asset, will make a predictable contribution to earnings over the ten-year term of the leaseback. Further, the financial position of Specialty Paperboard is marginally stronger in view of the overstatement of liabilities represented by the liability classification of the deferred gain on the sale leaseback.

Purchased Technology

Companies occasionally purchase the in-process technology of other firms. For example, 3Com Corp. acquired in-process technology for $132 million as part of its 1994 acquisitions of Synernetics, Inc., and Centrum Communications, Inc. 3Com also licensed in-process wireless technology from Pacific Monolithics, Inc. Because the "technology is still under development . . . $2.4 million of the $2.5 million cost of obtaining this license represented in-process technology and was charged to operations."[59] Amgen, Inc., also acquired in-process technology valued at $116 million as part of the 1994 acquisition of Synergen, Inc. Amgen noted that it expensed research and development costs as incurred and that "payments related to the acquisition of technology rights, for which development work is in-process, are expensed and considered a component of research and development."[60]

Expenditures such as those made by 3Com and Amgen for in-process technology are considered to be research and development costs and must be expensed as incurred under current GAAP requirements.[61] Amgen points out that the value assigned to purchased in-process technology "was evaluated through analysis of data concerning each of Synergen's product candidates."[62] While it may be true that recovery of an investment in in-process technology is subject to a higher-than-average degree of uncertainty, it is not plausible that its expected value is zero. This, however, is the valuation assigned under current GAAP. Firms with substantial purchases of in-process technology have additional off-balance-sheet value which, like other off-balance-sheet asset and liability values, should become part of the earnings of future periods. Such off-balance-sheet value adds to financial flexibility.

Business Combinations Accounting

Business combinations of various forms—mergers, consolidations, asset acquisitions, and stock acquisitions—are accounted for using either the purchase or pooling-of-interests methods.

Purchase versus Pooling-of-Interests

Under the purchase method, the cost of the combination is assigned to the assets and liabilities of the acquired firm on the basis of their respective fair values. Any excess of cost, or purchase price, over the fair value of the identifiable net assets is assigned to goodwill. In the case of an excess of fair value of the net assets over cost, negative goodwill is recognized.[63] Under the pooling-of-interests method, the assets and liabilities of the acquired firm are not marked to fair value. Rather, both the acquired and acquiring firms continue to carry their assets and liabilities at their historical book values.

The purchase method is used for most combinations, mainly because of the large number of restrictive criteria that must be satisfied to qualify for use of the pooling method. Recent survey results from the American Institute of Certified Public Accountants reveal the use of the pooling method in only 21 out of 200 business combinations identified in the annual survey.[64]

Implications for Position Analysis

There is a greater likelihood of unrecognized value when a firm has employed mainly the pooling-of-interests method. Both the acquiring and acquired firms continue to carry their assets and liabilities at book value, and no goodwill is recognized. However, when the purchase method has been the predominant method employed, then the assets and liabilities of the acquired firm will have been marked to fair value. This reduces the likelihood of significant differences between fair and book value of the assets and liabilities of the acquired firm. However, the assets and liabilities of the acquiring firm, which remain at historical cost, continue to have significant potential for valuation differences.

Cooper Industries, Inc., called the effect of accounting for business combinations to the attention of its shareholders, in its comments on the effects of inflation, as follows:

> Finally, many of the assets and liabilities included in Cooper's Consolidated Financial Position were recorded in business combinations that were accounted for as purchases. At the time of such acquisitions, the assets and liabilities were adjusted to a fair market value and, therefore, the cumulative long-term effect of inflation is reduced.[65]

The presence of significant amounts of goodwill is often seen to weaken a balance sheet. In the past, there was substantial resistance to the write-off of goodwill in cases where the acquisition giving rise to the goodwill did not perform up to expectations. As a result of SEC pressure, firms are now routinely reporting that they are subjecting the recoverability of goodwill to regular evaluation. For example, Carpenter Technology Corp. disclosed the following:

> The company's policy is to record an impairment loss against goodwill in the period when it is determined that the carrying amount of the asset may not be recoverable. This determination includes evaluation of factors such as current market value, future asset utilization, business climate and future cash flows expected to result from the use of the net assets.[66]

Negative Goodwill and Position Analysis

The case of negative goodwill brings with it a significant likelihood that assets will be either undervalued or written off completely, just as in the case of purchased in-process technology. When the fair value of the net assets—assets minus liabilities—acquired in a combination accounted for as a purchase exceed the purchase price, we have a case of negative goodwill. The implication is that a bargain purchase has been achieved. GAAP requires that the negative goodwill reduce the initially assigned fair values of the acquired noncurrent assets, with the exception of investments in marketable securities. If these assets are reduced to zero and negative goodwill still remains, then the remaining negative goodwill is amortized to income, increasing earnings on a straight-line basis.[67]

This GAAP treatment is motivated by both the concept of historical cost and the rejection of the implicit concept of a bargain purchase that is part of a negative goodwill transaction. An example may help to clarify this. Performance Food Group Co. acquired certain assets with a fair market value of approximately $1,352,000 from Loubat-L. Frank, Inc., for $820,000. Performance Food Group reported that the transaction resulted in negative goodwill of $351,000. The emergence of the negative goodwill and the apparent write-down of acquired assets are summarized in Exhibit 7.18.

Exhibit 7.18 Negative Goodwill and Asset Valuations in a Business Combination: Performance Food Group Co., 1993 (thousands of dollars)

Fair value of assets acquired	$1,352
Purchase price	820
Initial negative goodwill	532
Final negative goodwill	351
Implied write-down of noncurrent assets to zero	$ 181

Source: Performance Food Group Co., annual report, January 1994, p. 20.

In applying GAAP, the Loubat acquisition resulted in recording the acquired assets at the net amount of $1,171,000 [$1,352,000 – $181,000] rather than their fair market value of $1,352,000. However, the $1,171,000 is still $351,000 greater than the cost of $820,000 to Performance. Because not all of the $532,000 of initial negative goodwill was absorbed in the asset write-down ($351,000 remains), it follows that the noncurrent assets were written down to zero. Had the initial negative goodwill been less than $181,000, the inferred fair value of the noncurrent assets, then the assets would not have been reduced to zero.

Position analysis, in the face of negative goodwill transactions, should evaluate whether assets exist that do not appear on the balance sheet, such as in the Performance Food Group example, or whether assets have been recorded at well below their fair values. The strength of consolidated financial position and financial flexibility are enhanced in such cases.

Overstated Credit-Loss Reserves

During the 1980s the great concern with credit-loss reserves of banks and savings and loans was that they were understated. To the extent that this was true, it followed that the earnings and net assets, or equity, of banks and savings and credit-related assets were overstated. With the great banking recovery of the 1990s, more recent concern has been that credit-loss reserves are overstated, creating the opposite result to the case of understatement.

Premier Bancorp, Inc. represents a case of overstatement of credit-loss reserves. In 1993 and 1994, Premier reported negative provisions for possible credit losses of $12.5 million and $7.8 million, respectively.[68] The reserve overstatement resulted in an understatement of Premier's shareholders' equity. Shareholders' equity is a central gauge of financial strength because it is the major element of bank regulatory capital requirements. Note, once again, that in this case of an asset understatement, the undervaluation eventually made its way into earnings.

Off-Balance-Sheet Lease Obligations

Only lease commitments that meet certain GAAP criteria are recorded as obligations on the balance sheet.[69] The leases that are recorded on the balance sheet are called capital leases, and those that are not are called operating leases. Many would argue that most operating leases are the economic equivalent of debt. As such, it is claimed that they should be treated as obligations by recording them as liabilities on the balance sheet and by treating them as debt in judging a firm's financial leverage.

Whereas the presence of off-balance-sheet or appreciated on-balance-sheet assets increases financial flexibility in difficult times, the opposite is true in the case of off-balance-sheet liabilities. A case in point would be large multilocation retail operations that decide to close selected stores. Examples include firms such as Kmart Corp., Phar-Mor, Inc., Food Lion, Inc., and a number of restaurant operations. In discussing the costs of store closures under its 1993 restructuring plan, Kmart explained that lease obligations for closed stores represented one of the significant elements of its restructuring charge.[70] At January 25, 1995, Kmart's $721 million restructuring reserve included $468 million of lease obligation costs.[71]

Food Lion, Inc., was also affected by store closings. In 1993, Food Lion recorded a $170 million charge to cover the cost of store closings, of which $55 million covered the present value of remaining rent payments on leased stores closed.[72]

In the cases of both Kmart and Food Lion, the majority of their leases represented off-balance-sheet operating leases. The costs they each accrued as a result of store-closing decisions illustrate that, while not recorded as liabilities when the commitments are made, subsequent closings bring significant obligations into the balance sheet and place associated charges into the income statement. The presence of operating lease commitments should be seen as reducing financial flexibility and creating a potential negative effect on future earnings.

EXAMPLE: PHILIP MORRIS COMPANIES, INC.

The discussion up to this point has focused on individual topics in isolation. It is useful to summarize the effect of off-balance-sheet assets and liabilities as well as assets and liabilities with unrecognized appreciation or depreciation. This summary parallels to some extent the sustainable earnings base worksheet of Chapter 6. However, here the analysis is much less extensive because the candidates for inclusion are generally far fewer. Information drawn from the 1994 annual report of Philip Morris Companies, Inc. is presented in Exhibit 7.19. The focus of this summary is the potential effect on shareholders' equity.

The data in Exhibit 7.19 are designed to illustrate an approach to summarizing balance sheet information about assets and liabilities that have a potential effect on future earnings and financial flexibility. The items included do not necessarily exhaust all possibilities from the Philip Morris statements. A brief description of the items included and the associated reasoning follow:

An overfunded pension plan. The pensions plans of Philip Morris were overfunded by $1.425 billion against the projected benefit obligation. If this overfunding is realized in the future in the form of reduced pension contributions and lowered pension expense, then it has the potential to add $515 million to earnings and shareholders' equity.

An undervalued LIFO inventory. The LIFO inventory of Philip Morris is undervalued by $870 million. If fully liquidated, this could add $539 million to shareholders' equity. Future earnings and shareholders' equity would be increased.

Unrecorded deferred tax liabilities. Deferred tax liabilities on the accumulated earnings of foreign subsidiaries are sometimes not recorded. This is the case with some of the Philip Morris foreign subsidiaries. Philip Morris disclosed $287 million of such unrecorded deferred tax liabilities on "$5.1 billion of accumulated

Exhibit 7.19 Revision of Shareholders' Equity for Off–Balance-Sheet Assets and Liabilities and for Undervalued or Overvalued Assets and Liabilities, Philip Morris Companies, Inc., 1994 (millions of dollars)

Reported shareholders' equity		$12,786
Add		
Tax adjusted unrecognized pension overfunding		
Excess of assets over projected benefit obligation	1,425	
Prepaid pension cost	594	
Unrecognized overfunding	831	
× (1 − combined 38% tax rate) =	.62	515
Tax adjusted LIFO reserve		
LIFO reserve	870	
× (1 − combined 38% tax rate) =	.62	539
Deduct		
Off-balance-sheet deferred tax liabilities		(287)
Revised shareholders' equity		$13,553

Source: Philip Morris Companies, Inc., annual report, December 1994, pension data, p. 36, and LIFO data, p. 33.

earnings of foreign subsidiaries that are expected to be permanently reinvested abroad." These additional taxes would become payable if these earnings were eventually repatriated.[73] Earnings and shareholders' equity would be reduced.

Inclusions and exclusions in the preceding analysis, as well as computational details, can certainly be debated. For example, additional tax-adjusted assets of $340 million would be added to revised equity if overfunding were gauged against the accumulated rather than the projected benefit obligation. Inclusion of the additional overfunding, with a much larger tax adjustment, would have been in order if a liquidation scenario were being considered. Moreover, the deduction of the unrecorded deferred tax liability could be challenged on the basis that its actual realization may be too remote. Finally, Philip Morris has $19.7 billion of goodwill on its 1994 balance sheet. Bankers routinely deduct goodwill, as well as other intangibles, from shareholders' equity in computing measures of tangible net worth.

Nevertheless, our view is that a firm with an excess of off-balance-sheet assets and undervalued assets or overvalued liabilities over off-balance-sheet liabilities and overvalued assets and undervalued liabilities has additional financial flexibility. In the case of Philip Morris, this extra off-balance-sheet value adds a potential $767 million to its shareholders' equity. This makes it possible to respond to setbacks and take advantage of opportunities on a timely basis, and in general increases the likelihood that management will sustain the firm's profitability.

SUMMARY

The main topic of this chapter has been how the analysis of financial position can contribute to the formation of more reliable earnings expectations and, as a result, reduce the level of earnings surprises. A key goal of position analysis is the identification of additional off-balance-sheet value or obligations. The existence of the former increases financial flexibility, whereas the presence of the latter reduces it. Financial flexibility increases the likelihood that the firm will have or be able to secure the resources necessary to exploit opportunities on a timely basis, survive difficult times, and as a result sustain profitability over the long term.

Some of the topics discussed in this chapter are rather technical. However, we hope the real examples included will bring the financial significance of these topics within the reach of most readers. A more detailed discussion of each main topic in this chapter is given in the appendix.

Exhibit 7.20 provides a listing of balance sheet conditions and relations that can be used as guidance when conducting balance sheet analysis. The exhibit columns show (1) the balance sheet condition or relation, (2) the management action or other external development that can cause earnings to be affected, and (3) the nature of the potential earnings or shareholders' equity effect.

Exhibit 7.20 Listing for Balance Sheet Analysis

Condition or Relationship	Potential Development	Potential Earnings or Equity Effect*
Investments		
1. Available-for-sale investments with market value in excess of cost	Management elects to sell the securities	Increase in earnings no effect on equity
2. Available-for-sale investments with market value below cost	Management elects to sell the securities	Decrease in earnings no effect on equity
3. Equity-accounted investment with market value below the equity-method valuation	Management judges that the decline in market value is "other than temporary" and obliged to write down the investment	Decrease
4. Equity-accounted investment with market value in excess of the equity-method valuation	Management elects to sell part or all of the investment	Increase
5. Equity-accounted investment with market value below the equity-method valuation	Management elects to sell part or all of the investment	Decrease
Deferred taxes		
6. Deferred tax asset position with no valuation allowance	Deterioration of current and future profitability calling for establishment of valuation allowance	Decrease
7. Deferred tax asset position with a partial or complete valuation allowance	Improvement or deterioration in current or future profitability calling for either decrease or increase in valuation allowance, respectively	Increase or decrease in earnings Increase or decrease in equity
8. Deferred tax asset where GAAP calls for recognition of the benefit or provision in shareholders'equity	Improvement or deterioration in likelihood of realization of the deferred tax benefit	No effect on earnings increase or decrease in equity
9. Deferred tax valuation allowance is reduced	Loss or tax credit carryforward, previously written off in full expires unutilized	No effect

Exhibit 7.20 *(continued)*

Condition or Relationship	Potential Development	Potential Earnings or Equity Effect*
LIFO inventories		
10. Current cost of LIFO inventories exceeds book carrying value	LIFO inventory quantities are reduced	Increase
11. Current cost of LIFO inventories is less than the book carrying value of the LIFO inventories	LIFO inventory quantities are reduced	Decrease
13. LIFO is employed	Current cost of LIFO inventories declines	Increase
14. LIFO is employed	Current cost of LIFO inventories increases	Decrease
Pension and other postretirement and postemployment benefits		
15. Overfunded pension plans	Plans are terminated	Increase
16. Underfunded pension plans	Plans are terminated	No effect
17. Pension plans	Assumed rates of return are reduced	Decrease
18. Pension plans	Assumed rates of return are increased	Increase
19. Pension plans	Discount rates are reduced	Increase
20. Pension plans	Discount rates are increased	Decrease

*Unless noted, the effect on both earnings and equity are the same.
[a]The effects cited here are expressed in comparison to FIFO as the alternative.

REFERENCES

Comiskey, E. E. "Assessing Financial Quality: An Organizing Theme for Credit Analysts," *Journal of Commercial Bank Lending,* December 1982, pp. 32–47.

Comiskey, E. E. and C. W. Mulford. "Investment Decisions and the Equity Accounting Standard," *Accounting Review,* July 1986, pp. 519–525.

————. "The Equity Reporting Standard: Its Importance to Management Investment Decisions," *Accounting Horizons,* June 1988, pp. 67–72.

————. "Income Tax Disclosures: Their Role in Credit Analysis, Part I," *Commercial Lending Review,* Winter 1991/92, pp. 15–31.

————. "Income Tax Disclosures: Their Role in Credit Analysis, Part II," *Commercial Lending Review,* Spring 1992, pp. 17–25.

————. "Interpreting Pension Disclosures: A Guide for Lending Officers," *Commercial Lending Review,* Winter 1993/94, pp. 48–65.

————. "Understanding Pension Cost: A Guide for Lending Officers," *Commercial Lending Review,* Spring 1994, pp. 35–50.

————. "Evaluating Deferred Tax Assets: Some Guidance for Lenders," *Commercial Lending Review,* Summer 1994, pp. 12–25.

————. "Deferred Tax Asset Valuation Allowances: A Survey of Large Bank's Allowance Decisions," *Bank Accounting and Finance,* Spring 1995, pp. 3–18.

Comiskey, E. E., and C. A. Tritschler. "On or Off the Balance Sheet—Some Guidance for Credit Analysts," *Journal of Commercial Bank Lending,* October 1980, pp. 23–36.

ENDNOTES

1. General Motors Corp., annual report, December 1993, p. 38.
2. Norfolk Southern Corp. annual report, December 1994, p. 46.
3. LCI International, Inc., annual report, December 1994, p. 36.
4. Press release, The Seagram Company Ltd., Montreal, November 29, 1995, p. 4.
5. Statement of Financial Accounting Standards (SFAS) No. 106, "Employers' Accounting for Postretirement Benefits Other Than Pensions" (Norwalk, Conn.: Financial Accounting Standards Board, December 1990).
6. SFAS No. 109, "Accounting for Income Taxes" (February 1992).
7. SunTrust Banks, Inc., annual report, December 1994, p. 44.
8. SFAS No. 115, "Accounting for Certain Investments in Debt and Equity Securities" (May 1993).
9. Illinois Tool Works, Inc., annual report, December 1993, p. 33.
10. "Reporting Income, Cash Flows, and Financial Position of Business Enterprises," Proposed Statement of Financial Accounting Concepts (Stamford, Conn.: Financial Accounting Standards Board, 1981), para. 25.
11. D. E. Kieso and J. J. Weygandt, *Intermediate Accounting,* 8th ed. (New York: Wiley, 1995), p. 190.
12. Accounting Principles Board, Opinion No. 18, "The Equity Method of Accounting for Investments in Common Stock" (New York: American Institute of Certified Public Accountants, May 1971).
13. Redeemable preferred shares, an equity instrument, are defined as debt securities under SFAS No. 115, para. 137.
14. SFAS No. 115, para. 7.
15. Peterborough Savings Bank, annual report, December 1994, p. 19.
16. SFAS No. 115, para. 12(a).
17. BankAmerica Corp., annual report, December 1994, p. 52.
18. SFAS No. 115 does not include option contracts, financial futures contracts, forward contracts, and lease contracts within the definition of debt security. SFAS No. 115, para. 137.
19. The Wiser Oil Co., annual report, December 1993, pp. 19 and 23.
20. Chemed Corp. first-quarter report to shareholders, April 1995.
21. Guidance is found in Accounting Principles Board, Opinion No. 18, "The Equity Method of Accounting for Investments in Common Stock." The ultimate test for use of the equity method is whether or not the share holding, regardless of its size, provides the investor with the capacity to exercise significant influence over the investee.

22. It is possible, though not common, for the cost of an investment to be exceeded by the share of the fair value of assets acquired. This may create a negative goodwill balance that will be amortized and increase earnings rather than decrease them, as in the case of positive goodwill.
23. Chemed Corp., annual report, December 1993, p. 20.
24. Chemed Corp., annual report, December 1994, p. 24.
25. Kmart Corp., annual report, January 1994, p. 31.
26. Amdahl Corp., annual report, December 1993, p. 16.
27. SFAS No. 109, "Accounting for Income Taxes," para. 17.
28. Amdahl Corp., annual report, December 1993, p. 28.
29. UNR Industries, Inc., annual report, December 1994, p. 18.
30. Chad Therapeutics, Inc., earnings release, August 9, 1994.
31. SFAS No. 109, "Accounting for Income Taxes," para. 21, calls for the consideration of tax-planning strategies in determining the amount of valuation allowance required. Tax-planning strategies are actions that a firm "ordinarily might not take, but would take to prevent an operating loss or tax credit carryforward from expiring unused."
32. National Steel Corp. annual report, December 1993, p. 36.
33. National Steel Corp., Form 10-K annual report to the Securities and Exchange Commission, December, 1994 p. 55.
34. Ibid., p. 56.
35. Certain changes in ownership can place annual limitations on the use of both loss and credit carryforwards. Internal Revenue Code, Section 382. The applicability of such limitations is often cited as the basis for valuation allowances recorded against net operating loss and tax credit carryforwards.
36. Securities and Exchange Commission, Regulation S-X, Rule 5-02.6.
37. American Institute of Certified Public Accountants, *Accounting Trends and Techniques* (1994), p. 160.
38. *Accounting Trends and Techniques,* p. 161.
39. SEC, Regulation S-X, Rule 5-02.6.
40. Pennzoil Co. not included in Exhibit 7.10, is an example of this type of disclosure. Pennzoil Co. annual report, December 1994, p. 37.
41. Chevron Corp. reported losses from LIFO liquidations in each year from 1992 to 1994. The losses resulted from the fact that "inventories were liquidated at higher than then-current costs." Chevron Corp., annual report, December 1994, p. 29. Declining petroleum prices probably explain this atypical result.
42. The disclosure of the effects on earnings of LIFO liquidations is a requirement of the Securities and Exchange Commission. SEC, *Staff Accounting Bulletin No. 40.*
43. SFAS No. 106, "Employers' Accounting for Postretirement Benefits Other Than Pensions" (November 1992), and SFAS No. 112, "Employers' Accounting for Postemployment Benefits" (December 1992).
44. SFAS No. 87, "Employers' Accounting for Pensions" (December 1985).
45. Ibid., para. 24.
46. Ibid., para. 77.
47. Ibid., summary.
48. SFAS No. 87, paras. 36–37.
49. The full remainder of $20,529 was deducted from shareholders' equity without any offsetting tax benefit. This resulted from the fact that Grossman's wrote off all of its

deferred tax assets through a valuation allowance under the requirements of SFAS No. 109.

50. The Board considered but rejected basing the liability on the projected versus accumulated benefit obligation. SFAS No. 87, para. 149.

51. For guidance on federal income and excise taxes, see the Internal Revenue Code, Section 4980.

52. Teledyne, Inc., annual report, 1993, p. 25.

53. SFAS No. 106, "Employers' Accounting for Postretirement Benefits Other Than Pensions" (December 1990), para. 112.

54. General Motors Corp., annual report, December 1993, p. 38.

55. Union Camp Corp., annual report, December 1993, p. 36.

56. Champion International Corp., annual report, December 1993, p. 31.

57. SFAS No. 28, "Accounting for Sales with Leasebacks" (May 1979).

58. Specialty Paperboard, Inc., annual report, December 1994, p. 24.

59. 3Com Corp., annual report, December 1994, pp. 33–34.

60. Amgen, annual report, 1994, p 34.

61. SFAS No. 2, "Accounting for Research and Development Costs" (October 1974).

62. Amgen, Inc., annual report, 1994, p. 35.

63. Accounting Principles Board, Opinion No. 16, "Business Combinations" (August 1970).

64. *Accounting Trends and Techniques,* p. 58.

65. Cooper Industries, Inc., annual report, December 1993, p. 35.

66. Carpenter Technology Corp., annual report, December 1994, p. 34.

67. Accounting Principles Board, Opinion No. 16, "Business Combinations" and No. 17, "Intangible Assets" (August 1970).

68. Premier Bancorp, Inc., annual report, December 1994, p. 29.

69. SFAS No. 13, "Accounting for Leases" (November 1976).

70. Kmart Corp., annual report, January 1995, p. 19.

71. Ibid, p. 20. This obligation only includes U.S. general merchandise operations.

72. Food Lion, Inc., annual report, December 1994, pp. 17–18.

73. Philip Morris Companies, Inc., annual report, December 1994, p. 36. The case for not requiring firms to record deferred tax liabilities on permanently reinvested earnings of foreign subsidiaries turns mainly upon the complex and hypothetical nature of the necessary calculations. See SFAS No. 109, paras. 169–173.

Chapter 8

Overstated Revenue

Future Now, Inc., Cincinnati, said it restated its first-quarter results to reflect the exclusion of barter credits and certain contract revenues that were incorrectly booked in the period. The restatement cut its net income in the quarter to $1 million, or 14 cents a share, from the $2.2 million, or 30 cents a share, that was first reported.[1]

Revenue is a useful measure of the level of a firm's overall business activity. It receives prominent attention, being displayed as the first line, the "top line," on a firm's income statement. The importance of the revenue number cannot be overemphasized, since much of the rest of what is reported on the income statement, including whether there is a profit or a loss, is dependent on it.

For many transactions across different industries, accounting standards guiding the timing of revenue recognition are not specific as to when revenue should be recognized, leaving much to the judgment of management.[2] As a result, revenue might be recognized at different points in a transaction's life with significant consequences for the amount of income reported. For example, depending on the circumstances surrounding the transaction, the nature of the goods or services being provided, and management judgment, revenue might be recognized at the time an order is placed by a customer, during the production process, at the time of shipment of the goods or providing of services, after acceptance of the goods by the customer, after all return privileges have expired, or even after collection of the amount billed. Consider the effect on income if revenue is recognized at the time an order is placed and that order is later canceled. Earnings would clearly fall short of expectations dependent on order-based revenue.

Unfortunately, many investors and creditors are not clear as to when in the life of its sales or service transactions a firm recognizes revenue. This lack of basic knowledge as to the timing and appropriateness of a firm's revenue recognition policy is a prescription for an earnings surprise.

Consider the following revenue recognition practices taken from the footnotes of the annual reports of three software companies, published during 1991 and early 1992.

From the annual report of BMC Software, Inc.:

> Revenue from the licensing of software is recognized upon the receipt and acceptance of a signed contract or order.[3]

From the annual report of Autodesk, Inc.:

Revenue from sales to distributors and dealers is recognized when the products are shipped.[4]

From the annual report of Computer Associates International, Inc.:

Product license fee revenue is recognized after both acceptance by the client and delivery of the product.[5]

Note how the timing of revenue recognition varied for these firms. BMC Software recognized revenue upon receipt and acceptance of a signed contract or order, the software had likely not been shipped at that point. Autodesk waited until the software was shipped. And Computer Associates International postponed recognition until delivery and acceptance by its client. At the time, all companies were, in the view of their managements, fulfilling the requirements for revenue recognition under then extant generally accepted accounting principles. One firm, BMC Software, was clearly more aggressive than the other two in its approach to revenue recognition. This aggressiveness resulted in reported income with a more tentative quality, more likely to produce an earnings surprise.

Today, accounting standard setters have tightened considerably the permitted policies for software revenue recognition. No longer can software revenue be recognized in advance of shipment. Moreover, if there is substantial uncertainty as to a customer's acceptance of the product, revenue recognition must be postponed until the uncertainty has passed.[6] This change in accounting principles moved BMC Software to adopt the following revenue recognition policy:

Revenue from the licensing of software, including upgrade revenue, is recognized when both the company and the customer are legally obligated under the terms of the respective agreement and the underlying software products have been shipped.[7]

The policies of Autodesk and Computer Associates International already fulfilled the updated requirements for revenue recognition and were left unchanged.

The potential effect of a firm's revenue recognition policy on reported income and stockholders' equity can be seen quite readily in the case of American Software, Inc. In fiscal years prior to 1991, American Software recognized revenue in advance of shipment. The company described its former revenue recognition policy for standard software sales as follows:

Upon entering into a licensing agreement for standard proprietary software, the company recognized eighty percent (80%) of the licensing fee upon delivery of the software documentation (system and user manuals), ten percent (10%) upon delivery of the software (computer tapes with source code), and ten percent (10%) upon installation.[8]

In its 1991 fiscal year, the company changed its revenue recognition policy to the following:

> Licensing fees in connection with licensing agreements for standard proprietary software are recognized upon delivery of the software.[9]

The change was made retroactive to 1989, the earliest year presented for comparison purposes with the firm's 1991 results. With retroactive treatment, retained earnings as of the beginning of fiscal 1989 were restated to incorporate the cumulative effect of the change on the firm's net income. As a result of the change, retained earnings, which represents cumulative life-to-date net income net of dividends paid, was reduced from $34.1 million to $28.6 million, a reduction of $5.5 million, or 16%. Total shareholders' equity was reduced by the same amount, from $55.3 million to $49.8 million. This reduction in retained earnings and shareholders' equity was due to nothing more than a change in the firm's policy of revenue recognition.

While in the software industry generally accepted accounting principles for revenue recognition are now reasonably tight, in many other revenue situations accounting principles are not so specific. Much is left to management judgment as to the amount and timing of revenue to be recognized. In the majority of cases, this judgment is applied reasonably, resulting in revenue that is properly recorded. There are exceptions, however, where revenue is recognized prematurely, or worse, fictitiously. Such inappropriate approaches to revenue recognition result in revenue and earnings that are subject to subsequent downward adjustment and have the potential to produce an earnings surprise.

REVENUE RECOGNITION POLICIES

To be recognized, revenue must first be earned. For revenue to be earned, a firm must have completed all activities required to entitle it to the benefits represented by the revenue and an exchange transaction must have taken place—an exchange of rights and privileges. In addition to the revenue's having been earned, however, recognition also requires the revenue amount to be either realized through collection or realizable through an enforceable claim for collection.[10]

Sales Revenue

For companies selling products, the point of recognition is typically the time of delivery to the customer. At that point, the company has earned the revenue and has an enforceable claim for collection. The Leather Factory, Inc., for example, a company that manufactures, distributes, imports, and exports leather goods and accessories, states its revenue recognition policy as follows:

> Sales are recorded when goods are shipped to customers.[11]

In the company's view, the earnings process is complete upon shipment. Assuming the sales price is realized or realizable, revenue recognition is appropriate at that time.

Many firms that sell products and recognize revenue upon customer delivery make no mention of their revenue recognition policies in their financial statements. Included in this group are firms such as the retailers, restaurants, and grocery chains that sell directly to the public. Here, the presumption is that the earnings process is complete at the time of sale. For example, the 1993 annual reports of such firms as the maternity clothing retailer A Pea in the Pod, Inc., El Chico Restaurants, Inc., and Quality Food Centers, Inc., do not indicate the revenue recognition policies employed. Such firms recognize revenue at the time their respective goods are sold. Sun Television and Appliances, Inc., a retailer of consumer electronics and appliances, is an exception. The company states its revenue recognition policy for product sales succinctly:

> Revenues from the sale of merchandise are recognized at the time that the customer accepts physical possession of the merchandise.[12]

Sales with Rights of Return

When the customer has the right to return goods purchased, the point at which the earnings process is complete becomes somewhat unclear. Possibilities include the time of sale or after the return privilege has expired. For normal returns, as in retail exchanges and refunds, generally accepted accounting practice maintains that the earnings process is complete, permitting revenue recognition, at the time of sale. However, the sale should be recorded net of a provision for estimated returns, determined using returns experience from prior periods. The revenue recognition policy for Borland International, Inc., provides a good example:

> Revenue from the sale of software products, including sales to distributors and retail dealers, is recognized upon shipment, and allowances for estimated future returns and exchanges are provided at that time based on the company's return policies and the company's historical experience.[13]

In some industries, returns constitute a much higher percent of sales than in others. Examples include sales by publishers, manufacturers, or distributors to retail outlets of hardcover books, perishable foods, recorded music, and toys. Here, one possibility for revenue recognition is to record the sale, net of estimated returns, at the time of shipment. The problem that arises is that prior return experience may not be indicative of future returns. Another possibility is to record the shipment as a delivery on consignment and postpone revenue recognition completely until after the recipient resells the delivered goods. Such a practice, however, may unduly delay revenue recognition to a point considerably after the earnings process is complete.

In industries with a high ratio of returns to sales, accounting standards permit recognition of revenue at the time of sale provided the sale price is fixed, payment is not contingent on resale of the goods by the buyer, the buyer has the risk of loss and is economically separate from the seller, and returns can be estimated.[14] For example, Thomas Nelson, Inc., a publisher of inspirational books, states its policy regarding sales returns as follows:

> Provision is made for the estimated effect of sales returns where right-of-return privileges exist. Returns of products from customers are accepted in accordance with standard industry practice. The full amount of the returns allowance (estimated returns to be received net of inventory and royalty costs) is shown, along with the allowance for doubtful accounts, as a reduction of accounts receivable in the accompanying financial statements.[15]

Houghton Mifflin Co., another publisher, simply states that estimated returns are provided for at the time of sale. Presumably the requirements for revenue recognition are fulfilled at that time:

> A provision for estimated returns, consisting of the sales value less related inventory value and royalty costs, is made at time of sale.[16]

A contrast to the policies noted here is provided by Big Rock Brewery Ltd., a Canadian firm. The company states its revenue recognition policy as follows:

> Revenue is recognized at the time of shipment as the gross sales price charged to the purchaser. Product, which is returned due to expired shelf life and for which the customer is given credit, is netted against gross sales.[17]

Note how the company does not include a provision for estimated returns at the time of shipment. Rather, returns are accounted for as they occur. In using this policy, the company leaves itself open for large unaccounted-for returns in future periods.

As noted, one of the requirements for revenue recognition when returns constitute a large proportion of sales is that the sale price be fixed. The sale price is not fixed when the seller offers its customers price protection—the right to a refund for price declines on goods held by them in inventory. One would expect, then, that when price protection is offered, revenue would not be recognized until after the goods are resold by the company's customer. It is only at that point that the true earnings effect of the price protection clause can be determined.

Cypress Semiconductor, Inc., provides a good example of such a policy:

> Revenue from product sales direct to customers is recognized upon shipment. Certain of the company's sales are made to distributors under agreements allowing certain rights of return and price protection on merchandise unsold by the distributors. Accordingly, the company defers recognition of sales and profit on such sales until the merchandise is sold by the distributors.[18]

As described in the note, when shipments are made allowing rights of return and price protection, the company defers or postpones recognition of the revenue and profit on the sale until after the goods have been sold by its customers, the distributors. This policy appears to be in keeping with the letter of the accounting standard for such transactions.

One last example of sales with rights of return is provided in the following contrast between the revenue recognition practices of two computer makers, International Business Machines Corp. and Amdahl Corp. IBM describes its revenue recognition practice for the sale of hardware as follows:

> Revenue is recognized from hardware sales or sales-type leases when the product is shipped. . . . Reserves are established to provide for instances where customer acceptance does not take place and for other potential price adjustments.[19]

Amdahl provides the following policy:

> Revenues from equipment sales and sales-type leases are generally recognized when the equipment has been shipped and installed, and financing arrangements have been completed.[20]

Note that IBM recognizes sales revenue at the time of shipment, while Amdahl waits until the completion of installation and financing arrangements. IBM does provide for potential returns and price protection. The company is, however, taking a more aggressive stance, recognizing revenue earlier in the transaction cycle, than is Amdahl. Later, if returns increase markedly, or higher than expected price adjustments are needed, a greater portion of IBM's earnings would be subject to downward adjustment.

Service Revenue

Service firms recognize revenue when services have been performed and are billable. Included in this category are such firms as Omnicom Group, Inc., the advertising firm, and The Multicare Companies, Inc., a provider of long-term skilled nursing care and specialty medical services. Omnicom Group provides the following statement of its revenue recognition policy:

> Substantially all revenues are derived from commissions for placement of advertisements in various media and from fees for manpower and for production of advertisements. Revenue is generally recognized when billed. Billings are generally rendered upon presentation date for media, when manpower is used, when costs are incurred for radio and television production, and when print production is completed.[21]

While the firm provides its clients with various services, revenue is recognized as these services are provided and billed. The Multicare Companies recognizes revenue as follows:

Revenues consist of services paid for by patients and amounts for services provided that are reimbursable by certain third-party payors. Medicare and Medicaid revenues are determined by various rate setting formulas and regulations. Final determinations of amounts paid by Medicaid and Medicare are subject to review or audit. In the opinion of management, adequate provision has been made for any adjustment that may result from these reviews or audits. To the extent that final determination may result in amounts which vary from management estimates, future earnings will be charged or credited.[22]

Here, too, revenue is recognized as services are provided. Note how the company deals with the potential for unrealizable amounts related to Medicare and Medicaid reimbursement formulas. A provision for loss is recorded based on estimated amounts.

Some product sales firms also earn revenue from the providing of services. Sun Television and Appliances, mentioned earlier, can be included in this category. In addition to retailing consumer electronics and appliances, the company sells extended service contracts. Revenue from these contracts is deferred or postponed at the time of contract sale and recognized as earned over the lives of the service contracts. Such deferred revenue is reported as a current liability. The company owes its customers the promised service. The following policy statement is provided:

The company sells service contracts which extend beyond the manufacturers' warranty period, usually with terms of coverage (including the manufacturers' warranty period) between 12 and 60 months. Revenues from the sale of service contracts, net of direct selling expenses, are deferred at the time of sale and amortized on a straight-line basis over the lives of the contracts.[23]

A final service provider case is Delta Air Lines, Inc. The company provides the following revenue recognition policy note:

Passenger ticket sales are recorded as revenue when the transportation is provided. The value of unused tickets is included in current liabilities as air traffic liability.[24]

The company earns revenue by providing air service. Tickets paid for in advance are excluded from revenue and are reported as deferred revenue, termed air traffic liability. While this treatment is straightforward, what is less so is Delta's policy regarding frequent flyer miles. The company makes the following statement regarding its frequent flyer program:

The company sponsors a travel incentive program whereby frequent travelers accumulate mileage credits that entitle them to certain awards, including free travel. The company accrues the estimated incremental cost of providing free travel awards under its Frequent Flyer program when travel award levels are achieved. The accrued incremental cost is recorded in current liabilities.[25]

Note that the company states that it accrues the incremental cost of providing free travel when travel award levels are achieved. However, if an airline ticket entitles its holder to current air travel and to a portion of a free ticket for future air travel, then it would seem that Delta has not earned all of the revenue indicated by the ticket price when current air service is provided. A more appropriate revenue recognition practice would be to defer a portion of the ticket price representing the free miles earned and to recognize that revenue later when the free air service is provided. As an example, if Delta offers a free coach-class ticket for 25,000 miles of paid air travel, then a 5,000 mile round-trip ticket entitles its holder to 20% of a free ticket. When Delta fulfills its obligation to the ticket holder by providing 5,000 miles of air travel, it does not fulfill its obligation for 20% of an additional round-trip ticket. Accruing the incremental cost of providing free travel when travel award levels are achieved falls short of this objective.

Delta is not alone in its revenue recognition practice for frequent flyer miles. The policy of accruing only the incremental cost of providing free travel is widespread among air carriers. Such widespread acceptance does not make it right, however. Strict adherence to the revenue recognition principle would call for deferral of the portion of each ticket's sales price representing the amount of free travel earned.

Revenue from the Use of Company Assets

Included in this revenue category would be such items as interest, rent, and license royalties. Such revenue is recognized as time passes and the assets are used.

King World Productions, Inc., provides a useful example of the recognition of license royalties. In its 1991 annual report, King World Productions, which licenses such television programs as Wheel of Fortune, Jeopardy!, The Oprah Winfrey Show, and Inside Edition, described the accounting policy for license revenue that it had employed in years prior to 1994:

> Historically, King World has followed a practice of recognizing license fees from the distribution of first-run syndicated television properties at the commencement of the license period and as each show was produced (even though the particular show may not have been broadcast by a television station for several months).[26]

Given the noncancelable nature of its license agreements, King World Productions had recognized the related revenue when the respective shows were produced, even though they might not have been broadcast for a considerable period after that. In the view of the company, the earnings process was complete at that time.

In its 1994 report, the company changed its approach to license fee revenue recognition. It began recognizing revenue as each show was made available to its licensees via satellite transmission. While the change was made to help reduce quarter-to-quarter fluctuations in license fee revenue, the new approach also seems to defer revenue recognition until the earnings process is complete.

A special type of revenue that should be included in this category is franchise revenue. Such revenue includes initial franchise fees, or amounts due from the sale of franchise agreements and from continuing franchise royalties. Consider the following note from the 1993 annual report of International House of Pancakes (IHOP), Inc.:

> Revenue from the sale of franchises is recognized as income when IHOP has sub-stantially performed all of its material obligations under the franchise agreement, and the franchisee has commenced operations. Continuing service fees, which are a percentage of the net sales of franchise operations, are accrued as income when earned.[27]

This note describes well an appropriate accounting policy for initial franchise fees and franchise royalties. The company is recognizing both types of franchise revenue when earned. For its initial franchise fee, the company helps the franchisee to, "lo-cate the site, obtain rights to the site, construct an IHOP restaurant, train the crew, open, and then franchise the restaurant."[28] Given all the services the company pro-vides for its initial franchise fee, it is apparent that this fee is not earned until after the restaurant is open and the franchisee has commenced operations. It is at that point that the company recognizes the initial franchise fee revenue. Franchise royalties, termed continuing service fees in the note, are based on a percentage of franchisee sales. This revenue is earned and recognized as restaurant sales are logged by fran-chised units.

Another example of franchise-related revenue includes the revenue earned by Right Management Consultants, Inc., a provider of career management and human resource consulting. The company describes its revenue recognition practices as follows:

> Royalties from the members of the company's franchise network arise from agree-ments made with affiliates, which generally operate exclusively in designated re-gions based on location. The terms of these agreements require the affiliate to provide services under the company's service marks in accordance with programs and stan-dards developed by the company. Affiliate royalties are 10% of each affiliate's gross receipts and are recorded when the affiliate bills its customers for services.[29]

The company has earned and records franchise royalties when its consulting affili-ates bill their customers for services.

When Collectibility Is in Doubt

Earlier it was noted that in addition to being earned, revenue recognition requires either collection of the revenue amount or an enforceable claim for collection. Most companies assume that amounts billed are collectible and record revenue when the earnings process is complete. They deal with the potential for noncollectibility by charging against income a portion of the amounts due. Out-standing receivables are reported net of this estimate of uncollectible amounts determined using prior-year collection experience and a review of the quality of outstanding receivables. Estimates of uncollectible amounts are later adjusted based on actual collection results. Home Nutritional Services, Inc., provides a good example:

> A provision for doubtful accounts is made for revenues estimated to be uncollectible and is adjusted periodically based upon the company's evaluation of current industry conditions, historical collection experience, and other relevant factors which, in the opinion of management, deserve recognition in estimating the allowance for uncollectible accounts.[30]

For some transactions, collectibility is so uncertain that the entire concept of realizability must be called into question. In such cases, revenue should be not recognized when earned but when collected. Only then can the true realizability of the revenue amount be judged.

The installment method provides a valid revenue recognition technique for situations involving collection of the sale price in a series of installment payments where collectibility of those installments is in doubt at the time of the sale. This method permits recognition of a portion of the gross profit on sale equal to the percentage of the sale price collected. Typical of the kinds of transactions for which the installment method is appropriate are real estate sales where the seller has provided purchase money financing and the buyer's ability or willingness to pay are called into question. This uncertainty may be due to a lack of financial strength on the part of the buyer or to an insignificant down payment that calls into question the buyer's true commitment to the deal.

Collectibility of the sale amount may also be called into question where the purchaser is a government agency and each installment payment is subject to a new appropriation by a potentially different administration. The 1993 annual report of Florida East Coast Industries, Inc., provides a good example:

> In 1988, the company entered into an agreement with the Florida Department of Transportation (DOT) for the sale of approximately 20.7 miles of abandoned 100-foot-wide right-of-way. The total sales price of $35,525,000 was divided into six segments. The DOT made an initial payment of $10,000,000 and issued an executory note for $25,525,000 at an interest rate of 9.01%. As the payments from DOT were received, the liens on the pro rata portion of the succeeding segments were removed and related gains recognized. Principal and interest payment of $6,250,000 was received in 1989, a payment of $8,857,000 was received in 1990, and a final payment of $16,371,326 was received in 1991. The land sale gains recognized amounted to $15,018,000, $6,884,000, $3,923,000, and $9,574,000 in 1991, 1990, 1989, and 1988, respectively.[31]

In this transaction, Florida East Coast Industries sold land to the Florida Department of Transportation for $35,525,000. The company collected a down payment of $10,000,000 and provided installment financing for the balance. A portion of the land sale gain was recognized with the down payment and as each installment was collected. In addition to these gains, interest income was also recognized on the note as it accrued and was collected.

PREMATURE REVENUE RECOGNITION

Premature revenue is revenue that is recognized too soon. Usually such revenue is recognized before the earnings process is complete, though on occasion early recognition may be the result of recording revenue before realizability is established. Regardless of the cause, earnings that include such revenue have a tentative quality and are subject to future adjustment. Such an adjustment results in a charge to earnings, or a possible restatement, and a downward adjustment to assets and shareholders' equity.

Examples of Premature Revenue Recognition

Before looking carefully at the numbers and developing financial early warnings to detect the potential existence of premature revenue recognition, a few preliminary examples are provided. These examples are designed to help clarify when revenue should be recognized by providing useful contrasts from the practices observed earlier. For example, in the BMC Software case, cited earlier, revenue was being recognized at the time of receipt of a signed contract or order. This is an example of premature revenue recognition. While at the time an order was placed the company had not completed the earnings process, it was nonetheless recording revenue and accounts receivable for amounts due. To gain an appreciation for the premature nature of the revenue in this case, one need only consider the company's customers, who would likely not consider BMC Software to have a valid claim for payment at that point. As noted earlier, BMC Software is no longer using this policy. In recent years, the company has changed its method to require shipment before revenue is recognized.

Jiffy Lube International, Inc., provides a good example of the importance to revenue recognition of determining when revenue is earned and realized or realizable. Jiffy Lube, the operator of quick oil-change centers, which is now owned by Pennzoil Co., began as a franchiser. The company collected initial franchise fees for franchises sold and franchise royalties based on outlet sales. The company also collected a fee for the sale of what were termed area development rights. These rights granted prospective franchisees exclusive access to particular territories. The company recognized revenue from these area development rights up front on the basis that the fee was nonrefundable and that the company had completed the earnings process by granting the franchisee the prescribed area. However, based on other services promised by Jiffy Lube as part of its area development agreement, it does not appear that the earnings process was complete at that time. That is, in addition to providing the franchisees with exclusive areas, Jiffy Lube also provided them with training and advertising support services as units were opened. In 1988 the company was ordered by the Securities and Exchange Commission to change its accounting practice for fees related to area development rights. In particular, the SEC maintained that these fees were not earned up front and should not be recognized at that time.

Rather, the SEC held that revenue from area development rights should be recognized over the period that the ancillary services were provided.

Regarding the realizability of Jiffy Lube's revenue, it was later learned that Jiffy Lube accepted promissory notes for a substantial portion of its franchise fees and royalties. Recording revenue in such a situation was permissible, assuming the outstanding notes were collectible. In the case of Jiffy Lube, collectibility was an issue because many of the franchised outlets were losing money and had poor financial prospects. One could argue that revenue should have been recognized only as collections on those notes were made.

PerSeptive Biosystems, Inc., a manufacturer of purification and analysis equipment for the biotechnology industry, employed a strategy of shipping unordered equipment to companies on a trial basis. Each machine came with an offer, "Pay nothing for it now and return it later if you don't like it."[32] Such a practice may be questionable strategically. However, the appropriate revenue recognition policy seems clear. There was no basis whatsoever for recognition of revenue when such unordered goods were shipped. Rather, these shipments were nothing more than inventory transfers between locations.

PerSeptive's 1993 annual report provides the following accounting policy for revenue recognition related to equipment sales:

> The company recognizes revenue from product sales upon shipment from the company's warehouse.[33]

If the company were in fact recognizing revenue when unordered equipment was shipped, it would be a violation of generally accepted accounting principles. In November 1994, when asked about its revenue recognition practices, the company's management responded as follows:

> The company recognizes revenue only on machines that have been shipped against a customer's binding commitment to pay.[34]

Later in 1994, PerSeptive Biosystems restated results for much of the two previous fiscal years because of improperly recorded sales and other accounting errors. Among the reasons for the restatement, the company provided the following explanation:

> Some sales were reversed because they were made on a contingent basis . . . or because they were based on oral orders prior to receipt of written purchase orders. In addition . . . some units were shipped with incomplete documentation.[35]

Apparently, in the case of PerSeptive Biosystems, some shipments of equipment were being recognized as revenue even when destinations were to "customers" that had not placed orders. The company attributed the practice to rapid growth and the fact that it "outgrew its internal control systems."[36] Regardless of the reason, the practice was a clear violation of the requirement that before revenue is recognized it must be earned and realized or realizable. No valid claim can exist against a customer for unordered goods. Interestingly, the company's 1994 annual report, released after the restatement, includes new language in the revenue recognition policy note. The note now reads as follows:

> The company recognizes revenue upon shipment of its products to the customer. Significant future obligations, such as satisfaction of subjective or more than perfunctory customer-mandated performance criteria, and sales-related contingencies, such as unilateral rights to return product, delay revenue recognition until the obligation is satisfied or the contingency is resolved.[37]

The company is now acknowledging the need for resolution of key uncertainties, including potential customer returns, before revenue is recognized. Trial-basis shipments would not fulfill these criteria.

In the paragraphs that follow, we look carefully at three examples of premature revenue recognition. Here we examine not only each company's revenue recognition policy but also reported balance sheet and income statement amounts. Our objective is to develop financial early warnings of earnings surprises caused by premature revenue recognition practices. The first two examples, Knowledgeware, Inc., and The Topps Co., were developed after the fact. These companies reported losses that were due in large part to premature revenue recognition in earlier periods. We examined their financial statements in the years and quarters preceding the losses in an effort to identify key warning signs. The third firm, Global Resources, Inc., has not reported a loss or an earnings surprise. In fact, Global Resources' results continue to be very promising. However, our reading of the company's policy note and its financial statements suggest it may be a surprise waiting to happen. Only time will tell.

Example: Knowledgeware, Inc.

In its 1991 annual report, Knowledgeware, Inc., a software company, described its revenue recognition practices as follows:

> Revenues are derived from the licensing and development of computer software products, sale of software service agreements, licensing of technology, and on-going consulting and education activities. Revenues are recognized at the time of software shipment for product license agreements. Revenues from sales of service agreements are deferred and recognized ratably over the lives of the agreements. Other revenues are recognized as services are performed or technology rights transferred.[38]

The policy sounds appropriate; revenue was being recognized as earned. What is not stated are the terms for payment that were being offered.

In late 1991 the company announced that it was expecting to post a loss for the quarter ending September 30th. This loss was noteworthy in that it was the first since the firm had gone public in 1989. One of the revelations provided by the company was that it was offering some of its customers up to one year to pay open accounts. Such terms call into question the realizability of its sales. Realizability is especially questionable when the product being sold, such as software, has a short technological life. Questions of realizability notwithstanding, the company was recognizing revenue at the time of shipment. In 1991 five class-action lawsuits were filed against the firm and its chairman, Fran Tarkenton, which claimed, among other things, that the company had misled shareholders by recognizing revenue prematurely.

Selected account balances from the company's income statement and balance sheet for the years ending June 30, 1990 and 1991, are provided in Exhibit 8.1. The 1991 annual report provided much reason for investors in the company to be optimistic. Revenue had nearly doubled, and net income had increased by over 50%. There seemed to be little to indicate the impending loss that would be reported for the quarter ending September 30, 1991. There were, however, some troubling signs.

Prior to collection, recorded revenue results in open accounts receivable (A/R) on the balance sheet. When revenue is recognized prematurely, whether before the earnings process is complete or before realizability has been established, these open receivables take longer to collect. The accounts receivable balance grows. As the proportion of revenue that is recognized early increases, percentage increases in accounts receivable exceed percentage increases in revenue. The Knowledgeware data bear this out. In the year ending June 30, 1991, the company's revenue increased by 88% while accounts receivable increased by 172%. The company was clearly recognizing revenue that was not being collected.

Another way to look for signs of premature revenue recognition is to calculate the ratio accounts receivable days (A/R days). A/R days provides a measure of the length of time it will take a firm to collect its ending accounts receivable balance. As such, it has more intuitive meaning than a comparison of the percentage increase in accounts receivable with the percentage increase in revenue. Calculated as accounts receivable divided by revenue-per-day (revenue divided by 360), A/R days was running at 82 days and 119 days, respectively, at June 30, 1990 and 1991.[39]

Increases in accounts receivable at rates that are faster than increases in revenue and growth in A/R days do not necessarily mean that a firm is employing prema-

Exhibit 8.1 Knowledgeware, Inc., Selected Account Balances, Years Ending June 30, 1990 and 1991 (thousands of dollars)

	1990	1991
Revenue	$66,229	$124,277
A/R, net of allowance for doubtful accounts	$15,119	$ 41,171
Net income	$ 9,764	$ 15,328

Source: Knowledgeware, Inc., annual report, June 1991.

ture revenue recognition practices. They do, however, indicate that something is potentially wrong. Customers are taking longer to pay. In the case of Knowledgeware, the average customer was taking nearly four months to settle. Some were shorter, but some were much longer. For a high-growth technology firm, four months is unusually long. At the time, software firms on average were collecting accounts receivable in about 64 days.[40] While larger firms took a bit longer, Knowledgeware was clearly on the high side. Why is that? Is management aware of it? Have credit standards been relaxed in an effort to boost revenue? Are customers having financial difficulties? Has the company changed its revenue recognition practices? Is revenue recognized when earned and realizable? Answers to questions such as these are necessary in formulating expectations about future performance.

The A/R days statistic can be skewed to the high side when applied to annual results for a high-growth firm such as Knowledgeware. The ratio uses end-of-period accounts receivable in its calculation, which includes amounts due for more recent revenue transactions. The revenue number employed, however, includes activity from earlier in the year when business activity was running at a much lower rate. As a result, accounts receivable will appear to be high relative to revenue. One way to address this measurement constraint is to calculate A/R days using quarterly amounts. This approach will relate more recent revenue activity with ending accounts receivable balances. Quarterly measures are also beneficial in that they can provide earlier, more sensitive indicators of potential problems.

Selected quarterly statistics for Knowledgeware for the fiscal year ending June 30, 1991, are provided in Exhibit 8.2, together with statistics for the September 1991 quarter during which the company reported its first loss. Note that in the March and June quarters immediately preceding the drop in revenue and earnings for September 1991, accounts receivable was clearly growing more rapidly than revenue. In those quarters, accounts receivable increased 14% and 70%, respectively, while revenue increased 4% and 31%, respectively. This greater increase in accounts receivable relative to revenue was showing up as an increase in A/R days. Calculated using quarterly revenue, A/R days was 71 days in March and 92 days in June. While these statistics, adjusted now for the high growth rate of Knowledgeware, appear much better than the statistics cited earlier, relative to the industry average of 64 days, the measures were still high and growing rapidly. There was clearly reason for concern. Note how revenue dropped off markedly and was accompanied by a net loss in the September 1991 quarter. This sudden drop suggests that in the March and June quarters, the company employed premature revenue recognition practices to "borrow" revenue in advance from September. That is, revenue that should have been recognized in September 1991, when realizability was assured, was recognized in earlier quarters.

Example: The Topps Co.

The Topps Co. is a marketer of collectible trading cards featuring sports figures, and television and movie characters. The company also produces and distributes bubble

Exhibit 8.2 Knowledgeware, Inc., Selected Quarterly Statistics, Year Ending June 30, 1991, and Quarter Ending September 30, 1991 (thousands of dollars)

	Fiscal Year 1991				
	Sept	Dec.	Mar.	June	Sept. 1991
Revenue	$23,517	$29,658	$30,797	$40,305	$21,598
Percent increase (decrease) in revenue from previous quarter	5%	26%	4%	31%	(46)%
A/R, net of allowance for doubtful accounts	$19,718	$21,283	$24,282	$41,171	$28,479
Percent increase (decrease) in A/R from previous quarter	30%	8%	14%	70%	(31)%
A/R days based on 90-day quarter	75	65	71	92	119
Net income (loss)	$2,532	$3,134	$4,399	$5,263	$(4,872)

Source: Knowledgeware Inc., annual report. Data obtained from Disclosure, Inc., *Compact D/SEC: Corporate Information on Public Companies Filing with the SEC* Bethesda, Md.: Disclosure, Inc., December 1992).

gum and other candy products. The company sells its trading card products to wholesalers and retailers. These customers, who represent about 70% of the company's sales, have the right to return unsold cards. The company's 1992 annual report described its accounting policy with respect to the return privilege as follows:

Estimated losses expected in connection with sales returns are accrued in the period in which the related sales are recorded.[41]

The company's revenue recognition policy is to record revenue and accounts receivable at the time of shipment. At that time, returns are estimated and a loss and related liability, termed allowance for estimated losses on sales returns, are recorded. The amount of the loss and liability recorded is an estimate of the lost revenue, less the residual value of the returned cards, if any, plus any costs estimated to be incurred in administering the returns. Later, when cards are returned and the actual loss is known, that amount can be deducted from the liability.

Selected account balances from the company's income statement and balance sheet for 1991 and 1992 are provided in Exhibit 8.3. The exhibit reveals some troubling signs. During the year ending February 29, 1992, a revenue increase of 5% was accompanied by an increase in accounts receivable of 62%. This increase in accounts receivable translated into an increase in A/R days to 42 days from 27 days the previous year. At the same time, the allowance for estimated losses on sales returns was reduced to $8,375,000, or 24% of accounts receivable, from $8,818,000 or 41% of

Exhibit 8.3 The Topps Co. Selected Statistics, Years Ending March 2, 1991, and February 29, 1992 (thousands of dollars)

	1991	1992
Revenue	$290,006	$303,187
Percent increase (decrease) in revenue from previous year	18%	5%
A/R, net of allowance for doubtful accounts	$ 21,621	$ 35,081
Percent increase (decrease) in A/R from previous year	17%	62%
Allowance for estimated losses on sales returns	$ 8,818	$ 8,375
Allowance for estimated losses on sales returns as percentage of A/R	41%	24%
A/R days	27	42
Net income	$ 54,119	$ 54,474

Source: The Topps Co. annual report, February 1992.

accounts receivable, the previous year. It seems unusual that as accounts receivable grew, fewer returns were to be expected.

When one examines statistics for subsequent quarters of 1992, shown in Exhibit 8.4, the negative evidence mounts. During the May and August quarters, revenue continued to grow much as it had in the previous two fiscal years. Moreover, the rapid buildup of accounts receivable noted in the previous two years continued, and even accelerated. As a result, A/R days increased to 57 during the August quarter. A revenue decline was experienced in the November quarter. Accounts receivable was unchanged from the same quarter in the previous year. A/R days declined to 48. While a decline in A/R days to 48 in the November 1992 quarter is an improvement from the 57 days noted in August, it is actually an increase from the 41 days it took to collect outstanding accounts receivable in the November 1991 quarter. During the entire period under review, the allowance for estimated losses on sales returns remained at around $8,500,000. Something was not right.

In December 1992 company management was asked about the unusual increase in accounts receivable and whether management was concerned about higher-than-normal returns. Management replied as follows:

> No . . . Topps still gets paid every 21 days . . . receivables appear to be rising only because Topps has been shipping nearly 50% of its cards in the final few weeks of each quarter, leaving huge receivables on the books at quarter's end. . . . Topps changed its shipping schedules in the past year. . . . The increased receivables are really just an accident of bookkeeping timing.[42]

Terms of 21 days were generally consistent with the A/R days figure of 27 calculated for the year ending March 2, 1991. A/R days were as low as 20 in the May 1991 quarter, jumped to 45 in August, and remained around 40 days in the November 1991

Exhibit 8.4 The Topps Co., Inc. Selected Quarterly Statistics, 1992 (thousands of dollars)

	1992		
	May	Aug.	Nov.
Revenue	$76,433	$83,758	$62,609
Percent increase (decrease) in revenue from same quarter, previous year[a]	12%	10%	(15%)
A/R, net of allowance for doubtful accounts	$44,838	$52,716	$33,632
Percent increase (decrease) in A/R from same quarter, previous year	195%	38%	0%
A/R days based on 90-day quarter	53	57	48
Net income	$12,504	$16,505	$11,414

Source: Data obtained from Disclosure, Inc., *Compact D/SEC: Corporate Information on Public Companies Filing with the SEC* (Bethesda, Md.: Disclosure, Inc., December 1992 and December 1993).

[a]Because of the seasonal nature of the company's business, quarterly revenue and accounts receivable increases are calculated using the same quarter of the previous year.

and February 1992 quarters. As noted in Exhibit 8.3, A/R days were calculated at 42 days for the year ending February 29, 1992.

A change in shipping schedules could give, at least for a while, the impression of an alarming increase in accounts receivable. This may have happened during the August 1991 quarter, when A/R days increased to the 40's from the 20's. One could determine if the company were still collecting accounts receivable in 21 days by calculating A/R days as of the end of one month using only sales for that month. However, such data are hard to obtain and are typically unavailable for public companies.

After a year's worth of changed shipping schedules, growth in accounts receivable should not be high relative to sales growth when compared with the previous year's bloated receivables. In the case of Topps, however, problems with accounts receivable appeared to be continuing for more than a year. For example, in Exhibit 8.4, a 10% increase in revenue in the August 1992 quarter as compared with August 1991, a quarter when A/R days was already running at 45, was matched with a 38% increase in accounts receivable. Accounts receivable were continuing to grow faster than revenue, with A/R days now up to 57. Topps' problems appeared to be more fundamental than a change in its shipping schedule.

Inquiries to some of Topps' customers showed just how pervasive its problems might have been. These customers found Topps' explanation of the increase in accounts receivable, "hard to swallow." They noted that Topps cards were selling much more slowly than they had in previous years and that they were intending to return much more merchandise than in the past. For some cards, the return rate would be 30% higher. Topps' allowance for estimated losses on sales returns, which had not been increased as sales had grown, was potentially insufficient to absorb a substantial increase in returns.

In January 1993, about a month after the inquiries of Topps' management mentioned earlier, the company circulated the following news release:

> The Topps Company (TOPP-Nasdaq) today announced that shipments of sports cards during the fourth quarter ending February 27, 1993, will be significantly lower than the company anticipated. As a result of lower shipments as well as the company's decision to increase provisions for obsolescence and returns, the company will report a net loss for its fourth quarter.[43]

In March 1993 the company reported financial results for the fourth quarter ending February 27, 1993. Revenue for the quarter had fallen to $40,358,000 and the company reported a net loss of $21,386,000. In hindsight, given its inability to estimate returns, it appears the company may have been recording revenue earlier than it should. At a minimum, when collections slowed, the return allowance should have been increased to provide for a potential increase in returns. The astute financial statement reader would have become concerned about developments at the company many months prior to the January 1993 news release. At a minimum, firm-level financial developments should have indicated the need to seek evidence from the outside to corroborate management's explanation for the increase in accounts receivable. In the case of Topps, such evidence was provided by interviews with some of the company's customers. These interviews would have served as the basis for anticipating a decline in earnings and an avoidance of an earnings surprise.

Example: Global Resources, Inc.

Global Resources, Inc., provides recreational travel opportunities for individuals interested in prospecting for gold. The company describes its business as follows:

> The company's principal business activities consist of the promotion and sale of an "Alaska trip," a recreational gold mining expedition to the company's Cripple River property located near Nome, Alaska, and the sale of LDMA/AU memberships which entitle members to engage in recreational prospecting on its Burnt River (Baker County, Oregon), Junction Bar Place (Siskiyou County, California), and Land Mine (White County, Georgia) properties. The company has also signed a mutual use agreement with Lost Dutchman's Mining Association, under which members of either LDMA/AU or Lost Dutchman's Mining Association would be entitled to engage in recreational prospecting on certain of each other's properties.[44]

Our particular interest in the company focuses on the sale of the prospecting memberships. The company describes its revenue recognition policy for the sale of these memberships as follows:

The company has sold memberships primarily on an installment basis. Memberships include contracts that give purchasers recreational prospecting and mineral rights to the company's land and undivided interests in the land and facilities. The contracts are generally non-interest-bearing, unsecured, and provide for a down payment and monthly installments of $25 for periods of up to ten years. Sales revenue is recognized upon execution of a sales contract, expiration of the refund period, and receipt of cumulative payments of at least 10% of the sales price. Cumulative payments received on contracts where the refund period has not expired, or which are less than 10% of the original contract amount, are recorded as deposits. Deposits are fully refundable for sixty days. The contracts are discounted over the contractual repayment period at a discount rate of 2% over the prime rate.[45]

According to the company's annual report to the SEC for the year ended December 1993, memberships sell for $3,500, though a discount of $1,000 is given for a $250 down payment and payments of $25 per month. In addition, there is a yearly maintenance fee of $96 that commences once the initial membership fee is paid. As of December 31, 1993, a total of 1,500 memberships had been sold.

If we assume that most members take the discount, the membership fee of $2,500 will be paid with a $250 down payment and 90 monthly installment payments of $25 ($300 annually for seven and a half years). As noted in its revenue recognition policy, the company recognizes the full contract amount, net of a discount representing the time value of money, as revenue upon execution of the contract, expiration of the refund period (60 days), and receipt of cumulative payments of at least 10% of the sale price. Using this formula and assuming timely payments, a member has paid $300 ($2,200 is still due) after 60 days when the refund period expires. That is, $250 down and two monthly payments of $25. Since this is more than 10% of the $2,500 discounted sale price, it appears that the company recognizes the contract amount, net of the interest discount, as membership revenue at that time.

We calculate the interest discount to be approximately $700 per contract. That is, after a down payment of $250 and two installments of $25, $2,200 is still owed on the contract. This amount will be paid in 88 monthly installments of $25. Using an 11% discount rate or, as stated by the company, 2% over the prime rate, assumed here to be 9%, the present value of these 88 monthly installments of $25 is approximately $1,500. This is $700 less than the remaining contract balance of $2,200. At the 60-day mark after a contract is signed, membership revenue would thus be recognized in the amount of $1,800, the $1,500 discounted amount remaining to be collected plus $300 collected in the down payment and the first two monthly installments. The $700 deferred interest income discount is netted against the contract amount and is recognized over the term of the membership agreement. Also netted against the contract amount is an allowance for cancellations equal to about 8% of the total amount due.

Selected account balances for Global Resources for 1992 and 1993 are provided in Exhibit 8.5, and for nine months 1993 and 1994, in Exhibit 8.6.

According to the financial results reported in Exhibits 8.5 and 8.6, the company appears to be on a roll. Membership sales revenue and net income are up dramati-

cally. In a press release, the company described its results for the third quarter ended
September 30, 1994, as follows:

> Management of Global Resources, Inc. (Nasdaq: GLRS), an Alaskan corporation,
> today announced the company had significant increases in revenues and earnings
> for the third quarter ended September 30, 1994, compared to the third quarter of
> 1993. Revenues for the third quarter of 1994 were up 37% to $965,534 from
> $707,065 for the third quarter of 1993. Net income was up 450% to $259,316 or
> $.18 per share from $47,674 or $.04 per share. . . .
>
> Global has had several straight years of increased earnings and revenues. This
> trend is expected to continue. The company had a significant number of member-

Exhibit 8.5 Global Resources, Inc., Selected Account Balances, Years Ending
December 31, 1992 and 1993 (thousands of dollars)

	1992	1993
Membership sales	$ 560	$ 701
Membership contracts receivable	$ 614	$1,090
Less: Unearned interest	120	226
Less: Allowance for cancellations	49	86
Membership contracts receivable, net	$ 445	$ 778
Total assets	$2,296	$3,020
Stockholders' equity	$1,552	$1,975
Net income	$ 153	$ 403

Source: Global Resources, Inc., annual report, December 1993.

Exhibit 8.6 Global Resources, Inc., Selected Account Balances, Nine Months
Ending September 30, 1993 and 1994 (thousands of dollars)

	1993 Nine Months	1994 Nine Months
Membership sales	$ 611	$1,568
Membership contracts receivable	$ 913	$2,654
Less: unearned interest	195	611
Less: allowance for cancellations	69	218
Membership contracts receivable, net	$ 649	$1,825
Total assets	$2,836	$4,308
Stockholders' equity	$1,891	$2,764
Net income	$ 387	$ 784

Sources: Global Resources, Inc., annual report, December 1993, and quarterly report to
the Securities and Exchange Commission, September 1994.

ship sign ups in the first nine months of 1994 and is projecting significant growth to continue throughout the year and into 1995.[46]

These glowing reports and optimistic prospects notwithstanding, the company's revenue recognition policy for membership sales, which now represent nearly 60% of total revenue and are growing rapidly in importance, gives much cause to pause and reflect. What is the likelihood of collection of a $2,200 receivable through installments of $25 per month? At 8% of the gross receivable amount, does the allowance for cancellations provide sufficiently for poor collection experience? Will the company's collection experience worsen after a year or two when its members have had an opportunity to visit a property once or twice? Having started in 1991, the sale of memberships is a reasonably new activity for the company. Does the company have sufficient collection experience on these long-term contracts to determine an appropriate allowance for cancellations?

These questions cannot be answered now. The company is, however, at significant risk for an earnings surprise if its collection experience worsens. Note that by September 30, 1994, net membership contracts receivable composed 42% of total assets and 66% of shareholders' equity. The sale of memberships had grown to become the company's largest single asset. An unexpected increase in cancellations could strike a significant blow to the company's balance sheet and net worth.

While not available from public disclosures, information on the company's collection experience, including the number of contracts that are late, would be useful. Any weakening in the company's collection experience would be an important indicator that earnings may be about to decline significantly. Another indicator would be an increase in membership contracts receivable that is perceptibly greater than the increase in membership sales revenue.

At present, the company's financial statements do not manifest any obvious problems with its collection experience. In our view, the best early warning indicator for Global Resources remains the company's policy of revenue recognition for membership sales. We think that it is aggressive and may result in revenue being recognized prematurely. In our opinion, an installment basis, which ties revenue recognition to collections, would be more appropriate in instances such as this where the contract covers an extended period and there is no collateral on which to foreclose.

FICTITIOUS REVENUE RECOGNITION

The revenue recognition criteria of earned and realized or realizable revenue offer managements considerable latitude in deciding whether and when revenue should be recognized. Recognizing revenue at a point that may seem premature has more to do with management judgment than with a conscious decision to violate generally accepted accounting principles. The more aggressive that judgment becomes, the earlier recognition may be considered. Thus, premature revenue recognition should not necessarily be viewed as fictitious or fraudulent. However, the line between premature and fictitious recognition is only a matter of degree. What may have seemed simply premature revenue recognition at the time may in hindsight appear to have had a fraudulent intent.

The examples reviewed to this point involve premature, not fictitious, revenue recognition. We now turn our attention to revenue recognized fictitiously.

Fictitious revenue recognition entails recognizing revenue without regard to whether it will materialize. At the time revenue is recognized, there is a fraudulent intent designed to deceive financial statement readers. Because it is nonexistent, fictitious revenue results in the overstatement of earnings, assets, and shareholders' equity. Earnings expectations that are based on these statements are erroneous and subject to disappointment later, when the charade is exposed.

Because fictitious revenue affects key amounts on the balance sheet as well as on the income statement, using these statements together can be helpful in identifying when fictitious revenue is being recognized. The analyst who carefully and regularly reviews both statements and stays well informed on company, industry, and economic developments can improve markedly the likelihood that he or she will not be misled by revenue recognized fictitiously.

Examples of Fictitious Revenue Recognition

As we did in the previous section, we begin by providing some preliminary examples. We then turn our attention to two major frauds involving fictitious revenue recognition: MiniScribe Corp., and Comptronix Corp.

Sequoia Systems, Inc., manufactures fault-tolerant computer systems. In fiscal 1991 the company overstated revenue and net income by about 8% and 60%, respectively. Among the actions taken by the company was the shipment of computer systems against canceled purchase orders. This activity was brought to light by a disgruntled customer who was billed for a canceled order and contacted the SEC.

Some of the same statistics that worked in identifying premature revenue recognition would be helpful in uncovering the fictitious revenue of Sequoia Systems. For example, in recognizing revenue related to canceled orders, the company would boost accounts receivable. As a result, this balance would increase faster than sales and would move A/R days higher. Whether these measures would be sensitive enough to pick up the fiction sufficiently early is unclear. However, it is possible that the disgruntled customer helped uncover the fraud before it got out of hand.

Flight Transportation, Inc. was an air charter carrier. The company overstated tourist charter revenue by 62% in 1980 and 54% in 1981 by recording flights that were not made. In this case, the president of another air charter company was helpful in uncovering the deception. Flight Transportation was offering to acquire that president's company. In his view, Flight Transportation did not have the physical capacity to generate the amount of air charter revenue that it was reporting. In fact, it was later learned that in its fiscal 1980, the company claimed to have made 120 flights, 12 during the first three quarters of the year and 108 during the final quarter.

In the case of Flight Transportation, calculating revenue per plane would have been helpful in noting that something was awry. The lesson to be learned here is that revenue should always be compared with some measure of physical capacity. The appropriate measure of physical capacity to use, however, will vary by company. For example, it might be revenue per employee, or revenue in relation to fixed assets or total assets. We will find this statistic particularly helpful in the Comptronix case.

In the paragraphs that follow, we look carefully at two additional examples of fictitious revenue recognition. We perform an in-depth study of the company's financial statements, our objective being to develop financial early warnings of earnings surprises caused by such revenue recognition practices.

Example: MiniScribe Corp.

MiniScribe Corp. designed, manufactured, and marketed a broad range of small disk drives used in personal computers and workstations. The early 1980s was a period of rapid growth for the company. Revenue increased from under $9 million in 1982 to over $124 million in 1984. In 1985 revenue declined somewhat, to $114 million, still a significant increase over the amount reported as recently as 1982. During the years between 1982 and 1985, however, profitability was somewhat elusive. In fact, during that period, the company reported an operating loss in every year except 1983.

According to its financial statements for the fiscal year ended December 31, 1986, the company was back on the growth track. Revenue increased to $185 million, and the company reported net income of $22.7 million. The market price of its common stock had quintupled over the previous 18 months, and all seemed well. In fact, the company was rushing to finish a prospectus to sell $97.7 million in bonds to help finance its cash needs, which ostensibly were related to its rapid growth.

As it turns out, MiniScribe's revenue growth and profits were fictitious, invented by management to help boost the share price and sell the bonds. The glowing results for 1986 were later restated and reduced, from revenue and net income as originally reported of $185 million and $22.7 million, respectively, to restated amounts of $178 million and $12 million. After that, the company never gained a secure financial footing and filed for bankruptcy court protection in 1990.

Court documents later showed that the company had taken numerous steps to artificially boost revenue and income. For example, the company recorded revenue on shipments of disk drives that customers had not ordered and counted as sales for 1986 certain shipments that really took place early in fiscal 1987. The company also recorded inadequate reserves for customer returns and uncollectible accounts and took other steps to increase net income, including the spreading of costs over future years that should have been expensed immediately and the reduction in a reserve for employee bonuses.

Our focus is on the steps taken by MiniScribe to boost 1986 revenue and net income through inappropriate revenue recognition practices and insufficient reserves for returns and uncollectible accounts. Selected information from the company's annual account balances for the fiscal years ended December 31, 1985 and 1986, are provided in Exhibit 8.7.

In its annual report, the company also provided the following revenue recognition and inventory reserve policy notes:

> Revenue is generally recognized upon shipment of products to customers. A reserve for gross margins has been recorded based upon inventory levels at distributors.[47]
>
> In 1985, the company increased its reserve for excess inventory as a result of a general decline in the demand for micro-Winchester drives and severe price competition. In 1986, this reserve was reduced by $2.1 million as a result of a general improvement in demand and the ability of the Company to sell the inventory at higher prices than had been anticipated.[48]

On the surface, the financial results reported for fiscal 1986 provide much reason for optimism. In reviewing Exhibit 8.7, we note that in 1986 net sales increased 62%; gross margin, or gross profit as a percent of net sales, improved to over 25% from about 2%; and the company reported significant net income after a sizable loss the previous year. There was, however, plenty of information here to give the careful financial statement reader reason to be concerned.

The company's revenue recognition note specified that revenue was recognized at the time of shipment. Given the high-tech nature of the company's product line, returns could potentially be very high. The earnings impact of these returns was accounted for by providing a "reserve for gross margins." That is, an estimate of the gross profit associated with potential returned merchandise was charged against earnings through an increase in cost of sales and a reduction in inventory. This reserve for excess inventory was increased or decreased based on inventory levels at the company's distributors. An underestimate of the sales return implications of in-

Exhibit 8.7 MiniScribe Corp., Selected Account Balances, Years Ending December 31, 1985 and 1986 (thousands of dollars)

	1985	1986
Net sales	$113,951	$184,861
Cost of sales	111,445	137,936
Gross profit	$ 2,506	$ 46,925
Net income (loss)	$(16,773)	$ 22,711
Accounts receivable	$ 16,793	$ 40,502
Less: Allowance for doubtful accounts	752	736
Accounts receivable, net	$ 16,041	$ 39,766
Inventories	$ 22,501	$ 45,106

Source: MiniScribe Corp., annual report, December 1986.

ventory levels at these distributors would result in an overstatement of gross profit and net income.

The company stated that in 1985, the reserve for excess inventory was increased because of declining demand and severe price competition. As a result of an increase in this reserve, gross profit suffered that year. According to the company, conditions improved markedly in 1986. Returns were predicted to fall below prior-year levels and a smaller excess inventory reserve was needed. The reduction in the reserve added $2.1 million to gross profit in 1986. However, other account balances provided a story that was inconsistent with the rosy conditions highlighted in this inventory reserve footnote.

Exhibit 8.7 indicates that while net sales increased 62% in 1986, accounts receivable increased 141%, pushing A/R days to 77 days from 51. If the shipments reflected in sales were valid, the company should have enforceable claims against its customers. The explosion in accounts receivable suggests this may not be the case. Note too that while accounts receivable was increasing, the company's estimate of uncollectible accounts was being reduced. As a percent of gross accounts receivable, the allowance for doubtful accounts was reduced to just under 2% in 1986 from approximately 4.5% in 1985.

Also of concern is the inventory balance. Normally, inventory would not play a direct role in a fiction involving revenue recognition. It did in the MiniScribe case because of the approach used by the company to account for returns. That is, rather than netting returns from sales and accounts receivable, the company provided for returns with a charge against cost of sales and a reduction in inventory. Inventory was reported net of that reserve for returns. If the correct level of returns were accounted for, this approach would provide an appropriate measure of gross profit, net income, and current assets. The significant growth in inventory suggests, however, that a sufficient reserve for returns was not being provided. In 1986 inventory increased over 100%. Inventory days, calculated as inventory divided by cost of sales per day (cost of sales divided by 360) increased to 118 days from 73. Something was wrong. If demand, as stated by the company, were improving, inventory should not be increasing so rapidly.

The careful analyst would be concerned about the apparent inconsistencies noted in the MiniScribe disclosures provided for 1986. Growth in receivables and inventory did not reconcile with reported sales, gross profit, and net income. An explanation from management was needed, together with corroborating evidence from third parties. For example, management might attribute the high level of A/R days to a high level of shipments at year-end. Such shipments would show up in the ending balance of accounts receivable. Revenue calculated across the year, however, would understate the level of activity being experienced at year-end. As a result, A/R days would be skewed to the high side. Similarly, the high level of inventory days might be explained as the result of a buildup needed to meet anticipated increases in demand. Inquiries of one or two of the company's customers could corroborate the company's claims. For example, is demand for the company's disk drives improving? Similarly, are prices being charged rising? Finally, are customers planning to return fewer units than in the past? Such queries would quickly shed much light on the company's claims and provide sufficient time to avoid an impending earnings decline.

Example: Comptronix Corp.

Few financial frauds have involved as much active financial statement manipulation as did the financial chicanery attempted by the management of the electronics manufacturer Comptronix Corp. The financial fiction involved many financial statement accounts and was carried out with the involvement of several individuals. It lasted for a period that exceeded two years, from fiscal 1989 until late in the fiscal year ended December 31, 1992.

The fraud began around the time that the company lost a sizable customer and management decided to put in place a profit-boosting scheme rather than report income that would be displeasing to Wall Street. The plan began not with fictitious revenue, but with an artificial increase in gross profit achieved with an artificial addition to inventory. That is, the company simply recorded an increase in inventory and a reduction in cost of sales. The "adjustment," which was carried out regularly, usually on a monthly basis, increased current assets and gross profit. To help prevent an analyst from identifying unusual inventory growth as a potential problem area, management also moved some of the bogus inventory to the equipment account. Fake invoices for equipment purchases were prepared to make it appear as though equipment additions were actually being made. Phony sales were also recorded to reduce inventory and boost profits further. These sales were supported by fake accounts receivable. Finally, in order to show collections of accounts receivable that did not really occur, the company wrote checks payable to vendors for nonexistent equipment purchases. These checks were not endorsed by the equipment vendors and were actually deposited in the company's own bank account as a simultaneous increase and reduction in the cash account. No change in cash actually occurred. But the cash activity, an increase and a decrease, made it appear that accounts receivable were being collected and cash was being used to pay for equipment purchases. When asked about this unusual arrangement, which required participation by the company's bank, a bank spokesperson said the deposit arrangement was "used to accomplish a legitimate business purpose" when a customer for the company's electronics equipment was also a vendor.[49] If an equipment vendor to Comptronix was also a Comptronix customer, a special account at the bank was used to "reconcile the difference."[50] That is, Comptronix wrote a check, which was then used to post activity to both companies' accounts, that of Comptronix and its customer. When the activity was posted to the accounts of Comptronix, the company was able to show an increase in cash and a reduction in accounts receivable for the collection, and then a reduction in cash and an increase in equipment for the equipment purchase.

It is clear that Comptronix management was aware of how the analysis of certain financial statement accounts might raise difficult questions about the company's performance. In particular, the managers were concerned about overstatement of accounts receivable and inventory. By parking overstatements of at least a portion of these accounts in the equipment account, management hoped to reduce, if not eliminate, such inquiries. Exhibit 8.8 presents selected account balances for Comptronix for the five years leading up to and including December 31, 1991.

Among the information provided in Exhibit 8.8, data for 1987 and 1988 were reported by the company before the financial fraud. The years 1989, 1990, and 1991 include fraudulent amounts and were reported prior to discovery of the fraud in 1992. The information presents an interesting picture of a profitable, high-growth company. For example, net sales increased at a compound annual rate of 64% between 1987 and 1991, while over that same period, net income increased at a compound annual rate of 101%.

A casual review of Exhibit 8.8 provides little to suggest the presence of misreported amounts, though there are some potential signs. Consider, for example, accounts receivable, inventory, and accounts payable. In 1991, accounts receivable was little changed, even while net sales increased nearly $32 million that year. One explanation is that these increased sales were for cash. The company was not likely making cash sales. Another explanation, short of calling the unusual account balance change a financial fiction, was that in 1991 the company addressed problems with customer accounts that had developed in 1990. Looking at two other accounts, in 1991, accounts payable was also little changed, even as inventory increased nearly $8 million. Because inventory is typically purchased on open account, the inventory and accounts payable balances tend to move in tandem. A sizable increase in inventory with no accompanying change in accounts payable suggests the unlikely possibility that the company was paying for inventory with cash. Again, short of calling the increase in inventory a fictional event, the company may have been paying accounts too slowly in 1990 and addressed that situation in 1991. In hindsight, we know

Exhibit 8.8   Comptronix Corp., Selected Account Balances as Originally Reported, Years Ending December 31, 1987–1991 (thousands of dollars)

	1987	1988	1989	1990	1991
Net sales	$14,251	$29,255	$42,420	$70,229	$102,026
Cost of sales	12,187	24,943	36,726	59,330	85,404
Gross profit	$ 2,064	$ 4,312	$ 5,694	$ 10,899	$16,622
Net income	$311	$ 1,020	$ 1,470	$ 3,028	$ 5,071
Accounts receivable	$ 2,139	$ 9,310	$ 4,704	$12,013	$ 12,625
Inventory	$ 3,669	$ 8,963	$ 7,481	$20,660	$ 28,532
Property, plant, and equipment, net	$ 4,497	$ 7,075	$18,804	$26,627	$ 38,720
Accounts payable	$ 1,114	7,287	$ 3,360	$ 8,445	$ 8,531

Source: Data obtained from Disclosure, Inc., *Compact D/SEC: Corporate Information on Public Companies Filing with the SEC* (Bethesda, Md.: Disclosure, Inc., December 1992). Amounts reported are before restatement for fraud-related inaccuracies.

that some of the balances reported in Exhibit 8.8 were fictitious and potential explanations ring hollow. In an effort to find other signs of fictitious reporting, selected statistics calculated using the information provided in Exhibit 8.8 are reported in Exhibit 8.9.

In first reviewing the statistics in Exhibit 8.9, it is clear that company management took great care to cover its tracks. Given the pervasive nature of the fraud that had been carried out, there are not as many signs of its existence as one might expect. For example, earlier it was noted that the small increase in accounts receivable in 1991, given a $32 million increase in net sales that year, was suspect. In Exhibit 8.9 year-to-year changes in accounts receivable do not match well the increases in net sales in any of the years. However, when one considers A/R days, the account bal-

Exhibit 8.9   Comptronix Corp., Selected Statistics, Years Ending December 31, 1987–1991

	1987	1988	1989	1990	1991
Percent increase in net sales	–	105%	45%	66%	45%
Percent increase (decrease) in A/R	–	335%	(49)%	155%	5%
A/R days	54	115	40	62	45
A/R days, industry average	55	54	52	51	49
Percent increase (decrease) in inventory	–	144%	(17)%	176%	38%
Inventory days	108	129	73	125	120
Inventory days, industry average	78	79	79	74	76
Net sales divided by property, plant, and equipment, net	3.2	4.1	2.3	2.6	2.6
Net sales divided by property, plant, and equipment, net, industry average	7.3	8.5	8.6	8.9	8.5
Net sales divided by property, plant, and equipment, net, industry 75th percentile	3.7	4.7	5.0	4.7	4.8
Percent increase (decrease) in AP	–	554%	(54)%	151%	1%
A/P days[a]	33	105	33	51	36
A/P days, industry average	38	34	33	33	34

Source: Statistics calculated from data provided in Exhibit 8.8. Industry statistics taken from Robert Morris Associates, *Annual Statement Studies* (Philadelphia: Robert Morris Associates, 1992), pp. 164–165.
[a]Accounts payable days, or accounts payable divided by cost of sales per day.

ance changes do not seem so questionable. That is, during the fraud years of 1989, 1990, and 1991, A/R days hovered near the industry average. Similarly, as noted earlier, accounts payable changed very little in 1991 as inventory increased about $8 million. Once again, when viewed in context of other fraud years, the company's A/P days was never much out of line with the industry average.

According to the statistics provided in Exhibit 8.9, the company did appear to be carrying a higher level of inventory than one would expect. Note that while the industry average for inventory days tended to hover in the high 70's, Comptronix often took around 120 days to move inventory. A surplus inventory does not make sense for a high-growth firm. One would expect such a firm to have the opposite problem, difficulty in meeting demand. At a minimum, management should have been questioned about the inventory.

As noted earlier, when sales grow extremely fast and are booked late in a fiscal year, the inventory days statistic computed using annual amounts can be biased on the high side. Calculating it using the most recent month's or quarter's sales figures, rather than an annual amount, can adjust for this bias. We recalculated inventory days using quarterly net sales for each of the March, June, September, and December 1991 quarters. Monthly data were not available. We found the inventory days figure to hover in the 102–136 range, still very high by industry standards.

One statistic in Exhibit 8.9 stands out as being especially questionable. It is net sales divided by net property, plant, and equipment. Note that in the fraud years, 1989, 1990, and 1991, this figure for Comptronix ranged between 2.3 and 2.6, down from 4.1 in 1988. During this period, the industry average ranged between 8.5 and 8.9. While a heavy investment in land or buildings would skew this statistic to the low side, the bulk of the company's investment in property, plant, and equipment was in equipment. Thus, Comptronix appeared to have over three times the equipment of the average firm, and nearly twice as much as the low end in the industry, the 75th percentile. Interestingly, this is the opposite problem noted in Flight International discussed earlier. That company had more charter revenue than its planes could reasonably produce. Because the management of Comptronix had moved fictitious inventory and collections for fictitious sales to the property, plant, and equipment account, that account balance had become overstated.

What is clear from the Comptronix case is that when a company overstates revenue, one or more accounts on the balance sheet must also be overstated. Because cash is so easy to verify, that account will typically not be misstated. Accounts receivable is a likely target. Accounts receivable recorded this way will increase faster than revenue and lead to a buildup in A/R days. Inventory is another possibility, but much like accounts receivable, falsely reporting inventory will result in inventory increases that exceed increases in revenue and inventory days that give the appearance of slow-moving goods. Moreover, fictitious inventory that is not accompanied by a similar misstatement of accounts payable will give the impression of inventory purchases that are paid for with cash. The property, plant, and equipment account is less sensitive to detection of misstatement. When revenue is fictitiously recorded, a company can hide fraudulent amounts there for longer periods. Financial statement readers should be cautious and seek clear explanations when property, plant, and equipment appear out of line relative to revenue.

Because the Comptronix fraud has now been cleaned up, we have company account balances available that have been restated to remove any fraudulent effects. These corrected balances can be used to identify specifically the financial statement effect of the company's fraudulent activity. Selected restated account balances and statistics are provided in Exhibit 8.10.

In Exhibit 8.10, note that while net sales are still up, their growth is not as phenomenal as had been previously reported. In 1989, 1990, and 1991, the company inflated net sales by $5,145,000, $6,785,000, and $13,272,000, respectively. Apparently, each year, the amount by which net sales was inflated had to increase to give the impression of continuing high growth. With an accompanying understatement of cost of sales, the company overstated gross profit by $5,814,000, $7,823,000, and $11,603,000 in 1989, 1990, and 1991, respectively.

Interestingly, accounts receivable as restated is no different than originally reported. A/R days are a bit higher, however, because of the reduction in net sales. Similarly, restated accounts payable is only slightly different than the amounts originally reported.

The two balance sheet accounts that were affected most by the company's fraud were inventory and property, plant, and equipment. Over the years 1989, 1990, and

Exhibit 8.10 Comptronix Corp., Selected Account Balances and Statistics as Restated, Years Ending December 31, 1987–1991 (dollar amounts in thousands)

	1987	1988	1989	1990	1991
Net sales	$14,251	$29,255	$37,275	$63,444	$88,754
Cost of sales	12,187	24,943	37,395	60,368	83,735
Gross profit	$ 2,064	$ 4,312	$ (120)	$ 3,076	$ 5,019
Percent increase in net sales	–	105%	27%	70%	40%
Net income (loss)	$ 311	$ 1,020	$(3,524)	$(3,647)	$(3,225)
Accounts receivable[a]	$ 2,139	$ 9,310	$ 4,704	$12,013	$12,625
A/R days	54	115	45	68	51
Inventory	$ 3,669	$ 8,963	$ 7,175	$17,926	$21,271
Inventory days	108	129	69	107	91
Property, plant, and equipment, net	$ 4,497	$ 7,075	$13,856	$15,846	$20,303
Net sales divided by property, plant, and equipment, net	3.2	4.1	2.7	4.0	4.4
Accounts payable	$ 1,114	$ 7,287	$ 3,752	$ 9,102	$ 8,531
A/P days	33	105	36	54	37

Source: Comptronix Corp., annual report, December 1992, pp. 17–18.
[a] Accounts receivable were unchanged from amounts originally reported.

1991, inventory was overstated by $306,000, $2,734,000, and $7,261,000, respectively. Restated inventory days, while still high, were reduced considerably and were much closer to inventory averages. During those same years, net property, plant, and equipment was overstated by $4,948,000, $10,781,000, and $18,417,000, respectively. Once restated, net sales divided by net property, plant, and equipment was still low by industry standards but close to the 75th percentile.

When carefully executed with collusion among management personnel, financial frauds are difficult to uncover. This was seen in the Comptronix case, which surprised many investors and creditors. After learning of the fraud, one analyst who followed the company noted, "I've spent nearly 3 $1/2$ years covering this company. . . . I'm completely washed out right now."[51] Still, it is clear that even the best fraud leaves some tracks in the financial statements. A careful reading of them with pointed questions of management when selected amounts seem out of line would go far toward avoiding an earnings surprise by alerting the reader that something was potentially wrong.

RECOGNIZING REVENUE UNDER LONG-TERM CONTRACTS

Long-term contracts involve revenue recognition under special circumstances. Because of its special and technical nature, the subject is addressed here separately. Further technical background is available in the appendix.

We refer here to long-term contracts in the construction industry, such as those of general building, heavy earth moving, dredging, demolition, and specialty contracts such as mechanical, electrical, paving, and environmental. Also included are contracts to design and build ships or transport vessels; to design, develop, manufacture, or modify complex aerospace or electronic equipment; and contracts for services performed by architects, engineers, or architectural design firms. Excluded from this section are sales by manufacturers of goods produced in standard manufacturing operations; sales or supply contracts to provide goods from inventory or from homogeneous, continuing production; service contracts of health clubs, correspondence schools, and similar consumer-oriented organizations that provide their services over extended periods of time; and magazine subscriptions.

Two alternatives are available for recognizing revenue under long-term contracts: the percentage-of-completion method and the completed-contract method. The first method, percentage-of-completion, is used when the contractor can make reasonably dependable estimates of the extent of progress toward completion, contract revenue, and contract costs. This is the preferred method, assuming the contract clearly specifies the enforceable rights and obligations of all parties, the consideration to be exchanged, and the manner and terms of settlement, and that all parties to the contract can be expected to perform their contractual obligations. The completed-contract method is, in effect, the default method, used in cases where the conditions for use of the percentage-of-completion method are not met.

Under the percentage-of-completion method, revenue is recognized as progress toward completion of the contract is made. Progress provides a measure of the earnings process, permitting recognition of revenue as it is earned. It might be measured in different ways, for example, based on labor hours worked, direct materials employed, or machine hours logged. However, costs incurred as a percentage of total estimated contract costs is the most commonly used measure of progress toward completion. Consider, for example, the following policy note from the annual report of Serv-Tech, Inc., an oil-service contractor:

> Revenues from fixed-price and modified fixed-price contracts are recognized on the percentage-of-completion method, measured primarily by the percentage of costs incurred to date to estimated total costs for each contract. This method is used because management considers total costs to be the best available measure of progress on the contracts.
>
> Contract costs include all direct material and labor costs and those indirect costs related to contract performance, such as indirect labor, supplies, tools, and repairs.[52]

Under the completed-contract method, no revenue is recognized until the contract is complete. It is only at completion that the contractor can be certain of the amount of revenue earned under the contract. In its 1985 report, Wedtech, Inc., a defense contractor, provided the following revenue recognition note:

> Revenue under U.S. Government contracts in process are recognized under the percentage-of-completion method of accounting whereunder the estimated revenue is measured by the percentage that costs incurred to date bears to the latest estimated total costs of the contract less revenue recognized in previous periods.[53]

In subsequent developments surrounding the firm, certain members of Wedtech's management pleaded guilty to a scheme that included illegally inflating the company's earnings. As was later determined, the company improperly used percentage-of-completion accounting because its defense contracts could be unilaterally rescinded or reduced in size. If Wedtech had recognized revenue on a contract that was later reduced in size, the firm would have been forced to reverse some of the revenue previously recorded. Given the nature of the contracts it was party to with the U.S. government, Wedtech should have been using the completed-contract method. With this method the company would not have run the risk of having to reverse previously recognized revenue because no revenue would have been recorded until the project was complete and all the facts of the case were known.

Our discussion of revenue recognition under long-term contracts focuses on the percentage-of-completion method. It is much more prevalent than completed-contract accounting and, given the estimates that are employed in its application, can potentially result in sizable earnings surprises.

Under the percentage-of-completion method, cumulative contract revenue is calculated by multiplying total contract price by the percent of contract completion. Using contract costs, the percent of contract completion is measured by dividing contract costs incurred by total estimated contract costs. Cumulative contract revenue is thus computed as follows:

$$\text{Cumulative contract revenue} = \text{Total contract price} \times \frac{\text{Contract costs incurred}}{\text{Total estimated contract costs}}$$

Revenue for any one period is computed by subtracting revenue recognized on the contract in prior periods from this cumulative contract revenue.

In examining the formula for cumulative contract revenue, it should be noted that the percent of contract completion, contract costs incurred divided by total estimated contract costs, is increased, permitting revenue recognition, in one of two ways. It is increased either through cost incurrence, the formula's numerator, or by changing total estimated contract costs, the denominator. Thus, simply through incurring costs, it is possible to record an increased percent of contract completion and contract revenue. As a guard against premature recognition of contract revenue due to, for example, cost overruns, total estimated contract costs must be continually reviewed and revised. These revisions alter the completion percentage and potentially lead to the reporting of contract losses when revenue recognized in prior periods exceeds cumulative contract revenue. These losses are to be reported as soon as they become known. Consider the following Serv-Tech, Inc., disclosure:

> Provisions for estimated losses on uncompleted contracts are made in the period in which such losses are determined. Changes in job performance, job conditions, and estimated profitability may result in revisions to costs and income, which are recognized in the period in which the revisions are determined.[54]

Thus, because of the importance of estimates in determining the percent of contract completion, employment of the percentage-of-completion method lends a tentative quality to contract revenue. Reported amounts are always subject to adjustment. Moreover, this extensive use of estimates means that contract revenue is open to manipulation by unscrupulous managements.

While contract revenue recognition is based on costs incurred, customer billings are based on contract specifications and physical completion benchmarks. As a result, contract revenue recognized will typically differ from amounts billed. For example, a construction contract for a building might specify that the building is 15% complete, permitting billing of 15% of the contract price, when the architectural work is complete, the land is graded, and the foundation is poured. At that point, the company may have incurred more or less than 15% of total costs, resulting in revenue recognition that differs from the amount billed.

When contract revenue is recognized in excess of customer billings, the excess is reported as a current asset, titled either "costs plus estimated gross profit in excess of billings" or, more simply, "unbilled receivables." Both titles are consistent with the notion that the contractor has a receivable for revenue earned and recognized in excess of amounts billed. The asset classification indicates that progress toward completion for accounting purposes, which is based on costs incurred, is more advanced than amounts recovered through billings based on physical completion tied to contract benchmarks. When customer billings exceed contract revenue recognized, the excess is reported as a current liability, titled either "billings in excess of costs plus estimated gross profit" or "deferred revenue." Here the contractor has unearned income for amounts billed in excess of amounts earned. The liability classification indicates that amounts recovered through billings based on physical completion tied to contract benchmarks are more advanced than progress toward completion for accounting purposes based on costs incurred.

The following note comes from the Serv-Tech disclosures. Except for use of the term *estimated earnings* in place of *estimated gross profit*, the terminology is the same as that just described:

> The asset "costs and estimated earnings in excess of billings on uncompleted contracts" represents revenues recognized in excess of amounts billed. The liability "billing in excess of costs and estimated earnings on uncompleted contracts" represents billings in excess of revenues recognized.[55]

Gundle Environmental Systems, Inc., provides a descriptive revenue recognition policy note for long-term contracts:

> Revenues from installation contracts are recognized on the percentage-of-completion method, measured by the percentage of lining material deployed and installed to date to the total estimated lining material to be installed for each contract. Management considers this method to be the best available measure of progress on these contracts.[56]

Gundle Environmental manufactures and installs lining material used to help ensure the environmental integrity of landfill sites. Because the volume of material used in the installation process provides a valid measure of progress toward completion, management uses it, rather than costs incurred, for this purpose.

Exhibit 8.11 provides a summary for Gundle Environmental of the costs incurred on contracts in process, estimated earnings recognized, and the overbilled and underbilled status of its contracts at fiscal year-end.

At year-end 1994, cumulative contract revenue was $26,809,000, consisting of costs incurred of $24,447,000 plus estimated earnings or gross profit of $2,362,000. Of this cumulative revenue amount, $25,301,000 had been billed, leaving $1,508,000 unbilled on all contracts. The $1,508,000 is a net figure, composed of $2,025,000 for contracts on which costs and estimated earnings exceeded billings and $517,000 for contracts for which billings exceeded cost and estimated earnings.

For Gundle Environmental, costs and estimated earnings in excess of billings (net) or unbilled receivables, made up 9% and 6% of cumulative in-process contract revenue at March 31, 1993 and 1994, respectively. That is, at the end of fiscal 1994, a greater proportion of the company's cumulative contract revenue had been trans-

Exhibit 8.11 Summary of Overbilled and Underbilled Contracts: Gundle Environmental Systems, Inc., at March 31, 1993 and 1994 (thousands of dollars)

	1993	1994
Costs incurred on contracts in progress	$17,872	$24,447
Estimated earnings, net of losses	2,489	2,362
	20,361	26,809
Less: Billings to date	18,583	25,301
	$1,778	$ 1,508
Included in the accompanying balance sheet under the following captions:		
Costs and estimated earnings in excess of billings on contracts in progress	$ 2,075	$ 2,025
Billings in excess of costs and estimated earnings on contracts in progress	(297)	(517)
	$ 1,778	$ 1,508

Source: Gundle Environmental Systems, Inc., annual report, March 1994, p. 20.

lated into physical completion as represented by amounts billed than at the end of fiscal 1993. As will be seen in subsequent illustrations, these proportions, and the relations between underbilled and overbilled contract amounts should be carefully monitored. While not the case with Gundle, it is potentially a cause for concern when unbilled receivables compose an increasing proportion of cumulative contract revenue. Consider, for example, the case of Dycom Industries, Inc.

Exhibit 8.12 provides a summary of Dycom Industries' overbilled and underbilled contracts at fiscal year.

Note that at year-end 1990, unbilled receivables of $11,112,255 grew to 24% of cumulative in-process contract revenue of $46,999,891. This was an increase from 13% of cumulative in-process contract revenue in 1989. In addition, unbilled receivables grew at a rate of 66% in 1990, which was faster than the 39% rate of revenue increase for the year.[57] As a result of costs incurred, the company recognized revenue at a rate faster than contract benchmarks have enabled it to bill. Such a development was likely appropriate given the company's contracts, cost activity, and billing cycle. Moreover, the increase in unbilled receivables was an insignificant 3% of total revenue recognized that year. However, taking note of unbilled receivables as a percent of cumulative contract revenue, and of the percent change in unbilled receivables as compared with the percent change in contract revenue, is important in ensuring a company is not experiencing significant cost overruns or misapplying the percentage-of-completion method. Stirling Homex Corp. is a case in point.

Stirling Homex provides a good example of how the percentage-of-completion method can be abused, permitting revenue recognition even as contract problems or completion benchmarks prohibit recovery of costs incurred through billing. Though the case dates to the early 1970s, its lessons are still valid.

Exhibit 8.12   Summary of Overbilled and Underbilled Contracts: Dycom Industries, Inc., 1989 and 1990

	1989	1990
Costs incurred on contracts in progress	$44,201,458	$39,414,332
Estimated earnings thereon	8,203,203	7,585,559
	52,404,661	46,999,891
Less: Billings to date	45,722,695	35,887,636
	$ 6,681,966	$11,112,255
Included in the accompanying balance sheets under the following captions:		
Costs and estimated earnings in excess of billings	$ 7,188,611	$11,787,317
Billings in excess of costs and estimated earnings	(506,645)	(675,062)
	$ 6,681,966	$11,112,255

Source: Dycom Industries, Inc., annual report, July 1990. Data obtained from Disclosure, Inc., *Compact D/SEC: Corporate Information on Public Companies Filing with the SEC* (Bethesda, Md.: Disclosure, Inc., December 1992).

Stirling Homex Corp. manufactured and installed modular housing units under contract for the Department of Housing and Urban Development. The company employed percentage-of-completion accounting and commenced profit recognition on modular home contracts when units were assigned to specific purchase contracts. In the year ended July 31, 1971, company revenue was up 63% and net income had increased 60% from the previous year. A careful examination of the balance sheet, however, showed an alarming increase in unbilled receivables.

At fiscal year-end 1971, the company was reporting unbilled receivables, or cost incurred plus estimated gross profit in excess of billings, in three different places. The details are presented in Exhibit 8.13. In the consolidated balance sheet, unbilled receivables were included with both current assets and noncurrent assets. In addition, the company included unbilled receivables with the assets of an unconsolidated financing subsidiary, which was reported on its balance sheet as an investment. During 1971 total unbilled receivables increased $28,651,654, to $33,278,024 from $4,626,370 in 1970.

Recall that the percentage-of-completion method permits revenue recognition on the basis of costs incurred. Billings are based on physical completion benchmarks as identified in the contract. When revenue is recognized that is not billed, the balance in unbilled receivables increases. Usually, there are valid reasons for the increase, such as the timing of cost incurrence and billing. It is possible, however, that unusual increases in unbilled receivables are due to cost overruns that are not billed, or to the potential misapplication of the percentage-of-completion method. For example, estimates of total contract costs may be misstated, resulting in an incorrect percentage of completion. As a result, unbilled receivables will make up a higher percentage of cumulative contract revenue, and the rate of growth in unbilled receiv-

Exhibit 8.13 Unbilled Receivables: Stirling Homex Corp., Years Ending July 31, 1970 and 1971 (thousands of dollars)

	1970	1971
Current assets: Unbilled contract receivables	$4,626,370	$24,633,799
Noncurrent assets: Long-term portion of contract receivables—unbilled	–	$ 3,694,225
Investment in unconsolidated subsidiary: Accounts receivable—unbilled	–	$ 4,950,000
Total unbilled receivables	$4,626,370	$33,278,024

Source: Stirling Homex Corp, annual report, July 1971.

ables will exceed the rate of growth in contract revenue. When such developments are noted, satisfactory explanations should be obtained.

In the case of Stirling Homex, data were not available to calculate unbilled receivables as a percent of cumulative contract revenue. We were, however, able to compare the percent increase in unbilled receivables with the percent growth in contract revenue. During 1971 total unbilled receivables increased 619%. That year, contract revenue was up approximately 63%. The rapid increase in unbilled receivables relative to the growth in contract revenue was clearly a sign for concern.

Stirling Homex filed for bankruptcy in July 1972. As the story unfolded, it was determined that the company was storing over 9,000 completed modular homes, worth over $35 million, in open fields in several states awaiting customer purchases that never came. Later it was learned that the company's contracts were little more than unenforceable letters of intent to buy. The company could not bill its customers because it had no valid claim on which to enforce payment. It continued manufacturing the housing units, incurring costs, and under the percentage-of-completion method, recognizing revenue. In the absence of billing, unbilled receivables continued to grow.

Had Stirling Homex employed the completed-contract method, revenue recognition would have been postponed until the company had realizable, enforceable contracts. With this method, revenue overstatement would have been avoided. Instead of recording unbilled receivables, costs incurred on manufacturing would have been carried as unsold inventory.

INCENTIVES FOR OVERSTATED REVENUE

There are many reasons a firm's management may choose to employ recognition practices that overstate revenue. Obvious ones include the following:

- Higher management compensation resulting from bonuses tied to reported earnings

- Higher stock price resulting in reduced cost of equity capital, and for management, increased market value of ownership stakes in company shares and options
- More slack in debt covenants from higher earnings, working capital, retained earnings, and stockholders' equity
- Lower apparent firm risk due to higher reported equity, resulting in reduced cost of debt capital

There may also be a hidden agenda beyond the obvious direct benefits of overstated revenue. Higher current revenue and accompanying earnings can mask a multitude of operating sins, helping to paper over weak financial performance until better times arrive. One must question whether such better times will actually arrive. By overstating revenue, management may be able to postpone difficult decisions that should be faced. These difficult decisions may include responses to questions such as the following:

- Have changes in customer tastes, or new, more intense competition fundamentally altered demand for the company's products or services?
- Have the operating environment and cost structure of the company changed, necessitating important adjustments in company operations?
- Are production inefficiencies necessitating cost control and new investment in state-of-the-art production technology?
- Are operating inefficiencies necessitating reductions in selling, general, and administrative expense?

The failure to face difficult decisions early may have ominous long-term consequences. Solid, financially secure, profitable companies with bright futures and growing demand need not take steps to overstate revenue.

SUMMARY

To be recognized, revenue must be earned and realized or realizable. As the nature of revenue transactions differ, the definition of earned and realized or realizable can vary markedly, affecting the timing of revenue recognition. While accounting standards provide considerable guidance for some industries, determining when to recognize revenue in others depends greatly on management judgment. In most situations, that judgment is properly applied and revenue is recognized appropriately. There are situations, however, where that judgment can be questioned.

When revenue is recognized prematurely, transactions that will likely be fully realized are taken into account early. With fictitious revenue, amounts are recorded without regard to even the existence of a transaction. Corporate earnings are directly dependent on the amount of revenue recognized. Whether revenue is recognized that is premature or fictitious, the stage is set for an earnings surprise when the true facts of the situation become known.

The careful financial statement reader will take steps to assess the likelihood that revenue is not overstated. The checklist in Exhibit 8.14 is designed to be a memory jogger to help the investor or creditor judge the likelihood that financial statements include overstated revenue that might result in a material, negative earnings surprise. Checklist questions are designed to be thought-provoking, forcing the financial statement reader to consider all aspects of the financial statements and footnotes. Most of the questions require a very short answer, sometimes only a yes or no.

Using examples provided in the chapter, it should be clear with each question which response is indicative of an increased potential for overstated revenue. While the questions are not specifically designed to provide potential dollar amounts of earnings surprises, in those cases where dollar amounts are deemed appropriate, they can be derived using points raised in the chapter in combination with the circumstances that exist in the situation under review.

Cursory use of the checklist will not suffice. Each question must be considered in detail. The chapter should be reviewed if the implications of a particular question for detecting overstated revenue are not understood.

While the checklist is useful in identifying situations of increased likelihood of overstated revenue, it should not be viewed as an all-encompassing, fool-proof test. Rather, it is a single tool in a larger arsenal used in a careful financial statement review program.

Exhibit 8.14 Checklist for Financial Early Warnings: Overstated Revenue

A. What is the company's revenue recognition policy?
   1. Before delivery or performance?
      a. Is it really earned?
   2. At delivery or performance?
      a. Is there a right of return or price protection?
         i. Has the company provided adequately for returns or price adjustments?
      b. Does the company offer separate letters offering the right of return or price protection not contained in the actual sale contract?
   3. After delivery or performance and full customer acceptance?
B. Was there a change in the revenue recognition policy?
   1. Did the change result in earlier revenue recognition?
C. Are there any unusual changes in revenue reported in recent quarters?
   1. What is revenue for each of the last four to six quarters?
   2. Does any one quarter show unusual activity not explained by seasonal factors?
   3. How do quarterly changes in revenue compare with the industry or selected competitors?
D. Does the company have the physical capacity to generate the revenue reported?
   1. What is revenue per appropriate measure of physical capacity for each of the last four to six quarters?

Exhibit 8.14   *(continued)*

2. How does the company compare with the industry or with selected competitors?
   a. Possible measures of revenue per physical capacity:
      i. Revenue per employee
      ii. Revenue per dollar of fixed assets
      iii. Revenue per dollar of total assets
E. Are there signs of overstated accounts receivable?
   1. Compare the percentage rate of change in accounts receivable with the percentage rate of change in revenue for each of the last four to six quarters.
      a. What are the implications of differences in the rates of change in accounts receivable and revenue?
   2. Compute A/R days for each of the last four to six quarters.
      a. What are the implications of changes noted in A/R days over the last four to six quarters?
      b. How does the absolute level of A/R days and changes therein compare with the industry and selected competitors?
F. Does the company use the percentage-of-completion method for long-term contracts?
   1. Is management experienced in applying the method?
   2. Has the company reported losses in prior years from cost overruns?
   3. Depending on data availability, compute unbilled receivables as a percentage of cumulative contract revenue for each of the last four to six quarters.
      a. What are the implications of the percentage and its trend?
   4. Compare the percentage rate of change in unbilled receivables with the percentage rate of change in contract revenue for each of the last four to six quarters.
      a. What are the implications of differences between the rates of change in unbilled receivables and contract revenue?

Note: Where the checklist requires calculations using financial statement amounts, quarterly data are recommended in order to achieve a more timely identification of overstated revenue.

For firms with strong seasonal activity, quarterly amounts should be compared with amounts for the same quarter in the previous year.

For some contractors, quarterly data may give misleading signals. For example, certain key contract benchmarks may not have been met during the quarter, limiting amounts billed over that short of a time frame.

If quarterly data are not available, or if quarterly data give misleading signals, annual data can be used. Three or more years of data should provide a sufficient number of data points to get a meaningful indicator of potential problems.

ENDNOTES

1. *The Wall Street Journal*, November 15,1994, p. A10.
2. General accounting guidance on the definition, measurement, and reporting of revenues and gains is provided in Statement of Financial Accounting Concepts No. 5,

"Recognition and Measurement in Financial Statements of Business Enterprises" (Stamford, Conn.: Financial Accounting Standards Board, December 1984), and Statement of Financial Accounting Concepts No. 6, "Elements of Financial Statements (December 1985).

3. BMC Software, Inc., annual report, March 1991, p. 42.
4. Autodesk, Inc., annual report, January 1992, p. 28.
5. Computer Associates International, Inc., Annual report, March 1992, p. 20.
6. Statement of Position 91-1, "Software Revenue Recognition" (New York: American Institute of Certified Public Accountants, 1991).
7. BMC Software, Inc., annual report, March 1994. Information obtained from Disclosure, Inc., *Compact D/SEC: Corporate Information on Public Companies Filing with the SEC* (Bethesda, Md.: Disclosure, Inc., March 1995).
8. American Software, Inc., annual report, April 1991, p. 39.
9. Ibid., p. 38.
10. This guidance for revenue recognition is provided in Statement of Financial Accounting Concepts No. 5, "Recognition and Measurement in Financial Statements of Business Enterprises" (December 1984).
11. The Leather Factory, Inc., annual report, December 1993, p. 16.
12. Sun Television and Appliances, Inc., annual report, February 1994, p. 10.
13. Borland International, Inc., Form 10-K annual report to the Securities and Exchange Commission, March 1993, p. 26.
14. Statement of Financial Accounting Standards No. 48, "Revenue Recognition When Right of Return Exists" (Stamford, Conn.: Financial Accounting Standards Board, 1981).
15. Thomas Nelson, Inc., annual reort, March 1994. Information obtained from Disclosure, Inc., *Compact D/SEC: Corporate Information on Public Companies Filing with the SEC* (Bethesda, Md.: Disclosure, Inc., March 1995).
16. Houghton Mifflin Co., annual report, December 1993. Information obtained from Disclosure, Inc., *Compact D/SEC: Corporate Information on Public Companies Filing with the SEC* (Bethesda, Md.: Disclosure, Inc., March 1995).
17. Big Rock Brewery Ltd., annual report, March 1994, p. 10.
18. Cypress Semiconductor, Inc., annual report, January 1994, p. 23.
19. International Business Machines Corp., annual report, December 1993, p. 36.
20. Amdahl Corp., annual report, December 1993, p. 18.
21. Omnicom Group, Inc., Form 10-K annual report to the Securities and Exchange Commission, December 1993, p. F-7.
22. The Multicare Companies, Inc., annual report, December 1993, p. 19.
23. Sun Television and Appliances, Inc., annual report, February 1994, p. 10.
24. Delta Air Lines, Inc., annual report, June 1993, p. 25.
25. Ibid, p. 25.
26. King World Productions, Inc., annual report, August 1991. Information obtained from Disclosure, Inc., *Compact D/SEC: Corporate Information on Public Companies Filing with the SEC* (Bethesda, Md.: Disclosure, Inc., March 1995).
27. International House of Pancakes, Inc., annual report, December 1993, p. 22.
28. Ibid, p. 6.
29. Right Management Consultants, Inc., annual report, December 1993. Information obtained from Disclosure, Inc., *Compact D/SEC: Corporate Information on Public Companies Filing with the SEC* (Bethesda, Md.: Disclosure, Inc., March 1995).

30. Home Nutritional Services, Inc., annual report, December 1991, p. 21.
31. Florida East Coast Industries, Inc., annual report, December 1993. Information obtained from Disclosure, Inc., *Compact D/SEC: Corporate Information on Public Companies Filing with the SEC* (Bethesda, Md.: Disclosure, Inc., March 1995).
32. *The Wall Street Journal*, November 8, 1994, p. B1.
33. PerSeptive Biosystems, Inc., annual report, September 1993, p. 26.
34. *The Wall Street Journal*, November 8, 1994, p. B1.
35. Ibid., p. B1.
36. Ibid., p. B1.
37. PerSeptive Biosystems, Inc., Form 10-K annual report to the Securities and Exchange Commission, September 1994, p. F-7.
38. Knowledgeware, Inc., annual report, June 1991, p. 29.
39. To simplify the calculations somewhat, we used a 360-day year.
40. Robert Morris Associates, *Annual Statement Studies* (Philadelphia: Robert Morris Associates, 1991), pp. 736–737.
41. The Topps Co., annual report, February 1992, p. 12.
42. Roula Khalaf, "Card Glut," *Forbes*, December 21, 1992, p. 89.
43. The Topps Co., press release, January 25, 1993.
44. Global Resources, Inc., annual report, December 1993, p. 22.
45. Ibid., p. 23.
46. Global Resources, Inc., press release, November 17, 1994.
47. MiniScribe Corp., Form 10-K annual report to the Securities Exchange Commission, December 1986, p. F-6.
48. Ibid, p. F-8.
49. *The Wall Street Journal*, December 14, 1992, p. B4.
50. Ibid., p. B4.
51. *The Wall Street Journal*, November 27, 1992, p. A3.
52. Serv-Tech, Inc., annual report, December 1993, p. 29.
53. Wedtech, Inc., Form 10-K annual report to the Securities Exchange Commission, December 31, 1985, p. 47.
54. Serv-Tech, Inc. annual report, December 1993, p. 29.
55. Ibid., p. 29.
56. Gundle Environmental Systems, Inc., annual report, March 1994, pp. 19–20.
57. The rate of revenue increase was calculated using revenue as reported on the income statement.

Chapter 9

Understated Expenses

This year's results will include a pre-tax charge of $2.1 million from a change in accounting, said Pat L. Ross, chief financial officer. Under that change, 50-Off [Stores, Inc.] wrote off all unamortized preopening store costs for the year in the just-ended fourth quarter. In the future, the company said it will write off preopening costs as incurred, rather than in the first 12 months, as it had been doing.[1]

In Chapter 8 our focus was on the early detection of overstated revenue. Our premise was that to the extent revenue is overstated, whether through premature or fictitious recognition, earnings are also overstated and subject to potential decline, and consequently, an earnings surprise. In this chapter, we direct our attention to expenses. In particular, we examine those expenses that begin as capitalized expenditures, or assets, and are subsequently charged to expense through amortization. Examples include such capitalized expenditures as preopening costs of retailers, costs incurred in developing landfill space, and software development costs. Managements capitalize these and many other similar expenditures under the premise that they will benefit future periods. In so doing, their effect on earnings is postponed to subsequent years.[2] In those situations where amortization has been insufficient, as in the 50-Off Stores, Inc., example, significant one-time charges to earnings must be taken.

Earnings that are calculated after excluding such capitalized expenditures are subject to unexpected declines in two situations. In the first, management is aggressive in its capitalization decision, reporting costs as assets that should have been expensed. Later, when it is determined that such expenditures carry no future benefit, they are written off with an accompanying income statement charge. In the second, the initial amount capitalized is appropriate, but the assumed benefit period is too long. Here again, earnings are subject to an additional charge when amounts that should have been expensed in previous years are written off.

Since our interest here is in assets that are subject to systematic amortization, we exclude understated expenses related to such assets as inventory and investments. Understated expenses associated with liabilities are also excluded. Both subjects are taken up in Chapter 10, Misreported Assets and Liabilities.

AGGRESSIVE COST CAPITALIZATION

For retailers and other establishments such as restaurants that sell goods and services directly to the public, store preopening costs, or costs incurred in preparing a new outlet for business, can be a significant component of operating expense. Such preopening costs include many types of expenditure. Typical examples are costs incurred in site selection, hiring and training of employees, preopening supplies and promotions. For one unnamed retailer, we learned that even the costs incurred in providing a grand-opening party were included in the preopening cost designation.

The extent to which these costs benefit future periods can be debated. There is clearly no consensus in practice. Consider the following accounting practices for store preopening costs taken from the accounting policy notes of selected retailers and restaurant companies.

From the annual report of Bob Evans Farms, Inc.:

> Expenditures related to the opening of new restaurants, other than those for capital assets, are charged to expense when incurred.[3]

From the annual report of Sun Television and Appliances, Inc.:

> Costs of opening new stores are capitalized and amortized on a straight-line basis over the twelve-month period following the store opening.[4]

From the annual report of Lechter's, Inc.:

> Preopening costs are capitalized and amortized over a period of 24 months from the date operations commenced.[5]

From the annual report of Cash America International, Inc.:

> Preopening costs associated with the establishment of new stores are capitalized and expensed over three years.[6]

From the annual report of Ryan's Family Steak Houses, Inc.:

> Preopening costs represent certain costs incurred before a restaurant is opened, primarily employee training costs, and are amortized straight line over a five-year period commencing the date the restaurant opens.[7]

In reviewing these accounting policies, it can be seen that there is much disagreement over how to account for preopening costs. Some companies take a somewhat conservative view and charge these costs to expense when incurred. Others are more aggressive and report them as assets, charging a portion of the amount capitalized to expense each year over an amortization period. As in the examples provided, these amortization periods might range to as much as five years. The longer the amortization period chosen, the lower the amount of annual expense reported. If it is later determined that the capitalized costs are not providing a future benefit, for example, if the new location is subsequently closed, any unamortized costs must be written off. The amount of the resulting charge to earnings for the closure is accordingly increased.

Consider, for example, the 50-Off Stores example referred to in the chapter opening quotation. In the company's January 1994 annual report, the following accounting policy change for preopening costs was announced:

> Effective at the beginning of fiscal 1994, the company changed its accounting policy for preopening store costs, which consist primarily of advertising, occupancy, and payroll expenses, to expense such costs as incurred. Prior to the change, the company capitalized such costs and amortized them over a twelve-month period following the month of store opening.[8]

On the company's January 1993 balance sheet, a total of $5,156,947 in capitalized preopening costs were carried as an asset, comprising 7% of total assets. In 1994, when the company changed its policy to one of expensing preopening costs, that $5,156,947 was written off, resulting in an after-tax charge of $3,403,585. Even before the write-off for store preopening costs, the company reported a loss of $5,512,261. Thus, there were already significant problems at the company. The decision to change its policy for preopening costs was arguably made to allow the company to put all its bad news in a single year and keep the $5,156,947 in preopening costs from reducing pre-tax earnings in its fiscal 1995. Whatever the reason for the change, the previous practice of cost capitalization resulted in an increased loss for fiscal 1994 and helped lead to an earnings announcement that surprised analysts.

An example of a company going in the other direction with its capitalization policy is Value Merchants, Inc. Consider the following statement:

> Included in prepaid expenses and other current assets at February 1, 1992, is $1,334,000 of preopening costs. The company changed its amortization period for store preopening costs from amortizing these costs over the remaining periods in the fiscal year in which new stores are opened to amortizing these costs over the first 12 months after new stores are opened.[9]

One can question why the company chose a new policy that leads to higher earnings and assets. Was it simply to provide an earnings boost? One cannot question, however, the earnings effect it provided. In the year ended February 1, 1992, the company's change in accounting for preopening costs added approximately 10% to pre-tax earnings.

Two of the companies previously mentioned also recently changed accounting policies for preopening costs. In its annual report for fiscal 1993, Lechter's made the following statement:

Prior to fiscal 1992, preopening costs were capitalized and amortized over a period of 24 months from the date operations commenced. Beginning with new stores opened in fiscal 1992, the company established an amortization period for these costs of twelve months.[10]

Similarly, in its 1993 annual report, Ryan's Family Steak Houses noted:

In 1992, the amortization period of preopening costs, which commences on the date a restaurant opens, was changed from five years to one year in order to better reflect the estimated period of the related economic benefits and to be more consistent with industry practice.[11]

These changes are consistent with a general reduction in the variation of accounting practice for preopening costs. That variation has not, however, been eliminated.

As can be seen, there are no hard-and-fast rules dictating accounting practice for store preopening costs. Such variations in practice, however, are not limited to preopening costs. Similar differences can be found with other items, such as expenditures incurred in developing landfill space or software development costs. We examine accounting practices in a representative sample of such costs. While our scope limits the number of such items we can address individually, the ones examined should provide the background needed to deal with all types of capitalized costs.

While specific accounting guidance can be found for certain costs such as software development, most direction as to whether to expense or capitalize cash expenditures is provided by the matching principle. This principle is very broad and provides ample room for the application of judgment. In addition, even in those situations where specific guidance can be found, there remains much room for management judgment and the reporting of differing results in situations that appear to be similar. Managements may take an aggressive or conservative stance regarding cost capitalization policies. Those that take an aggressive position report results more likely to yield an earnings surprise if subsequent developments move against them.

The Matching Principle

Guidance in the timing of expense recognition is provided by the matching principle. The matching principle maintains quite simply that expense should follow revenue. That is, to the extent it is reasonable and practicable to do so, costs incurred in earning revenue should be matched with, or recognized with, the associated revenue. Examples include inventory costs and commissions paid a salesperson. Inventory costs are charged to cost of sales when the inventory is sold. In this way, inventory costs are matched with the related revenue. Similarly commissions, such as on life insurance, paid in the generation of sales revenue, are expensed when the related sales revenue is recognized. While with inventory costs the cash expenditure likely precedes expense recognition, in the case of sales commissions, expense recognition likely occurs before the related amounts are paid. In both instances, however, it is the timing of revenue recognition and not cash payment that dictates when the expense should be recognized.

Consider the following example from the annual report of Arctco, Inc., a manufacturer of snow mobiles and watercraft:

> The company provides for estimated warranty costs as charges to current operations at the time of sale.[12]

Arctco's warranty policy helps to sell its products. Accordingly, warranty costs are matched with revenue and recognized in the same period. Warranty costs, like commissions, typically entail the recognition of expense before payment. Nonetheless, it is the matching principle that prescribes the timing of that expense recognition.

For many cash expenditures, it is not practical to match expense recognition with revenue. In such situations, expenditures are allocated as expense charges against those future periods that benefit from the expenditures. Here expenditures incurred are first capitalized, that is, given asset treatment, and then amortized as expense against future periods. Examples include the depreciation of property, plant, and equipment and the amortization of intangible assets. From the annual report of Top Air Manufacturing, Inc.:

> Amortization on patents is computed by straight-line method, primarily over a six-year period.[13]

The company initially capitalizes certain expenditures related to acquisition of patents and then amortizes them over the six years expected to benefit from the expenditures. Such a policy does not specifically relate the patent expenditure to specific revenue, but rather to the periods over which revenue is expected to be generated.

When expenditures are made for which no future benefit can be identified, immediate expense or loss recognition is appropriate. Examples include general and administrative expense and maintenance and repairs expense. The following footnote taken from the annual report of American Power Conversion, Inc., shows a distinction between two types of expenditure related to property, plant, and equipment accounts: maintenance and repairs, which are expensed as incurred, and major renewals and betterments, which are capitalized:

> Maintenance and repairs are charged to costs and expenses as incurred. Major renewals and betterments are added to property, plant, and equipment accounts at cost.[14]

In some instances, difficulty in determining whether or not expenditures will benefit future periods lead accounting principles to favor the expensing option. Research and development expenditures are a case in point. Even though companies incur research and development expenditures with the expectation of generating future benefits, these costs are expensed as incurred.[15] As noted in the Microframe, Inc., annual report:

Research and development costs are expensed as incurred.[16]

Similarly, advertising and marketing expense has no clear-cut future benefit and is expensed as incurred.

While superficially it may appear that the matching principle provides sufficient guidance for determining when expense should be recognized, much is left to management judgment. When cash expenditures are made, management must determine whether future revenue or future periods might benefit and the length of time of that benefit. There are no strict guidelines to indicate specifically which expenditures should be recorded as assets and over which periods those assets should be expensed. Estimates are necessary. Similarly, management must use estimates to measure and record costs incurred in earning revenue when no related cash expenditure has as yet been made. Here liabilities are recorded, reflecting estimates of future payments due.

Judgment employed in applying the matching principle is evident in the following excerpts from the accounting policy note of the Homestake Mining Co.:

Exploration costs, including those incurred through joint ventures, are expensed as incurred.

Preoperating and development costs relating to new mines and major programs at existing mines are capitalized. Ordinary mine development costs to maintain production are expensed as incurred.

Depreciation, depletion, and amortization of mining properties, mine development costs and major plant facilities is computed principally by the units-of-production method based on estimated proven and probable ore reserves. Proven and probable ore reserves reflect estimated quantities of economically recoverable reserves which can be recovered in the future from known mineral deposits. Such estimates are based on current and projected costs and prices. Other equipment and plant facilities are depreciated by straight-line or accelerated methods principally over estimated useful lives of three to ten years.

Property evaluation: Recoverability of investments in operating mines is evaluated annually. Estimated future net cash flows from each mine are calculated using estimates of proven and probable reserves, estimated future prices (considering historical and current prices, price trends and related factors) and operating capital and reclamation costs on an undiscounted basis. Reductions in the carrying value of each mine are recorded to the extent the remaining investment exceeds the estimate of future net cash flows.

Recoverability of the carrying values of non-operating properties is evaluated annually based upon estimated future net cash flows from each property determined as described above using estimates of contained mineralization, which represent estimated mineralization expected to be classified as proven and probable reserves, based upon geological delineation to date, upon completion of a feasibility study.

... Reductions in the carrying value of each property are recorded to the extent that the company's carrying value in each property exceeds its estimate of future net cash flows.

Reclamation costs and related accrued liabilities, which are based on the company's interpretation of current environmental and regulatory requirements, are accrued and expensed over the operating life of the mine, principally by the units-of-production method.[17]

In reviewing the policy note excerpts, it can be seen that the company is expensing immediately certain expenditures, such as exploration costs and ordinary mine development costs. Other costs, such as preoperating and development costs, mining properties, and major plant facilities, are capitalized and amortized. In addition, the realizability of costs capitalized to operating mines and nonoperating properties is evaluated annually, and these investments are reduced, with accompanying charges to income, for portions expected to be unrealized. Finally, estimates of the future costs of reclamation of mining properties is expensed while the mines are operated, even though payment will not occur until after mining ceases.

As noted, our interest here is in cash expenditures that are expected to benefit future periods. Specifically, we focus on cost capitalization and its subsequent amortization. Assets not subject to amortization, and liabilities arising from expenses incurred in advance of payment, are examined elsewhere.

Capitalizing Membership Acquisition Costs

CUC International, Inc., provides a useful example of how a company's cost capitalization policy can lead to future losses. The company offers membership-based shopping services that consumers access from their homes. Excerpts from the company's balance sheet for 1987 and 1988 are provided in Exhibit 9.1.

The company's accounting policy notes describe its accounting policies with respect to these assets as follows:

Exhibit 9.1 Cost Capitalization: CUC International, Inc., Selected Account Balances, Years Ending January 31, 1987 and 1988 (thousands of dollars)

	1987	1988
Noncurrent assets		
Deferred membership charges, net	$ 13,112	$ 22,078
Prepaid solicitation costs	4,915	17,089
Prepaid commissions	8,127	6,267
Total capitalized costs	$ 26,154	$ 45,434

Source: CUC International, Inc., annual report, January 1988, p. 18.

Deferred membership charges, net: Deferred membership charges comprise (in thousands):

January 31	1987	1988
Deferred membership income	$(43,205)	$(52,834)
Unamortized membership acquisition costs	56,311	74,912
Deferred membership charges, net	$ 13,112	$ 22,078

The related membership fees and membership acquisition costs have been between $30 and $39 per individual member during the years ended January 31, 1988 and 1987. In addition, the annual renewal costs have remained between 10% and 20% of annual membership fees for the same period.

Renewal costs consist principally of charges from sponsoring institutions and are amortized over the renewal period. Individual memberships are principally for a one-year period. These membership fees are recorded, as deferred membership income, upon acceptance of membership, net of estimated cancellations, and prorated over the membership period. The related initial membership acquisition costs are recorded as incurred and charged to operations as membership fees are recognized, allowing for renewals, over a three-year period. Such costs are amortized commencing with the beginning of the membership period, at the annual rate of 40%, 30%, and 30%, respectively. Membership renewal rates are dependent upon the nature of the benefits and services provided by the company in its various membership programs. Through January 31, 1988, membership renewal rates have been sufficient to generate future revenue in excess of deferred membership acquisition costs over the remaining amortization period.

Amortization of membership acquisition costs, including deferred renewal costs, amounted to $44.6 million, $35.5 million, and $20.2 million for the years ended January 31, 1988, 1987, and 1986, respectively.

Prepaid solicitation costs: Prepaid solicitation costs consist of initial membership acquisition costs pertaining to membership solicitation programs that were in process at year end. Accordingly, no membership fees had been received or recognized at year end.

Prepaid commissions: Prepaid commissions consist of the amount to be paid in connection with the termination of contracts with the company's field sales force ($4.9 million and $5.8 million at January 31, 1988 and 1987, respectively) and the termination of special compensation agreements with an officer and former officer ($1.3 million and $1.6 million at January 31, 1988 and 1987, respectively). The amount relating to the termination of the field sales force is being amortized, using the straight-line method, over eight years and the amount relating to the termination of the special compensation agreement is being amortized ratably over ten years.[18]

In this note, deferred membership charges, net, represent capitalized costs of acquiring new members for the company's shopping services, net of deferred membership income. That is, costs incurred in obtaining new members, which likely include promotional and administrative expenses, are capitalized. Subtracted from them on the balance sheet are the individual membership fees collected from these new members. Interestingly, the deferred membership fees were amortized to income over the one-year membership period. Meanwhile, allowing for renewals, the membership acquisition costs were amortized over a three-year period. Other costs capitalized by the company included the costs of general solicitation of new members, which had not as yet been fruitful, and commissions paid to a terminated field sales force.

There is a future benefit associated with the costs incurred in acquiring a new member. At a minimum, the company is certain of recovering at least a portion of its costs through the membership fee received. Whether those new members would stay for three years, justifying the company's three-year amortization period for its deferred membership acquisition costs, is an open question. The future benefit of other capitalized costs seems to be even more dubious. There are no new members associated with prepaid solicitation costs. Its capitalization represents little more than reporting general marketing costs as an asset. Similarly, the prepaid commissions seem to represent payment for past acts with little, if any, identifiable benefit. Calling these expenditures assets is a stretch.

In the year ending January, 1988, CUC International reported pre-tax earnings of $31,440,000. Had the company followed a policy of expensing when incurred all three capitalized costs, pre-tax earnings would have been reduced by $28,909,000 to $2,531,000.[19] In the following year, the company reported a pre-tax loss of $14,640,000. Causing the loss was the following item:

> In the fourth quarter of fiscal 1989, the company accelerated the amortization of membership acquisition costs from the three-year policy of 40%, 30%, and 30%, respectively, to a twelve-month period (straight-line method). The change was made to amortize the costs over a period that coincides with the initial membership period as opposed to the estimated renewal period and to ensure recoverability on a more conservative basis. The unamortized membership acquisition costs as of January 31, 1989, have been determined on this basis. The effect of this change in estimate resulted in an accumulated charge to operations for the year ended January 31, 1989, of $58.9 million.[20]

The company was aggressive in its cost capitalization policy in 1988 and earlier. While it was not now changing what costs it would capitalize, it was revising its estimate of the future periods expected to benefit from these expenditures. As a result, earnings in 1988 and earlier were overstated. In moving to a new, more conservative outlook on the recoverability of some of these costs, the company took a significant earnings charge. Earnings expectations formulated on earlier reported results would have been disappointed.

Identifying Aggressive Cost Capitalization

In accordance with the matching principle it is appropriate to capitalize certain expenditures expected to provide identifiable future benefits. When costs are capitalized in an aggressive fashion, however, earnings may yield a surprise. The question is, How can one identify aggressive cost capitalization?

One useful technique is to compare the capitalization policies of the company with those of competitors and other companies in the industry. Is the company capitalizing costs that other companies expense? Or does it expense more, taking a more conservative approach?

As an example, America Online, Inc., a provider of communication, information, and entertainment services to consumers who are subscribers to its information network, provides the following policy note for costs incurred in writing new subscriptions:

> Subscriber acquisition costs are deferred and charged to operations over a 12 or 18 month period (straight-line method) beginning the month after such costs are incurred. These costs, which relate directly to subscriber solicitations, principally include printing, production, and shipping of starter kits and the costs of obtaining qualified prospects by various targeted direct marketing programs.[21]

The company carries $26,392,000 in deferred subscriber acquisition costs on its June 1994 balance sheet, up from $6,890,000 in 1993. It anticipates that these costs will be recovered through membership subscriptions and renewals. In contrast, CompuServe, Inc., a subsidiary of H&R Block, Inc., and competitor to America Online, expenses these costs as incurred.[22] Had America Online followed a similar policy, the company's 1994 pre-tax earnings of $10,042,000 would have instead been a pre-tax loss of $9,460,000.

Both companies, America Online and CompuServe, are employing practices that are within the guidelines of the matching principle. However, when one compares America Online's policy to that of CompuServe, the former is clearly taking a more aggressive approach. If the realizability of its deferred subscriber acquisition costs is later called into question, the company's earnings will suffer.

While comparing a company's capitalization policy with those of competitors and others in the industry is one useful approach for identifying aggressive cost capitalization, it is possible that other firms chosen for comparison are also taking an aggressive stance. Accordingly, one should give serious consideration to what the capitalized costs represent. Do they represent identifiable assets with utility separate and apart from the company? That is, do they have an ascertainable market value? Or do they represent little more than bookkeeping entries, whose value, if any, is tied to the fortunes of the company? If the capitalized costs represent identifiable assets, then capitalization would seem to be appropriate, though they should not be carried at amounts that exceed the total, undiscounted cash flows expected to be realized from the asset.[23] However, if the costs have no separable and identifiable value, then capitalization can be considered somewhat aggressive and the careful financial statement reader should be on the alert. If at some future date the company faces financial difficulties, those previously capitalized costs may be taken as a cumulative charge against income.

The practice of most lenders in dealing with goodwill is consistent with the view that goodwill has no utility separate and apart from the company. In computing a company's net worth, lenders typically deduct goodwill, the price paid in an acquisition in excess of the fair market value of identifiable net assets acquired, from shareholders' equity. The end result is tangible net worth, void of the effects of the intangible asset, goodwill.

Just because capitalization is permitted, or not specifically excluded, by generally accepted accounting principles, does not necessarily make it appropriate. Even aggressive cost capitalization is typically within the guidelines of generally accepted accounting principles. It is a matter of degree. Most managements take a conservative stance and charge costs to expense when it is unclear if future periods will benefit. The optimism of some managements, however, leads them to take an aggressive stance and assign a higher likelihood than is perhaps warranted to the benefits to be derived from costs incurred. For example, the previous capitalization policy of 50-Off Stores would likely be defended on the grounds that it was consistent with generally accepted accounting principles. Such support, however, did not stop the company from later changing its policy and taking a significant earnings charge with an accompanying loss.

As one additional example of differing practices permitted by generally accepted accounting principles, consider the accounting for oil and gas exploration expenditures. Companies in this industry can employ one of two permitted practices. The first, the full-cost method, permits capitalization of all exploration expenditures, even unsuccessful ventures, under the premise that bearing the cost of dry holes is necessary to finding commercially viable reserves. Apache Corp. provides the following description of its policy for exploration expenditures:

> The company uses the full-cost method of accounting for its investment in oil and gas properties. Under this method, the company capitalizes all acquisition, exploration, and development costs incurred for the purpose of finding oil and gas reserves, including salaries, benefits, and other internal costs directly attributable to these activities.[24]

In contrast, the second permitted practice, the successful-efforts method, permits capitalization of exploration expenditures associated with successful projects only. As reported by St. Mary Land & Exploration Co.:

> The company follows the successful-efforts method of accounting for its oil and gas properties. Under this method of accounting, all property acquisition costs and costs of exploratory and development wells are capitalized when incurred, pending determination of whether the well has found proved reserves. If an exploratory well has not found proved reserves, the costs of drilling the well are charged to expense.[25]

Both companies are employing accounting practices that are permitted by generally accepted accounting principles.[26] Apache Corp., however, is capitalizing costs that

St. Mary Land & Exploration charges to expense. These capitalized costs will be charged to income later, either through amortization or as a write-off.

Capitalized Costs and the Balance Sheet

The examples reviewed here should provide an important reminder of the effects that capitalized costs can have on the balance sheet. When costs incurred are capitalized, they are reported on the balance sheet as assets. Classification as either current or noncurrent assets depends on the anticipated timing of the assets' realization. These costs will later find their way to the income statement, either through amortization as expense or through a write-off in the event that amounts capitalized are no longer deemed to be realizable.

In the case of 50-Off Stores, the company took a one-time charge in the year ending January 28, 1994 and wrote off capitalized preopening costs that had accumulated to $5,156,947. Similarly, at June 30, 1994, American Online carried as assets deferred subscriber acquisition costs in the amount of $26,392,000. While this amount has not been written off, in the event of financial difficulties, it is a substantial looming charge.

Disclosures provided by Continental Medical Systems, Inc., a provider of rehabilitation services, help dramatize the effects that capitalized costs have on the balance sheet and the income statement. Among the company's assets, which totaled $468.2 million at June 30, 1992, was "deferred costs, new facilities." The company's footnotes provide the following information:

Deferred costs, new facilities: Deferred costs, new facilities comprise the following (in thousands):

	June 30, 1991	June 30, 1992
Deferred development costs	$10,063	$11,899
Preopening costs	25,684	39,264
Total	35,747	51,163
Less: Accumulated amortization	6,734	14,862
Total	$29,013	$36,301

The company defers costs incurred to obtain government approvals and other expenses related to the development of rehabilitation facilities. For facilities owned by third parties and leased by the company, deferred costs are amortized over the lease term, principally 10 years. For internally developed and owned facilities, these costs become part of the fixed asset and are amortized over its estimated useful life. In the event that any projects are abandoned, their respective costs are charged to operations.

Start-up expenses ("preopening costs") incurred prior to the opening of new facilities are capitalized and amortized on a straight-line basis over periods of 24 to 60 months upon the commencement of operations.[27]

The company's capitalization policies for costs incurred in the opening of new rehabilitation centers have resulted in the addition of new assets to the balance sheet in the amount of $51,163,000 at June 30, 1992. Of this amount, $14,862,000 had been amortized. Note that the company is amortizing these expenses over periods of up to ten years and more for costs related to the development of new facilities and up to 60 months for certain preopening costs. In the event that a new facility is abandoned, any related capitalized costs are charged to operations. Such charges associated with abandoned facilities can be substantial. For example, during 1993, the company recorded a special charge of $14.6 million to write off costs capitalized on approximately 30 development projects that were subsequently abandoned.

In anticipating earnings surprises, one must continually keep an eye on the balance sheet, considering what assets are being accumulated there and what those assets represent. At a minimum, capitalized costs represent future charges against income. If those costs are not fully recovered, there will be insufficient revenue to offset those charges and a net loss will result.

Taking an Aggressive Position

Chambers Development Co., provides solid waste management services, including the development and operation of solid waste landfill sites. Until a few years ago, the company capitalized the costs of obtaining landfill permits. The following information was provided in its 1990 annual report:

> *Property and equipment:* Landfill disposal sites, including land and related landfill preparation and improvement costs, are stated at cost. Landfill preparation and improvement costs are amortized as consumed during the useful lives of the sites.
> *Deferred costs:* Deferred costs include debt issuance costs and development costs for waste collection and security guard service contracts.[28]

In reviewing these asset descriptions, it can be seen that the company included certain capitalized costs on its balance sheet. The amount of capitalized costs in the deferred costs caption was clear. The balance sheet reported an asset with that title in the amount of $27.6 million, which was net of amounts amortized. The amount of capitalized costs included in the landfill disposal sites caption, however, was unclear. At year-end 1990, the company simply reported a single sum in the amount of $383.6 million, which included land costs along with other undisclosed capitalized expenditures. Little other information was provided about the nature and amount of the costs capitalized into this caption.

A careful analysis of the Chambers Development financial statements for 1990 would indicate the need to study both captions more carefully. Given the general lack of descriptive information in the company's annual report, management would need to be questioned regarding the nature and amount of costs capitalized, especially to the landfill disposal sites account.

In subsequent revelations concerning the company it was learned that the landfill disposal sites account included costs capitalized by Chambers that its competitors, companies such as Browning-Ferris Industries, Inc., and WMX Technologies, Inc., were charging to expense immediately. These expenditures included such items as, "portions of executives' salaries for time spent on developing projects such as new landfills. In addition, the company delayed recognizing some public relations and legal costs as well as executive travel expenses."[29]

By early 1992 the future benefits to be provided by the capitalized expenditures were being questioned. Moreover, the amounts involved had reached levels that were uncomfortably high. The company's accountants refused to sign off on its 1991 results unless the amounts in question were written off. Company management went along and agreed to restate the company's results for 1991 to exclude those capitalized costs. Pre-tax earnings for the year were reduced by a write-off of capitalized expenses that totaled nearly $50 million. Net income was reduced from a previously reported $49.9 million to a revised $1.5 million. Accompanying the earnings adjustment was a drop in the company's share price by approximately 63%. Clearly many investors were surprised by these developments.

In hindsight it seems easy to say that the Chambers Development situation should have been expected. We do not think that such an assessment would have been easy in the years before the write-down. Chambers Development was employing accounting practices that were not necessarily outside the boundaries of generally accepted accounting principles. In addition, the company provided very little information to help the reader determine the extent of its capitalization practices. However, the company did indicate that it was capitalizing certain landfill development costs. Its competitors were charging these same costs to expense immediately. Accordingly, the Chambers practice should have been considered aggressive. When such aggressive capitalization practices are employed, earnings are at a heightened risk for occasioning a surprise. This is not to say that an earnings surprise must happen. But any financial developments that move against the company in a concerted way can expose the aggressive tactics and call for an adjustment. With these thoughts in mind, a creditor or equity investor reading the Chambers financial statements could at least have been forewarned that such a development was a possibility.

Before leaving the Chambers Development case, let us consider what catalysts might precipitate a change in management judgment that would result in a sudden write-down. When management takes an aggressive position with respect to cost capitalization, what causes it to change? In the case of Chambers Development, it was the company's auditors. In years prior to the write-down year, this group was likely uncomfortable with the company's capitalization practices. However, given that these practices were not clearly outside the boundaries of generally accepted accounting principles, they signed off. Finally, when capitalized amounts reached levels that could not be justified, the auditors insisted on a change. In those cases where the auditors do not force a change, it is likely that financial developments will. A general decline in business activity or the loss of a single large customer could alter management's optimism and precipitate a change. More cynically, if a year is going poorly, management might consider cleaning up the balance sheet by writing off much of what had been capitalized in prior years. Such an act sets the stage for much better reported performance in future years. Even a change in executive management might be reason to see a change in capitalization policies. Why not write those capitalized costs off and blame the prior administration? The balance sheet that remains would be one without those capitalized costs and would help the company report higher earnings in future years.

Capitalizing Software Development Costs

Earlier it was noted that because of the uncertainty surrounding the realizability of research and development expenditures, those costs are expensed as incurred. Accounting principles, however, do permit capitalization of costs associated with one type of research and development activity—that associated with the development of computer software for eventual sale or licensing.[30] Accounting principles for software development costs permit capitalization under the premise that the realizability of amounts spent on software development can be determined earlier and more accurately than spending on other research and development projects. As noted by a financial executive of a computer software company, "The key distinction between our spending [on software development] and R&D is recoverability. We know we are developing something we can sell."[31]

Accounting principles for software development costs maintain that costs incurred in creating computer software products should be charged to research and development expense as incurred until technological feasibility has been established for the software under development. Once technological feasibility is reached, subsequent software development costs should be capitalized. These capitalized costs are reported as noncurrent assets and are amortized to expense over the estimated useful lives of the software products.

Technological feasibility is defined as that point at which all the necessary planning, designing, coding, and testing activities have been completed to the extent needed to establish that the software product in question can meet its design specifications. Essentially, it will do what it was designed to do.

The following note provided by PeopleSoft, Inc., is informative for understanding the accounting for software development costs:

> The company capitalizes certain costs, consisting of salaries, related payroll taxes and benefits, and an allocation of indirect costs incurred internally in developing computer software products. Costs incurred prior to the establishment of technological feasibility are charged to product development expense. . . . Upon general release of the product to customers, capitalization ceases and such costs are amortized on a product by product basis over periods not exceeding three years.[32]

As would be expected, determining when technological feasibility is reached requires management judgment. As a result, different companies capitalize software development costs to varying degrees. When higher proportions of software development costs are capitalized, current earnings benefit. These capitalized costs will, however, weigh on future earnings through increased amortization. Moreover, they raise the likelihood of future losses through write-downs when the realizability of previously capitalized costs is questioned.

The cases of three software companies dramatize the differences that exist in the proportions of software development costs being capitalized. Consider, first, the case of Microsoft Corp. The company provided the following accounting policy note in its 1993 annual report:

> Research and development costs are expensed as incurred. Financial accounting rules requiring capitalization of certain software development costs do not materially affect the company.[33]

Thus, the company capitalizes none of its software development costs. Of course, this is not to say that Microsoft has had no software products that have reached technological feasibility. A more likely explanation is that the company is sufficiently profitable that its earnings can handle the full expensing of software development costs.

A second software company example is provided by System Software Associates, Inc. The company provided the following disclosure in its 1993 annual report:

> *Software costs:* Purchased software is capitalized and stated at cost. The company capitalizes software development costs in accordance with SFAS No. 86. Amortization of capitalized costs is computed using an estimated useful life of five years or a period based upon anticipated revenues, whichever provides the greater amortization.
> Capitalized software costs are summarized as follows (in millions):

	Oct. 31, 1992	Oct. 31, 1993
Purchased software	$ 2.2	$ 4.7
Internally developed software	25.3	39.6
Total	27.5	44.3
Accumulated amortization	(10.7)	(17.0)
Net capitalized software costs	$ 16.8	$27.3

Purchased software and accumulated amortization at October 31, 1993, reflect $1.7 million and $.7 million, respectively, related to the combination of Elke Corp. Additionally, purchased software and accumulated amortization include a write-off of $.3 million in 1993.

Amortization of capitalized software charged to cost of license fees aggregated $5.9 million, $4.3 million, and $2.7 million during 1993, 1992, and 1991, respectively.[34]

In reviewing these disclosures, we see that the company capitalized $14.3 million in additional software development costs during 1993 ($39.6 million less $25.3

million). During that same year, the company's income statement, which is not provided here, reported research and development expense, or software costs that were expensed when incurred and not capitalized, of $23.0 million. This amount excludes amortized software costs, which are charged to cost of license fees. Thus, during 1993, the company incurred total software development costs in the amount of $37.3 million ($14.3 million plus $23.0 million), of which $14.3 million, or 38%, were capitalized.

As an aside, other disclosures made by the company provide an example of the accounting treatment accorded capitalized software costs that are deemed not to be recoverable from future revenue. In 1993 the company wrote off $0.3 million of unrecoverable software costs with a direct charge to earnings.

The third software company example is that of American Software, Inc. The company provided the following disclosures in its 1993 annual report:

> The company capitalizes computer software development costs by project, commencing when technological feasibility for the respective product is established and concluding when the product is ready for general release to customers. The company capitalized computer software development costs totaling $8,610,918, $7,924,027, and $6,065,154 in 1993, 1992, and 1991, respectively. Capitalized computer software development costs are being amortized using the straight-line method over an estimated useful life of three years. Amortization expense was $4,793,398, $4,341,490, and $2,151,547 in 1993, 1992, and 1991, respectively.
>
> The company incurred research and development costs totaling approximately $5,078,000, $4,645,000, and $3,852,000, which were expensed in 1993, 1992, and 1991, respectively.[35]

During 1993, American Software incurred $13,688,918 in software development costs of which $8,610,918 were capitalized and $5,078,000, the amount of research and development costs reported for the year, were expensed. Thus, the company capitalized 63% of the software development costs it incurred, or $8,610,918 out of $13,688,918.

From the examination of the capitalization policies of three software companies, a considerable range of capitalization rates is seen. As noted, in 1993, Microsoft capitalized none of its software development expenditures, whereas System Software and American Software capitalized 38% and 63%, respectively. The effect on earnings can be significant. For example, in 1993, American Software reported pre-tax earnings of $6,744,711. As noted, during that year, the company capitalized software development costs of $8,610,918 and amortized previously capitalized software costs of $4,793,398. Had the company expensed all of its software development costs that year, pre-tax earnings would have been reduced by $3,817,520 ($8,610,918 less $4,793,398), or 57%.

A high proportion of software costs capitalized may indicate an aggressive management position with regard to realizability of future benefits. Future earnings are more subject to an earnings charge in the event of financial difficulties. In analyzing software firms, careful consideration is needed of the extent to which software development costs have been capitalized and the degree to which those costs are realizable.

Capitalizing Interest Costs

Generally accepted accounting principles require the capitalization of interest incurred on monies invested in assets under construction.[36] While interest should be capitalized to any asset that requires a time period to get ready for its intended use, the amount of interest involved in most such cases is immaterial. Thus interest is normally capitalized only in those situations involving an extended construction period.

The asset under construction might be an item of inventory if the project is one that is to be sold. For example, a homebuilder would capitalize interest incurred on houses being built for sale while they are under construction. Consider, for example, the following accounting policy note provided by D. R. Horton Custom Homes, Inc.:

> In addition to direct land acquisition, land development, and housing construction costs, inventory costs include interest and real estate taxes, which are capitalized in inventory during the development and construction periods.[37]

Alternatively, the asset under construction might be a property or equipment item if the project is one that is to become part of a company's fixed asset base. Examples here include the construction costs of new plant facilities or advance payments made to manufacturers by airlines in conjunction with aircraft acquisitions. Delta Air Lines, Inc., provides the following policy note:

> Interest attributable to funds used to finance the acquisition of new aircraft and construction of major ground facilities is capitalized as an additional cost of the related asset. Interest is capitalized at the company's weighted average interest rate on long-term debt or, where applicable, the interest rate related to specific borrowings. Capitalization of interest ceases when the property or equipment is placed in service.[38]

In all situations, the amount of interest capitalized is the amount of interest that could have been avoided if the construction project had not been undertaken. As a result, capitalized interest can include interest on borrowings specific to the construction project or other, unrelated borrowings. Had the company not undertaken this new construction project, the monies invested in it could have been used to repay those other unrelated borrowings. The amount of interest capitalized is, however, limited to the amount of interest incurred. Thus, except in limited industry settings, such as with regulated utilities, there is no capitalization of the implied costs of equity funds.

Interest is capitalized during the period in which an asset is being constructed and readied for its intended use. Once the asset is ready for use, interest capitalization is discontinued. That is, even if the inventory item is not sold or the new fixed asset is not yet placed in service, their completion and availability is sufficient to warrant discontinuation of interest capitalization.

When a completed asset is placed in service, capitalized interest is charged against income. The expense is recorded either through cost of sales in the case of constructed inventory or through depreciation expense over the asset's estimated useful life in the case of constructed items of property, plant, and equipment. For example, Oriole Homes Corp. provides the following disclosure:

> During the years 1993, 1992, and 1991 respectively, the company capitalized interest in the amount of $9,997,908, $6,944,173, and $7,147,527 and expensed as a component of cost of goods sold $10,036,456, $7,685,554, and $5,318,689.[39]

For Oriole Homes, interest capitalization actually resulted in lower income during the years 1992 and 1993. That is, during those years, the company expensed more capitalized interest from prior years through cost of sales than new amounts capitalized. For example, in 1993, the company capitalized $9,997,908 but expensed through cost of sales $10,036,456.

While interest capitalization is to be continued during construction, if capitalization were to result in the cost of an asset exceeding its net realizable value, or the amount for which an asset could be sold less the costs of sale, then capitalization is to be stopped. This net realizable value, or NRV, rule provides a natural limit on the amount of interest that can be capitalized and helps to prevent overcapitalization. Companies should periodically compare the total costs of their construction projects with net realizable value to confirm that interest capitalization should be continued. This is an especially important step in those situations where there have been construction delays and cost overruns. The failure to discontinue interest capitalization when costs of a project exceed net realizable value can lead to future asset write-downs.[40]

Returning to D. R. Horton Custom Homes, a homebuilder that carries capitalized interest in its inventory account, we provide the following note:

> Inventories are stated at the lower of cost (specific identification method) or net realizable value.[41]

Note that while the company capitalizes interest costs to its home inventory account, it takes steps to ensure that its accumulated inventory costs do not exceed net realizable value.

Because interest capitalization is required by generally accepted accounting principles, it should not be considered, in and of itself, an aggressive capitalization policy. However, just because companies are required to capitalize interest under generally accepted accounting principles does not necessarily mean that the policy cannot lead to potential problems or earnings surprises. Consider, for example, the case of Alumax, Inc., an aluminum company.

Alumax capitalizes interest during the construction period of new or major additions to existing aluminum production facilities. On the company's income statement for 1991, 1992, and 1993, the summary of other income (expense), as presented in Exhibit 9.2, was reported.

Exhibit 9.2   Interest Cost Capitalization: Alumax, Inc., Other Income (Expense), Years Ending December 31, 1991–1993 (millions of dollars)

	1991	1992	1993
Interest expense	$(68.2)	$(95.6)	$(79.2)
Interest capitalized	39.6	41.7	0

Source: Alumax, Inc., annual report, December 1993, p. 31.

In the exhibit it can be seen that the company incurred interest expense in amounts ranging from $68.2 million in 1991 to $95.6 million in 1992. In addition, in 1991 and 1992, the company capitalized significant amounts of that interest, increasing pre-tax profits. In 1993, however, because of completion of its recent plant construction projects, the company ceased capitalizing interest. As a result, no interest was capitalized that year, providing no offset to interest expense. Moreover, while not disclosed separately, any interest capitalized in prior years was now being amortized to expense. Thus, while capitalization provided a pre-tax earnings boost of around $40 million in 1991 and 1992, no such earnings boost was provided in 1993. Earnings expectations for 1993 that assumed a continuation of the earnings-increasing effect of interest capitalization, as in 1991 and 1992, would have been optimistic. Moreover, as part of a restructuring of its mill products, extrusions, and architectural products businesses in 1993, the company recorded a pre-tax charge of $91.8 million. Included in this charge was $10 million in asset write-downs. While not disclosed separately, these asset writedowns likely included interest capitalized to fixed assets in prior years.

Emphasizing the earnings effect that a discontinuation of interest capitalization can have is the example of Union Camp Corp. In 1992 net income fell to $76.2 million, from $124.8 million in 1991. Among the reasons provided for the decline in income was the following explanation:

In comparing 1992 earnings with 1991, about two-thirds of the earnings decrease was attributable to higher interest expense due to a lower level of capitalized interest following the completion of the mill modernization and expansion program in 1991.[42]

Thus, a discontinuation of interest capitalization can have a significant effect on reported income.

Chambers Development provides another case in point. We examined the capitalization policies of Chambers Development earlier when our focus was on landfill development costs. Chambers also provides a good example of the potential pitfalls associated with interest capitalization. Even after Chambers announced that it was restating its results for 1991 to remove nearly $50 million in capitalized landfill development costs, some analysts were not convinced that the company had fully faced up to its overcapitalization problem. They noted that the company had also been capitalizing interest on its development expenditures. On the surface such a practice is appropriate. However, by writing off these development expenditures, any interest capitalized on them would need to be written off as well. In addition, future interest capitalized should be reduced.

Ultimately, Chambers Development did face up to the need to remove capitalized interest from its balance sheet. In a highly unusual move, the company restated its 1991 results a second time. Net income that had been reported originally at $49.9 million and was restated once to $1.5 million, was restated a second time to a loss of $72.2 million. Other items besides capitalized interest were called into question and adjusted here. Nonetheless, the removal of previously capitalized interest formed an important part of the new restatement.

EXTENDED AMORTIZATION PERIODS

Costs are capitalized when future periods are expected to benefit from amounts incurred. Accordingly, once capitalized, these costs are charged to expense over those future years. The process of expensing these costs is termed amortization, and typically a straight-line method is used whereby equal expense charges are taken in each year expected to benefit. In this section, we look for early warnings in the amortization of all long-lived assets, including those arising from capitalized costs. Examples of other long-lived assets include property, plant, and equipment accounts as well as an important intangible, goodwill.

Generally accepted accounting principles provide no specific guidance as to an appropriate period over which to amortize long-lived assets. As a result, management judgment is needed in choosing the proper period. This decision provides management with much discretion over reported results. The longer the amortization period chosen, the lower the annual expense amount, and the higher pre-tax earnings become.

Differences of opinion among managements regarding the amortization or depreciation periods for property, plant, and equipment items is evident in the following accounting policy notes. All the companies are from a single industry: medical supplies and devices.

From the annual report of Centocor, Inc.:

Depreciation is provided using the straight-line method over the estimated useful lives of the assets, which range from 3 to 31 years. Leasehold improvements are depreciated over the applicable lease period or their estimated useful lives, whichever is shorter.[43]

From the annual report of Cordis Corp.:

The lives used in calculating provisions for depreciation and amortization of the principal assets using the straight-line method are as follows:[44]

Building and improvements   10–30 years
Leasehold improvements   10–20 years
Machinery and equipment   3–10 years

From the annual report of U.S. Surgical Corp.:

Depreciation and amortization is provided using the straight-line method over the following estimated useful lives:[45]

Buildings   40 years
Molds and dies   5–7 years
Machinery and equipment   3–10 years
Leasehold improvements   10–30 years

In reviewing the footnote disclosures it becomes apparent that all three companies are using different periods to expense buildings, equipment, and other capitalized costs. For example, while Centocor apparently uses an amortization period of 31 years for its buildings, U.S. Surgical amortizes buildings over periods of up to 40 years. Similarly, while Cordis Corp. employs an amortization period of 10–20 years for leasehold improvements, U.S. Surgical uses 10–30 years.

The effect of amortization or depreciation periods chosen can have significant effects on pre-tax earnings. Consider, for example, the property, plant, and equipment account balances for U.S. Surgical provided in Exhibit 9.3.

Applying an amortization period of 40 years (the company's stated useful life) to the average cost of buildings account, an average amortization period of 6 years (the company reports the use of 5–7 years) to the average cost of molds and dies, and average amortization periods of 6.5 years (3–10 years is used) and 20 years (10–30 years is used), respectively, to the average cost of machinery and equipment and

Exhibit 9.3   Amortization and Depreciation: United States Surgical Corp., Selected Account Balances, 1992 and 1993 (millions of dollars)

	1992	1993
Land	$ 18.6	$ 20.7
Buildings	150.3	163.4
Molds and dies	128.3	114.3
Machinery and equipment	262.6	306.6
Leasehold improvements	127.5	147.1
Total	687.3	752.1
Less: Allowance for depreciation and amortization	159.2	159.9
Total	$ 528.1	$ 592.2

Source: United States Surgical Corp., annual report, December 1993, p. 7.

leasehold improvements would yield a total depreciation and amortization charge of $74,788,000 for 1993.[46]

If the company were to reduce its amortization period for buildings to 30 years, for molds and dies to 4 years, for machinery and equipment and leasehold improvements to 4.5 years and 15 years, respectively, a depreciation and amortization charge of $107,951,000 would result for 1993. This revised depreciation charge, recomputed using asset depreciation and amortization periods that are consistent with what its competitors are using, yields an income statement charge that is $33,163,000 higher. Pre-tax earnings would be reduced accordingly, or in the case of United States Surgical in 1993, the pre-tax loss would be increased. The $33,163,000 depreciation difference is 24% of the company's reported pre-tax loss of $137,400,000 for 1993.

While the choice of an amortization period or useful life can have a significant effect on pre-tax earnings, it also affects asset book values. That is, when amortization periods are lengthened, depreciation and amortization expense amounts are reduced, leaving greater asset book values on the balance sheet. Moreover, this balance sheet effect is cumulative, boosting asset book values each year through reduced amortization.

In Chapter 3, disclosures of the amortization periods for goodwill obtained from the annual reports of four medical instruments companies were provided. Because those differences help highlight the impact of management judgment on amortization periods, the disclosures are reproduced here. Recall that generally accepted accounting principles require amortization of goodwill but permit companies to choose their amortization periods. Amortization periods of any length are allowed as long as they do not exceed a 40-year maximum. Consider the following examples.

From the annual report of Biomet, Inc.:

Excess acquisition costs over fair value of acquired net assets (goodwill) are amortized using the straight-line method over periods ranging from eight to ten years.[47]

From the annual report of Diagnostic Products, Inc.:

The excess of cost over net assets acquired is being amortized over 20 years using the straight-line method.[48]

From the annual report of Allergan, Inc.:

Goodwill represents the excess of acquisition costs over the fair value of net assets of purchased businesses and is being amortized on a straight-line basis over periods from ten to thirty years.[49]

From the annual report of Healthdyne, Inc.:

The excess of cost over net assets of businesses acquired is being amortized using the straight-line method over periods of up to 40 years.[50]

Note how the managements of each of these companies have different expectations regarding the future periods expected to benefit from amounts paid for companies acquired in excess of the market values of their identifiable net assets. As a result, amortization periods range from as few as 8 years to as many as 40.

The impact of judgment on the selection of amortization periods is also evident from the following disclosures provided by three computer software firms.

From the annual report of Autodesk, Inc.:

> Costs incurred in the initial design phase of software development are expensed as incurred. Once the point of technological feasibility is reached, direct production costs (programming and testing) are capitalized. Certain software technology rights acquired are also capitalized. Capitalized software is amortized ratably as revenues are recognized, but not less than on a straight-line basis over two-to-ten-year periods.[51]

From the annual report of Bolt, Beranek & Newman:

> The company capitalizes purchased software technology and certain internally developed computer software costs to be sold or otherwise marketed to customers. Costs incurred internally after establishing technological feasibility and before general release of a computer software product, are amortized over 3 years. Costs incurred for purchased software technology are amortized over periods up to 7 years.[52]

From the annual report of Caere Corp.:

> The company capitalizes software development costs incurred subsequent to determining a product's technological feasibility. Such costs are amortized on a straight-line basis over the estimated useful life of the product, generally two to three years.[53]

Here again, amortization periods vary from as little as two to as many as ten years with differing effects on earnings and asset book values.

Earlier it was noted that the effect of an extended amortization period or useful life has a cumulative effect on asset book values. Asset book values are boosted each year by the reduced depreciation and amortization charges that a longer amortization period provides. All long-lived assets, including property, plant, and equipment, identifiable intangibles, and goodwill, whether held for use or sale, are subject to write-down and an accompanying impairment loss when their balance sheet amounts are value-impaired. A determination of when an asset is value-impaired varies depending on the asset. Long-lived assets to be held for use are value-impaired when their book values exceed the future cash flows expected from their use. These assets are to be written down to their fair market value, or the amount at which they could be purchased or sold in a current arm's-length transaction that is not a forced liquidation. Long-lived assets that are held for sale are value-impaired when their book values exceed net realizable value, or the amounts for which the assets are expected to be sold less the estimated costs of sale.[54] By limiting the amounts at which asset book values can be carried, potential losses on these assets, either through use or sale, are not postponed to subsequent periods. A postponement of such losses would be tantamount to carrying the losses as assets on the balance sheet.

When a long-lived asset is value-impaired, a write-down and accompanying charge to income are needed. Accounting principles call this loss an impairment loss. Companies use different names for the charge, though asset write-down, special charge, and impairment loss are commonly used. Such write-downs are also often effected as part of a broader restructuring of a company's operations. In these cases, the impairment loss is included as part of a restructuring charge.

For example, in its fiscal 1992, Integrated Device Technology, Inc., provided the following disclosure:

> In fiscal year 1992, the company recorded $4.5 million of charges to net income relating to the abandonment of IDT's original wafer processing facility and a reorganization of the company's management structure. In addition, due to changes in the market during the second fiscal quarter, the company revised its estimated useful lives and future realizable values of certain assets. These charges included a $7.2 million write-down of excess inventory to its net realizable value and $5.4 million of write-offs and changes in useful lives of underutilized capital assets.[55]

The company is recording special charges to income for numerous items, including write-downs of the book values of depreciable assets. Note that useful lives chosen originally for selected assets were, in hindsight, too long. As a result, asset book values were left on the balance sheet that were too high relative to the amounts expected to be realized from them, necessitating the write-downs.

Another example is provided by Bassett Furniture Industries, Inc.:

> In the first quarter of 1990, the company recorded a provision for restructuring charges of $14.3 million ($11.2 million net of tax, or $1.38 per share).
> The restructuring plan was designed to bring the Casegood Division's plant capacity in line with market demands and to lower inventory positions in order to improve its competitive positioning, asset utilization, and work force efficiency.
> The provision for restructuring charges included primarily the costs to phase out the oldest Casegood plant, eliminate marginal suites, and write off related unproductive assets.[56]

Like Integrated Device Technology, Bassett Furniture is writing down assets that have become value-impaired.

Historically, inflation has helped to alleviate the need for asset write-downs. As prices generally rise, cash flows and the market values of corporate assets are pulled up and tend to exceed their historical cost-based book values. More recently, with disinflation and deflation in many industries, net realizable values are falling, sometimes rapidly. If we add to this stable-to-declining price environment the extremely rapid technological advances that tend to render fixed-asset and intangible-asset investments obsolete, future losses from asset impairments are more likely.

An extended amortization period is one that leads to insufficient amortization and depreciation charges while an asset is in service. As under-amortization or depreciation of the asset slows the reduction in its book value, the likelihood increases that the cash flows expected to be received from the asset might be exceeded by that asset's book value. Value impairment and an asset write-down become more likely. A "catch-up" is needed in the form of an asset write-down to make up for insufficient depreciation and amortization charges in prior years. In effect, earnings were overstated in prior years.

As a case in point, in 1987, General Motors Corp. lengthened the estimated service lives of its plant and equipment. This change reduced 1987 depreciation and amortization charges by $1.2 billion. The company reported net income of $3.6 billion that year. In 1990, 1991, and 1992, the company reported significant losses. Contributing to the losses were a series of restructuring charges described in the company's 1992 annual report as follows:

> The 1992 operating results include a special restructuring charge of $1,237.0 million . . . primarily attributable to redundant facilities and related employment costs at Hughes. The special charge comprehends a reduction of Hughes worldwide employment over the July 1992 through December 1993 time period, a major facilities consolidation, and a re-evaluation of certain business lines that no longer meet Hughes' strategic objectives.
>
> In 1991, 1990, and 1986, special restructuring charges of $2,820.8 million, $3,314.0 million, and $1,287.6 million, respectively, were made to provide for the closing of plants and other restructuring costs.[57]

It can be reasonably argued that a portion of the restructuring charges reported by General Motors in these years was attributable to useful lives that were too long for the company's plant and equipment.

Signs that a company may be a candidate for an asset write-down as the result of an extended amortization period are found in the amortization periods used to expense fixed and intangible assets. What useful lives has the company chosen? The appropriateness of the useful lives employed should be given careful consideration in light of the company's operating circumstances. Do they make sense? Does it seem reasonable that the company might benefit from the assets over the periods indicated? Or is it more likely that before the useful lives selected are complete, changing business conditions will require new directions and investments. In such a setting, old book values that remain on the balance sheet may need to be written down.

In considering the appropriateness of the amortization periods employed, a comparison with the useful lives used by competitors and other companies in the industry would be helpful. Companies that select useful lives consistently longer than their competitors' may face asset write-downs later.

Unfortunately, as seen earlier, amortization periods or useful lives are typically not well disclosed. Recall, for example that Centocor provides depreciation, "using the straight-line method over the estimated useful lives of the assets, which range from 3 to 31 years."[58] It is difficult to determine what amortization period is being employed when information on useful lives is presented in such a vague fashion.

One useful technique for determining a company's amortization period is to compute an average amortization period or useful life for its collective depreciable asset base. For example, Micron Technology, Inc., a manufacturer of semiconductors, provides the following depreciation policy:

> Depreciation is computed using the straight-line method over the estimated useful lives of 5 to 30 years for buildings and 2 to 5 years for equipment.[59]

Exhibit 9.4 provides detail of the company's property, plant, and equipment account.

Using the information in the exhibit, we can calculate the company's overall average useful life by first calculating its depreciable asset base. This is the average cost of its property, plant, and equipment accounts excluding land and construction in progress. At September 30, 1993, that figure is $796.4 million ($828.6 million less $7.5 million less $24.7 million), and at September 30, 1994, it is $1,085.5 million ($1,162.1 million less $7.9 million less $68.7 million). The average depreciable asset base is thus $941.0 million, or the simple average of $796.4 million and $1,085.5 million. During 1994, the company reported depreciation and amortization expense on these assets of $140.3 million.[60] Given that the company uses the straight-line method and assuming no significant salvage value, the resulting average useful life is 6.7 years. That is, at the rate of $140.3 million per year, it will take 6.7 years to fully expense a depreciable base of $941.0 million.

The 6.7 years figure is actually on the low end for companies in the semiconductor industry. *The Value Line Investment Survey* reports an average annual depreciation rate of 11.2% for the 18 companies it includes in the semiconductor industry.[61] The average useful life is the reciprocal of this depreciation rate. That is, if a company depreciates 11.2% of an asset per year, it will take 8.9 years, or 1 divided by

Exhibit 9.4 Calculating Average Amortization Period: Micron Technology, Inc., Property, Plant, and Equipment, Years Ending September 30, 1993 and 1994 (millions of dollars)

	1993	1994
Land	$ 7.5	$ 7.9
Buildings	217.6	260.0
Equipment	578.8	825.5
Construction in progress	24.7	68.7
Total	828.6	1,162.1
Less: Accumulated depreciation and amortization	390.8	498.6
Total	$ 437.8	$ 663.5

Source: Micron Technology, Inc., annual report, September 1994, p. 22.

0.112, to totally depreciate the asset. Thus, Micron Technology is writing its depreciable assets off more quickly, over an average period of 6.7 years, compared to the 8.9 years that is the industry average. As a result, Micron Technology is less susceptible to an earnings surprise resulting from an impairment loss.

The average useful life calculation is rather crude and depends on key assumptions, namely, that all companies used for comparison have a similar long-lived asset mix. That is, companies with heavy investments in buildings will naturally have longer average useful lives than companies that lease their buildings. Also, use of the straight-line method of depreciation is assumed. If a company uses an accelerated method of depreciation, it will tend to report higher depreciation expense in the early part of an asset's useful life. This will give a misleading reading of a relatively shorter useful life.

Provided the necessary data are available, calculations of average useful lives can be extended to different asset groups. Continuing the Micron Technology example, the company's balance sheet reports product and process technology, net, in the amount of $69.7 million and $48.2 million, respectively, at the end of fiscal 1993 and 1994. The company reports the following information in its notes:

> Amortization of capitalized product and process technology costs charged to operations was $40.9 million in 1994; $26.2 million in 1993; and $10 million in 1992. Accumulated amortization was $100.4 million and $59.5 million as of September 1, 1994, and September 2, 1993.[62]

Adding accumulated amortization of $59.5 million to the asset's book value of $69.7 million at year-end 1993 yields a computed asset cost of $129.2 million. Performing a similar calculation at year-end 1994, that is, adding accumulated amortization of $100.4 million to the asset's book value of $48.2 million yields a computed asset cost of $148.6 million. Finding the average of $129.2 million and $148.6 million yields an average asset cost of $138.9 million. As disclosed in its footnote, the company amortized $40.9 million of this average asset cost during 1994, implying an average useful life of 3.4 years. That period seems reasonable and appears to take into account the rapid technological advances that are part of this high-tech industry.

Closely related to the capitalized technology costs of Micron Technology are capitalized software development costs. Recall that computer software companies can capitalize research and development costs on software products once technological feasibility has been reached. Those capitalized software development costs are then amortized to expense when marketing of the software product begins. Amortization is typically taken using the straight-line method over the estimated useful lives of the software products.[63]

Recall that System Software capitalizes approximately 38% of its software development costs. At year-end 1992 and 1993, the total of the company's capitalized software costs were $27.5 million and $44.3 million, respectively. The average total cost was thus $35.9 million during 1993. During that year, the company amortized $5.9 million of these costs, implying an average amortization period for these software costs of six years ($35.9/$5.9). The company reports use of a five-year amortization period. The discrepancy is likely due to an increase in amounts capitalized during the final months of the fiscal year. Amounts capitalized late in the year tend to skew the calculated average amortization period to the high side. That is, while amounts capitalized late in the year increase the costs capitalized, they do not increase ratably the amount of amortization expense recorded.

System Software's stated amortization period of five years for software costs could be argued as being long. New products and releases that come to market continually might render older software products obsolete before five years elapse.

A good example of an extended amortization period is provided by the Vista Resources case discussed in Chapter 3. Recall that as recently as 1989, Vista Resources was not amortizing goodwill acquired prior to 1971 because, in the opinion of management, it had not decreased in value.[64] The company reported goodwill on the balance sheet in the amount of $1.7 million.

By not amortizing goodwill, the company was taking the position that it had an infinite useful life. The asset was, however, one that could potentially become value-impaired, necessitating a write-down. The write-down came in 1990. That year, the company took a special charge to write the asset off because, in the opinion of management, it no longer had value. That charge helped to push the company into a loss position for the year. Had the company been amortizing a portion of its goodwill each year, that special charge could have been reduced, if not eliminated.

SUMMARY

Under the matching principle, cost capitalization is permitted when future periods are expected to benefit from expenditures incurred. Amounts capitalized are reported as assets and are amortized over those future years. Deciding whether future periods will benefit from costs incurred relies much on management judgment. As a result, different capitalization policies are employed in what would appear to be similar situations. Some companies take a conservative stance and expense amounts incurred. Others, more optimistic regarding the extent to which future periods will benefit from expenditures incurred, take a more aggressive stance and capitalize many of the items expensed by others. In the latter case, future earnings will be negatively affected if costs capitalized in previous years are not realized and must be written off.

Once costs are capitalized, management must select the time period that will benefit. The resulting amortization period is the asset's expected useful life. The annual charge to income for depreciation and amortization expense depends on that useful life. The longer the life, the smaller the annual expense amount becomes.

When amortization periods are extended, insufficient annual charges for depreciation and amortization are taken. Asset book values build up. At some point, the asset becomes value-impaired and a write-down is needed. That write-down or impairment loss is in effect a catch-up adjustment for inadequate expense charges in prior years.

The incentives for managements to understate expenses are much the same as those underlying overstated revenue. Understated expenses lead to higher earnings, which can mean higher management compensation and share price along with lower apparent firm risk and cost of capital.[65] By understating expenses, managements may be inflating earnings to postpone difficult decisions in the hope that better times arrive. Future losses are inevitable as income statement charges are recorded to make the company's balance sheet more representative of economic realities.

Careful analysis of financial performance and position requires an appreciation and understanding of cost capitalization and amortization policies and their implications for future results. Earnings expectations formed without such information are at greater risk of an earnings surprise. Exhibit 9.5 provides a checklist that will help the investor or creditor anticipate earnings surprises arising from understated expenses.

Exhibit 9.5   Checklist for Financial Early Warnings: Understated Expenses

---

Aggressive Cost Capitalization
A. For cost capitalization generally:
  1. What are the company's policies with respect to cost capitalization?
      a. Is the company capitalizing costs that competitors or other companies in the industry expense?
      b. Does the company expense more, taking a more conservative approach?
      c. What do capitalized costs represent?
          i.   An identifiable asset with an ascertainable market value?
          ii. Not an identifiable asset, whose market value, if any, is tied to the general fortunes of the company?
  2. Do capitalized costs exceed net realizable value?
B. For companies incurring software development costs:
  1. What proportion of software development costs incurred are being capitalized?
  2. How does this percentage compare with competitors or other companies in the industry?
C. For companies capitalizing interest costs:
  1. Should capitalization of interest costs be discontinued?
      a. Is the asset under construction complete and available for its intended use?
      b. Do costs incurred on the asset under construction give an indication of exceeding net realizable value?
          i.   Have there been construction delays?
          ii. Have there been cost overruns?
D. For companies incurring oil and gas exploration expenditures:
  1. Does the company use the successful-efforts method (expensing option) or the full-cost method (capitalization option) to account for exploration expenditures?
  2. Do costs capitalized appear to be realizable?
E. A policy of capitalizing the following costs should be considered very aggressive, potentially at odds with generally accepted accounting principles:
  1. Advertising, marketing, and promotion costs

   2. Costs incurred to acquire new members or subscribers unless costs can be linked with new sign-ups
   3. Costs incurred on internally conducted research and development activities (software development excluded; can be capitalized after technological feasibility has been reached)
F. Has the company shown evidence in the past of being aggressive in its capitalization policies?
   1. Is there an example of a prior-year write-down of capitalized costs that, in hindsight, should not have been capitalized?

Extended Amortization Periods

A. Has the company selected extended amortization and depreciation periods for capitalized costs?
   1. As data permit, how does the calculated average amortization period for long-lived assets compare with competitors or other firms in the industry?
      a. Calculated as average asset costs, excluding land and construction-in-process, divided by the annual amount of depreciation or amortization expense
      b. Can be calculated for property, plant, and equipment accounts and other capitalized costs, including technology-related assets like software development costs
B. Be particularly alert for extended amortization periods in the following situations:
   1. Company's industry is experiencing price deflation
   2. Company in an industry that is experiencing rapid technological change
   3. Company has shown evidence in the past of employing extended amortization periods
      a. Is there an example of a prior-year write-down of assets that became value-impaired?

ENDNOTES

1. *The Wall Street Journal*, February 16, 1994, p. C6.
2. General accounting guidance on the definition and measurement of expenses and losses and on when such items should be reported as assets is provided in Statement of Financial Accounting Concepts No. 5, "Recognition and Measurement in Financial Statements of Business Enterprises" (Stamford, Conn.: Financial Accounting Standards Board, December 1984), and Statement of Financial Accounting Concepts No. 6, "Elements of Financial Statements" (December 1985).
3. Bob Evans Farms, Inc., annual report, April 1994, p. 20.
4. Sun Television and Appliances, Inc., annual report, February 1994, p. 10.
5. Lechter's, Inc., annual report, January 1991, p. 17.
6. Cash America International, Inc., annual report, December 1993, p. 18.
7. Ryan's Family Steak Houses, Inc., annual report, January 1991, p. 19.
8. 50-Off Stores, Inc., Form 10-K annual report to the Securities and Exchange Commission, January 1994, p. F-7.
9. Value Merchants, Inc., annual report, February 1992, p. 25.
10. Lechter's, Inc., annual report, January 1993, p. 11.

11. Ryan's Family Steak Houses, Inc., annual report, December 1993, p. 15.
12. Arctco, Inc., annual report, March 1993, p. 16.
13. Top Air Manufacturing Co., annual report, May 1992, p. 8.
14. American Power Conversion, Inc., annual report, December 1993, p. 45.
15. Statement of Financial Accounting Standards (SFAS) No. 2, "Accounting for Research and Development Costs" (Stamford, Conn.: Financial Accounting Standards Board, October 1974).
16. Microframe, Inc., Form 10-K annual report to the Securities and Exchange Commission, March 1994, p. F-8.
17. Homestake Mining Co., annual report, December 1993, pp. 33–34.
18. Ibid., p. 22.
19. The Increase in expense is calculated as the increase in unamortized membership acquisition costs of $18,595,000, which excludes the deferred membership income portion, plus the increase in prepaid solicitation costs of $12,174,000 less the decline in prepaid commission of $1,860,000.
20. CUC International, Inc., annual report, January 1989, p. 22.
21. America Online, Inc., annual report, June 1994, p. 23. Statement of Position No. 93-7, "Reporting on Advertising Costs" (New York: American Institute of Certified Public Accountants, 1993), does permit capitalization of direct-response advertising where customers can be shown to have responded specifically to the advertising. This statement lends support to America Online's capitalization policy.
22. *Forbes*, October 24, 1994, pp. 74–75.
23. SFAS No. 121, "Accounting for the Impairment of Long-Lived Assets and for Long-Lived Assets to Be Disposed of " (March 1995).
24. Apache Corp., annual report, December 1993, p. 26.
25. St. Mary Land & Exploration Co., annual report, December 1993, p. 26.
26. SFAS No. 19, "Financial Accounting and Reporting by Oil and Gas Producing Companies" (December 1977) required use of the successful-efforts method. The effective date of that standard was indefinitely suspended by SFAS No. 25, "Suspension of Certain Accounting Requirements for Oil and Gas Producing Companies" (February 1979). As a result, use of either the successful-efforts or the full-cost method was effectively permitted.
27. Continental Medical Systems, Inc., annual report, June 1992, p. 30.
28. Chambers Development Co., annual report, December 1990, p. 44.
29. Chambers Development Switches Accounting Plan," *The Wall Street Journal*, March 19, 1992, p. B4.
30. Refer to SFAS No. 86, "Accounting for the Costs of Computer Software to be Sold, Leased, or Otherwise Marketed" (August 1985).
31. As reported in D. Kieso and J. Weygandt, *Intermediate Accounting*, 8th ed. (New York: Wiley, 1995), p. 593.
32. PeopleSoft, Inc., Form 10-K annual report to the Securities and Exchange Commission, September 1991, p. F-6.
33. Microsoft Corp. annual report, June 1993, p. 34.
34. System Software, Inc., annual report, October 1993, p. 40.
35. American Software, Inc., annual report, April 1993, p. 36.
36. SFAS No. 34, "Capitalization of Interest Cost" (October 1979).
37. D. R. Horton Custom Homes, Inc., annual report, September 1993, p. 20.
38. Delta Air Lines, Inc., annual report, June 1993, p. 25.

39. Oriole Homes Corp., annual report, December 1993, p. 12.
40. SFAS No. 121, "Accounting for the Impairment of Long-Lived Assets and for Long-Lived Assets to Be Disposed of" (March 1995) amended SFAS No. 34. Effective for fiscal years beginning after December 1995, SFAS No. 121 indicates that long-lived assets to be held and used, including those under construction for which interest is being capitalized, are value impaired, necessitating a discontinuation of interest capitalization, when the asset's cost exceeds the future cash flows expected to result from the use and eventual disposition of the asset.
41. D. R. Horton Custom Homes, Inc., annual report, April 1993, p. 20.
42. Union Camp Corp., annual report, December 1993, p. 26.
43. Centocor, Inc., annual report, December 1992, p. 19.
44. Cordis Corp., annual report, June 1993, p. 38.
45. United States Surgical Corp., annual report, December 1993, p. 6.
46. This calculated amount of depreciation and amortization is provided for the sake of argument and is not intended to equal the actual amount of depreciation and amortization reported for the year. The company reported actual depreciation and amortization expense of $83,200,000. This amount includes approximately $17,500,000 in amortization of other assets that is not included in the amount of depreciation and amortization expense estimated here. Other differences are due to the rough estimates that were used in calculating average useful lives and to the fact that no salvage value was employed in our estimates.
47. Biomet, Inc., annual report, May 1993, p. 17.
48. Diagnostic Products, Inc., annual report, December 1993, p. 23.
49. Allergan, Inc., annual report, December 1993, p. 34.
50. Healthdyne, Inc., annual report, December 1993, p. 26.
51. Autodesk, Inc., annual report, January 1993, p. 29.
52. Bolt, Beranek & Newman, Inc., annual report, June 1993, p. 27.
53. Caere Corp., annual report, December 1993, p. 18.
54. SFAS No. 121, "Accounting for the Impairment of Long-Lived Assets and for Long-Lived Assets to Be Disposed of " (March 1995).
55. Integrated Device Technology, Inc., annual report, April 1992. Information obtained from Disclosure, Inc., *Compact D/SEC: Corporate Information on Public Companies Filing with the SEC* (Bethesda, Md.: Disclosure, Inc., December 1992).
56. Bassett Furniture Industries, Inc., annual report, November 1990, footnote H.
57. General Motors Corp., annual report, December 1992. Information obtained from Disclosure, Inc., *Compact D/SEC: Corporate Information on Public Companies Filing with the SEC* (Bethesda, Md.: Disclosure, Inc., September 1993).
58. Centocor, Inc., annual report, December 1992, p. 19.
59. Micron Technology, Inc., annual report, September 1994, p. 20.
60. Depreciation and amortization expense is reported as a noncash expense on the company's cash flow statement. This amount differs from the change in accumulated depreciation and amortization as reported in Exhibit 9.4 because of dispositions of property, plant, and equipment items during the year.
61. *The Value Line Investment Survey: Ratings and Reports* (New York: Value Line Publishing, April 28, 1995), pp. 1056–1073.
62. Micron Technology, Inc., annual report, September 1994, p. 22.
63. SFAS No. 86, "Accounting for the Costs of Computer Software to be Sold, Leased, or Otherwise Marketed" (August 1985). SFAS No. 86 permits straight-line amorti-

zation provided the percent of capitalized software costs amortized for a year exceeds the percent of software revenue generated by the product for that year to the total estimated software revenue to be generated by the product.

64. Generally accepted accounting principles permit this exception. In particular, refer to Accounting Principles Board, Opinion No. 17, "Intangible Assets" (New York: American Institute of Certified Public Accountants, August 1970).

65. Though much academic work on efficient markets could be seen as challenging the soundness of the share price, risk, and cost of capital arguments.

Chapter 10

Misreported Assets and Liabilities

Crown Crafts, Inc., today announced financial results for the fourth quarter and fiscal year ended March 28, 1993. As anticipated, the company achieved record annual net sales and net earnings. Full-year net earnings per share declined slightly due to higher average shares outstanding and an unanticipated fourth-quarter inventory write-down. . . .

Both fourth-quarter and full-year operating results were negatively impacted by an unanticipated inventory write-down of approximately $1.4 million at the company's comforters and accessories facilities in Roxboro, N.C.

"The fourth-quarter inventory write-off in Roxboro reduced net earnings per share by about $0.10 for both the quarter and the full fiscal year," stated Michael H. Bernstein, Crown Crafts' president and chief executive officer. "Our conclusion, after reasonable investigation, is that a significant portion of the inventory shortage is probably the result of theft."[1]

As demonstrated by Crown's inventory loss, the importance of the close relation between the balance sheet and the income statement cannot be overemphasized. This relation was highlighted in Chapter 9, where the focus was on capitalized costs and long-lived assets. It can be extended, however, to include all assets reported on the balance sheet, as well as liabilities.

When assets are reported at amounts exceeding what can be expected to be realized through their use or sale, loss recognition is being postponed. The balance sheet reports these future losses as components of assets. These so-called assets, or postponed losses, will be recognized later, either through a write-down or a loss on sale.

Consider, for example, the following description of a restructuring charge provided by Tektronix, Inc.:

In 1990, the company provided for restructuring charges of $80.0 million for costs associated with downsizing of operations, consolidating facilities and the disposal, either through sale or abandonment, of certain product lines. The charges included severance costs, commitments to third parties, product line disposal costs, write-off of intangible assets and relocation costs.[2]

The company is recording an $80 million restructuring charge associated with a general downsizing of operations. Included in the charge are costs associated with the disposal of certain product lines, which would likely include inventory write-downs, and the write-off of intangible assets. It is difficult to say precisely when these inventory items and intangible assets became value-impaired. Probably, they were value-impaired for some time prior to their write-down. During that time, the company was carrying postponed losses on its balance sheet as assets. Stated another way, these assets were being overvalued.

Similarly, when liabilities are reported at amounts below the present value of what will be needed to satisfy existing claims, they are undervalued. The balance sheet does not include the full valuation of claims against the reporting firm. At a future date, when the company recognizes the full amount of its obligations, a special charge or loss will be needed.

For example, the 1993 annual report of Athanor Group, Inc., provided the following discussion:

> During the year ended October 31, 1992, a provision of $200,000 was recorded to other income (expense) relating to the estimated cost to remediate the perchloroethlyene contamination in the subsurface soil below Alger. This provision is included with other accrued liabilities at October 31, 1992. It is estimated that this remediation will take approximately two years.
>
> During the year ended October 31, 1993, an additional provision of $50,000 was recorded to other income (expense) relating to the estimated cost to remediate the perchloroethlyene contamination in the subsurface soil below Alger. This increased the provision, included with other accrued liabilities, to $250,000 at October 31, 1993.[3]

The company had an obligation to remediate the contaminated soil below its manufacturing plant. This obligation existed when the contamination occurred. An estimate of the cost of remediation was recorded as a liability, presumably when the problem was first discovered. That first provision was the company's best estimate of the total amount needed to correct the problem, but the estimate was insufficient. An increase in the liability was needed, with an additional charge to income. Prior to the recording of that second charge, the liability was undervalued. Moreover, depending on the actual costs of remediation, the liability may still be undervalued.

As with other financial statement items, the reporting of assets and liabilities requires the application of management judgment. Amounts reported as assets must be continually evaluated in light of their realizability. Claims, too, must be constantly assessed to determine whether amounts reported as liabilities are sufficient. This use of judgment in the preparation of financial statements leaves room for error. Moreover, in some instances, it leaves room for intentional misreported amounts.

In this chapter, we continue our search for evidence of understated expenses. We do so by employing the close link that exists between assets and liabilities as reported on the balance sheet and associated expenses as reported on the income statement. We seek to anticipate charges against income—expenses and losses—by uncovering evidence that assets may be overvalued or liabilities undervalued.

OVERVALUATION OF ASSETS

In Chapter 9, we searched for understated expenses associated with capitalized costs and long-lived assets subject to amortization. Here our focus is on assets not subject to annual amortization. In particular, we consider three asset accounts: accounts receivable, inventory, and investments.

Accounts Receivable

The balance sheet item "accounts receivable" is useful in uncovering overstated revenue. Premature or fictitious revenue recognition typically yields an uncollectible buildup in the accounts receivable balance. A careful examination of accounts receivable should also be made even when revenue is properly recognized. Even though it was considered collectible at the time of sale, such revenue may later prove to be uncollectible. Expenses are understated when an insufficient provision has been made for these uncollectible amounts.

Accounts receivable is reported at net realizable value, the amount of cash expected to be received upon collection. Accordingly, amounts due are reported after subtracting an estimate of uncollectible accounts. This estimate, also known as an allowance for doubtful accounts or a reserve for doubtful accounts, arises with the recording of an expense, the provision for doubtful accounts. Note that the allowance for doubtful accounts is a balance sheet account. It is a contra-asset or negative-asset account subtracted from accounts receivable in valuing them at net realizable value. When uncollectible accounts are written off, they are charged against this allowance for doubtful accounts. In contrast, the provision for doubtful accounts, also called bad-debt expense, is an income statement expense account recorded when the balance in the allowance for doubtful accounts is increased.

When revenue is recognized, some portion will likely prove to be uncollectible. The matching principle calls for recording an estimate of these uncollectible amounts in the same time period that the revenue is recognized. In this way, one cost of extending credit, uncollectible accounts, is matched with revenue.

When a company's estimate of uncollectible accounts is determined to be insufficient, such that the accounts receivable balance exceeds net realizable value, a write-down and an accompanying loss or charge against income is needed. This loss will typically exceed the normal annual provision for doubtful accounts. Consider the following discussion taken from Intellicall, Inc.'s annual report:

In the fourth quarter of 1992 new management began a broad assessment of the company's product and service offerings relative to competing manufacturers and service providers, the company's relationship with its customers, declining sales of pay telephones and call processing systems, declining call revenue from pay telephones and call processing systems, and the magnitude of uncollected call traffic upon which the company had previously advanced revenues to its customers. Based on that assessment, management determined that the value of several categories of assets was significantly impaired, that a strategic restructuring of the company's business arrangements with certain of its customers is necessary in order to revitalize the health of the company's core business, and that the company will be required to forgo or defer collection of significant amounts of receivables, primarily related to advances made on uncollected call revenue and customer receivables.

Accordingly, for the fourth quarter of 1992, the company recorded reserves of approximately $8.5 million against receivables for advances on uncollected call traffic, amounts owed to local exchange carriers for uncollected call traffic, and receivables from the sale and licensing of pay telephones and call processing systems.[4]

In previous periods, Intellicall had not provided sufficiently for uncollectible accounts. As a result, a significant charge or expense was needed in one year. The amount, $8.5 million, helped to increase the company's pre-tax loss to $29.6 million in 1992.

In searching for overstated revenue, one series of steps recommended in Chapter 8 was to look for signs of overstated accounts receivable. These steps consisted of comparing the percentage change in accounts receivable with the percentage change in revenue and evaluating the level of and changes in accounts receivable days, or A/R days, in light of similar measures for the industry and selected competitors. These same steps can be employed when checking for accounts receivable that may be reported in excess of net realizable value. There are, however, some subtle differences. For example, with overstated revenue, the amount of reported revenue is typically increasing. With overvalued accounts receivable, however, it is not unusual to have declining revenue. Falling revenue implies declining demand for a company's products and services, and indicates potential inroads by competitors. It is also a potential sign of industry weakness that may be affecting not only the company but also its customers, weakening their ability to pay. Moreover, the company may be selling to less creditworthy customers in an attempt to maintain previous revenue levels. All such factors lead to reduced collectibility of accounts receivable.

We do not want to imply that, in the absence of premature or fictitious recognition, rising revenue implies collectible accounts receivable. While increasing revenue does imply demand strength, it can indicate that higher credit risks are being taken. Thus, even when revenue is rising, other checks on the collectibility of accounts receivable should be made.

In the case of Intellicall, quarterly revenue peaked at $62 million in September 1991. Revenue fell in December and in each quarter of 1992. By the fourth quarter of that year, quarterly revenue had fallen below $30 million. The company had been slow in responding to changes in its industry, a miscalculation that would prove difficult to overcome.

Home Nutritional Services, Inc.

Home Nutritional Services, Inc., a provider of home health care services, enjoyed six years of consistent growth in revenue and earnings. That growth continued into its seventh year, 1992. Selected quarterly statistics for 1992 are provided in Exhibit 10.1. Revenue at Home Nutritional Services continued to grow during 1992 and increased faster than increases in accounts receivable. As a result, A/R days was improving slightly. The very high level of A/R days was cause for concern, however, especially considering how the company's collection experience compared with other companies in its industry.

For example, in 1992, median A/R days for the home health care services industry was running at approximately 61. Sometimes industry statistics are not directly comparable. In such situations, it helps to use for comparison purposes the statistics of a competitor. Data for a competitor, T^2 Medical, Inc., are provided in Exhibit 10.2. Note that while Home Nutritional was taking approximately five months to collect outstanding receivables, T^2 Medical was collecting accounts receivable in less than two months, better than the industry median of about two months.

In order to obtain an estimate of the dollar amount of Home Nutritional's accounts receivable that were potentially uncollectible and at risk for a write-down, a target level for A/R days is needed. The industry median of 61 days could be used for this purpose, as could the mid 50's reading for Home Nutritional's competitor T^2 Medical. Alternatively, another measure, determined in discussion with Home Nutritional's management, might be appropriate. That is, it would be helpful to know management's view as to a desirable level for A/R days. Assume that in 1992, 90 days would have been an acceptable collection period for Home Nutritional's accounts receivable.

To reduce A/R days from 145 to 90 for September 1992 would require a reduction of 55 days. Dividing revenue of $33,253,000 for the September quarter by 90 translates into daily revenue of $369,500. Multiplying $369,500 by 55 days indicates

Exhibit 10.1   High A/R Days: Home Nutritional Services, Inc., Selected Statistics, Quarters Ending March 31, June 30, and September 30, 1992 (thousands of dollars)

	1992		
	Mar.	June	Sept.
Revenue	$28,972	$30,530	$33,253
A/R, net of allowance for doubtful accounts	$50,005	$51,943	$53,736
A/R days based on 90-day quarter	155	153	145
Net income	$ 3,103	$ 2,340	$ 1,454

Source: Home Nutritional Services, Inc., annual report, December 1992. Data obtained from Disclosure, Inc., *Compact D/SEC: Corporate Information on Public Companies Filing with the SEC* (Bethesda, Md.: Disclosure, Inc., September 1993).

Exhibit 10.2 Lower Comparative A/R Days: T² Medical, Inc., Selected Statistics, Quarters Ending March 31, June 30, and September 30, 1992 (thousands of dollars)

	1992		
	Mar.	June	Sept.
Revenue	$54,832	$59,840	$80,524
A/R, net of allowance for doubtful accounts	$32,784	$33,246	$34,542
A/R days based on 90-day quarter	54	50	39
Net income	$12,419	$14,717	$21,235

Source: T² Medical, Inc., annual report, September 1992. Data obtained from Disclosure, Inc., *Compact D/SEC: Corporate Information on Public Companies Filing with the SEC* (Bethesda, Md.: Disclosure, Inc., September 1993).

that $20,323,000 of accounts receivable were at risk for a write-down. If at the end of the September quarter, the company were to record a special provision for doubtful accounts in the amount of $20.3 million, accounts receivable and A/R days would be reduced to $33,413,000 and 90 days, respectively.

Upon release of its December 1992 results, Home Nutritional Services made the following announcement:

Home Nutritional Services, Inc. (Nasdaq: HNSI), today announced financial results for the fourth quarter and fiscal year ended Dec. 31, 1992.

Revenues for the year grew 27% to $129 million. Net earnings, before giving effect for an after-tax charge due to restructuring and a special provision for doubtful accounts receivable totaling $10.9 million, were $8.3 million, or $.70 per share, compared with 1991 earnings of $11.4 million, or $.97 per share.

During the year, the company relocated its corporate headquarters from Parsippany, NJ, to Marietta, GA, added a second major reimbursement center, and restructured its operations as a result of changes in reimbursement patterns that have been occurring in the home infusion therapy industry. As a result, after-tax restructuring charges totaling $4.2 million were incurred. In addition, changes in the reimbursement patterns of indemnity insurance carriers developed late in the year and necessitated a special provision for doubtful accounts of $6.7 million after-tax. These charges resulted in the company incurring a net loss for both the fourth quarter and for the year of $.83 and $.22 per share, respectively.[5]

The company noted that changes in reimbursement patterns of indemnity insurance carriers resulted in a slowing in its collections and the need for a special provision for doubtful accounts. In other words, insurance companies were paying smaller percentages of amounts billed by the company. It was not an inability, but rather an unwillingness, on their part to pay amounts billed. Accordingly, amounts reported as due were no longer collectible in their entirety. These changes were showing up as increases in A/R days. At the time, neither the home health care industry nor the company's competitors were manifesting similar difficulties.

In adjusting to a new market realism, Home Nutritional recorded a special provision for doubtful accounts. This provision was reported as $6.7 million after-tax. In the company's annual report for the year ending December 31, 1992, this provision was reported to be $11 million before taxes. Accounts receivable was reduced by this same amount.

An $11 million reduction in accounts receivable for September 1992 reported in Exhibit 10.1 would reduce A/R days to approximately 116. While down from the 145 days shown in the exhibit, 116 days is still high and exceeds our 90 day assumed target. Either management had faced up to its collection problems and viewed 116 days as an appropriate target, or those collection problems had not been totally dealt with. Interestingly, by the end of 1993, A/R days was up to 134 days. Thus, it appeared that another write-down might be necessary. We cannot know the outcome, however, because the company was acquired in early 1994.

Urcarco, Inc.

Urcarco ran a chain of used car lots. The company provided sales and on-site financing support to customers who typically could not obtain financing from traditional sources. Through its fiscal year ending June 30, 1990, the company experienced significant growth in revenue and net income. Gross margins earned on car sales and interest rates charged on outstanding loan contract balances were more than enough to cover the company's loan losses, providing a significant return to shareholders.

With the recession of 1990-1991, however, car sales slowed and collection problems began to grow. Financial statistics are provided in Exhibit 10.3. Urcarco's problems developed and compounded quickly. They were very much in evidence at the end of the December quarter. Notice the increase in late contracts as a percent of contracts outstanding and in the percent of contracts repossessed. In the December quarter, on an annual basis, the company repossessed 36% of its cars. Moreover, borrowers were late with their payments on 8% of the contracts that had not been repossessed.

Evidence of a slowing economy was the primary warning that the company might have difficulty in collecting its receivables. By December 1990 the economic environment was not robust and the U.S. economy was slipping into recession. And while the company had increased its provision for doubtful accounts as a percent of sales, the allowance for doubtful accounts as a percent of gross accounts receivable was still only 10%. This was no higher than it had been in earlier quarters, when economic conditions were much better.

The question can be asked as to whether the company should have reported pre-tax profit for the December 1990 quarter. Increasing the allowance for doubtful accounts percentage just to 11%, a level at which it had been in previous quarters, would have required an additional provision for doubtful accounts of $1,754,000. Since the company reported pre-tax income of only $1,077,000 that quarter, such an increase in the provision for doubtful accounts would have put the company into a loss position.

Exhibit 10.3   Increasingly Uncollectible Accounts: Urcarco, Inc., Selected Statistics, Year Ending June 30 and Quarters Ending September 30 and December 31, 1990 (thousands of dollars)

	1990		
	Year-end June 30	Sept.	Dec.
Sales	$150,417	$ 52,788	$ 43,615
Gross accounts receivable	126,559	158,902	175,353
Beginning allowance for doubtful accounts	3,470	14,450	16,165
Provision for doubtful accounts	26,928	9,154	12,333
Write-offs of uncollectible accounts	(15,948)	(7,439)	(10,386)
Ending allowance for doubtful accounts	14,450	16,165	18,112
Net accounts receivable	$112,109	$142,737	$157,241
Pre-tax income	$ 24,059	$ 10,195	$1,077
No. of additional cars financed	18,692	6,002	4,737
No. of contracts outstanding	18,165	21,767	23,597
No. of contracts late	1,067	1,606	1,952
No. of repossessions	4,094	1,547	2,301
Late contracts % of contracts outstanding	6%	7%	8%
Annualized repossession % of contracts outstanding plus repossessions	18%	26%	36%
Provision for doubtful accounts % of sales	18%	17%	28%
Allowance for doubtful accounts % of gross accounts receivable	11%	10%	10%

Sources: Urcarco, Inc., annual report, June 1990, and Form 10-Q quarterly reports to the Securities and Exchange Commission, September 1990 and December 1990.

In March and June 1991 quarters, Urcarco's sales declined markedly, to $40,690,000 and $18,831,000, respectively. As the company came to grips with these sales declines and its collection problems, it reported pre-tax losses in those quarters of $22,324,000 and $36,174,000, respectively. By November 1992 the company was out of the car sales business and had redirected its attention to operating consumer lending offices.

Inventory

While inventory levels may be raised to meet anticipated increases in demand, an unexplained buildup in the inventory account can have many downside implications. Inventory represents the cost of unsold goods. As these costs accumulate, the risk that goods on hand may be slow-moving or obsolete increases. With increases in this risk comes the heightened chance that management may need to address its inventory problems with a write-down and an accompanying charge to income. Such a write-down is needed when the cost of inventory exceeds the cost to replace it. More than a needed inventory write-down, however, an inventory buildup may indicate the company has other, more fundamental problems with its products or markets. Additionally, in some isolated instances, an inventory buildup may indicate the reporting of fictitious inventory. Here, certain costs have been erroneously capitalized to inventory, or physical counts have been overstated, either in error or through fraudulent intent.

In this section, we discuss early warning indicators related to inventory. Our objective is to anticipate earnings surprises caused by inventory write-downs. These write-downs might be the result of something as simple as slow-moving and obsolete goods or of something more complicated, such as erroneous inventory reporting.

Obsolete Inventory and Other Fundamental Problems

A good example of what causes an inventory-related earnings surprise is provided by Machine Technology, Inc., a company in the semiconductor industry. In its year ending August 31, 1988, Machine Technology recorded a pre-tax charge of $1,777,212, which it described as a nonrecurring inventory write-down. The company provided the following description of the charge:

> During the fourth quarter, 1988, the company re-evaluated its inventories because of changes in its sales mix toward newer, more technologically advanced products. Accordingly, inventories were reduced to account for excess quantities related to its older product lines.[6]

Some of Machine Technology's products had become technologically obsolete. The company reduced the balance sheet valuation of its inventory and took a charge against income for $1,777,212. As a result of this charge and other restructuring costs, it reported a pre-tax loss in 1988 of nearly $6 million. Selected financial statistics for Machine Technology are provided in Exhibit 10.4.

In 1987 the company's inventory days was nearly 300. At the time, other companies in the semiconductor industry were carrying inventory in the 75–100 day range, with 126 days representing the poorest performing firms in the industry.[7] The company's gross margin was about on par with other firms in the industry.

Carrying inventory for 300 days is a potentially significant problem, especially when the inventory is technologically advanced, as was the case here. In 1988, Machine Technology was forced to take an inventory write-down to address the obsolescence of its inventory. This write-down, which as noted totaled $1,777,212, had the effect of reducing the company's inventory days to 226 in 1988. That is, the decline in inventory days during 1988 was not necessarily an improvement in the company's performance but rather the result of a write-down of obsolete goods.

It should be noted that an inventory write-down has the effect of improving future years' profitability. When inventory is written down, there is less inventory on the balance sheet to be taken to cost of sales, improving future years' profitability. For Machine Technology, gross margin improved to 41% in 1989, the first year after the

Exhibit 10.4 High Inventory Days: Machine Technology, Inc., Selected Statistics, Years Ending August 31, 1986–1988 (thousands of dollars)

	1986	1987	1988
Net sales	$15,372	$17,774	$20,799
Cost of sales	9,461	12,155	14,064
Gross profit	$ 5,911	$ 5,619	$ 6,735
Gross margin	38%	32%	32%
Inventory	$ 9,071	$10,032	$ 8,819
Inventory days	345	297	226

Source: Machine Technology, Inc., annual report, August 1988. Data obtained from Disclosure, Inc., *Compact D/SEC: Corporate Information on Public Companies Filing with the SEC* (Bethesda, Md.: Disclosure, Inc., September 1993).

inventory write-down, from 32% in 1988. If fundamental problems were not addressed, however, this improvement in profitability would be short-lived.

Machine Technology appeared to have a persistent inventory problem that was seemingly not due to the obsolescence of a single product line. In 1989 and 1990 inventory days remained over 200 days. Such persistent problems suggest that the company was facing other, more fundamental difficulties. On February 5, 1992, the company circulated the following press release:

> Machine Technology, Inc., in announcing a restructuring concentrated principally in its engineering departments, said it will take a pre-tax operating charge of about $150,000 to $200,000.[8]

Then on March 24, 1992, the following announcement was made:

> Machine Technology said the rate of incoming orders has continued to decline due to the continued weakness in the semiconductor processing equipment market and in the overall economy. Gary Hillman, president, said that because of this, "regaining positive operating results during the balance of the fiscal year is unlikely."[9]

The company lost money in 1992. It lost money again in 1993 and, with continuing declines in revenue, in 1994 as well. The persistent inventory days problem was an indicator of an impending inventory write-down. But even more, it was an early indicator of other problems for the company. There was something fundamentally wrong that was not being explained by general economic or industry weakness. In our view, the problems appeared to be either with the products the company was producing or with the markets it served.

Another recent example of a company with inventory problems is CompUSA, Inc. In 1994 the company was forced to auction off, at a significant loss, $7.6 million in defective notebook computers. The company apparently provided for the loss on this sale as part of a $9.9 million restructuring charge reported in its June 1994 income statement. In reviewing prior-year financial statements, we noted that inventory days increased from 55 days in 1991 to 61 days in 1992 and to 63 days in 1993, the year before the inventory write-down. The company's inventory levels were growing. In 1993 the median inventory days figure for retailers of computers and software was 39.[10] Thus, CompUSA did appear to be having inventory difficulties. After the write-down and the likely benefit of other restructuring actions, in June 1994, inventory days for the company was a much more manageable 52.

One last example, Tektronix, was mentioned earlier. The company included a write-down of its inventory as part of an $80 million restructuring charge in 1990. Inventory days reached 95 days in 1988, up from 83 in 1987. They were running at 93 days in 1989. After the reported restructuring charge in 1990, the company's inventory days were at 82.

Fictitious Inventory

When companies need instant profits, inventory chicanery is arguably one of the easiest ways to obtain it. While reporting fictitious inventory does not boost revenue, it does boost the level of gross profit reported on that revenue, and accordingly, net income. Gross profit is calculated by subtracting cost of sales from revenue. In computing cost of sales, ending inventory is subtracted from goods available for sale, or the sum of beginning inventory and purchases made during the year. Thus, steps taken to overstate ending inventory result automatically in understated cost of sales. Moreover, the inclusion of fictitious amounts in ending inventory improves the balance sheet by raising the levels of current assets and shareholders' equity.

For managements that are so inclined, there are several ways that fictitious inventory might be reported. For example, the quantity or number of inventory units on hand might be overstated. Documented examples of such practices include actions by Phar-Mor, Inc., F&C International, Inc., Leslie Fay Companies, Inc., and the following actions of Laribee Wire Manufacturing Co.:

> Shipments between plants were recorded as stocks located at both plants. Some shipments never left the first plant, and documentation supposedly showing they were being transferred to the second plant "appeared to be largely fictitious," the report to the court found. And 4.5 million pounds of copper rod, supposedly worth more than $5 million, that Laribee said it was keeping in two warehouses in upstate New York would have required three times the capacity of the buildings, the report said.[11]

In the case of Laribee Manufacturing, inventory quantities were miscounted, and some items were double-counted by reporting their existence at two separate locations. A similar example was provided to us by an astute lender who was conducted to different pasture lands to observe the cattle that served as security for his loan. All seemed fine until the second or third location, when he felt that he actually recognized a particular animal. As it turned out, he was observing many of the same cattle in different locations. Company management was taking great pains to quickly move cattle between locations in an effort to give the impression that it had a larger herd than it actually did.

Besides overstating the quantity of units on hand, increasing the dollar value of inventory is a way to report fictitious inventory. Comptronix Corp. provides an example where such fictitious inventory was reported along with fraudulent revenue. At Comptronix, the reporting of fictitious inventory became almost routine. Every month, corporate officers inflated inventory and decreased cost of sales, boosting net income.

A third alternative for reporting fictitious inventory is more indirect. Here inventory is overstated by intentionally avoiding a needed write-down of slow-moving or obsolete goods that are value-impaired. Companies raising income in this way include Laribee Wire Manufacturing Co. and MiniScribe Corp. In the case of MiniScribe, the company boosted profit for 1986 by reducing a reserve for slow-moving goods that had been increased the previous year:

> In 1985, the company increased its reserve for excess inventory as a result of a general decline in the demand for micro-Winchester drives and severe price competition. In 1986, this reserve was reduced by $2.1 million as a result of a general improvement in demand and the ability of the company to sell the inventory at higher prices than had been anticipated.[12]

There was no general improvement in business conditions that warranted a $2.1 million reduction in the reserve for excess inventory. The boost it provided to net income was fictitious in nature.

The question that must be (and has been) asked when discussing fictitious inventory reporting is, Where were the auditors? Why do such frauds go undetected? We devote Chapter 13 to the auditor's role in detecting fraudulent financial reporting. For now, suffice it to say that the auditor's responsibility is to gather sufficient evidence to enable him or her to express an opinion on the fairness of presentation of the financial statements generally. Such an opinion does not include a guarantee that fraud is absent.

In a financial statement audit, auditors are not asked to look specifically for evidence of fraud. For example, they do not test signatures for forgeries or examine documents for authenticity. Requirements that such steps be taken would unduly expand the scope of audits and make them prohibitively expensive. Rather, auditors are asked to be diligent in their audit steps and to increase those steps as deemed necessary when potential evidence of fraud is uncovered. When financial frauds entail collusion among different management personnel, so as to render normal internal controls inoperative, they can go undetected by these normal audit procedures.

Whether inventory is overstated by raising the physical count or the dollar valuation of goods on hand, or by avoiding a write-down, the financial statement effect is the same. Inventory is overstated with an accompanying understatement of cost of sales. As a result, gross profit and net income are overstated, as are current assets and shareholders' equity.

Such fictitious amounts ultimately must be reversed. A reversal would likely entail a restatement of erroneous amounts reported in prior years. Of course, restatement and correction of the financial fiction requires its discovery. Depending on the extent of management participation in the fraud and the dollar magnitude of the amounts involved, this can take years. But at some point, through the actions of management or of the company's auditors, or through business failure, it will come to light.

It is important to note that early warning indicators are helpful in detecting inventory overstatement whether or not fraudulent financial reporting is present. For example, an indicator of the potential need for an inventory write-down is an unexplained increase in inventory days. Inventory is increasing faster than cost of sales. This increase in inventory may be due to slow-moving goods or to the inclusion of fictional amounts in the inventory account. Either way, inventory days is increased above norms appropriate for the company, its industry, or its competitors.

While gross margin is a useful indicator for anticipating inventory write-downs, traditional inventory problems and fictional inventories affect gross margin differently. In the presence of traditional inventory problems, such as slow-moving or obsolete goods, gross margin tends to be depressed. Even though inventory may be overstated and eventually subject to a write-down, the poor business conditions and price weakness that often accompany slow-moving or obsolete goods tend to reduce gross margin. Gross margin may improve once inventory is written down, though as we saw earlier, this improvement may be illusory, and is probably temporary. In contrast, gross margin tends to improve in the presence of fictitious inventory reporting. That is, increases in inventory reduce cost of sales and increase gross profit. Gross margin, or gross profit as a percent of revenue, is also increased. Of course, improving gross margins are never a sure sign that fictitious inventories are being reported. It is unusual, however, to have improving gross margins at the same time that inventory days are increasing. When both conditions are present, the investor or creditor should give careful consideration to the reason. Growth is a possibility. The company may be accumulating inventory to accommodate anticipated growth needs. But if those growth needs do not materialize, the company may find itself overstocked and ripe for a write-down.

Consider the case of Leslie Fay Companies, Inc., a manufacturer of women's clothing.[13] As the facts of the case have become known, there were several types of fraudulent activity taking place at the company, primarily in 1991 and 1992 but beginning as early as 1990. These acts included falsified revenue, including the reporting of sales shipments made after the end of reporting periods and shipments made to a company-owned storage site. They also included the reporting of borrowings and the proceeds from the sale of a division as sales revenue and an inappropriate delay in the write-off of uncollectible loans. Our interest in Leslie Fay here, however, is on acts taken to misrepresent inventory and cost of sales.

In 1992, Leslie Fay saw its sales sagging because of high prices and out-of-date styles. To counter these difficulties, the company gave its buyers mark-down money, in the form of merchandise discounts, and ultimately cut prices 20%. While these were not fraudulent acts, what was fraudulent was overstating the number of garments produced. This enabled the company to reduce its cost of sales by leaving a higher proportion of production costs in inventory. In this way, the company was able to maintain profit margins even as sale prices and revenue declined. While changing fundamentals may have caused the company to resort to fraudulent reporting, the real surprise occurred when investors and creditors learned that earlier results had been fabricated. A significant loss was reported as fictitious results reported in prior years were corrected.

In the Leslie Fay case, the financial early warning was the fact that the company's published financial results were inconsistent with its known financial difficulties. A company that must resort to significant mark-downs in an effort to counter a sales slow-down would be expected to report declining sales revenue and gross margins and an increase in inventory days. As will be seen, the company's gross margin held up fine even as sale prices were reduced through mark-downs. In addition, slowing sales did not result in an increase in its inventory days figure.

Selected annual financial statistics for Leslie Fay are provided in Exhibit 10.5. As noted, the fraud at Leslie Fay began as early as 1990 and continued into 1991 and 1992. It was uncovered late in 1992, after the company had reported results for the nine months ending September 1992 but before annual results for the year were released. The data presented in the exhibit include 1989, a year prior to the financial fraud, and two full years within the fraud period, 1990 and 1991. Note that after discovery of the fraud, the company was forced to restate prior-year amounts that were determined to be in error. The data in Exhibit 10.5 are as originally reported, without restatement.

The annual results give little outward appearance of financial difficulties. Sales in 1991 are about 2% below sales for 1990, but both years are above 1989. There was a small decline in gross margin, but nothing that would seem to be consistent with significant financial difficulties. Moreover, inventory days, at 78 in 1991, are much improved over prior years.

Fraudulent activities at Leslie Fay became more pronounced during 1992. Quar-

Exhibit 10.5   Leslie Fay Companies, Inc., Selected Statistics, Years Ending December 31, 1989–1991 (thousands of dollars)

	1989	1990	1991
Net sales	$ 786,257	$ 858,768	$ 836,564
Cost of sales	536,736	589,359	585,050
Gross profit	$ 249,521	$ 269,409	$ 251,514
Gross margin	32%	31%	30%
Inventory	$ 121,149	$ 147,899	$ 126,799
Inventory days	81	90	78

Source: Leslie Fay Companies, Inc., annual report, December 1991.

terly results for March, June, and September 1992 are presented in Exhibit 10.6. Because Leslie Fay's results are seasonal, the previous year's quarterly results are also presented, for comparison.

During 1992, Leslie Fay was having significant difficulty in selling its clothing. Some retailers had cut orders by as much as 15% because the company's dresses were not selling. Buyers at some of these retailers report that Leslie Fay's CEO called them regularly imploring them to take more of his company's merchandise. Accompanying these pleas came offers of mark-down money in the form of cash or discounts on future orders if the retailers later had to mark down goods that were not selling. One retailer reported receiving as much as $1 million in mark-down money. Such mark-downs affect a company's profitability by effectively reducing its sale prices and its gross margin.

As 1992 progressed, it became apparent that fall orders were running well behind prior year levels. As a final tack in addressing these demand problems, Leslie Fay announced in September 1992 that it would reduce prices by 20% on future orders in an effort to boost demand. This latest move alarmed many retail analysts, who viewed it as sufficient to push the company into a loss position. However, it was not until early 1993, when the company announced that the fraud was taking place, that the world was informed of the problems at Leslie Fay.

Given what was known about the market performance of Leslie Fay, its reported results as provided in Exhibit 10.6 made little sense. In the March and June periods, while sales were down, gross margin and inventory days either remained unchanged or improved in 1992 from 1991. It was not until late in 1992, during the September quarter, that gross margin and inventory days begin to deteriorate.

Exhibit 10.6 Leslie Fay Companies, Inc., Selected Statistics, Quarters Ending March 31, June 30, and September 30, 1991–1992 (thousands of dollars)

	March		June		September	
	1991	1992	1991	1992	1991	1992
Net sales	$244,844	$210,543	$171,113	$156,242	$249,234	$239,292
Cost of sales	169,103	145,091	123,971	111,697	168,082	167,127
Gross profit	$ 75,741	$ 65,452	$ 47,142	$ 44,545	$ 81,152	$ 72,165
Gross margin	31%	31%	28%	29%	33%	30%
Inventory	$130,646	$112,401	$151,610	$132,391	$114,902	$138,621
Inventory days	70	70	110	107	62	75

Sources: Data obtained from Leslie Fay Companies, Inc., Form 10-Q quarterly reports to the Securities and Exchange Commission, March 1992, June 1992, and October 1992. Some supplementary information was obtained from Disclosure, Inc., *Compact D/SEC: Corporate Information on Public Companies Filing with the SEC* (Bethesda, Md.: Disclosure, Inc., December 1992).

Company management was altering reported amounts in an effort to give investors and creditors what they wanted. In terms of inventory fraud, this was done by inflating claimed production quantities even as actual quantities were reduced. This action enabled the company to include a smaller proportion of total inventory costs in cost of sales when sales were made, inflating gross margin. It also permitted the company to leave a greater proportion of inventory costs on the balance sheet. Inventory days were not increased, however, because actual production was reduced, limiting total inventory costs.

It is unclear how long such a scheme could have been maintained. At some point, auditors would note that stated inventory quantities were not on hand. However, such a discovery could have been postponed in a fraud such as this one, which involved the falsification of inventory count tags. Fortunately, it did not go on for long, as management made its announcement and the fraud became known.

Other Inventory Issues

Our focus to this point has been on identifying financial early warnings related to overstated inventory. The remainder of this section addresses miscellaneous inventory topics and their related financial early warnings.

LIFO and the Fourth-Quarter Earnings Surprise

The basic mechanics of the LIFO, or last in, first out, inventory method were described in Chapter 7. A more detailed discussion is provided in the appendix. Our interest here is on LIFO as it affects interim financial statements.

LIFO is an annual inventory method. Accordingly, the official LIFO reserve adjustment, which adjusts inventory and cost of sales to LIFO, is made at year-end. It is at this time that all actual purchase information and price change data for the full year are known.

Interim LIFO adjustments are made using estimates. Companies must estimate what the annual rate of price change in inventory will be. Each quarter is considered an integral part of the full year. Unusual price swings during interim periods that may reverse later in the fiscal year, caused by seasonal factors for example, should be excluded when LIFO adjustments are made for those quarters. Instead, LIFO adjustments for any one quarter should be made based on that quarter's estimated contribution to the full year's annual rate of inflation. As noted in the annual report of Safeway Stores, Inc.:

> The LIFO charge to cost of goods sold for the first 36 weeks of each year is based upon estimated annual inflation ("LIFO Indices"). Actual LIFO Indices are calculated during the fourth quarter of the year based upon a statistical sampling of inventories. Accordingly, fourth-quarter pre-tax earnings were increased by $9.2 million, $10.2 million, and $7.7 million in 1993, 1992, and 1991, respectively.[14]

As the company notes, cost of goods sold or cost of sales for the first 36 weeks or three quarters is calculated using estimates of annual inflation. Actual price changes are used, based on a statistical sampling technique, to calculate the annual LIFO adjustment after year-end. That the company is reporting an earnings increase in the fourth quarter of each year indicates that annual rates of inflation were overestimated during the year.

Fourth-quarter results for LIFO firms depend on the level of accuracy used in the calculation of the LIFO reserve adjustment during the year. In the case of Safeway Stores, pre-tax earnings for the fourth quarter were boosted by between 8%–10% because of an overestimation of annual inflation rates during the year. While this might have been a pleasant surprise, the surprises are not always pleasant. In addition, they can become much more significant, especially when the financial statements of very small companies are being analyzed.

Many small LIFO firms providing compiled financial statements make their LIFO reserve adjustments only at year-end.[15] Thus, while the company is a LIFO firm for annual reporting purposes, during interim periods the income statement is effectively on a FIFO (first in, first out) basis. As a result, cost of sales is lower than it should be, while gross profit and pre-tax earnings are higher. The unsuspecting reader of such financial statements will be unpleasantly surprised when all of a year's increase in the LIFO reserve is taken into account in the fourth quarter. Any improvement in performance that is related to the failure to make interim LIFO reserve adjustments will be eliminated in that fourth quarter.

As an example, we can relate the story of a lender who was surprised when a small-company customer reported annual results that were much below what he had expected, given the customer's first three quarterly reports. The customer was using the LIFO method for annual reporting and tax purposes but reported on a FIFO basis during the year. Apparently because of significant price increases across the year, sharp year-end increases in the LIFO reserve and cost of sales were required. Gross profit was affected negatively.

Users of interim financial statements, especially those of small, nonpublic companies, should confirm with management whether LIFO adjustments have been made for interim periods. Such adjustments will change the LIFO reserve account during interim periods. Thus, one way to determine if an interim LIFO adjustment has been made is to ascertain whether the LIFO reserve account has changed during an interim period. Alternatively, the interim period's gross margin can be compared with the prior year's annual gross margin. An improvement in the interim gross margin over the prior year's annual profit rate may be due to better performance, or it may be explained by the lack of an interim LIFO reserve adjustment.

A Changing Inventory Mix: A Precursor of Falling Sales?

Top Air Manufacturing, Inc., is a manufacturer of farm equipment. After peaking at $5.3 million in 1990, sales declined slightly, to $5.0 million in 1991 and $4.7 million in 1992. At year-end 1991 and 1992, the company reported the inventory composition provided in Exhibit 10.7.

Among the three components of inventory, raw materials, work in process, and finished goods, a manufacturer has greatest control over raw materials. It is easier to shut off the flow of inventory coming into the company at the receiving dock than to reduce it once it is placed in process. Once in process, inventory will likely be carried through to finished goods, which must be held until sold.

In examining Exhibit 10.7, note the drop in raw materials inventory in 1992. As a percent of total inventory, raw materials declined to less than 3% from over 7% in 1991. The significant drop in raw materials may indicate that management anticipates continuing, perhaps even accelerating, sales declines.

Sales did decline at Top Air Manufacturing. For the six months ending in November, sales in 1992 were down approximately 49% from the same period 1991. On a more pleasant note, sales recovered later that year. For 1993, sales of $4.9 million were reported, up about 4% from 1992.

Inventory Theft and the Unexpected Inventory Write-down

The quotation at the beginning of this chapter, concerning Crown Crafts, Inc., mentioned that the company's "inventory shortage is probably the result of theft." It is difficult to anticipate an earnings surprise resulting from theft. Amounts involved may accumulate over time and typically are not large enough in any one year to warrant such a write-down. In most instances, theft or shrinkage flows into cost of sales as just another cost of doing business. In the case of Crown Crafts, however, it would seem that $1.4 million in comforters would have been noticed.

In any event, answers to a few questions may help in anticipating inventory theft. For example, what controls are in place to guard against theft? Do they seem adequate? Indications that inventory is left unattended in an open warehouse would obviously be a sign for concern. When physical inventory is taken, how does it compare with the books? Do the books consistently exceed the physical count by a significant amount? A lower physical count could be due to theft. Finally, Are the books adjusted, or are differences dismissed as errors in taking the physical inventory? By ignoring the physical count, one may be ignoring shrinkage through theft.

Exhibit 10.7   Changing Inventory Composition: Top Air Manufacturing, Inc., Years Ending May 31, 1991 and 1992

	1991	1992
Raw materials	$ 113,236	$ 35,091
Work in process	96,001	181,388
Finished goods	1,370,795	955,499
Total inventory	$1,580,032	$1,171,978

Source: Top Air Manufacturing, Inc., annual report, May 1992.

Investments

The fundamentals of investment accounting and reporting were discussed in Chapter 7.[16] A more detailed background is provided in the appendix. Our focus here is on identifying financial early warnings for the following investment situations: debt securities held to maturity, nonmarketable debt and equity securities, debt securities and marketable equity securities that are available for sale, and investments accounted for under the equity method. Our position is not that these assets are misreported. Rather, the vagaries of generally accepted accounting principles open the income statement up to sudden potentially significant and unexpected losses.

Debt Securities Held to Maturity

Investments in debt securities held to maturity are carried at cost adjusted for any unamortized premium or discount. When a company carries a portfolio of debt securities held to maturity, there is the risk of a write-down and an accompanying charge to income if the market value of one or more investments is less than cost. Such a write-down would not be made if the market value decline were considered to be temporary. For example, a decline in market value due to a rise in interest rates generally would not justify a write-down. Consider, however, a market value decline due to credit difficulties of the debt issuer. As long as management judges the market value decline to be a temporary phenomenon, a write-down is not necessary. However, if at some point management judges the decline in market value to be other than a temporary event, then a write-down and a charge to income must be made. In so doing, market value declines across several years may be taken to income in one year.

As an example, consider Presidential Life Corp., which carried its junk-bond portfolio at amortized cost. Certain securities in that portfolio, including Circle K Corp., Eastern Airlines, Inc., and Southland Corp., had registered significant declines in market value. The company had judged these declines to be temporary and had not effected a write-down. The Securities and Exchange Commission disagreed, judging the market value declines of these troubled companies to be other than temporary events. Presidential Life was forced to restate its results for 1989 to include a write-down of these investments to market value.

When a company carries a portfolio of debt securities at amortized cost, to the extent possible the investor or creditor should be cognizant of the market values of those investments. In situations where cost exceeds market value, there is the risk of a future write-down and income statement charge.

As another example, consider Berkshire Hathaway, Inc.'s investment in USAir, Inc. Berkshire Hathaway owned preferred stock in USAir. This investment was not separately disclosed in Berkshire's 1993 report. It appears, however, that the company included it with redeemable preferred shares carried at cost. While not a debt security, the redemption feature of this preferred issue gave it an effective maturity date, enabling the company to classify it as held-to-maturity.

At December 31, 1993, Berkshire Hathaway disclosed gross unrealized losses on redeemable preferred stocks of $90.1 million. These losses, which appeared to include declines in the market value of the company's investment in USAir, were considered to be temporary, not necessitating a write-down. During 1994, however, USAir's stock price declined by another 67%. In March 1995, Berkshire Hathaway made the following announcement:

> Berkshire Hathaway, Inc., the investment firm run by multibillionaire Warren Buffett, reported yesterday that profit fell 28% last year because of a plunge in the value of its stake in USAir, Inc. . . .
>
> Closely held Berkshire said profit fell to $494.8 million, or $420 a share, from $688.1 million, or $595 a share, in 1993. The firm did not report revenue or quarterly results.
>
> The 1994 profit included a pre-tax charge of $268.5 million in the fourth quarter to reflect the drop of Berkshire's investment in USAir, based in Arlington County, VA.
>
> Berkshire estimated USAir preferred stock it originally bought for $358 million was worth $89.5 million at the end of the third quarter.[17]

Apparently Berkshire Hathaway now viewed this market value decline as being other than temporary. As a result, the company recorded a $268.5 million pre-tax charge. It should be noted that this entire market value decline did not occur during 1994. Some of it was accumulated in prior years. However, in those prior years, the declines were viewed as temporary and were not taken to income.[18]

Nonmarketable Equity Securities

Like debt securities held to maturity, investments in equity securities that are not readily marketable are carried at cost. These investments might include positions held in private companies or in public companies for which there are fewer than three market makers. For example, an investment in a closely held stock issue would be included in this designation. As with debt securities held to maturity, these investments are not written down for a decline in market value unless the decline is viewed as being other than temporary. Here again, the income statement is at risk for a special charge to reduce to market investments in nonmarketable equity securities.

Debt Securities and Marketable Equity Securities Available for Sale

Investments in debt securities and marketable equity securities that are available for sale are reported at market value. Increases and decreases in these market values are included as direct additions to or subtractions from shareholders' equity. Thus, while these securities are held, resulting gains and losses bypass the income statement.

When these securities are sold, or when a decline in market value is considered to be other than temporary, the loss that has accumulated in shareholders' equity is taken to the income statement. Thus, the investor or creditor should be aware of any accumulation of these losses within shareholders' equity. If they are not recovered through market value appreciation, they will eventually reduce reported income and retained earnings, though because shareholders' equity was already reduced for the losses, income statement recognition of them will result in no net change in shareholders' equity.

For example, at December 31, 1992, Overseas Shipholding, Inc., reported investments in marketable equity securities carried at $67,485,000. The cost of these securities was $78,336,000.[19] The difference, an unrealized loss in the amount of $10,851,000, was subtracted from shareholders' equity. Some or all of this loss would be taken to income if the company were to sell any of the investments before their market values recovered. Alternatively, if the market value decline on any of the company's investments were considered to be other than temporary, the loss on that investment would also be recognized in the income statement.

Our focus here has been on the potential impact of investment losses on income. Note that when a company includes in shareholders' equity sizable gains on its available-for-sale investments, the very nature of equity is changed. That is, reported shareholders' equity has traditionally been viewed as the ultimate hedge against financial difficulties. However, by including investment gains in shareholders' equity, the financial strength afforded by shareholders' equity becomes tied, at least in part, to the whims of the financial markets.

Investments Accounted for under the Equity Method

Investments accounted for under the equity method include equity positions that are of sufficient magnitude to provide the investor with significant influence over the affairs of the investee. As discussed in Chapter 7 and the appendix, these investments are accounted for at cost plus the investor's share of investee net income, less the investor's share of any dividends paid by the investee.

Investments accounted for using the equity method are not reported at market value unless a decline in market value is considered to be other than temporary. As an example, Gerber Scientific, Inc., held 21% of the common stock of Boston Digital Corp. Gerber used the equity method to account for its investment. At April 30, 1990, the company carried its investment at $2,584,000.[20] At the time, the market value of this investment was $1,599,000. The company viewed this market value decline as a temporary condition and accordingly did not record a provision for loss. As with other investments, if management were to change its view and regard the market value decline as other than temporary, or if the investment were to be sold, an income statement loss would be recorded.

UNDERVALUATION OF LIABILITIES

Liabilities are probable future sacrifices of corporate resources or services made to settle present obligations. For reporting purposes, liabilities are valued at the present value of the resources or services to be provided to settle those obligations. When reported at amounts less than present value, liabilities are undervalued. The amount of this undervaluation represents a future expense or loss. Recognition will take place when the liability is ultimately settled or when its balance is adjusted to present value. Accordingly, earnings expectations formed without consideration of the potential income effect of an undervalued liability will be overly optimistic and subject to an earnings surprise.

Financing-Related Obligations

Most financing-related liabilities are properly valued, and accordingly do not represent a potential future charge against earnings. Included in this category are such liabilities as credit line obligations and the current and noncurrent portions of notes and bonds payable. It should be noted, however, that when longer-term notes and bonds were issued at rates that exceed current market rates of interest, a loss may be reported in the event of early retirement. This loss would be the result of a prepayment penalty or a premium paid to repurchase the bonds on the open market. While such a loss would be reported as an extraordinary item, it would nonetheless reduce net income and shareholders' equity.[21]

For example, during 1993, Act III Broadcasting, Inc., conducted a refinancing. The company described the effect on financial results for the year as follows:

> On December 22, 1993, the company refinanced a substantial portion of its outstanding debt. As a result of the retirement of certain loans and the redemption of Senior Preferred Stock, a prepayment premium of $9,000,000 was incurred and certain deferred financing charges and original issue discounts associated with the retired debt were charged against income. These charges are reflected as an extraordinary item.[22]

On its income statement for 1993, the company reported a net loss of $15.9 million, of which $12.6 million was an extraordinary loss resulting from the refinancing. The extraordinary loss comprised a debt prepayment penalty of $9 million and remaining unamortized original issue discounts. Those discounts had reduced the proceeds from borrowing and book value of the original debt and had boosted the issue's effective interest rate. Accounting standards call for their amortization over the repayment term. In refinancing that debt, the company was forced to write off the entire original issue discount as part of the extraordinary charge to income.

Act III Broadcasting also included as part of its extraordinary loss the write-off of deferred financing charges incurred at the time the retired loans were issued.

Such charges include costs to issue the debt, including, for example, registration and underwriting costs, and accounting and legal fees. The company capitalized these costs and proceeded to amortize them as an increase in interest expense over the debt's term. This treatment is appropriate given that such fees increase the debt issue's cost and should be reflected as an increase in interest expense over the borrowing period. When the underlying debt is terminated early, however, these deferred costs must be written off, adding to the extraordinary loss. Thus, when companies report deferred charges associated with long-term borrowings, the deferred charges represent potential significant charges to income in the event of early debt termination. An example is provided in the financial statements of Ackerley Communications, Inc.

In 1993, Ackerley Communications reported net income of $2.3 million. Included in its calculation was an extraordinary loss in the amount of $0.6 million, which the company described as follows:

> On October 1, 1993, the company completed a refinancing of its senior indebtedness (the "Refinancing") to obtain more favorable repayment terms respecting its senior indebtedness and to provide the company with liquidity both in the near term and the long term. . . .
>
> As a result of the Refinancing, the company wrote off deferred costs of $0.6 million related to the Old Credit Agreement and certain Subordinated Note Agreements.[23]

In originally obtaining its senior indebtedness, the company incurred certain debt issue costs. These costs were deferred and were reported as assets on the balance sheet. With the refinancing, the original debt issue was removed from the balance sheet and the related deferred costs were written off as an extraordinary charge.

Outside of extraordinary losses due to early debt retirement, most earnings surprises related to liabilities are from two general areas. The first, called operating-related obligations, consists of accrued expenses payable and accounts payable. The second, a broad category termed contingent liabilities, includes many types of potential obligations, such as legal and environmental obligations, and liabilities associated with financial derivatives.

Operating-Related Obligations

Accrued Expenses Payable

Accrued expenses payable is a liability for expenses recognized that have not been paid. Examples include amounts due for unpaid selling, general, and administrative expenses, such as wages, employee-related sick pay and vacation pay, warranties, utilities, and insurance. Interest expense could also be included. However, because it is reasonably easy to calculate the appropriate amount of interest expense given a company's outstanding loan balances and relevant interest rates, interest expense and accrued interest payable will not be dealt with here.

Accrued expenses payable is typically a short-term obligation. Because of its short time frame, its discounted present value amount differs very little from the total dollar amount due. Accordingly, unless the amount of the discount is considered to be material, it is not reported at present value.

When operating-related expenses are underaccrued, future earnings are subject to higher-than-normal expense levels. These additional expenses are recorded when an underaccrued liability balance is increased or when a related payment is made for which no such liability exists. Reported earnings will suffer.

A good indicator of underaccrued expenses is the trend in accrued expenses payable. A declining trend indicates that payments exceed new expense accruals. This may be expected to happen over short periods of time or in a scaling back of operations. However, for most firms, the balance in accrued expenses payable should be steady to increasing.

It would seem that if the scale of a company's operations is changing, whether increasing or decreasing, for example because of growth, decline, or even seasonal factors for interim periods, a good test for underaccrued expenses would be to compare the percent change in accrued expenses payable with the percent change in revenue. For example, in this test, the percent increase in accrued expenses payable that was exceeded by the percent increase in revenue could be due to an underaccrual of expenses. The problem with such a test is that changes in accrued expenses payable cannot be related accurately to overall changes in business activity. Revenue might increase, but through efficiencies gained, operating expenses may not increase at the same rate. In such a setting, accrued expenses payable would not be expected to increase at the same rate as revenue.

Thus, the trend in accrued expenses payable remains a better indicator of an underaccrual of operating expenses. A declining balance, especially as business activity remains steady or increases, should be examined carefully. Why are payments exceeding new expense accruals?

MiniScribe Corp. provides a useful example. In 1986, as net sales increased 62% to $184.9 million, accrued warranty expense payable declined from $2,083,000 to $1,374,000. One would expect that as sales increased, warranty accruals should increase as well. Even more suspect was the significant decline in the warranty liability. Soon after the release of the company's 1986 results, the financial fraud at MiniScribe was uncovered. While fictitious revenue and bogus inventory accounting were the primary culprits, underaccruals of expense also were prominent misstatements.

Accounts Payable

Unlike accrued expenses payable, accounts payable does not arise from the recording of unpaid operating expenses. For the most part, increases in accounts payable are due to the purchase of inventory for which payment has not been made. Like accrued expenses payable, accounts payable is short-term and is not discounted to present value. When accounts payable is understated, inventory purchases are potentially understated as well. Note that purchases of inventory can be understated even as an accurate physical count results in a properly stated ending inventory balance. As a result, in understating inventory purchases, goods available for sale are understated. If ending inventory is reported accurately and goods available for sale are understated, cost of sales will be understated. Later, when the unrecorded inventory purchases are discovered and recorded, a charge to income must be taken, resulting in lower earnings, though if the purchase misstatement relates to prior years, the correcting adjustment is taken to retained earnings.

When inventory purchases and accounts payable are misstated, usually the amounts involved are too small relative to cost of sales to have a significant effect on gross margin or A/P days. A more sensitive early warning indicator can be developed employing the relation that exists between inventory and accounts payable.

As noted, most accounts payable transactions are for the purchase of inventory. Accordingly, changes in accounts payable should closely track, in percentage terms, changes in inventory. This was not the case at Collins Industries, Inc.

Selected annual and quarterly statistics from the ambulance maker's financial statements are provided in Exhibits 10.8 and 10.9.

In reviewing Exhibit 10.8, note that in 1992 gross margin is relatively stable at 14% and A/P days are up slightly from 1991. Neither statistic gives any indication of the potential existence of unrecorded inventory purchases. This is not surprising since, as noted, amounts involved would likely not be material relative to cost of sales, an expense used in the calculation of gross margin and A/P days. Note, however, that inventory increased 23% in 1992, while accounts payable increased only 4%. Such a development should be looked at carefully. Growth in inventory that exceeds growth in accounts payable requires cash payments for inventory to exceed inventory purchases. Over short periods management may take such steps in an ef-

Exhibit 10.8 Inventory and A/P Relation: Collins Industries, Inc., Selected Statistics, Years Ending October 31, 1991 and 1992 (thousands of dollars)

	1991	1992
Sales	$145,590	$148,234
Cost of sales	125,879	127,707
Gross profit	$ 19,711	$ 20,527
Gross margin	14%	14%
Inventory	$ 23,997	$ 29,555
Increase in inventory	–	23%
Accounts payable	$ 15,673	$ 16,356
Increase in accounts payable	–	4%
A/P days	45	46

Source: Data as originally reported, before restatement, obtained from Collins Industries, Inc., annual report, October 1992.

Exhibit 10.9   Inventory and A/P Relation: Collins Industries, Inc., Selected Quarterly Statistics, April 30, July 31, and October 31, 1992 (thousands of dollars)

	1992		
	April	July	October
Inventory	$26,663	$28,164	$29,555
Increase in inventory	–	6%	5%
Accounts payable	$17,535	$18,010	$16,356
Increase (decrease) in accounts payable		3%	(9)%

Source: Data obtained from Disclosure, Inc., *Compact D/SEC: Corporate Information on Public Companies Filing with the SEC* (Bethesda, MD.: Disclosure, Inc., March 1993).

fort to reduce A/P days even as inventory balances are increased. These actions may be needed to keep good credit terms with vendors.

In the quarterly data provided in Exhibit 10.9, however, changes in accounts payable relative to changes in inventory appear even more unusual. In the July quarter, accounts payable increased 3% while inventory increased 6%. Then, in October, accounts payable actually declined by 9% even while inventory increased another 5%. These developments should provide reason for a much closer look. Typically, accounts payable is not expected to decline as inventory is increased. At a minimum, comments from management should be obtained. Are these developments part of a concerted plan? To what level are they planning to reduce accounts payable?

Collins Industries was later forced to restate its financial results for fiscal 1992. Net income for the year was overstated by approximately 72%. Among the reasons for the restatement was the failure to record supplier invoices in the October 1992 quarter. As a result, inventory purchases and accounts payable were understated, overstating gross profit.

Contingent Liabilities

A contingent liability is an obligation that is not certain. Generally accepted accounting principles require that an estimated loss from a contingency should be recorded by a charge against income and the establishment of a balance sheet liability when two conditions are met. The first requires that information available prior to the issuance of the financial statements indicates that it is *probable* that a liability has been incurred at the date of the financial statements. The second requires that the amount of the loss can be *reasonably estimated*.[24] Examples of contingencies that meet both requirements would include a warranty obligation and an anticipated litigation loss from a judgment entered by the courts against a company. Another example would include environmental damage caused by a company once the cost of remediation could be estimated. Lindsay Manufacturing Co. provides a good example. The following discussion was taken from the financial overview section of the company's annual report:

> Charges of $3.2 million ($2.9 million in the fourth quarter) were included in FY90's cost of sales to reserve for the anticipated cost of an environmental remediation at Lindsay's manufacturing facility. The total balance sheet reserve for this remediation was $3.5 million at year-end.
>
> Environmental contamination at the manufacturing facility occurred in 1982 when a drill, operated by a sub-contractor installing groundwater monitoring wells, punctured a silt and sand lens and an underlying clay layer beneath a clay-lined waste lagoon. The puncture caused acid and solvent leachate to enter the sand and gravel aquifer.
>
> Since 1983, Lindsay has worked actively with the Nebraska Department of Environmental Controls (NDEC) to remediate this contamination by purging and treating the aquifer. In October 1989, the Environmental Protection Agency (EPA) added Lindsay to the list of priority Superfund sites. In 1988, sampling which was performed in connection with an investigation of the extent of aquifer contamination, revealed solvent contamination (volatile organic compound) in the soil and shallow groundwater in three locations at and in the vicinity of the plant. Under a 1988 agreement with the EPA and NDEC, Lindsay has conducted and financed a Remedial Investigation/Feasibility Study (RI/FS). This study was completed in June 1990. Lindsay believes that other than the above mentioned, there is no other soil or groundwater contamination at the manufacturing facility.
>
> In September 1990, the EPA issued its Record of Decision (ROD) selecting a plan for completing the remediation of both contaminations. The plan selected for aquifer remediation was in line with Lindsay's expectations. However, the plan for remediation of the soil and shallow groundwater contamination proposes a higher degree of remediation than the company had previously expected. Therefore, Lindsay recognized the additional $2.9 million accrual in the fourth quarter.
>
> Lindsay believes that the current reserve is sufficient to cover the estimated total cost for complete remediation of both the aquifer and soil and shallow groundwater contaminations, net of expected recovery from Lindsay's insurer, under the ROD as it now stands. Lindsay believes that its insurer should cover costs associated with the contamination of the aquifer that was caused by the puncture of the clay layer in 1982. If the EPA or NDEC require remediation which is in addition to or different from that presently proposed, this estimate could increase or decrease, depending on the nature of the change.[25]

Lindsay's accrual for this contamination was reported at a nominal dollar amount for years. In fact, even though the problem first surfaced in 1982, a balance sheet liability of only $315,000 was reported as late as 1989. Then, based on new information obtained in 1990, that liability was increased to $3,454,000. Note that there was no question regarding the probability that a loss had been incurred. The only dispute focused on the amount of loss to be accrued. Accordingly, it should be noted that the amount of contingent loss accrued is based on the best estimate at the balance sheet date and is always subject to change. With those changes come new income statement charges and potentially lower earnings.

Most loss contingencies do not meet the requirements of being probable and reasonably estimated. For example, in the case of a lawsuit, it may only be reasonably possible and not probable that a loss has been incurred. Such an obligation would not be accrued. Rather, the nature of the contingency and, if possible, the amount involved would be disclosed in the notes. If a reasonable estimate of the amount cannot be made, then the contingency would be described in the notes in general terms with the explanation that no amount can be estimated.

Clearly, there is room for judgment in determining which loss contingencies are probable versus reasonably possible. In practice, examples of loss contingencies that tend not to be accrued but rather disclosed in the notes include the following:

1. Guarantees of indebtedness of others
2. Obligations of commercial banks under stand-by letters of credit, constituting commitments to provide financing under certain circumstances
3. Guarantees to repurchase receivables that have been sold or assigned
4. Income tax disputes from prior years
5. Pending lawsuits with uncertain outcomes
6. Losses associated with potential environmental damage before an amount can be estimated

The following note from the annual report of Original Italian Pasta Products Co. provides a good example of a contingent liability for which no amount has been accrued:

> In 1989, a complaint was filed against the company alleging that the company had used the "Trios" trademark and had breached the license agreement . . . through the improper use of the Trios name. The trial was held on January 24, 1991, and judgment was entered for the company. The Trios filed an appeal on April 17, 1991. No estimate of the probable outcome of the appeal can be determined at this time. The company intends to vigorously contest this claim on appeal.[26]

The company has not accrued a loss because it is not probable that a loss has been incurred, and if it has, it is not possible to estimate a loss amount.

Alcan Aluminum Co., Inc., discloses the following item as a contingent liability. Note that while the contingent liability amount can be estimated, it is not considered to represent a probable loss. Accordingly, no liability has been accrued:

> In addition, there are guarantees for the repayment of approximately $13 million of indebtedness by related companies. Alcan believes that none of these guarantees is likely to be invoked.[27]

Interestingly, some assets expose a firm to sizable contingent liabilities and potential earnings charges. For example, the footnotes of Personal Diagnostics, Inc., a firm that provides precision-machine manufacturing, included the following discussion of the company's off–balance sheet market risk:

> At September 30, 1992, the company has open future positions for silver and gold. The gains or losses are recognized in income as they occur. The contract amounts, while appropriately not recorded in the financial statements, reflect the extent of the company's market risk which at September 30, 1992, totaled $3,637,000.[28]

This statement was part of the company's financial instruments disclosure. Generally accepted accounting principles require that companies disclose the extent, nature, and terms of financial instruments with off–balance sheet credit and market risk.[29] For Personal Diagnostics, these open futures positions in silver and gold were speculative in nature, creating market risk. They were not needed as hedges of the prices of raw materials used in production. With total assets of $12.2 million and shareholders' equity of $8.7 million at September 30, 1992, a total exposure to loss of $3.6 million was significant for the company. While these positions could also result in significant gain for the company, one must question why it had strayed so far from its apparent business purpose.

As another example of an investment position that created a risk of loss, consider the financial statements of Bay Tact Corp. The company's balance sheet for 1993 reported marketable securities in the amount of $192,360. In the footnotes it was learned that these investments were carried at market value less an amount due on margin.[30] The total market value of the investment portfolio was $283,662, from which margin debt of $91,302 was subtracted, resulting in the net investment balance of $192,360 as reported on the balance sheet. Also disclosed was the cost of the total investment portfolio, $286,647.

By investing on margin, the risk of investment loss was increased dramatically. At first glance, the balance sheet implied that the total risk of loss was the amount reported there, $192,360. From the notes, however, it was learned that the total risk of loss was actually the full cost of the portfolio, $286,647. This was a sizable sum given that the company's total assets at December 31, 1993, were $801,607 and total shareholders' equity was $521,794. Actually, firm management may have also realized this. According to the company's 1994 annual report, no investments were carried on margin and the investment portfolio had been scaled back significantly.

In reviewing financial statements it must be remembered that all firms are subject to contingent liabilities. Most of these contingencies are not reported on the balance sheet. Instead, their existence and, if possible, estimates of their amount are disclosed in the footnotes. Thus, careful analysis requires a complete reading of the notes, including information on contingencies. A full understanding of the issues gained from the notes and from discussions with management, as needed, provide a basis for estimating the firm's total exposure. A worst-case scenario should be considered and the financial strength of the company weighed on that basis.

In our discussion of contingent liabilities, two situations where supposed assets created loss exposure for the firm were included. Both involved financial instruments. The Bay Tact case involving investments on margin was straightforward. The investment portfolio was reported net of the amount of margin debt. The risk of loss associated with market fluctuations was equal to the total investment cost reported in the footnotes. The Personal Diagnostics example, however, was a bit different. Here the company provided an estimate of its total exposure to loss from financial derivatives, namely, futures positions in silver and gold. In recent years, financial derivatives, including interest rate swaps and futures tied to foreign currencies, have resulted in significant unexpected losses for many firms. Because of the magnitude of these losses and their prominent exposure in the financial press, that subject is given additional attention.

Financial Derivatives

Derivatives are financial instruments that derive their value from other, underlying financial contracts or indices. One example of a financial derivative provided in Chapter 2 is a stock call option, giving its holder the right to buy stock in a specified company at an established price and by an established date. In this instance, the option derives its value from its terms and the value of the underlying stock. Another example includes a long position in a foreign currency futures contract. Such a position provides a cash settlement to its holder or requires a cash payment from its holder based on changes in the market value of the foreign currency underlying the contract. A third example is an interest rate swap. Here a firm with variable-rate debt, concerned about the likelihood and effect of rising interest rates, swaps or trades interest payments with a fixed-rate debt firm that may not share the same concerns. Each firm continues to make its own interest payments, but payments are made between the firms to settle net differences resulting from changing interest rates.

There are many other kinds of financial derivatives. The three mentioned here are representative of the range of products available. We continue to refer to them in our discussion of accounting and disclosure practices for derivatives.

Disclosure Requirements for Derivatives

Several recent accounting pronouncements require specific accounting disclosures for financial instruments, including financial derivatives. SFAS No. 105 focuses on those financial instruments that create off–balance sheet market risk and credit risk.[31] According to the standard, market risk is the risk of loss associated with market price fluctuations. In contrast, credit risk is the amount of loss an entity would incur if any party to a financial instrument failed to perform according to the terms of the contract. Since there was no risk of contractual default by another firm or counterparty with futures contracts, the futures positions, or exchange-traded contracts, in gold and silver held by Personal Diagnostics did not carry credit risk. They did, however, create market risk for the company that was much greater than the actual amount of cash invested in the contracts at the balance sheet date. It was this off–balance sheet market risk, reported to be $3,637,000, that Personal Diagnostics disclosed in the notes to its financial statements.

Of the three representative financial derivatives mentioned earlier, only the foreign currency futures contract and the interest rate swap agreement are off–balance sheet instruments. An investment in a stock call option is reported on the balance sheet and does not create off–balance sheet risk. Thus, because of its focus on off–balance sheet risk, SFAS No. 105 is not applicable for the stock call option.[32] Instead, the provisions of SFAS No. 115, discussed in Chapter 7, would be relevant.[33]

The disclosure requirements of SFAS No. 105 include the face or notional amount of the contract and its nature, terms, and the amount of potential loss from the contract due to market risk and credit risk. In addition, for those financial instruments creating credit risk for the firm, disclosure requirements include the amount of loss that the firm would incur if a party to the contract defaulted and collateral, if any, proved to be worthless.

Both the foreign currency futures contract and the interest rate swap have off–balance sheet market risk. An estimate of the potential loss from market fluctuations would be necessary for both. However, only the interest rate swap has a contractual counterparty creating risk of default, or credit risk. Thus, disclosure of the potential loss resulting from default by another party would be needed for that agreement only.

Dell Computer Corp. entered into certain interest rate swap agreements. The company described its positions as follows:

> The company also employs a variety of interest rate derivative instruments to more efficiently manage its principal, market and credit risks as well as to enhance its investment yield. Derivative instruments used include interest rate swaps, written and purchased interest rate options and swaptions (options to enter into interest rate swaps). Interest rate differentials to be paid or received on interest rate swaps which are designated to specific borrowings are accrued and recognized as an adjustment to interest expense as interest rates change. Realized gains or losses on terminated interest rate swap positions designated to specific borrowings are recognized as an adjustment to interest expense over the remaining life of the obligations. Interest rate derivative instruments that are not designated to a specific asset or liability are considered investment derivatives and are accounted for on a mark-to-market basis, with realized and unrealized gains or losses recognized as incurred and included as a component of financing and other income in the consolidated financial statements.[34]

In this note, the company reports that it has certain interest rate swap agreements outstanding and provides a description of how it uses those swaps. As noted, some of the swaps are designated to, or matched with, specific borrowings and used to alter the interest expense pattern of those borrowings. As the company explains, "Interest rate differentials to be paid or received on interest rate swaps which are designated to specific borrowings are accrued and recognized as an adjustment to interest expense as interest rates change."[35] Other interest rate swap agreements are used as investment (speculative) vehicles where mark-to-market or market-value accounting is used: "Interest rate derivative instruments that are not designated to a specific asset or liability are considered investment derivatives and are accounted for on a mark-to-market basis, with realized and unrealized gains or losses recognized as incurred and included as a component of financing and other income in the consolidated financial statements."[36] Like other financial derivatives, swaps can be used to hedge other financial risks or they can be used as investments. More will be said later about the accounting practices used for these instruments, which depend on whether they are designated as hedges of other financial risks faced by the firm.

To fulfill other disclosure requirements for its swap agreements, Dell provided the following discussion:

> At January 30, 1994, and January 31, 1993, the company had outstanding interest rate derivative contracts with a total notional amount of $355 million and $180 million, respectively. Interest rate derivatives generally involve exchanges of interest payments based upon fixed and floating interest rates without exchanges of underlying notional amounts. Consequently, the company's exposure to credit loss is significantly less than the stated notional amounts. The company's investment policy limits the weighted average maturity of its investment derivative portfolio to a maximum of three years and limits the maturity of individual positions to a maximum of five years. At January 30, 1994, the weighted average maturity of the investment derivative portfolio was 1.8 years.
>
> The value of the company's investment derivatives arise principally from changes in interest rates. At January 30, 1994, the value of company's short-term and derivative investment portfolio is subject to movements in United States, Canadian, Japanese and European interest rate markets and, generally, would be adversely effected by increases in market rates of interest. Since January 30, 1994, the value of the company's short-term and investment derivative portfolios has decreased as a result of interest rate increases in these markets. If interest rate market conditions as of March 2, 1994, prevail, the company's investment income, included as a component of financing and other, will be adversely affected by the recognition of realized and unrealized losses.[37]

Here the company provides the total contract or notional amount of its swaps and provides additional discussion about the nature of its swap agreements, including a comment on its existing market risk. Interestingly, the company has alerted the reader of its financial statements to the potential for significant derivatives-related losses. Also included is a general discussion about its underlying credit risk. A more detailed discussion about the existing credit risk is provided in the following discussion:

> All of the company's foreign exchange and interest rate derivative instruments involve elements of market and credit risk in excess of the amounts recognized in the financial statements. The counterparties to financial instruments consist of a number of major financial institutions. In addition to limiting the amount of agreements and contracts it enters into with any one party, the company regularly moni-

tors its positions with and the credit quality of the financial institutions which are counterparties to these financial instruments, and it does not anticipate nonperformance by the counterparties.[38]

A second recent accounting standard that also includes disclosure requirements for financial derivatives is SFAS No. 107, "Disclosures about Fair Value of Financial Instruments." The scope of SFAS No. 107 is broad, including most financial assets and liabilities, both on and off the balance sheet. For example, that scope would include the currency futures contract and the interest rate swap mentioned above.

SFAS No. 107 requires that, for financial instruments with available market quotes, those market quotes should be used in valuation. For those financial instruments for which there are no market quotes available, estimates of market value should be made and disclosure provided of the method used to make the estimates.

Continuing the Dell Computer example, the company provided the following information to fulfill its market value disclosure requirements:

The estimated fair value amounts disclosed under SFAS No. 107 "Disclosures about Fair Value of Financial Instruments" have been determined by the company using available market information and appropriate valuation methodologies as described below. However, considerable judgment is necessary in interpreting market data to develop estimates of fair value. Accordingly, the estimates presented herein are not necessarily indicative of the amounts that the company could realize in a current market exchange. Changes in assumptions could significantly affect the estimates. Cash, accounts receivable, short-term borrowings, accounts payable and accrued liabilities are reflected in the financial statements at fair value because of the short-term maturity of these instruments. The estimated fair values of the company's other financial instruments as of January 30, 1994, and January 31, 1993, are as follows (in thousands):

	1993		1994	
	Carrying Amount	Fair Value	Carrying Amount	Fair Value
Short-term investments	$ 80,367	$ 80,367	$333,667	$333,667
Long-term debt	–	–	(100,000)	(105,500)
Foreign currency hedging instruments				
Foreign exchange forward contracts	(23,661)	(23,661)	(81)	(81)
Foreign currency option contracts	38,533	38,533	8,035	8,035
Interest rate derivative instruments				
Interest rate swaps designated to long-term debt	–	–	–	(1,170)

	1993		1994	
	Carrying Amount	Fair Value	Carrying Amount	Fair Value
Unmatched interest rate derivatives				
Interest rate options and swaptions	(5,550)	(5,550)	(2,444)	(2,444)
Interest rate swaps	–	–	812	812

The fair values of short-term investments, long-term debt, and interest rate derivative instruments were estimated based upon quotes from brokers. Foreign exchange forward contracts fair values are estimated using market quoted rates of exchange at the applicable balance sheet date. The estimated fair value of foreign currency option contracts is based on market quoted rates of exchange at the applicable balance sheet date and the Black-Sholes options pricing model.[39]

Accounting Requirements for Derivatives

Our focus has been on disclosure requirements for financial derivatives. Accounting requirements dictate how gains and losses arising from financial derivatives are recorded. In particular, accounting requirements specify if these gains and losses are recognized in income as they accrue or if they are deferred in some way to later periods.

The Financial Accounting Standards Board is working on a standard to prescribe accounting requirements for financial derivatives. As of this writing, however, no accounting standard has specified a preferred accounting method for financial derivatives. Thus, accounting for gains and losses that arise is not officially standardized. However, some guidance is provided by SFAS No. 52, "Foreign Currency Translation," and SFAS No. 80, "Accounting for Futures Contracts."[40] While these standards were not designed for all financial derivatives, accounting methods in practice seem to apply their guidelines.[41] A more detailed discussion of their provisions is provided in the appendix.

Financial derivatives are accounted for generally using mark-to-market accounting. Individual positions are reported at fair market value with gains and losses recognized in income. This treatment is applied whether the financial derivatives are held for investment or as a hedge of a firm's other exposed positions. If held as a hedge, the gains and losses recognized in income would be approximately equal to and offset gains and losses derived from the firm's other exposed positions.

For example, a U.S. firm with outstanding long-term debt that is denominated in yen would incur foreign currency losses if the yen were to appreciate against the dollar. Those foreign currency transaction losses would be reported in income. If that same firm hedged its yen-denominated debt with the purchase of a yen-based foreign currency futures contract, that futures contract would generate gains as the yen appreciated. Those gains would also be reported in income and would offset the losses on the yen-denominated debt.

Red Eagle Resources Corp. uses futures contracts to hedge the market risk associated with oil and natural gas. The company provided the following description of its practices in its quarterly report for the nine months ended September 30, 1994:

> The company entered into futures contracts to hedge the market risk caused by fluctuations in the price of crude oil and natural gas. These contracts involve settlements of the difference between the fixed value and market value of crude oil and natural gas prices. All realized and unrealized gains or losses on the contracts are included in current results of operations. The company recorded a loss for the nine months ended September 30, 1994, of $2.1 million including a loss of $78,000 before income taxes for the three months ended September 30, 1994. The company will record a gain of $42,000 for the month of October 1994. No further gains or losses are anticipated.[42]

Note that gains and losses on the company's hedges are included in income and are likely designed to offset increases and decreases in gross margin caused by changes in spot prices of crude oil and natural gas.

Some financial derivatives are designated as hedges of anticipated transactions, including firm commitments and forecasted transactions for which there is no current firm commitment. If a U.S. firm has a pound-based contract to sell goods to a British customer, the U.S. firm has a pound-based commitment. That firm could sell a pound-based foreign currency futures contract to hedge its anticipated receivable from the British firm. Gains and losses on the futures contract during the commitment period before the sale is completed would be deferred and recognized later as part of the profit on the sale. After the sale is recorded, and assuming that the futures contract is still held, new gains and losses on it would be recognized in income as they accrue and would offset gains and losses on the pound-based receivable.

Cedar Group, Inc., provides the following example of deferral of gains and losses associated with the hedge of a foreign currency commitment:

> The company uses forward foreign exchange contracts primarily to offset the effects of foreign currency fluctuations related to expected foreign-denominated receivables and payables transactions and also to hedge firm sale and purchase commitments. Gains or losses on forward foreign exchange contracts which hedge an identifiable foreign currency commitment are deferred and recognized as the related transactions are settled.[43]

Note how the company has identified its forward foreign exchange contracts as hedges of expected foreign-denominated receivables and payables and of firm sale and purchase commitments. Resulting gains and losses on the forward contracts were not recognized currently but were deferred and recognized when the related transactions were settled.

In a similar way, a company that is negotiating a variable-rate long-term debt financing might choose to swap its future variable-interest payment stream for a fixed-payment stream even before the debt financing deal is closed. Gains and losses on the interest rate swap during the period before the debt financing is closed would be deferred and recognized as a component of interest expense over the term of the borrowing.

Derivatives and the Risk of Loss

Financial derivatives came into existence as a means for firms to hedge financial risk. Managements that are adept at handling business risk, for example, risk associated with product demand, production flow, or even employee relations, may be less inclined to deal with risk associated with the financial markets that can affect the market values of company assets and liabilities. Such managements can use financial derivatives to hedge financial risk and create a more stable earnings stream.

In an effort to increase corporate earnings, other managements choose to invest in financial derivatives that are not hedges. They create open positions with the intent of deriving financial gain. In some cases, with a near gambling mentality, managements use borrowed money to increase the gain potential of financial derivatives. The potential for gain is increased markedly when leverage is employed with financial instruments that are inherently risky to begin with; the risk of loss is increased as well.

Investors who take speculative positions in financial derivatives that are not hedges serve a useful purpose. Through their activity they increase the liquidity of the derivatives markets and provide a ready market for those wishing to use them as hedges. In recent years, however, the amount of speculative activity in financial derivatives has increased markedly. During this time, some managements may have devoted too much of their firms' time and financial resources to financial derivatives. They have strayed from their stated business purposes and exposed their firms and shareholders to undue risk. Consider the following examples.

Dell Computer Corp., in its financial derivatives disclosures provided earlier, included the following statement:

> Since January 30, 1994, the value of the company's short-term and investment derivative portfolios has decreased as a result of interest rate increases in these markets. If interest rate market conditions as of March 2, 1994, prevail, the company's investment income, included as a component of financing and other, will be adversely affected by the recognition of realized and unrealized losses.[44]

Soon after the company published this statement in its annual report, the magnitude of the expected losses from derivatives was publicly announced:

> Dell computer Corp.'s stock tumbled 12% after the company estimated it would incur losses from derivatives for the quarter ending May 1. The projected paper loss, which some analysts pegged at between $5 million and $15 million, comes amid a string of derivatives-related hits in recent weeks.[45]

The magnitude of Dell's derivatives-related losses may not seem sufficient to warrant a 12% decline in the price of the company's stock. However, many investors recalled more significant losses incurred by the firm in foreign currency trading just two years earlier. In late 1992 the company had lost tens of millions of dollars in currency trading, which prompted an inquiry by the Securities and Exchange Commission.

In its 1994 annual report, Procter & Gamble Co. described how it uses options on interest rate swaps "to manage the company's overall risk profile and reduce interest expense." The company noted that its options activity includes writing or selling options, described as follows (dollar amounts in millions):

> When using written option contracts, the company receives a premium in exchange for providing a counterparty the right to enter into a swap. Gains and losses on such options are recognized currently. The notional amounts of such instruments were $1,094 and $845 at June 30, 1994 and 1993, respectively. The fair values were $40 at June 30, 1994, and $14 at June 30, 1993, reflecting the approximate cost to terminate the options.[46]

When writing or selling an option, one's risk is effectively unlimited, much as it is in taking a short position in common stock. If the company had other offsetting positions, however, or could use the written options to hedge other interest rate exposure, these written options would be risk-reducing as opposed to risk-increasing.

Procter & Gamble was not using these options exclusively for the purpose of reducing risk. As stated by the company (dollar amounts in millions):

> The option portions of the two out-of-policy leveraged interest rate swaps entered into during 1994 were closed in the January-March quarter. The related $157 charge in the quarter to close these options is reflected in other income/expense, net. Leveraged options can magnify the effect of interest rate changes. At June 30, 1994, no such instruments were in our portfolio and it is the company's intent not to enter such leveraged contracts in the future.[47]

Thus, during 1994, the company had taken some very aggressive positions. These positions were increased in size and made even more risky using leverage. These positions were taken not to reduce interest rate risk but to increase it markedly, with the intent of generating significant gains. With such aggressive positions, however, comes the risk of loss. Such a loss was incurred.

The disturbing investment actions taken during 1994, prompted the company to provide the following "statement of financing philosophy" in its annual report:

> The derivatives write-off, which resulted in a $102 million charge [after-tax] to third-quarter earnings, warrants special comment to our shareholders.
> Procter & Gamble is in the business of developing and marketing consumer products of superior value in a broad range of categories. The financing objective is in support of this business. Our philosophy about the use of financial instru-

ments is to manage risk and cost. Our policy on derivatives is not to engage in speculative leveraged transactions.

The company has taken steps to substantially increase the oversight of the company's financial activities, including the formation of a Risk Management Council.

The council's role is to insure that the policies and procedures approved by the Board of Directors are being followed within approved limits, that transactions are properly analyzed prior to implementation, and that they are regularly monitored once implemented.

The Risk Management Council goes well beyond normal corporate operating controls. With these new procedures in place, the shareholders of the corporation can be assured that the company's management has taken the appropriate steps so that the situation which led to the third-quarter write-off will not happen again.[48]

Unfortunately, companies like Dell Computer and Procter & Gamble were not alone in their ventures into financial derivatives speculation. During the early 1990s, several companies experienced significant losses related to speculative activities. They include Air Products and Chemicals, Inc., which lost $113 million pre-tax on leveraged interest rate and currency swaps, Gibson Greetings, Inc., which lost $20 million pre-tax on leveraged interest rate swaps, and Mead, Inc., which lost $12 million, also on leveraged interest rate swaps. While the reported losses seem to have subsided, there will undoubtedly be similar events with other companies in the future. The investor or creditor should be prepared to employ available disclosures, such as those made available by SFAS Nos. 105, 107, and 115, in determining if a company under review is at risk for loss. Disclosures made available from a recently published accounting standard, SFAS No. 119, should also be helpful.

Expanded Disclosure Requirements for Financial Derivatives

SFAS No. 119, "Disclosure about Derivative Financial Instruments and Fair Value of Financial Instruments," was issued to provide more disclosures about financial derivatives.[49] The Financial Accounting Standards Board felt that additional disclosures were needed because of the increasing importance of those instruments and the need by investors and creditors for more information about them. SFAS No. 119 extended its scope to include all financial derivatives, including those with on–balance sheet and off–balance sheet risk. Recall that while an investment in a stock call option is a financial derivative, it does not have off–balance sheet risk. Accordingly, the disclosure requirements of SFAS No. 105 are not applicable. With SFAS No. 119, the Financial Accounting Standards Board specifies disclosure requirements for all financial derivatives, regardless of whether they have on–balance sheet or off–balance sheet risk.

In addition to expanding the scope of SFAS No. 105, SFAS No. 119 increases the disclosure requirements for financial derivatives. For example, in addition to providing information about the nature and terms of financial derivatives, including market risk and credit risk, it requires information on their leverage or risk multiplier features. It also requires disclosure of the purpose for which financial derivatives are held, including whether they are for investment or trading purposes or for other than trading. If held for trading purposes, the net gains or losses arising from trading activities must be reported. If held for other than trading purposes, such as hedging, the objectives for holding or issuing the financial derivatives and strategies for achieving those objectives must be disclosed together with how related gains and losses are reported.

SFAS No. 119 is effective for fiscal years ending after December 15, 1994. Accordingly, it was not effective for the financial statement examples provided here. Thus, more information should be available in the future for those firms that were less forthcoming about their derivatives positions. In particular, more information on the leverage or multiplier effects employed with their financial derivatives should be provided.

Analyzing Financial Statements with Open Derivatives Positions

Firms that invest or speculate in financial derivatives that do not serve as hedges of other exposed positions create a risk of loss. When an investment in a financial derivative is reported on the balance sheet, as with a stock call option, the risk of loss is equal to the amount at which the investment is reported. However, as noted earlier, many financial derivatives create off–balance sheet risk. Here, because the risk of loss is much greater than any amount reported on the balance sheet, the firm is effectively subject to a contingent liability. Depending on the movement of financial markets, the firm may report a loss on its off–balance sheet investment.

The American Institute of Certified Public Accountants (AICPA) has developed a series of detailed questions that are designed to help managements and boards of directors of different companies gain a better understanding of their entity's derivatives activities. These questions are useful in gaining insight into how managements are attempting to get more control over the derivatives investing that is occurring in their firms.

1. Has the board established a clear and internally consistent risk management policy, including risk limits (as appropriate)?

    Are our objectives and goals for derivatives activities clearly stated and communicated? To what extent are our operational objectives for derivatives being achieved? Are derivatives used to mitigate risk or do they create additional risk? If risk is being assumed, are trading limits established? Is the entity's strategy for derivatives use designed to further its economic, regulatory, industry, and/or operating objectives?

2. Are management's strategies and implementation policies consistent with the board's authorization?

    Management's philosophy and operating style create an environment that influences the actions of treasury and other personnel involved in derivatives activities. The assignment of authority and responsibility for derivatives transactions sends an important message. Is that message clear? Is compliance with these or related policies and procedures evaluated regularly? Does the treasury function review itself, or is it evaluated, as a profit center?

3. Do key controls exist to ensure that only authorized transactions take place and that unauthorized transactions are quickly detected and appropriate action is taken?

    Internal controls over derivatives activities should be monitored on an ongoing basis, and should also be subject to separate evaluations. Who is evaluating controls over derivatives being identified and reported upstream? Are duties involving execution of derivatives transactions segregated from other duties (for example, the accounting and internal audit functions)?

4. Are the magnitude, complexity, and risks of the entity's derivatives commensurate with the entity's objectives?

    What are the entity's risk exposures, including derivatives? Internal analyses should include quantitative and qualitative information about the entity's derivatives activities. Analyses should address the risks associated with derivatives, which include:

    - Credit risk (the possible financial loss resulting from a counterparty's failure to meet its financial obligations)
    - Market risk (the possible financial loss resulting from adverse movements in the price of a financial asset or commodity)
    - Legal risk (the possible financial loss resulting from a legal or regulatory action that could invalidate a financial contract)
    - Control risk (the possible financial loss resulting from inadequate internal control structure)

    Are our derivatives transactions standard for their class (that is, "plain vanilla") or are they more complex? Is the complexity of derivatives transactions inconsistent with the risks being managed? The entity's risk assessment should result in a determination about how to manage identified risks of derivatives activities. Has management anticipated how it will manage potential derivatives risks before assuming them?

5. Are personnel with authority to engage in and monitor derivative transactions well qualified and appropriately trained?

    Who are the key derivatives players within the entity? Is the knowledge vested only in one individual or a small group? The complexity of derivatives activities should be accompanied by development of personnel. For example, do employees involved in derivatives activities have the appropriate technical and professional expertise? Are other employees being appropriately educated before they become involved with derivatives transactions? Does the entity have personnel that have been cross-trained in case of the absence or departure of key personnel involved with derivatives activities? How do we ensure the integrity, ethical values, and competence of personnel involved with derivatives activities?

6. Do the right people have the right information to make decisions?

What information about derivatives activities are we identifying and capturing, and how is it being communicated? The information should address both external and internal events, activities, and conditions. For example, are we capturing and communicating information about market changes affecting derivatives transactions and about changes in our strategy for the mix of assets and liabilities that are the focus of risk management activities involving derivatives? Is this information being communicated to all affected parties?

Are the analysis and internal reporting of risks the company is managing and the effectiveness of its strategies comprehensive, reliable, and well designed to facilitate oversight? The board should consider derivatives activities in the context of how related risks affect the achievement of the entity's objectives—economic, regulatory, industry, or operating. For example, do derivatives activities increase the entity's exposure to risks that might frustrate, rather than further, achievement of these objectives?

Do we mark our derivatives transactions to market regularly (and, if not, why not)? Do we have good systems for marking transactions to market? Have the systems been tested by persons independent of the derivatives function? Do we know how the value of our derivatives will change under extreme market conditions? Is our published financial information about derivatives being prepared reliably and in conformity with generally accepted accounting principles?[50]

AICPA's questions about financial derivatives are excellent and should help an investor or creditor get a clearer picture of a firm's use of derivatives and the potential for loss. Because they have more access to corporate operating information, creditors would be more likely than investors to obtain answers to these questions. However, for investors and those creditors unable to obtain this sort of information, an increasing amount of information is available in a company's general-purpose financial statements. As we have seen, significant disclosure requirements have evolved to provide details about the financial derivatives held by firms. These disclosures include insight on market risk and credit risk, on the purpose of the financial derivatives, on its market value and the amount at which it is reported on the balance sheet.

When a firm has positions in financial derivatives, at a minimum answers to the following questions should be obtained. These questions can be answered from the company's general-purpose financial statements. First, why has the firm entered into the contracts? Are they serving as hedges? Or were the positions taken for investment purposes? Second, does it make sense for the company to be taking positions in financial derivatives? Third, does management have the expertise to do it? And finally, what is the total amount of exposure to loss faced by the firm? Is that risk of loss on the balance sheet or off the balance sheet? What would happen to assets and shareholders' equity if the total exposure to loss were to be realized?

SUMMARY

Assets are overvalued when their book values exceed amounts that can be expected to be realized through their use or sale. The amount of this overvaluation is a loss that has not been recognized. Because it is carried on the balance sheet, it implies the existence of a future benefit. When the lack of a future benefit is ultimately acknowledged, an income statement charge will be recorded. Potentially overvalued assets include accounts receivable, inventory, and investments. Each of these is not subject to an automatic reduction each year through amortization.

Liabilities are undervalued when they are reported at amounts less than the present value of the resources or services to be used in their settlement. As with overvalued assets, undervalued liabilities represent future charges to income. Balance sheet liabilities that may represent future charges include financing-related obligations such as notes and bonds payable, and operating-related obligations, including accrued expenses payable and accounts payable. Another category of liability, contingent liabilities, may be on or off the balance sheet. A contingent liability is reported on the balance sheet when it is probable that a liability has been incurred and its amount can be estimated. If both of these conditions are not met, the obligation is relegated to footnote disclosure. It is only through a careful examination of the notes that the potential effect on earnings of these contingencies can be gained.

A special kind of contingent liability that has created sizable losses for many companies in recent years arises through the use of financial derivatives. These instruments provide companies with a useful avenue for reducing financial risk. Managements have awakened to the availability of derivatives such as swaps, options, futures, and the like, and have embraced them. Unfortunately, some managements have chosen to use these instruments for purposes of speculation and have exposed their firms and shareholders to significant risk of loss.

Recent accounting pronouncements have markedly improved the availability of information on companies' derivatives positions. Proper use of this information should help the investor or creditor avoid earnings surprises caused by unsuspected speculation in financial derivatives.

A checklist for misreported assets and liabilities is provided in Exhibit 10.10. A careful review of the questions contained there should be helpful in avoiding unexpected shocks to net income.

Exhibit 10.10 Checklist for Financial Early Warnings: Misreported Assets and Liabilities

---

Overvaluation of Assets

A. Is the allowance for doubtful accounts sufficient to cover future collection problems?
   1. Compute A/R days for each of the last four to six quarters.
      a. Is the trend steady, improving, or worsening?
      b. Is the overall level high when compared with competitors or other firms in the industry?
   2. What amount of accounts receivable are at risk for a write-down?
      a. By what amount would the allowance for doubtful accounts need to be increased, reducing net accounts receivable, such that A/R days would be more in line with a target based on prior years, competitors, or the industry?
         i. Calculate as target A/R days reduction multiplied by revenue per day.
B. Have economic conditions for the company's customers worsened recently?
   1. Are company sales declining?
   2. Are there other general economic reasons to expect that customers are, or may be, having difficulties?
C. Are sales growing rapidly?
   1. Has the company changed its credit policy?
      a. Is credit being granted to less creditworthy customers?
   2. Have payment terms been extended?
D. Are inventories overstated because of inclusion of nonexistent inventories or by the reporting of true quantities on hand at amounts that exceed replacement cost?
   1. Compute gross margin and inventory days for the last four to six quarters.
      a. Is the trend steady, worsening, or improving?
      b. How do the statistics compare with competitors and other firms in the industry?
         i. Before making comparisons with competitors, make sure that the same inventory methods (LIFO, FIFO, etc.) are being used.
   2. Do ongoing company events and fortunes suggest problems with slackening demand for the company's products?
      a. Are sales declining?
      b. Have raw materials inventories declined markedly as a percentage of total inventory?
   3. Are prices falling, suggesting general industry weakness and an increased chance that inventory cost may not be recoverable?
   4. Is the company in an industry that is experiencing rapid technological change, increasing the risk of inventory obsolescence?
   5. Has the company shown evidence in the past of inventory overvaluation?
      a. Is there an example of a prior-year write-down of inventory that became value-impaired?
   6. Does the company use the FIFO method?
      a. Companies that use FIFO run a greater risk that inventory costs may exceed replacement costs.

E. Does the company employ the LIFO inventory method for at least a portion of its inventory?
    1. Are LIFO adjustments being made for interim periods?
        a. Has the LIFO reserve account remained unchanged during interim periods?
        b. If the LIFO reserve account has been adjusted during interim periods, does the estimate of inflation used appear reasonable?
        c. How does gross margin for interim periods compare with prior years' annual results?
        d. Do increased gross margins suggest the influence of undisclosed LIFO liquidations?
F. What is the nature of the company's environment with respect to inventory controls?
    1. Do controls to guard against theft seem adequate?
    2. When a physical inventory is taken, how does the amount compare with the books?
        a. Do the books consistently exceed the physical count by a significant amount?
        b. Are the books adjusted, or are differences dismissed as errors in taking the physical inventory?
G. For debt securities held until maturity, and nonmarketable equity securities:
    1. Is there evidence of a nontemporary decline in market value?
H. For debt securities and marketable equity securities that are available for sale:
    1. Are investment losses included in shareholders' equity that might be taken to income?
        a. Might the designation of these losses be changed to other than temporary?
        b. Is sale of one or more investments imminent?
    2. Has shareholders' equity been buoyed by substantial write-ups to market value?
I. For investments accounted for under the equity method:
    1. Is there evidence of a nontemporary decline in market value?

Undervaluation of Liabilities
A. Are coupon or stated interest rates on long-term notes and bonds payable significantly higher than the current level of rates?
B. What are the prospects for early termination of this debt leading to an associated extraordinary loss?
C. Accrued expenses payable
    1. What is the trend in accrued expenses payable?
    2. Does an improvement in selling, general, and administrative expense as a percentage of sales revenue reflect true operating efficiencies?
D. Accounts payable
    1. Compute accounts payable in days for each of the last four to six quarters.
        a. Is the trend steady, worsening, or improving?
        b. How does the statistic compare with competitors' and other firms in the industry?
    2. How does the percent change in accounts payable compare with the percent change in inventory?

E.   Contingent liabilities
1.   What unrecognized contingencies are noted in a careful reading of the footnotes?
2.   Given an understanding of the company's business dealings, is there reason to believe that an unrecognized contingent liability exists?
3.   Does the company have speculative investment positions?
     a.   Is the risk of loss limited to an amount reported on the balance sheet?
     b.   Is the risk of loss reported off the balance sheet in the footnotes?
4.   Special questions related to financial derivatives
     a.   Why has the firm taken the position?
          i.   Is it a hedge or a speculation?
          ii. Does it make sense for the company to be taking positions in financial derivatives?
     b.   Does management have the expertise to properly take the positions taken?
     c.   What is the off–balance sheet exposure to loss?
          i.   What would happen to assets and shareholders' equity if the total exposure to loss were to be realized?

REFERENCES

Comiskey, E. E. and C. W. Mulford, "Investment Decisions and the Equity Accounting Standard," *Accounting Review,* July 1986, pp. 519–525.
———. "Risks of Foreign Currency Transactions: A Guide for Loan Officers," *Commercial Lending Review,* Summer 1990, pp. 44–60.
———. "The Impact of Globalization on Management and Financial Reporting." In T*he Portable MBA—Accounting and Finance*, ed. Leslie J. Livingstone, (New York: John Wiley, 1992), ch. 17.
———. "The Influence of Accounting Principles on Management Investment Decisions." *Accounting Horizons,* June 1988, pp. 67–72.
Comiskey, E. E., C. W. Mulford, and D. H. Turner, "Interest Rate Swap Accounting Practices." In *Handbook of Bank Accounting and Finance*, eds. Larry D. Crumbley, Nicholas G. Apostolou, and George Simonton, (New York: Shepherds'/McGraw-Hill, 1989), ch. 40.
Mulford, C. W., "The Importance of a Market Value Measurement of Debt in Leverage Ratios—Replication and Extensions." *Journal of Accounting Research,* Autumn 1985, pp. 897–906.
Ronen, J., A. Saunders, and A. Sondhi, eds. *Off–Balance Sheet Activities* (New York: Stern School of Business, New York University, 1990).

ENDNOTES

1.   Crown Crafts, Inc., press release, May 5, 1993.
2.   Tektronix, Inc., annual report, May 1991, p. 23.
3.   Athanor Group, Inc., annual report, October 1993, p. 35.
4.   Intellicall, Inc., annual report, December 1992. Information obtained from Disclo-

sure, Inc., *Compact D/SEC: Corporate Information on Public Companies Filing with the SEC* (Bethesda, Md.: Disclosure, Inc., March 1994).

5. Home Nutritional Services, Inc., press release, March 3, 1993.

6. Machine Technology, Inc., annual report, August 1988. Information obtained from company's annual report, August 1989, p. 21.

7. Robert Morris Associates, *Annual Statement Studies* (Philadelphia: Robert Morris Associates, 1991), pp. 162–163.

8. Machine Technology, Inc., press release, February 5, 1992.

9. Ibid., March 24, 1992.

10. Robert Morris Associates, *Annual Statement Studies* (Philadelphia: Robert Morris Associates, 1993), pp. 544–545.

11. *The Wall Street Journal*, December 14, 1992, p. A1.

12. MiniScribe Corp., Form 10-K annual report to the Securities and Exchange Commission, December 1986, p. F-6.

13. "Dressmaker Leslie Fay Is an Old-Style Firm That's in a Modern Fix," *The Wall Street Journal*, February 23, 1993, pp. A1 and A8.

14. Safeway Stores, Inc., annual report, December 1993. Information obtained from Disclosure, Inc., *Compact D/SEC: Corporate Information on Public Companies Filing with the SEC* (Bethesda, Md.: Disclosure, Inc., March 1995).

15. Differences among compiled, reviewed, and audited financial statements are discussed in Chapter 13.

16. The relevant accounting standard is Statement of Financial Accounting Standards (SFAS) No. 115, "Accounting for Certain Investments in Debt and Equity Securities" (Norwalk, Conn.: Financial Accounting Standards Board May 1993).

17. Excerpts taken from an article in the *Richmond Times-Dispatch* as carried on *Dow Jones New Retrieval* (New York: Dow Jones & Co., March 14, 1995).

18. As subsequently disclosed in the company's December 1994 annual report, in early 1994 the investment in USAir preferred was reclassified to available-for-sale status from held-to-maturity. Accordingly, during 1994, losses accrued on this investment were charged against shareholders' equity. However, these losses were still excluded from income until it was determined in March 1995 that the market value decline in USAir was other than temporary.

19. Overseas Shipholding, Inc., annual report, December 1992.

20. Gerber Scientific, Inc., annual report, April 1990.

21. Prepayment penalties may also be incurred, resulting in extraordinary income statement losses, when current market rates of interest exceed the rates in existence when longer-term notes and bonds were issued. However, the likelihood of early termination is reduced in such a setting.

22. Act III Broadcasting, Inc., annual report, December 1993. Information obtained from Disclosure, Inc., *Compact D/SEC: Corporate Information on Public Companies Filing with the SEC* (Bethesda, Md.: Disclosure, Inc., March 1995).

23. Ackerley Communications, Inc., annual report, December 1993. Information obtained from Disclosure, Inc., *Compact D/SEC: Corporate Information on Public Companies Filing with the SEC* (Bethesda, Md.: Disclosure, Inc., March 1995).

24. Refer to SFAS No. 5, "Accounting for Contingencies" (March 1975).

25. Lindsay Manufacturing Co., annual report, August 1990, pp. 14–15.

26. Original Italian Pasta Products Co., annual report, June 1993, pp. 11–12.

27. Alcan Aluminum Co., annual report, December 1993. Information obtained from

Disclosure, Inc., *Compact D/SEC: Corporate Information on Public Companies Filing with the SEC* (Bethesda, Md.: Disclosure, Inc., March 1995).

28. Personal Diagnostics, Inc., Form 10-K annual report to the Securities and Exchange Commission, September 1992, p. F-8.

29. As required by SFAS No. 105, "Disclosure of Information about Financial Instruments with Off–Balance Sheet Risk and Financial Instruments with Concentrations of Credit Risk" (March 1990).

30. The company's investment portfolio was reported at market value under SFAS No. 115, "Accounting for Certain Investments in Debt and Equity Securities" (May 1993).

31. SFAS No. 105, "Disclosure of Information about Financial Instruments with Off–Balance Sheet Risk and Financial Instruments with Concentrations of Credit Risk" (March 1990).

32. Our focus is on long positions in stock options. Because they create off–balance sheet market risk, or the risk of loss beyond any investment balance, options written, or short positions in stock options, are subject to the disclosure requirements of SFAS No. 105.

33. SFAS No. 115, "Accounting for Certain Investments in Debt and Equity Securities" (May 1993).

34. Dell Computer Corp., annual report, January 1994, pp. 29–30.

35. Ibid., p. 29.

36. Ibid., p. 30.

37. Ibid., p. 34.

38. Ibid., p. 34.

39. Ibid., p. 34.

40. SFAS No. 52, "Foreign Currency Translation" (December 1981), and SFAS No. 80, "Accounting for Futures Contracts" (August 1984).

41. Early indications are that a new accounting standard for financial derivatives will be close to the guidance already provided by SFAS No. 52 and SFAS No. 80. Thus, no drastic changes in accounting for gains and losses arising from derivatives are expected.

42. Red Eagle Resources, Inc., Form 10-Q quarterly report to the Securities and Exchange Commission, September 1994, p. 7.

43. Cedar Group, Inc., annual report, September 1994. Information obtained from Disclosure, Inc., *Compact D/SEC: Corporate Information on Public Companies Filing with the SEC* (Bethesda, Md.: Disclosure, Inc., March 1995).

44. Dell Computer Corp., annual report, January 1994, p. 34.

45. *The Wall Street Journal*, April 22, 1994, p. B10.

46. Procter & Gamble Co., annual report, September 1994, p. 23.

47. Ibid., p. 23.

48. Ibid., p. 5.

49. SFAS No. 119, "Disclosure about Derivative Financial Instruments and Fair Value of Financial Instruments" (October 1994).

50. As included in *New Developments Summary* (New York: Grant Thornton & Co.), July 25, 1994.

Chapter 11

Cash Flow Warnings

Though my bottom line is black, I am flat upon my back,
My cash flows out and customers pay slow.
The growth of my receivables is almost unbelievable;
The result is certain—unremitting woe!
And I hear the banker utter an ominous low mutter,
"Watch cash flow."[1]

This poem captures well the purpose of cash flow analysis. Profit, or net income as reported on the income statement, provides an important measure of performance. However, in the absence of cash flow, profit does not pay the bills. Interest and dividend payments, required principal reductions on term debt, and capital expenditures for replacement of plant and equipment consumed in operations and expansion cannot be made without cash. Cash provided by operating activities, also known as operating cash flow, is a primary source of cash to meet these needs.

In the absence of operating cash flow, cash from other sources can be used to cover corporate cash requirements. For example, needed cash can be obtained from on-hand balances or nonrecurring asset sales, new debt or equity financing, or from an outside guarantor. However, these nonoperating sources of cash flow can be relied upon only in the short run. In the long run, operating cash flow is the only reliable source of cash available to meet recurring corporate needs. It is a continuing source of cash, it is within management's control and accordingly can be earmarked for corporate needs, and it does not expose the firm to additional risks associated with new financings.

The cash flow statement, which reports operating cash flow, provides important information to investors and creditors. In particular, it provides information about differences in the timing of revenue and expense recognition under generally accepted accounting principles and associated cash inflows and outflows. Recall that revenue is recognized when earned and realized or realizable. Expenses incurred in earning that revenue are recognized, or matched, with that revenue. In the absence of a direct link between revenue earned and expenses incurred, expenses are matched with the periods that benefit from their incurrence. This timing of revenue and expense recognition is known as accrual-basis accounting.

However, there is no requirement that revenue be collected before it is recognized. Similarly, expenses need not be paid before they are recorded. Thus, under accrual-basis accounting, reported net income will not, except by coincidence, be equal to operating cash flow. This latter measure of performance, also known as cash-basis accounting, is simply the sum of operating cash receipts less operating cash payments and interest paid.

Cash-basis accounting is appealing in its simplicity and in the measure of performance it provides. Operating cash flow provides very direct information about the ability of a firm to pay its bills, to pay financing costs such as interest and dividends, to repay debt, and to make capital expenditures. In addition, the Financial Accounting Standards Board has stated that an objective of financial reporting is to provide information to investors and creditors that is useful in assessing the amounts, timing, and uncertainty of prospective cash receipts from dividends or interest and the proceeds from the sale, redemption, or maturity of securities or loans. According to the Board,

> The prospects for those cash receipts are affected by an enterprise's ability to generate enough cash to meet its obligations when due and its other cash operating needs, to reinvest in operations, and to pay cash dividends.[2]

Why, then, has the Financial Accounting Standards Board embraced accrual-basis accounting over cash-basis accounting?

According to the Board, accrual-basis accounting provides a better measure of the future cash-generating capacity of a firm than does information on current cash flows. Consider the following statement:

> Information about enterprise earnings and its components measured by accrual accounting generally provides a better indication of enterprise performance than information about current cash receipts and payments. Accrual accounting attempts to record the financial effects on an enterprise of transactions and other events and circumstances that have cash consequences for an enterprise in the periods in which those transactions, events, and circumstances occur rather than only in the periods in which cash is received or paid by the enterprise. Accrual accounting is concerned with the process by which cash expended on resources and activities is returned as more (or perhaps less) cash to the enterprise, not just with the beginning and end of that process. It recognizes that the buying, producing, selling, and other operations of an enterprise during a period, as well as other events that affect enterprise performance, often do not coincide with the cash receipts and payments of the period.[3]

As an example, assume that a firm starts with one asset, cash. Assume also that in the very next transaction, the firm uses that cash to purchase inventory. If an income statement were to be prepared at that point using cash-basis accounting, it would show a use of cash, in effect, a net cash loss. This loss would not consider the cash flow generating capacity of the inventory. Said cash flow would be generated when that inventory was sold and the sale price collected. The reported use of cash on a cash-basis income statement would not be a good indicator of the company's ability to generate future cash flow. Under accrual-basis accounting, no income or expense would be reported. The purchase of inventory is simply a shift of assets and would not be considered as reducing the firm's ability to generate future cash flow.

The purchase of equipment provides another example. Under true cash-basis accounting, purchases of all assets, including equipment, would appear as cash expenses. Such treatment gives no acknowledgment to the future benefit and cash generating capacity resulting from their purchase. Accrual-basis accounting spreads the cost of those assets over their useful lives, charging a portion as expense to each period that benefits.

LINKING THE STATEMENT OF CASH FLOWS WITH OTHER STATEMENTS

In previous chapters, we stressed the importance of the relation between the balance sheet and the income statement in anticipating earnings surprises. We noted that when costs are capitalized aggressively or amortization periods extended, when assets are overvalued or liabilities undervalued, the result will be a charge to income in some future period as balance sheet misstatements inevitably are revealed and corrected. As a result of the relation between these two statements, selected balance sheet accounts were shown to be useful in helping to predict those earnings charges. A third statement, the statement of cash flows, which prominently displays operating cash flow, is also closely linked with the other two. When properly used, it also provides a fruitful hunting ground for potential earnings surprises.

In understanding how the statement of cash flows, the income statement, and the balance sheet are linked, one need only recognize that under accrual-basis accounting, unrealized income statement items result in changes in noncash balance sheet accounts. For example, unrealized or uncollected revenue increases the accounts receivable account reported on the balance sheet. Expenses paid in advance (of being incurred or consumed) increase accounts such as prepaid expenses, inventory, and property, plant, and equipment. In both cases, net income will exceed operating cash flow by the amount of the increase in the related balance sheet asset accounts. Similarly, revenue collected in advance of being earned increases the deferred or unearned revenue account reported on the balance sheet. And expenses incurred in advance of payment increase such liabilities as accrued expenses payable. Here, operating cash flow will exceed net income by the amount of the increase in the related liability accounts.

In this way, the cash flow statement is related to the income statement and the balance sheet. If an income-related transaction is realized or settled, it will affect both the income statement and cash flow. If unrealized, it will affect the income statement and a noncash balance sheet account.

Negative operating cash flow is a useful flag in our search for early warnings of earnings surprises. Steps taken to recognize revenue prematurely, to overcapitalize costs, to extend amortization periods, or to report assets at overvalued amounts will increase income but not operating cash flow. Later, if these asset balances are not realized, they will result in write-downs and charges to income. For example, as discussed in Chapter 8, the software company Knowledgeware, Inc., recognized revenue even in situations where customers were being permitted up to one year to pay. This revenue was unrealized, resulting in increases in accounts receivable and income that exceeded operating cash flow. Later, collectibility of these accounts receivable was shown to be questionable, resulting in a downward adjustment to income. Similarly, as discussed in Chapter 9, Chambers Development Co. aggressively capitalized landfill development costs. This led to an increase in a balance sheet account and contributed to net income's exceeding operating cash flow. Here, too, income was later reduced to remove these overcapitalized costs. Undervaluing liabilities will also increase income without an accompanying increase in operating cash flow. Again, if required payments exceed the amount of liabilities accrued, additional charges to income will be needed. An example was provided in Chapter 10 for MiniScribe Corp. The company reduced its accrual for warranty expenses, resulting in a decline in its balance sheet liability for warranties. While increasing income, this underaccrual did not increase operating cash flow. For this and other reasons, the company's earnings were subsequently restated to report a loss.

The lack of operating cash flow is a useful indicator of potential future charges to income. It is, however, a very rough indicator and must be used with caution. For example, in growth situations, companies can for many years generate substantial profit while consuming cash in operations. In such situations, negative operating cash flow is not necessarily followed by losses and special charges to earnings. In contrast, a company in decline can generate ample amounts of cash flow even as operations falter. This result is often due to substantial noncash charges, such as depreciation, and the liquidation of working capital. Here, positive operating cash flow is often followed by losses and special charges to income. Further, even when operating cash flow is giving valid signals of future earnings difficulties, the signals can be very crude. That is, negative operating cash flow does not readily pinpoint the specific area of potential earnings difficulty. Without careful analysis, it is difficult to determine if the problems are related to inventory, accounts receivable, or some other asset or liability account.

In this chapter, we use operating cash flow as an early indicator of future earnings problems. The cash flow analysis employed is also used to pinpoint the specific areas of potential earnings problems.

THE STATEMENT OF CASH FLOWS

Generally accepted accounting principles require companies to provide a statement of cash flows as part of a full set of general-purpose financial statements.[4] This statement is designed to measure the change in cash and cash equivalents over a reporting period. Here cash equivalents are highly liquid, debt-type instruments with original maturities of three months or less and are viewed the same as cash. An example cash flow statement for Scientific Technologies, Inc., for 1994 is provided in Exhibit 11.1. Note how the cash flow statement separates changes in cash and cash equivalents into three major categories: operating cash flow, investing cash flow, and financing cash flow. The statement sums to the actual change in cash and cash equivalents during the year. The beginning and ending balances in cash and cash equivalents are equal to the amounts reported on the balance sheet.

Cash Flows from Operating Activities

Cash provided by operating activities, or operating cash flow, consists of the cash effects of transactions that enter into the determination of net income, such as cash receipts from sales of goods and services and cash payments to suppliers and employees for acquisitions of inventory and operating expenses. This operating cash flow can be viewed as the cash flow counterpart of net income from continuing

Exhibit 11.1   Indirect-Method Cash Flow Statement: Scientitic Technologies, Inc., Year Ending December 31, 1994 (thousands of dollars)

	1994
Cash flows from operating activities	
Net income	$ 3,698
Adjustments to reconcile net income to cash provided by operating activities	
Depreciation and amortization	337
Changes in assets and liabilities	
Accounts receivable, net	(1,841)
Inventories	(652)
Receivable from parent company	675
Trade accounts payable	670
Accrued expenses	590
Other	(98)
Cash flows from operating activities	3,379
Cash flows from investing activities	
Property and equipment	(1,041)
Sale (purchase) of short-term investments	809
Cash flows from investing activities	(232)
Cash flows from financing activities	
Payments on debt	(50)
Reissuance of treasury stock	4
Dividends	(957)
Cash flows from financing activities	(1,003)
Change in cash and cash equivalents	2,144
Cash and cash equivalents at beginning of year	103
Cash and cash equivalents at end of year	$ 2,247

operations measured on the accrual basis. Except for an isolated exception or two, the cash flow consequences of those items that go into the calculation of net income from continuing operations are included in operating cash flow. For example, interest paid, which might be viewed as a financing-related expenditure, is included in the operating section. Also, interest expense is deducted in computing net income. In contrast, dividends, which are considered a distribution of profits and not a component of net income, are excluded from the operating section of the cash flow statement and reported in the financing section.

An important exception to the symmetry that exists between the definition of net income and cash provided by operating activities is gains and losses from the sale of investments and property, plant, and equipment. This exception is important because of its frequency of occurrence. Gains and losses on sales of investments and property, plant, and equipment are included in net income from continuing operations, but proceeds from their sale are excluded from operating cash flow and reported with investing cash flow.

There are other exceptions to this symmetry that occur less frequently. For example, the operating component of discontinued operations is excluded from net income from continuing operations. However, its cash flow consequences are reported with cash provided by operating activities. That is, cash flows from operating activities includes cash provided by continuing operations and the operating component of discontinued operations. We exclude these other exceptions from the discussion that follows. When we refer to net income, we mean net income from continuing operations excluding discontinued operations, extraordinary items, and the cumulative effect of changes in accounting principle.

The operating section of the cash flow statement does not report actual cash inflows and outflows. For example, using the cash flow statement shown in Exhibit 11.1, one cannot say how much cash the company collected from customers or how much cash was paid to suppliers and employees. That cash flow statement is presented in the indirect-method format. Such a format begins with net income and reconciles to cash from operating activities. The reconciliation requires an identification of all noncash expenses, such as depreciation and amortization and the inclusion of changes in all operating-related balance sheet accounts. These account changes represent items of income or expense whose associated cash flow differs from their timing of recognition in income. For example, an uncollected sale results in an increase in accounts receivable. The sale is included in net income. The increase in accounts receivable that it causes must be subtracted from net income in calculating operating cash flow.

Two operating cash flow items important to lenders and other financial statement users that are not reported in an indirect-method cash flow statement are interest and income taxes paid. It is important to know the amount of interest paid to determine whether the company is able to service the interest component of its debt with operating cash flow. And because income taxes can make up 40% or more of pre-tax profit, it is important to know the amount of the current year's tax provision that was actually paid in cash. Given the importance of these two items, generally accepted accounting principles require their separate disclosure even though they are not part of an indirect calculation of cash provided by operating activities.

Cash Flows from Investing Activities

Cash provided by or used in investing activities includes investments in, and the proceeds from sale of, debt and equity investments, and property, plant, and equipment accounts. Note that investments in long-lived assets are reported in the investing section, whereas cash income from those investments is reported in the operating section. For example, the purchase of a delivery truck is reported in the investing section. Collections from delivery customers are reported in the operating section. Similarly, an investment in bonds or loans is included in investing cash flows, whereas interest income on them is reported with operating cash flow.

Cash Flows from Financing Activities

Cash provided by or used in financing activities consists of borrowings and repayments of debt, and the issue and repurchase of stock. Dividends on that stock are also reported here, but interest on debt is included in the operating section.

It seems a bit inconsistent to report interest paid as an operating item and dividends as a financing item. However, that inconsistency is needed to maintain symmetry with the definition of net income. Net income is defined as amounts available for shareholders after senior claims, including those of debt-holders, have been covered. Thus, interest, a claim of debt-holders, is subtracted in computing net income. Dividends, however, are a payment to shareholders, a distribution of profits available for them. Thus, dividends are not subtracted in measuring net income. In this way, net income consists of earnings available for all shareholders, common and preferred. Similarly, cash provided by operating activities consists of cash flow available for all shareholders after interest claims of debt-holders have been covered.

Direct-Method Format

An alternative format for the operating section of the cash flow statement, which is also permitted and encouraged under generally accepted accounting principles, is the direct-method format. This method differs from the indirect method in that actual cash receipts and disbursements, rather than an indirect reconciliation of net income to operating cash flow, are reported. The investing and financing sections of the cash flow statement are the same for the direct method as for the indirect method. The operating section of the Scientific Technologies cash flow statement is presented in the direct-method format in Exhibit 11.2.

The cash flow statement in Exhibit 11.2 does not start with net income. Rather, it starts with actual cash receipts and then subtracts cash disbursements. The end

Exhibit 11.2   Direct-Method Cash Flow Statement (Operating Section): Scientific Technologies, Inc., Year Ending December 31, 1994 (thousands of dollars)

	1994
Cash flows from operating activities	
Cash received from customers	$ 24,274
Interest received and other cash income	685
Cash paid to suppliers and employees	(19,107)
Income taxes paid	(2,466)
Interest paid	(7)
Cash flows from operating activities	$ 3,379

Source: Amounts computed, as shown, using data reported in Exhibit 11.1.

result is cash provided by operating activities of $3,379,000. This is the same amount of operating cash reported on the indirect-method cash flow statement in Exhibit 11.1.

An additional requirement for companies using direct-method cash flow statements is a supplementary disclosure of the reconciliation of net income to cash provided by operating activities. That reconciliation is done in the operating activities section of the indirect-method cash flow statement. It starts with net income and adjusts for noncash expenses and other operating balance sheet account changes to compute cash provided by operating activities.

The majority of companies use indirect-method cash flow statements. In fact, probably only 1 company in 100 or less currently provides a direct-method cash flow statement. One possible reason is the requirement that a reconciliation of net income to cash provided by operating activities supplement a direct-method cash flow statement. In effect, both reports must be provided where an indirect-method cash flow statement alone would suffice.

In performing cash flow analysis, we employ the indirect-method cash flow statement because our primary interest is in identifying noncash income statement amounts. These noncash items will appear as balance sheet account changes in the operating section of the indirect-method cash flow statement.[5]

"CREATIVITY" IN CLASSIFYING CASH FLOWS

Before proceeding with our discussion of how cash flow analysis can be used to avoid earnings surprises, we make a few points about "creativity" in classifying cash flows to improve *apparent* cash flow performance. The choice of category—deciding whether to report an item in the operating, investing, or financing section—can itself make a difference in results, and overstate the apparent capacity to generate operating cash flow. Typically, this is done by classifying operating uses of cash as investing items, but it can involve a cross-classification with the financing section as well. As a result, operating cash flow is apparently improved.

Consider the classification of software development costs. The majority of software companies classify capitalized software development costs as uses of cash in the investing section. However, this is only their classification of capitalized software development costs. Any software development costs that are expensed when incurred would appear as operating uses of cash. Thus, Microsoft Corp., a company that capitalizes none of its software development costs, classifies all costs incurred on software development as an operating use. In contrast, American Software, Inc., a company that capitalizes over 60% of its software costs, includes a much smaller proportion of costs incurred on software development in the operating section.

As another example, consider the cash flow classification of the preopening costs of retailers. Most retailers classify preopening costs incurred as operating uses of cash. However, in its cash flow statement for the year ending January 31, 1993, 50-Off Stores, Inc., classified $7.7 million of preopening costs as an investing item. That year, the company reported $10.3 million in operating cash flow. Had the company classified its preopening costs as an operating item, operating cash flow would have been reduced to $2.6 million ($10.3 million less $7.7 million). Interestingly, in 1994, 50-Off Stores changed its cash flow classification for preopening costs to report them as operating items. That year, the company reported a use of cash from operating activities in the amount of $2.8 million.[6]

In 1990, Seitel, Inc., a company that develops and markets seismic data, reported a use of cash from operating activities of $4.8 million. Included in the operating section that year was a $15.0 million use of cash for the acquisition and development of seismic data. In 1991 the company changed its classification of seismic data acquisition and development to include it in the investing section. The 1990 cash flow statement was restated in the company's 1991 annual report to include the seismic data item as an investing action. As a result, the company's 1990 operating cash flow was transformed from a $4.8 million use of cash to a $10.2 million source.[7] What a difference cash flow classification can make!

One last example demonstrates a "creative" technique for boosting operating cash flow. In 1992, Value Merchants, Inc., a retailer, was growing rapidly and consuming significant amounts of operating cash flow in the process. On its February 1992 balance sheet, the company included $6.1 million of outstanding checks with accounts payable.[8] The logic here was that since the checks had not cleared, the accounts payable were still outstanding. Most companies would likely report such checks as a subtraction from cash on hand. However, since increases in accounts payable are reported as operating sources of cash, by including the outstanding checks with accounts payable Value Merchants was able to boost its operating cash flow. As an alternative form of presentation, Value Merchants could also have reported the outstanding checks as a bank overdraft under the premise that if the checks were to clear and if the company did not have sufficient deposits to meet them, the bank would provide the necessary financing. Had this been done, financing cash flow, instead of operating cash flow, would have been increased.

A company using this latter approach is Ag Services of America, Inc. On its February 1994 balance sheet, the company reported "excess of outstanding checks over bank balance" as a current liability, separate and apart from accounts payable. The change in that account during the year was reported as a financing item on the company's statement of cash flows.

Cash flow classification can affect a company's apparent ability to generate operating cash flow. Before analyzing cash flows, investors and creditors should make sure that they agree with the classification of various items among the three sections: operating, investing, and financing activities. The analysis of operating cash flows discussed in this chapter, together with references provided at the end of the chapter, should be helpful in this regard.

ANTICIPATING TRENDS IN NET INCOME AND OPERATING CASH FLOW

Our purpose for performing cash flow analysis is to anticipate earnings surprises. In this regard, the cash flow statement is useful in helping to anticipate special charges against earnings due to asset write-downs and liability accruals.

As noted, the cash flow statement reports account changes representing items of income or expense whose cash flow effects differ from their timing in the measurement of income. When net income exceeds operating cash flow, the company may be recognizing income in advance of realization. That income results in increases in operating-related balance sheet assets. Alternatively, expenses may be accrued, resulting in increases in operating related liabilities. Here, operating cash flow will exceed income. There are limits to how far these account balances can go. At some point, realization becomes questionable and write-downs ensue. Or liabilities are reduced as far as they can be taken and new accruals are necessary. When asset write-downs are taken or additional liabilities accrued, earnings are reduced.

Analyzing cash flow to identify candidates for earnings surprises is not as simple, however, as identifying firms that generate income in excess of operating cash flow. Nor can one always be reassured when operating cash flow exceeds income. Either alternative may be a natural development at key points in the firm's life cycle.

With the exception of cash flows associated with debt and equity financing, the lifetime earnings of a company will be equal to its lifetime cash flows. For purposes of analysis, however, that lifetime of business activity must be broken down into shorter segments. Periods of time consisting of a quarter or a year are the norm. Over these short periods, profits and cash flow will likely be unequal, not only in amount but often in sign as well. One company may report net income that exceeds operating cash flow, and another operating cash flow that exceeds net income.

At first, it may seem that differences between net income and operating cash flow are random, caused by no particular underlying factor. While natural period-to-period business events may lend a random appearance to differences between net income and cash flow, there are other broader, more pervasive trends at work. In particular, a company's life cycle helps to explain observed differences between net income and operating cash flow.

A Company's Life Cycle

Net income and operating cash flow have certain characteristic relations as a company moves through the normal stages of its life cycle: start-up, growth, maturity, and decline. For example, a firm in the early growth phase of its life cycle may be profitable but typically consumes operating cash. Because of the purchase of inventory and increases in accounts receivable, items that consume cash but are not expensed, operating cash flow is less than net income. Or, for example, during maturity, as growth rates decline to sustainable levels and additions to accounts receivable and inventory level off, a company will likely generate ample amounts of cash. Then, cash flow may exceed the amount of net income reported.

Considering a company's stage in its life cycle, we can form an opinion as to what relation between net income and cash flow to expect. If a company diverges significantly from the expected characteristic relation, there is reason to investigate further. For example, while it is not unusual for a growth firm to generate net income that exceeds cash flow, it is less likely that a mature firm would suddenly do so. It would be even more unusual if that mature firm's cash flow turned negative, even as the firm remained profitable. The sources of that profitability would have to be examined carefully.

Knowing a company's stage in its life cycle is helpful in anticipating future developments. For example, in the late stages of maturity, sales may start to decline. The company would begin liquidating current assets acquired in prior years. Operating cash flow would exceed net income. The general desirability of cash flow notwithstanding, investors or creditors should not feel reassured by these larger cash flows. As operations falter, there may be the need to record special charges for slow-moving inventory or to anticipate the costs of plant consolidation. If a company's stage in its life cycle is decline, these special charges should not be a surprise. A graphical depiction of a company's life cycle is provided in Exhibit 11.3.

In Exhibit 11.3, the life cycle of a company is divided into four segments: start-up, growth, maturity, and decline. A graph of net income and operating cash flow is drawn through each of those segments. Both net income and operating cash flow begin in negative territory, depicting net losses and negative operating cash flow. At the start of the growth segment, net income becomes positive while operating cash flow is still negative. At later stages of growth, operating cash flow also becomes positive. Net income exceeds operating cash flow until the later stages of maturity, when cash flow exceeds net income. Both net income and operating cash flow remain positive until the late stages of decline, when both become negative again. A more detailed description of each life cycle segment follows.

Start-up

It is not unusual for a company to lose money in the early stages of its life. Here, the company incurs costs associated with organization, development of its products or

Exhibit 11.3 A Company's Life Cycle

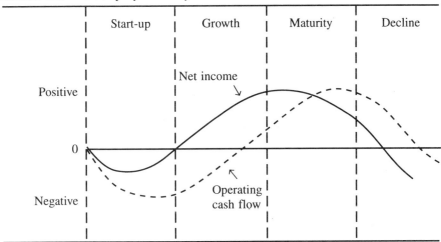

Source: E. Comiskey and C. Mulford, "Anticipating Trends in Operating Profits and Cash Flows," *Commercial Lending Review*, Spring 1993, p. 42.

services, and promotion and distribution. These expenses typically exceed any revenue the company may be generating. While the company is generating net losses, it is likely consuming even more operating cash, because certain expenditures do not appear as expenses on the income statement. For example, amounts expended to purchase or manufacture inventory would not be expensed. In addition, a portion of the revenue that is recognized would likely result in an increase in accounts receivable.

Research Frontiers, Inc., is investigating electrically operated devices to control the amount of light that is transmitted through glass. The amounts incurred for research and development, especially when combined with other costs incurred in promoting the company's devices to potential manufacturing licensees, have for several years exceeded any revenue generated, resulting in sizable start-up losses.

During these early years of its existence, Research Frontier's operating cash flow has also been negative. The company has little in the way of noncash expenses such as depreciation. And, while it does not have inventory requirements, as a result of increases in accounts receivable and other current assets the company has in recent years consumed more operating cash than the amount of net losses reported. A summary of the company's losses and cash consumed in operations over the last several years is provided in Exhibit 11.4.

While in 1990 and 1993 the loss reported by the company was marginally greater than the cash consumed in operations, collectively across the five years, the amount of cash consumed in operations was much greater than the net loss reported. Such a development is to be expected for a start-up firm.

Exhibit 11.4 A Start-up Firm—Net Loss and Negative Operating Cash Flow: Research Frontiers, Inc., Years Ending December 31, 1990–1994 (thousands of dollars)

	1990	1991	1992	1993	1994
Revenue	$485	$352	$278	$207	$575
Net loss from continuing operations	(747)	(1,043)	(1,354)	(1,817)	(2,924)
Cash used in operating activities	(605)	(1,072)	(1,401)	(1,691)	(4,395)

Sources: Data obtained from Research Frontiers, Inc., annual report, December 1992, and Disclosure, Inc., *Compact D/SEC: Corporate Information on Public Companies Filing with the SEC* (Bethesda, Md.: Disclosure, Inc., June 1995).

Research Frontiers is a good example of a start-up firm. This start-up status can continue for several years and, in our view, lasts until the company generates sufficient revenue to report positive net income. At that point, the firm most likely enters the growth stage of its life cycle.

Growth

At the start-up firm becomes more established, its revenue increases sufficiently to offset its expenses, and the company begins to report a profit. However, as continued increases in inventory and accounts receivable are needed to support the growth in sales, the amount of income reported will probably continue to exceed any cash flow realized. In fact, it is not unusual for growth firms to report net income and negative operating cash flow. Consider, for example, Apogee, Inc. Financial results for the company are presented in Exhibit 11.5.

Exhibit 11.5 A Growth Firm—Net Income (Loss) and Negative Operating Cash Flow: Apogee, Inc., Years Ending December 31, 1991–1994 (thousands of dollars)

	1991	1992	1993	1994
Revenue	$1,070	$1,651	$6,626	$33,473
Net income (loss) from continuing operations	(627)	(1,372)	(2,831)	387
Cash used in operating activities	(592)	(1,224)	(3,091)	(4,772)

Source: Apogee, Inc., annual report, December 1994. Data obtained from Disclosure, Inc., *Compact D/SEC: Corporate Information on Public Companies Filing with the SEC* (Bethesda, Md.: Disclosure, Inc., June 1995).

Apogee operates outpatient mental health practices. The company's revenue increased markedly in 1994 and was sufficient that year to permit Apogee to report a profit after many years of start-up losses. Even as the company moved to profitability, however, its operating cash flow remained decidedly negative. Like Research Frontiers, Apogee did not carry inventory. The company did, however, see its accounts receivable increase markedly in 1994. This increase in accounts receivable was the main reason the company reported negative operating cash flow that year.

Apogee, Inc., fits the characteristics of a growth firm. Revenue is increasing, the company is profitable, and net income exceeds operating cash flow. While operating cash flow is still negative for Apogee (Exhibit 11.5), growth firms can, and many do, report positive operating cash flow. A good example is the high-growth restaurant chains, such as Apple South, Inc., Boston Chicken, Inc., and Outback Steakhouse, Inc. These firms have both earnings and positive operating cash flow in the face of dramatic growth. This is possible because little cash is consumed by increases in inventory or accounts receivable.

Maturity

In the mature segment of its life cycle, a firm's revenue continues to grow, but growth is much slower and more sustainable. One cannot say precisely when a company leaves the growth segment and enters maturity. Because the characteristic relation between net income and operating cash flow is no different for a firm in late growth and in early maturity, an exact specification is for all practical purposes unnecessary.

What is important to note about this stage is that firms can operate profitably and generate ample amounts of operating cash flow for extended periods. It is a relatively stable segment of the life cycle. In early maturity, as in late growth, net income may exceed operating cash flow. However, as revenue growth continues to slow, net income growth may stall. At some point, in the absence of any strategic changes, revenue may even begin to decline. Net income remains positive but begins a descent. As current assets such as accounts receivable and inventory are liquidated, operating cash flow may move above net income. Just as with growth comes investment in current assets, with maturity comes their liquidation. An example of a mature firm is presented in Exhibit 11.6.

American Consumer Products, Inc. manufactures and sells specialty hardware consumer and pet products. As can be seen in Exhibit 11.6, the company's revenue is growing, but not rapidly. The company is profitable, but profits are flat to declining. Even as net income declines, however, the company is able to generate significant amounts of operating cash. These are all normal characteristics of a mature firm. In the later stages of maturity, when profitability is becoming somewhat precarious, operating cash flow may be very strong. However, that may be fleeting unless significant corporate changes are made.

Exhibit 11.6 A Mature Firm—Net Income and Positive Operating Cash Flow: American Consumer Products, Inc., Years Ending December 31, 1990–1994 (thousands of dollars)

	1990	1991	1992	1993	1994
Revenue	$92,911	$95,361	$99,189	$102,734	$106,748
Net income from continuing operations	1,240	517	1,217	317	421
Cash provided by operating activities	2,646	2,293	2,659	2,108	4,053

Source: American Consumer Products, Inc., annual report, December 1994. Data obtained from Disclosure, Inc., *Compact D/SEC: Corporate Information on Public Companies Filing with the SEC* (Bethesda, Md.: Disclosure, Inc., June 1995).

Decline

In the decline segment of the life cycle, the revenue decreases that began in late maturity continue and may even accelerate. Net income continues to decline, though it may remain positive. Operating cash flow probably exceeds net income as the liquidation of current assets continues.

At some point in this decline in business activity, it may become apparent to management that the company's investments in accounts receivable, inventory, and property, plant, and equipment will not be realized. Asset write-downs ensue. In addition, in an attempt to cut costs and move them more in line with the company's lower level of revenue, certain restructuring actions may be taken. For example, plants may be consolidated and part of the work force terminated. As a result of restructuring actions and asset write-downs, special charges are taken to income, resulting in a net loss.

The asset write-downs and restructuring actions are typically not accompanied by concurrent cash payments. As a result, operating cash flow may remain positive, even as the company reports significant losses. Later, as revenue declines continue, losses may become so large that noncash expenses and liquidations of current assets are not sufficient for the company to report positive operating cash flow. The company has reached an ominous point. It is late in its life cycle and is reporting losses and negative operating cash flow.

Exhibit 11.7 provides an example of a firm in decline that may have corrected its problems. A. T. Cross Co., a maker of writing instruments and accessories, appeared to fit well the description of a company in decline. Revenue and net income peaked in 1989 at $247.4 million and $36.0 million, respectively. Since then, through 1993, both amounts were on a steady downward march. The figures reached bottom in the year ending December 31, 1993. That year, the company recorded several nonrecurring charges to income and reduced income from continuing operations to as little as $519,000. After discontinued operations and extraordinary items, the com-

Exhibit 11.7 A Declining Firm—Declining Net Income and Positive Operating Cash Flow: A. T. Cross Co., Inc., Years Ending December 31, 1990–1994 (thousands of dollars)

	1990	1991	1992	1993	1994
Revenue	$209,633	$205,248	$187,130	$164,606	$177,136
Net income from continuing operations	27,223	21,187	12,773	519	10,534
Cash provided by operating activities	32,767	26,304	26,396	24,940	26,851

Source: A. T. Cross Co., Inc., annual report, December 1994. Data obtained from Disclosure, Inc., *Compact D/SEC: Corporate Information on Public Companies Filing with the SEC* (Bethesda, Md.: Disclosure, Inc., June 1995).

pany reported a net loss that year of $43.5 million. Consistent with our expectations, operating cash flow remained positive and well above the reduced net income figures during all years presented.

While it is still early, based on information available in February 1996, the steps taken by the firm to correct its difficulties may have worked. For the year ended December 31, 1995 A. T. Cross reported revenue of $191.1 million and net income of $13.4 million.[9] If the improvements are lasting, it would illustrate that companies can become vigorous again, improving their positions on the life cycle.

Using a Company's Stage in Its Life Cycle to Anticipate Earnings Surprises

Earlier we noted that to anticipate earnings surprises we need to investigate carefully those situations where net income and operating cash flow differ from the characteristic relations expected, given the current stage of a firm in its life cycle. Heldor Industries, Inc., is a case in point. After peaking at $103.5 million in 1984, revenue for the maker of vinyl-lined swimming pools began a long decline. Selected financial statistics for the company for 1987, 1988, and 1989 are provided in Exhibit 11.8.

Exhibit 11.8 A Declining Firm—Net Income (Loss) and Negative Operating Cash Flow: Heldor Industries, Inc., Years Ending October 31, 1987–1989 (thousands of dollars)

	1987	1988	1989
Revenue	$98,507	$96,962	$91,226
Net income (loss) from continuing operations	138	656	(4,043)
Cash used in operating activities	(458)	(80)	(1,301)

Source: Heldor Industries, Inc., annual report, October 1989, pp. 9 and 11.

Heldor's revenue was down in 1987 and 1988. During both years, the company was able to maintain a minimum level of profitability. The company would seem to fit our description of a company in decline. Such a company would be expected to report operating cash flow that exceeds net income. However, as seen in Exhibit 11.8, Heldor was consuming cash. Upon closer examination of the company's cash flow statement, we noted that this use of cash was due to a substantial decline in accounts payable and accrued liabilities and to significant increases in accounts receivable and inventory. These developments were inconsistent with the natural progression of a company in decline. While some decline in accounts payable and accrued liabilities would be expected as revenue declines, an $8.1 million decline as reported by Heldor in 1987 seemed unusual. Further, a $2 million increase in accounts receivable and a $3.2 million increase in inventory in 1988 were very much out of the ordinary.

The developments underlying the use of cash in 1987 and 1988 were providing a warning of even greater earnings difficulties to come. The decline in accrued liabilities may indicate that the company had been underaccruing expenses in an effort to report positive net income. At some point, additional accruals would be needed. Also, the increases in accounts receivable and inventory gave warning of the potential for future write-downs.

Heldor's earnings difficulties were apparent in 1989. That year, as revenue continued to decline, net income turned to a significant net loss. Interestingly, the company's use of operating cash that year was less than the net loss reported and was consistent with what we would expect for a declining firm.

We have noted that knowing a company's stage in its life cycle is helpful for anticipating future developments. For example, by positioning A. T. Cross Co. in 1993 in the decline segment, we expected operating cash flow to exceed net income, as it did. But we know that for a declining company, we should not feel secure about significant amounts of operating cash being generated. If strategic changes were not made, earnings would likely turn to losses and eventually operating cash flows would turn negative.

Understanding a company's stage in its life cycle, and the characteristic relations between net income and operating cash flow, can provide a useful broad indicator of potential earnings difficulties. The tool is, however, somewhat crude. It will not pinpoint where earnings difficulties might occur. Without additional analysis, one cannot say if a company might report an earnings surprise because of an inventory charge or because of an additional expense accrual. For example, with Heldor, we had to look at the details of the cash flow statement to determine that accounts payable and accrued liabilities were declining or that accounts receivable and inventory were increasing. In the next section, we provide cash flow analysis tools to better determine where earnings difficulties are likely to occur.

CASH FLOW ANALYSIS

In analyzing cash flows, we seek to find the determinants of operating cash flow surpluses or shortages. Those determinants, which can be segregated into growth, changes in operating profitability, and changes in operating efficiency, can help locate causes of earnings surprises.

Growth

Growth in revenue has a pervasive effect on all aspects of operating cash flow. Increasing revenue provides cash flow, while increases in associated expenses, such as cost of sales and certain variable selling, general, and administrative expense consume cash. Assuming a positive operating profit margin (revenue less cost of sales and selling, general, and administrative expense, all as a percent of revenue), the net effect of revenue growth should be an increase in operating cash flow.

However, growth also affects key balance sheet accounts. With growth in revenue comes the need for increased investments in accounts receivable and inventory, less the offsetting effects of increased financing provided by vendors in the form of accounts payable. Thus, it cannot be readily known whether growth in revenue will lead to an increase in operating cash flow. It depends on the rate of growth, the firm's operating profit margin, and its accounts receivable, inventory, and accounts payable requirements.

Shortages of operating cash flow due to growth are not necessarily precursors of earnings surprises. When those shortages do occur, they are likely due to increases in the current asset accounts. In later years, assuming the firm remains viable, those current assets should be realized and provide cash flow when growth stabilizes at more sustainable levels. It is only when the firm does not remain viable and realizability of those current asset accounts is put in doubt that earnings surprises become a greater possibility. However, by then, other early warnings would have become prominent.

Changes in Operating Profitability

Changes in operating profitability—in particular, decreases in gross margin or increases in selling, general, and administrative expense as a percent of revenue—have a very direct effect on operating cash flow. A decline in gross margin indicates that more of the cash generated by revenue transactions is being consumed in paying for inventory. Similarly, an increase in selling, general, and administrative expense as a percent of revenue indicates that more revenue dollars are being spent on these operating items.

Changes in operating profitability—in particular, *declines* in profitability—also have implications for future profit rates. On the surface, a decline in gross margin will have an obvious adverse effect on current year's net income, as will an increase in selling, general, and administrative expense as a percent of revenue (henceforth SGA%). However, forecasting whether a current decline in operating profitability will lead to earnings surprises due to additional declines in profitability in future years requires careful study and a determination of why profit rates declined.

In our review of trend-based and analyst-based earnings surprises in Chapter 2, we saw situations in which declines in operating profitability might affect future earnings. We also saw reference to the future implications of current-year declines in operating profitability in our survey of lenders, summarized in Chapter 4. We combined our own observations with the items noted in Chapters 2 and 4. A summary of those situations where we consider declining profit margins likely to be precursors of future earnings surprises is presented in Exhibit 11.9. There are undoubtedly others, but we feel that the items mentioned provide a useful, representative set. In some situations, declines in operating profitability are not likely to be precursors of future earnings surprises. We summarize these in Exhibit 11.10.

Exhibit 11.9   Declines in Operating Profitability Likely to Be Precursors of Earnings Surprises

Declines in gross margin
Caused by price cutting to maintain volume as competition increases or demand declines.
  • Competitive pressures tend to continue and intensify.
  • Inventory may be slow-moving or obsolete.
Caused by volume declines with stable prices.
  • Inventory may be slow-moving or obsolete.
  • Excess capacity may exist and need to be written down.
Caused by higher fixed costs associated with increased capacity that exceeds market requirements.
  • Increased capacity may become excess capacity and need to be written down.
Caused by changing product mix to products with lower gross margins.
  • Change in product mix may not be temporary and may get worse.
Caused by general cost increases not passed along as higher prices.
  • Competitive pressures may be limiting ability to recover cost increases.
Caused by special inventory write-down for slow-moving or obsolete goods.
  • Remaining inventory may also be slow-moving or obsolete.

Increases in selling, general, and administrative expense as a percent of revenue (SGA%)
Caused by increased marketing and advertising expenses to maintain unit volume.
  • Inventory may be slow-moving or obsolete.
Caused by a special operating expense provision for asset write-downs, or underaccrued expenses, or a corporate restructuring.
  • Such nonrecurring events often recur.
Caused by an increase in administrative costs associated with additional infrastructure to handle anticipated revenue increases.
  • Revenue increases may not materialize.
Caused by decreases in revenue.
  • Cost structure has high component of fixed costs that affects earnings more as revenue declines continue.
Caused by increased legal expenses.
  • Legal battles take management's time away from company affairs.
Caused by increased customer service expense.
  • Company is not well received in the marketplace.

Exhibit 11.10 Declines in Operating Profitability Not Likely to Be Precursors of Earnings Surprises

---

Declines in gross margin
Caused by price cutting to increase volume.
- While gross margin may decline, total gross profit is increased.
- In long run, economies of scale may result in increased gross margin.

Caused by higher fixed costs associated with increased capacity that exceeds market requirements.
- Order backlog and likely future orders indicate that increased capacity will not become excess capacity.

Caused by changing product mix to products with lower gross margins.
- Change in product mix was due to an isolated event, such as a single large order.

Caused by general cost increases not passed along as higher prices.
- Competitive pressures do not limit ability to raise prices.
- Price increases are typically timed at certain points in the year.

Caused by special inventory write-down for slow-moving or obsolete goods.
- Inventory written down is characteristically different from primary product lines.

Caused by adverse foreign currency movements.
- Foreign currencies may move against the firm in one year and in its favor in another.

Caused by increased costs associated with new product development.
- Not necessarily a future expense to the extent these costs are viewed as discretionary.

Caused by lower gross margin of acquired company.
- Not necessarily a reason for margins to decline further.

Increases in selling, general, and administrative expense as a percent of revenue (SGA%)
Caused by increased marketing and advertising expenses to raise unit volume.
- In long run, revenue and operating profit are increased.

Caused by an increase in administrative costs associated with additional infrastructure to handle anticipated revenue increases.
- Order backlog and likely future orders indicate that additional infrastructure is needed.

Caused by increased legal expenses.
- Litigation has ended.

Caused by increased expenses of acquired company.
- Not necessarily a reason for selling, general, and administrative expenses to increase further.

Caused by increased customer service expense.
- Company is well received in the marketplace, and increased expenses help solidify that perception.

Cash flow shortages due to declines in operating profitability may signal an earnings surprise. When such declines are noted, the investor or creditor should give careful consideration to their cause. If such changes are due to factors noted in Exhibit 11.9, then the likelihood of a future earnings surprise is increased.

Changes in Operating Efficiency

Changes in operating efficiency have very direct implications for operating cash flow. Our interest focuses on three key areas of operating efficiency that affect operating cash flow: accounts receivable, inventory, and accounts payable. Changes in operating efficiency related to two of these, accounts receivable and inventory, are also important indicators of a future earnings surprise. Changes in efficiency related to the third item, accounts payable, have important cash flow implications and must be analyzed in understanding changes in operating cash flow. However, notwithstanding the Collins Industries, Inc., example discussed in Chapter 10, changes in operating efficiency related to accounts payable typically do not have implications for earnings surprises.[10]

To understand how a change—more specifically, a decline—in operating efficiency affects cash flow and has implications for future earnings, consider the following points. A decline in the rate of accounts receivable collection, measured by an increase in A/R days, results in a reduction in operating cash inflows. As unrealized accounts receivable increases, so does the likelihood of a write-down of the accounts receivable and a charge to earnings. An increase in the level of inventory carried, measured by an increase in inventory days, results in higher cash outflows for that inventory. As inventory balances build, the probability of an inventory write-down is increased. While, as noted, changes in efficiency related to accounts payable tend not to imply future earnings problems, cash flow analysis would be incomplete without including its effects. An increase in the rate at which accounts payable are settled, measured by a decrease in A/P days, results in higher cash outflows. Similarly, a decrease in their rate of settlement, measured by an increase in A/P days, results in lower cash outflows.

Using Cash Flow Analysis to Find Causes of Earnings Surprises

Cash flow analysis is performed to find the determinants of operating cash flow surpluses or shortages. Once these determinants are identified, expectations can be formed about future operating cash flow. Some of the determinants have implications for future earnings difficulties and provide signals of potential earnings surprises. As discussed, examples include, in some instances, changes in gross margin, SGA%, and changes in operating efficiency. Other determinants of operating cash flow surpluses or shortages have less direct implications for future earnings. However, the effects of these determinants, such as growth or changes in efficiency related to accounts payable, must also be identified in order to perform a complete cash flow analysis. By including them, one is better able to understand why a company has generated a cash flow surplus or shortage.

Our focus is on analyzing operating cash flow in order to anticipate earnings surprises. Most investors and creditors analyze operating cash flow to determine if the firm is generating sufficient amounts to meet current and expected future needs. Operating cash flow is the only reliable long-term source of cash to meet cash needs such as interest and dividend payments, required principal reductions on term debt, and replacement capital expenditures. When operating cash is insufficient to meet these needs, the firm must obtain that cash from other sources. At first, that cash might come from on-hand balances or nonrecurring asset sales. Later, if cash needs continue, additional borrowings and equity infusions might be needed. Obtaining cash from borrowings and equity infusions exposes the firm to new risks. New debt financing increases interest charges and principal requirements. New equity financing leads to earnings dilution. In addition, there is always the risk that new sources of cash might not be available, or if available, at very high cost. Thus, in an indirect sense, the inability to generate positive operating cash flow may have negative implications for future earnings. As a result, in our analysis of operating cash flow, we seek the determinants of cash flow surpluses and shortages with two objectives in mind: first, to pinpoint potential sources of future earnings surprises, and second, to anticipate the future capacity of the firm to generate operating cash flow.

Example: Scientific Technologies, Inc.

To demonstrate how the determinants of operating cash flow surpluses and shortages are measured, we return to Scientific Technologies, Inc. As shown in the company's cash flow statement in Exhibit 11.1, Scientific Technologies generated $3,379,000 in operating cash during 1994. This operating cash covered interest payments of $7,000, and was sufficient to pay dividends of $957,000 and to replace property, plant, and equipment consumed in operations. An estimate of the amount needed to replace that property, plant, and equipment is the amount of depreciation and amortization recorded, $337,000. To our knowledge, the company had no required principal reductions on long-term debt during the year.

In 1994, Scientific Technologies looks very sound on a cash flow basis. However, what about next year? Is the company likely to continue generating sufficient operating cash to meet its needs? By identifying the determinants of the operating cash flow surplus, we will be better prepared to answer that question.

To begin, we need some descriptive ratios for the company. A schedule of selected financial information is provided in Exhibit 11.11. Growth, defined here as an increase in revenue, affects operating cash flow in different ways. As revenue grows, keeping operating profitability and efficiency measures unchanged, we expect an increase in gross profit and in selling, general, and administrative expense. The increase in gross profit has a positive effect on operating cash flow, while an increase in selling, general, and administrative expense would consume more cash. With growth in revenue, we also expect increases in accounts receivable and inventory, which consume cash, and in accounts payable, which is a source of cash. The effects of these operating cash flow determinants are summarized in Exhibit 11.12.

In isolating the cash flow effects of growth we assumed that profitability and efficiency determinants were unchanged. If we allow for changes from one year to the next in profitability and efficiency, they too will change cash flows. For example, an increase in gross margin has positive effects, while increases in selling, general,

Exhibit 11.1   Scientific Technologies, Inc., Selected Financial Information, 1993–1994

	1993	1994	Increase (Decrease)
Operating cash flow	$ 3,359,000	$ 3,379,000	$ 20,000
Revenue	$18,617,000	$26,115,000	$7,498,000
Cost of sales	8,893,000	12,323,000	3,430,000
Gross profit	$ 9,724,000	$13,792,000	$4,068,000
Revenue per day[a]	$ 51,713.89	$ 72,541.67	$20,827.78
Cost of sales per day[a]	$ 24,702.78	$ 34,230.56	$ 9,527.78
Gross margin	52.232%	52.813%	.581%
Selling, general, and administrative expenses[b]	$ 5,729,000	$ 7,729,000	$ 2,000,000
SGA%	30.773%	29.596%	(1.177)%
Accounts receivable	$ 2,945,000	$ 4,786,000	$1,841,000
A/R days[c]	56.948	65.975	9.027
Inventory	$ 1,715,000	$ 2,367,000	$ 652,000
Inventory days[d]	69.425	69.149	(.276)
Accounts payable	$ 878,000	$ 1,548,000	$ 670,000
A/P days[d]	35.542	45.223	9.681

Source: Scientific Technologies, Inc., annual report, December 1994. Note: Ratios are carried out to three places to lessen rounding effects on cash flow calculations.
[a]Calculated as revenue and cost of sales, respectively, divided by 360. A 360-day year was employed to simplify the calculations.
[b]Research and development in the amounts of $1,023,000 and $1,370,000 in 1993 and 1994, respectively, are included in selling, general, and administrative expense.
[c]Calculated as accounts receivable divided by revenue per day.
[d]Calculated as inventory and accounts payable, respectively, divided by cost of sales per day.

Exhibit 11.12   Effects of Revenue Growth on Operating Cash Flow

Cash Flow Determinant Affected by Revenue Growth	Cash Flow Effect[a]
Gross profit	Positive
Selling, general, and administrative expense	Negative
Accounts receivable	Negative
Inventory	Negative
Accounts payable	Positive

[a]Positive and negative cash flow effects refer, respectively, to increases and decreases in operating cash flow. A decline in revenue would produce effects exactly opposite to the ones shown in this column.

and administrative expense have negative effects on cash flow. With respect to efficiency, increases in A/R days and inventory days have negative effects on cash flow because of the higher amounts of operating cash flow invested in them. Decreases in these measures, a sign of improved efficiency, have positive effects on cash flow. In contrast, an increase in A/P days has a positive effect on cash flow, as the firm uses more vendor financing. A decrease in A/P days has a negative effect on cash flow. The cash flow effects of changes in profitability and efficiency are summarized in Exhibit 11.13.

To calculate the cash flow effects of growth on gross profit and selling, general, and administrative expense during 1994, we multiply the growth in revenue during 1994 by the prior year's, or 1993's, profitability measures. In a similar fashion, the cash flow effects of growth on accounts receivable is computed by multiplying the growth in revenue per day during 1994 by A/R days for 1993. And the cash flow effects of growth on inventory and accounts payable are computed by multiplying the growth in cost of sales per day during 1994 by inventory days and A/P days, respectively for 1993. These calculations are presented in Exhibit 11.14.

Revenue at Scientific Technologies grew $7,498,000, or 40.3%, in 1994. A company that grows at such a rapid rate often consumes much operating cash. In such a situation, the calculations in Exhibit 11.14 would result in a significant negative amount. This occurs as the cash provided by the growth-induced increase in gross profit in excess of increases in selling, general, and administrative expense is insufficient to cover additional amounts committed to accounts receivable and inventory less increases in accounts payable.

The higher a company's profitability rate, and the lower its required commitments to accounts receivable and inventory, the faster it can grow and still provide

Exhibit 11.13   Effects of Changes in Operating Profitability and Efficiency on Operating Cash Flow

Cash Flow Determinant Affected by Changes in Profitability and Efficiency	Cash Flow Effect[a]
Increase in gross margin	Positive
Decrease in gross margin	Negative
Increase in SGA%	Negative
Decrease in SGA%	Positive
Increase in A/R days	Negative
Decrease in A/R days	Positive
Increase in inventory days	Negative
Decrease in inventory days	Positive
Increase in A/P days	Positive
Decrease in A/P days	Negative

[a]Positive and negative cash flow effects refer, respectively, to increases and decreases in operating cash flow.

Exhibit 11.14   Scientific Technologies, Inc., Cash Effects of Growth: 1994

Cash Flow Determinant Affected by Revenue Growth	Computations	Cash Flow Effect Source (Use)
Increase in revenue effect on gross profit	$7,498,000 × 52.232%	$3,916,355

Increase in revenue effect
  on selling, general, and
  administrative expense
	$7,498,000 × 30.773%	(2,307,360)

Increase in revenue per day effect on accounts receivable	$20,827.78 × 56.948	(1,186,100)
Increase in cost of sales per day effect on inventory	$9,527.78 × 69.425	(661,466)
Increase in cost of sales per day effect on accounts payable	$9,527.78 × 35.542	338,636
Total cash flow effects of growth		$ 100,065

positive operating cash flow. Scientific Technologies' gross margin of 52.232% in 1993 less its SGA% of 30.773% that year left an operating profit margin of 21.459%.[11] If this operating profit margin were maintained in 1995, and assuming no significant changes in the investments needed in accounts receivable and inventory relative to the level of revenue, growth of more than 40% could be achieved, and the company would continue generating positive operating cash flow. As one looks ahead to future years, Scientific Technologies should be able to grow at very high rates and still provide positive operating cash flow. For this company, growth does not appear to be a reason to forecast future operating cash shortages. The usefulness of the calculations provided in Exhibit 11.14 is in revealing that point. Scientific Technologies can grow at significant rates and still provide positive operating cash flow.

To calculate the cash flow effects of changes in profitability, we multiply the change in the gross margin and SGA% during 1994 by the current year's, or 1994's, revenue. The cash flow effects of changes in efficiency in collecting accounts receivable is computed by multiplying the change in A/R days during 1994 by 1994's revenue per day. Similarly, the cash flow effects of changes in inventory and accounts payable efficiency are calculated by multiplying the change in inventory days and A/P days during 1994, respectively, by cost of sales per day in 1994. These calculations are presented in Exhibit 11.15.

In measuring the cash effects of growth in 1994, operating profitability and efficiency levels in 1993 were assumed to be held constant in 1994. In measuring the cash effects in 1994 of changes in operating profitability and efficiency, we allow those profitability and efficiency rates to change. Thus, all the calculations presented in Exhibit 11.15 include a change in profitability or efficiency from 1993 to 1994.

Several points should be noted in reviewing Exhibit 11.15. An increase of 0.581% in gross margin provided $151,728, and an improvement of 1.177% in SGA% pro-

Exhibit 11.15 Cash Effects of Changes in Operating Profitability and Efficiency: Scientific Technologies, Inc., 1994

Cash Flow Determinant Affected by Changes in Profitability and Efficiency	Computations Increase (Decrease)	Cash Flow Effect Source (Use)
Increase in gross margin effect on gross profit	.581% × $26,115,000	$151,728
Decrease in SGA% effect on selling, general, and administrative expense	(1.177%) × $26,115,000	307,374
Increase in A/R days effect on accounts receivable	9.027 × $72,541.67	(654,834)
Decrease in inventory days effect on inventory	(.276) × $34,230.56	9,448
Increase in A/P days effect on accounts payable	9.681 × $34,230.56	331,386
Total cash flow effects of changes in operating profitability and efficiency		$145,102

vided $307,374. That is, the company was able to generate $459,102 ($151,728 + $307,374) more in cash flow during 1994 because of these improvements in profitability. Also on a positive note, a decline of 0.276 in inventory days increased operating cash flow in 1994 by the amount of $9,448. The increase in A/R days of 9.027 days is a sign of concern. During 1994, A/R days increased to nearly 66 days from just under 57 days. The net result was a use of cash in the amount of $654,834. The company generated $654,834 less in operating cash in 1994 than it would have if A/R days had remained unchanged from 1993. The investor or creditor would want to gain assurances that this was not the beginning of a protracted slow-down in the rate of collection of accounts receivable. Such a slow-down could be a precursor of a future earnings surprise because of a write-down of accounts receivable. The company's A/R days in 1991 and 1992 were running at 58 and 64 days, respectively. Thus, the 66 days figure in 1994 is not significantly out of line. Nonetheless, it needs to be watched carefully. If the company were to reduce its A/R days back toward the mid-50's, it would free up the incremental cash invested in accounts receivable during 1994. The 9.681 increase in A/P days to just over 45 days from a bit under 36 days provided $331,386 in additional operating cash. The company has effectively borrowed an additional $331,386 from its vendors. While this shows up as positive operating cash flow, a reduction in A/P days back to the 30-day range would require the use of cash of a similar amount. Looking at the total cash flow effects of changes in operating profitability and efficiency, we can see that collectively these changes served to increase operating cash flow by $145,102 in 1994.

In order to help demonstrate what the calculations in Exhibits 11.14 and 11.15 are showing, consider one more illustration, shown in Exhibit 11.16. In the exhibit, we show that the cash flow effects of growth and of changes in operating profitability and efficiency can be related to actual changes noted in the income statement and balance sheet items analyzed. The exhibit reconciles the beginning with ending balances. Only insignificant rounding differences remain unexplained. For example, gross profit increased from $9,724,000 in 1993 to $13,792,000 in 1994. An increase in gross profit, in the absence of any other account changes, is a source of cash. That source can be attributed to growth in the amount of $3,916,355 and to an increase in gross margin in the amount of $151,728. Selling, general, and administrative expense increased from $5,729,000 in 1993 to $7,729,000 in 1994. This is a use of cash due to growth of $2,307,360 less $307,374 due to an improvement in the SGA%. Accounts receivable increased from $2,945,000 to $4,786,000 during 1994. This use of

Exhibit 11.16   Reconciling Cash Effects of Growth and Changes in Profitability and Efficiency to Changes in Selected Income Statement and Balance Sheet Items: Scientific Technologies, Inc., 1994

	Change During 1994
Income statement item	
Gross profit, 1993	$ 9,724,000
Cash effect of growth	+3,916,355
Cash effect of change in gross margin	+151,728
Rounding differences	−83
Gross profit, 1994	$13,792,000
Selling, general, and administrative expense, 1993	$ 5,729,000
Cash effect of growth	+2,307,360
Cash effect of change in SGA%	−307,374
Rounding differences	+14
Selling, general, and administrative expense, 1994	$ 7,729,000
Balance sheet item	
Accounts receivable, 1993	$ 2,945,000
Cash effect of growth	+1,186,100
Cash effect of change in A/R days	+654,834
Rounding differences	+66
Accounts receivable, 1994	$ 4,786,000
Inventory, 1993	$ 1,715,000
Cash effect of growth	+661,466
Cash effect of change in inventory days	−9,448
Rounding differences	−18
Inventory, 1994	$ 2,367,000
Accounts payable, 1993	$ 878,000
Cash effect of growth	+338,636
Cash effect of change in A/P days	+331,386
Rounding differences	−22
Accounts payable, 1994	$ 1,548,000

cash is due to growth of $1,186,100 and to an increase in A/R days of $654,834. Similarly, inventory increased from $1,715,000 to $2,367,000 during 1994 because of growth of $661,466 less the cash savings from a decline in inventory days of $9,448. Finally, accounts payable increased from $878,000 to $1,548,000 during 1994. This is a source of cash due to growth in the amount of $338,636 and to an increase in A/P days of $331,386.

There was little in our analysis of Scientific Technologies' cash flows to suggest a potential earnings surprise. The accounts receivable item needs to be watched, but that account does not currently appear to be a problem. With our cash flow analysis, we better understand the determinants of the company's positive operating cash flow and are better prepared to anticipate how that cash flow might appear in future years.

Example: Cincinnati Microwave, Inc.

Cincinnati Microwave, Inc., a maker of high-technology electronic communications devices reported revenue of $64.7 million in 1994, up from $58.5 million in 1993. Revenue in 1992 was $51.3 million. Profits, however, have been elusive. The company reported losses in each of the last three years, amounting to $8.8 million in 1992, $1.3 million in 1993, and $10.3 million in 1994. The reporting of losses is reason enough to be concerned about the firm's future prospects. However, cash flow analysis provides other reasons to be concerned. Selected financial information for the company is provided in Exhibit 11.17.

Cincinnati Microwave consumed operating cash of $3,133,000 during 1994. Thus, the company was not able to meet such needs as interest and principal payments. These needs were met with new long-term borrowing and on-hand cash balances.

On the surface, the company's operating cash performance in 1994 appears to be a significant improvement from the use of $6,801,000 from operations in 1993. By identifying the cash effects of growth, operating profitability, and operating efficiency, we can better determine whether 1994 was a true improvement over 1993. The cash effects of growth are presented in Exhibit 11.18, and the cash effects of changes in operating profitability and efficiency are presented in Exhibit 11.19.

Revenue at Cincinnati Microwave increased $6,247,000, or 10.7%, in 1994. By keeping operating profitability and efficiency determinants of cash flow fixed at 1993 levels, the cash effects of this growth can be computed. As presented in Exhibit 11.18, the cash effects of growth summed to an overall use of operating cash in the amount of $1,626,437. While growth in gross profit was a source of cash, increases in selling, general, and administrative expense, accounts receivable, and inventory were uses of cash. An increase in accounts payable accompanying the growth in revenue and cost of sales was a source of cash.

Looking ahead to 1995 cash flow, unless changes in profitability and efficiency are made, continued growth in revenue at rates comparable to 1994, or higher, will result in additional cash needs for the company. This situation contrasts with that of Scientific Technologies, where the mix of profitability and efficiency determinants

Exhibit 11.17   Cincinnati Microwave, Inc., Selected Financial Information, 1993 and 1994

	1993	Increase 1994	(Decrease)
Operating cash flow	$(6,801,000)	$(3,133,000)	$ 3,668,000
Revenue	$58,461,000	$64,708,000	$ 6,247,000
Cost of sales	39,778,000	50,359,000	10,581,000
Gross profit	$18,683,000	$14,349,000	$(4,334,000)
Revenue per day	$162,391.66	$179,744.44	$ 17,352.78
Cost of sales per day	$110,494.44	$139,886.11	$ 29,391.67
Gross margin	31.958%	22.175%	(9.783)%
Selling, general, and administrative expense[a]	$21,767,000	$24,373,000	$ 2,606,000
SGA%	37.233%	37.666%	.433%
Accounts receivable	$ 3,636,000	$ 5,137,000	$ 1,501,000
A/R days	22.390	28.579	6.189
Inventory	$ 7,299,000	$ 9,159,000	$ 1,860,000
Inventory days	66.057	65.474	(.583)
Accounts payable	$ 3,884,000	$ 8,627,000	$ 4,743,000
A/P days	35.151	61.671	26.520

Source: Cincinnati Microwave, Inc., annual report, December 1994. Data obtained from Disclosure, Inc., *Compact D/SEC: Corporate Information on Public Companies Filing with the SEC* (Bethesda, Md.: Disclosure, Inc., June 1995).
[a]Includes research and development expense in the amounts of $8,117,000 and $8,449,000, respectively, in 1993 and 1994.

Exhibit 11.18   Cash Effects of Growth: Cincinnati Microwave, Inc., 1994

Cash Flow Determinant Affected by Revenue Growth	Computations	Cash Flow Effect Source (Use)
Increase in revenue effect on gross profit	$6,247,000 × 31.958%	$ 1,996,416
Increase in revenue effect on selling, general, and administrative expense	$6,247,000 × 37.233%	(2,325,946)
Increase in revenue per day effect on accounts receivable	$17,352.78 × 22.390	(388,528)
Increase in cost of sales per day effect on inventory	$29,391.67 × 66.057	(1,941,526)
Increase in cost of sales per day effect on accounts payable	$29,391.67 × 35.151	1,033,147
Total cash flow effects of growth		$(1,626,437)

Exhibit 11.19   Cash Effects of Changes in Operating Profitability and Efficiency: Cincinnati Microwave, Inc., 1994

Cash Flow Determinant Affected by Changes in Profitability and Efficiency	Computations Increase (Decrease)	Cash Flow Effect Source (Use)
Decrease in gross margin effect on gross profit	(9.783%) × $64,708,000	$(6,330,384)
Increase in SGA% effect on selling, general, and administrative expense	.433% × $64,708,000	(280,186)
Increase in A/R days effect on accounts receivable	6.189 × $179,744.44	(1,112,438)
Decrease in inventory days effect on inventory	(.583) × $139,886.11	81,554
Increase in A/P days effect on accounts payable	26.520 × $139,886.11	3,709,780
Total cash flow effects of changes in operating profitability and efficiency		$(3,931,674)

permitted that firm to handle growth in revenue in the 40% range and still generate positive operating cash flow.

Exhibit 11.19 does not provide evidence of progress in Cincinnati Microwave's ability to improve profitability and efficiency. The company's gross margin percent declined 9.783% of revenue in 1994 from 1993. That decline in profitability alone cost the company $6,330,384 in operating cash. Stated differently, had the company maintained the same gross margin in 1994 as in 1993, it would have generated $6,330,384 more in operating cash. This is a very negative signal and could be a precursor of a continued weakening in gross margin in future years. More information would be needed from management to determine if this decline in gross margin was a warning of a future earnings surprise. A small increase in the SGA% also added to the company's cash requirements in 1994.

During 1994, A/R days increased 6.189 days. This slowing in collection cost the company $1,112,438 in operating cash. An increase in A/R days often indicates potential collection problems and the possibility of a write-down in accounts receivable. However, given that A/R days were still under 29 in 1994, a future write-down of accounts receivable does not appear likely at present. Inventory days decreased slightly, providing $81,554 in cash.

An important component of the company's operating cash flow in 1994 was the increase in A/P days by 26.520 days to over 61 from 35 days in 1993. This management action provided $3,709,780 in cash. The company has effectively borrowed $3.7 million from its vendors to help pay for cash shortages arising elsewhere. It is not known what terms Cincinnati Microwave's vendors were offering, though the company may be reaching the limits of those terms. If A/P days are kept unchanged in 1995, the company will not have the additional $3.7 million from accounts payable to meet its operating needs. Moreover, if vendors require that A/P days be reduced, such a reduction will be an additional use of cash.

Any improvement in Cincinnati Microwave's cash flow performance in 1994 from 1993 appears to be illusory. It was primarily due to an increased level of borrowing from company vendors. Exhibit 11.20 provides a reconciliation of our cash flow calculations with changes in the underlying income statement and balance sheet accounts.

Exhibit 11.20 Reconciling Cash Effects of Growth and Changes in Profitability and Efficiency to Changes in Selected Income Statement and Balance Sheet Items: Cincinnati Microwave, Inc., 1994

	Change During 1994
Income statement item	
Gross profit, 1993	$18,683,000
Cash effect of growth	+1,996,416
Cash effect of change in gross margin	−6,330,384
Rounding differences	−32
Gross profit, 1994	$14,349,000
Selling, general, and administrative expense, 1993	$21,767,000
Cash effect of growth	+2,325,946
Cash effect of change in SGA%	+280,186
Rounding differences	−132
Selling, general, and administrative expense, 1994	$24,373,000
Balance sheet item	
Accounts receivable, 1993	$ 3,636,000
Cash effect of growth	+388,528
Cash effect of change in A/R days	+1,112,438
Rounding differences	+34
Accounts receivable, 1994	$ 5,137,000
Inventory, 1993	$ 7,299,000
Cash effect of growth	+1,941,526
Cash effect of change in inventory days	−81,554
Rounding differences	+28
Inventory, 1994	$ 9,159,000
Accounts payable, 1993	$ 3,884,000
Cash effect of growth	+1,033,147
Cash effect of change in A/P days	+3,709,780
Rounding differences	+73
Accounts payable, 1994	$ 8,627,000

SUMMARY

In the long-run, operating cash flow is the most reliable source of cash to meet recurring needs such as interest and dividend payments, principal reductions on term debt, and replacement capital expenditures. An inability to generate operating cash may be a sign of problems and a precursor of earnings surprises. Much depends, however, on the reasons for the operating cash flow shortages. If those shortages are due to rapid growth, assuming continued viability, they should self-correct in later years as growth subsides to more sustainable levels. However, if the shortages are due to other, more fundamental problems, such as declining operating profitability or efficiency, the prognosis is less optimistic. Such problems may be forecasting future declines in operating profitability or write-downs of accounts receivable or inventory.

The analysis skills identified in this chapter should be helpful in identifying the determinants of operating cash flow surpluses and shortages. When these determinants are identified, the investor or creditor will be in an improved position to ascertain whether an earnings surprise may be in the offing.

A checklist for cash flow warnings is provided in Exhibit 11.21. The questions will help users anticipate cash flow–related earnings surprises.

Exhibit 11.21   Checklist for Financial Early Warnings: Cash Flow
_____

Indirect-method cash flow statement
A. Consider the appropriateness of the classification of items to the operating, investing, and financing sections.
   1. Are operating uses of cash included with investing or financing activities?
B. Are operating cash flows, measured after interest paid, sufficient to cover dividends, required principal reductions on long-term debt, and replacement capital expenditures?
   1. For required principal reductions, use the current portion of long-term debt at the beginning of the year.
   2. For replacement capital expenditures, use depreciation expense as an approximation.
C. If not from operations, where has the company obtained the cash to meet its needs?
   1. New borrowings
      a. What are the implications for future interest and principal payments?
      b. What is the likelihood of default on these required payments?
   2. New equity
      a. What is the dilutive effect on earnings available for existing equity holders?
   3. Cash on hand
      a. Will the company have access to the cash it needs for other strategic plans?

Exhibit 11.21 *(continued)*

Company's Life Cycle
A. Where is the company currently in its life cycle?
   1. Start-up
   2. Growth
   3. Maturity
   4. Decline
B. How does the relation between the company's net income and operating cash flow compare with expectations based on its life cycle stage?

Determinants of Cash Flow Surplus or Shortage
A. Identify the determinants of the observed cash flow surplus or shortage.
   1. Growth
      a. What are the implications of current growth-related cash flow determinants for future operating cash flows?
   2. Nongrowth determinants
      a. Changes in operating profitability
         i. Does a decrease in gross margin warn of future earnings difficulties?
         ii. Does an increase in SGA% warn of future earnings difficulties?
      b. Changes in operating efficiency
         i. Does an increase in A/R days warn of a future write-down?
         ii. Does an increase in inventory days warn of a future write-down?
         iii. What is the contribution of changes in A/P days to operating cash flow?

REFERENCES

Beach, R., "Cash Flow vs. 'Cash Flow.'" *Commercial Lending Review*, Winter 1985–1986, p. 48–52.

Comiskey, E. E., and C. W. Mulford. "Anticipating Trends in Operating Profits and Cash Flow." *Commercial Lending Review*, Spring 1993, pp. 38–48.

———. "Finding the Causes of Changes in Cash Flow," *Commercial Lending Review*, Summer 1992, pp. 21–40.

———. "Understand the Reasons Behind Changes in Cash Flow," *Commercial Lending Review*, Winter 1992–1993, pp. 29–43.

Comiskey, E. E., S. Gulbrandsen, and C. W. Mulford. "Improving the Accuracy of Computer-Generated Cash-Flow Statements," *Commercial Lending Review*, Summer 1991, pp. 11–27.

Porter, M., *Competitive Strategy: Techniques for Analyzing Industries and Competitors* (New York: Free Press, 1980).

ENDNOTES

1. H. S. Bailey, Jr., "Watch Cash Flow," *Publishers Weekly*, January 13, 1975, p. 34.
2. Statement of Financial Accounting Concepts No. 1, "Objectives of Financial Re-

porting by Business Enterprises" (Stamford, Conn.: Financial Accounting Standards Board, November 1978). Reprinted in *Accounting Standards Original Pronouncements*, vol. 2 (Norwalk, Conn.: Financial Accounting Standards Board, 1994), pp. 1014–1015.

3. Ibid., p. 1016.
4. Statement of Financial Accounting Standards (SFAS) No. 95, "Statement of Cash Flows" (Stamford, Conn.: Financial Accounting Standards Board, November 1987).
5. A third cash flow statement format that is popular with lenders combines the direct- and indirect-method formats. It is useful in determining whether a company can service its debt. Refer to R. Beach, "Cash Flow vs. 'Cash Flow,'" *Commercial Lending Review*, Winter 1985–1986, p. 51. An example is also provided in E. Comiskey, S. Gulbrandsen, and C. Mulford, "Improving the Accuracy of Computer-Generated Cash-Flow Statements," *Commercial Lending Review*, Summer 1991, p. 13.
6. 50-Off Stores, Inc., annual report, January 1993, p. 14 and 10-K annual report to the Securities and Exchange Commission, January 1994, p. F-6.
7 Seitel, Inc., annual report, December 1990, p. 20, and December 1991, p. 20.
8. Value Merchants, Inc., annual report, February 1992, p. 25.
9. Data obtained from A. T. Cross Co., press release dated February 6, 1996.
10. Changes in the rate of accounts payable payments can have indirect implications for future earnings. For example, a disgruntled vendor might put a company on a cash basis, effectively cutting it off from its supply. This would negatively affect sales and earnings. However, our interest here is on identifying implications of more direct earnings effects.
11. Note that cash flow calculations are very sensitive to rounding. Thus, while we typically do not carry profitability and efficiency ratios out to three places, we do so here to minimize these rounding effects.

Chapter 12

Managed Earnings

In the past decade, GE's earnings have risen every year, although net income fell in 1991 and 1993 because of accounting changes related to post-retirement benefits. The gains, ranging between 1.7% and 17%, have been fairly steady— especially for a company in a lot of cyclical businesses. As a result, GE almost seems able to override the business cycle.

How does GE do it? One undeniable explanation is the fundamental growth of its eight industrial businesses and 24 financial-services units. "We're the best company in the world," declares Dennis Dammerman, GE's chief financial officer.

But another way is "earnings management," the orchestrated timing of gains and losses to smooth out bumps and, especially, avoid a decline. Among big companies, GE is "certainly a relatively aggressive practitioner of earnings management," says Martin Sanakey, a CS First Boston, Inc., analyst.[1]

As indicated by the chapter opening quotation, an impression exists that earnings at General Electric Co. are managed toward a smoother, increasing trend. In especially good years, earnings are reduced and stored for use in bad years. When those disappointing years arrive, a boost is provided from earnings stored in prior years.

Earnings management is the active manipulation of accounting results for the purpose of creating an altered impression of business performance. In some cases, current-year earnings are boosted at the expense of future years. Such earnings-boosting actions might be taken in an effort to increase income-based bonuses, meet debt covenants, or raise share prices. For example, a lengthening of the useful lives of depreciable assets reduces current-year depreciation charges and raises net income. Total assets and shareholders' equity are also reported at higher amounts. Future-year income is reduced as depreciation of those assets continues for a longer time. In other cases, companies find that current-year earnings are already at or above desired levels, and steps are taken to reduce them in order to reserve income for future years. Income-based bonuses that have reached their maximum for the year, or a desire to maintain a smoother, ever-increasing earnings stream, provide understandable incentives. The use of accelerated depreciation methods or the overaccrual of expenses would achieve this objective, as would the postponement of one-time gains. The General Electric case appears to fit the second category of earnings management. However, as noted later, earnings management at GE, as well as at certain other companies, does serve a valid, useful purpose.

In this chapter, we look at both types of earnings management activity: earnings management to boost current-year income at the expense of future years, and earnings management to reduce current-year earnings.

BOOSTING CURRENT-YEAR PERFORMANCE

We have illustrated the use of earnings management techniques to boost current-year performance in several chapters of this book. In Chapter 3, we referred to such practices as the aggressive application of accounting principles. While judgment calls and estimates are required in the preparation of financial statements, some managements use these estimates to put a consistently positive spin on their companies' results. In effect, the earnings reported in the current year are borrowed from future years. In Chapter 8, we focused on overstated revenue and provided numerous examples where managements had increased current-year earnings through the premature recognition of revenue. Premature revenue was defined as revenue recognized early, either before the earnings process was complete or before realizability was established. Through such recognition practices, revenue that belonged to future years was used to improve current-year income. An example provided was that of The Topps Co., which had optimistically underestimated the level of sales returns, boosting current-year income. Later, the company determined that its estimate of those returns was insufficient and that an increased provision for obsolescence and returns was needed.

In Chapter 8, we also provided examples of fictitious or fraudulent revenue recognition. Fictitious revenue is revenue recognized without regard to whether it will materialize. In effect, it is nonexistent revenue, recognized with a willful intent to conduct a material deception. Earnings management entails a change in the timing of income reporting. Either earnings are moved from future years to the current year or current-year earnings are pushed into the future. Steps taken to report fraudulent results, including fictitious revenue recognition, do not entail, for the most part, a temporal move of earnings from one year to the next. Instead, these steps result in the reporting of totally fictitious or nonexistent income. Accordingly, we exclude fraudulent income reporting and fictitious revenue from our definition of earnings management.

In Chapter 9, we looked at examples of understated expenses. As with premature revenue recognition, the understatement of expenses boosts current-year earnings. The income of future years is reduced with higher expense charges. One method used to understate current-year expenses is aggressive cost capitalization. Examples noted include the preopening costs of retailers, membership acquisition costs, software development expenses, and landfill development costs. In the latter category, Chambers Development Co. had capitalized many costs that its competitors routinely expensed, such as executive officers' salaries, public relations expenses, legal costs, and travel. These actions boosted income, but future years suffered when those capitalized costs were written off. Another approach for understating current-year expenses is through the use of extended amortization periods. Here, assets subject to depreciation and amortization are afforded useful lives that are, in hindsight, too long.

Depreciation and amortization expense charges are reduced currently at the expense of future years. An example noted was that of Vista Resources, Inc., a company that did not amortize goodwill. By not amortizing goodwill, the company implied that it had a useful life of infinite length. Future-year income was reduced when that useful life was ultimately shown to be too long and the goodwill was written off.

In Chapter 10, we saw examples of the excessive valuation of assets not subject to amortization, including accounts receivable, inventory, and investments. Here, assets are carried at valuations exceeding realizable amounts. For example, the allowance for doubtful accounts might be underprovided, or a write-down may be postponed for obsolete inventory or an investment whose market value has declined below cost. In all these cases, the postponement of an income charge boosts current earnings. Future earnings will be reduced when these balance sheet accounts are adjusted. In a similar fashion, current-year income would be boosted by an undervaluation of liabilities. Earnings in future years are reduced when liabilities are increased as needed. Lindsay Manufacturing Co. provides a good example of this latter situation. The company underaccrued the liability for the cleanup of a contaminated site. Earnings were later reduced when that liability was increased to the needed level.

All these examples and the others discussed in Chapters 8, 9, and 10, excluding those found to involve a fraudulent intent, can be included within the topic broadly defined as earnings management. They consist of various steps taken to boost current-year income at the expense of future years.

Two other approaches are used to improve current-year performance that should be included in our discussion of earnings management. The first is the discretionary use of accounting changes. Such changes in accounting principles and estimates are often done at management's discretion for little other reason than to improve current-year income. For example, as discussed at length in Chapter 7, changes in the estimated amount needed for the valuation allowance against deferred tax assets can be used to boost income. The second is through timed management actions. Here, earnings are boosted through the recognition of one-time gains, such as gains on the sale of appreciated land or investments, or through LIFO liquidations, as discussed in Chapter 7. Another way by which income can be boosted through timed management actions is by the postponement of expenses.

Discretionary Accounting Changes

As discussed in Chapter 5, there are two general types of accounting changes: changes in principle and changes in estimate. Changes in accounting principle entail the change from one accepted accounting principle to another. The most common form of accounting treatment for such changes is to show the cumulative effect of the change on net income of prior years as a single amount, net of income taxes, in the income statement in the year of change. The current-year effect of the change is reported in the body of the income statement and is not highlighted. Footnote disclosure in the year of the accounting principle change is the only detail provided of the current-year effect. For example, a change from an accelerated method of depreciation to the straight-line method for selected equipment items would constitute a change in accounting principle. The difference in accumulated depreciation between the two methods would be calculated as of the beginning of the year of the change. That amount, net of income taxes, would be reported in the body of the income statement as a change in accounting principle. The current-year difference in depreciation expense between the two methods would be included with other costs and expenses on the income statement. Only a footnote would detail that current-year effect.

A less common form of treatment for accounting principle changes is the retro-active-effect approach whereby prior-year financial statements are restated to a new accounting principle as if it had been in effect all along. Here the cumulative income effect of the change is adjusted to retained earnings and is not reported as a component of net income. Unless called for use specifically by a new accounting principle, this type of treatment is reserved for those accounting changes that have very pervasive, material effects on the financial statements taken as a whole. Examples include a change from the LIFO to the FIFO method of inventory costing and a change between the percentage of completion and completed contract methods for long-term contract accounting.

Changes in accounting estimate are very common. Financial statements are a collection of estimates, where management judgment is needed in measuring balance sheet and income amounts. For example, estimates are used in determining the useful lives of equipment accounts, their residual values, the portion of accounts receivable that will not be collected, the interim effects of price changes on LIFO inventory, and the present value of pension obligations. The need to change these estimates arises frequently. There is no separate income statement disclosure of their effect. However, when material, their effect on current-year income is disclosed in a footnote.

We noted in Chapter 5 that in recent years accounting changes have been dominated by the requirements to adopt new financial accounting standards promulgated by the Financial Accounting Standards Board. There still remain, however, many accounting changes that are not driven by the actions of the FASB. These are discretionary accounting changes.

Discretionary accounting changes refer to changes in accounting principle or estimate that are not called for by accounting standard setters. They are made at the discretion of management. Some of these discretionary changes are needed periodically for a continued fair presentation of financial results and position over time. Companies, circumstances, and industries change. For example, Battle Mountain Gold Co. provided the following note regarding a change in accounting principle:

Effective January 1, 1990, the company changed its method of accounting for exploration expenditures. With the exception of lease costs incurred to acquire mineral rights, the company, under the newly adopted method, charges all exploration and pre-development evaluation expenditures to expense as incurred. Previously, all exploration costs that could be identified with specific projects were initially capitalized. They were subsequently charged to expense only through the abandonment, impairment or depletion of those projects. Lease costs continue to be accounted for as under the previous method.

Both methods are acceptable accounting practice. However, the company considers the newly adopted method preferable because it improves the comparability of the company's operating results and financial position with industry peers, the majority of whom are applying similar methods. It also results in a more conservative reporting of the company's assets.

The cumulative income effect of this change for periods ending prior to January 1, 1990, was $33.8 million, net of a $12.2 million income tax benefit. The effect is shown separately on the company's consolidated statement of income for the year ended December 31, 1990. The adoption of the new method resulted in a reduction in 1990 net income before the cumulative effect of the change in accounting method of $3.4 million, or $.05 per share.[2]

This is a good example of a discretionary change in accounting principle. The company changed its method of accounting for the costs of exploring for new reserves from capitalizing those costs to expensing them as incurred. It was noted that both accounting methods were acceptable under generally accepted accounting principles. The company chose this new method, even though it resulted in lower income and assets, because it improved the comparability of its operating results and financial position with that of other companies in the industry. Note that the change was made as of the beginning of 1990. The cumulative effect on years prior to 1990, $33.8 million, was reported in the 1990 income statement. The effect on 1990 earnings was not reported separately on the income statement but was disclosed in the footnote.

Many discretionary changes are tactically timed and used for the primary purpose of improving reported results. The resulting "improvements" are only in reported results. Actual economic performance has probably not improved. In fact, economic fundamentals may have deteriorated. The reported financial effects of the accounting change may be designed to buy time and provide cover until fundamentals improve. The appearance of improved results may direct attention away from declining fundamentals and delay timely action by management.

A good example of a series of discretionary accounting changes, both in accounting principle and estimate, that may have been timed to postpone bad news, is provided by General Motors Corp. In 1987 the company extended the useful lives of plant, equipment, and tools, a change in accounting estimate, increasing pre-tax income that year by $1,237 million. Also in 1987, General Motors Acceptance Corp. (GMAC), the company's consolidated finance subsidiary, changed the rate of depreciation of automobiles on lease to retail customers. This added an additional $255 million to consolidated net income. Then, in 1988, the company began capitalizing certain manufacturing overhead costs to inventory that had previously been expensed as incurred. The current-year effect of this change in accounting principle was to increase pre-tax income by approximately $524 million.

Did the accounting changes at General Motors hide developing bad news? Consider that while the company's net income of $4,856 million in 1988 was followed with net income of $4,224 million in 1989, net losses in 1990 and 1991 were $1,986 million and $4,453 million, respectively.[3]

Also providing boosts to income through accounting changes in principle and estimate was Value Merchants, Inc. A change in accounting principle was described by the company as follows:

> Effective February 4, 1990, the company changed its inventory valuation method to absorb certain direct warehouse expenses in inventory values. This new method, which was accounted for as a change in accounting principle, was made to better approximate the expenditures and charges directly incurred in bringing inventories to their existing location and condition. The change was also made to minimize the differences between inventories for financial reporting and tax purposes created by the Tax Reform Act of 1986 by adopting certain aspects of the new inventory capitalization method established by the Internal Revenue Service. The cumulative effect of this change for periods prior to February 4, 1990, of $721,000, or $.12 per share (net of income taxes), is included in net income for fiscal 1990 in the consolidated statements of income. For fiscal 1990, the effect due to this change was to increase income before cumulative effect of accounting change on prior years by approximately $606,000, or $.10 per share.[4]

In this example, the company described how it began capitalizing certain warehouse expenses to inventory. These expenses likely included such costs as utilities and insurance on the warehouse, and payroll costs of warehouse workers. Using consistency with tax accounting was a curious justification for the change. Our tax laws are designed to raise federal revenue and meet certain social objectives and not to provide measures of income that are theoretically sound from an investor's or creditor's point of view. On their income statements, most companies charge to expense the kinds of expenditures that must be capitalized for tax purposes as highlighted by the Tax Reform Act of 1986. With this change, Value Merchants appeared to be moving away from general practice. The current-year effect of the change added $606,000, or 11%, to income from continuing operations in 1991.

In the following year, the company effected a change in accounting estimate, described as follows:

> Included in prepaid expenses and other current assets at February 1, 1992 is $1,334,000 of preopening costs. The company changed its amortization period for store preopening costs from amortizing these costs over the remaining periods in the fiscal year in which new stores are opened to amortizing these costs over the first 12 months after new stores are opened.[5]

Here the company changed its estimate of the length of time over which benefit is presumed to be received from preopening costs incurred. The change added $1,334,000, or 9%, to pre-tax income in 1992.

Before its bankruptcy, 1992 was the last year that Value Merchants reported a profit. The company lost nearly $8 million the following year and was in bankruptcy proceedings by December 1993. The impression remains that accounting changes made in the years prior to the bankruptcy were part of an unsuccessful attempt to provide a false sense of security about the company's prospects for growth and prosperity.

Other examples of changes in accounting estimate providing boosts to current-year income are provided by Continental Airlines, Inc., and Alumax, Inc. In 1993, Continental Airlines changed its estimate of unearned income, termed air traffic liability. This account represents the value of tickets sold for which air transportation has not yet been provided. The change increased revenue by $75 million.[6] During the 1993 reporting period, operating income was $95.5 million, including the change. Thus, a significant component of the company's income was derived from the change in estimate. At Alumax, 1993 operating income before a $91.8 million restructuring charge was a loss of $19.3 million. However, that loss was lessened by an $18.4 million reduction in depreciation expense due to a change in the estimated service lives of certain production facilities.[7]

Companies must provide a theoretical justification for discretionary changes in accounting principle. In the General Motors example, the change was justified on the grounds that it provided a better matching of costs with revenue. Value Merchants justified its change by saying that it provided an approximation of the total costs incurred in bringing inventories to their existing location and condition. The company also justified the change on the grounds that it minimized differences between financial and tax reporting created by tax reform. Common justifications for changes in accounting principle are that the new method provides a better matching of expenses with revenue, or that the new method makes the firm's results more comparable with other companies in the industry. Often, such justifications are little more than standard boiler-plate. The real reason may be only to improve reported results. Moreover, just because a new method is consistent with general industry practice should not be viewed as automatic justification. If the new method is preferable, why was the old method originally selected? Further, while changes toward industry practice may improve comparisons with other firms, they hamper prior-year comparisons for the same firm.

Similar justifications are not needed for changes in accounting estimate. It is understood that financial statements are built on a collection of estimates. As these estimates change, reported income must be adjusted. However, as with changes in accounting principle, changes in estimate may also be timed to give short-term boosts to income.

All accounting changes, but especially those that boost current-year income at the expense of future years, should be carefully examined. There are situations where a new method results in higher income, has more theoretical support, and is consistent with industry practice. For example, a move to begin capitalizing a portion of software costs might make sense for a company, such as Microsoft Corp., that has always expensed them. Generally accepted accounting principles call for such treatment, and expensing all such costs could be viewed as being overly conservative.

However, when such a change is made, the investor or creditor should be aware that a portion of the current year's income is the result of an accounting change. Income from continuing operations after deducting the current-year effect of the accounting change should be used in making comparisons with prior years in judging current-year performance. If current-year income, once adjusted to remove the effects of the accounting change, is somewhat disappointing, the implication is that the change may have been done solely for an earnings boost. Expectations about future years' results should likely be revised downward accordingly.

Timed Management Actions

Management has discretion not only over the accounting principles and estimates it employs but also over the timing of its operating decisions. Through the timing of management actions, a more positive light can be shed on current-year earnings. For example, appreciated land held for years by a company could be sold, generating a gain, when that gain is needed. The sale date can be timed, assuming a buyer is available, to offset an emerging dip in earnings. The market value of the land and the corresponding gain have likely increased over many years. In timing the date of sale, the company is able to move those gains from prior years to the current year. In this instance, earnings are not borrowed from the future but rather are moved to the current year from the past. Nonetheless, the gain on sale was not really produced in the current year.

Raychem Corp. provides an example of just this sort of action. In 1992 the company's pre-tax earnings were pushed into a loss position by a provision for restructuring and divestitures that totaled $43.3 million. To help offset this special charge, the company sold a piece of land that generated a gain of $31.6 million. With this gain, the company's pre-tax earnings were once again in the plus column.[8]

As another example, in 1993, Eastman Kodak Co.'s income from continuing operations was boosted by 7% from a gain on the sale of assets. Unfortunately, this gain was not disclosed in the company's annual report. As a result, in looking toward 1994, and using 1993 as a base, analysts were somewhat optimistic in their forecasts.

For a third example, we return to GE. In 1993 the company used a $1,430 million gain on the sale of an aerospace unit to Martin Marietta Corp. to offset the negative effects on earnings of a $1,011 million pre-tax restructuring charge. That year, income from continuing operations increased to $4,424 million from $4,305 million, an increase that would not have been possible without the nonrecurring gain.[9]

Another way for management to time its actions in order to boost current-year income is through the postponement of certain operating expenses. In particular, two expenses that can be readily postponed in an effort to improve current-year performance are advertising costs and research and development. Under generally accepted accounting principles, both expenditures are expensed as incurred. Given this required treatment, both items affect current-year earnings directly. By postponing their incurrence, earnings can be increased or losses reduced. Unfortunately, such actions are a short-term fix and are taken at the expense of future operations. A company might lose market share through the postponement of advertising expenses. Similarly, a technical edge might be lost through a reduction in research and development.

As an example, Aero Systems Engineering, Inc., designs and constructs turbine engine test equipment. In 1993 the company reported revenue and net income of $27.8 million and $2.6 million, respectively. That year, expenditures on research and development totaled $636,000. In 1994 revenue declined to $25.2 million and the company reported a loss of $1.2 million. A careful check of the income statement indicates that in 1994 the company reduced its research and development expenditures by 50%, to $318,000. While this action reduced the company's pre-tax loss by $318,000, it may also affect its technological edge. In fact, the company may have to spend more than $318,000 to regain technical leadership that may have been lost.[10]

As with discretionary accounting changes, temporary current-year boosts to income arising through timed management actions tend to lessen critical evaluations of performance. They help managements buy time while results improve. Unfortunately, the time purchased can be expensive if it means that needed actions are postponed while problems fester.

Warnings from Boosted Current-Year Performance

Companies with significantly improving fortunes do not need to enhance reported results with discretionary accounting changes or with tactically timed actions. Thus, generally speaking, discretionary moves designed to boost earnings can be viewed in and of themselves as potential early warnings of future earnings difficulties. Earnings boosted in this way are borrowed from other years. The result is income that is not sustainable. Further, earnings-increasing acts typically increase asset book values, or result in their slower decline, increasing the potential need for subsequent asset write-downs. When expectations are developed using reported earnings that include the effects of income-increasing discretionary accounting changes or timed management actions, the chances for surprise are increased. To avoid this outcome, the sustainable earnings worksheet of Chapter 6 is designed to facilitate the adjustment of results by removing the nonrecurring items that may be created by earnings management.

REDUCING CURRENT-YEAR PERFORMANCE

Companies can reduce current-year income and store earnings for future years in two main ways. The first, most prevalent, approach is through a change in estimate. Typically, this change results in increased expenses in the current year or near term. For example, by reducing the useful lives of assets, a more rapid write-off of their acquisition costs can be achieved. Expense charges are increased near-term and reduced in future years. Alternatively, a company can determine that an asset is value-impaired, necessitating a direct write-down and charge to income. Such a charge provides a convenient one-year reduction in income. Another way to increase current-year expense is through the creation of special reserves. Examples include an overstatement of such contra-asset accounts as the allowance for doubtful accounts or, for banks, the allowance for loan loss, and the reserve for inventory obsolescence. Heightened expense charges are needed to increase these reserves, reducing current-year income. Later, if and when income is needed, expenses can be reduced through decreases in these reserves. Current-year expenses can also be increased through the overaccrual of liabilities. Examples include heightened warranty expenses, self-insurance, and tax liabilities.

For example, in 1991, Fruit of the Loom, Inc., reported interest income of $49.4 million arising from a court-ordered refund of federal income taxes. To offset this windfall, the company recorded $10.2 million "to provide for certain obligations and other matters related to former subsidiaries" and $39.2 million "to write down the company's investment in Acme Boot to its then market value."[11] It seems almost unbelievable that the special charges totaled $49.4 million, an amount that was exactly equal to the interest income windfall. Their timing and amount suggest strongly that the company was taking steps to offset the one-time gain. Before the gain and special charges, income from continuing operations was up 44% in 1991. By writing the investment down and providing for certain obligations, the company was effectively storing earnings for future years.

As another example, in 1993, Kellogg Co. reported a $65.9 million gain from the sale of its British carton-container division and its Argentine snack food business. Reducing this gain were pre-tax charges of $64.3 million from the write-down of "certain assets in Europe and North America."[12] As in the Fruit of the Loom example, this asset write-down, in effect a change in estimate, appears to be timed to offset the one-time gain. Future earnings will be increased through reduced amortization charges of those assets that have been written down. The Kellogg story is a bit less clear, however. Before the gain on the sale of its British division and Argentine business, the company's 1993 income from continuing operations was little changed from 1992. Thus, while the company took steps to help ensure a smooth income stream, we cannot say whether the special charges were used to offset the gain, or the gain was used to offset the charges. It is also possible that both naturally occurred in 1993 and just happened to be about equal in amount.

A third example is provided by Merck & Co. In its 1993 annual report, the company disclosed the following:

In 1993, other income, net, includes a gain of $148.8 million from the company's sale of its Calgon Water Management business. This gain was largely offset by a $78.8 million provision for environmental costs and a $60.0 million provision for the funding of the Merck Company Foundation.[13]

Given the discretionary nature of the special charges, especially the provision for funding of the Merck Company Foundation, we are inclined to believe that, like Fruit of the Loom, Merck was using special charges to offset the one-time gain on its sale of Calgon.

A second, less prevalent, approach for reducing current-year income is through timed management actions. Here, expenditures, such as advertising and research and development are accelerated to reduce current-year income. Alternatively, an asset whose market value has fallen below cost and that has not been written down, might be sold, resulting in a loss. Cooper Industries, Inc., provides a good example that includes just such a loss. The example also includes changes in estimate. Exhibit 12.1 was constructed with data from the company's 1993 annual report.

Note that in 1993 the company reported a gain of $273.8 million from the initial public offering (IPO) of stock in a subsidiary. Offsetting this gain was a loss on the sale of Cameron Forged Products Co. and selected asset write-downs and liability accruals. The loss and special charges reduced the one-time gain to zero.

It can be argued that some steps taken to manage earnings are inherently good. For example, earnings management might be used to smooth income toward a more sustainable level, much as we adjusted earnings for nonrecurring items in Chapter 6. It is our preference to see earnings reported without the effects of earnings management. However, when steps are taken to smooth income toward a more sustainable level, we do not find the practice to be totally objectionable. Here, management is attempting to inform its financial statement users of recurring profit and not mislead them with false results. The problem with such income-smoothing activities is that financial statement users may not know when management's intent has changed. We have seen several examples of earnings management that might be included in this "good" variety. Depending on the circumstances, the examples provided for General Electric, Fruit of the Loom, Kellogg, Merck, and Cooper Industries would seem to fit this description.

Exhibit 12.1 Nonrecurring Income: Cooper Industries, Inc., Year Ending December 31, 1993 (millions of dollars)

	1993
Gain from IPO of 90.4% of stock in Belden, Inc.	$ 273.8
Loss on sale of Cameron Forged Products	(65.0)
Productivity improvement and consolidation programs	(126.0)
Reduction in carrying value of machinery and equipment and other assets related to the production of transformers	(65.0)
Reduction in carrying value of capitalized software	(17.8)
Total (before tax)	–

Source: Cooper Industries, Inc., annual report, December 1993, p. 26.

Warnings from Reduced Current-Year Performance

Many see nothing wrong with using increased expenses or timed actions to reduce current-year earnings. A more conservative light is shed on net income and the balance sheet. However, one must remember that even though it results in conservative financial statements, action taken to reduce current-year performance is active earnings manipulation. Earnings become what management says they should be, not necessarily the result of actual performance. During difficult times, earnings stored from prior years are used to buy time before difficult decisions must be made. The smoothing effect of earnings stored from prior years can give a false sense of security during downturns, an impression that the firm is operating profitably. The real problem arises when conditions do not improve, the firm exhausts its special reserves, and outsiders become painfully aware of problems that may have existed for some time. At this stage, it may be too late for timely action to fix problems.

When steps are taken to reduce current-year performance, the likelihood of a near-term earnings surprise is reduced. Management is communicating that earning power is strong. However, the risk of an earnings surprise increases markedly when a company begins including in the current year earnings generated in prior years. For example, there might be a sudden reduction in the allowance for doubtful accounts, an inventory obsolescence reserve, or depreciation expense due to an increase in estimated useful lives or salvage values. Alternatively, accrued liabilities might be reduced. Looked at from another angle, there may be an improvement in gross margin or the SGA% for no apparent reason. These are indications that management was unhappy with the company's performance and felt the need to add earnings from another year. They were disappointed with the company's earnings and the likelihood increases that others might be disappointed in the future.

The Big Bath

Closely related to steps taken to reduce current-year performance is the "big bath": a company uses wholesale asset write-downs and liability accruals to turn what appears to be a poor quarter or year into a rout. Such an action permits the company to get all the bad news behind it. It is then positioned for increased future earnings through lower cost of sales and depreciation charges and lower liability accruals. Such a tactic can be especially useful to a new management team because the bad results can be blamed on a prior administration.

The benefits of a big bath can be illusory. The problem that arises is that the next several years may appear better than they really are. An impression of sustainable earnings at higher levels may be gained through the observance of higher gross margins and improved expense ratios. This improved performance may not be real, which may become apparent as the effects of the big bath begin to wear off.

A big bath is not a sign of strength. It is often taken when strategic and structural changes are needed. Often it takes the form of a restructuring charge and is essentially an admission of corporate problems and past mistakes. Such an admission may in and of itself be a positive sign. However, admitting a problem and taking a charge to correct it is one thing. Comprehending the total scope of the problem and recognizing its total effect is something else. Special charges associated with a big bath in one year are frequently the precursors of additional charges in future years.

As an example, consider Agway, Inc. In 1992 the marketer of fresh fruits and vegetables made the following announcement:

> In 1992, the company initiated "Customer Driven: 1995. Focusing on the 21st Century" (the "Project") to restructure the company to better focus on its members and customers and to re-engineer the company's business processes to improve future profitability. These restructuring measures included a reduction in personnel; plants; stores; and adjustments to net realizable values of certain assets which were disposed; and resulted in a pre-tax restructuring charge of $75 million in the fourth quarter of fiscal 1992, the amount estimated at that time to be necessary to accomplish Project goals.[14]

The restructuring charge of $75 million was significant for the company and resulted in a net loss of $58.8 million for 1992. In 1993 the company returned to profitability. However, by 1994, the company once again reported a net loss.

SUMMARY

Earnings are managed for different reasons. Operating below plan, some companies take steps to boost current-year income. This might be done to increase management bonuses, meet debt covenants, or maintain share prices. Typically these earnings increases are obtained at the expense of future earnings through premature revenue recognition, aggressive cost capitalization, extended amortization periods, excessive asset valuations, or undervaluation of liabilities. Other approaches used include accounting changes and timed management actions. Other companies find that current earnings are already at or above desired levels and take a variety of steps to reduce them.

Investors and creditors should be aware that when earnings are managed, up or down, a company may not be reporting its true performance. Thus, impressions gained and judgments made using those earnings can be biased. There are exceptions where earnings management may be desirable: when the objective is to inform of sustainable earnings rather than mislead.

Exhibit 12.2 presents a checklist for managed earnings. The checklist's questions will help users anticipate earnings surprises related to earnings management.

Exhibit 12.2 Checklist for Financial Early Warnings: Managed Earnings

---

Boosting Current-Year Performance
A. Have accounting tactics been used to increase current-year income?
   1. Premature revenue recognition
   2. Aggressive cost capitalization
   3. Extended amortization periods
   4. Excessive asset valuation
   5. Undervaluation of liabilities
B. Has current-year income been increased through the use of discretionary accounting changes?
   1. Are there changes in accounting principle disclosed on the income statement and notes?
      a. What is the current-year effect of the change on income?
   2. Are there changes in accounting estimate disclosed in the notes?
      a. What is the current-year effect of the change on income?
   3. How is the company doing in the absence of the effects of accounting changes?
   4. Have the accounting changes resulted in asset book values whose realizability may be questioned?
      a. Has the likelihood of a future write-down of these assets been increased?
   5. What does the change do to comparisons of results with prior years?
   6. Has management been known to boost earnings with discretionary accounting changes in the past?
C. Has management timed actions to boost current-year income?
   1. Is there evidence of significant nonrecurring gains on asset sales?
   2. Have expenses been postponed?
      a. Research and development
         i. Has the absolute dollar amount of research and development declined significantly?
         ii. What are the implications for the company's research agenda?
      b. Advertising expenses
         i. If the SGA% declined, what was the reason for the decline?
            • Did a short-term reduction in advertising play a role?
         ii. If the SGA% declined, is the decline a long-term improvement?

Reducing Current-Year Performance
A. Has the company used changes in accounting estimates to reduce current-year income?
   1. Reduced useful lives of assets
   2. Reduced realizable values of assets necessitating write-downs
   3. Increased reserves or contra-asset accounts
   4. Overaccrued liabilities
B. Have timed management actions been used to reduce current-year income?
   1. Sale of assets at a loss
   2. Increased discretionary expenses
C. Is the company reporting income earned in prior years?
   1. Sudden reductions in reserves or contra-asset accounts
   2. Declines in accrued liabilities

Exhibit 12.2 *(continued)*

---

   3. Unexpected improvements in gross margin or SGA%
D. Has the company taken a big bath in recent periods?
   1. Has current performance benefited as a result?
   2. How will performance look when the benefits of the big bath wear off?
E. Did earnings management result in more sustainable earnings?

REFERENCES

Ayres, F. "What Managers Need to Know: Making the Bottom Line Look Better May Have a Negative Result," *Management Accounting*, March 1994, pp. 27–29.

Barefield, R., and E. E. Comiskey. "The Smoothing Hypothesis: An Alternative Test." *Accounting Review*, April 1972, pp. 291–298.

Rosenzweig, K., and M. Fischer. "Is Managing Earnings Ethically Acceptable?" *Management Accounting*, March 1994, pp. 31–34.

Schipper, K. "Commentary on Earnings Management." *Accounting Horizons*, December 1989, pp. 91–102.

ENDNOTES

1. *The Wall Street Journal*, November 3, 1994, p. A1.
2. Battle Mountain Gold Co., annual report, December 1990, pp. 38–39.
3. Information obtained from General Motors Corp., annual report, December 1988, and from Disclosure, Inc., *Compact D/SEC: Corporate Information on Public Companies Filing with the SEC* (Bethesda, Md.: Disclosure, Inc., March 1994).
4. Value Merchants, Inc., annual report, February 1992, p. 29.
5. Ibid., p. 25.
6. Continental Airlines, Inc., annual report, December 1993, p. 38.
7. Alumax, Inc., annual report, December 1993, p. 36.
8. Raychem Corp., annual report, June 1993, p. 23.
9. *The Wall Street Journal*, November 3, 1994, p. A6, and General Electric Co., annual report, December 1994, p. 26.
10. Aero Systems Engineering, Inc., December 1993 annual report. Data obtained from Disclosure, Inc., *Compact D/SEC: Corporate Information on Public Companies Filing with the SEC* (Bethesda, Md.: Disclosure, Inc., June 1995).
11. Fruit of the Loom, Inc., annual report, December 1993, p. 38.
12. Kellogg Co., annual report, December 1993, p. 17.
13. Merck & Co., annual report, December 1993, p. 48.
14. Agway, Inc., annual report, December 1994. Information obtained from Disclosure, Inc., *Compact D/SEC: Corporate Information on Public Companies Filing with the SEC* (Bethesda, Md.: Disclosure, Inc., June 1995).

Chapter 13

The Role of Accountants and Auditors

Where were the auditors?

"Where were the auditors?" has been an all too common outcry in recent years as companies suffered sudden earnings declines, or other signs of financial deterioration, and then quickly fell into the embrace of our country's system of bankruptcy laws. Especially troublesome has been the proximity between unexpected declines and so-called clean or unqualified audit opinions. The term *audit failure* has sometimes been used to describe cases of bankruptcy that have closely followed the issuance of clean audit opinions. These events have raised questions about the role of auditors and the reliance that is to be properly placed on financial statements with which outside auditors or accountants are associated.

This chapter outlines the different levels of association that outside accountants and auditors can have with financial statements. Included is a brief overview of the process preceding the issuance of the accountant's or auditor's report. This is designed to help users of financial statements develop a better sense of the assurance afforded by the different levels of accountant or auditor association with financial statements. Reference is both to accountants and to auditors because the association of outside accountants, typically CPAs, with financial statements is not always in the capacity of auditor. For example, an outside accountant specifically disclaims the performance of any auditing procedures when engaged to compile financial statements for a client and to render a compilation report. The CPA is providing accounting, not auditing, services in this circumstance.

In addition to the various activities of outside accountants and auditors, their role in detecting fraudulent financial reporting is reviewed. Fraudulent financial reporting is a significant source of earnings surprises. The accountants' and auditors' key role in preventing or detecting earnings surprises makes them clearly important to the overall thrust of this book.

The emphasis here on outside accountants and auditors should not be taken to imply that in-house accountants and auditors have no role to play in preventing earnings surprises. A competent team of accountants and internal auditors is critical to the design and maintenance of systems of internal controls that make possible the production of reliable financial statements. Moreover, effective systems of internal controls are critical to the prevention and detection of financial fraud. The focus here is on outside accountants and auditors because their role in the avoidance of earnings surprises is often less well understood and recently much more the subject of contention.

THE SEVERAL ROLES OF OUTSIDE ACCOUNTANTS AND AUDITORS

The primary levels of association by outside accountants and auditors with financial statements are (1) compilation, (2) review, and (3) audit. The scope of their role at each level and the assurance provided are discussed in this section. To place these levels of association in perspective, it is useful to consider the conventional view that the role of an auditor is to reduce "information risk." Robertson has defined information risk as "the risk (probability) that the financial statements distributed by the company will be materially false and misleading."[1]

The scope of activities involved in the case of compilations and reviews is substantially narrower than in the case of audits. In fact, the outside accountant or auditor is not functioning as an auditor as such when performing a compilation or review engagement. The extent to which information risk is reduced when these services are provided is unclear. However, it is reasonable to assume some degree of reduction in information risk with compilation or reviews if the alternative is simply company-prepared financial statements.

In terms of the theme of this book, the likelihood of earnings surprises should be reduced if, regardless of the level of involvement of outside accountants or auditors, there is some degree of reduction of information risk. A decidedly lower level of information risk reduction is implicit in the case of compilations and reviews, based upon the results of the lender survey discussed in Chapter 4. Examples of relevant financial early warnings provided by lenders included providing only compiled financial statements, and going from audited to reviewed, or reviewed to compiled, statements.

We discuss standards for the performance of compilation and review services and standards for the performance of audits separately.

Compilation and Review Services

Authoritative guidance for compilation and review services is provided by the Accounting and Review Services Committee of the American Institute of Certified Public Accountants (AICPA). This committee issues Statements on Standards for Accounting and Review Services. These statements apply to work on unaudited financial statements of nonpublic companies.

Compilation Engagements

The Accounting and Review Services Committee describes the objective of an engagement to compile financial statements as follows:

> Presenting in the form of financial statements information that is the representation of management (owners) without undertaking to express any assurance on the statements. [2]

The committee has also outlined in general terms what the accountant performing a compilation must do, and is not required to do, in a compilation engagement. Key summary requirements include the following:[3]

- The accountant should possess a level of knowledge of the accounting principles and practices of the industry in which the entity operates that will enable him to compile financial statements that are appropriate in form for an entity operating in that industry.
- The accountant should possess a general understanding of the nature of the entity's business transactions, the form of its accounting records, the stated qualifications of its accounting personnel, the accounting basis on which the financial statements are to be presented, and the form and content of the financial statements.
- The accountant is not required to make inquiries or perform other procedures to verify, corroborate, or review information supplied by the entity.
- Before issuing the report, the accountant should read the compiled financial statements and consider whether such financial statements appear to be appropriate in form and free from obvious material errors. In this context, the term *error* refers to mistakes in the compilation of the financial statements, including arithmetical or clerical mistakes, and mistakes in the application of accounting principles, including inadequate disclosures.

Notice that the performance of activities that are a traditional part of the auditing process are not required. For example, the accountant is not required to review the client's systems of internal controls, confirm its cash and accounts receivable balances, or perform analytical procedures.

The accountant renders a review report upon completion of the compilation engagement. A standard compilation report is presented in Exhibit 13.1. Each page of the financial statements compiled by the accountant should include the statement "see accountant's compilation report."

Modifications of the Standard Compilation Report

It is very common for the client to request that the statement of cash flows and all notes be omitted. This is permitted as long as such omission is clearly indicated in

Exhibit 13.1   Standard Compilation Report

I have compiled the accompanying balance sheet of XYZ Company as of December 31, 19—, and the related statements of income, retained earnings, and cash flows for the year then ended, in accordance with Statements of Standards for Accounting and Review Services issued by the American Institute of Certified Public Accountants.

A compilation is limited to presenting in the form of financial statements information that is the representation of management. I have not audited or reviewed the accompanying financial statements and, accordingly, do not express an opinion or any other form of assurance on them.

Source: *Codification of Statements on Standards for Accounting and Review Services* (1995), AR section 100.14.

the compilation report and the omission is not, to the accountant's knowledge, motivated by the intention to mislead potential users. Assuming that the motivation is not to mislead, then the standard compilation report is modified as shown in Exhibit 13.2.

The accountant may become aware that information provided by the client is incorrect, incomplete, or otherwise unsatisfactory for the purpose of compiling financial statements. "In such circumstances, the accountant should obtain additional or revised information. If the entity refuses to provide additional or revised information, the accountant should withdraw from the compilation engagement."[4]

Further, an accountant engaged to perform a compilation may become aware of departures from generally accepted accounting principles that have a material impact

Exhibit 13.2   Modified Standard Compilation Report

I have compiled the accompanying balance sheet of XYZ Company as of December 31, 19—, and the related statement of income and retained earnings for the year then ended, in accordance with Statements of Standards for Accounting and Review Services issued by the American Institute of Certified Public Accountants.

A compilation is limited to presenting in the form of financial statements information that is the representation of management. I have not audited or reviewed the accompanying financial statements and, accordingly, do not express an opinion or any other form of assurance on them.

Management has elected to omit substantially all of the disclosures and the statement of cash flows required by generally accepted accounting principles. If the omitted disclosures and the statement of cash flows were included in the financial statements, they might influence the user's conclusions about the company's financial position, results of operations, and cash flows. Accordingly, these financial statements are not designed for those who are not informed about such matters.

Source: *Codification of Statements on Standards for Accounting and Review Services* (1995), AR section 100.21.

on the client's financial statements. "If the financial statements are not revised, the accountant should consider whether modification of the standard report is adequate to disclose the departure."[5] An example of a modification of the standard compilation report to disclose a departure from generally accepted accounting principles is provided in Exhibit 13.3. Only the revised second paragraph of the standard report and a separate additional paragraph are provided in the exhibit; the first and third paragraph of the standard report (Exhibit 13.2) remains unchanged.

Review Engagements

Unlike a compilation engagement, a review is designed to provide the accountant "with a reasonable basis for expressing limited assurance that there are no material modifications that should be made to the financial statements in order for the statements to be in conformity with generally accepted accounting principles."[6]

The knowledge required in a compilation engagement of the client, its business, its industry, and its accounting practices is also called for in a review. However, beyond this the accountant relies on inquiries and analytical procedures to develop the basis for expressing limited assurance on the reviewed statements. The *Codification of Statements on Standards for Accounting and Review Services* maintains that the accountant's inquiry and analytical procedures should generally consist of those enumerated in Exhibit 13.4.

Analytical procedures "involve comparisons of recorded amounts, or ratios developed from recorded amounts, to expectations developed by the auditor."[7] Examples of sources of information used to form these expectations include the following:[8]

- Financial information for comparable prior period(s), giving consideration to known changes

Exhibit 13.3 Modified Compilation Report for a Departure from Generally Accepted Accounting Principles

---

A compilation is limited to presenting in the form of financial statements information that is the representation of management. I have not audited or reviewed the accompanying financial statements and, accordingly, do not express an opinion or any other form of assurance on them. However, I did become aware of a departure from generally accepted accounting principles that is described in the following paragraph.

As disclosed in note X to the financial statements, generally accepted accounting principles require that land be stated at cost. Management has informed me that the company has stated its land at appraised value and that, if generally accepted accounting principles had been followed, the land account and stockholders' equity would have decreased by $500,000.

Source: *Codification of Statements on Standards for Accounting and Review Services* (1995), AR section 100.40.

- Anticipated results—for example, budgets, or forecasts including extrapolations from interim or annual data
- Relations among elements of financial information within the period
- Information regarding the industry in which the client operates—for example, gross margin information
- Relations of financial information with relevant nonfinancial information

Exhibit 13.4 Inquiries and Analytical Review Procedures in Review Engagements

1. Inquiries concerning the entity's accounting principles and practices and the methods followed in applying them.
2. Inquiries concerning the entity's procedures for recording, classifying, and summarizing transactions, and accumulating information for disclosure in the financial statements.
3. Analytical procedures designed to identify relationships and individual items that appear to be unusual:
   a. Comparison of the financial statements with statements for comparable prior period(s).
   b. Comparison of the financial statements with anticipated results, if available (for example, budgets and forecasts).
   c. Study of the relationships of the elements of the financial statements that would be expected to conform to a predictable pattern based on the entity's experience.
4. Inquiries concerning actions taken at meetings of stockholders, board of directors, committees of the board of directors, or comparable meetings that may affect the financial statements.
5. Reading the financial statements to consider, on the basis of information coming to the accountant's attention, whether the financial statements appear to conform with generally accepted accounting principles.
6. Obtaining reports from other accountants, if any, who have been engaged to audit or review the financial statements of significant components of the reporting entity, its subsidiaries, and other investees.
7. Inquiries of persons having responsibility for financial and accounting matters concerning:
   a. Whether the financial statements have been prepared in conformity with generally accepted accounting principles.
   b. Changes in the entity's business activities or accounting principles or practices.
   c. Matters as to which questions have arisen in the course of applying the foregoing procedures.
   d. Events subsequent to the date of the financial statements that would have a material effect on the financial statements.

Source: *Codification of Statements on Standards for Accounting and Review Services (1995), AR section 100.27.*

Many of the activities listed in Exhibit 13.4 would be part of a standard audit engagement. The inquiries and analytical procedures are standard elements of an audit program. However, omitted from the listing in the exhibit are standard features of a complete audit program, such as evaluation of the systems of internal control, evaluation of control risk, tests of accounting records, documentation of transactions, confirmation of accounts receivable and cash balances, and so on.

After the procedures outlined in Exhibit 13.4 have been performed, the accountant issues a review report that states the following:[9]

- A review was performed in accordance with Statements of Standards for Accounting and Review Services issued by the American Institute of Certified Public Accountants.
- All information included in the financial statements is the representation of the management of the entity.
- A review consists principally of inquiries of company personnel and analytical procedures applied to financial data.
- A review is substantially less in scope than an audit, the objective of which is the expression of an opinion regarding the financial statements taken as a whole and, accordingly, no such opinion is expressed.
- The accountant is not aware of any material modifications that should be made to the financial statements in order for them to be in conformity with generally accepted accounting principles, other than those modifications, if any, indicated in the report.

An example of a standard review report is provided in Exhibit 13.5.[10] Unlike a compilation report (Exhibit 13.1), the review report is designed to express limited assurance that there are no material modifications that should be made to the financial statements in order for them to be in conformity with generally accepted accounting principles.

Modifications of the Standard Review Report

The accountant conducting a review may become aware of a departure from generally accepted accounting principles that is material. If the statements are not revised, then "the accountant should consider whether modification of the standard report is adequate to disclose the departure."[11] If modification is sufficient, then the departure should be disclosed in a separate paragraph, along with the effects of the departure on the financial statements, if the effects have been determined by management. "The accountant is not required to determine the effects of the departure if management has not done so, provided the accountant states in the report that such determination has not been made."[12] An example of a modified standard review report is provided in Exhibit 13.6. Only the modified third paragraph of the standard report (Exhibit 13.5) and an additional paragraph are included in Exhibit 13.6.

Exhibit 13.5   Standard Review Report

I have reviewed the accompanying balance sheet of XYZ Company as of December 31, 19—, and the related statements of income, retained earnings, and cash flows for the year then ended, in accordance with Statements of Standards for Accounting and Review Services issued by the American Institute of Certified Public Accountants. All information included in these financial statements is the representation of the management of XYZ Company.

A review consists principally of inquiries of company personnel and analytical procedures applied to financial data. It is substantially less in scope than an audit in accordance with generally accepted auditing standards, the objective of which is the expression of an opinion regarding the statements taken as a whole. Accordingly, I do not express such an opinion.

Based on my review, I am not aware of any material modifications that should be made to the accompanying financial statements in order for them to be in conformity with generally accepted accounting principles.

Source: *Codification of Statements on Standards for Accounting and Review Services* (1995), AR section 100.35.

Audits

A traditional element of the auditor's role is the responsibility to reduce the likelihood that financial statements will be materially false and misleading. An earnings surprise is likely in cases where statements prove to be materially false and misleading. Larry Konrath, in his auditing textbook, offers the following view of the varying

Exhibit 13.6   Modified Standard Review Report

Based on my review, with the exception of the matter described in the following paragraph, I am not aware of any material modifications that should be made to the accompanying financial statements in order for them to be in conformity with generally accepted accounting principles.

As disclosed in note X to the financial statements, the company reports its inventory following the uniform cost capitalization rules of the Tax Reform Act of 1986. As a result, the inventory value includes general and administrative costs. Generally accepted accounting principles call for inventory to include direct labor, direct materials, and manufacturing overhead, but not general and administrative expenses. The effects of this departure on financial position, results of operations, and cash flows have not been determined.

Source: *Codification of Statements on Standards for Accounting and Review Services* (1995), AR section 100.39-40.

degrees of assurance provided by compilations, reviews, and audits regarding the fairness of the financial statements:

> To summarize, a *compilation* offers *no assurance;* a *review* offers *limited assurance;* and an *audit* offers *reasonable assurance* regarding fairness of the financial statements.[13]

In principle, the likelihood of an earnings surprise resulting from information risk should rank as follows, from highest to lowest information risk:

1. Company-prepared statements
2. Compiled statements
3. Reviewed statements
4. Audited statements

Konrath takes the position that a compilation offers no assurance. This assessment is probably too negative. An outside accountant, even in a compilation engagement, can potentially detect some deviations from generally accepted accounting principles. He or she, just by being present, may also have a subtle influence over the discipline exercised by the firm in the production of its financial information. While varying somewhat according to the nature of the client, the quality of the outside accountant, and other factors, some reduction in information risk should be achieved even from a compilation engagement. There appears to be general agreement that reviews provide a more substantial reduction in information risk.

The purpose of this section, dealing with audited financial statements, is to (1) provide a summary of the scope of the audit process in relation to compilations and reviews, (2) review the various types of audit reports, and (3) distill some auditing research that indicates the role auditing can play in the detection of fraudulent financial reporting.

The Auditing Process and Generally Accepted Auditing Standards

The scope of activity in an audit is considerably greater than that of the accountant's activity in either a compilation or a review. The discussion here is aimed at providing a general sense of the differences between the requirements of an audit and the requirements of compilations and reviews. Guidance for the auditing process is provided by the Auditing Standards Board of the American Institute of Certified Public Accountants (AICPA). The Board issues Statements on Auditing Standards.

Generally Accepted Auditing Standards

On the most general level, auditing activity is guided by a set of Generally Accepted Auditing Standards. These standards do not focus on auditing procedures but rather

on the auditor's professional qualities and the judgment exercised in the performance of the audit and in rendering the audit report. The Standards of Field Work
provide a sense of the expanded activities involved in an audit engagement as
compared with a compilation or review engagement. The Standards of Field Work
are as follows:

1. The work is to be adequately planned, and assistants, if any, are to be properly
    supervised.
2. A sufficient understanding of the internal control structure is to be obtained to
    plan the audit and to determine the nature, timing, and extent of tests to be
    performed.
3. Sufficient competent evidential matter is to be obtained through inspection,
    observation, inquiries, and confirmations to afford a reasonable basis for an
    opinion regarding the financial statements under audit.[14]

Note that the second and third field work standards make reference to tests,
inspections, and confirmations. These are all elements of the process of accumulating "sufficient competent evidential matter" in a audit, as was not the case with
compilations and reviews.

Once sufficient competent evidential matter has been developed, the Standards
of Reporting become applicable. These include the following:

1. The report shall state whether the financial statements are presented in accor-
    dance with generally accepted accounting principles.
3. The report shall identify those circumstances in which such principles have not
    been consistently observed in the current period in relation to the preceding period.
3. Informative disclosures in the financial statements are to be regarded as reason-
    ably adequate unless otherwise stated in the report.
4. The report shall either contain an expression of opinion regarding the financial
    statements, taken as a whole, or an assertion to the effect that an opinion cannot
    be expressed. When an overall opinion cannot be expressed, the reasons therefor
    should be stated. In all cases where an auditor's name is associated with finan-
    cial statements, the report should contain a clear-cut indication of the character
    of the auditor's work, if any, and the degree of responsibility the auditor is tak-
    ing.[15]

Various Forms of Audit Reports

An example of the standard unqualified audit report is provided in Exhibit 13.7.
Departures from the standard unqualified audit report or opinion shown in Exhibit
13.7 include the addition of explanatory information, and qualified opinions, adverse
opinions, and disclaimers of opinion.

Exhibit 13.7   Standard Unqualified Audit Report

We have audited the accompanying balance sheets of XYZ Company as of December 31, 19— and 19—, and the related statements of income, retained earnings, and cash flows for the years then ended. These financial statements are the responsibility of the company's management. Our responsibility is to express an opinion on these financial statements based on our audits.

We conducted our audits in accordance with generally accepted auditing standards. Those standards require that we plan and perform the audit to obtain reasonable assurance about whether the financial statements are free of material misstatement. An audit includes examining, on a test basis, evidence supporting the amounts and disclosures in the financial statements. An audit also includes assessing the accounting principles used and significant estimates made by management, as well as evaluating the overall financial statement presentation. We believe that our audits provide a reasonable basis for our opinion.

In our opinion, the financial statements referred to above present fairly, in all material respects, the financial position of XYZ Company as of December 31, 19— and 19—, and the results of its operations and its cash flows for the years then ended in conformity with generally accepted accounting principles.

Source: *Codification of Statements on Auditing Standards* (1995), AU section 508.08.

1.   *Explanatory language added to the auditor's standard report.* Explanatory language, generally in the form of an added paragraph, may be required for a variety of reasons. The addition of such explanatory language does not change the unqualified character of the auditor's report. The following are selected examples of circumstances that may require explanatory language:

(a)   There has been a change in accounting principles or the method of their application.

(b)   The auditor's opinion is based in part on the report of another auditor.

(c)   The financial statements are affected by uncertainties concerning future events, the outcome of which cannot be reasonably estimated at the date of the auditor's report.

(d)   The auditor may add an explanatory paragraph to emphasize a matter regarding the financial statements.[16]

The most common case that calls for adding explanatory language is accounting changes. Information from the annual survey conducted by the American Institute of Certified Public Accountants disclosed 829 references to a lack of consistency in 1993 from the audit reports of 417 companies.[17] This very high number reflects the several important new accounting standards issued in recent years: Statements of Financial Accounting Standards (SFAS) Nos. 106, 109, 112, and 115. An example of an explanatory paragraph prompted by accounting changes made by Norfolk Southern Corp. follows:

As discussed in note 1, the company changed its methods of accounting in 1993 by adopting the provisions of the Financial Accounting Standards Board's Statement 109, Accounting for Income Taxes; Statement 106, Employers' Accounting for Postretirement Benefits Other Than Pensions; and Statement 112, Employers' Accounting for Postemployment Benefits.[18]

Information on the nature and number of cases involving the addition of explanatory language because of the existence of uncertainties is provided in Exhibit 13.8. Roughly 5% of the firms covered by the survey had audit reports that added explanatory language dealing with uncertainties. Here is an example from Terex Corp. of a short explanatory paragraph dealing with an uncertainty:

As discussed in note O to the consolidated financial statements, the company is required to make significant principal repayments during 1995 and is currently seeking to refinance its long-term obligations.[19]

Note O contained details on the maturing obligations and the company's plans for refinancing them. The addition of the explanatory paragraph and the tone of note O (it ends with the statement that "there is no assurance that the company will be able to conclude any of such financings"[20]) indicates that the auditors had some degree of uncertainty about whether the company was a going concern. However, the audit opinion remained unqualified.

The audit report of ERLY Industries, Inc., similarly remained unqualified with the addition of the following paragraph, declaring that "conditions raise substantial doubt about its [the company's] ability to continue as a going concern":

The accompanying financial statements have been prepared assuming that the company will continue as a going concern. The company has incurred substantial operating losses in each of the two years ended March 31, 1993, has a consolidated working capital deficit of approximately $44 million and has a consolidated deficiency in assets at March 31, 1993. In addition, the company is in default on certain bank debt covenants. These conditions raise substantial doubt about its ability to continue as a going concern. Management's plan is described in note 2. The

Exhibit 13.8 Audit Opinions with Explanatory Language Added Because of the Presence of Uncertainties

	1991	1992	1993
Litigation	16	18	18
Going concern	17	17	8
Other	6	7	6
Total uncertainties	39	42	32
Total companies	32	35	29

Source: *Accounting Trends and Techniques*, 48th ed. (New York: American Institute of Certified Public Accountants, 1994), p. 543.

financial statements do not include any adjustments that might result from the outcome of this uncertainty.[21]

The addition of an explanatory paragraph in situations like this is called for by the *Codification of Statements on Auditing Standards:*

> If management believes and the auditor is satisfied that it is probable that a material loss will occur, but management is unable to make a reasonable estimate of the amount or range of potential loss and thus has not made an accrual in the financial statements, the auditor should add an explanatory paragraph to his report because of the matter involving uncertainty.[22]

While the ERLY audit report is technically unqualified, the added explanatory paragraph contains information that a statement user would want to incorporate into the formation of an earnings expectation. These disclosures are relevant in efforts to avoid earnings surprises.

2. *A qualified opinion.* Opinions may be qualified in the following cases:
    (a) There is a lack of sufficient competent evidential matter, or there are restrictions on the scope of the audit that have led the auditor to conclude that she cannot express an unqualified opinion, and she has concluded not to disclaim an opinion.
    (b) The auditor believes, on the basis of the audit, that the financial statements contain a departure from generally accepted accounting principles, the effect of which is material, and she has concluded not to express an adverse opinion.[23]

When a qualified opinion is rendered, the reasons for the qualification must be outlined in an explanatory paragraph preceding the opinion paragraph of the audit report. The opinion paragraph of the report should include qualifying language, such as *except for* or *with the exception of,* plus a reference to the explanatory paragraph.

Departures from unqualified opinions are rare under current auditing standards. The annual survey of the American Institute of Certified Public Accountants found none in the 1993 statements reviewed for the 1994 edition of *Accounting Trends and Techniques* and only one the previous year. The public companies in this survey do not want to receive a qualified opinion. Therefore, they will cooperate with auditors and ensure that there are neither scope limitations nor departures from generally accepted accounting principles.

While increasingly rare, qualified opinions are not extinct. Union Bank, a California state-chartered bank and a 71% owned subsidiary of the Bank of Tokyo Ltd., received a qualified audit opinion in 1994 and in several prior years, because of a departure from generally accepted accounting principles. The auditors were Arthur Andersen LLP. The additional explanatory paragraph and modified opinion paragraph are presented in Exhibit 13.9.

Exhibit 13.9   Qualified Audit Opinion Due to a Departure from Generally Accepted Accounting Principles: Union Bank

---

As more fully described in note 2 to the financial statements, the bank has charged goodwill directly to shareholders' equity. Generally accepted accounting principles require that goodwill be recorded as an asset and amortized to expense over future periods.

In our opinion, except for the effect of the accounting treatment of goodwill as discussed in the preceding paragraph, the financial statements referred to above present fairly, in all material respects, the consolidated position of Union Bank and subsidiaries as of December 31, 1994 and 1993, and the results of their operations and their cash flows for each of the three years in the period ended December 31, 1994, in conformity with generally accepted accounting principles.

Source: Union Bank, annual report, December 1994, p. 62.

3.   *An adverse opinion.* The departure of Union Bank from generally accepted accounting principles was considered sufficiently material by the bank's auditors to require a qualified opinion but not an adverse opinion. If even more material, the departure from generally accepted accounting principles could lead to an adverse opinion. In judging materiality, consideration must be given to "the significance of the item to a particular entity (for example, inventories to a manufacturing company), the pervasiveness of the misstatement . . . and the effect of the misstatement on the financial statements taken as a whole."[24]

An adverse opinion is rendered when an auditor has completed an audit and reached the conclusion that the statements do not present fairly the financial position or the results of operations or cash flows in accordance with generally accepted accounting principles. When an adverse opinion is rendered, the auditor adds two additional paragraphs to the standard audit report: a paragraph containing all the substantive reasons for the adverse opinion, and a paragraph describing the principal effects on financial position, results of operations, and cash flows, if practicable.[25] Finally, the opinion paragraph would be modified to read as follows:

In our opinion, because of the effects of the matters discussed in the preceding paragraphs, the financial statements referred to above do not present fairly, in conformity with generally accepted accounting principles, the financial position of XYZ Company or the results of operations or its cash flow for the years then ended.[26]

4.   *A disclaimer of opinion.* "A disclaimer of opinion states that the auditor does not express an opinion on the financial statements."[27] The basis for a disclaimer is an audit whose scope is not sufficient to provide the basis for the expression of an opinion. When disclaiming an opinion, the auditor abides by the following:

(a)   States in a separate paragraph why the audit did not comply with generally accepted auditing standards.

(b)   Does not identify procedures that were followed nor include the scope paragraph of the auditor's standard report.

(c) Discloses any other reservations regarding fair presentation or conformity with generally accepted accounting principles.[28]

An example of a disclaimer of opinion is provided in Exhibit 13.10. Only the paragraph describing the nature of the scope limitation and the disclaimer paragraph are included. Recall from (b) in the preceding list that the scope paragraph of the standard audit report would not be included when a disclaimer is rendered. Omission of the scope paragraph is designed to ensure that a recitation of the audit's scope does not "overshadow the disclaimer."[29]

The recent effort by Price Waterhouse to audit records of the U.S. House of Representatives provides a prominent example of a disclaimer of opinion due to scope limitations. Information on the audit published by *The Wall Street Journal* suggests that the absence of records and an effective internal control structure represented the key scope limitations that led to a disclaimer.[30] Examples included the following:

- There was no system for tracking the types of assets under lease or the terms and costs associated with lease agreements.
- Lack of information about equipment the House owned made it difficult to detect the loss or theft of equipment.
- Weaknesses in the House's computer security meant that unauthorized individuals could have accessed financial applications and made unauthorized changes.
- Clerks in the Office of Finance had the capability of changing the vendor name on a payment about to be made, so that the payment could have gone to whomever they chose.

AUDITORS AND FRAUDULENT FINANCIAL REPORTING

As noted at the beginning of this chapter, fraudulent financial reporting is a potentially significant source of earnings surprises. The activities of outside accountants

Exhibit 13.10   Disclaimer of an Audit Opinion Due to Scope Limitations

The company did not make a count of its physical inventory in 19— or 19—, stated in the accompanying financial statements at $_____ as of December 31, 19—, and at $_____ as of December 31, 19—. Further, evidence supporting the cost of property and equipment acquired prior to December 31, 19—, is no longer available. The company's records do not permit the application of other auditing procedures to inventories or property and equipment.

Since the company did not take physical inventories and we were not able to apply other auditing procedures to satisfy ourselves as to inventory quantities and the cost of property and equipment, the scope of our work was not sufficient to enable us to express, and we do not express, an opinion on these financial statements.

Source: *Codification of Statements on Auditing Standards* (1995), AU section 508.72.

and auditors play a key role in avoiding earnings surprises by reducing the level of information risk. Again, information risk is the probability that the financial statements distributed by the company will be materially false and misleading. The balance of this chapter focuses on the role of outside auditors in the detection of fraudulent financial statements. In the process, information is provided that should prove useful to nonauditors who evaluate the likelihood that financial statements may misrepresent the financial performance or position of firms.

The Nature and Incidence of Fraudulent Financial Reporting

Fraudulent financial reporting has been defined in the *Report of the National Commission on Fraudulent Financial Reporting* as "intentional or reckless conduct, whether act or omission, that results in materially misleading financial statements."[31] The report did not focus on other types of potentially fraudulent behavior, such as embezzlement, violation of environmental or product safety regulations, and tax fraud, because the commission did not believe that such acts would "necessarily cause the financial statements to be materially inaccurate."[32]

These views of the commission are supported by a fraud survey conducted by KPMG Peat Marwick. Of the 12 individual types of fraudulent acts that resulted in losses, false financial statements was ranked third by average loss per company. However, if the category of patent infringement, for which there were only two instances reported, is excluded, then false financial statements tied for the top spot with credit card fraud. The average loss suffered from false financial statements was $1.3 million per reporting company. The average loss per reporting company for the other nine types of fraud was $310,000.[33]

Auditing Standards and Auditors' Responsibility for Detecting Fraudulent Financial Reporting

Guidance for auditors relative to the responsibility to detect fraudulent financial reporting is found principally in Statement of Auditing Standards No. 53, "The Auditor's Responsibility to Detect and Report Errors and Irregularities" (April 1988). As the title suggests, the scope of this statement is broader than fraudulent financial reporting. However, errors can also lead to earnings surprises and are therefore of interest. Further, a consideration of the nature of errors sharpens the understanding of fraudulent behavior.

Errors and Irregularities, and Statement No. 53

Errors are the result of *unintentional* misstatements or omissions. Examples could include incorrect accounting estimates resulting from oversight or misinterpretation of facts, and mistakes in the application of accounting principles relating to amount, classification, manner of presentation, or disclosure.[34] Irregularities, as described in

Statement No. 53 are *"intentional* misstatements or omissions of amounts or disclosures in financial statements."[35] Irregularities, according to Statement No. 53, include fraudulent financial reporting as well as misappropriations of assets or defalcations.

Examples of irregularities that could be considered fraudulent financial reporting include the following:

- Manipulation, falsification, or alteration of accounting records or supporting documents from which financial statements are prepared
- Misrepresentation or intentional omission of events, transactions, or other significant information
- Intentional misapplication of accounting principles relating to amounts, classification, manner of presentation, or disclosure.[36]

Auditors' Responsibility to Detect Errors and Fraudulent Financial Reporting

The basic responsibility of the auditor to detect errors and fraudulent financial reporting, called irregularities in Statement No. 53, is found in the following:

> The auditor should assess the risk that errors and irregularities may cause the financial statements to contain a material misstatement. Based on that assessment, the auditor should design the audit to provide reasonable assurance of detecting errors and irregularities that are material to the financial statements.[37]

Statement No. 53 acknowledges that irregularities involving forgery and collusion may not be discovered by a properly designed and executed audit.[38] Moreover, it is important for statement users to note that the standard to which the auditor is held is one of reasonable assurance. Audits that would rise much above this threshold would quickly become uneconomic: the incremental reduction in information risk would not justify the added auditing costs. Audits can only provide reasonable assurance; they cannot guarantee that all material errors or fraudulent financial reporting will be discovered.

Assessing Audit Risk and the Likelihood of Material Misstatements

Auditors must assess the risk that the financial statements will contain material misstatements as part of their audit planning. Statement No. 53 provides the auditor with guidance for this risk assessment, guidance that is equally useful for statement users who are interested in assessing the likelihood of earnings surprises. Useful risk assessment factors have been grouped by management, operating and industry, and engagement characteristics (see Exhibit 13.11). In using these factors, the auditor is cautioned that "the factors . . . should be considered in combination to make an overall judgment; the presence of some factors in isolation would not necessarily indicate increased risk."[39]

Exhibit 13.11   Characteristics to Be Considered in the Assessment of Audit Risk

Management Characteristics
  1. Management operating and financing decisions are dominated by a single person.
  2. Management's attitude toward financial reporting is unduly aggressive.
  3. Management (particularly senior accounting personnel) turnover is high.
  4. Management places undue emphasis on meeting earnings projections.
  5. Management's reputation in the business community is poor.

Operating and Industry Characteristics
  1. Profitability of entity relative to its industry is inadequate or inconsistent.
  2. Sensitivity of operating results to economic factors (inflation, interest rates, unemployment) is high.
  3. Rate of change in entity's industry is rapid.
  4. Direction of change in the entity's industry is declining, with many business failures.
  5. Organization is decentralized without adequate monitoring.
  6. Internal or external matters that raise substantial doubt about the entity's ability to continue as a going concern are present.

Engagement Characteristics
  1. Many contentious or difficult accounting issues are present.
  2. Significant difficult-to-audit transactions or balances are present.
  3. Significant and unusual related party transactions not in the ordinary course of business are present.
  4. Nature, cause (if known), or amount of known and likely misstatements detected in the audit of prior period's financial statements is significant.
  5. It is a new client with no prior audit history, or sufficient information is not available from the predecessor auditor.

Source: *Codification of Statements on Auditing Standards* (1995), AU section 316.10.

In addition, the Accounting Standards Division of the American Institute of Certified Public Accountants issues periodic *Audit Risk Alerts,* which contain information dealing with the assessment of the risk of material misstatement. The 1994 issue of *Audit Risk Alerts* provided the guidance listed in Exhibit 13.12. The *Audit Risk Alert* also identified incentives and opportunities that might predispose management to fraudulent financial reporting. Examples of incentives included the following:

• A substantial portion of executives' compensation depends on operating results.
• The entity is being put up for sale.
• Management is undertaking an aggressive acquisition program using the entity's stock.
• There are indications that the entity will fall short of meeting its own and securities analysts' forecasts of earnings.[40]

Exhibit 13.12   Indicators of the Risk of Materially Misleading Financial Statements

1. Recent significant sales of the entity's stock by insiders.
2. Reported allegations of management impropriety by employees.
3. Recent changes in accounting principles that favorably affect reported earnings.
4. Sales of real estate with complex or unusual terms.
5. Unusually large increases in year-end sales to a single or a few customers.
6. Dramatic increases in sales and receivables along with increases in gross profit margins totally inconsistent with past experience or industry averages.
7. Certain sales of merchandise that are billed to customers prior to delivery and held by the seller (bill-and-hold transactions).
8. Significant and unexpected increases in inventories (particularly, in-transit inventories).
9. Judgmental allowances (for example, bad debt, inventory obsolescence, or product warranty) consistently estimated at or near the low end of reasonableness.
10. Delays in producing documents requested by the auditor.
11. Unusual and material related-party transactions.
12. A significant number of postclosing adjustments that increase reported income.

Source: *Audit Risk Alert—1994* (New York: American Institute of Certified Public Accountants, 1994), p. 17.

A board dominated by a chief executive, a weak control environment, a blatant disregard of auditors' recommendations to improve controls, and weak accounting and financial personnel were examples provided in the *Audit Risk Alert* of conditions that provide the opportunity for fraudulent financial reporting. Further extensive guidance on assessing the risk of fraudulent financial reporting can be found in Appendix F, "Good Practice Guidelines for Assessing the Risk of Fraudulent Financial Reporting," of the *Report of the National Commission on Fraudulent Financial Reporting*.[41]

This chapter opened by posing the question, "Where were the auditors?" The discussion about the nature of audits makes it clear that auditors have a responsibility to assess the risk of financial fraud or irregularities by, among other things, determining if conducive conditions, motivation, and attitude are present. If these factors are present, the audit program must be modified to deal with these circumstances. Auditors not doing this raise the likelihood that fraudulent financial reporting will go undetected. The section that follows provides evidence on auditors' detection of fraudulent financial reporting.

Evidence on Auditors' Detection of Fraudulent Financial Reporting

Recent auditing research has shed light on auditors' detection of material irregularities in financial statements—their nature, frequency, and detectability. Especially useful results are found in a work by Loebbecke, Eining, and Willingham.[42]

Assessing the Risk of Material Management Fraud

The research results reported by Loebbecke, Eining, and Willingham were obtained through an assessment model of the risk of material management fraud, summarized in Exhibit 13.13. This model suggests that the likelihood of management fraud is zero if conducive conditions, motivation, and attitudes are not present. Loebbecke and Willingham tested the model against 51 management fraud cases that had been the subjects of Securities and Exchange Commission Accounting and Auditing Enforcement Releases.[43] They concluded that all three components of the model—conditions, motivation, and attitudes—were present in 71% of the 51 management fraud cases.[44]

The Model and the Survey Results

Continued development of the assessment model took the form of a survey of 277 audit partners of KPMG Peat Marwick. Of the 277 partners, 165 had been on audit engagements where material irregularities were encountered; the other 112 had had no experience with material irregularities. Of the 165 partners included in the survey, 121 responded.

The 121 respondents reported a total of 354 irregularities. Of these, 55% were cases of management fraud and 45% were cases of defalcation. Eighty percent of the management fraud cases were considered material to the financial statements, compared with 36% for the defalcations. These results are consistent with the KPMG

Exhibit 13.13 Assessment of the Risk of Material Management Fraud: Assessment Model Approach

$P(MI) = f(C, M, A)$

where

MI	=	material irregularities
C	=	degree to which conditions are such that a material management fraud could be committed
M	=	degree to which the person or persons in positions of authority and responsibility in the entity have a reason and motivation to commit fraud
A	=	degree to which the person or persons in positions of authority and responsibility in the entity have an attitude or set of ethical values such that they would allow themselves (or even seek) to commit fraud;

and where

If C or M or A = 0, then $P(MI) = 0$

Source: J. K. Loebbecke, M. M. Eining, and J. J. Willingham, "Auditors' Experience with Material Irregularities: Frequency, Nature, and Detectability," *Auditing: A Journal of Practice and Theory,* Fall 1989, p. 5.

Peat Marwick fraud survey results discussed earlier. The cases of management fraud were most prevalent in the manufacturing, transportation, and high-technology and communications companies. A breakdown of the irregularities by nature of deceptive action is provided in Exhibit 13.14.

The averages per occurrence shown in the exhibit indicate that the typical irregularity involves the use of more than a single deceptive action. The first eight items in Exhibit 13.14 would appear to fit the standard definition of fraudulent financial reporting, and the remaining three represent defalcations. Other detail on the survey revealed that management fraud was typically committed by top management and defalcations by persons at all levels in the organization.[45]

Substantive tests of details were the most effective type of audit procedure in revealing irregularities, followed by analytical tests of specific accounts, and the study and evaluation of internal control.

The 121 survey respondents were also asked for more detailed information about

Exhibit 13.14   Classification of Irregularities by Deceptive Action

	All Respondents		Defalcations		Management Fraud	
	No.	% of 354	No.	% of 158	No.	% of 196
1. Assets overvalued or incorrectly valued	168	47.7%	55	35.3%	113	57.7%
2. Revenue or other credits recognized improperly	73	20.7	16	10.3	57	29.1
3. Specious accounting judgments made	59	16.8	11	7.1	48	24.5
4. Transactions/events not recorded	122	34.7	61	39.1	61	31.1
5. Transactions in the wrong period	38	10.8	5	3.2	33	16.8
6. Expenses recorded incorrectly	86	24.4	44	28.2	42	21.4
7. Disclosures omitted or misleading	47	13.4	6	3.8	41	20.9
8. Liabilities understated	1	.3	1	.6	0	0
9. Misappropriation of funds	17	4.8	16	10.1	1	.5
10. Theft of cash receipts	3	.8	3	1.9	0	0
11. Falsified and altered records	10	2.8	5	3.2	5	2.6
Total	624		223		401	
Average per occurrence	1.8		1.4		2.0	

Source: J. K. Loebbecke, M. M. Eining, and J. J. Willingham, "Auditors' Experience with Material Irregularities: Frequency, Nature, and Detectability," *Auditing: A Journal of Practice and Theory,* Fall 1989, p. 11.

Note: Numbers and percentages are based on the number of irregularities. These totaled 354. The actions taken by perpetrators in connection with the irregularities totaled 624.

one of the irregularities they encountered. Respondents were asked to provide information in several forms on the indicators ("red flags") of the irregularities. A compressed version of the substantial amount of detail in the Loebbecke, Eining, and Willingham study is provided in Exhibit 13.15. Only the survey results relating to management fraud are presented there because they are far more likely than defalcations to have a material impact on the financial statements and to contribute to earnings surprises. All items are simply listed by their relative frequency; an additional classification system used by Loebbecke, Eining, and Willingham (primary, secondary, and tertiary) is not employed. Readers are referred to the original study for more detail.

SUMMARY

Outside accountants and auditors contribute to the avoidance of earnings surprises by reducing information risk. The reduction of information risk is greatest in the case of audits and lowest in the case of compilations.

Most audit reports as such are not very informative because, in the vast majority of cases, they are simply in the standard unqualified format. However, special atten-

Exhibit 13.15 Indicators of Management Fraud by Assessment Model Component

	Frequency
I. Conditions Allowing the Commission of an Irregularity	
1. Management operating and financial decisions are dominated by a single person or a few persons who generally act in concert.	74
2. The company has a weak control environment.	47
3. The company has a significant number of difficult-to-audit transactions.	31
4. The company is in a period of rapid growth.	26
5. There are inadequacies in the company's accounting system.	25
6. There are accounts that are material to the financial statements for which extensive judgment is involved in determining their balances.	22
7. The company has entered into a significant transaction or transactions with one or more related parties.	17
8. The company has entered into one or an aggregation of transactions that have a material effect on the financial statements.	16
9. Complex calculations are required for significant accounts in the financial statements.	11
10. A conflict of interest exists within the company and/or its personnel.	11
11. The company has significant assets subject to misappropriation.	10
12. The company has inexperienced management.	10
13. Organization is decentralized without adequate monitoring.	9
14. The client is a new client with no prior audit history, or sufficient information is not available from predecessor auditor.	6
15. Management turnover is high.	5
16. Other.	7

Exhibit 13.15 *(continued)*

	Frequency
II. Motivation for the Commission of an Irregularity	
1. Management places undue emphasis on meeting earnings projections.	32
2. Profitability relative to the industry is inadequate or inconsistent.	31
3. There are adverse conditions in the client's industry.	27
4. The company is in a period of rapid growth.	26
5. The client's industry is declining, with many business failures.	20
6. The company is subject to significant contractual commitments.	18
7. The rate of change in the client's industry is rapid.	17
8. Operating results are highly sensitive to economic factors.	17
9. The company is having solvency problems.	17
10. Management personnel perceive their job is threatened by poor performance.	10
11. Compensation arrangements are based on recorded performance.	9
12. The company is confronted with adverse legal circumstances.	8
13. Company holdings represent a significant portion of management's personal wealth.	8
14. Management personnel display a strong need for increased personal wealth.	4
15. The company has a planned public offering or other action to raise capital.	4
16. Management displays a propensity to take undue risks.	4
17. Other.	11
III. Attitudes Allowing the Commission of an Irregularity	
1. The company has a weak control environment.	47
2. Management places undue emphasis on meeting earnings projections	32
3. Management displays an overly aggressive attitude toward financial reporting.	29
4. Management has lied to the auditor or has been overly evasive.	28
5. The auditor's experience with management indicates a degree of dishonesty.	23
6. Management has engaged in frequent disputes with the auditors.	14
7. Client personnel exhibit strong personality anomalies.	9
8. The client places undue pressure on the auditors.	8
9. Client displays significant disrespect for regulatory bodies.	8
10. Management's reputation in the business community is poor.	6
11. Management turnover is high.	5
12. The client has engaged in opinion shopping.	5
13. Top management is considered to be highly unreasonable.	5
14. Client management displays a significant lack of moral fiber.	5
15. Management displays a propensity to take undue risks.	4
16. Other.	9

Source: J. K. Loebbecke, M. M. Eining, and J. J. Willingham, "Auditors' Experience with Material Irregularities: Frequency, Nature, and Detectability," *Auditing: A Journal of Practice and Theory,* Fall 1989, p. 15–20.

tion should be given to any audit report with deviations from this format. Even here, though, most cases involving deviations from the standard format—usually taking the form of an additional explanatory paragraph—will simply report on changes in accounting policy. Most such changes involve mandatory adoptions of new Statements of Financial Accounting Standards issued by the Financial Accounting Standards Board. The effect of such changes is always thoroughly disclosed and discussed in several different locations in audited financial statements.

Audit reports including separate paragraphs dealing with significant uncertainties, especially when the expression "substantial doubt" is employed, should be given special attention. In particular, notes referred to in these reports should be read and carefully considered. Qualified and adverse opinions are a rarity.

A variety of information has been distilled and discussed in this chapter on (1) indicators of the risk of materially misleading financial statements, (2) characteristics considered in the assessment of audit risk, (3) the classification of irregularities by deceptive action, and (4) indicators of fraudulent financial reporting. This is provided in the hope that it will be a useful addition to the tools provided in earlier chapters for attempting to avoid earnings surprises.

Finally, it should be clear that users of financial statements cannot assume the absence of fraudulent financial reporting simply because outside auditors have rendered a clean audit report. The coexistence of fraudulent financial reporting and unqualified audit reports may represent a failure on the part of the auditor. However, audits are designed, and priced, to provide only reasonable assurance and are not guarantees. As a result, serious users of financial statements must make some degree of independent effort to gauge the likelihood that financial statements will misrepresent the financial performance and position of firms. This is an essential step in the total process of avoiding earnings surprises.

ENDNOTES

1. J. C. Robertson, *Auditing* (Homewood, Ill.: Richard D. Irwin, 1993), p. 12.
2. *Codification of Statements on Standards for Accounting and Review Services* (New York: American Institute of Certified Public Accountants, 1995), AR section 100.04.
3. Ibid., AR section 100.09-13.
4. Ibid., AR section 100.19-21.
5. Ibid., AR section 100.39-40.
6. Ibid., AR section 100.24.
7. *Codification of Statements on Auditing Standards* (New York: American Institute of Certified Public Accountants, 1995), AU section 329.05.
8. Ibid., AU section 329.05.
9. Ibid., AR section 100.32.
10. *Codification of Statements on Standards for Accounting and Review Services*, AR section 100.35.
11. Ibid., AR section 100.39.
12. Ibid., AR section 100.40.

13. L. F. Konrath, *Auditing Concepts and Applications,* 2d ed. (St. Paul, Minn.: West Publishing, 1993), p. 665.
14. *Codification of Statements on Auditing Standards,* AU section 150.02.
15. Ibid., AU sections 150.02 and 504.01.
16. Ibid., AU section 508.11.
17. *Accounting Trends and Techniques,* 48th ed. (New York: American Institute of Certified Public Accountants, 1994), p. 549.
18. Norfolk Southern Corp., annual report, December 1993, p. 55.
19. Terex Corp., Form 10-K annual report to the Securities and Exchange Commission, December 1994, p. F-2.
20. Ibid., p. F-29.
21. *Accounting Trends and Techniques,* p. 566 (quoting from the March 31, 1993, annual report of ERLY Industries, Inc.).
22. *Codification of Statements on Auditing Standards,* AU section 508.25. A new auditing standard, SAS No. 79, *Amendment to SAS No. 58, Reports on Audited Financial Statements* (February 1996), may reduce the frequency with which uncertainty related explanatory paragraphs appear.
23. Ibid., AU section 508.38.
24. *Codification of Statements of Auditing Standards*, AU section 508.50.
25. Ibid., AU section 508.68.
26. Ibid., AU section 508.69.
27. Ibid., AU section 508.70.
28. Ibid., AU section 508.71.
29. Ibid., AU section 508.71.
30. "Mismanager's Journal," *The Wall Street Journal,* July 20, 1995, p. A12.
31. *Report of the National Commission on Fraudulent Financial Reporting* (October 1987), p. 2.
32. Ibid., p. 2.
33. *Fraud Survey Results 1993* (New York: KPMG Peat Marwick, 1993), pp. 8–9.
34. *Codification of Auditing Standards,* AU section 316.02.
35. Ibid., AU section 316.03.
36. Ibid., AU section 316.03.
37. Ibid., AU section 316.05.
38. Ibid., AU section 316.07.
39. Ibid., AU section 316.10.
40. Ibid., p. 16.
41. *Report of the National Commission on Fraudulent Financial Reporting,* pp. 153–163.
42. J. K. Loebbecke, M. M. Eining, and J. J. Willingham, "Auditors' Experience with Material Irregularities: Frequency, Nature, and Detectability," *Auditing: A Journal of Practice and Theory,* Fall 1989, pp. 1–28.
43. J. K. Loebbecke and J. J. Willingham, "Review of SEC Accounting and Auditing Enforcement Releases." Unpublished working paper (1988).
44. "Auditors' Experience with Material Irregularities," p. 5.
45. Ibid., p. 11.

Appendix

Topical Accounting Guides

Deriving maximum benefit from the discussions in this book is aided by a solid background in the fundamentals of financial accounting. For some, this will have been acquired in a formal academic setting, and for others through on-the-job experience. This appendix provides concise reviews of a number of relevant topics that are at a somewhat advanced level. The objective of these guides is to provide a quick reference source for those who need additional grounding in the selected topical areas and to ensure the accessibility of the material in this book.

LONG-TERM CONTRACT REPORTING

It is common to think that long-term contract reporting is relevant only to construction contractors. However, an annual survey of financial statements conducted by the American Institute of Certified Public Accountants (AICPA) reveals that each year about 125 companies, out of the 600 surveyed, disclose an accounting policy used to account for long-term contracts. Long-term contract reporting extends well beyond the construction industry to industries such as aerospace, consulting, ship repair, and ship building. The 1993 survey by the AICPA revealed 91 firms using the percentage-of-completion method (POC), 27 the units-of-delivery method, and 4 the completed-contract (CC) method to account for long-term contracts.[1] We focus here on outlining the operation of the POC method and contrasting its results with the results obtained under CC.

The CC method is used infrequently, it simply involves booking profit on contracts only upon completion. The units-of-delivery method is similar to POC and is described in the accounting policy note of Stewart & Stevenson Services, Inc., as follows: "Substantially all of the revenues of the Tactical Vehicle Systems segment are recognized under the units-of-delivery method, whereby sales and estimated average cost of the units to be produced . . . are recognized as units are substantially completed."[2]

The requirements of generally accepted accounting principles (GAAP) for contract reporting are principally found in Statement of Position 81-1 of AICPA.[3] The expectation is that the POC method will be used if reasonably dependable estimates can be made of progress toward completion, contract revenues, and contract costs. In addition, the following two conditions must be satisfied: (1) the contract clearly specifies the rights and obligations of the parties, and (2) both parties can be expected to satisfy their obligations.

Contract-Reporting Terminology

A number of terms, largely unique to contract reporting, are defined here:

- *Contracts-in-process.* A current asset, a form of receivable, where contract costs and estimated profits are accumulated on contracts-in-process. In the case of the completed contract method, the balance includes only contract costs and not estimated profits.
- *Billings.* A contra account deducted from contracts-in-process where amounts billed customers on contracts-in-process are accumulated until contract completion.
- *Retainage.* That portion of contract receivables that is generally not collectible until contract completion and acceptance. This entire balance is typically included in current assets even though collection in some cases may not occur for a number of years.
- *Unbilled receivables.* The excess of contracts-in-process (costs plus estimated earnings) over billings. This balance sheet disclosure is also referred to as cost plus estimated earnings in excess of billings. Under the completed-contract method, this balance is simply referred to as cost in excess of billings.
- *Unearned revenue or advance billings.* The excess of billings over contracts-in-process. This balance sheet disclosure is also referred to as billings in excess of cost plus estimated earnings.
- *Estimated earnings.*

$$\frac{\text{Cumulative contract costs}}{\text{Estimated total contract costs}} \times \begin{array}{c} \text{Estimated total} \\ \text{contract profit} \end{array} - \begin{array}{c} \text{Profit recognized} \\ \text{in previous periods} \end{array}$$

If total profit recognized in previous periods exceeds estimated total contract profit, then the result of the computation will be a loss for the current period. In this case, the overall contract is profitable, but earnings recognized to date have simply been excessive. This could be the result of the combination of a fixed-price contract and an unexpected increase in costs. This loss is absorbed in the current period because it is considered to be the result of a change in an estimate. However, if total contract costs, both incurred to date and yet to be incurred, plus estimated earnings recognized to date exceed the total contract price, then there will be a loss over the balance of the contract period. This loss must also be recognized currently.

An Illustration of Contract Reporting

Reporting a contract under both the POC and CC methods is illustrated in Exhibit A.1. This example employs the cost-to-cost method of estimating stage of completion. That is, stage of completion is computed as the ratio of (1) costs incurred to date, to (2) the most recent estimate of total costs upon completion of the project. Some firms use other input-related measures or measures of output. For example, the number of labor hours, an input measure, is often used in ship-repair contracts. Miles of highway laid is an example of an output measure of progress.

A frequent concern with the POC method is that overly optimistic projections of contract costs and performance will result in recognizing excessive profits in early periods that result in significantly reduced profits, or even losses, in later periods. For example, assume that costs to complete the contract in Exhibit A.1 turn out to be $35,000 instead of the expected amount of $25,000. This means that the estimated stage of completion at the end of year 1 was overstated. Instead of the contract's

Exhibit A.1   Contract Reporting under the Percentage-of-Completion and Completed-Contract Methods

Data: A two-year, $80,000 contract. Construction costs: $60,000 ($35,000 in year 1 and $25,000 in year 2). At the end of year 1, the estimated cost to complete is $25,000. There were no cost overruns. Thus, the contract is 35/60 complete at the end of year 1 and 60/60 complete at the end of year 2. Billings: $45,000 in year 1 and $35,000 in year 2. Collections: $40,000 in years 1 and 2.

	Percentage of Completion		Completed Contract	
	Year 1	Year 2	Year 1	Year 2
Income statement				
Revenue	$46,667[a]	$33,333[a]	–	$80,000
Construction expense	35,000[b]	25,000[b]	–	60,000
Gross profit	$11,667[c]	$ 8,333[c]	–	$20,000
Balance sheet (end-of-year)				
Accounts receivable	$5,000[d]		$5,000[d]	
Costs plus estimated earnings in excess of billings	1,667[e]		–	
Billings in excess of contracts-in-process	–		10,000[f]	

[a] 35/60 × $80,000 = $46,667; and 60/60 × $80,000 – $46,667 = $33,333.
[b] Contract costs incurred during the year.
[c] 35/60 × ($80,000 – $60,000) = $11,667; and 60/60 × ($20,000) – $11,667 = $8,333.
[d] $45,000 – $40,000 (billings minus collections) = $5,000.
[e] $46,667 – $45,000 (cost plus estimated earnings in excess of billings) = $1,667.
[f] $45,000 – $35,000 (billings minus costs incurred) = $10,000.

being 35/60 complete, it was only 35/70 complete. The expectation at the end of year 1 was that profits of 25/60 × $20,000, or $8,333, would be reported in year 2. Instead, a loss of $1,667 [$33,333 − $35,000] would be recognized. The actual year 2 costs of $35,000 are charged against the remaining contract revenue of $33,333 recognized in year 2.

Under POC, the balance sheet at the end of year 1 would include, as current assets, both the $5,000 account receivable and the $1,667 balance of contracts-in-process in excess of billings. Recall that the contracts-in-process balance is made up of $35,000 of contract costs plus the $11,667 of gross profit recognized in year 1. Deducting the billings of $45,000 yields the $1,667 balance that would appear on the balance sheet. In the typical case, a firm will have multiple contracts-in-process, and some will be underbilled (contracts-in-process exceeds billings to date) and others will be overbilled (billings to date exceed contracts-in-process). The net balance of underbilled contracts would be included in current assets, and the net balance of overbilled contracts would be included in current liabilities.

The reliability of the POC method depends upon the capacity of firms to estimate and control contract costs effectively. The recognition of profits as progress is made on the contract is consistent with the principle of accrual accounting. Under the CC method, all profit is simply recorded in the period in which the contract is completed. Financial statements under the CC method are generally of far less value in judging the periodic financial performance of firms.

Contract-Reporting Uncertainties

The multiyear nature of many contracts creates a higher level of uncertainty than is typical for most revenue recognition circumstances. Companies attempt to deal with this heightened uncertainty by the manner in which they implement the POC method.

Delayed Start of POC

For example, in some cases, POC is implemented with a delayed start. That is, estimated earnings are recognized only after the project achieves a sufficient level of progress. Avondale Industries, Inc., a firm involved with marine construction and repair, does not start recognition of POC profits until "progress reaches a point where contract performance is sufficient to estimate final results with reasonable accuracy."[4]

Recognition of Disputed Amounts

It is common for final amounts due under long-term contracts to be disputed. In such cases, there are differences of opinion regarding the degree of certainty of eventual success required to justify recognition of the disputed amounts as revenue. Practice varies. Blount, Inc., reported that it recognizes contract revenue for claims against owners resulting, for example, from changes or delays deemed to be the responsibility of the owners and not Blount, only when the amounts are awarded or resolved.[5] Alternatively, Avondale Industries recognizes disputed amounts as revenue when collection is "probable."[6]

INVENTORY-REPORTING ALTERNATIVES

The treatment of inventory accounts by manufacturing and retailing companies can have a major effect on both earnings and financial position. There is considerable diversity in inventory methods currently in use. However, the four principle methods are the following:

- *First in, first out (FIFO).* Units sold are costed at the earliest costs of goods available. The most recent inventory costs remain in inventory.
- *Last in, first out (LIFO).* Units sold are costed at the latest costs of goods available. The earliest inventory costs remain in inventory.
- *Weighted average.* Units sold are costed at the average costs of goods available. The average inventory costs remain in inventory.
- *Specific identification.* Records are kept of actual costs for each unit in stock. Units sold are costed at these amounts, leaving specific costs in inventory.

Information on the relative use of each of these methods is provided in Exhibit A.2 from the annual financial statement survey conducted by the AICPA. The data in the exhibit are based upon a survey of 600 companies. The total inventory methods employed exceed 600 each year because many firms employ more than one inventory method. For example, only 17 of the 348 firms disclosing the use of LIFO employed it for all their inventories. Where the industry sample sizes are large enough to be meaningful, some of the most significant users of LIFO were found in the paper products, petroleum, rubber products, grocery stores, and machinery, equipment, and supplies industries. Less frequent users were found

Exhibit A.2 Inventory Cost Determination

	No. of Companies			
	1990	1991	1992	1993
First in, first out (FIFO)	411	421	415	417
Last in, first out (LIFO)	366	361	358	348
Average cost	195	200	193	189
Other	44	50	45	42

Source: *Accounting Trends and Techniques* (Jersey City, N.J.: American Institute of Certified Public Accountants, 1994), p. 160.

in industries such as electronic equipment, controls, instruments, medical equipment, drugs, and cosmetics.

Exhibit A.2 reveals that LIFO and FIFO are the most popular inventory accounting methods. A comparison of these two methods provides the focus for this discussion. In deciding between the use of LIFO and FIFO, a number of factors are generally considered:

- *Matching of costs and revenue.* LIFO is generally seen to provide the superior matching of costs with revenue in that it matches the most recent inventory costs against revenue. This is seen to be especially important in periods when inventory replacement prices are rising.
- *Tax considerations.* LIFO yields a higher cost of sales in periods of rising prices, reducing taxable earnings and tax payments, and increasing cash flow.
- *Income smoothing.* By matching current costs with revenue, LIFO generally produces a smoother earnings stream than FIFO. This does, however, assume the absence of LIFO liquidations.
- *LIFO liquidations.* LIFO liquidations result when inventory quantities are reduced and earlier, typically lower, costs are charged to cost of sales, resulting in increased earnings.
- *Inventory valuation.* LIFO tends to undervalue inventory, in relation to current replacement cost, after a lengthy inflationary period.
- *Financial statistics.* LIFO reduces working capital, increases inventory turnover (where turnover is computed by dividing cost of sales by average inventory), lowers inventory days, lowers gross profit and stockholders' equity, and increases financial leverage.

Typically, the first three factors in this list would be considered to be beneficial aspects of the use of LIFO, and the last three, neutral or negative. LIFO liquidations, discussed later, generally result in unsustainable increases in earnings. Further, when the liquidations increase taxable earnings, they result in additional cash payments for income taxes. Undervaluation of inventory could cause statement users to underestimate a firm's liquidity or the strength of its current position. Statement users, should they not give proper consideration to the effect of LIFO on financial performance and position, could misjudge the real financial strength or operating efficiency of the LIFO firm.

Application of the LIFO Method

Introductions to LIFO and FIFO typically do not address the combination of using LIFO for reporting purposes and FIFO or average cost for internal reporting and control. FIFO is often used for internal reporting purposes, and the books are adjusted to a LIFO basis at the end of each reporting period. This adjustment is usually facilitated through use of the LIFO reserve account.

Role of the LIFO Reserve

The LIFO reserve is a contra-inventory account. The account accumulates the difference between inventory valued at FIFO, which approximates current or replacement cost, and inventory valued at LIFO. For balance sheet reporting, the LIFO reserve is subtracted from the FIFO inventory to yield the LIFO inventory amount. Cost of sales based upon FIFO is adjusted for the change in the LIFO reserve during the accounting period to yield cost of sales at LIFO. The data in Exhibit A.3 illustrate the operation of the LIFO reserve.

The LIFO reserve is simply the difference in inventory valuation under LIFO versus FIFO. The beginning of the year LIFO reserve was zero because the LIFO and FIFO inventory values were the same. However, at the end of the year, inventory measured at FIFO is $3,000 versus $2,000 at LIFO. Cost of sales is $9,000 on a FIFO basis and $10,000 under LIFO. Recall that it is assumed that FIFO is used for internal reporting purposes. The adjustment of cost of sales and inventory from FIFO to LIFO is accomplished by adjusting the balance in the LIFO reserve account to its $1,000 balance at the end of reporting period. This is accomplished by an entry to increase both cost of sales and the LIFO reserve (+ denotes an account balance increase and – denotes an account balance decrease):

Account	Debit	Credit
Cost of goods sold (+)	1,000	
LIFO reserve (+)		1,000

This entry increases cost of sales from $9,000 under FIFO to $10,000 under LIFO and simultaneously adjusts the ending inventory to the correct LIFO value by adding $1,000 to the LIFO reserve. Recall that the LIFO reserve is subtracted from the FIFO inventory valuation to yield the LIFO amount:

Ending inventory at FIFO	$3,000
Less: Ending LIFO reserve	1,000
Ending inventory at LIFO	$2,000

Exhibit A.3   LIFO and FIFO Inventories and the LIFO Reserve

	FIFO Inventory	LIFO Inventory	LIFO Reserve
Beginning inventory	$ 2,000	$ 2,000	$0
Plus: Purchases	10,000	10,000	
Goods available for sale	12,000	12,000	
Less: Ending inventory	3,000	2,000	1,000
Cost of sales	$ 9,000	$10,000	

The relation between cost of sales under FIFO versus cost of sales under LIFO in this example provides a useful rule to gauge the effect of changing prices on LIFO results: increases in the LIFO reserve, caused by rising inventory costs, increase LIFO cost of sales. Decreases in the LIFO reserve, caused by falling inventory costs or declining inventory quantities, reduce LIFO cost of sales. Therefore, LIFO earnings are less than those under FIFO when the LIFO reserve increases, but LIFO earnings are greater than FIFO earnings when the LIFO reserve declines.

An example of a reduction in a LIFO reserve caused by the combination of a decline in inventory costs and a LIFO liquidation is provided by the inventory disclosures of Wyman-Gordon Co. Wyman-Gordon disclosed differences between its inventories valued at LIFO and FIFO, which approximates current replacement cost, of $33,448,000 and $41,365,000 at the end of 1993 and 1992, respectively. It identified the composition of the approximately $8 million LIFO reserve decrease during 1993 as follows:[7]

$$\text{LIFO reserve decrease of \$8 million} = \begin{cases} \text{\$5.5 million from LIFO liquidations} \\ \text{\$2.5 million from deflation} \end{cases}$$

With the LIFO liquidations, undervalued (LIFO cost below replacement value) inventory is eliminated, and the deflation (replacement values declining) narrows the difference between LIFO and FIFO valuations of the remaining inventory. Both of these conditions contribute to the reduction in the LIFO reserve.

Nature and Effect of LIFO Liquidations

As noted, a LIFO liquidation occurs when inventory quantities are reduced and earlier, typically lower, costs are included in cost of sales. Financial statement disclosures, at least for public companies, include the effect of LIFO liquidations on earnings.[8] The effect of a liquidation on pre-tax results is the difference between the actual cost of sales and the amount that would have resulted had the reduced inventory quantities been replaced at prevailing (current) costs. The following example illustrates the isolation of the effect of a LIFO liquidation:

Cost/Quantity Data	Quantity	Cost/Unit
Beginning inventory	10	$2.00
Purchases	30	$3.00
Sold	35	

In this example, five more units were sold than were replaced during the year. Assume that the replacement cost of these additional units would have been $3. Cost of sales computed using the LIFO method is $100: $(30 \times \$3) + (5 \times \$2)$. Had the five additional units sold been replaced during the year, cost of sales would have been

$105: (35 × $3). The dollar effect of the LIFO liquidation is thus $5, increasing pre-tax earnings by $5 and after-tax earnings by $3 (assuming a 40% combined state and federal tax rate). The SEC requirement calling for disclosure of material gains from LIFO liquidations reflects the view that the LIFO liquidation benefit is nonrecurring and that statement users should know of its contribution to earnings in order to evaluate earnings properly.

The LIFO Reserve and Financial Position

In addition to disclosure of the effect of LIFO liquidations, the SEC requires disclosure of differences between the LIFO value of inventories and their replacement value. The SEC permits the use of FIFO as an approximation of replacement value. The size of the LIFO reserve, assuming that replacement value exceeds LIFO value, is a measure of additional value that is not recorded on the balance sheet. Some firms, such as Phillips Petroleum Co., make it a point to highlight this fact: "The company's short-term liquidity position at December 31, 1994, was stronger than indicated because the current costs of the inventories were approximately $427 million greater than their last in, first out (LIFO) carrying value."[9]

INTEREST CAPITALIZATION

Generally accepted accounting principles require that interest incurred be capitalized, or added to an asset's carrying value, when assets require an extended period of construction or other development before they are ready for sale or use.[10] Examples of items on which interest is commonly capitalized include

- The construction of residential housing
- The construction of new plant facilities
- Advance payments made in conjunction with the acquisition of aircraft
- Poultry raised for egg production, but only up to the point when they start laying eggs

In principle, avoidable interest, that is the amount of interest that could have been avoided if the project had not been undertaken, is the amount capitalized. This amount is assumed to be approximated by the following computation:

Capitalized interest = Average accumulated expenditures × Interest rate × Construction period

Interest capitalization ceases when the asset is ready for sale or use. Further, the amount of interest capitalized may not exceed the actual interest incurred during the period. In addition, interest capitalization is discontinued if further capitalization of interest would result in the asset's book value exceeding its net realizable value. The relevant interest rate is the actual rate incurred on money borrowed specifically to finance construction. However, as commonly occurs, if accumulated expenditures exceed such specific borrowings, then the average interest rate on all other borrowings is applied.

The logic behind the interest capitalization requirement is that assets should be recorded at their cost. Here, cost is seen to include funding costs associated with a period of construction or development. They are part of the cost required to bring the asset to a condition where it can either be offered for sale or placed in use. If the asset is sold, then the capitalized interest is included in cost of sales. Alternatively, the previously capitalized interest is included in depreciation expense if the asset is placed in use rather than sold. An illustration of the computation of capitalized interest is provided in Exhibit A.4.

The interest accrual and the interest capitalization for the example in Exhibit A.4 are recorded as follows (+ denotes an account balance increase and – denotes an account balance decrease):

Account	Debit	Credit
Interest expense (+)	146,000	
Cash (–)		146,000
Assets under development (+)	109,000	
Interest expense (–)		109,000

Exhibit A.4 Determination of Interest to Be Capitalized

Data: $1 million of average accumulated expenditures across the year. Project financed in part with $600,000 of specific borrowings at 12%. Remainder of accumulated expenditures of $400,000 funded from other borrowings consisting of a mortgage note of $600,000 at 9% and a $200,000 bank note payable at 10%.

Weighted interest rate on	$600,000	× .09	=	$54,000
nonspecific borrowings:	200,000	× .10	=	20,000
	$800,000			$74,000
	$74,000/$800,000		=	9.25%
Total interest incurred:	$600,000	× .12	=	$72,000
	$600,000	× .09	=	54,000
	$200,000	× .10	=	20,000
				$146,000
Interest capitalized:				
Specific borrowing of $600,000 × .12			=	$72,000
Balance of $400,000 × .0925			=	37,000
				$109,000

The income statement for this example will include net interest expense of $37,000 [$146,000 – $109,000]. It is common to display the amount of capitalized interest on the face of the income statement in cases where capitalized interest is material in amount. For example, the 1994 annual report of Delta Air Lines, Inc., discloses its capitalized interest within the "other income (expense)" section of its income statement (millions of dollars):[11]

	1992	1993	1994
Other income (expense)			
Interest expense	(221)	(239)	(304)
Interest capitalized	70	62	33

The entire interest of $146,000 in computational example of Exhibit A.4 would have been capitalized if the accumulated cost of assets under development had been equal to or greater than the total borrowings of $1,600,000. UDC Homes, Inc., provides an example (1993) of complete capitalization of all interest incurred. An excerpt from its note on housing interest is shown in Exhibit A.5.

TAX ACCOUNTING: FOUNDATIONS

Income taxes are accounted for on an accrual basis like all other revenue and expense. Accounting for income taxes is heavily influenced by two important factors: (1) There are generally two income calculations, one for shareholder (book) reporting and another for tax-return purposes. Differences between generally accepted accounting principles and tax law cause book and tax return earnings to diverge. (2) The disparity between book and tax return income is explained by temporary and permanent differences between revenue and expense included in the book versus tax-return income calculations.

Most temporary differences result from recognizing revenue and expense items in different periods in the books versus the tax return. Typical sources include accounting for

Exhibit A.5 Capitalization of All Interest Incurred: UDC Homes, Inc., 1991–1993 (thousands of dollars)

	1991	1992	1993
Interest costs incurred	$30,072	$26,450	$36,968
Less: Interest capitalized	(30,013)	(26,413)	(36,968)
Interest expensed	$ 59	$ 37	–

Source: UDC Homes, Inc., annual report, December 1993, p. 14.

- Depreciation
- Long-term contracts
- Bad debts
- Warranties
- Restructuring charges
- Installment sales
- Sale/leasebacks
- Leases
- Foreign currency gain/losses

Permanent differences result from such items as

- Nondeductible goodwill amortization
- Tax-exempt interest income
- Premiums on employee life insurance where the company is the beneficiary
- Tax exempt portion of dividends
- The nondeductible portion of meals and entertainment expense
- Interest incurred to invest in tax-exempt securities
- Excess tax depletion

To achieve matching and to avoid misstatement of book earnings, deferred taxes are recorded on all temporary differences. However, deferred taxes are not generally recorded on permanent differences, thus resulting in effective tax rates that differ from statutory levels.

The following pre-tax book and tax return earnings, along with the data on temporary and permanent differences shown in Exhibit A.6, are used to illustrate the effect on tax accounting of both temporary and permanent differences.

Depreciation in the tax return exceeded that deducted in computing book earnings by $1,500. Generally, depreciation is recorded on the books using the straight-line method. Accelerated methods, or shorter useful lives, are typically used in the tax return. Hence, an additional $1,500 of depreciation is deducted from book earnings to arrive at tax return earnings. Moreover, $1,000 of tax-exempt income is included in book earnings that is not included in the tax return. It is similarly deducted in reconciling book to tax return earnings. The depreciation effect is a temporary

Exhibit A.6   Basic Tax Accounting Example

Book earnings before taxes	$5,000
Excess of tax return over book depreciation	(1,500)
Tax-exempt interest	(1,000)
Tax return earnings before taxes	$2,500

difference and will result in recording a deferred tax provision and associated deferred tax liability. The tax-exempt interest is a permanent difference and will reduce the total tax provision and effective tax rate.

At a combined federal and state income tax rate of 40%—35% federal and 5% state—taxes would be recorded as follows (+ denotes an account balance increase and – a denotes an account balance decrease):

Account	Debit	Credit
Current tax provision (+)	1,000[a]	
Cash(–)		1,000
Deferred tax provision (+)	600[b]	
Deferred tax liability (+)		600

[a]($2,500 × .40).
[b]($1,500 × .40).

Of the book profit of $5,000, only $4,000 is subject to tax because $1,000 is tax-exempt interest income. The tax provision, or tax expense, on the taxable portion of the book profit is $1,600 [$1,000 current tax expense + $600 of deferred tax expense] and is deducted in the shareholder income statement to arrive at net income.

On the face of the income statement, or in the tax note, the total tax provision will be divided into two components: the current and deferred tax provision:

Total tax provision	
Current	$1,000
Deferred	600
	$1,600

It is important to note that the current portion of the provision is based upon tax return profit and the deferred provision is based upon the temporary differences. For statement users concerned with cash flows, the focus should be on the current provision. The tax return results and the associated current tax provision determine tax payments or refunds.

In an indirect-basis statement of cash flows, the deferred tax would be added to net income in arriving at cash flow from operating activities. In the direct-basis statement of cash flows, the increase in the deferred tax liability is deducted from the total tax provision in computing taxes paid.

It is typical for firms to have more than a single temporary or permanent difference. In such cases, the note disclosures become somewhat more complex. Further illustration of tax accounting and associated disclosures is based upon the example in Exhibit A.7. Of the book profit of $5,000, $4,300 is subject to tax, either currently or in the future. The computation of the $4,300 taxable portion is as follows:

Reported pre-tax profit	$5,000
Less tax-exempt interest	(1,000)
Plus nondeductible goodwill amortization	300
Book profit subject to tax	$4,300

The accrual of income taxes on the books is based upon that portion of the book profit that will ultimately be subject to tax. While properly included in the computation of book pre-tax earnings, the tax-exempt interest is not subject to tax and is excluded from book earnings, *but only for the purpose of computing the tax provision.* Similarly, the nondeductible goodwill amortization is added back to book earnings.[12]

At a combined federal and state income tax rate of 40%, taxes would be recorded as follows:

Account	Debit	Credit
Current tax provision (+)	1,440[a]	
Taxes payable (+)		1,440
Deferred tax asset (+)	320[b]	
Deferred tax provision (−)		320
Deferred tax provision (+)	600[c]	
Deferred tax liability (+)		+600

[a]($3,600 × .40).
[b]($800 × .40).
[c]($1,500 × .40).

A typical set of tax disclosures for these data would be made up of the following four elements:

1. The breakdown of the total tax provision into current and deferred components:

Current tax provision	$1,440
Deferred tax provision	280
Total tax provision	$1,720

Exhibit A.7 Enriched Tax Accounting Example

Book earnings before taxes	$5,000
Excess of tax return over book depreciation	(1,500)
Excess of book over tax return warranty expense	800
Tax-exempt interest	(1,000)
Nondeductible goodwill amortization	300
Tax-return earnings before taxes	$3,600

Where applicable and material, this breakdown will also classify the provisions into state, federal, and foreign elements.

2. The tax effects of temporary differences comprised by the deferred tax (assets) and liabilities:

Excess of tax return over book depreciation	$600
Excess of book over tax return warranty expense	(320)
Net deferred tax liability	$280

3. Components of deferred tax provision:

Excess of tax return over book depreciation	$600
Excess of book over tax return warranty expense	(320)
Total deferred tax provision	$280

Schedules 2 and 3 contain the same amounts only because this is the initial year of existence of the firm. In subsequent years, the composition of the deferred tax assets and liabilities would change by the new deferred tax provisions. The deferred tax assets and liabilities are cumulative balances, whereas the deferred tax provision elements are only for a single year.

4. Tax reconciliation schedule:

Tax at statutory federal rate	$1,750	35.0%
State income taxes net of federal benefit	250	5.0
Tax reduction due to nontaxable interest	(400)	(8.0)
Tax increase due to nondeductible goodwill amortization	120	2.4
Total tax provision and effective tax rate	$1,720	34.4%

The third of the disclosures, the breakdown of the deferred tax provision by types of temporary differences, is not required by SFAS No. 109, "Accounting for Income Taxes." Rather, SFAS No. 109 calls for the detailing of cumulative deferred tax assets and liabilities by type of temporary difference or tax carryover. However, pre–SFAS 109 practice, prompted by requirements of the SEC, included this breakdown, and many firms continue to include it in among their tax disclosures.

TAX ACCOUNTING: CARRYOVERS, DEFERRED TAX ASSETS AND THE VALUATION ALLOWANCE

Deferred Tax Assets: Deductible Temporary Differences, and Loss and Tax Credit Carryovers

SFAS No. 109 requires that deferred tax assets be recorded for all "deductible" temporary differences as well as loss and tax credit carryovers. Deductible temporary differences result in reductions in tax return profits upon their reversal. Reversal of a deductible temporary difference occurs when, for example, an asset write-down taken earlier in the book income statement is deducted in computing taxable income in the tax return. Loss carryovers shield future profits from taxation, whereas tax credit carryovers reduce future taxes directly.

Deductible Temporary Differences

In the case of deductible temporary differences, it is common to write-down assets in the book income statement prior to their actual disposition. Assume that a book write-down of $100,000 is taken to write-down assets to their disposal value. This deduction will be taken in the tax return when the assets are actually disposed of and the loss realized. The $100,000 is an "originating" temporary difference. This adjustment would be recorded as follows:

1. The asset is written down and a $100,000 deduction is taken in the book income statement:

Account	Debit	Credit
Provision for asset write-down (+)	100,000	
Asset (−)		100,000

2. The tax-saving potential of the deduction is recognized on the books (40% tax rate):

Account	Debit	Credit
Deferred tax asset (+)	40,000	
Deferred tax provision (−)		40,000

These entries result in a net reduction in book earnings of $60,000. The $100,000 write-down is offset in part by the $40,000 deferred tax benefit recognized. The tax consequence of this transaction is recognized in the period in which the write-down is recognized on the books. Recognition on the books is not delayed. Matching is achieved through this application of accrual techniques to the accounting for income taxes.

The preceding temporary difference will reverse when the asset is actually sold and the realized loss becomes deductible in the tax return. Assume that the asset's carrying value, after the write-down, is equal to the sale proceeds of $300,000. The sale and effect on deferred taxes would be recorded as follows:

3. The sale of the asset is recorded:

Account	Debit	Credit
Cash (+)	300,000	
Asset (–)		300,000

4. The temporary difference reverses and the deferred tax asset is amortized:

Account	Debit	Credit
Deferred tax provision (+)	40,000	
Deferred tax asset (–)		40,000

The entry to record the asset's sale results in no loss being recognized on the books—it was recognized in the prior year upon the write-down of the asset. However, the loss of $100,000 is now taken in the tax return. The temporary difference has now reversed, and an additional deduction, beyond that available in the books, is taken in the tax return. Again, this example illustrates a deductible temporary difference. In the year of reversal, results in the tax return are less than those in the books by $100,000, the asset write-down taken earlier in the books. The amortization of the deferred tax asset puts a $40,000 deferred tax provision into the income statement to match against the $100,000 excess of pre-tax book over tax return earnings. Book earnings exceed those in the tax return because the tax return results now bear the burden of the $100,000 loss.

The principal sources of deferred tax assets are expenses that are recognized on the books before they are available in the tax return. Other temporary differences giving rise to deferred tax assets would be a case where income is recognized in the tax return prior to its recognition on the books. An example of this category would be a sale and leaseback transaction. The gains from such transactions are included in the tax return in the year of sale but deferred, in whole or in part, on the books. They are then amortized into future book earnings over the term of the leaseback. Book profit is less than tax return profit upon origination of this temporary difference. As a result, a deferred tax asset would be recorded just as in the case of the preceding asset write-down. The temporary difference reverses when the deferred gain is amortized into book earnings. As this occurs, the deferred tax asset is amortized.

Loss and Tax Credit Carryovers

Examples of loss and tax credit carryovers and their associated carryback and carryforward periods include the following:

Loss and Tax Credits	Carryback and Carryforward Periods
• Net operating losses	Back 3 and forward 15 years
• Capital losses	Back 3 and forward 5 years
• Alternative minimum tax credits	Unlimited carryforward
• Foreign tax credits	Back 2 and forward 5 years

The following example illustrates accounting for deferred tax assets related to loss and tax credit carryovers. A firm incurs a loss of $1,000. In the three carryback years the firm earned $400 and paid taxes of $160. The full potential tax saving associated with the loss, assuming a flat 40% tax rate, is $400 [40% × $1,000]. Of this benefit, $160 would be a refund that results from carrying back $400 of the loss against profits in the three-year carryback period. The balance of the benefit, $240, would be realized by carrying forward $600 of the loss to shield future profits from taxation. The tax saving of this carryforward is reported as a deferred tax asset in the amount of $240. These tax benefits would be recorded as follows:

Account	Debit	Credit
Income tax refund receivable (+)	160	
Deferred tax asset (+)	240	
Current tax provision (–)		160
Deferred tax provision (–)		240

The income statement in the loss year appears as follows:

Loss before tax	$(1,000)
Tax provision	
Current tax benefit	160
Deferred tax benefit	240
Total	400
Net loss	$ (600)

To complete this illustration, assume that this firm has pre-tax earnings of exactly $600 in the year following the loss. The required accounting and the income statement would be as follows:

Account	Debit	Credit
Deferred tax provision (+)	240	
Deferred tax asset (–)		240

The income statement:

Income before taxes	$600
Deferred tax provision	(240)
Net income	$360

The deferred tax asset is realized because it shields the $600 of taxable income from taxation. Because of the $600 carryforward, there is no taxable income in the tax return and therefore no current tax provision.[13] However, book earnings are $600, and a deferred tax provision of $240 is matched against these earnings. The tax benefit of the loss carryforward was *recognized* on the books in computing the after-tax loss of the prior year. The tax benefit of the loss carryforward, represented by the deferred tax asset, is *realized* in the current year because the $600 loss carryforward shields the $600 of taxable income in the tax return.

Deferred Tax Assets and the Tax Valuation Allowance

The relatively new standard governing tax accounting made major changes in the treatment of deferred tax assets. This standard, SFAS No. 109, relaxes former restrictions on recording deferred tax assets and requires that deferred tax assets be recorded for all deductible temporary differences as well as loss and credit carryforwards.[14] However, the standard then requires that an evaluation be made of the likelihood that the deferred tax assets will be realized. Realization of deferred tax assets requires future tax return profits. Therefore, assessing the likelihood of realization of deferred tax assets requires firms to evaluate their future profitability.

Assessing the Realizability of Deferred Tax Assets

Statement No. 109 requires that a valuation allowance be established if the likelihood is greater than 50% that some or all of a firm's deferred tax assets will not be realized.[15] This adjustment increases the deferred tax provision and reduces the gross deferred tax assets to the net amount that is expected to be realized.

Sources of Taxable Income

Realization of deferred tax assets associated with either deductible temporary differences or tax benefit carryforwards requires taxable income of a sufficient amount, in the right time period, and of the right nature. Loss and tax credit carryforwards require that taxable income be earned prior to their expiration. Moreover, the utilization of capital loss carryforwards requires future capital gain income. Statement No. 109 identifies possible sources of taxable income as[16]

- Future reversals of existing taxable temporary differences
- Future taxable income exclusive of reversing temporary differences
- Taxable income in prior carryback year(s)

Tax Planning Strategies

Statement No. 109 also includes tax-planning strategies as sources of taxable income to be considered in assessing the likelihood of realization of deferred tax assets. Tax-planning strategies are actions a firm might not ordinarily take but would to prevent, for example, a tax benefit carryforward from expiring unused. Examples cited in the statement include[17]

- A sale-leaseback transaction that includes the full realized gain in taxable income in the year of the sale
- A sale structured such that all income is included in taxable income in the year of sale rather than over future years, as it would be under the installment sale alternative
- A switch from tax-exempt to taxable investments
- A change designed to convert income from ordinary to capital gain status to avoid expiration of an unused capital loss carryforward

Examples of tax-planning strategies disclosed by a number of companies include (1) realization of capital gains on appreciated securities (Aetna), (2) a change in depreciation methods (Bethlehem Steel), (3) capitalization for tax purposes of software expenditures (IBM), (4) adjustments of pension plan contributions (Bethlehem Steel), and (5) a switch from LIFO to FIFO (Federal Mogul). Each of these strategies are designed to put taxable income into the tax return to ensure realization of the tax-saving potential underlying deferred tax assets.

Positive and Negative Evidence in Assessing Realizability

Statement No. 109 calls for the consideration of all available evidence, both positive and negative, in assessing realizability of deferred tax assets.[18] Examples provided in the statement include the following:

Positive Evidence
- Existing contracts or firm sales backlog that will produce taxable income
- Appreciated assets that could be sold to produce taxable income
- A strong earnings history exclusive of the events that created the tax loss carryforward or deductible temporary difference combined with evidence that the loss is not likely to be recurring

Negative Evidence
- A history of carryforwards expiring unused
- Losses expected in early future years
- A short initial or remaining carryback or carryforward period

Operation of the Valuation Allowance

After recording all their deferred tax assets, firms must assess realizability as outlined in the preceding sections. If it is decided that some or all of these assets are unlikely to be realized, with a likelihood of greater than 50%, then that portion must be written off through a deferred tax valuation allowance. As an example, the disclosure of the deferred tax assets and liabilities of Mycogen Corp. is provided in Exhibit A.8.

Mycogen recorded a valuation allowance sufficient to reduce its net deferred tax assets to the amount of its deferred tax liabilities. It is very common to see this result. It suggests that a portion of the deferred tax assets, equal in amount to the deferred tax liabilities, will be realizable because the reversal of the deferred tax liability will increase tax return income. Unlike deductible temporary differences, which reduce tax return earnings when they reverse, taxable temporary differences underlie deferred tax liabilities. They increase tax return earnings, relative to those reported in the books, when they reverse.

Mycogen is an agricultural biotechnology company that experienced net losses of $77 million over the three years ending December 31, 1993. Further, it had an accumulated retained earnings deficit of $101 million. Its federal tax loss and credit carryforwards begin to expire in 1997 if they had not been previously utilized. Also, in its state of California, loss and tax credit carryforwards usable in its California tax returns began expiring in 1994. For these and other reasons, Mycogen recorded the valuation allowance disclosed in Exhibit A.8 and stated that it was "due to the uncertainty surrounding the future realization of favorable tax attributes."[19]

To the extent that Mycogen earns tax return profits in the future, or its profit prospects improve, it will become possible to recognize these currently off–balance sheet tax benefits.

Exhibit A.8 Disclosure of Deferred Tax Assets, Liabilities, and Valuation Allowance: Mycogen Corp., 1993 (thousands of dollars)

	1993
Deferred tax assets	
Net operating loss carryforwards	$ 12,135
Capitalized research expenditures	4,658
Tax basis of inventory greater than book	4,648
Research credit carryforwards	3,388
Other items with tax basis greater than book	2,209
Total deferred tax assets	27,038
Less: Valuation allowance	(25,737)
Net deferred tax assets	1,301
Net deferred tax liabilities	(1,301)
Net deferred taxes	$ –

Source: Mycogen Corp., annual report, 1993, p. 42.

When a firm records a valuation allowance for a deferred tax asset but later realizes the tax saving associated with the underlying deductible temporary difference, or loss or tax credit carryforward, both the valuation allowance and the tax provision will be reduced. Selected portions of the tax disclosures of Outboard Marine Corp., in Exhibit A.9, illustrate this circumstance.[20] Notice that Outboard Marine's valuation allowance was reduced by approximately $16 million (Part A of Exhibit A.9) and that this in turn lowered the company's effective tax rate by 29.2 percentage points (Part B of Exhibit A.9).

Outboard Marine stated, "The change in the valuation allowance from 1993 to 1994 is primarily due to deductible deferred tax assets which reduced income tax expense for the current year."[21] Outboard's accounting treatment for the realization of this deferred tax asset would be as follows (millions of dollars):

Exhibit A.9   Effect of a Reduction in a Tax Valuation Allowance: Outboard Marine Corp., 1993 and 1994 (millions of dollars)

	1993	1994
Part A. Partial deferred tax asset and liability schedule:		
Deferred tax assets		
Litigation claims	$ 16.5	$ 14.6
Product warranty	9.4	9.0
Marketing programs	8.3	7.7
Postretirement medical programs	43.8	43.1
Restructuring	38.8	12.9
Loss carryforwards	25.6	39.7
Other	33.3	38.2
Valuation allowance	(130.0)	(113.9)
Total deferred tax assets	$ 45.7	$ 51.3
Part B. Tax-rate reconciliation schedule (1992 omitted)		
At statutory rate	(34.7%)	35.0%
State taxes, net of federal benefit	.5	3.0
Tax effect of non-U.S. subsidiary earnings (loss) taxed at other than U.S. rate	.5	(6.2)
Tax benefit not provided on foreign operating losses	1.7	–
Tax effect of goodwill amortization and write-offs	7.1	5.4
U.S. tax benefit not realized	27.7	–
Reversal of valuation allowance	–	(29.2)
Federal benefit of prior years state income taxes paid	(.1)	.6
Other	.5	.6
Actual provision	N.M.[a]	9.2%

Source: Outboard Marine Corp., annual report, September 1994, pp. 28–29.
[a]Outboard Marine labeled this as N.M., not meaningful, because the pre-tax result is a loss of $159.9 million and the effective tax rate on the loss is a positive 3.2%.

Account	Debit	Credit
Valuation allowance (–)	16	
Deferred tax asset (–)		16

The deferred tax asset has been realized, and both its balance and that of the associated valuation allowance are eliminated. Net income is increased because the deduction in the tax return of the associated deductible temporary difference reduces tax return earnings and with it the current tax provision.

Realization of the deferred tax asset would not have increased 1994 earnings if Outboard had not recorded a valuation allowance against this deferred tax asset. If the asset were recognized and not subsequently written off through the valuation allowance, then the tax saving of the deductible temporary difference would have increased Outboard's book earnings for the year in which the temporary difference originated. In this case, the entry to record the realization of this deferred tax asset would be as follows (millions of dollars):

Account	Debit	Credit
Deferred tax provision (+)	16	
Deferred tax asset (–)		16

Realization of the tax savings through the reduction of earnings in the tax return lowers the current tax provision. However, this expense reduction would be offset by the deferred tax provision recorded upon amortization of the deferred tax asset. Thus, realization would have no effect on current-year earnings because the tax benefit had already been recognized in the year of origination.

The Tax Valuation Allowance and Accounting Flexibility

The tax valuation allowance feature of the new tax accounting standard introduces an important new area in financial reporting where judgment must be exercised by management. The expectation is that firms will operate in good faith to comply with both the letter and spirit of Statement No. 109, in which the valuation allowance feature was introduced. However, it is also clear that the valuation allowance feature of the standard opens up a significant new avenue for earnings management. Some firms will probably find this irresistible.

It should be a fairly simple matter to argue that a valuation allowance, established earlier in more difficult times, is now overstated because prospects have improved. A reduction in the valuation allowance will produce a dollar-for-dollar increase in earnings. In these cases, the tax reconciliation schedule is the key disclosure. It will identify the amount by which taxes have been reduced and earnings increased, exactly as revealed in Part B of Exhibit A.9.

FOREIGN CURRENCY ACCOUNTING ISSUES

Foreign currency accounting matters can be divided into two categories: transaction reporting and translation reporting. The majority of foreign currency transactions result from activities such as buying or selling abroad with the purchase or sale denominated in a foreign currency. For example, a U.S. firm sells to a German customer and invoices the German firm in the German mark (DM). Other foreign currency transactions may result from entering into foreign currency contracts such as futures, options, forwards, and swaps, where these may be employed in either hedging or investment (speculative) applications. Translation reporting involves restating the financial statements of foreign branches or subsidiaries into U.S. dollars for purposes of either consolidation or the application of the equity method of accounting.

Transaction Reporting

The requirements of generally accepted accounting principles call for the remeasurement of foreign currency assets and liabilities into their U.S. dollar equivalent when financial statements are prepared.[22] Whether such remeasurements result in transaction gains or losses depends upon whether the foreign currency balance is an asset or liability and whether the foreign currency appreciated or depreciated against the dollar. Reference is often made to the nature of the foreign currency exposure, that is, whether it is asset or liability exposure. Exposure creates the possibility of transaction gains or losses when foreign currency assets and liabilities are remeasured into U.S. dollars. The examples that follow outline the nature of transactional reporting for (1) an unhedged sale, (2) a hedged purchase transaction, (3) a hedged purchase commitment, and (4) a currency speculation.

The effects of exposure, changes in the value of the foreign currency, and the emergence of foreign currency gains or losses are summarized in Exhibit A.10. A gain results when a foreign currency asset is denominated in a currency that appreciates. Alternatively, a loss results if a firm has a liability denominated in a foreign currency that appreciates. In this case, additional dollars will be required to purchase the foreign currency needed to retire the obligation.

Exhibit A.10   Exposure, Exchange Rate Movements, and Transaction Gains or Losses

Movement of the Foreign Currency	Nature of Exposure	
	Asset	Liability
Appreciates	Gain	Loss
Depreciates	Loss	Gain

An Unhedged Sale Transaction

On November 1, 19X1, USA Co. ships goods to German Co. and invoices it 100,000 DM (German marks). USA Co. collects the account receivable on January 15, 19X2. The November 1, December 31, and January 15 exchange rates are $0.6452, $0.7034, and $0.6754, respectively. These rates are expressed in the direct manner, with the foreign currency expressed in terms of dollars. That is, the mark is worth $0.6452 on November 1, $0.7034 on December 31, and $0.6754 on January 15. Alternatively, it costs $0.6452 to purchase one mark on November 1, $0.7034 on December 31, and $0.6754 on January 15. On balance, the mark appreciated against the dollar over the period November 1, 19X1, to January 15, 19X2. USA Co.'s accounting period ends on December 31. The accounting for this foreign currency transaction is shown in Exhibit A.11.

The sale-date exchange rate is used to record the sale. The year-end, or "current," rate is used to remeasure the mark account receivable into dollars. This ensures that results for the year are on a full-accrual basis. Because the mark appreciated, a gain is recorded. Upon collection at January 15, 19X2, the mark has depreciated since the end of the 19X1, and a foreign exchange loss is recorded. However, on balance an overall transaction gain of $3,020 [gain of $5,820 in 19X1 less a loss of $2,800 in 19X2] was realized on this transaction.

Transactions such as these are frequently hedged so that the potential for gain or loss is removed, either in whole or in part. The gain or loss from the balance sheet exposure is offset by a loss or gain on the hedging position. The next example illustrates the hedge of foreign currency liability exposure.

Exhibit A.11   Accounting for an Unhedged Foreign Currency Sale

Account	Debit	Credit
Recording the sale (November 1, 19X1)		
Accounts receivable (+)	64,520[a]	
Sales revenue (+)		64,520
Remeasuring the German mark account receivable at year-end (December 31, 19X1)		
Accounts receivable (+)	5,820[b]	
Foreign exchange gain (+)		5,820
Recording collection of the account receivable (January 15, 19X2)		
Foreign currency (+)	67,540[c]	
Foreign exchange loss (+)	2,800[d]	
Accounts receivable (−)		70,340

[a]100,000 DM × $.6452.
[b]100,000 DM × ($.7034 − $.6452).
[c]100,000 DM × $.6754.
[d]100,000 DM × ($.7034 − $.6754).

A Hedged Purchase Transaction

Import Co. purchases electronic equipment from a Japanese supplier and is invoiced 10 million yen (¥) on November 15, 19X1. The yen account payable is due on December 15, 19X1. At November 15, 19X1, the spot exchange rate is ¥84.780 under the indirect convention of expressing the yen rate, or $0.01180 following the direct convention. In practice, the yen is usually expressed in indirect-rate form. The computations in this section use the direct-rate form because it is computationally more convenient. Import Co. is concerned that the dollar might depreciate against the yen by the time it must acquire the yen to pay off its account payable. This would cause the dollars required to obtain the needed yen to increase and result in an exchange loss.

Import decides to hedge its yen exposure. It enters into a forward contract on November 15, 19X1, to acquire ¥10 million on December 15, 19X1, at a forward rate ¥84.408. Expressed in direct form, the spot rate is $0.01180 at November 15, 19X1, and the 30-day forward rate is $0.01185 (1/84.408). The forward rate is at a premium to the spot because it costs $0.01180 to acquire one yen in the spot market but $0.01185 to acquire one yen in the 30-day forward market.

A forward contract is an arrangement to exchange currencies at an agreed price on a future date. Unlike exchange-traded instruments, forwards can be tailored to a user's requirements in terms of both amount and duration. This arrangement locks in the cost to Import Co. of acquiring the yen. Should the dollar depreciate against the yen, Import will record a loss on its accounts payable position (liability exposure in the yen), but this loss will be offset by a gain on its forward contract (asset exposure in the yen). This emergence of offsetting gains and losses is the essence of a hedge. This example assumes that Import hedges its entire exposure and that the hedge is perfect, that is, the gains and losses offset exactly. The accounting for these transactions is shown in Exhibit A.12.

On December 15, 19X1, Import Co. acquires the ¥10 million under the forward contract for the agreed amount of $118,500. The spot value of the yen depreciated to $0.01177 between November 15 and December 15. Thus, there is a foreign exchange loss recorded upon acquisition of the ¥10 million; the yen were acquired at the forward rate $0.01185 but have a spot value of only $0.01177. The premium on the forward is charged to financial expense, and a gain is recorded on the payment of the account payable. The forward contract premium would have been amortized if the contract had spanned more than a single accounting period. These transactions are shown in Exhibit A.12.

The operation of the hedge is demonstrated by the $300 loss on the forward contract offset by the $300 gain on the payment of the accounts payable. Without the hedge, Import Co. would have realized a transaction gain of $300 and had a total cash disbursement of $117,700 to pay off the account payable originally recorded at $118,000. With the hedge, Import disbursed total cash of $118,500. This difference in cash disbursement of $800 is made up of the $500 forward contract premium and the $300 transaction loss.

Exhibit A.12   Accounting for a Hedged Foreign Currency Purchase

Account	Debit	Credit
Recording the purchase in dollars (November 15, 19X1)		
Purchases (+)	118,000[a]	
Accounts payable (+)		118,000
Recording the forward contract (November 15, 19X1)		
Forward Contract (+)	118,000	
Premium on forward contract (+)	500[b]	
Due to exchange broker (+)		118,500[c]
Recording payment of forward contract (December 15, 19X1)		
Due to exchange broker (−)	118,500	
Cash (−)		118,500
Recording receipt of foreign currency (December 15, 19X1)		
Foreign currency (+)	117,700[d]	
Transaction loss (+)	300	
Forward contract (−)		118,000
Recording charge-off of contract premium (December 15, 19X1)		
Financial expense (+)	500	
Premium on forward contract (−)		500
Recording payment of yen account payable (December 15, 19X1)		
Accounts payable (−)	118,000	
Foreign currency (−)		117,700
Transaction gain (+)		300

[a] ¥ 10,000,000 × $.01180.
[b] ($.01185 − $.01180) × ¥10,000,000.
[c] ¥10,000,000 × $.01185.
[d] ¥10,000,000 × $.01177.

This result does not imply that Import Co. made an unwise decision by hedging. The hedge eliminated the possibility of large losses that could have resulted if there had been no hedge and the dollar had suffered a sharp decline in value. It is somewhat analogous to purchasing flight insurance and then surviving the flight safely. Most would probably not consider the cost of the insurance to have been a waste of money.

A Hedged Purchase Commitment

Firms sometimes enter into commitments to make purchases of goods some time in advance of the actual purchase and delivery. Depreciation of the dollar during the commitment period will increase the dollar cost of the goods. To protect against this possibility, firms enter into hedges during the commitment period.

Copy Co. enters into a firm purchase commitment with Precision Ltd., a Japanese electronics firm. Precision will manufacture and sell Copy Co. a color copying machine for which Copy Co. holds patents. The commitment is made on November 1, 19X2, and the machines are to be shipped and Copy invoiced ¥100 million on January 15, 19X3. The invoice will be payable on March 15, 19X3. At the commitment date, the spot value of the yen is $0.01115.

Copy Co. hedges the exposure by buying exchanged-traded yen futures contracts. Should the yen appreciate, this long position (asset exposure in the yen) will create a gain to offset the increased dollar cost of the copying machines. Should the yen depreciate, then a loss will result from the futures contracts but will be offset by the reduced dollar cost of the machines. Therefore, a hedge is created. If, instead of its liability exposure, Copy had made sales to Japanese customers and invoiced them in yen, creating asset exposure, then a hedge using futures contracts would have required selling yen futures contracts. A gain on this short futures contract position would result if the yen depreciated. This gain would offset the loss on the accounts receivable exposure. A summary of currency movements, futures position, i.e., long or short, and resulting gains and losses is provided in Exhibit A.13.

The recording of Copy Co.'s purchase of futures contracts and provision of margin on November 15, 19X2, is shown in Exhibit A.14. Copy purchased eight yen futures contracts. Each contract represents ¥12.5 million. A $20,000 margin deposit with the broker is required, and commissions are ignored. The margin deposit is designed to ensure the availability of funds to cover losses, if incurred. In this case, the standard denomination of the yen futures contract is ¥12.5 million and therefore eight contracts provide the amount ¥100 million, which is exactly equal to the yen purchase commitment. A determination of the appropriate number of contracts can be a complex matter and goes beyond the scope of the explanation here. This simplified approach assumes that buying contracts that simply equal the yen commitment is the appropriate strategy.

By the end of 19X2, the yen had appreciated in value, and the futures contracts have risen in market value by $100,000. This gain is deferred because the futures contracts are serving as a hedge. The act of deferral of either gains or losses in this hedge application of futures contracts is an example of hedge accounting. The purchase has not yet been recorded, and there is no loss to offset this gain if it were included in the income statement. This is why the gain is deferred. The deferred gain

Exhibit A.13 Currency Movements and Gains or Losses on Futures Contracts

	Futures Position	
Movement of the Futures Currency	Long	Short
Appreciates	Gain	Loss
Depreciates	Loss	Gain

Exhibit A.14   Accounting for a Hedged Foreign Currency Purchase Commitment

Account	Debit	Credit
Recording the purchase of futures contracts and		
* provision of margin (November 15, 19X2)*		
Futures margin account (+)	20,000	
Cash (–)		20,000
Recording the gain on futures contracts		
* (December 31, 19X2)*		
Futures margin account (+)	100,000	
Deferred futures gain (+)		100,000
Recording the purchase (January 15, 19X3)		
Purchases (+)	1,190,000	
Accounts payable (+)		1,190,000[a]
Recording the loss on futures contracts		
* (January 15, 19X3)*		
Deferred futures gain (–)	25,000	
Futures margin account (–)		25,000
Recording and adjustment of net deferred futures		
* gain against cost of purchase (January 15, 19X3)*		
Deferred futures gain (–)	75,000	
Purchases (–)		75,000[b]

[a]¥100,000,000 × $.01190.
[b]Original deferred gains of $100,000 less subsequent loss of $25,000.

will be deducted from the amount of the purchase when it is recorded. The gain on the futures contracts increases the margin account balance and is recorded as shown in Exhibit A.14. Deferred futures gain is a balance sheet account and is analogous to deferred or unearned income. It would be classified in the liabilities section of the balance sheet.

The copy machines are shipped, and Copy Co. is invoiced ¥100 million on January 15, 19X3. A reversal in the value of the yen resulted in a loss of $25,000 between the end of 19X2 and January 15, 19X3. The spot value of the yen on January 15, 19X3, is $0.01190. The subsequent accounting steps are shown in Exhibit A.14.

The cost of the copy machines would have increased during the commitment period if Copy Co. had not hedged this exposure. The spot rate for the yen increased from $0.01115 to $0.01190 between commitment and purchase date, increasing the purchase price by $75,000 [($0.01190 – $0.01115) × ¥100 million]. This cost increase of $75,000, a part of the *initial* recorded cost of the purchases, is exactly offset by the net deferred gain of $75,000 from the futures contracts.

Copy Co. now has ¥100 million of on–balance sheet liability exposure in the yen. If the futures contracts are retained, they will provide continued protection against increases in the value of the yen until the accounts payable are paid off. If the futures contracts are sold, then Copy Co. will receive the balance in its futures account and its yen exposure will be unhedged.

A Currency Speculation

A currency speculation involves taking a position in a currency, usually through one of the same instruments employed in hedging. However, in taking a position there is no offsetting exposure, and the position does not function as a hedge. Our example of a speculation involves the use of currency options. The creation of gains and losses on currency option contracts, whether calls, which grant the right to buy the currency, or puts, which grant the right to sell the currency, are summarized in Exhibit A.15.

A loss results if the foreign currency appreciates when the investor (speculator) has invested in a put. The right to sell a currency at a fixed price, the strike price, is worth less when the currency's market value rises. Alternatively, if the currency's value depreciates, the option's value rises and a gain results. The effect of appreciation and depreciation is the opposite in the case of call options. Appreciation in the foreign currency creates a gain on the call option because the right to purchase a currency at a fixed price is worth more when the currency's value has risen in the market. Depreciation in the option currency creates the opposite result.

Assume that Thrill Co. invests $100,000 in currency call options on the Swiss franc. The call option investment would be recorded as follows:

Account	Debit	Credit
Investment in call options (+)	100,000	
Cash (−)		100,000

Upon expiration of the option contract, the Swiss franc has appreciated in value and the contract is worth $125,000. The sale of the call option contract and the associated gain are recorded as follows:

Account	Debit	Credit
Cash (+)	125,000	
Investment in call options (−)		100,000
Gain (+)		25,000

Exhibit A.15 Currency Movements and Gains or Losses on Currency Options

	Option Position	
Movement of the Option Currency	Put	Call
Appreciates	Loss	Gain
Depreciates	Gain	Loss

Thrill Co. was on the right side of this currency movement and realized a gain. If, instead, the Swiss franc had depreciated below the call strike price, then the option contract would have expired without value. However, Thrill's loss on the option is limited to its investment in the contract.

Translation of Foreign Currency Statements

The statements of foreign subsidiaries must be restated, i.e., translated, into dollars before they can be consolidated with those of their U.S. parent or before the equity method can be applied. There are two different methods under U.S. GAAP that are used in translation: the current-rate method and the temporal method.

The current-rate method is used most frequently, and is applied in cases where the foreign subsidiary operates in other than a highly inflationary country and in a relatively autonomous manner. *Highly inflationary* is defined as cumulative inflation of 100% or more over the most recent three-year period. Key features of translation under the current-rate method are as follows:

- All assets and liabilities of the foreign subsidiary are translated at the current or year-end exchange rate.
- All revenues and expenses are translated at the average exchange rate for the year.
- Paid-in capital is translated at the historical exchange rate existing when the shares were issued.
- Retained earnings comprises translated income statement amounts and has therefore already been subject to translation.
- Dividends are translated at the declaration-date rate of exchange.
- The translation adjustment (gain or loss) resulting from this process is reported as part of shareholders' equity. If a subsidiary is sold, the translation adjustment is included in the computation of the gain or loss on the sale.

The inclusion of the translation adjustment in shareholders' equity rather than in income is a key feature of the current-rate method. Under previous GAAP, SFAS No. 8, translation adjustments were included in the income statement as gains or losses.[23] This introduced a degree of volatility to earnings that was strongly objected to by firms. The current standard, SFAS No. 52, keeps translation gains or losses out of the income statement in those cases where the all-current translation method is applicable.

Key differences between the current-rate and temporal methods include the following:

- The temporal method is applied in cases where the subsidiary operates in a highly inflationary economy or does not operate in an independent and autonomous manner from its U.S. parent. In these cases, the functional currency of the subsidiary is generally held to be the U.S. dollar and not the local (foreign) currency.

• Assets and liabilities carried at current prices are translated using the current rate and those carried at historical prices, such as inventory and property, plant, and equipment, are translated at the exchange rates that existed when these items were recorded. In almost all cases, this means that monetary assets and liabilities, e.g., cash, accounts receivable, accounts payable, notes payable, are translated at the current rate, and nonmonetary items such as inventory and property, plant, and equipment are translated at historical rates.

• Revenue is translated at the average exchange rate for the year.

• Costs or expenses, such as cost of sales or depreciation, are translated at the same historical rates as their associated assets, i.e., inventory and property, plant, and equipment.

• Costs and expenses not related to inventory and property, plant, and equipment are translated at the average exchange rate for the year.

• The translation gain or loss is included in the income statement and not in shareholders' equity.

Technically, the temporal method is a translation procedure. However, its application is referred to as remeasurement when the foreign subsidiary's functional currency is the U.S. dollar. Remeasurement implies that the translation of balances at exchange rates that existed when the balances originated yields the same outcomes as if the transactions had taken place in dollars.

Examples of the application of each of these translation methods are provided next.

Illustrations of Statement Translation

Illustrations of both the all-current and temporal translation methods are based upon the following information:

• French Subsidiary is formed in January 1, 19X1 with an initial share issue that raised FF 1 million.

• Selected exchange rates for the French franc are

At January 1, 19X1	$.20
Average for 19X1	$.19
At December 31, 19X1	$.18

• All of French Subsidiary's fixed assets were acquired when the exchange rate was $0.20.

• Ending inventory was acquired at the average rate for the year of $0.19.

• Depreciation of FF 400,000 was included in selling, general, and administrative expense.

All-Current Translation

The trial balance of French Subsidiary with FF balances translated to dollars under the current-rate method is presented in Exhibit A.16.

Following the all-current method, the translation of French Subsidiary's trial balance has applied the current rate ($0.18) to all assets and liabilities, the average rate ($0.19) to revenue and expenses, and the historical rate ($0.20) to paid-in capital. Prior to translation, French Subsidiary's trial balance was in balance. But, after translation and prior to consideration of the cumulative translation adjustment, the trial balance has total credit account balances that exceed the debit account total by $23,000. The trial balance is restored to balance by adding this $23,000 as the cumulative translation adjustment in the trial balance.

While appearing to be only a "plug" number, which restores the equality of the debit and credit account balances, the $23,000 has a financial interpretation and can be computed directly. French Subsidiary represents asset exposure in the French franc for its parent. Its balance sheet has an excess of FF assets over FF liabilities. Therefore, when the French franc depreciates, a reduction in value, a translation adjustment, results. This reduction in value would be realized if the subsidiary were liquidated at its book value amounts.

The translation adjustment can also be computed directly as follows (in thousands):

Exhibit A.16　Trial Balance Translated under the All-Current Method: French Subsidiary (currency amounts in thousands)

	FF	Rate	US$
Debit balance accounts			
Cash	200	.18	36
Accounts receivable	400	.18	72
Inventory	460	.18	83
Property, plant, and equipment, net	2,000	.18	360
Cost of sales	1,200	.19	228
Selling, general, and administrative expense	500	.19	95
Tax provision	240	.19	46
Cumulative translation adjustment	–	–	23
Total	5,000		943
Credit balance accounts			
Accounts payable	500	.18	90
Notes payable	1,200	.18	216
Common stock	1,000	.20	200
Retained earnings	0	–	0
Sales	2,300	.19	437
Total	5,000		943

Cumulative translation adjustment:				$23
Beginning net assets:	FF $1,000 \times (\$.18 - \$.20)$	=	20	
Net income:	FF $360 \times (\$.19 - \$.20)$	=	3	$23

The $20,000 component is the decline in the translated value of the beginning shareholders' equity or net assets. The $3,000 element represents the additional decline in net assets due to the continued depreciation in the French franc from the rate of $0.19 used in the translation of the income statement accounts to the $0.18 used in the translation of all assets and liabilities.

The translated income statements and balance sheets based upon the translated trial balances in Exhibit A.16 are presented in Exhibit A.17.

A desirable feature of translation under the current-rate method is preservation in the translated income statement and balance sheet of the relations found in the foreign currency financial statements. For example, the gross profit percentage in both the FF and dollar income statements is 48% and the ratio of total liabilities to total shareholders' equity is 1.25 to 1.

At the end of 19X1, the cumulative translation adjustment represents a reduction of shareholders' equity. It will be adjusted each year to reflect the cumulative

Exhibit A.17   Translated Income Statement and Balance Sheet under the All-Current Method: French Subsidiary (currency amounts in thousands)

	FF	Rate	US$
Income statements			
Sales	2,300	.19	437
Cost of sales	1,200	.19	228
Gross profit	1,100	–	209
Selling, general, and administrative expense	500	.19	95
Profit before taxes	600	–	114
Tax provision	240	.19	46
Net income	360		68
Balance sheets			
Cash	200	.18	36
Accounts receivable	400	.18	72
Inventory	460	.18	83
Property, plant, and equipment	2,000	.18	360
Total assets	3,060		551
Accounts payable	500	.18	90
Notes payable	1,200	.18	216
Common stock	1,000	.20	200
Retained earnings	360	–	68
Cumulative translation adjustment	–	–	(23)
Total liabilities and stockholders' equity	3,060		551

effect of the translation process on shareholders' equity. Generally, it will reduce shareholders' equity further if the French franc continues to depreciate. If it instead appreciates, then the balance could eventually become an addition to equity. The cumulative translation adjustment becomes part of the computation of a realized gain or loss should all or a significant portion of the underlying subsidiary be sold.

Temporal Translation or Remeasurement

Translation or remeasurement under the temporal rule takes place where the local currency in not the functional currency of the subsidiary. This is held to be the case where the local country has a highly inflationary economy, i.e., cumulative inflation of approximately 100% or more over the most recent three-year period. "For an entity with operations that are relatively self-contained and integrated within a particular country, the functional currency generally would be the currency of that country."[24] In this case, the all-current method would apply. Otherwise, the temporal remeasurement procedure would be used.

Leslie Fay Companies, Inc., is an example of a company using the temporal method for a subsidiary located in Hong Kong because the U.S. dollar, the reporting currency of its parent, and not the Hong Kong dollar, the local country's currency, was judged to be the functional currency. This was because the subsidiaries were financed by U.S. dollar advances, and all their sales were to their U.S. parent. Under SFAS No. 52, Leslie Fay's Hong Kong subsidiary was seen as "a direct and integral component or extension of the parent company's operations."[25] In this case, the temporal or remeasurement method is applied. Remeasurement following the temporal method puts the Hong Kong subsidiary's statements into U.S. dollars. In this case, SFAS No. 52 declares, "If a foreign entity's functional currency is the reporting currency, remeasurement into the reporting currency obviates translation."[26]

In the following case, translation would follow remeasurement under the temporal method:

- Malaysian subsidiary of a U.S. parent with the Singapore dollar as its functional currency.
- Remeasurement into the Singapore dollar would take place following the temporal method.
- Translation following the all-current method would take the Singapore dollar statements from the functional currency, Singapore dollar, into the reporting currency, the U.S. dollar.

Application of the temporal rule is designed to achieve results that simulate those that would have been produced if the underlying transactions had taken place in dollars. This is achieved by translation using exchange rates that existed when the transactions took place. Hence, use of the term *temporal.*

Illustration of the temporal method for French Subsidiary starts with the translated trial balance provided in Exhibit A.18. Unlike all-current translation, inventory and property, plant, and equipment are translated at the rates that existed when these balances came onto the books. Further, the depreciation is translated using the same rate, $0.20, employed to translate the associated property, plant, and equipment balance.

The temporal translation alters the exposure of the subsidiary's statements to changing exchange rates from that under the all-current method. Asset exposure existed under the all-current method because assets exceed liabilities translated with the current rate. With the temporal method, liabilities translated using the current rate exceed assets translated with the current rate. With liability exposure in a currency against which the dollar appreciated, a remeasurement, or translation, gain resulted. The number of dollars that would be required to discharge this net liability position is reduced by the strengthening of the dollar.

The income statement and balance sheet of French Subsidiary are provided in Exhibit A.19. Because of its liability exposure under the temporal method, a remeasurement gain of $25,000 resulted. This gain is included in the income statement under the temporal method. It would be deducted from net income in an indirect-basis cash flow statement because it is an unrealized, noncash gain. Net income is $89,000 versus $68,000 under the all-current translation method. This difference in net income can be reconciled as follows:

Exhibit A.18 Trial Balance Translated under the Temporal Method: French Subsidiary (currency amounts in thousands)

	FF	Rate	US$
Debit balance accounts			
Cash	200	.18	36
Accounts receivable	400	.18	72
Inventory	460	.19	87
Property, plant, and equipment, net	2,000	.20	400
Cost of sales	1,200	.19	228
Selling, general, and administrative expense	100	.19	19
Depreciation expense	400	.20	80
Tax provision	240	.19	46
Total	5,000		968
Credit balance accounts			
Accounts payable	500	.18	90
Notes payable	1,200	.18	216
Common stock	1,000	.20	200
Retained earnings	0	–	0
Sales	2,300	.19	437
Translation gain	–	–	25
Total	5,000		968

Exhibit A.19   Translated Income Statement and Balance Sheet under the Temporal Method: French Subsidiary (currency amounts in thousands)

	FF	Rate	US$
Income statement			
Sales	2,300	.19	437
Cost of sales	1,200	.19	228
Gross profit	1,100	–	209
Selling, general, and administrative expense	100	.19	19
Depreciation expense	400	.20	80
Remeasurement gain	–	–	(25)
Profit before taxes	600	–	135
Tax provision	240	.19	46
Net income	360		89
Balance sheet			
Cash	200	.18	36
Accounts receivable	400	.18	72
Inventory	460	.19	87
Property, plant, and equipment	2,000	.20	400
Total assets	3,060		595
Accounts payable	500	.18	90
Notes payable	1,200	.18	216
Common stock	1,000	.20	200
Retained earnings	360	–	89
Total liabilities and stockholders' equity	3,060		595

Net income under the all-current method		$68,000
Plus: Remeasurement gain	$25,000	
Less: Increase in SG&A expense due to depreciation translation at $.20 versus $.19 under all-current: 400,000 FF × (.20 – .19)	(4,000)	21,000
Net income under the temporal method		$89,000

The remeasurement gain of $25,000 results mainly from the shrinkage in the translated value of the FF 1,200,000 notes payable: FF 1,200,000 × (0.20 − 0.18) = $24,000.

INVESTMENTS IN EQUITY SECURITIES

The requirements governing accounting for investments in equity securities are found in Accounting Principles Board Opinion No. 18 and SFAS Nos. 94 and 115.[27] Statement No. 94 deals with consolidated financial statements, an important topic, but a detailed treatment is beyond the scope of this appendix. The coverage here is organized by size of investment holding as a percentage of shares outstanding, the key factor in determining accounting treatment. Holdings of less than 20% are discussed first, followed by holdings of 20%–50%. Consolidation is normally required when holdings of voting shares exceed 50%.

Holdings of Less than Twenty Percent

The accounting requirements for marketable equity securities (common and preferred shares, stock options, etc.) holdings of less than 20% are provided in SFAS No. 115. The accounting treatment turns on the classification of the investment. The three classifications and the associated accounting treatments are summarized in Exhibit A.20. While our focus is on equity securities, this standard deals with both debt and equity securities, and this scope is evident in the classifications. The percentage holding thresholds do not apply to debt securities.

Held-to-Maturity Classification

With the possible exception of certain issues of redeemable preferred stock, equity securities have no maturity, and therefore this classification is not relevant for them. Rather, this classification applies to debt instruments with a stated maturity. Such investments are simply recorded and carried at their amortized cost until their maturity. However, a write-down would be required if the financial position of the issuer of the debt declined and the loss of value were judged to be other than temporary.

Exhibit A.20 Investment Classifications and Accounting Treatments under SFAS No. 115

Classification	Holding Intent	Accounting Treatment
Held-to-maturity	Firm has the intent and ability to hold the investment to maturity.	Carried on the books at amortized cost. Declines in value are only recognized if they are considered to be other than temporary.
Trading	Bought and held for the purpose of sale in the near term.	Carried at market value with gains or losses included in earnings.
Available-for-sale	Held for neither trading nor as long-term investment.	Carried at market value with appreciation or depreciation included in shareholders' equity.

Trading Classification

Holdings of debt securities and marketable equity securities are accounted for as trading securities if the intent is to hold for short periods before sale. Assume that $100,000 is invested in marketable common stock of a large public company. The firm holding the stock is anticipating release of good news about earnings prospects in the near future and plans to sell the securities when the release causes a rise in the stock price. The purchase is made on December 1, 19X1, and the shares are sold on February 1, 19X2. The market value of the shares is $125,000 at December 31, 19X1 and $80,000 when they were sold (the news proved to be disappointing) on February 1, 19X2. Entries to record these transactions are shown in Exhibit A.21.

The hoped for good news was not forthcoming. The eventual sale was for $20,000 less than the initial investment, even though an unrealized gain of $25,000 was recognized at the end of 19X1. Current tax-accounting regulations require recording a deferred tax provision on the unrealized gain recorded at the end of 19X1. The unrealized gain results in a book carrying value for the investment that exceeds the tax carrying value (usually termed *basis*) by $25,000. The deferred tax on this temporary difference, at a combined federal and state tax rate of 40%, would be recorded at year-end as follows:

Account	Debit	Credit
Deferred tax provision (+)	10,000[a]	
Deferred tax liability (+)		10,000

[a]$25,000 × .40.

With this adjustment, the effect on 19X1 net income is an increase of $15,000.

Exhibit A.21 Accounting for Trading Securities

Account	Debit	Credit
Recording the purchase of stock (December 1, 19X1)		
Trading portfolio (+)	100,000	
Cash (−)		100,000
Recording change in value of stock (December 31, 19X1)		
Trading portfolio (+)	25,000	
Unrealized gain on trading portfolio (+)		25,000
Recording the sale of stock (February 1, 19X2)		
Cash (+)	80,000	
Realized loss on trading portfolio (+)	45,000	
Trading portfolio (−)		125,000

The deferred tax liability would be removed or adjusted upon either subsequent sale or further revaluations of the investment.

This example involved recognition of an unrealized gain at year-end. An unrealized loss would have been recorded if the investment had instead fallen by $25,000. In that case, a deferred tax asset of $10,000 would have been recorded on the temporary difference that resulted.

Available-for-Sale Classification

Generally, holdings of marketable equity securities that represent less than 20% of outstanding shares are classified as available-for-sale under the requirements of SFAS No. 115. Recall that the held-to-maturity classification is not applicable because equity securities generally have no maturity. The trading classification would also be unusual because commercial and industrial firms typically do not purchase equity investments for trading purposes. Occasionally, a less than 20% holding of voting shares would provide the investor with the ability to exercise significant influence over the investee company. If so, then the equity method of accounting would be applied and Accounting Principles Board Opinion No. 18 would be applicable.

Assume that on July 1, 19X1, a firm invests $80,000 for less than 1% of the shares of a publicly traded company. At year-end, December 31, 19X1, the shares have fallen in value to $50,000. SFAS No. 115 requires that this investment be adjusted to market value and that the unrealized loss be deducted directly from shareholders' equity. The accounting for this investment would be as follows:

Account	Debit	Credit
Available-for-sale portfolio (+)	80,000	
Cash (–)		80,000

Account	Debit	Credit
Unrealized loss (+)	30,000	
Available-for-sale portfolio (–)		30,000

This revaluation gives rise to a $30,000 temporary difference on which a deferred tax asset must be recorded. The loss is only recorded for shareholder reporting purposes. No loss is available for tax purposes until the investment is sold and the loss becomes realized. The deferred tax asset represents the tax-saving potential of the loss. The offsetting credit to the deferred tax provision reduces the decline in shareholders' equity to the net amount of $18,000 (pre-tax loss of $30,000 less a potential tax benefit of $12,000 based upon a combined tax rate of 40%). The deferred tax is recorded as follows:

Account	Debit	Credit
Deferred tax asset (+)	12,000	
Deferred tax provision (–)		12,000

The after-tax, unrealized loss of $18,000 would appear as a deduction in shareholders' equity.

Appreciation of the investment by $30,000 at the end of 19X1 would have required a write-up of $30,000 and the recording of a deferred tax liability of $12,000. An after-tax, unrealized gain of $18,000 would appear in shareholders' equity.

Holdings of 20%–50%

Holdings of from 20%–50% of the voting shares of a company, which provide the investor with the capacity to exercise significant influence over the investee, are accounted for using the equity method. The provisions of SFAS No. 115 do not apply in this case. SFAS No. 115, and the market-value reporting requirement, apply if a 20%–50% holding does not provide the investor with significant influence.

The Equity Method

The equity method is a miniature version of consolidation and is often referred to as a one-line consolidation. The equity method yields the same earnings and shareholders' equity totals as would a conventional consolidation. The investor's share of earnings or losses is recognized, and the investment balance increased or decreased, under the equity method. Dividends received are treated as a partial liquidation of the investment position and are recorded as a reduction in the investment and not as income.

Our illustration of the equity method is based upon the following information:

- A 20% voting interest is acquired for $10 million at the beginning of 19X1.
- The amount invested is equal to 20% of the market value of the net assets of the investee company.
- The investee company has net income of $6 million in 19X1.
- A total dividend of $1 million was paid by the investee company.

The entries required to apply the equity method to this information in the case of no goodwill are shown in Exhibit A.22.[28] At year-end, the investment will have risen by $1 million: the $1.2 million share of equity earnings less the $200,000 dividend received. The undistributed earnings of $1 million, in addition to increasing the investment, would be deducted from the net income of the investor in the investor's indirect-basis statement of cash flows. While $1.2 million is included in the investor's

Exhibit A.22 Accounting by Equity Method for an Investment Not Including Goodwill (thousands of dollars)

Account	Debit	Credit
Recording the investment (January 1, 19X1)		
Equity investment (+)	10,000	
Cash (−)		10,000
Recording share of 19X1 earnings		
Equity investment (+)	1,200	
Equity earnings (+)		1,200
Recording dividend received		
Cash (+)	200	
Equity investment (−)		200

earnings, only $200,000 is supported by a cash inflow. Therefore, the $1 million undistributed amount is deducted from net income in arriving at net cash from operating activities.

In the case including goodwill, assume the same information as before except that the investor's share of the market value of the investee's net assets, 20%, only amounts to $8 million. The extra $2 million is goodwill and amortized as part of the application of the equity method.[29] A ten-year amortization period is assumed. Goodwill is amortized as part of the application of the equity method. The entries to account for the investment in this case are shown in Exhibit A.23.

Exhibit A.23 Accounting by Equity Method for an Investment Including Goodwill (thousands of dollars)

Account	Debit	Credit
Recording the investment (January 1, 19X1)		
Equity investment (+)	10,000	
Cash (−)		10,000
Recording share of 19X1 earnings		
Equity investment (+)	1,200	
Equity earnings (+)		1,200
Recording amortization of goodwill		
Equity earnings (−)	200	
Equity investment (−)		200
Recording dividend received		
Cash (+)	200	
Equity investment (−)		200

With the goodwill amortization, the net equity earnings and investment are reduced by $200,000. Notice that the goodwill is not disclosed in a separate account but is simply part of the equity investment balance. Moreover, the goodwill amortization is deducted directly from equity earnings.

The Equity Method and Market Value

Investments in marketable equity securities will be carried at market value if SFAS No. 115 applies and not the equity-accounting requirements of Accounting Principles Board Opinion No. 18. An equity-accounted investment is written up in response to profitable operations of the investee. This may move the investments carrying value closer to market value than would be the case if it were carried at original cost. However, there are many cases where great disparities still exist between carrying value under the equity method and market value. Recent prominent examples are the holdings of Kmart Corp. in Coles Myer Ltd., of Seagram Co. in E. I. du Pont de Nemours and Co., and of Chemed Corp. in Omnicare, Inc. In each of these cases, the equity method was (Seagram has now disposed of its investment in Du Pont, Kmart disposed of its investment in Coles Myer, and Chemed reduced its holding in Omnicare to less than 20%) employed. Nevertheless there were tremendous excesses of market value, amounting to billions of dollars in the case of Seagram/Du Pont, over the equity-accounting investment balance. In contrast, there are also cases where the market value is well below the equity-accounting investment balance.

ACCOUNTING FOR LEASES

The topic of accounting for leases can be broken down into the requirements for lessees (users of assets) and for lessors (owners of assets). The classifications of leases on the lessee side are capital leases and operating leases. On the lessor side, the classifications are finance (or direct-finance) leases and operating leases. In addition, manufacturers or dealers, as lessors, may have sale-type leases. Finally, sale/leaseback transactions are a combining of a sale and a lease.

Lessee Accounting

The key determinant of the accounting treatment applied to leases is whether the lease agreement is the economic equivalent of a purchase. If so, then the lease is accounted for as the acquisition of an asset and the incurrence of an obligation. This is termed treating the agreement as a capital lease. The alternative classification is as an operating lease. Here, neither asset nor liability is recorded and the annual lease expense is simply equal to the lease payment. SFAS No. 13, "Accounting for Leases," includes the following criteria to determine whether a lease is to be accounted for as a capital lease:[30]

- The lease transfers title at its expiration.
- The lease contains a bargain purchase option.
- The lease term is for 75% or more of the useful life of the leased asset.
- The present value of the minimum lease payments is 90% or more of the fair value of the leased asset.

A lease agreement that satisfies one or more of these criteria is to be accounted for as a capital lease. Otherwise, the operating lease treatment is applied. Illustration of each of these accounting treatments is based upon the follow lease data:

- The lease has a term of five years and the leased asset also has a useful life of five years.
- The lease does not transfer title at its expiration.
- There is no bargain purchase option.
- The annual year-end lease payment is $10,000, and the implicit interest rate in the lease contract, used to determine present value, is 10%.

This lease would be treated as a capital lease because its term equals 100% of the useful life of the leased asset. Illustration of the capital lease accounting treatment, for the first year only, is provided in Exhibit A.24.

Accounting for the lease would have followed the operating-lease method if it had not met one or more of the lease classification criteria. This would simply have involved an entry each year charging lease expense for $10,000:

Exhibit A.24   First-Year Capital Lease Accounting Treatment

Account	Debit	Credit
At lease inception		
Leased asset (+)	37,908	
Lease obligation (+)		37,908[a]
First payment		
Lease obligation (−)	6,209	
Interest expense (+)	3,791[b]	
Cash (−)		10,000
Amortization of leased asset		
Leased asset amortization (+)	7,582	
Leased asset (−)		7,582[c]

[a]Present value of five $10,000 annual lease payments discounted at 10%.
[b]$37,908 × .10.
[c]$37,908/5.

Account	Debit	Credit
Lease expense (+)	10,000	
Cash (–)		10,000

Exhibit A.25 shows the complete five-year schedule associated with the accounting for the capital lease. Exhibit A.26 shows the annual expense differences between the capital and operating lease treatments. In most cases where the capital lease method is used in the books, the equivalent of the operating lease method is used in the tax return. As a result, the differences between capital and operating lease expenses are temporary differences and require the recording of deferred taxes. For example, in year 19X1, book expense exceeds that in the tax return by $1,373. A deferred tax asset would be recorded to recognize, in 19X1, the tax-saving potential of this extra expense. It will become a realized benefit when this extra expense is deducted in the tax return and produces a tax saving. A deferred tax asset, at a combined tax rate of 40%, would be recorded in 19X1 as follows:

Exhibit A.25   Complete Capital Lease Amortization Schedule

Date	Annual Payment	Interest (a)	Obligation Reduction (b)	Obligation Balance (c)
Jan. 1, 19X1	–	–	–	$37,908
Dec. 31, 19X1	$10,000	$ 3,791	$ 6,209	31,699
Dec. 31, 19X2	10,000	3,170	6,830	24,869
Dec. 31, 19X3	10,000	2,487	7,513	17,356
Dec. 31, 19X4	10,000	1,736	8,264	9,092
Dec. 31, 19X5	10,000	908	9,092	0
Total	$50,000	$12,092	$37,908	

(a) 10% × prior year amount in column (c).
(b) Annual payment less amount in column (a).
(c) Prior-year balance less amount in column (b).

Exhibit A.26   Annual Expense Differences: Capital Versus Operating Lease Treatments

Year	Capital	Operating	Difference
19X1	$11,373	$10,000	$1,373
19X2	10,752	10,000	752
19X3	10,069	10,000	69
19X4	9,318	10,000	(682)
19X5	8,488	10,000	(1,512)
Total	$50,000	$50,000	0

Account	Debit	Credit
Deferred tax asset (+)	549[a]	
Deferred tax provision (−)		549

[a]$1,373 × .40.

Deferred tax assets would also be recorded in 19X2 and 19X3 as additional temporary differences emerged. The deferred tax assets would be amortized in 19X4 and 19X5 as the temporary differences reversed.

Exhibits A.24 and A.25 reveal the effect of the operating and capital lease treatments on expense recognition and lease obligations. Lessees typically do not want an agreement to be treated as a capital lease. Exhibit A.24 shows that a capital lease requires putting additional long-term obligations on the lessee's balance sheet. This increases leverage as computed by such ratios as debt-to-equity and also reduces return on asset ratios because of the increase in assets under capital lease accounting. Moreover, Exhibit A.26 shows that expense recognition is accelerated under the capital lease treatment. These appear to be the major reasons for the strong preference to avoid lease structures that require the capital lease treatment. On the other hand, lessors typically prefer finance lease classification, the lessor's equivalent of a capital lease.

Lessor Accounting

Typically, the terminology on the lessor side of lease transactions refers to finance leases and operating leases rather than to capital leases and operating leases. The *finance lease* term emphasizes the financing nature of leasing transactions.

Lessors must compare their lease contracts to the same set of four criteria used by lessees. That is, (1) title transfer, (2) bargain purchase option, (3) lease term of 75% or more of asset useful life, and (4) lease present value of 90% or more of leased asset's fair value. In addition to these, lessors must consider two additional features:

- Is collectibility of payments reasonably predictable?
- Are there any important uncertainties regarding costs to be incurred by the lessor under the lease?

If collectibility of payments is not predictable or performance of the lessor is not complete, then treatment as an operating lease may be necessary.

Finance Lease Treatment

If a lease arrangement (1) meets at least one of the first four criteria, (2) collectibility is reasonably predictable, and (3) there are no important uncertainties regarding costs to be incurred, then the lease will be accounted for as either a finance or sale-type lease. Failure of the lease to qualify for finance lease treatment will require operating lease accounting. A comparison of a lessor's accounting for a finance lease and an operating lease is provided in Exhibits A.27–A.29. The same lease arrangement illustrated for the lessee in Exhibits A.24–A.26 is used to illustrate lessor reporting: five-year lease term and asset useful life, $10,000 annual lease receipt, 10% interest rate, and no bargain purchase option. In addition, this example assumes, for simplicity, that there is no residual value at the end of the lease term, and that the asset cost the lessor $37,908 to purchase.

Notice that the cost of the equipment is removed from the balance sheet of the lessor and replaced with the net investment in leases. Net investment in leases is

Exhibit A.27   Finance Lease Accounting Treatment by a Lessor

Account	Debit	Credit
At lease inception		
Lease payments receivable (+)	50,000	
Equipment (−)		37,908
Unearned finance income (+)		12,092[a]
First lease receipt		
Cash (+)	10,000	
Lease payments receivable (−)		10,000
Recognition of unearned income		
Unearned income (−)	3,791[b]	
Finance income (+)		3,791

[a]$50,000 − $37,908.
[b]($50,000 − $12,092) × 10%.

Exhibit A.28   Finance Lease Amortization Schedule

Date	Annual Receipt	Finance Income (a)	Net Investment Reduction (b)	Net Investment Balance (c)
Jan. 1, 19X1	–	–	–	$37,908
Dec. 31, 19X1	$10,000	$3,791	$6,209	31,699
Dec. 31, 19X2	10,000	3,170	6,830	24,869
Dec. 31, 19X3	10,000	2,487	7,513	17,356
Dec. 31, 19X4	10,000	1,736	8,264	9,092
Dec. 31, 19X5	10,000	908	9,092	0
Totals	$50,000	$12,092	$37,908	

(a) 10% × prior year amount in column (c).
(b) Annual receipt minus amount in column (a).
(c) Prior year balance minus amount in column (b).

Exhibit A.29 Annual Income Differences: Finance Versus Operating Lease Treatments

Year	Finance	Operating	Difference
19X1	$ 3,791	$ 2,419	$1,372
19X2	3,170	2,419	751
19X3	2,487	2,418	69
19X4	1,736	2,418	(682)
19X5	908	2,418	(1,510)
Total	$12,092	$12,092	0

measured as the difference between the lease payments receivable and the balance of the unearned finance income account. It is this amount upon which the earned finance income is based. While removed from the shareholder books, the leased asset is generally still owned by the lessor and depreciated in its tax return.

Operating Lease Treatment

If the preceding lease had not qualified as a finance lease, then it would have been accounted for as an operating lease. No entry would have been made upon inception of the lease agreement, and subsequent accounting would simply involve recognition of the lease receipt as revenue and depreciation on the leased asset as expense. Depreciation expense is recorded because, unlike in the finance lease case, the leased asset in not removed from the lessor's books. The following entries are recorded for lease revenue and depreciation expense, both at the end of each year over the term of the lease:

Account	Debit	Credit
Cash (+)	10,000	
Lease revenue (+)		10,000

Account	Debit	Credit
Depreciation expense (+)	7,582[a]	
Accumulated depreciation (+)		7,582

[a]$37,908/5.

Exhibit A.28 shows the complete five-year schedule associated with the accounting for this finance lease. Exhibit A.29 shows the annual income differences between the finance lease and operating lease treatments. Income under a finance lease is recognized on a more accelerated basis than under an operating lease. The schedule of income recognized in Exhibit A.28 shows a decline across time as the net investment in the lease declines. Lease profit under the operating lease is generally recognized in a straight-line pattern. These profit differences are disclosed in Exhibit A.29.

Temporary differences, calling for the recording of deferred taxes, will be required if the finance lease method is used in the books and the operating lease method in the tax return. Because book profit under the finance lease treatment exceeds tax return results under the operating lease treatment, a deferred tax provision and deferred tax liability will be recorded. Entries to record deferred taxes in two representative years, 19X1 and 19X4, respectively, are as follows:

In 19X1:

Account	Debit	Credit
Deferred tax provision (+)	549[a]	
Deferred tax liability (+)		549

[a]$1,372 × .40.

In 19X4:

Account	Debit	Credit
Deferred tax liability (−)	273[a]	
Deferred tax provision (−)		273

[a]$682 × .40

Book earnings exceed those in the tax return from 19X1 to 19X3, and a deferred tax provision and associated deferred tax liability are recorded on this originating temporary difference. However, in 19X4, the temporary differences begin to reverse, with the process completed in 19X5. In these two years the deferred tax liabilities are reduced.

Sale-Type Leases

Leases that otherwise qualify as finance leases may be accounted for as if a sale had occurred. The sale-type lease treatment is applied where the fair value of the leased asset and the lessor's cost differ significantly, i.e., a manufacturer's or dealer's profit margin exists.

Assume the same information used in the preceding examples with the exception that the lessor is the manufacturer of the leased asset and the lessor's cost is $30,000. The present value of the lease receipts, $37,908, approximates the fair value of the leased asset and is treated as the amount of the sale. The initial recording of the sale-type lease would be as follows:

Account	Debit	Credit
Lease payments receivable (+)	50,000	
Sale (+)		37,908
Unearned finance income (+)		12,092
Cost of sales (+)	30,000	
Inventory (−)		30,000

This treatment results in the immediate recognition of gross profit of $7,908, the sale amount of $37,908 less the cost of sales of $30,000. The unearned finance income is recognized over the lease term in exactly the same manner as if the lease were simply a finance lease (see Exhibit A.28). Sale-type lease treatment is applied to such items as computer software, computers, and hospital equipment.

Sale and Leaseback Transactions

A sale-type lease involves the lessor as seller, but a sale/leaseback transaction involves a lessee as seller. Airlines are among the more active types of firms engaging in sale/leasebacks. As the name implies, this transaction first involves the sale of an asset followed by its immediate leaseback. Accounting guidance for these transactions is found in SFAS No. 28.[31]

SFAS No. 28 permits recognition of gains in the year of the sale/leaseback in some cases. For example, if the leaseback is considered to be minor, then all the gain on the sale may be included in earnings in the year of sale. In all other cases, some or all of the gain is deferred and amortized into earnings, usually as a reduction of lease expense, over the lease term.

Complete Gain Deferral

The amount of gain recognized immediately and the amount deferred depend on the size of the gain in relation to the present value of the leaseback. Profit can be recognized immediately to the extent that it exceeds the present value of the lease agreement. The following information is used to illustrate accounting for a sale/leaseback transaction, which is summarized in Exhibit A.30:

- A retailer sells and leases back store properties.
- Carrying value of the properties is $2.2 million.
- Sale price is $5.9 million and the gain is therefore $3.7 million.
- The lease term is 20 years, and the leaseback is classified as an operating lease.

Exhibit A.30   Accounting for a Sale/Leaseback Transaction (thousands of dollars)

Account	Debit	Credit
Recording the sale transaction		
Cash (+)	5,900	
Properties (−)		2,200
Deferred sale/leaseback gain[a] (+)		3,700
Recording deferred taxes		
Deferred tax asset (+)	1,480[b]	
Deferred tax provision (−)		1,480
Recording the year-end lease payment		
Lease expense (+)	601	
Cash(−)		601
Amortizing deferred sale/leaseback gain		
Deferred sale/leaseback gain (−)	185[c]	
Lease expense (−)		185
Amortizing the deferred tax asset		
Deferred tax provision (+)	74[d]	
Deferred tax asset (−)		74

[a]Immediate gain-recognition test:

Total gain	$3,700
Less: Present value of the leaseback	5,900
Excess of present value over gain	$(2,200)

No gain can be recognized in the year of sale because the present value of the leaseback exceeds the total gain on the sale.
[b]$3,700 × .40.
[c]$3,700/20.
[d]$185 × .40.

- The present value of the leaseback is equal to the sale price of $5.9 million.
- Annual lease payments are $601,000.

The deferred sale/leaseback gain is amortized over the 20-year lease term and reduces net lease expense to $416,000 per year. A temporary difference arises because the gain is included in the tax return in the year of sale but is deferred in the books. The excess of tax return over book profit of $3,700,000 gives rise to a deferred tax asset of $1,480,000 based on a combined tax rate of 40%. The temporary difference reverses at the rate of $185,000 each year as this amount of deferred gain ($3,700,000/20 years) is amortized through the book income statement. Book profit exceeds that in the tax return by $185,000 during each year of the lease term because the sale/leaseback gain is amortized through the book income statement. This calls for a corresponding amortization each year of the deferred tax asset in the amount of $74,000.

Partial Gain Deferral

Some gain could have been recognized in the year of sale, and less deferred, if the leaseback period in this example had been significantly shorter. This would result if the lease present value became less than the total gain. Then, gain equal to this difference would be recognized in the year of sale and only the remainder would be deferred. Assume that a shortened leaseback resulted in a lease present value of only $3 million. The entry in the year of the sale/leaseback would then have been as follows (thousands of dollars):

Account	Debit	Credit
Cash (+)	5,900	
Properties (−)		2,200
Recognized gain on sale (+)		700[a]
Deferred sale/leaseback gain (+)		3,000

[a]Total gain on the sale of properties

($5,900 − $2,200)	$3,700
Present value of leaseback	3,000
Excess of gain over lease-back present value	$ 700

The logic of limiting immediate gain recognition is to preclude immediate recognition of gain that could be seen as having been "financed" through the leaseback transaction. In the end, the full gain is ultimately recognized in the book income statement. However, the timing of the recognition of these gains can include (1) all in the year of sale, (2) part in the year of sale and part over the lease term, and (3) all the gain recognized over the term of the lease.

ACCOUNTING FOR PENSIONS

Pension accounting and related disclosures are guided mainly by SFAS No. 87, "Accounting for Pensions."[32] Defined benefit plans create the key issues from an accounting and financial reporting perspective. These plans define the benefit that must eventually be paid to the employee and not simply a contribution that the employer or plan sponsor will make on behalf of employees.

Characteristics of Pensions and Their Reporting Treatment

The Employee Retirement Income Security Act of 1974 (ERISA) made major legal changes designed to ensure that employees' pension rights and benefits were protected. Funding was made mandatory for tax-qualified plans, and limitations were imposed on the period of service that could be required before employees' pension benefits became vested. Vesting ensures that employees will receive a pension benefit upon retirement even if they leave the current employer prior to retirement. Further, the employees' security is aided by the insurance feature that is part of ERISA. The Pension Benefit Guaranty Corp. (PBGC) was established to ensure a maximum, "guaranteed" benefit. It is funded by a per capita premium levied on plan sponsors. In the event that a pension plan is terminated in an underfunded condition, the PBGC can bring a claim against the sponsoring firm for up to 30% of its net assets. This is a powerful claim because it has the same standing as a tax lien.

There are funding requirements under current pension law that call for employers to make contributions to their pension funds. In addition, in some defined-benefit plans employees also are required to make contributions. Benefits ultimately received under a defined-benefit plan are generally related to average compensation levels close to retirement. Typical examples would base pension benefits on the average compensation for the last five years of service or the average compensation for the five highest out of the last ten years of employment.

The plan sponsor accrues the cost of pension benefits earned during the year by its employees. An accrued liability will result if the contribution made to the pension fund is less than the pension cost accrued. A prepaid pension asset will result in the opposite case. Unless a pension plan is underfunded, these differences between cost accruals and pension fund contributions will be the only sources of pension assets or liabilities on the books of the plan sponsor. The pension cost accrual will be the only pension-related item in the sponsor's income statement.

Pension Plan Disclosures

The financial statements and related information on the pension plan are footnote disclosures to the financial statements of the plan sponsor. An example of the equivalent of the balance sheet of a pension plan is provided in Exhibit A.31.

Pension Plan Financial Position

The financial position, or funded status, of the Union Bank plan in Exhibit A.31 is judged by the relation of plan assets to two different measures of plan obligations. Notice that the plan assets are reported at fair or market value. The plan assets exceed both the accumulated and projected benefit obligations. The accumulated benefit obligation is the actuarial present value of benefits earned to date. It is based upon historical pay levels. The projected benefit obligation incorporates estimates of future wage increases. If the plan's benefits were not pay-related, then the accumulated and projected obligations would be the same. This plan's other disclosures reveal an expected rate of increase in salary levels of 5.75% for 1993.

Based upon the projected benefit obligation, the Union Bank pension plan is overfunded by $28,639,000. However, the balance sheet of Union Bank shows a prepaid pension cost asset of only $26,644,000. The items disclosed between the

Exhibit A.31 Statement of Pension Plan Funded Status: Union Bank, Years Ending December 31, 1992 and 1993 (thousands of dollars)

	1992	1993
Accumulated benefit obligation		
Actuarial present value of benefits for services rendered to date		
Vested	$(143,437)	$(168,730)
Nonvested	(16,452)	(17,392)
Total	(159,889)	(186,122)
Projected benefit obligation	(217,978)	(233,076)
Fair value of plan assets	232,168	261,715
Projected benefit obligation less than plan assets	14,190	28,639
Prior service cost not yet recognized in net periodic pension cost	13,927	11,768
Unrecognized net gain due to change of assumptions and experience different from assumptions made	(2,888)	(12,958)
Unrecognized transition asset at January 1, 1986, being recognized over 13.4 years	(954)	(805)
Prepaid pension costs included in other assets	$ 24,275	$ 26,644

Source: Union Bank, annual report, December 1993, pp. 48–50.

excess funding of $28,639,000 and the prepaid pension cost of $26,644,000 reconcile the funded status of the pension plan to the pension asset carried on the balance sheet of the plan sponsor, Union Bank. Only the prepaid pension cost balance is included on the balance sheet of the plan sponsor.

The $1,995,000 difference between the plan overfunding and the prepaid pension cost is due to three different items that have been recognized in determining the funded status of the pension plan but not in the financial statements of the plan sponsor:

1. *Prior period cost not yet recognized in net periodic pension cost.* Pension benefits are sometimes changed with retroactive effect. In most cases, the changes involve improved benefits and the result is an immediate increase in the pension obligations. The pension standard does not require that this increase in pension obligation be recognized immediately in the computation of pension cost by the plan sponsor. Rather, this amount is amortized over the remaining service life of the affected employees as an addition to pension cost. The decline of $2,159,000 [$13,927,000 – $11,768,000] in this balance in 1993 is an addition to pension cost. The $11,768,000 is added to the overfunded amount in the pension fund in moving toward the pension asset balance on the plan sponsor's books. This increase in pension obligation was recognized by the pension fund but not in the pension cost computations of the plan sponsor. This causes the pension asset of

the plan sponsor to exceed the overfunded amount of the pension fund by the $11,768,000.

2. *Unrecognized net gain due to change of assumptions and experience different from assumptions made.* Many assumptions are made in the process of computing pension cost and obligations. For example, the computation of pension cost requires an assumption as to the rate of return on pension assets. If the actual return exceeds or falls short of this expectation, this difference has an immediate impact on the funded status of the pension plan. However, this excess or shortfall in return is not given immediate recognition in the financial statements of the plan sponsor. This plan has performed above its expectations (actuarial assumptions) in recent years. At the end of 1993, $12,958,000 more assets were recognized in the pension plan than were recognized in the computation of net periodic pension cost on the books of Union Bank. This amount is, therefore, deducted from the overfunded amount shown by the pension plan's statements ($28,639,000) in reconciling to the pension asset ($26,644,000) shown on the balance sheet of Union Bank. The bank's pension asset is lower than the overfunded amount on the pension plan's statements because of this unrecognized gain.

3. *Unrecognized transition asset at January 1, 1986, being recognized over 13.4 years.* The Union Bank pension plan was overfunded when SFAS No. 87 was initially adopted in 1986. This statement requires that underfunded or overfunded amounts at adoption be recognized in the computation of pension cost over the remaining service life of the employees covered by the plan. Again, these additional assets are already included in the fair value of plan assets and are reflected in the overfunded status of the plan. Since an unrecognized amount of $805,000 remains, this amount is yet to be reflected in the plan sponsor's prepaid pension asset. Therefore, this $805,000 is deducted from the overfunded amount of the pension plan to arrive at Union Bank's pension asset. The adjustment for this item makes the reconciliation complete.

Net Periodic Pension Expense or Cost

The reconciliation items in Exhibit A.31 also affect the computation of net periodic pension expense. Their effect is revealed by the display of the elements of net periodic pension expense for the Union Bank plan in Exhibit A.32. Pension rate assumptions are also provided in the exhibit. The key items in Exhibit A.32 are explained here and related to associated balances in Exhibit A.31:

1. *Service cost.* This is the increase in the projected benefit obligation resulting from the additional pension benefits earned by Union Bank employees during the year. This amount, as is true of almost all others in the pension disclosures, is the result of calculations performed by actuaries.

2. *Interest on projected benefit obligation.* This element of net pension cost reflects

Exhibit A.32 Components of Net Periodic Pension Expense: Union Bank, Years Ending December 31, 1991–1993 (thousands of dollars)

	1991	1992	1993
Service cost—present value of benefits earned	$9,650	$10,494	$10,654
Interest cost on projected benefit obligation	13,992	15,537	16,246
Less: Return on assets			
Actual return	(29,501)	(14,857)	(22,213)
Gains (losses) in excess of expected return on assets	16,053	(846)	4,747
Expected return on assets	(13,448)	(15,703)	(17,466)
Amortization of prior service cost	2,159	2,159	2,159
Amortization of transition asset	(149)	(149)	(149)
Net periodic pension expense	$12,204	$12,338	$11,444
Assumptions used in accounting			
Discount (settlement) rate	8.00%	8.00%	7.75%
Rate of increase in salary levels	6.00	6.00	5.75
Expected return on assets	8.00	8.00	7.75

Source: Union Bank, annual report, December 1993, pp. 48–50.

the increase in the projected benefit obligation due to the passage of an additional year. The projected benefit obligation is measured at present value. Therefore, moving one year closer to the cash outflows increases their present value by interest. While only an approximation, notice that multiplication of the projected benefit obligation at the end of 1992 ($217,978,000) in Exhibit A.31 by the discount rate at the end of 1992 (8.00%) in Exhibit A.32 approximates the 1993 interest on projected benefit obligation:

$218 million × 0.08 = $17 million [versus $16 million in Exhibit A.32]

The difference of about $1 million could reflect a small difference in discount rate actually used in computing interest, in view of the change in rate from the end of 1992 to the end of 1993. Also, the approximation uses, as the 1993 beginning projected benefit obligation, the ending amount from 1992. This number would change across the year as new benefits are earned, payments are made that reduce the project benefit obligation, or actuarial assumptions (for example, the reduction in the assumed rate of increase in salary levels to 5.75%) are changed.

3. *Actual and expected return on plan assets.* Actual return on plan assets is computed as follows:

Actual return (loss) on pension plan assets	=	Fair value of plan assets at end of year
	−	Fair value of plan assets at beginning of year
	−	Contributions to pension plan during year
	+	Benefit payments from pension plan during year

The expected return is based upon plan assets at the beginning of 1993 ($232,168,000) and the expected return on assets (8.00%) at the end of 1992:

$232 million × 0.08 = $18.6 million [versus $17.5 in Exhibit A.32]

This is only an approximation because assets flow in and out during the year as a result of payments and possible contributions. These would also affect the expected return.

In computing pension expense, credit is only taken for the expected and not the actual return. This is clear from the Union Bank disclosure in Exhibit A.32. The expected return of $17,466,000, and not the actual return of $22,213,000, is deducted from service cost and interest in arriving at net pension expense. The difference between actual and expected return is deferred and would only be included in the computation of net pension cost if it exceeded 10% of the larger of pension assets or the projected benefit obligation. The basis for this treatment is to smooth out the annual pension cost and not have it fluctuate wildly as a result of fluctuations in year-to-year pension fund returns.

4. *Amortization of prior service cost.* The increase, or rarely decrease, in the projected benefit obligation from retroactive improvements or reductions in benefits is amortized over the remaining working lifetime of those affected by the change. Amortization in this case simply refers to being included in the computation of net pension expense by the plan sponsor. Nothing was recognized on the books of Union Bank when the benefits were retroactively improved. Therefore, there is nothing on Union Bank's books to amortize. Nonetheless, *amortization* is the term used for this pension expense element. Note that the prior service cost is amortized on a straight-line basis in the amount of $2,159,000 per year and that it increases net pension expense.

5. *Amortization of transition asset.* Union Bank's pension plan was overfunded when it adopted SFAS No. 87. Overfunding for this purpose is measured as the excess of plan assets over the projected benefit obligation. A transition obligation would be amortized, increasing pension expense if the plan had been underfunded upon adoption of SFAS No. 87.

Union Bank's income statement for 1993 would include the $11,444,000 net pension expense.

Recognition of Underfunded and Overfunded Amounts by the Plan Sponsor

One of the most important features of SFAS No. 87 is the requirement that the plan sponsor record an obligation in cases where its pension plans are underfunded. There is no comparable provision permitting immediate recognition of the excess assets of overfunded plans.

Liability Recognition and Underfunded Plans

SFAS No. 87 requires firms to record an obligation equal to the difference between plan assets and the accumulated benefit obligation. This is the additional minimum pension liability requirement of SFAS No. 87. While an offsetting charge against earnings or shareholders' equity might have been expected, SFAS No. 87 calls instead for recognition of an intangible pension asset. The goal of the Financial Accounting Standards Board was to ensure that liabilities were recorded when pensions were underfunded. There was substantial resistance by the business community to reducing either earnings or shareholders' equity as part of the liability recognition process. A failure by the Board to require charges against earnings or shareholders' equity, even though shareholders' equity is reduced in some cases, appears to have been a compromise solution.

Limits on Recognition of Pension Intangible Assets

SFAS No. 87 does place limits on the portion of the recorded liability than can be matched by the recording of a pension intangible asset. This limit is the sum of unrecognized or unamortized prior service cost and of the transition obligation. The logic, at least as it relates to prior service cost, is that a retroactive increase in benefits may simultaneously create an asset as well as a liability. The growth in the projected benefit obligation is clearly a result of retroactive benefit increases. The emergence of an offsetting asset is based upon a presumption that employee productivity would improve as a result of the improvement in benefits.

We illustrate now the application of the additional minimum pension liability. For the case where no unrecognized prior service cost or transition obligation exists, the following information applies:

- Accumulated benefit obligation $1,000,000
- Plan assets at fair value 800,000
- Minimum pension liability required 200,000
- Pension accrual on the sponsor's balance sheet prior to the adjustment 50,000
- Required additional minimum pension adjustment $ 150,000

The entries for adjusting minimum pension liability and for deferred taxes at a 40% rate are as follows:

Account	Debit	Credit
Shareholders' equity—		
underfunded pension loss (–)	150,000	
Pension liability (+)		150,000

Account	Debit	Credit
Deferred tax asset (+)	60,000	
Deferred tax provision (−)		60,000

All the liability adjustment of $150,000 is charged against shareholders' equity because there is neither unrecognized prior service cost nor unrecognized transition obligation. The reduction in shareholders' equity is offset in part by the $60,000 deferred tax benefit recorded on this temporary difference. The minimum liability adjustment is recorded in the books but not in the tax return. A deferred tax asset is created here just as it is when a warranty liability is accrued in the books but not in the tax return.

For the case where unrecognized prior service cost and a transition obligation totaling $80,000 exists, all other information being the same as for the first case, the entries are as follows:

Account	Debit	Credit
Shareholders' equity—		
unfunded pension loss (−)	70,000	
Intangible pension asset (+)	80,000	
Pension liability (+)		150,000

Account	Debit	Credit
Deferred tax asset (+)	28,000[a]	
Deferred tax provision (−)		28,000

[a]$70,000 × .40.

The net reduction in shareholders' equity in the first case was $90,000. In this second case the reduction is only $42,000, a difference of $48,000. This results from the presence of the unrecognized prior service cost and transition obligation of $80,000. This reduced the after-tax charge against shareholders' equity by $80,000 × (1 − 0.40) = $48,000.

The preceding entry is recorded on the shareholder books only and thus a temporary difference results. The originating temporary difference is $70,000, the net difference between the book and tax return basis of the recorded intangible asset, $80,000, and the pension liability, $150,000. Generally accepted accounting principles call for recording a deferred tax asset in this circumstance.

The minimum pension liability is adjusted at the end of each successive accounting period as the pension plan becomes more or less overfunded. As the liability is increased or decreased, the associated pension intangible assets, reduction in shareholders' equity, and deferred tax assets are also adjusted. The pension intangible asset is not amortized through the income statement as an element of pension expense.

Asset Recognition and Overfunded Plans

Assets may not simply be recorded on the books of the sponsor of an overfunded pension plan. However, the process of measuring periodic pension cost results in gradual recognition of overfunding. For example, pension cost is reduced by the amortization of overfunding that exists upon adoption of SFAS No. 87. Reducing pension expense increases net income and with it the shareholders' equity or net assets of the plan sponsor. This result is illustrated by the Union Bank disclosures in Exhibit A.32. Amortization of an overfunded position upon adoption of SFAS No. 87 has reduced pension expense by $149,000 each year since its adoption in 1986.

Actual pension returns may exceed expected returns to the point that such accumulated gains exceed 10% of the higher of plan assets or the projected benefit obligation. At this point, a portion of such excess is amortized as a reduction in pension expense. Similarly, a significantly overfunded condition results in the recognition of an increased level of expected return. This reduces net pension expense, sometimes to the point of creating net pension income. For example, R. R. Donnelley & Sons Co., had significantly overfunded pension plans for each of the years 1992–1994. As a result, the company disclosed net pension income of $16.3 million, $13.9 million, and $13.7 million in 1992, 1993, and 1994, respectively.[33] Interestingly, the growth in asset prepaid pension cost was exactly equal to net pension income in each of these three years. After its computation, the net pension income for 1994 was recorded with the following entry (millions of dollars):

Account	Debit	Credit
Prepaid pension costs (an asset) (+)	13.7	
Pension income (+)		13.7

Other Pension-Type Benefit Plans

Similar financial reporting and disclosure standards apply to postretirement benefits other than pensions and to postemployment benefits. The postretirement benefits include such items as medical and life insurance.[34] Postemployment benefits, received during a period between the end of employment and the beginning of retirement, include such items as wage or benefit continuation, severance pay, job training, and disability benefits.[35]

In the past, these benefits were typically not accrued over the relevant period of service of the covered employees. They were simply accounted for on a cash or as-paid basis. Moreover, they were not funded. The absence of funding was due in part to the inability to deduct amounts as funded for tax purposes. In some cases, the effects of adopting these standards was dramatic. For example, in adopting the requirements of SFAS No. 106, "Employers' Accounting for Postretirement Benefits Other Than Pensions," General Motors Corp. increased its 1992 loss by $20.8 billion.[36] In addition to the effect on previous years, there is an incremental increase in future costs as a result of adopting accrual accounting for these benefits. Again, for General Motors, this resulted in an incremental increase that reduced net income for 1993 by $1.5 billion.

ENDNOTES

1. *Accounting Trends and Techniques* (Jersey City, NJ.: American Institute of Certified Public Accountants, 1994), p. 398.
2. Stewart and Stevenson Services, Inc., annual report, January 1994, p. 36.
3. "Accounting for Performance of Construction-Type and Certain Production-Type Contracts" (1981).
4. Avondale Industries, Inc., annual report, December 1994, p. 20.
5. Blount, Inc., annual report, February 1992, p. 26.
6. Avondale Industries, Inc., annual report, December 1994, p. 20.
7. Wyman-Gordon Co., annual report, December 1993, p. 24.
8. A Securities and Exchange Commission (SEC) requirement. *Staff Accounting Bulletin No. 40,* which applies only to public companies, calls for firms to "disclose the amount of income, if material, that has been recorded because a LIFO inventory liquidation has taken place."
9. Phillips Petroleum Co., annual report, December,1994, p. 31.
10. Statement of Financial Accounting Standards SFAS No. 34, "Interest Capitalization" (Stamford, Conn.: Financial Accounting Standards Board, October 1979).
11. Delta Air Lines, Inc., annual report, June 1994, p. 24.
12. For goodwill acquired after August 10, 1993 in an asset acquisition transaction, its cost is generally amortizable for income tax purposes on a straight-line basis over 15 years. *Internal Revenue Code,* Section 197(a). This new treatment applies to most intangibles.
13. We simplify the tax treatment somewhat but capture the essence of the accounting.
14. SFAS No. 109, "Accounting for Income Taxes" (February 1992).
15. Ibid., para. 17.
16. Ibid., para. 21.
17. Ibid., paras. 21 and 46–47.
18. Ibid., paras. 20–24.
19. Mycogen Corp., annual report, 1993, pp. 41–42.
20. Outboard Marine Corp., annual report, September 1994, pp. 28–29.
21. Ibid., pp. 28–29.
22. Most of the GAAP requirements for both transaction and translation reporting are found in SFAS No. 52, "Foreign Currency Translation" (December 1981).
23. SFAS No. 8, "Accounting for the Translation of Foreign Currency Transactions and Foreign Financial Statements" (October 1975).
24. SFAS No. 52, para. 6.
25. Ibid., para. 6.
26. Ibid., para. 10.
27. Accounting Principles Board, Opinion No. 18, "The Equity Method of Accounting for Investments in Common Stock" (New York: American Institute of Certified Public Accountants, March 1971); SFAS No. 94, "Consolidation of All Majority-Owned

Subsidiaries" (October 1987); and SFAS No. 115, "Accounting for Certain Investments in Debt and Equity Securities" (May 1993).

28. Income tax issues can become somewhat involved in the case of intercorporate investments and are not dealt with in this example.

29. If other assets of the investee had values different from their book values, then revaluations of these items would come first, with goodwill then amounting to the residual.

30. SFAS No. 13, "Accounting for Leases" (November 1976), para. 7.

31. SFAS No. 28, "Accounting for Sales with Leasebacks" (May 1979).

32. SFAS No. 87, "Employers' Accounting for Pensions" (December 1985).

33. R. R. Donnelley and Sons, annual report, December 1994, p. 37.

34. Details are found in SFAS No. 106, "Employers' Accounting for Postretirement Benefits Other Than Pensions" (December 1990).

35. Details are found in SFAS No. 112, "Employers' Accounting for Postemployment Benefits" (November 1992).

36. General Motors Corporation, 1993 Annual Report, p. 38.

Company Index

A

America Online, Inc., 254, 256

American Building Maintenance Industries, Inc., 99

American Business Products, Inc., 20

American Consumer Products, Inc., 339

American Management Systems, Inc., 35

American Power Conversion, Inc., 249

American Software, Inc., 55, 203, 261, 334

Amgen, Inc., 190

Amoco Corp., 114, 151, 178

Amtran, Inc., 96

Analog Devices, Inc., 20, 32

Analogic Corp., 35

Anheuser-Busch Companies, Inc., 20

Apache Corp., 35, 255

Apogee, Inc., 338

Applied Magnetics Corp., 35

Arch Petroleum, Inc., 20

Arctco, Inc., 249

Argosy Gaming Co., 95, 100

Armstrong World Industries, Inc., 117, 180

Arvin Industries, Inc., 35, 45

ARX, Inc., 20

AST Research, Inc., 1, 5, 61

Astrosystems, Inc., 20

Athanor Group, Inc., 280

Atlantic Richfield Co., 35

Autodesk, Inc., 203, 268

Avery International, Inc., 35

Avon Products, Inc., 106

Avondale Industries, Inc., 403

Axciom Corp., 20

B

Bairnco Corp., 35

Baltimore Gas and Electric Co., 35

Bank of Tokyo Ltd., 387

BankAmerica Corp., 165

Bankers Trust New York Corp., 14

Bassett Furniture Industries, Inc., 58, 269

Battle Mountain Gold Co., 363

Baxter International, Inc., 95

Bay Tact Corp., 307

Becton, Dickinson and Co., 20, 96

Belden, Inc., 370

Bell Atlantic Corp., 20, 35

Berkshire Hathaway, Inc., 297

Best Lock Corp., 20

Big Rock Brewery Ltd, 206

Bindley Western Industries, Inc., 35

Bio-Medicus, Inc., 36

Biocraft Labs, Inc., 20

Biogen, Inc., 107

BioLogic Systems, Inc., 20

Biomet, Inc., 54, 267

Blount, Inc., 403

BMC Software, Inc., 203, 212

Bob Evans Farms, Inc., 246

Boise Cascade Corp., 95

Bolt, Beranek & Newman, Inc., 36, 44, 268

Borland International, Inc., 205

Boston Chicken, Inc., 158

Boston Digital Corp., 299

Bristol-Myers Squibb Co., 36

Brock Exploration Corp., 20

Brooklyn Union Gas Co., 20

Browning-Ferris Industries, Inc, 56, 258

Subject Index

A

Accounting changes
  changes as an early warning, 81–82
  changes in estimates, 103–104, 362–367
  changes in principles, 101–102, 362–367
    cumulative effect implementation, 101
    incremental effects, 102–103, 363
    retroactive restatement
      implementation, 101, 204
  characterized, 101
  disclosure, 102–103
  discretionary, 363
  earnings management applications, 364–367
  examples, 102–103, 247–248, 363–367
Accounting Principles Board (APB)
  Opinions
  APB No. 13, 201
  APB No. 16, 201
  APB No. 17, 65, 201, 278
  APB No. 18, 164, 199, 436
  APB No. 30, 118
Accounting and Review Services
  Committee of the American Institute
  of CPAs, 376
Accounting Trends and Techniques 99, 102, 177, 386–387, 398, 404, 460
Accounts payable (A/P) days, 230
  early warnings, 303–304
  relationship to future earnings, 346
Accounts receivable
  accounts receivable (A/R) days, 12, 68, 72, 215–216, 219, 282–285

allowance for doubtful accounts, 281–282
bad debt expense or provision for doubtful
  accounts, 281–282, 284–286
Accrual-basis accounting cash-flow
  relationship, 326–328
Aggressive cost capitalization, 246
  identifying agressive capitalization, 253–254
  landfill development costs, 257–258
  membership acquisition costs, 251–253
  preopening costs, 246–248
Assets
  off-balance sheet assets
    deferred tax assets, 162, 173–174
    purchased technology, 190
  under or overvalued assets, 162–164, 186
    accounts receivable, 281–282
    intangible assets, 280
    inventory, 279, 286–288, 408
    investments, 162–163, 297–299
    land, 189
    lender early warning, 68
    loans, with overstated loss reserves, 193
    pensions, 181, 186
    property, 164
Audits
  audit failure, 10
  audit risk alerts, 391–393
  audit risk assessment, 391–392
  audit risk indicators, 393
  change in auditor as an early warning, 81
  earnings surprises and information risk, 395